ADULT LEARNING DISORDERS

A Neuropsychologist's Handbook

Barbara Uzzell, Series Editor

Adult Learning Disorders: Contemporary Issues
Lorraine E. Wolf, Hope E. Schreiber, and Jeanette Wasserstein

ADULT LEARNING DISORDERS

CONTEMPORARY ISSUES

EDITED BY
LORRAINE E. WOLF
HOPE E. SCHREIBER
JEANETTE WASSERSTEIN

Psychology Press
Taylor & Francis Group
New York   Hove

Psychology Press
Taylor & Francis Group
270 Madison Avenue
New York, NY 10016

Psychology Press
Taylor & Francis Group
27 Church Road
Hove, East Sussex BN3 2FA

© 2008 by Taylor & Francis Group, LLC

Printed in the United States of America on acid-free paper
10 9 8 7 6 5 4 3 2 1

International Standard Book Number-13: 978-1-84169-419-1 (Hardcover)

Visit the Taylor & Francis Web site at
http://www.taylorandfrancis.com

and the Psychology Press Web site at
http://www.psypress.com

Contents

Part 4: Life Outcomes

About the Editors

Lorraine E. Wolf, Ph.D., is the Director of Disability Services at Boston University. She holds a doctorate in clinical neuropsychology from the City University of New York and has more than 20 years of experience working with children, adolescents, and adults. She has taught experimental psychology, assessment, and neuropsychology at the undergraduate and graduate levels.

Dr. Wolf has published and presented extensively on issues for students with attention and learning disorders, psychiatric disabilities, and autism spectrum disorders. She holds faculty appointments in psychiatry and in rehabilitation sciences at Boston University. She was a coeditor (with Dr. Wasserstein) of *Adult Attention Deficit Disorders: Brain Mechanisms and Life Outcomes* (2001, New York Academy of Sciences) and is the senior coauthor of *Asperger Syndrome in Higher Education: A Professional Guide*, to be published by Autism Asperger Publishing Company in 2008. Dr. Wolf's research interests include the neuropsychology of attention disorders, cognitive deficits in schizophrenia, and effective services for students with autism spectrum and other psychiatric disabilities in higher education.

Hope Schreiber, Psy.D., ABPP/CN, has been interested in neurodevelopmental disorders in children, adolescents, and adults through over 20 years of clinical experience in inpatient, outpatient, and teaching-hospital contexts. Dr. Schreiber directed the Neuropsychology Service at Charles River Hospital in Wellesley, Massachusetts. She currently works as the neuropsychologist for the Psychiatry Department at Tufts–New England Medical Center in Boston, and directs the College Learning Disorders/Attention

Deficit/Hyperactivity Disorder (LD/ADHD) Program, serving colleges and universities throughout New England.

Jeanette Wasserstein, Ph.D., has been a neuropsychologist for more than 25 years. She directed Neuropsychology Services at The Mount Sinai School of Medicine and The New School for Social Research. Currently she is in full-time private practice and is also part of the psychiatry faculty at the medical school. Throughout her career, she has been interested in the diagnosis and treatment of neurodevelopmental disorders over the life span. Dr. Wasserstein has published in various areas but is perhaps best known for her work with adult ADHD.

List of Contributors

Katherine Barboza
New School for Social Research
New York, New York

Jane Holmes Bernstein
Children's Hospital—Boston
Boston, Massachusetts

Chris Coleman
University of Georgia
Athens, Georgia

Anne Daniels
Harvard University
Cambridge, Massachusetts

Erika Geetter
Boston University
Boston, Massachusetts

Jeffrey W. Gilger
Purdue University
W. Lafayette, Indiana

Jordan Grafman
National Institute of Neurological
   Disorders and Stroke
Bethesda, Maryland

Noel Gregg
University of Georgia
Athens, Georgia

Elena L. Grigorenko
Yale University
New Haven, Connecticut

Ruben C. Gur
University of Pennsylvania
   Medical Center
Philadelphia, Pennsylvania

Bonnie J. Kaplan
University of Calgary
Calgary, AB, Canada

Edith Kaplan
Boston University
Boston, Massachusetts

Kathryn Kniele
Medical University of
  South Carolina
Charleston, South Carolina

Frank Krueger
National Institute of Neurological
  Disorders and Stroke
Bethesda, Maryland

Kristen A. Lindgren
Boston University School of
  Medicine
Boston, Massachusetts

Jennifer Lindstrom
University of Georgia
Athens, Georgia

Allan H. Macurdy
Boston University
Boston, Massachusetts

Robert L. Mapou
Stixrud & Associates
Silver Springs, Maryland

Maria Mody
Massachusetts General Hospital
  and Harvard Medical School
Boston, Massachusetts

Deanna Morgan
The College Board
New York, New York

Celiane Rey-Casserly
Children's Hospital—Boston
Boston, Massachusetts

Byron P. Rourke
University of Windsor
Ontario, Canada

Janet Cohen Sherman
Massachusetts General Hospital
Boston, Massachusetts

Linda S. Siegel
University of British Columbia
Vancouver, BC, Canada

Ian S. Smythe
Ibis Creative Consultants, Ltd.
Sutton, United Kingdom

Gerry A. Stefanatos
Moss Rehabilitation Research
  Institute
Philadelphia, Pennsylvania

Helen Tager-Flusberg
Boston University School of
  Medicine
Boston, Massachusetts

Katherine D. Tsatsanis
Yale University
New Haven, Connecticut

Nehal P. Vadhan
Columbia University
New York, New York

Cheryl Weinstein
Harvard University Medical School
Boston, Massachusetts

Introduction

ALLAN F. MIRSKY

I am pleased and honored to have been asked by Drs. Wolf, Schreiber, and Wasserstein to write an introduction to this splendid volume. Perhaps they have called on me due to my august status in the field. "August" stems from the fact that I have been attempting, for better or for worse, to understand the neurobiological nature of deficits in attention and learning since 1952. I believe, therefore, that I may have published an article relevant to the thrust of this volume before any of the current contributors (Rosvold, Mirsky, Sarason, Branome, & Beck, 1956). Presumably, that confers on me a certain depth of knowledge and experience. I am quite satisfied that we have made substantial gains in our understanding of adult learning disorders since the 1950s, and the chapters in this volume attest to that.

Relevant to my persistent interest in deficits, learning, and the brain is the volume that I coedited with Jeanne Chall in 1978 (Chall & Mirsky, 1978). The planning for the work began in 1973, and it was proposed to be a yearbook on the neurosciences for educators, researchers, administrators, and teachers. Chall and I had a wonderful time recruiting the experts who contributed to that volume, including such eminent brain and educational researchers as Martha Denckla, Herman Epstein, Kenneth Heilman, Marcel Kinsbourne, Paul MacLean, and Rita Rudel. In the concluding section of the book, Chall and I opined as to what the future of education, as illuminated by developments in neuroscience, would be in the 21st century. While our work in 1978 did not address that these children would grow into adults, I believe it is of relevance to the current volume to see what we predicted would happen, 30 years ago:

> It is tempting to speculate on a possible future collaborative effort between educators and neuroscientists as we enter the twenty-first century. Conceivably, a new specialty of educational neuroscientist or educational neuropsychologist could emerge. ... Each child in the school system would, according to this scheme, be tested by this new professional.

The test battery of the twenty-first century would be the responsibility of a team of specialists including the educational neuroscientist. It would encompass behavioral and photographic analyses designed to identify motor patterns, cerebral dominance and related psycho- and physiomotor capacities; it might also include electrographic and sensory tests that would provide data about the relative maturity and efficiency of processing information in all relevant sensory modalities. Attentional capacities would be assessed by both behavioral and electrophysiological means, and the sources of attentional difficulties (if any) categorized and identified with respect to intra- as opposed to extra-cerebral causes. Brain size, maturity, and relative degree of myelinization in key areas would be assessed by means of noninjurious neuroradiological techniques (the progeny of today's computerized axial tomography scanners). Oxygen utilization in various brain regions at rest and during a variety of mental activities would be assessed by means of dynamic energy utilization techniques. Such methods currently exist and need only to be refined further. Brain neurohumoral balance and maturity would be assessed by means of biochemical assays performed on a few drops of urine and blood. Computer-assisted analyses of these data would enable the educational neuroscientist to perform an accurate assessment of the child's developmental stage, his particular strengths and weaknesses, the instructional materials he would best be able to handle, and the problem areas that would most likely to be encountered during his educational career. This program would permit the early identification, forecasting and remediation of educational difficulties; but more than that, it should help in the development of a pedagogical effort and program designed on the basis of how each child is growing and maturing, on each child's talents and weaknesses, and not on the basis of an average, normative set of values that fits any single pupil in a loose way. (Chall & Mirsky, 1978, pp. 377–378)

The contributions of the authors in this volume attest to the fact that the methodology to implement a large part of the program that Chall and I outlined in 1978 now exists, and a number of the chapters in this volume illustrate this convincingly. Many chapters highlight core biology and neuroscience, while others focus more on clinical issues. In particular, in the chapter by Gilger and Kaplan, there is a wistful mention of a diagnostic evaluation that is similar, if not as utopian, as the one that Chall and I prognosticated in 1978. Indeed, as many of the chapters stress, the clinical neuropsychological evaluation of learning disabilities (LD) may closely approximate the work of the educational neuroscientist we envisioned.

According to Gilger and Kaplan (this volume, Chapter 3),

> The ABD (atypical brain development) conceptualization highlights the importance of formulating treatment and research plans around the idea of peaks and valleys within persons and between people. This approach pertains to the psychometrically assessed phenotypes such as cognitive processing skills, as well as correlating behavioral phenotypes with brain phenotypes. Peaks and valleys may include both ends of the continua of skills, as well as morphological differences in the brain. Of course, practical constraints (time, money, local laws requiring labels, guarded clinical specialties, training, etc.) often preclude such thorough assessments in real-life settings. Certain theoretical and funding philosophies also limit (implicitly or explicitly) such an approach in the typical research setting.

I guess this means that, despite claims to the contrary, many a child will be left behind.

The use of magnetic resonance imaging (MRI) to evaluate brain growth and development is discussed in the contributions by Daniels, by Sherman, and by Tager-Flusberg, Lindgren, and Mody in their chapter (6) on the neuroanatomy of autism spectrum disorders. Relevant to this, as well, is the chapter by Kniele and Gur, which discusses the course of myelinization, especially as it impacts the differences between male and female brains. Gilger and Kaplan speculate, in their model of ABD, about the interaction of environmental effects and genetic timetables in producing a phenotype such as reading disability. Grigorenko discusses the contributions of functional neuroimaging to our understanding of learning disorders in adults.

In considering cognitive development and learning disorders, Sherman mentions the "Matthew Effect":

> Evidence indicates that while IQ remains relatively stable for normal learners, at least after age 5 (Sattler, 1992), for LD learners this may not be the case. Due to secondary effects of their academic deficit, LD individuals' difficulties can extend into other aspects of learning, resulting in a reduction of IQ scores over the course of development

> (Stanovich, 1986). This phenomenon, referred to as the "Matthew
> Effect" ("the rich get richer and the poor get poorer," from the gospel
> according to Matthew) provides an explanation for the progressive
> lowering of IQ scores in LD, stipulating that while the deficiency
> in LD may be focal, its impact may be more generalized, impeding
> learning in other academic areas as well as more general cognitive
> and processing skills. (Sherman, this volume, Chapter 1)

As I write these sentences, the national news is reporting a study emanating from McGill University and the National Institute of Mental Health (NIMH) that states MRIs indicate that the anterior cortex of highly intelligent children reaches its maximum thickness later than that of less intelligent children, and that this is "perhaps reflecting a longer developmental window for high-level thinking circuitry" (NIMH press release, March 29, 2006). Clearly, we have much to learn about the complex interactions between environment and biology.

An issue that Chall and I did not mention in 1978 but that strikes me as extremely salient is the issue of comorbidity. As Schreiber describes so persuasively in her chapter, persons referred for LD or attention-deficit/hyperactivity disorder (ADHD) often have other disorders (for example, depression or anxiety), of which impaired attention or learning capacity is just one symptom. Duncan and I (Mirsky & Duncan, 2001) emphasized that impaired attention could be a symptom of numerous disorders in addition to ADHD, including schizophrenia, undiagnosed seizure disorders, phenylketonuria (PKU), narcolepsy, uremia, a closed head injury, neurocysticercosis (*Taenia solium* or pork tapeworm infestation of the brain), or sleep breathing disorders. In some cases, treatment with stimulants—the preferred medication for ADHD—would be contraindicated and even dangerous for the patient. Schreiber also makes mention in her chapter of the report by Wilcott and Pennington (2000) of the genetic susceptibility locus for ADHD on chromosome 6p.

We previously noted (Mirsky & Duncan, 2001) that there are a number of disorders, in addition to ADHD, with putatively the same susceptibility locus on chromosome 6p; these include schizophrenia, juvenile myoclonic epilepsy (a type of "absence" epilepsy), narcolepsy, a genetic form of deafness (related, possibly, to auditory attention deficit), and kidney disease. In end-stage kidney disease (uremia), patients show deficits in attention and electroencephalograph (EEG) patterns reminiscent of an induced "absence-like" seizure disorder (Burns & Bates, 1998). (Grigorenko points out that susceptibility genes for developmental dyslexia have been identified on 6p.) Perhaps I will be accused of premature anatomizing or geneticizing of disorders, but it is alluring to speculate that there may be some type of susceptibility gene for impaired or altered attention on chromosome 6p that is shared by all these disorders—some gene whose normal products ensure competent transmission of information from brain stem to cortex.

Also worthy of discussion is the use of event-related brain potentials (ERP) in the diagnosis of disorders as well as response to treatment. There is, for example, abundant literature on the P300 (the "attention" component of the ERP) in ADHD, and the way in which it is affected by drug treatment (e.g., Klorman et al., 2002). Tager-Flusberg and colleagues discussed the alterations of the N100 and P300 components in auditory processing in autism. ERP analysis has also been shown to aid significantly in the moment-to-moment (millisecond by millisecond, actually) parsing of specific deficits in information processing that the patient manifests. An illustrative example of this is provided in a recent review of ERP studies in closed head injuries (Duncan, Kosmidis, & Mirsky, 2005). One of the salient points in that article concerns the particular vulnerability of auditory information processing after closed head injuries (as well as other disorders). This would seem to have particular salience to a consideration of the pathophysiology of learning disorders and, in particular, developmental dyslexia. Relevant, also, to the last point is the finding by Duncan and colleagues (1994) that the ERPs (including P300) of adult male dyslexics appear normal—except if there was a history of ADHD. Perhaps more research should include ERP analyses of learning disorders and the differential vulnerabilities of various stimulus modalities in adults.

In closing, I wish to thank the editors for their industry and scholarship in putting together this valuable collection of contributions to the study of adult learning disorders, and for giving me the pleasure of introducing the volume.

References

Burns, D. J., & Bates, D. (1998). Neurology and the kidney. *Journal of Neurology, Neurosurgery and Psychiatry, 65*, 810–821.

Chall, J. S., & Mirsky, A. F. (1978). *Education and the brain.* Chicago: University of Chicago Press.

Duncan, C. C., Kosmidis, M. H., & Mirsky, A. F. (2005). Closed head injury related information processing deficits: An event-related potential analysis. *International Journal of Psychophysiology, 58*, 133–157.

Duncan, C. C., Rumsey, J. M., Wilkniss, S. M., Denckla, M. B., Hamburger, S. D., & Odoupotkin, M. (1994) Developmental dyslexia and attention dysfunction in adults—Brain potential indexes of information-processing. *Psychophysiology, 31*, 386–401.

Klorman, R., Thatcher, J. E., Shaywitz, S. E., Fletcher, J. M., Marchione, K. E., Holahan, J. M., et al. (2002). Effects of event probability and sequence on children with attention-deficit/hyperactivity, reading, and math disorder. *Biological Psychiatry, 52*, 795–804.

Maziade, M., Merette, C., Cayer, M., Roy, M. A., Szatmari, P., Cote, R., et al. (2000). Prolongation of brainstem auditory-evoked responses in autistic probands and their unaffected relatives. *Archives of General Psychiatry, 57*, 1077–83.

Mirsky, A. F., & Duncan, C. C. (2001). A nosology of disorders of attention. In J. Wasserstein, L. Wolf, & F. F. LeFever (Eds.), *Adult attention deficit disorder: Brain mechanisms and life outcomes* (pp. 17–32). New York: Annals of the New York Academy of Science.

Rosvold, H. E., Mirsky, A. F., Sarason, I., Bransome, E. D., Jr., & Beck, L. H. (1956). A continuous performance test of brain damage. *Journal of Consulting Psychology, 20*, 343–350.

Wilcott, E. G., & Pennington, B. (2000). Comorbidity of reading disability and attention deficit/hyperactivity disorder: Differences by gender and subtype. *Journal of Learning Disabilities, 33*, 179–191.

PART 1

Development

CHAPTER 1

Normal and Learning Disabled (LD) Development of Academic Skills

JANET COHEN SHERMAN

Contents

The topic of this chapter, academic skill development in normal and learning disabled (LD) populations, focuses on two central concepts in the expression of developmental learning disabilities. The first concerns the developmental aspects of these disorders, an issue that is of particular importance when considering the expression of developmental learning disabilities in adulthood. The second concerns the normal development of academic skills, and how the acquisition of these skills differs in normal and LD populations. In considering these two central issues regarding academic skill learning, this chapter addresses the nature of the acquisition process across the developmental spectrum. Questions addressed include: What distinguishes LD and normal learners at different points in development? What factors account for differences in the learning process? What is the impact of educational practices and individual differences on academic skill acquisition? In addressing these questions, I argue that the nature of the difficulties that individuals with LD encounter in acquiring academic skills is best understood when academic skill acquisition is viewed from a developmental framework, one that accounts for both normal and atypical learning.

Definitions of Learning Disabilities

The Requirement for an IQ-Achievement Discrepancy

The definition of LD focuses on the basic notion that academic skill acquisition is "difficult" for this group of learners, as can be seen in the following:

> Learning Disabilities is a general term that refers to a heterogeneous group of disorders manifested by significant difficulties in the acquisition and use of listening, speaking, reading, writing, reasoning, or mathematical abilities. These disorders are intrinsic to the individual, presumed to be due to central nervous system dysfunction, and may occur across the life span. Problems in self-regulatory behaviors, social perception, and social interaction may exist with learning disabilities but do not by themselves constitute a learning disability. Although learning disabilities may occur concomitantly with other handicapping conditions (for example, sensory impairment, mental retardation, serious emotional disturbance) or with extrinsic influences (such as cultural differences, insufficient or inappropriate instruction), they are not the result of those conditions or influences. (National Joint Committee on Learning Disabilities, 1988)

Although this definition suggests that an individual has difficulty relative to some standard, it provides little information as to what that standard is.

However, as it is typically operationalized, the stipulation that the disability is "intrinsic to the individual" and "is not the result of [other] conditions or influences" is supported by a discrepancy between an individual's aptitude and his or her level of academic achievement. In the realm of clinical diagnosis, this "individual comparison standard" is supported by a significant discrepancy between IQ and academic achievement scores. Other definitions of LD—for example, the *Diagnostic and Statistical Manual of Mental Disorders* (4th ed., text rev.; *DSM-IV-TR*) criteria—require that individuals also meet a "group comparison standard," with difficulty in skill acquisition additionally supported by a significantly lower achievement level relative to a normative sample. "Learning disorders are diagnosed when the individual's achievement on individually administered, standardized tests in reading, mathematics, or written expression is substantially below that expected for age, schooling, and level of intelligence" (American Psychiatric Association, 2000).

Importantly, both definitions suggest that a particular relationship between academic achievement and IQ distinguishes LD learners. Other groups of learners, who may also have difficulties with academic skill acquisition, are not included in this definition because of their IQ level. For example, individuals with high IQ scores and substantially lower academic achievement scores may meet the individual comparison standard, with a discrepancy between IQ and achievement scores, but not the group comparison standard, with their achievement level not sufficiently low enough. Conversely, individuals with academic achievement levels deficient relative to group norms meet the group comparison standard but may not meet the individual comparison standard, with their IQ not sufficiently above their level of academic achievement. While the exclusion of these types of learners suggests that there is something distinct about learners who have difficulty acquiring academic skills in the face of a particular IQ score, evidence suggests that academic difficulties look quite similar in individuals with and without IQ-achievement discrepancies (Francis, Shaywitz, Stuebing, Shaywitz, & Fletcher, 1996; Gustafson & Samuelsson, 1999; Siegel, 1988, 1989; Stanovich, 1988; Vellutino, Scanlon, & Lyon, 2000). Moreover, the definition suggests that in contrast to the weak and negative relationship between IQ and achievement for LD learners, for normal learners there should be a strong and positive relationship between these two sets of scores. However, at least for reading, this is not the case, with IQ accounting for only 16 to 25% of the variance in normal reading achievement (Gustafson & Samuelsson, 1999).

While issues such as these have called the role of IQ in definitions of LD into question, it is clear that the intent of these definitions is to indicate that the academic skill deficit in LD is specific. In particular, by requiring a discrepancy between IQ and achievement, diagnostic criteria for LD attempt to exclude those individuals for whom a more generalized cognitive impairment can account for the "difficulty" in academic skill acquisition. However, as will be discussed in this chapter, what specifically distinguishes LD from normal learners may not be a particular relationship between aptitude and achievement but instead may be underlying differences in cognitive processing and the impact these have on the development of academic skills.

Developmental Considerations

The diagnostic criteria for LD suggest that, relative to normal learners, IQ and achievement levels remain static across development. However, evidence indicates that while IQ remains relatively stable for normal learners, at least after age 5 (Sattler, 1992), for LD learners this may not be the case. Due to secondary effects of their academic deficit, LD individuals' difficulties can extend into other aspects of learning, resulting in a reduction of IQ scores over the course of development (Stanovich, 1986). This phenomenon, referred to as the "Matthew Effect" ("the rich get richer and the poor get poorer," from the gospel according to Matthew), provides an explanation for the progressive lowering of IQ scores in LD, stipulating that while the deficiency in LD may be focal, its impact may be more generalized, impeding learning in other academic areas as well as more general cognitive and processing skills. Studies also provide evidence that expression of academic skill difficulty becomes more subtle later on in development (e.g., Denckla, 1993; Everatt, 1997). This results in LD learners achieving higher scores on some measures of academic achievement (e.g., single-word reading) while performance on other measures (e.g., reading rate, spelling), which often do not contribute to diagnosis, may remain impaired. Moreover, as a result of changes in academic demands across development, the nature of what constitutes "academic difficulty"—which is largely unspecified in LD definitions—is likely to change. A failure to consider these developmental factors, as well as the effects of remediation on academic skill development (Scarborough, 1984) can lead to exclusion of older LD learners, who may continue to have difficulty with academic skills, but may express this in ways that differ from learners at earlier stages of the acquisition process.

Beyond LD Definitions: An Alternative Focus

In the field of neuropsychology, individuals with impaired cognitive functioning are generally considered to fall into two broad classes of disorders: acquired impairments, in which an individual's cognitive disorder results from some event (i.e., disease, damage) that occurs after some period of (typically) normal development, and developmental impairments, in which there was never evidence for normal acquisition of a particular skill (Temple, 1997). Although impairment for an individual with an acquired disorder is determined relative to that individual's premorbid level of functioning, for individuals with developmental disorders, deficits in cognitive functioning are defined relative to developmentally matched peers, with acquisition of a particular skill different in some way for individuals with a developmentally based impairment than for normally developing individuals. Given that LD belongs to this latter class, defining the academic difficulty in this group requires a developmental model as the point of reference (e.g., Goswami, 2003; Thomas & Karmiloff-Smith, 2002). Developmental questions are best addressed by longitudinal studies that provide information about how underlying differences in cognitive abilities impact these learners' academic skills throughout the developmental process. While the majority of LD studies are cross-sectional, within the most well-studied class of LD, developmental dyslexia, there are now a number of studies that have examined LD learners longitudinally (e.g., Francis et al., 1996; Shaywitz et al., 1999; Snowling, Goulandris, & Defty, 1996). Studies that attempt to differentiate LD from normal learners at critical points in development—for example, initial and final states—also contribute to our understanding of the essentially developmental nature of these disorders (e.g., Bradley & Bryant, 1983; Bruck, 1985, 1992; Denckla, 1993; Pennington, Van Orden, Smith, Green, & Haith, 1990; Wagner & Torgesen, 1987), as do studies that compare LD with normal learners matched for academic skill level (e.g., Bruck, 1990, 1992; Snowling et al., 1996). These achievement-matched, rather than age-matched comparisons, provide information about whether LD learners differ from normal learners not just in the point in development at which they achieve academic skills but whether, even at the same level of academic achievement, they rely on different underlying cognitive processes. In the remainder of this chapter, I review findings from studies that provide information regarding the developmental learning process in LD and normal learners.

Distinguishing Normal and LD Learners at the Initial State

Although definitions of LD focus on difficulty in academic achievement, there is now considerable behavioral, neurological, and genetic evidence that LD learners can be distinguished from normal learners well before either group has even begun to learn an academic skill. Numerous cognitive studies indicate that dyslexic and normal learners differ in their phonological processing abilities at the "initial state" (see Adams, 1990, and Vellutino,

Fletcher, Snowling, & Scanlon, 2004, for a review). A recent review (Castles & Coltheart, 2004) indicates that over 40 longitudinal studies have investigated the relationship between young children's phonological awareness and later reading skills. While only some of these studies have looked at children who are truly nonreaders, raising questions about whether there is a causal link between early phonological awareness skills and later reading achievement, a number of studies have found that young LD children have a deficiency in phonological awareness, specifically in their ability to perceive and manipulate phonemes (individual sounds). Evidence in support of a connection between this early deficiency and later development of reading decoding skills includes findings that young children's knowledge of nursery rhymes (Maclean, Bryant, & Bradley, 1987), their ability to divide the sound stream into syllables (Vellutino & Scanlon, 1987), and their ability to detect rhyme and alliteration in "odd word out" tasks (e.g., hat, cat, let; sap, tan, sat) (Bradley & Bryant, 1983) are related to subsequent reading ability.

Behavioral studies also characterize early differences in other classes of LD. For those individuals diagnosed with nonverbal learning disorders, studies indicate that early difficulties in the development of fine motor skills (e.g., delayed acquisition of a pincer grasp) and in the development of spatial abilities (e.g., less interest and skill in playing with blocks and puzzles or engaging in drawing activities) differentiate this group of learners who go on to display difficulties in arithmetic skills, handwriting, and social cognition (Pennington, 1991).

Neurobiological studies also differentiate LD and normal learners at the initial state. In a hallmark study, Galaburda, Sherman, Rosen, Aboitiz, and Geschwind (1985) identified neuroanatomical differences in postmortem analyses of four male dyslexic brains (ages 14 to 32). The dyslexic brains were characterized by developmental anomalies consisting of neuronal ectopias and architectonic dysplasias primarily located in the left perisylvian regions as well as a lack of the typical pattern of asymmetry of the left and right planum temporale. The symmetry observed in the dyslexic brains was due to larger right planum than in normal brains, attributed to a failure of normal reduction of cortical cells that occurs during prenatal development.

Finally, studies indicate that differences between normal and LD learners are the result of genetic influences, with LD both familial and heritable, and with studies identifying certain genes as placing individuals at risk for the development of LD (e.g., Gilger & Kaplan, 2001; Grigorenko et al., 1997). Results indicate that children who are genetically at risk for developmental dyslexia can be distinguished early on from normal children, whether or not they go on to develop reading problems. Snowling (2001) followed genetically at-risk children (those with a parent with dyslexia) from ages 4 to 8. Her findings indicate that while early problems with speech and phonological awareness differentiated the subgroup of children (60%) who went on to develop reading problems from those who did not, weaknesses on tasks that required knowledge of sound–spelling correspondences (e.g., nonword reading and spelling) differentiated *all* of the genetically at-risk children from the normal readers. Based on this finding, Snowling proposed that there is an inherited tendency for difficulty in mapping between orthography and phonology but that this genetically inherited phonological weakness can be largely overcome by stronger early language skills.

Characterizing the Developmental Process in LD and Normal Learners

Viewing the process of academic skill acquisition as dynamic rather than static raises questions about what happens to these learners beyond the initial state. Even if normal and LD learners look different at early stages of development, it is possible that LD learners "catch up" to normal learners, with early differences reflecting a developmental delay. Conversely, these early differences in development may continue to influence the developmental process. These two possibilities, one a "developmental lag" and the other a "developmental deficit," have been directly compared to one another in longitudinal studies that use growth curve analyses of academic skill development in normal and LD learners (Francis et al., 1996; Jordan, Hanich, & Kaplan, 2003a; Shaywitz et al., 1999).

Studies of the growth of basic math skills in normal and MD (math disordered) learners indicate that the developmental pattern differs depending upon the specific aspect of number skill acquisition (e.g., Geary, 1993; Jordan et al., 2003a). For early procedural math skills, MD learners are distinguished from normal learners in their error rates and in their use of developmentally immature algorithms (for example, using immature counting principles, such as "adding all" to derive a sum, rather than the min principle, in which children "count on," starting from the larger number and counting on the smaller number to it). While MD learners use more immature procedures than normal learners early on (i.e., in first grade), these procedural differences largely disappear by second grade, supporting a model of developmental delay. However, these early procedural differences may nonetheless have a lingering effect. For normal learners, the efficient and early understanding of counting principles appears to contribute to a shift from the use of counting procedures to a direct retrieval of math facts from memory. For MD children, the shift to retrieval-based learning is one that is not simply delayed but instead disrupted, with MD children continuing to make many more errors in retrieving arithmetic facts than normal learners and doing so significantly

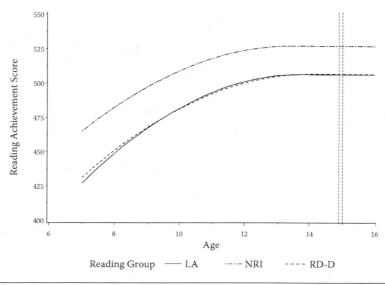

Figure 1.1 Estimated mean growth curves for the Woodcock-Johnson (1977) reading-cluster Rasch-scale score for the reading disabled-discrepancy (RD-D), reading disabled-low achievement (LA), and not reading impaired (NRI) groups. The curved lines show predicted achievement at each age by using mean growth parameters from the quadratic model with a plateau. The vertical reference lines are plotted at the estimated age at plateau for the NRI (left line) and disability (right line) groups. Reference lines for the LA and RD-D groups are coincident. The NRI group has a higher reading plateau but does not differ from the RD-D and LA groups in age at plateau. The disability groups do not differ from one another in reading plateau not in age at plateau. These data are consistent with a deficit model of reading disability. (Francis, Shaywitz, Shaywitz, Stuebing, & Fletcher; 1996 Copyright © 1996 by the American Psychological Association. Reprinted with permission.).

more slowly (Geary, 1993). Whether this retrieval deficit represents differences in these children's ability to retrieve facts from memory or in their actual fact representations, for this aspect of math acquisition, MD learners fail to catch up to normal learners, even with remediation. Moreover, studies have shown that not only do deficiencies in fact mastery persist, but they are also independent of other aspects of learning (e.g., reading and language abilities; Jordan, Hanich, & Kaplan, 2003b).

Studies that have used growth curve analyses to compare normal and reading-disordered (RD) learners provide evidence that reading disorders persist across development (e.g., Francis et al., 1996; Shaywitz et al., 1999). As can be seen in Figure 1.1 (Francis et al., 1996), results indicate that for all three groups of learners studied—normal learners, RD learners with an IQ-achievement score discrepancy, and RD learners without such a discrepancy—reading achievement summary scores from the Woodcock-Johnson Psychoeducational Test Battery (Word Identification,

Word Attack, and Passage Comprehension) increase across development and reach a plateau at about the same age. While duration of reading skill development is about the same for all groups, the most significant difference between the normal readers and the two RD groups is that those with disordered reading score lower than those with normal reading at every point of development. This result indicates that individuals with disordered reading not only start out with deficient reading skills but also never catch up to their normal reading peers. Moreover, as can also be seen in the figure, the developmental trajectories for the two RD groups studied are indistinguishable, suggesting that the relationship between IQ and achievement does not influence the development of reading skills. Note that for this growth curve analysis, the measure of reading included several components of the reading process, leaving questions as to whether there are different developmental trajectories for different aspects of reading, as has been found for math.

Characterizing the Final State of LD and Normal Learners

As discussed, definitions of LD describe the academic skill deficiency as specific. When we consider the "final state" of academic skill acquisition in LD learners, one important question is whether the deficit remains specific. As previously discussed, Stanovich (1986) has argued that as a result of the Matthew Effect, an initially specific academic deficiency may become more generalized later in development. Although there are differing results as to whether IQ scores are lowered over the course of development in LD (Bruck, 1990; Francis et al., 1996; Gottardo, Siegel, & Stanovich, 1997), studies suggest that academic deficits in adulthood may be more widespread than in childhood, with children who are disabled readers not only continuing to show reading deficits in adolescence and adulthood but also showing deficits in other academic skills (e.g., spelling, writing skills, grammar, organization, and math) (Bruck, 1985; Satz, Buka, Lipsitt, & Seidman, 1998; Spreen & Haaf, 1986). Moreover, comorbidity of LD—for example, RD and ADHD (attention-deficit/hyperactivity disorder) or RD and MD—may be the rule rather than the exception across development (Gilger & Kaplan, 2001).

At the same time as LD learners display deficits in more academic domains later in development, evidence also indicates that within a particular academic domain—for example, reading—there is an underlying core cognitive deficit that persists. Although a number of studies indicate that adult dyslexics' single-word reading skills often fall within the average range, their development of phonological processing abilities is limited, with a persistent phonological impairment supported by poor performance on

tasks that specifically require the individual to rely on phonological awareness, such as tests of pseudoword reading, phoneme deletion, spoonerisms,
and spelling (e.g., Gottardo et al., 1997; Hanley, 1997; Hatcher, Snowling,
& Griffiths, 2002; Pennington et al., 1990; Snowling, Nation, Moxham,
Gallagher, & Frith, 1997).

Utilizing developmentally based comparison methods, Bruck (1992)
demonstrated several important points regarding the persistence of the
phonological deficit in dyslexia and how this can account for differences in
reading achievement for normal and dyslexic readers. Bruck's results first
of all demonstrated that adult dyslexics' phonological awareness skills are
deficient not only for age but also for reading level, suggesting that even
when dyslexics read single words as accurately as their younger reading-
matched counterparts, the underlying process by which they recognize
written words differs from that of normal readers.

Second, her findings indicate that while dyslexics' phonological processing abilities are deficient relative to normal readers, the processes that
dyslexics rely on when reading are not "deviant" but instead are developmentally immature and, in particular, less completely specified than for
normal readers. Similar to much younger normal readers, adult dyslexics
achieve awareness of larger sublexical units, specifically, the syllable and
onset-rime (i.e., in the word *snap*, *sn* is the onset [the initial consonants]
and *ap* is the rime [the vowel and any consonants that follow the onset]),
but do not go on to develop awareness of smaller sublexical units, with continued deficient awareness at the level of phonemes (individual sounds).

Third, and likely related to their deficient phonological awareness, adult
dyslexic readers, unlike much younger normal readers, do not automatically activate orthographic information from phonetic information. This
finding was demonstrated by comparing normal and dyslexic readers' error
rates when asked to count or delete individual sounds (phonemes) from
spoken nonwords. Importantly, the adult dyslexics made more counting
errors than controls when the nonwords were nondigraph items (e.g., "tisk,"
in which there are an equal number of letters and sounds), suggesting that
they are less able to access orthography from phonology than are normal
readers. In contrast, the adult dyslexics made fewer counting errors than
reading-matched controls when the nonwords were digraph items (e.g.,
"leem" or "thoace," in which there are more letters than individual sounds).
For these items, the dyslexics' lower error rate also suggests that they are
less aware of orthographic structure than are normal readers, who err due
to consulting the nonword's orthography when making phonological judgments (e.g., when counting sounds in the nonword "leem," the normal
reader errs because the sound /e/ is represented by two letters, *ee*, and mis-
takenly responds "4" rather than "3"). Note that this difference in error rate

is likely not attributable to differences in spelling abilities (with dyslexics scoring above their achievement-matched controls on measures of word and nonword spelling) but rather suggests that, unlike normal readers, dyslexic readers do not automatically map between phonology and orthography, a critical process in the development of normal reading. Finally, developmental comparisons indicated that normal readers' performance on phonological tasks improved as a function of grade level, reaching adult level by grade 3. In contrast, neither age nor reading level significantly impacted dyslexic readers' performance on phonological awareness tasks. Based on the lack of developmental change in phonological awareness skills for the dyslexic readers, Bruck (1990, 1992) proposed that "arrested development" may best characterize the developmental process in dyslexia, with the adult dyslexics' phonological awareness skills similar to those of much younger children. This arrested development accounts for their failure to fully develop phonological abilities and an associated failure to automatically access orthography from phonology.

Results of neurobiological studies further support a fundamental and persistent phonological processing deficit in dyslexia (Larsen, Høien, Lundberg, & Ødegaard, 1990; Leonard et al., 2001; Shaywitz et al., 1998; Shaywitz et al. 2002; Temple, 2002; Temple et al., 2001). As can be seen in Figure 1.2 (Temple, 2002), a number of functional imaging studies, which have used different imaging techniques and different phonological tasks, converge on the finding of decreased activation in the left temporoparietal cortex in adult dyslexics relative to normal adult readers, an area that is considered pivotal in carrying out grapheme (print) to phoneme (sound) correspondences essential for normal reading decoding.

Studies have also reported a concomitant overactivation for dyslexics relative to normal readers in anterior regions (specifically left inferior frontal gyrus), possibly representing increased effort or compensation on the part of adult dyslexics when performing phonological analysis tasks (Shaywitz et al., 1998). While this "neural signature" (Shaywitz et al., 1998) could be the result of a lifetime of poor reading, imaging studies of childhood dyslexics replicate the activation patterns observed in adult dyslexics (e.g., Shaywitz et al., 2002; Temple, 2002; Temple et al., 2001), suggesting that the disruption is fundamental to the reading deficit in LD. In addition to the disruption in cortical areas involved in phonological processing, Temple et al. (2001) also found different activation patterns during an orthographic processing task (letter versus line matching) with normal but not dyslexic children showing activation in the occipital-parietal area. Finally, and parallel to behavioral studies, results of this study indicated that for normal and dyslexic children, brain activation patterns were unrelated to level of IQ.

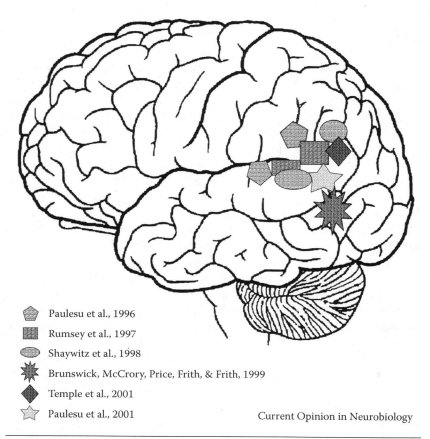

Paulesu et al., 1996

Rumsey et al., 1997

Shaywitz et al., 1998

Brunswick, McCrory, Price, Frith, & Frith, 1999

Temple et al., 2001

Paulesu et al., 2001

Current Opinion in Neurobiology

Figure 1.2 Neural disruption in phonological processing in dyslexia. Approximate anatomical locations where dyslexic groups showed less activity than normal reading control groups, during phonological processing of visual stimuli. Despite different methodologies (PET [⬠, ▦, ✴, ☆] and fMRI [⬭, ◆]), tasks (letter rhyme [⬠, ⬭, ◆], pseudoword processing [▦, ⬭, ✴, ☆], explicit and implicit tasks [✴, ☆]), analysis techniques (region of interest [⬭] and statistical parametric mapping [⬠, ▦, ✴, ◆, ☆]), ability levels (severely dyslexic [▦, ◆] and compensated [⬠, ✴, ☆]), age groups (children [◆] and adults [⬠, ▦, ⬭, ✴, ☆]), and languages [☆], all studies showed decreased activity in left hemisphere posterior language regions—temporoparietal cortex—in dyslexic subjects, as compared to normal reading subjects. (Reprinted from Temple, E. *Current Opinion in Neurobiology*, *12*, 179; Copyright © 2002. With permission from Elsevier.)

Reconsidering Differences Between the Normal and LD Learner: Ramifications for Academic Achievement

As the discussion thus far indicates, results of many experimental studies indicate that a core deficit in phonological processing discriminates normal readers from those with dyslexia. However, in considering the process of normal, fluent reading, one important question is whether, and to what extent, normal readers engage in phonological decoding when reading. While the answer to this question differs somewhat depending on the model of normal reading acquisition—a dual-route theory (e.g., Temple, 1997) or connectionist theory (e.g., Seidenberg & McClelland, 1989)—there is now considerable evidence that phonology does matter and, moreover, that normal phonological processing is what enables normal learners to go on to become highly fluent readers (Pennington, Lefly, & Van Orden, 1987). According to one model of normal reading (Share, 1995), the achievement of fluent word recognition, in which every word is not phonologically decoded but is recognized on the basis of stored information regarding its unique letter sequence, depends upon a "self-teaching device" in which children abstract relationships between spelling and sound patterns over the course of reading acquisition, ultimately allowing them to generalize to the thousands of words that they have not been explicitly taught to read. While this requires both phonological and orthographic processing, it appears that the ability to phonologically recode words (i.e., the ability to associate letters and sounds to identify novel words) is primary. Without this knowledge, or with phonologically underspecified representations that characterize dyslexic readers throughout development, the RD individual is precluded from becoming a highly fluent and efficient reader.

Uncovering this lack of fluency in adult LD learners requires clinical examinations that look beyond their performance on standardized measures developed for use with children and then extended into the adult population (Denckla, 1993). Further, in order to differentiate the adult LD learner from the normal learner, tasks must look not only at accuracy but also at rate of processing. Findings show that while accuracy levels (i.e., for single-word reading) may approach normal levels for adult dyslexics, rate of word reading as well as pseudoword reading remains extremely slow (e.g., Hatcher et al., 2002; Snowling et al., 1997). Given the changing and more significant academic processing demands in later adolescence and adulthood, it is often at this time that the dyslexics' more effortful processing has its most significant impact. Specifically, older dyslexics often have difficulties when they need to read and comprehend longer and more complex text, to take notes (which requires simultaneously listening to information, extracting its meaning, and rapidly transforming sound into print), and to synthesize and organize information when writing essays and papers (Simmons & Singleton, 2000). Clearly, these more complex tasks require more effortful processing for all learners, whether LD or normal. However, the dyslexic's lack of automaticity in performing the more basic aspects of reading and spelling makes these academic tasks all the more difficult. Empirical studies support this, indicating that for both LD and normal learners, word recognition abilities are the strongest predictor of reading comprehension (e.g., Perfetti, 1985).

In spite of their weak word recognition abilities, some dyslexics do go on to achieve relatively high (albeit generally not normal) levels of reading comprehension. In a study that compared dyslexic readers with relatively "good" and "poor" reading comprehension accuracy (with both groups showing a slow rate of reading), Bruck (1990) found that what differentiated the two groups was not their word decoding abilities but rather their performance on a test of oral receptive vocabulary knowledge (Peabody Picture Vocabulary Test, PPVT) and their childhood IQ scores. Results also suggested that all of the dyslexic readers relied more on contextual information to aid in the word identification process than did the younger reading-matched controls. Taken together, these results suggest that dyslexics utilize "top-down processing" in order to compensate for their deficient word recognition skills, relying on their higher-level language skills and on contextual information to bootstrap their weak word recognition skills (Bruck, 1990). However, studies indicate that utilizing this type of processing comes with a cost. In a study of reading comprehension in which words included in the passages were ones that the adult dyslexic could read, neither the dyslexics' reading rate nor their comprehension accuracy fell at normal levels (Simmons & Singleton, 2000). Differences between normal and dyslexic readers were most evident for longer passages and for inferential (rather than literal) comprehension questions, where the reader needs to refer to outside knowledge to interpret structural elements within the passages. With these greater demands placed on the dyslexic reader, who is already exerting more effortful processing even to read words that he or she recognizes, the adult dyslexic is left with diminished processing resources (e.g., working memory space) to devote to integration of information and inferential reasoning.

The model of a core cognitive deficit contributing to a reduction in cognitive processing resources for the dyslexic learner is one that may apply in other areas of LD as well. For MD learners, less-efficient math fact retrieval likely impacts their ability to solve more complex equations either as quickly or as accurately as normal learners. While this domain differs from reading in that it includes a number of different quantitative competencies, the learning of more complex mathematics depends upon proficiency in primary abilities involved in the appreciation of numbers (e.g., counting and arithmetic), with level of mastery achieved in childhood the best predictor of adult mastery of arithmetic skills (Geary, 2000).

Impact of Remediation and Education on Academic Skill Acquisition

While evidence indicates that there are underlying cognitive processing differences that distinguish the normal and LD learner, and that these deficits persist and impact academic skill learning throughout development, there is also evidence that educational practices and remediation impact the expression of LD. Although LD definitions stress that the academic difficulty cannot be accounted for by extrinsic factors, including "insufficient or inappropriate instruction," there is evidence that type as well as extent of educational instruction does impact academic skill development for LD and normal learners. For LD individuals, number of years of education is correlated with skill development. In the case of reading, continued exposure to demanding literacy tasks beyond adolescence results in continued skill development, although this is not the case for normal readers (Bruck, 1985). On the flip side, individuals exposed to limited education are deficient in their reading, with 50 to 85% of juvenile delinquents meeting the IQ-achievement discrepancy requirement for dyslexia due to low scores on measures of reading achievement (Gustafson & Samuelsson, 1999). For math, studies indicate that level of mastery achieved in the normal acquisition of secondary math skills (i.e., those taught in schools versus more inherent skills, such as a basic understanding of quantity and numerosity), is dependent on educational practices that vary across cultures and generations (Geary, 2000; Geary, Bow-Thomas, Liu, & Siegler, 1996). Acquisition of the base 10 concept, a difficult but critical math concept, is influenced by how number concepts are expressed in different languages. Specifically, children in Asian cultures, in which base 10 concepts are more transparently expressed in number words over 10 (e.g., with numbers such as 11 and 12 expressed as "ten one," "ten two," etc.), learn and apply this concept more readily and accurately than do children in cultures with European-based languages, where the concept is not directly expressed in number words (e.g., twelve, thirteen) (Geary et al., 1996). Evidence also shows that the extent to which normal adults retain math competencies is related to level of mathematical instruction achieved in school (with those individuals who studied math beyond basic calculus showing little loss of algebraic skills even at age 75), as well as extent of practice of quantitative procedures after leaving school (Geary, 2000).

Results of behavioral studies and studies of brain function also indicate that remediation impacts academic skill learning in LD. In several longitudinal studies of dyslexia, studies have found that early development of reading skills is influenced by specific training of phonological awareness and, moreover, that this type of training is superior to more general training procedures (Lyon & Moats, 1997). Results indicate that with this type of training, LD children improve their phonological decoding and single-word reading accuracy, although with less improvement in reading fluency and automaticity (Lyon & Moats, 1997; Torgesen et al., 2001). Thus, even with remediation efforts, findings suggest that LD and normal learners continue to exhibit differences in the ways in which they process information. Moreover, while a number of behavioral studies show that as a group, LD learners' academic functioning improves with remediation, this is not the case for all LD individuals. For example, Torgesen et al. (2001) found that 2 years following exposure to intensive 8-week phonologically based tutoring programs, approximately one-half to two-thirds of the children continued to exhibit "normalization" of their reading skills. An investigation of the variables that impacted children's response to treatment indicated that growth in reading skills correlated most highly with the children's attention and behavior ratings by their teachers, their general verbal ability, and the levels they had attained on component reading skills during the intervention period. Further, in support of critical language, and specifically in phonological abilities underlying the development of reading skills, Vellutino et al. (2000) found that young dyslexic readers response to remediation is predicted by their performance on tests that require phonological coding, including phonemic awareness, verbal memory, rapid automatized naming, and verbal association learning tasks, and not by either level of IQ or magnitude of IQ-achievement discrepancy. Moreover, results of this study indicated that the independence of IQ and growth in reading skills was true for normal readers as well as RD children.

Although a number of studies report improved academic achievement in LD as the result of intervention, study designs are limited, with a focus on short-term gains, and with few studies having appropriate control groups (Lyon & Moats, 1997). In a study that relied on retrospective methods, comparing adult dyslexics who received treatment in childhood to those who did not, Bruck (1985) surprisingly found little difference in reading achievement levels for the two groups, although those who received treatment showed better social and emotional adjustment and modestly better academic and occupational attainment. The lack of difference in reading achievement may be explained by the fact that the treated group had more severe reading impairment in childhood than the untreated group, with severity of childhood LD found to be the best predictor of academic skill development in adulthood (Bruck, 1985).

Further evidence that remediation promotes changes in the expression of LD is provided by results of brain activation studies. Not only have studies found changes in dyslexic children's brain activation patterns after exposure to different types of language-based interventions, with brain activation patterns after treatment more similar to those of normal readers (e.g., Aylward et al., 2003; Temple et al., 2003), but studies have also found that adult dyslexics with improved reading (i.e., "compensated" dyslexics) show different patterns of brain activation than adults with persistent reading difficulties and that both improved and nonimproved dyslexics show different brain activation patterns than normal adult readers. In this study, Shaywitz et al. (2003) found that relative to normal readers, compensated adult dyslexics show relative underactivation in posterior neural systems for reading (left parietotemporal and occipitotemporal regions) during word and nonword reading tasks, while showing greater activation during the nonword reading task than persistently poor readers in several other brain regions, including the right superior frontal and right middle temporal gyri and the left anterior cingulate. This finding suggests that the compensated dyslexics rely on processing strategies that differ from both normal and persistently poor readers. When reading words, the persistently poor readers, like the normal readers, showed activation in left posterior regions, although findings of connectivity analysis indicated that this site serves different functional roles for the two groups. Specifically, while the normal readers demonstrated connectivity between the left occipitotemporal seed region and left inferior frontal gyrus, a traditional language area, the impaired readers demonstrated connectivity between the seed region and areas associated with working memory and memory retrieval, specifically right prefrontal areas. This finding provides an interesting neuroanatomical analogy to findings of behavioral studies that indicate that LD readers are impaired relative to normal readers in basic underlying cognitive processes (i.e., phonological coding) and, as a result, utilize more effortful processing to recognize words.

Conclusions and Future Directions

In conclusion, findings of many recent studies indicate that basic cognitive processes differentiate LD and normal learners across the developmental spectrum. At this time, evidence comes mainly from studies of reading, with findings in this domain indicating that individuals with disordered reading can be distinguished from normal readers at initial and final states of development; that differences in a core component of reading acquisition—specifically, phonological coding—not only explain the underlying deficit in dyslexia but also account for how normal reading becomes highly fluent; and that differences in educational practices as well as individual differences impact how this core deficit is expressed. There are now several lines of evidence from behavioral, biological, and genetic studies to indicate that not only do LD learners differ from normal learners but that, within LD learners, some are also far more successful than others at overcoming their academic deficit in adulthood. These "successful LD" adults differ not only from their less successful counterparts but also from normal learners. As Denckla (1993) points out, "the real question to be answered about adults with learning disabilities is why have they not compensated for their cognitive deficits; or, if they have acquired basic academic skills, why have they not been able to use these skills?" (p. 121). Denckla proposes that the answer to this question is that a deficit in executive functioning precludes adults with LD from utilizing what they have learned. While executive functioning may, in fact, differentiate LD and normal learners (and, in the area of math LD, there is at least a subtype where this seems to be the case), this may not be because of an executive functioning deficit but instead may be because the academic task itself is different for the LD and normal learner. Specifically, because the LD learner, even when "successful," accomplishes basic academic tasks (whether reading words, retrieving basic math facts, or understanding important cues in social interactions) in a way that requires deliberate, conscious, and strategic processing rather than the automatic processes utilized by the normal learner, the LD learner may appear deficient in executive functioning, even when he or she is not.

Given that the ultimate goal of the psychologist and educator is to determine how LD learners can improve their academic skills, an important direction for future research is to understand what allows some LD learners to overcome their academic deficit relatively easily, while others remain almost "stubbornly" impaired. While studies indicate that level of LD severity may, in part, explain this difference, other factors outside the domain of academic learning also appear to impact learning. In particular, findings suggest that reliance on other cognitive factors, such as general language knowledge, attention, rote memory, and contextual information, may contribute to more successful learning. If, in fact, the more successful LD learner utilizes information outside of the domain of academic skill learning to bolster his achievement, then both assessment and remediation efforts need to look beyond academic achievement in order to identify those factors that promote academic skill learning. In doing so, it is important to appreciate that different cognitive processes underlie the learning processes for the LD and the normal learner. By understanding what is unique to the learning process for LD individuals, it may be possible to determine what factors may ultimately make the task of academic skill learning one that is less difficult for the LD learner, even if it is not the same as it is for the normal learner.

Acknowledgments

I gratefully acknowledge the invaluable assistance of Sara Shavel-Jessop and Lucila Halperin in the preparation of this manuscript.

References

Adams, M. J. (1990). *Beginning to read: Thinking and learning about print.* Cambridge, MA: MIT Press.

American Psychiatric Association. (2000). *Diagnostic and statistical manual of mental disorders* (4th ed., text rev.). Washington, DC: Author.

Aylward, E. H., Richards, T. L., Berninger, V. W., Nagy, W. E., Field, K. M., Grimme, A. C., et al. (2003). Instructional treatment associated with changes in brain activation in children with dyslexia. *Neurology, 61,* 212–219.

Bradley, L., & Bryant, P. E. (1983). Categorizing sounds and learning to read: A causal connection. *Nature, 301,* 419–421.

Bruck, M. (1985). The adult functioning of children with specific learning disabilities. In I. Sigel (Ed.), *Advances in applied developmental psychology* (Vol. 1, pp. 91–120). Norwood, ND: Ablex.

Bruck, M. (1990). Word-recognition skills of adults with childhood diagnoses of dyslexia. *Developmental Psychology, 26*(3), 439–454.

Bruck, M. (1992). Persistence of dyslexic's phonological awareness deficits. *Developmental Psychology, 28*(5), 874–886.

Brunswick, N., McCorory, E., Price, C. J., Frith, C. D., & Frith, U. (1999). Explicit and implicit processing of words and pseudowords by adult developmental dyslexics: A search for Wernicke's Wortschatz? *Brain, 122,* 1901–1917.

Castles, A., & Coltheart, M. (2004). Is there a causal link from phonological awareness to success in learning to read? *Cognition, 91,* 77–111.

Denckla, M. B. (1993). The child with developmental disabilities grown up: Adult residua of childhood disorders. *Behavioral Neurology, 11*(1), 105–125.

Everatt, J. (1997). The abilities and disabilities associated with adult developmental dyslexia. *Journal of Research in Reading, 20*(1), 13–21.

Francis, D. J., Shaywitz, S. E., Stuebing, K. K., Shaywitz, B. A., & Fletcher, J. M. (1996). Developmental lag versus deficit models of reading disability: A longitudinal, individual growth curves analysis. *Journal of Educational Psychology, 88*(1), 3–17.

Galaburda, A. M., Sherman, G. F., Rosen, G. D., Aboitiz, F., & Geschwind, N. (1985). Developmental dyslexia: Four consecutive patients with cortical anomalies. *Annals of Neurology, 18*(2), 222–233.

Geary, D. C. (1993). Mathematical disabilities: Cognitive, neuropsychological, and genetic components. *Psychological Bulletin, 114*(2), 345–362.

Geary, D. C. (2000). From infancy to adulthood: The development of numerical abilities. *European Child and Adolescent Psychiatry, 9,* II/11–II/16.

Geary, D. C., Bow-Thomas, C. C., Liu, F., & Siegler, R. S. (1996). Development of arithmetical competencies in Chinese and American children: Influence of age, language, and schooling. *Child Development, 67,* 2022–2044.

Gilger, J. W., & Kaplan, B. J. (2001). Atypical brain development: A conceptual framework for understanding developmental learning disabilities. *Developmental Neuropsychology, 20*(2), 465–481.

Goswami, U. (2003). Why theories about developmental dyslexia require developmental designs. *Trends in Cognitive Sciences, 7*(12), 534–540.

Gottardo, A., Siegel, L. S., & Stanovich, K. E. (1997). The assessment of adults with reading disabilities: What can we learn from experimental tasks? *Journal of Research in Reading, 20*(1), 42–54.

Grigorenko, E. L., Wood, F. B., Meyer, M. S., Hart, L. A., Speed, W. C., Shuster, A., et al. (1997). Susceptibility loci for distinct components of developmental dyslexia on chromosomes 6 and 15. *American Journal of Human Genetics, 60,* 27–39.

Gustafson, S., & Samuelsson, S. (1999). Intelligence and dyslexia: Implications for diagnosis and intervention. *Scandinavian Journal of Psychology, 40,* 127–134.

Hanley, J. R. (1997). Reading and spelling impairments in undergraduate students with developmental dyslexia. *Journal of Research in Reading, 20*(1), 22–30.

Hatcher, J., Snowling, M., & Griffiths, Y. M. (2002). Cognitive assessment of dyslexic students in higher education. *British Journal of Educational Psychology, 72,* 119–133.

Jordan, N. C., Hanich, L. B., & Kaplan, D. (2003a). A longitudinal study of mathematical competencies in children with specific mathematics difficulties versus children with comorbid mathematics and reading difficulties. *Child Development, 74*(3), 834–850.

Jordan, N. C., Hanich, L. B., & Kaplan, D. (2003b). Arithmetic fact mastery in young children: A longitudinal investigation. *Journal of Experimental Child Psychology, 85*(2), 103–119.

Larsen, J. P., Høien, T., Lundberg, I., & Ødegaard, H. (1990). MRI evaluation of the size and symmetry of the planum temporale in adolescents with developmental dyslexia. *Brain and Language, 39,* 289–301.

Leonard, C. M., Eckert, M. A., Lombardino, L. J., Oakland, T., Kranzler, J., Mohr, C. M., et al. (2001). Anatomical risk factors for phonological dyslexia. *Cerebral Cortex, 11,* 148–157.

Lyon, G. R., & Moats, L. C. (1997). Critical conceptual and methodological considerations in reading intervention research. *Journal of Learning Disabilities, 30*(6), 578–588.

Maclean, M., Bryant, P., & Bradley, L. (1987). Rhymes, nursery rhymes, and reading in early childhood. *Merrill-Palmer Quarterly, 33,* 255–281.

National Joint Committee on Learning Disabilities. (1988). *Collective perspectives on issues affecting learning disabilities: Position papers and statements.* Austin, TX: Pro-Ed.

Paulesu, E., Frith, U., Snowling, M., Gallagher, A., Morton, J., Frackowiak, R. S., et al. (1996). Is developmental dyslexia a disconnection syndrome? Evidence from PET scanning. *Brain, 119,* 143–157.

Pennington, B. F. (1991). *Diagnosing learning disorders: A neuropsychological framework.* New York: Guilford Press.

Pennington, B. F., Lefly, D. L., & Van Orden, G. C. (1987). Is phonology bypassed in normal or dyslexic development? *Annals of Dyslexia, 37,* 62–89.

Pennington, B. F., Van Orden, G. C., Smith, S. D., Green, P. A., & Haith, M. M. (1990). Phonological processing skills and deficits in adult dyslexics. *Child Development, 61,* 1753–1778.

Perfetti, C. A. (1985). *Reading ability.* New York: Oxford University Press.

Rumsey, J. M., Nace, K., Donohue, B., Wise, D., Maisog, J. M., & Andreason, P. (1997). A positron emission tomographic study of impaired word recognition and phonological processing in dyslexic men. *Archives of Neurology, 54,* 562–573.

Sattler, J. M. (1992). *Assessment of children* (3rd ed.). San Diego: Author.

Satz, P., Buka, S., Lipsitt, L., & Seidman, L. (1998). The long-term prognosis of learning disabled children: A review of studies. In B. Shapiro, P. J. Accardo & A. J. Capute (Eds.), *Specific Reading Disability: A View of the Spectrum* (pp. 223–248). Timonium, MD: York Press.

Scarborough, H. S. (1984). Continuity between childhood dyslexia and adult reading. *British Journal of Psychology, 75,* 329–348.

Seidenberg, M., & McClelland, J. (1989). A distributed, developmental model of word recognition and naming. *Psychological Review, 96,* 523–568.

Share, D. L. (1995). Phonological recoding and self-teaching: Sine qua non of reading acquisition. *Cognition, 55,* 151–218.

Shaywitz, S. E., Fletcher, J. M., Holahan, J. M., Shneider, A. E., Marchione, K. E., Stuebing, K. K., et al. (1999). Persistence of dyslexia: The Connecticut longitudinal study at adolescence. *Pediatrics, 104*(6), 1351–1359.

Shaywitz, S. E., Shaywitz, B. A., Fulbright, R. K., Skudlarski, P., Mencl, W. E., Constable, R. T., et al. (2003). Neural systems for compensation and persistence: Young adult outcome of childhood reading disability. *Biological Psychiatry, 54,* 25–33.

Shaywitz, S. E., Shaywitz, B. A., Pugh, K. R., Fulbright, R. K., Constable, R. T., Mencl, W. et al. (1998). Functional disruption in the organization of the brain for reading in dyslexia. *Proceedings of the National Academy of Sciences of the United States of America, 95*(5), 2636–2641.

Shaywitz, B. A., Shaywitz, S. E., Pugh, K. R., Mencl, W. E., Fulbright, R. K., Skudlarski, P., et al. (2002). Disruption of posterior brain systems for reading in children with developmental dyslexia. *Biological Psychiatry, 52,* 101–110.

Siegel, L. S. (1988). Evidence that IQ scores are irrelevant to the definition and analysis of reading disability. *Canadian Journal of Psychology, 42*(2), 201–215.

Siegel, L. S. (1989). IQ is irrelevant to the definition of learning disabilities. *Journal of Learning Disabilities, 22*(8), 469–478.

Simmons, F., & Singleton, C. (2000). The reading comprehension abilities of dyslexic students in higher education. *Dyslexia, 6,* 178–192.

Snowling, M. (2001). From language to reading and dyslexia. *Dyslexia, 7,* 37–46.

Snowling, M., Goulandris, N., & Defty, N. (1996). A longitudinal study of reading development in dyslexic children. *Journal of Educational Psychology, 88*(4), 653–669.

Snowling, M., Nation, K., Moxham, P., Gallagher, A., & Frith, U. (1997). Phonological processing skills of dyslexic students in higher education: A preliminary report. *Journal of Research in Reading, 20*(1), 31–41.

Spreen, O., & Haaf, R. G. (1986). Empirically derived learning disability subtypes: A replication attempt and longitudinal patterns over 15 years. *Journal of Learning Disabilities, 19*(3), 170–180.

Stanovich, K. E. (1986). Matthew effects in reading: Some consequences of individual differences in the acquisition of literacy. *Reading Research Quarterly*, *21*, 360–407.

Stanovich, K. E. (1988). Explaining the differences between the dyslexic and the garden-variety poor reader: The phonological-core-variable-difference model. *Journal of Learning Disabilities*, *21*(10), 590–604.

Temple, C. (1997). *Developmental cognitive neuropsychology*. Hove, UK: Psychology Press.

Temple, E. (2002). Brain mechanisms in normal and dyslexic readers. *Current Opinion in Neurobiology*, *12*, 178–183.

Temple, E., Deutsch, G. K., Poldrack, R. A., Miller, S. L., Tallal, P., Merzenich, M. M., et al. (2003). Neural deficits in children with dyslexia ameliorated by behavioral remediation: Evidence from functional MRI. *Proceedings of the National Academy of Sciences of the United States of America*, *100*(5), 2860–2865.

Temple, E., Poldrack, R. A., Salidis, J., Deutsch, G. K., Tallal, P., Merzenich, M. M., et al. (2001). Disrupted neural responses to phonological and orthographic processing in dyslexic children: An fMRI study. *NeuroReport*, *12*(2), 299–307.

Thomas, M., & Karmiloff-Smith, A. (2002). Are developmental disorders like cases of adult brain damage? Implications from connectionist modelling. *Behavioral and Brain Sciences*, *25*, 727–788.

Torgeson, J. K., Alexander, A. W., Wagner, R. K., Rashotte, C. A., Voeller, K. K. S., & Conway, T. (2001). Intensive remedial instruction for children with severe reading disabilities: Immediate and long-term outcomes from two instructional approaches. *Journal of Learning Disabilities*, *34*(1), 33–58, 78.

Vellutino, F. R., Fletcher, J. M., Snowling, M. J., & Scanlon, D. M. (2004). Specific reading disability (dyslexia): What have we learned in the past four decades? *Journal of Child Psychology and Psychiatry*, *45*, 2–40.

Vellutino, F. R., & Scanlon, D. M. (1987). Phonological coding, phonological awareness, and reading ability: Evidence from a longitudinal and experimental study. *Merrill-Palmer Quarterly*, *33*, 321–363.

Vellutino, F. R., Scanlon, D. M., & Lyon, G. R. (2000). Differentiating between difficult-to-remediate and readily remediated poor readers: More evidence against the IQ-achievement discrepancy definition of reading disability. *Journal of Learning Disabilities*, *33*(3), 223–238.

Wagner, R. K., & Torgeson, J. K. (1987). The nature of phonological processing and its causal role in the acquisition of reading skills. *Psychological Bulletin*, *101*(2), 192–212.

CHAPTER 2

Sex Differences in Brain Development and Learning Disability

KATHRYN KNIELE and RUBEN C. GUR

Contents

Boys are much more likely than girls to be identified as learning disabled and to be diagnosed with other psychiatric or developmental disorders. Controversy as to whether this discrepancy is biologically determined or whether it reflects sociocultural factors has sparked acute interest in the topic among parents, educators, and investigators in the social and biological sciences. For example, the lead article in the July 30, 2001, issue of *U.S. News and World Report* posed the question "Are Boys the Weaker Sex?" The answer was an emphatic "Yes!" At the elementary and high school levels, boys earn nearly 70% of the Ds and Fs doled out by teachers, though they make up less than half of the school-aged population (Mulrine, 2001). Nearly two thirds of students classified as learning disabled are male. Epidemiological estimates of the prevalence of dyslexia consistently cite higher rates of the disorder among boys than girls (Finnuci, Isaacs, Whitehouse, & Childs, 1983; Leiderman & Flannery, 1993; Neils & Aram, 1986), with some suggesting as much as a three- to fourfold increased prevalence of the disorder among boys (Finucci & Childs, 1981; Vogel, 1990). Males outnumber females approximately 10:1 among individuals with autism spectrum disorders (Bailey, Palferman, Heavey, & LeCouteur, 1998). Educators are keenly aware of the higher rate of attention-deficit/hyperactivity disorder (ADHD) among boys; the male-to-female ratio of ADHD diagnoses in referred samples ranges from 9:1 to 5:1 (Gaub & Carlson, 1997; Weiss & Hechtman, 1979) and from 1.5 to 2:1 in epidemiological studies (Arcia & Conners, 1998).

Sex is clearly an important factor to consider in understanding learning disabilities. However, the provocative question of whether boys are the "weaker sex" can be translated into the very legitimate research question "Why are neurodevelopmental disorders differentially expressed in boys as compared to girls?" The advent of neuroimaging and refinement of imaging procedures enabled visualization and volumetric measurement of brain structure. It is now possible to map patterns of neural activity to behavior and to observe changes in neural structure and function over time. Armed with these tools, we now know that brain development occurs differently in males and females. Sexually dimorphic neural development and its impact on brain structure, function, and neurophysiology appear to contribute to differential cognitive proficiencies among men and women. In this chapter, we examine how sex differences in brain development influence the expression of learning disabilities among boys and girls.

Normal Brain Development

Measuring Brain Development

Early investigations of brain development were limited to gross measures such as brain size, brain weight, and postmortem analyses of whole brains

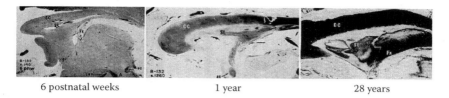

| 6 postnatal weeks | 1 year | 28 years |

Figure 2.1 Examples of the myelination process as they appear in Yakovlev's stained brain tissue for the corpus callosum. The corpus callosum is a large body of nerve fibers connecting the two cerebral hemispheres. The left-most section is from the brain of a baby at 6 postnatal weeks, the center shows a comparable section at 1 year, and the right-most picture shows the region at 28 years. Note the increased darkness of the banana-shaped corpus callosum, indicating increased myelination. (From Yakovlev & Lecours, 1967, Figure 19. With permission.)

or brain tissue. Paul Yakovlev and his colleagues at Harvard University produced the largest and most influential work regarding human brain maturation using staining techniques on postmortem brain tissue. That work culminated in the publication of a landmark chapter by Yakovlev and Lecours (1967) entitled "The Myelogenetic Cycles of Regional Maturation of the Brain"; it provides the foundation for much of what we know about human neurodevelopment across the life span (see Figure 2.1). However, inferences drawn from studies conducted during the early and middle parts of the 20th century are limited by serious methodological flaws, including gross variability in sampling procedures and significant sampling bias (i.e., dead brains were obtained from either very young or very old individuals with little representation of those in the middle years).

Neuroimaging methods (e.g., positron emission topography [PET] and magnetic resonance imaging [MRI]) developed in the 1970s and implemented in the 1980s yielded powerful tools for studying the living brain. By the 1990s, these methods had become the gold standard for assessing brain development, as they permit visualization and volumetric measurement of brain structure in living people. In recent years, functional magnetic resonance imaging (fMRI) has emerged as the state-of-the-art procedure for understanding brain-behavior relationships. Because fMRI enables observation of relationships between localized patterns of neural activity and behavior in near real time, it is possible to longitudinally track brain development and function over short- and long-term intervals. The emerging literature derived from structural and functional imaging studies, together with data obtained from neuropsychological studies of cognition in healthy and diseased individuals, confirms and elaborates on the findings of early research regarding the course of human brain development across the life span. Specifically, brain development appears to be a dynamic process that occurs over an extended period of time along a normal curve trajectory. As with all developmental processes, intra-individual (e.g., being male or female) and environmental factors influence this general trajectory such that the rate and pattern of development varies. However, there are universal and quantifiable markers of neural maturation. Among these, the two main indices of neural maturation are myelogenesis and synaptogenesis.

Myelogenesis, the progressive myelination of neural tracts, is considered to be the main index of neural maturation (Yakovlev & Lecours, 1967). Myelin is a fatty-like substance that forms an insulating sheath around the axon of some neurons in the central nervous system (CNS) and also around nerve fibers in the peripheral nervous system (PNS). Myelinated neurons appear white in color and are thus referred to as white matter (WM), whereas cell bodies and unmyelinated axons appear gray and are thus referred to as gray matter (GM). Myelin serves two primary functions. First, it acts as insulation for neurons, protecting nerves from interference from other neural impulses, similar to how rubber insulation around copper wires protects short-circuiting from other nearby wires. Second, myelin speeds nerve conduction. The more highly myelinated a nerve tract, the more quickly impulses travel along it. Thus, myelination promotes efficient transmission of neuronal signals across associative networks and along nerve tracts. The behavioral consequence is increased mental processing speed and improved reaction time. Conversely, demyelination of neural tracts results in loss of cognitive or motor functioning that is characteristic of certain neurodegenerative disorders such as Parkinson's disease.

During fetal development, the number of brain synapses—areas between neurons where chemical or electrical impulses are transmitted—increases exponentially. Synaptic density peaks by approximately the third year of life and stabilizes until age 5, at which time existing unused or weak synapses begin to die off. This natural elimination of neural connections is referred to as synaptogenesis and serves as another primary marker of brain maturation (Huttenlocher, 1979; Yakovlev & Lecours, 1967). During the "pruning" phase of synaptogenesis, which peaks during adolescence and continues until early adulthood, neurons and their connections that have not been consistently used during childhood "shrivel off" and are eliminated. The apparent purpose of this regressive pruning process is to optimize communication among remaining neural systems (Huttenlocher, 1979; Huttenlocher, de Courten, Garey, & van der Loos, 1982).

It is this refining of neural networks that enables proficiency in tasks and, perhaps more importantly, provides a neural mechanism by which experience may shape brain development. During the early stages of development, children demonstrate the most facilitated learning. For example, infants have the capacity to differentiate and imitate the sounds of all spoken languages. However, through repeated exposure to a single language, that ability to differentiate diminishes while learning of a native language continues. Neurally speaking, the synapses and neural pathways most frequently activated during growth are the ones that are preserved, while those that are infrequently used are eliminated through synaptogenesis. As such, synaptic pruning lies at the heart of the "nature versus nurture" debate that has persisted throughout the history of the life sciences. Appreciation of the complexity of brain development, and recognition that experience or "nurture" may indeed shape the neural structure and function of the brain, opens the door for a confluence of theories as to why psychopathology or other dysfunction occurs in some individuals but not others. Such an understanding may provide some explanation for why learning disabilities are more often observed and exhibited in boys than in girls.

The Pattern of Normal Brain Development

Elucidation of normal brain maturation is essential for understanding neurodevelopmental disorders. Brain development generally occurs in a standard fashion, though there is heterogeneity and remarkable sex differences in developmental trajectories. Neurodevelopment begins in utero; brain tissue and structures become well differentiated during fetal development. However, much of the maturational process occurs after birth, with increases in brain volume and maturation of neural tissue continuing into the third decade of life. The brain reaches roughly 80% of its adult weight by age 2 (Kretschmann, Kammradt, Krauthausen, Sauer, & Wingert, 1986) but does not reach its peak weight until about age 22 (Dekaban, 1978) (see Figure 2.2). Notably, while maturation is essentially complete by the early to mid-20s for both men and women, women tend to mature at a much more rapid rate (Caviness, Kennedy, Richelme, Rademacher, & Filipek, 1996). In addition, there are sex differences in the volumetric growth of certain brain regions. For example, hippocampal formation volume increases with age for females and amygdala volume increases with age for males (Giedd, Vaituzis, et al., 1996). These regional sex differences in development of subcortical structures are likely influenced by the sex hormones, as the amygdala contains a predominance of androgen receptors (Clark, MacLusky, & Goldman-Rakic, 1988; Sholl & Kim, 1989) while the hippocampus has a predominance of estrogen receptors (Morse, Scheff, & DeKosky, 1986).

As described previously, myelination and synaptogenesis serve as markers of brain development. Volumetric measurement of white matter (i.e., myelinated axons) and gray matter (i.e., unmyelinated axons and neural tissue) via neuroimaging procedures has promoted an understanding of

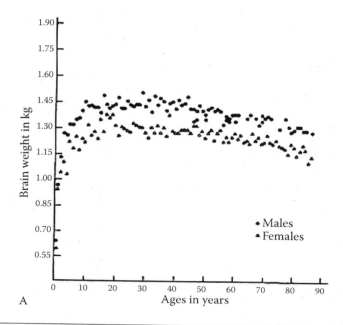

Figure 2.2 Brain weight (in kilograms) in relation to age based on about 10,000 autopsy reports. (From Dekaban, 1978, Figure 1. With permission)

how these processes contribute to changes in brain morphology and promote overall cognitive development. These MRI-based studies paved the way for creating three-dimensional models of neuroanatomy that allow us to visualize cortical and subcortical structures and to track changes in cerebral structure over time. Time-lapse sequences of normal brain development provide a powerful visual aid for understanding this process. There are now several online resources that provide access to these images. For example, the Proceedings of the National Academy of Sciences Web site (www.pnas.org) contains short videos of the process of brain development through adolescence (see Figure 2.3).

During fetal development, neuronal growth occurs uninhibited such that the number of synapses rises in exponential form, peaking at approximately age 2 or 3 (Matsuzawa et al., 2001) (see Figure 2.4). This peak level of synaptic density in children ranges from 50 to 100% greater than adult levels, depending upon the brain region (Jernigan & Tallal, 1990). While gray-matter volume increases early in childhood, it begins to decline as early as age 5 and then drops off precipitously around the time of puberty (Gogtay et al., 2004). The findings from structural and functional MRI investigations in pediatric populations reveal that gains in cognitive

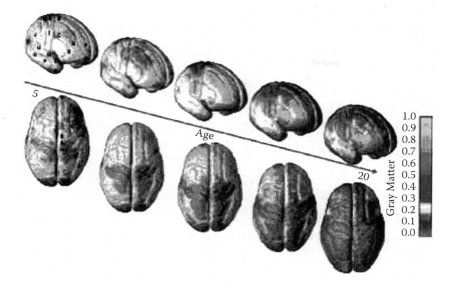

Figure 2.3 Constructed from MRI scans of healthy children and teens, the time-lapse "movie," from which the above images were extracted, compresses 15 years of brain development (ages 5 to 20) into just a few seconds. Gray matter wanes in a back-to-front wave as the brain matures and neural connections are pruned. Areas performing more basic functions mature earlier; areas for higher order functions mature later. (From Gogtay et al., 2004. With permission.)

capacity during childhood emerge in association with this gradual loss of gray matter (i.e., synaptogenesis) rather than the formation of new synapses (for review, see Casey, Giedd, & Thomas, 2000). Concurrently, myelination of neural tissue continues to occur through young adulthood (Jernigan, Trauner, Hesselink, & Tallal, 1991; Pfefferbaum et al., 1994; Caviness et al., 1996; Reiss, Abrams, Singer, Ross, & Denckla, 1996).

In one of the few available longitudinal studies of brain development during childhood and adolescence, Gogtay and colleagues (2004) obtained pre- and postpubertal structural brain images of 13 children over a 10-year period. Consistent with previously conducted cross-sectional imaging studies and earlier postmortem investigations, these investigators demonstrated that individual subregions of the human brain follow temporally distinct maturational patterns. Specifically, phylogenetically older areas of cortex (e.g., sensorimotor regions) develop first, followed by higher order association areas. These findings are consistent with prior findings showing regional patterns of maturation. Specifically, gray-matter dense subcortical regions (e.g., basal ganglia) decrease in volume during early childhood, particularly in males (Giedd, Snell, et al., 1996; Reiss et al.,

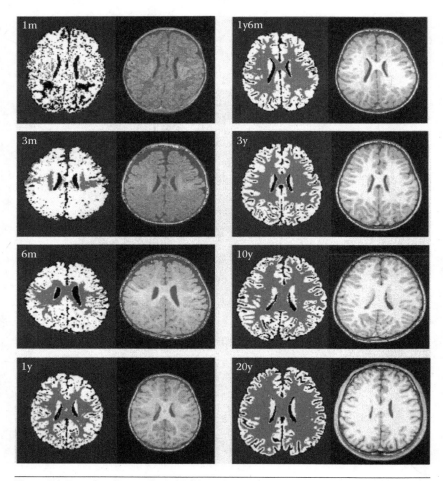

Figure 2.4 Examples of segmentation (left) and each original image (right). The segmented image shows gray matter (GM) in white, white matter (WM) in gray, and cerebrospinal fluid (CSF) in black. Note that WM starts in the sensorimotor area and expands throughout development but does not reach frontal regions until adulthood. (From Matsuzawa et al., 2001, Figure 1. With permission.)

1996) while cortical gray matter in the frontal and parietal cortices does not decrease until around the time of puberty (Giedd et al., 1999). White-matter volume changes also occur in regionally and temporally distinct patterns. The first area to become myelinated is the dorsal prefrontal cortex. Myelination of more ventral prefrontal regions (i.e., orbitofrontal cortex) occurs later and continues well into young adulthood (Matsuzawa et al., 2001; Reiss et al., 1996). In sum, myelogenesis and synaptogenesis take place concurrently, with myelination continuing from prenatal stages

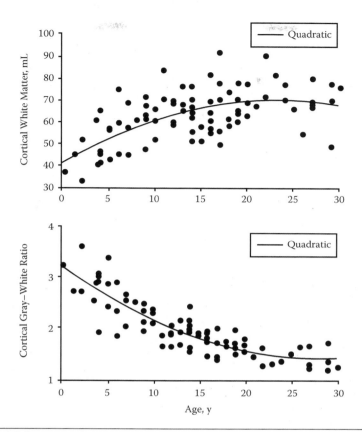

Figure 2.5 Association of age with the cortical white-matter volume (top panel) and with relative gray- to white-matter volume (bottom panel), showing that myelination and pruning are incomplete before the age of about 21. (From Pfefferbaum et al., 1994, Figure 3. With permission.)

through young adulthood, and synaptic pruning beginning around the time of middle childhood and completing by late adolescence (i.e., approximately age 18 to 20) (see Figure 2.5).

Findings from structural and functional imaging as well as early post-mortem studies are consistent with behavioral data on cognitive development. Clearly, brain development promotes emergence and refinement of cognitive abilities. The prefrontal sensorimotor cortex develops first, facilitating basic sensory (e.g., touch) and motor abilities. Maturation continues in the prefrontal and into the temporoparietal cortical regions, facilitating visual, auditory, and emotional cognitive processes. The brain areas that are latest to mature (e.g., association cortex and orbitofrontal regions) are associated with more complex cognitive abilities including language comprehension and expression, abstraction and reasoning, aspects of attention and memory, problem solving, planning, and impulse control. In the next section, we describe sex differences in brain development and how these are thought to relate to differential rates of learning disabilities in men and women.

Sex Differences in Neurodevelopment and Implications for Cognition

Review of the immense literature on sex differences in cognitive abilities points toward a male advantage for spatial relations, mathematical tasks, and gross motor functioning of approximately 1 standard deviation (Loring-Meier & Halpern, 1999; for reviews, see Masters & Sanders, 1993) and a female advantage for verbal fluency, basic language functions, and certain memory tasks of approximately ½ to 1 standard deviation (Halpern, 1992, 1997; Loring-Meier & Halpern, 1999; for reviews, see also Hines, 1990; Maccoby & Jacklin, 1974). The male advantage for spatial relations is evident as early as 3 months of age. For mathematical tasks, the advantage emerges as early as first grade but depends on age and complexity of the task (Geary, Saults, Liu, & Hoard, 2000). Specifically, the margin of the male advantage widens as the nature of mathematical tasks changes from basic computation to more visuospatial functions (e.g., geometry, calculus; Halpern & Tan, 2001). With regard to female-specific cognitive abilities, language develops earlier in females and this verbal advantage appears to remain throughout the life span (Halpern, 1992; Maccoby & Jacklin, 1974). Females obtain higher scores on tests of reading, writing, spelling, and literature (Hedges & Nowell, 1995; Stein, 1994; see Stanley, 1993). They also tend to perform better on essay-style examinations as compared to boys (Bridgeman & Moran, 1996; Halpern, Haviland, & Killian, 1998), presumably because of their more fully developed verbal expression and language comprehension abilities.

While males and females differ in their capacity for specific cognitive functions, debate continues as to whether there are identifiable sex differences in overall intelligence (IQ). The overwhelming evidence suggests that there is not a substantial difference in overall IQ between boys and girls (Court, 1983; Jensen, 1998; Mackintosh, 1996; Spearman, 1923; Terman, 1916). However, there does appear to be a small male advantage (i.e., approximately 4 points) on general intelligence tests, particularly at later ages (Lynn, 1992, 1994). Thus, it appears that this advantage is temporally tied to developmental factors (Colom & Lynn, 2004). Of course, an IQ score is a "fruit salad" that mixes in different specific abilities and the answer to the question of whether men and women will differ depends almost entirely on the choice of measures to be included in an IQ score.

Functional differences in cognitive abilities between the sexes have clear neurobiological underpinnings. Sex-typical differentiation of brain structures and neurophysiology has direct implications for understanding these differences in behavior. The size of certain brain structures is correlated with improved performance on tasks mediated by those structures. Predictably, different organization and localization of brain areas in men and women is also associated with sex-typical differences in cognitive proficiencies. Cognitive ability emerges in direct relationship to the degree of cerebral development. Thus, sex differences in the rate of neural maturation may help explain why boys are differentially diagnosed with learning disabilities (e.g., reading disability) at an earlier age than girls. Levels of circulating sex steroid hormones, namely estrogen and testosterone, are also clearly linked to cognitive abilities across the life span. Given this, the relationship between sex differences in brain development and resulting cognitive capacity may be best understood by examining: (a) differences in the organizing and activating effects of sex hormones during prenatal and postnatal development, (b) variability in rates of brain maturation, and (c) sexual dimorphism of the cerebral cortex.

Knowledge of sexual differentiation of brain structure, function, and neurophysiology may provide understanding as to why males and females differ with regard to particular cognitive abilities as well as why males manifest a higher prevalence of learning disabilities than females. The four major factors most often cited as causes of learning disabilities include: (a) structural brain abnormalities or damage, (b) abnormal cerebral lateralization, (c) maturational lag, and (d) environmental deprivation (Kolb & Whishaw, 1996). Of these, the first three are neurobiologically based; all three of these are confounded by sex-typical patterns of development, which are described below.

Androgen Influences on Brain Development and Function

The sex steroid hormones, testosterone and estrogen, exert profound influences on neurodevelopment and behavior beginning in the early stages of prenatal development and continuing throughout the life span. Animal and human studies confirm that the hormonal milieu of the perinatal environment directs sex-typical differentiation of brain structures that facilitate particular cognitive functions. Gonadal hormones are also associated with sex differences in lateralization of function in the central nervous system (Kimura, 1994), which has important implications for understanding sex differences in cognitive functioning. It has been proposed that differential expression of learning disabilities in males is tied to exposure to elevated testosterone levels during critical periods in brain development (Geschwind & Galaburda, 1985, 1987). Furthermore, the hormonal environment during fetal development permanently alters several neurotransmitter systems, resulting in higher overall levels of neuronal excitation in males but not females (McCarthy, Davis, & Mong, 1997). Surges in gonadal hormones during adolescence (i.e., puberty) activate reproductive maturation and mating behaviors, and influence cognitive functioning (see review in Susman, 1997). Later, decreases in circulating estrogen and testosterone are also associated with changes in cognitive functioning, particularly around the time of menopause for women (see Sherwin, 1999). In sum, gonadal hormones exert "organizational" influences on neural structure and functioning during prenatal and early postnatal development that facilitates sex-typical cognitive capacities and "activational" effects that influence behavior and cognition throughout the life span.

Prenatal, Critical Periods of Development   Perinatal hormones direct neural development. The male hormone, testosterone, is released during the early stages of embryonic development (i.e., between the 8th and 24th weeks of gestation), resulting in "masculinization" of the brain (Naftolin et al., 1975). This perinatal testosterone surge imparts permanent organizational effects on brain structure and neurophysiology that persists beyond the duration of the elevated hormone levels (Overman, 2004). There is a large body of research showing that pre- and perinatal hormones influence development of cortical asymmetries in humans (Kimura, 1994). Fetuses (both male and female) exposed to high levels of testosterone during gestation often fail to develop the typical left-greater-than-right lateralization pattern seen in normal development (Geschwind & Galaburda, 1987). The timing of cortical maturation also differs by gender and may be partially mediated by hormones. Testosterone, in particular, appears to be associated with myelogenesis (Martini & Melcangi, 1991). Testosterone and the aromatization of estrogen to testosterone facilitate speedier development of the orbital prefrontal cortex in males compared to females (see review in Breedlove, 1994). On the other hand, adult females have substantially larger volumes of frontal orbital cortex relative to amygdala volume compared to males, which may relate to their better ability to modulate physical aggression and possibly to their lower incidence of ADHD (Gur, Gunning-Dixon, Bilker, & Gur, 2002) (see Figure 2.6). However, high levels of perinatal testosterone are associated with slower development of the left hemisphere of the brain relative to the right in males (Geschwind & Galaburda, 1987). With regard to hormonal influences on neurochemistry, testosterone in males leads to increased gamma-aminobutyric acid (GABA), glutamate, and changes in glial morphology particularly in the amygdala and hypothalamus (McCarthy et al., 1997). Given that GABA acts as an excitatory neurotransmitter during early development, it is possible that

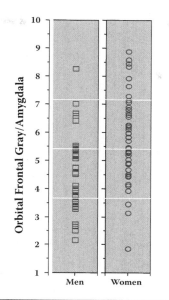

Figure 2.6 Scatterplots showing the distribution of the OARs (orbitofrontal to amygdala ratio) in men (squares) and women (circles). Dashed lines indicate cutoffs for the four equally spaced intervals from the smallest to the largest observed used in the Fisher exact test. Note how many more women have higher orbitofrontal volumes while men aggregate at the lower ratios. (From Gur et al., 2002b, Figure 3. With permission.)

enhanced GABA functioning in male brains may result in higher overall levels of neural excitation. It has been proposed that hyperactivity in boys may be a functional consequence of enhanced neural excitation in males (McCarthy et al., 1997).

Because we cannot manipulate the hormonal environment of developing human fetuses and newborns, much of what we know about hormonal influences on human brain development is derived from animal models of development and studies of neuroendocrine disorders in males and females. For example, male rats castrated at birth have female patterns of brain development in adulthood whereas females androgenized as neonates have male-like patterns as adults (Matsumoto & Arai, 1980, 1986; Nishizuka & Arai, 1981). Neuropsychological studies of children with congenital adrenal hyperplasia (CAH)—a condition characterized by overexposure to testosterone during prenatal development—also shed light on ways in which sex hormones during development influence cognitive abilities. Hines et al. (2003) compared the spatial abilities of 69 men and women with CAH and 59 healthy control individuals and found that females with CAH performed better than unaffected females and similarly to affected and unaffected males. Furthermore, a study of siblings with and without CAH found that CAH girls demonstrated a clear advantage on spatial tasks and tests of mechanical knowledge compared to their sisters. Interestingly, however, CAH boys demonstrated the reverse effect, namely a decrease in spatial abilities (Berenbaum, 2005). This suggests that either (1) the cognitive effects of androgens may be different on female than on male neurobiology or (2) the effect of hormones on behavior or cognition is quadratic in nature such that over or underexposure to the hormone results in deficits, while exposure to normal levels results in the typically observed cognitive advantage.

Gonadarche and Cognitive Development   Following the surge in testosterone immediately after birth, gonadal hormones remain relatively inert until gonadarche (i.e., puberty)—the period in development characterized by surges in sex steroid hormones. At the time of gonadarche, testosterone levels rise exponentially, resulting in a 26-fold increase in testosterone. Estrogen levels in females rise nearly 10-fold during puberty (see Ducharme & Forest, 1993). On average, puberty begins in early adolescence for girls and in middle adolescence for boys. This pubertal surge of hormones stimulates emergence of secondary sex characteristics and physical growth. Hormonal changes during puberty are also associated with further neural maturation. Although it is difficult to separate the effects of aging from pubertal influences on development because the two processes overlap, there is some evidence that gonadarche impacts both the rate and process of maturation independent of age. A structural MRI study performed by DeBellis and colleagues (2001) examined sex and age-related changes in neural development around the time of adolescence in a group of 118 boys and girls aged 6 to 17. They also investigated whether stage of puberty (Tanner staging) influenced development irrespective of age. Results showed robust age-related decreases in gray matter and increases in white-matter volume, as well as significant sex-by-stage interactions for cerebral GM and WM volumes, particularly in the corpus callosum of girls. This study was one of the first to demonstrate sex-by-age interactions in brain development, and provides support for the notion that hormones influence brain maturational processes.

Hormonal Influences on Cognition in Later Development   In women, natural fluctuations in reproductive hormones have been associated with changes in cognitive functioning. Menopause, the time in a woman's life span at which she has ceased having menstrual periods, is marked by a profound decrease in estradiol levels. Emergence of psychiatric and cognitive symptomatology is not uncommon at this time, suggesting that hormones regulate both mood and cognition at least to some degree. Well-designed studies have examined this question and the preponderance of evidence supports the hypothesis that estrogen maintains cognition, particularly language and memory functions, in women. We will not go into more detail about this here, other than to say that hormones clearly appear to have a lifelong impact on cognitive abilities in addition to the organizing and activating effects they produce during early development.

Rate of Development

Boys and girls mature at different rates both physically and neurodevelopmentally. Physical growth occurs at an equal pace until approximately age 9, at which time girls' growth accelerates and continues in advance of boys until around age 15. As boys reach puberty, the pattern reverses and the growth of girls decelerates relative to boys (Colom & Lynn, 2004). The pattern of neural maturation is more complicated, with marked interactions between age, sex, and rate of neural development. Girls appear to mature more rapidly than boys from birth through the age of 15. However, from the age of 16 onward, boys' growth accelerates and neural maturation continues somewhat longer into early adulthood for males than for females (Colom & Lynn, 2004; Gur, Gunning-Dixon, Turetsky, Bilker, & Gur, 2002). The dual process of myelogenesis and synaptic pruning occurs along different trajectories in males and females. Sex-related variability in the rate and density of myelination across brain regions may lend an understanding to how sex differences in the rate of neural maturation may influence expression and diagnosis of learning disabilities. As an index of maturation, myelination of neural tracts reflects proficiency in cognitive tasks. Recall that myelination of sensorimotor cortices occurs during infancy and early childhood, facilitating basic sensory (e.g., perception) and motor (e.g., manipulation of objects) abilities. Similarly, myelination of cortical language regions is associated with proficiency in verbal skills. Thus, it would seem that differential rates in myelination and synaptic pruning would directly influence the timing of emergence of certain cognitive abilities among boys and girls.

Cerebral gray-matter volume is greater in boys than girls in early childhood and reductions in gray-matter volume occur later in boys' development (DeBellis et al., 2001). In contrast, the process of myelination and synaptogenesis occurs earlier in girls, but the rate is slower. The result is that adult males have greater white matter and proportionately less gray matter than females (Gur et al., 1999; Gur, Gunning-Dixon, Turetsky, et al., 2002). These sex-by-age differences in GM versus WM distribution in adulthood are a direct result of differences in rates of myelination and synaptogenesis. DeBellis and colleagues (2001) demonstrated that the slope of changes in cerebral gray-matter and white-matter volume differs between males and females through childhood and adolescence. They observed a 19.1% reduction in GM among boys versus a 4.7% reduction in girls. In contrast, WM volume increased 45.1% in boys versus a 27.4% increase in girls.

Sex differences in the rate of brain maturation provide the foundation for several hypotheses as to why girls cognitively outperform boys, particularly early on in life. The maturational lag hypothesis suggests that delays in neural development among boys consequentially delays acquisition of complex skills such as language and attention, resulting in more frequent diagnosis of learning disabilities (e.g., disorders of reading and attention) among boys. Presumably, naturally occurring maturation processes, over time, produce a "catching up" phenomenon such that the LD is less apparent in adulthood because the brain regions responsible for the identified learning deficit have since fully developed. As such, maturational lag theories necessarily imply that sociocultural factors (i.e., expectancies regarding cognitive abilities in early childhood) also contribute to differential diagnosis of LD between boys and girls. For example, an individual would not be diagnosed with a reading disability in the second grade if we didn't expect him or her to have fully developed the necessary brain regions and cognitive abilities necessary for reading.

Maturational theories, while plausible, are not entirely supported by the available empirical evidence. For example, if delayed maturation "caused" dyslexia, one would expect that children diagnosed with dyslexia early in life would have a different symptom profile or would be entirely symptom-free in adulthood. This is clearly not the case. The symptoms of adult dyslexia are identical to symptoms observed in childhood dyslexia; additionally, diagnosis of dyslexia in late adolescence or early adulthood is not uncommon. Similarly, maturational lag theory fails to provide an adequate explanation for attention-deficit/hyperactivity disorder (ADHD). Although ADHD is characterized as a neurodevelopmental disorder that occurs at significantly higher rates in boys, 58 to 70% of children demonstrate persistent symptoms of ADHD through adulthood, and the underlying neuropathology remains constant from childhood into adulthood (McGough & Barkley, 2004).

Despite this, some remain strong proponents of maturational lag theory. For example, Lynn and colleagues propose that the small but consistent male advantage on IQ tests may be explained by maturational factors. These investigators argue that the male advantage on IQ tests emerges in parallel with accelerated physical and neural maturation among male adolescents, while the female advantage on IQ tests disappears as their rate of maturation slows (Colom & Lynn, 2004; Lynn, 1992; Lynn, 1994). This could support the theory that sex differences in the rate of brain maturation may explain sex-specific cognitive abilities. While it is likely that differential rates of maturation between the sexes may influence the timing of emergence of particular cognitive capacities, other factors such as sex differences in cerebral lateralization and environmental conditions may also contribute to diagnosis of learning disabilities in men and women.

Sexual Dimorphism of Cerebral Structure and Function

Volumetric Differences in Cortical and Subcortical Structures

Men's brains are approximately 8 to 12% larger than women's brains (DeBellis et al., 2001; Filipek, Richelme, Kennedy, & Caviness, 1994; Gur et al., 1999; Gur, Gunning-Dixon, Turetsky, et al., 2002a; Nopoulos, Flaum, O'Leary, & Andreasen, 2000; Passe et al., 1997; Rabinowicz, Dean, Petetot, & de Courten-Myers, 1999; Witelson, Glezer, & Kigar, 1995). The fact that women's brains are smaller than men's, though there is no significant difference in overall intellectual abilities, suggests the men's and women's brains work differently to process the same information and to produce the same behavior. Alternatively, regionally specific sex differences in the size of cortical and subcortical structures, relative to the size of the cerebrum (Goldstein et al., 2001), may also partially explain sex-typical cognitive proficiencies. The most consistent and robust findings from data obtained via imaging procedures are that women have: larger volumes of brain regions associated with language (Harasty, Double, Halliday, Kril, & McRitchie, 1997); larger hippocampi (Filipek et al., 1994; Giedd, Vaituzis, et al. 1996; Murphy et al., 1996); larger volume of caudate (Filipek et al., 1994; Murphy et al. 1996); larger volume of dorsolateral prefrontal cortex (Schlaepfer et al., 1995); and larger posterior corpus callosum (deLacoste-Utamsing & Holloway, 1982; Witelson, 1989). Men, on the other hand, typically have larger volumes relative to cerebrum size in limbic and paralimbic regions (Giedd, Vaituzis, et al., 1996; Goldstein et al., 2001), the hypothalamus (Swaab & Fliers, 1985; Allen, Hines, Shryne, & Gorski, 1989; Zhou, Hofman, Gooren, & Swaab, 1995), and perhaps the genu of the corpus callosum (Witelson, 1989).

These regionally specific sex differences in the size of brain regions appear to be directly related to sex-specific cognitive proficiencies. For example, the fact that women have larger areas of the brain associated with language functions may explain the female verbal advantage. In addition, larger callosal volume and increased callosal white-matter density in females may help to explain why problems with reading are less apparent in girls than boys. Women rely on a more diffusely distributed, and presumably more comprehensive network, of cerebral language processing compared to boys, whose language processing occurs primarily in left anterior brain regions (Shaywitz, Shaywitz, Pugh, Constable, & Skudlarski, 1995). However, results of studies attempting to link the size of brain structures to cognitive performance are equivocal (Hines, Chiu, McAdams, Bentler, & Lipcamon, 1992; Clarke & Zaidel, 1994). Thus, interpretation of differences in the size of brain structures must also take into account potential differences in cytoarchitecture or relative volume of difference given the known differences in the weight and volume of male and female brains. Initial studies investigating the relationship between brain size, sex, and volume of cortical and subcortical tissue found that brain-size sex differences are primarily attributable to white-matter volume, associated with better spatial performance (as discussed in Gur et al., 1999).

Distribution of Gray and White Matter

The most recent research shows that males have proportionately less gray matter and more white matter than do females (Passe et al., 1997; Gur et al., 1999), although the distribution of GM and WM varies during development as described previously. In a sample of 80 healthy men and women aged 18–45, our lab demonstrated that men have a higher overall percentage of cerebral WM, whereas women have higher percentages of GM (Gur et al., 1999). These differences were evident independent of overall cranial volume. Furthermore, in men, the percentage of GM in the left hemisphere was higher, whereas WM was distributed symmetrically. In contrast, women showed no hemispheric asymmetries in GM or WM. Rather, women appear to have a greater concentration of WM in the corpus callosum (Allen & Gorski, 1991; Highley et al., 1999; Nopoulos et al., 2000; Witelson, 1989), providing further evidence that females tend to have greater bilateral distribution of abilities across both cerebral hemispheres.

White-matter density represents the degree to which axons are myelinated and thus provides a secondary marker of how quickly neural impulses can travel. Nerve conduction velocity (NCV), the speed at which nerve impulses travel along neural pathways, has been extensively evaluated in human peripheral nerves (Reed, Vernon, & Johnson, 2004), with males demonstrating quicker impulse transmission along motor tracts. Only recently have investigators attempted to investigate NCV in the central nervous system. The first group to study NCV in the brain examined a group of 185 male and 200 female undergraduates and found reliable sex differences for NCV in the visual nerve pathway. Specifically, they found that visual nerve NCV is approximately 4% faster in males than females, despite overall greater head size (Reed et al., 2004). They also found that despite their greater physical size, male students had quicker reaction times across several different tasks than the female students (Reed et al., 2004). Further, they found that while male NCV increased with age, females showed no such increase and, in fact, showed a trend toward decreased NCV with age. This finding bolsters previous findings that brain maturation, and specifically myelination, continues in men later in life as compared to women, whose brains tend to lose white matter with age at faster rates. While this is only preliminary data, and whether or not NCV differs among men and women in other CNS pathways remains untested, it suggests that the advantage that men demonstrate in terms of visual acuity, greater reaction time to visual stimuli, and better eye-hand coordination may be explained in part by higher NCV in the visual nerve pathway. Furthermore, it may be that this faster NCV is directly related to the fact that male brains are more highly myelinated, thus giving rise to a biological advantage in NCV and performance on tasks reliant on speed of processing and reaction time.

Sexually Distinct Cerebral Lateralization of Structure and Function

Hemispheric asymmetry, or lateralization, is the degree to which each side of the brain is dominant for particular cognitive processes. The left cerebral hemisphere is primarily involved in language functioning; the right hemisphere is more involved in spatial processing (for review, see Springer & Deutsch, 1998). The typical pattern of human brain development results in left-hemisphere dominant lateralization of language function. However, the extent to which cognitive functions are lateralized depends on multiple factors (e.g., hormones) that regulate the rate and organization of neural growth during critical periods in development (Forget & Cohen, 1994). Observed sex-specific cognitive capacities (e.g., verbal, spatial, and mathematical skills) have traditionally been attributed to variations in hemispheric specialization of cognitive functions (Maccoby & Jacklin, 1974; Hiscock, Israelian, Inch, Jacek, & Hiscock-Kalil, 1995). Males exposed to high levels of testosterone during critical periods in development tend to demonstrate less asymmetry in hemispheric specialization and tend to show more lateralized functioning, with a greater proportion of right-hemisphere dominance (Geschwind & Galaburda, 1987). Conversely, females demonstrate more bilateral patterns of hemispheric processing (Hiscock et al., 1995). One study investigating sex differences in lateralized activation of the prefrontal cortex (PFC) and amygdala when viewing fearful faces found different patterns of lateralized cortical and subcortical brain activity in males and females. In males, activation within the dorsolateral PFC was bilateral in children, right lateralized in adolescents, and bilateral in adults. In contrast, women showed greater bilateral activation with age. There were no sex differences with regard to amygdala activation, but the same pattern occurred across genders—bilateral activation in children, right lateralized activation in adolescents, and then bilateral activation in adults (Kilgore & Yurgelun-Todd, 2004).

Sinistrality, or handedness, serves as a marker for brain organization and is thought to represent an individual's degree of lateral dominance (Levy & Reid, 1978). The central nervous system is organized such that each hemisphere of the brain controls the contralateral side of the body. Thus, right-handed persons typically have left-hemisphere language dominance, whereas only a small majority of left-handed persons have left-hemisphere language dominance. Several investigators have hypothesized that handedness, an indicator of brain organization, will correlate with the tests of cognitive abilities that typically show sex differences (as discussed in Bryden, McManus, & Bulman-Felming, 1994). However, there are significant sex-by-handedness interactions for particular cognitive functions. Halpern and colleagues (1998) evaluated the results of Medical College Admission Test scores by sex and handedness in over 174,000 individuals, finding that males and left-handers performed significantly better on the Sciences (Biological and Physical) portion of the test, while females and right-handers performed best on the Writing Sample portion of the test. These results support the notion that right-brain dominance, more frequently observed in males, is associated with better performance on mathematical and science-based tasks, whereas left-brain dominance is more frequently associated with better verbal abilities. Indeed, there are more males and more left-handers (especially left-handed males) among individuals with several types of mental retardation and with delayed and poor verbal abilities, including severe reading disabilities (Batheja & McManus, 1985; Pipe, 1990). Geschwind and Galaburda (1987) proposed a theory of learning disabilities based on the phenomenon that left-handed males with immune disorders seem to represent a disproportionate number of individuals with reading disabilities. Their theory is based on findings that males show greater deviance from the typical left-greater-than-right pattern of cerebral lateralization and that this appears to be mediated by the male hormone testosterone during prenatal development and postnatal maturation. While this theory is attractive because it provides a multifactorial (e.g., sinistral, hormonal, developmental) explanation of learning disabilities, it has been difficult to validate due to its sheer complexity (McManus & Bryden, 1991).

Specific Learning Disabilities and Their Relationship to Sex Differences in Neurodevelopment

Sex-typical patterns of normal and abnormal neurodevelopment appear to mediate cognitive capacity as well as the expression and subsequent diagnosis of learning disability. In particular, the cognitive deficits characteristic of dyslexia or reading disability may be mediated by sexually dimorphic neurodevelopment. The neurobiological bases of specific learning disability symptom complexes will be explored in later chapters (see section 2, Neurobiology and Specific Learning Disorders). However, the influence of sexual differentiation in brain development on manifest dyslexia is presented in brief below as an exemplar for understanding the impact of sexually dimorphic development.

Sex Differences in Development and Dyslexia

There is speculation that anomalies of asymmetry may be related to disruption in brain development and contribute to language-processing disorders. Anomalies in the organization of language centers in the brain during neurodevelopment are more prevalent among males than females (see Shultz et al., 1994). As such, it has been proposed that the reason for the exponential prevalence of language and reading disorders among males compared to females is somehow related to these differences in brain organization and impaired cerebral functioning. Congruency between structural abnormalities and functional impairment in male dyslexics may explain the higher proportion of males diagnosed with the disorder. However, it is important to recognize that boys are more often diagnosed with a number of neurodevelopmental and psychiatric disorders (Gualtieri & Hicks, 1985), presumably because the manifest symptoms of the disorder are more disruptive and generate greater attention to the problem. This may result in referral bias and, ultimately, a greater provision of diagnoses to boys.

Lambe (1999) provides a comprehensive review of the research on gender differences in brain development, functional organization, and activation, and parallels those to the functional impairments observed in boys and girls with dyslexia. The evidence supporting the hypothesis that sex differences in neuroanatomy and processing contribute to the phenomenon of a higher proportion of male dyslexics comes from postmortem studies of dyslexia in humans, in vivo structural and functional radiologic investigations of the brains of dyslexics, and from animal models of dyslexia and brain injury. The evidence to date suggests that dyslexia is causally related to abnormalities in brain development such as ectopias and cortical scars, particularly in the left, language-dominant areas of the brain. Male dyslexics demonstrate a higher number of these microscopic abnormalities compared to female dyslexics (Humphreys, Kaufmann, & Galaburda, 1990), male controls (Humphreys et al., 1990), and male and female controls (Galaburda & Kemper, 1979; Galaburda, Sherman, Rosen, Aboitiz, & Geschwind, 1985; Kaufmann & Galaburda, 1989). Animal models of dyslexia are concordant with results of postmortem studies and further support the notion of a sex-specific proclivity toward neuro-developmentally mediated dyslexia in males. For example, lesions in the medial geniculate nucleus of the thalamus lead to acoustic processing deficits in lesioned male rats but not in lesioned females (Fitch, Tallal, Brown, Galaburda, & Rosen, 1994; Fitch, Brown, Tallal, & Rosen, 1997; Herman, Galaburda, Fitch, Carter, & Rosen, 1997). More recently, brain-imaging studies provide evidence of sex differences in localization of function and differences in patterns of brain activation. Specifically, women showed greater bilateral activation of language areas of the brain as compared to men (Pugh et al., 1996; Shaywitz et al., 1995). Indeed, the expected left-greater-than-right pattern of asymmetry in the language areas of the cortex is often lacking in persons with dyslexia. This is particularly true in male dyslexics. As the left hemisphere is also specialized for distinguishing between sounds and sensory experience, left-hemisphere impairment or underdevelopment will impair language discrimination abilities (Tallal, Miller, & Fitch, 1993).

Summary and Future Directions

Sexually dimorphic development of the human brain contributes to development of sex-typical cognitive proficiencies, as well as the differential expression of learning disabilities in males and females. Mechanisms include the organizing and activating effects of hormones on pre- and postnatal development, sex differences in the rate of neural maturation, and male-female differences in size of cortical structures and lateralization of function. While sociocultural and other factors likely contribute to expressions of learning disabilities, the idea that sex differences in neurodevelopment may be related to diagnosis of learning disability has profound implications for educational policies and diagnostic procedures. Some school districts have already begun experimenting with single-sex classrooms at the elementary school level. In addition, some early childhood specialists advocate delayed entrance of boys into kindergarten in light of developmental differences between the sexes (Mulrine, 2001). Furthermore, psychoeducational evaluations performed in light of sex-by-age cognitive developmental interactions may result in more careful consideration of a diagnosis of learning disability.

Arguably the most exciting development in the area of understanding the neural basis of sex differences in neurodevelopment and developmental disabilities is the advance in genomics and the ability to link gene actions to behavioral endophenotypes. We are in the midst of a virtual transformation of the approach to behavioral research, where the links between traits and genetic variations can be tested and probed across human and animal species and placed in an evolutionary perspective. Future research on the topics discussed in this chapter will likely shift from the study of individual children and their diagnosed disorders to evaluation of whole families and the interaction between genetic predisposition and the environmental context. We will increasingly understand the action of specific genetic variants and how these variants are differentially shaped by stressors to result in clinically identifiable syndromes. Rigorous testing of specific hypotheses will be done through studies of genetically modified animal models, which can be more effectively examined through the life span. Sex differences will be more directly linkable to modulating effects of their chromosomal underpinnings, and we will better elucidate how sex hormones modulate neurodevelopment and its manifestation in healthy and dysfunctional behavior. Very likely, incorporation of ethologically based methods, which are increasingly influential in animal studies, will further enhance the depth of our understanding of the neurodevelopmental disorders and why they are so differently manifested in boys and girls.

References

Allen, L. S., & Gorski, R. A. (1991). Sexual dimorphism of the anterior commissure and massa intermedia of the human brain. *Journal of Comparative Neurology, 312*, 97.

Allen, L. S., Hines, M., Shryne, J. E., & Gorski, R. A. (1989). Two sexually dimorphic cell groups in the human brain. *Journal of Neuroscience, 9*, 497–506.

Arcia, E., & Conners, C. K. (1998). Gender differences in ADHD? *Journal of Developmental and Behavioral Pediatrics, 19*, 77–83.

Bailey, A., Palferman, S., Heavey, L., & LeCouteur, A. (1998). Autism: Phenotype in relatives. *Journal of Autism and Developmental Disorders, 28*, 369.

Batheja, M., & McManus, I. C. (1985). Handedness in the mentally handicapped. *Developmental Medicine and Child Neurology, 27*, 63–68.

Berenbaum, S. A. (2005, February). *Prenatal androgen effects on social and cognitive development.* Paper presented at the 33rd annual meeting of the International Neuropsychological Society. St. Louis, MO.

Breedlove, S. M. (1994). Sexual differentiation of the human nervous system. *Annual Review of Psychology, 45*, 389–418.

Bridgeman, B., & Moran, R. (1996). Success in college for students with discrepancies between performance on multiple-choice and essay tests. *Journal of Educational Psychology, 88*, 333–340.

Bryden, M. P., McManus, I. C., & Bulman-Felming, B. (1994). Evaluating the empirical support for the Geschwind-Behan-Galaburda model of cerebral lateralization. *Brain and Cognition, 26*, 103–167.

Casey, B. J., Giedd, J. N., & Thomas, K. M. (2000). Structural and functional brain development and its relation to cognitive development. *Biological Psychology, 54*, 241–257.

Caviness, V. S., Jr., Kennedy, D. N., Richelme, C., Rademacher, J., & Filipek, P. A. (1996). The human brain age 7–11 years: A volumetric analysis based on magnetic resonance images. *Cerebral Cortex, 6,* 726–736.

Clark, A. S., MacLusky, N. J., & Goldman-Rakic, P. S. (1988). Androgen binding and metabolism in the cerebral cortex of the developing rhesus monkey. *Endocrinology, 123,* 932–940.

Clarke, J. M., & Zaidel, E. (1994). Anatomical-behavioral relationships: Corpus callosum morphometry and hemispheric specialization. *Behavioral Brain Research, 64,* 185–202.

Colom, R., & Lynn, R. (2004). Testing the developmental theory of sex differences in intelligence on 12–18 year olds. *Personality and Individual Differences, 36,* 75–82.

Court, J. H. (1983). Sex differences in performance on Raven's Progressive Matrices: A review. *Alberta Journal of Educational Research, 29,* 54–74.

DeBellis, M. D., Keshavan, M. S., Beers, S. R., Hall, J., Frustaci, K., Masalehdan, A., et al. (2001). Sex differences in brain maturation during childhood and adolescence. *Cerebral Cortex, 11,* 552–557.

Dekaban, A. (1978). Changes in brain weights during the span of human life: Relation of brain weights to body heights and body weights. *Annals of Neurology, 4,* 345–356.

deLacoste-Utamsing, C., & Holloway, R. L. (1982). Sexual dimorphism in the human corpus callosum. *Science, 216,* 1431–1432.

Ducharme, J. R., & Forest, M. G. (1993). Normal pubertal development. In J. Bertrand, R. Rappaport, & P. C. Sizonenko (Eds.), *Pediatric endocrinology: Physiology, pathophysiology, and clinical aspects* (2nd ed., pp. 372–386). Baltimore, MD: Williams & Wilkins.

Filipek, P. A., Richelme, C., Kennedy, D. N., & Caviness, V. S., Jr. (1994). The young adult human brain: An MRI-based morphometric analysis. *Cerebral Cortex, 4,* 344–360.

Finnuci, J. M., & Childs, B. (1981). Are there really more dyslexic boys than girls? In A. Ansara, N. Geschwind, A. M. Galaburda, and N. Gartrell (Eds.), *Sex differences in dyslexia* (pp. 1–9). Towson, MD: Orton Dyslexia Society.

Finnuci, J. M., Isaacs, S. D., Whitehouse, C. C., & Childs, B. (1983). Classification of spelling errors and their relationship to reading ability, sex, grade placement and intelligence. *Brain and Language, 20,* 340–355.

Fitch, R. H., Brown, C. P., Tallal, P., & Rosen, G. D. (1997). Effects of sex and MK-801 on auditory processing deficits associated with developmental microgyric lesions in rats. *Behavioral Neuroscience, 111,* 404–412.

Fitch, R. H., Tallal, P., Brown, C. P., Galaburda, A. M., & Rosen, G. D. (1994). Induced cicrogyria and auditory temporal processing in rats: A model for language impairment? *Cerebral Cortex, 4,* 261–270.

Forget, H., & Cohen, H. (1994). Life after birth: The influence of steroid hormones on cerebral structure and function is not fixed prenatally. *Brain and Cognition, 26,* 243–248.

Galaburda, A., & Kemper, T. (1979). Cytoarchitectonic abnormalities in developmental dyslexia: A case study. *Annals of Neurology, 6,* 94–100.

Galaburda, A., Sherman, G., Rosen, G., Aboitiz, F., & Geschwind, N. (1985). Developmental dyslexia: Four consecutive patients with cortical anomalies. *Annals of Neurology, 18,* 222–233.

Gaub, M., & Carlson, C. L. (1997). Gender differences in ADHD: A meta-analysis and critical review. *Journal of the American Academy of Child and Adolescent Psychiatry, 36*, 1036–1045.

Geary, D. C., Saults, S. J., Liu, F., & Hoard, M. K. (2000). Sex differences in spatial cognition, computational fluency, and arithmetical reasoning. *Journal of Experimental Child Psychology, 77*, 337–353.

Geschwind, N., & Galaburda, A. M. (1985). Cerebral lateralization. Biological mechanisms, associations and pathology: I. A hypothesis and a program for research. *Archives of Neurology, 42*, 428–459.

Geschwind, N., & Galaburda, A. M. (1987). *Cerebral lateralization: Biological mechanisms, associations and pathology.* Cambridge: MIT Press.

Giedd, J. N., Blumenthal, J., Jeffries, N. O., Castellanos, F. X., Liu, H., Zijdenbos, A., et al. (1999). Brain development during childhood and adolescence: A longitudinal MRI study. *Nature Neuroscience, 2*, 861–863.

Giedd, J. N., Snell, J. W., Lange, N., Rajapakse, J. C., Casey, B. J., Kozuch, P. L., et al. (1996). Quantitative magnetic resonance imaging of human brain development: Ages 4–18. *Cerebral Cortex, 6*, 551–560.

Giedd, J. N., Vaituzis, A. C., Hamburger, S. D., Lange, N., Rajapakse, J. C., Kaysen, D., et al. (1996). Quantitative MRI of the temporal lobe, amygdala and hippocampus in normal human development: ages 4–18 years. *Journal of Comparative Neurology, 366*, 223–230.

Gogtay, N., Giedd, J. N., Lusk, L., Hayashi, K. M., Greenstein, D., Vaituzis, A. C., et al. (2004). Dynamic mapping of human cortical development during childhood through early adulthood. *Proceedings of the National Academy of Sciences, 101*, 8174–8179.

Goldstein, J. M., Seidman, L. J., Horton, N. J., Makris, N., Kennedy, D. N., Caviness, V. S., Jr., et al. (2001). Normal sexual dimorphism of the adult human brain assessed by in vivo magnetic resonance imaging. *Cerebral Cortex, 11*, 490–497.

Gualtieri, T., & Hicks, H. E. (1985). An immunoreactive theory of selective male affliction. *The Behavioral and Brain Sciences, 8*, 427–41.

Gur R. C., Gunning-Dixon, F., Bilker, W. B., & Gur, R. E. (2002). Sex differences in temporo-limbic and frontal brain volumes of healthy adults. *Cerebral Cortex, 12*, 998–1003.

Gur, R. C., Gunning-Dixon, F. M., Turetsky, B. I., Bilker, W. B., & Gur, R. E. (2002). Brain region and sex differences in age associated with brain volume: A quantitative MRI study of healthy young adults. *American Journal of Geriatric Psychiatry, 10*, 72–80.

Gur, R. C., Turetsky, B. I., Matsui, M., Yan, M., Bilker, W., Hughett, P., et al. (1999). Sex differences in brain gray and white matter in healthy young adults. *Journal of Neuroscience, 19*, 4065–4072.

Halpern, D. F. (1992). *Sex differences in cognitive abilities* (2nd ed.). Hillsdale, NJ: Lawrence Erlbaum.

Halpern, D. F. (1997). Sex differences in intelligence: Implications for education. *American Psychologist, 52*, 1091–1102.

Halpern, D. F., Haviland, M. G., & Killian, C. D. (1998). Handedness and sex differences in intelligence: Evidence from the Medical College Admission Test. *Brain and Cognition, 38*, 87–101.

Halpern, D. F., & Tan, U. (2001). Stereotypes and steroids: Using a psychobiological model to understand cognitive sex differences. *Brain and Cognition*, *45*, 392–414.

Harasty, J., Double, K. L., Halliday, G. M., Kril, J. J., & McRitchie, D. A. (1997). Language-associated cortical regions are proportionally large in the female brain. *Archives of Neurology*, *54*, 171–176.

Hedges, L. V., & Nowell, A. (1995). Sex differences in mental test scores, variability and numbers of high-scoring individuals. *Science*, *269*, 41–45.

Herman, A. E., Galaburda, A. M., Fitch, R. H., Carter, A. R., & Rosen, G. D. (1997). Cerebral microgyria, thalamic cell size and auditory processing in male and female rats. *Cerebral Cortex*, *7*, 453–464.

Highley, J. R., Esiri, M. M., McDonald, B., Roberts, H. C., Walker, M. A., & Crow, T. J. (1999). The size and fiber composition of the anterior commissure with respect to gender and schizophrenia. *Biological Psychiatry*, *45*, 1120–1127.

Hines, M. (1990). Gonadal hormones and human cognitive development. In J. Balthazart (Ed.), *Brain and behavior in vertebrates 1: Sexual differentiation, neuroanatomical aspects, neurotransmitters and neuropeptides* (pp. 51–63). Basel, Switzerland: Karger.

Hines, M., Chiu, L., McAdams, L. A., Bentler, P. M., & Lipcamon, J. (1992). Cognition and the corpus callosum: Verbal fluency, visuospatial ability and language lateralization related to midsagittal surface areas of callosal subregions. *Behavioral Neuroscience*, *106*, 3–14.

Hines, M., Fane, B. A., Pasterski, V. L., Mathews, G. A., Conway, G. S., & Brook, C. (2003). Spatial abilities following prenatal androgen abnormality: Targeting and mental rotations performance in individuals with congenital adrenal hyperplasia. *Psychoneuroendocrinology*, *28*, 1010–1026.

Hiscock, M., Israelian, M., Inch, R., Jacek, C., & Hiscock-Kalil, C. (1995). Is there a sex difference in human laterality? II. An exhaustive survey of visual laterality studies from six neuropsychology journals. *Journal of Clinical and Experimental Neuropsychology*, *17*, 590–610.

Humphreys, P., Kaufmann, W. E., & Galaburda, A. M. (1990). Developmental dyslexia in women: Neuropathological findings in three patients. *Annals of Neurology*, *28*, 727–738.

Huttenlocher, P. R. (1979). Synaptic density in human frontal cortex: Developmental changes and effects of aging. *Brain Research*, *163*, 195–205.

Huttenlocher, P. R., de Courten, C., Garey, L. J., & van der Loos, H. (1982). Synaptogenesis in human visual cortex: Evidence for synapse elimination during normal development. *Neuroscience Letters*, *33*, 247–252.

Jensen, A. R. (1998). *The G factor: The science of mental ability*. Westport, CT: Praeger.

Jernigan, T. L., & Tallal, P. (1990). Late childhood changes in brain morphology observable with MRI. *Developmental Medicine and Child Neurology*, *32*, 379–385.

Jernigan, T. L., Trauner, D. A., Hesselink, J. R., & Tallal, P. A. (1991). Maturation of human cerebrum observed *in vivo* during adolescence. *Brain*, *114*, 2057–2049.

Kaufmann, W., & Galaburda, A. (1989). Cerebrocortical microdysgenesis in neurologically normal subjects: A histopathologic study. *Neurology*, *39*, 238–244.

Kilgore, W. D., & Yurgelun-Todd, D. A. (2004). Sex-related developmental differences in the lateralized activation of the prefrontal cortex and amygdala during perception of facial affect. *Perceptual and Motor Skills, 99*, 371–91.

Kimura, D. (1994). Body asymmetry and intellectual pattern. *Personality and Individual Differences, 17*, 53–60.

Kolb, B., & Whishaw, I. Q. (1996). *Fundamentals of human neuropsychology* (4th ed.). New York: W. H. Freeman.

Kretschmann, H. J., Kammradt, G., Krauthausen, I., Sauer, B., & Wingert, F. (1986). Brain growth in man. *Bibliotheca Anatomica, 28*, 1–26.

Lambe, E. K. (1999). Dyslexia, gender and brain imaging. *Neuropsychologia, 37*, 521–536.

Leiderman, J., & Flannery, K. A. (1993). Male prevalence for reading disability is found in large sample free from ascertainment bias. *Society for Neuroscience Abstracts, 19*, 1462.

Levy, J., & Reid, M. (1978). Variations in cerebral organization as a function of handedness, hand posture in writing, and sex. *Journal of Experimental Psychology: General, 107*, 119–144.

Loring-Meier, S., & Halpern, D. F. (1999). Sex differences in visuospatial working memory: Components of cognitive processing. *Psychonomic Bulletin & Review, 6*, 464–471.

Lynn, R. (1992). Sex differences on the Differential Aptitude Test in British and American adolescents. *Educational Psychology, 12*, 101–106.

Lynn, R. (1994). Sex differences in brain size and intelligence: A paradox resolved. *Personality and Individual Differences, 17*, 257–271.

Maccoby, E., & Jacklin, C. (1974). *The psychology of sex differences.* Stanford: Stanford University Press.

Mackintosh, N. J. (1996). Sex differences and IQ. *Journal of Biosocial Science, 28*, 559–572.

Martini, L., & Melcangi, R. C. (1991). Androgen metabolism in the brain. *Journal of Steroid Biochemistry and Molecular Biology, 39*, 819–824.

Masters, M. S., & Sanders, B. (1993). Is the gender difference in mental rotation disappearing? *Behavior Genetics, 23*, 337–341.

Matsumoto, A., & Arai, Y. (1980). Sex dimorphism in "wiring pattern" in the hypothalamic arcuate nucleus and its modification by neonatal hormonal environment. *Brain Research, 190*, 238–242.

Matsumoto, A., & Arai, Y. (1986). Male-female differences in synaptic organization of the ventromedial nucleus of the hypothalamus in rats. *Neuroendocrinology, 42*, 232–236.

Matsuzawa, J., Matsui, M., Konishi, T., Noguchi, K., Gur, R. C., Bilker, W., et al. (2001). Age-related volumetric changes of brain gray and white matter in healthy infants and children. *Cerebral Cortex, 11*, 335–342.

McCarthy, M. M., Davis, A. M., & Mong, J. A. (1997). Excitatory neurotransmission and sexual differentiation of the brain. *Brain Research Bulletin, 44*, 487–495.

McGough, J. J., & Barkley, R. A. (2004). Diagnostic controversies in adult attention-deficit/hyperactivity disorder. *American Journal of Psychiatry, 161*, 1948–1956.

McManus, I. C., & Bryden, M. P. (1991). Geschwind's theory of cerebral lateralization: Developing a formal, causal model. *Psychological Bulletin, 110*, 237–253.

Morse, J. K., Scheff, S. W., & DeKosky, S. T. (1996). Gonadal steroids influence axon sprouting in the hippocampal dentate gyrus: A sexually dimorphic response. *Experimental Neurology, 94,* 649–651.

Mulrine, A. (2001). Are boys the weaker sex? *U.S. News and World Report, 131,* 40–47.

Murphy, D. G. M, DeCarli, C., McIntosh, A. R., Daly, E., Mentis, M. J., Pietrini, P., et al. (1996). Sex differences in human brain morphometry and metabolism: An in vivo quantitative magnetic resonance imaging and positron emission tomography study on the effect of aging. *Archives of General Psychiatry, 53,* 585–594.

Naftolin, F., Ryan, K. J., Davies, I. J., Petro, Z., White, R. J., & Wolin, L. (1975). The formation of estrogen by central neuroendocrine tissue. *Recent Progress in Hormone Research, 31,* 295–319.

Neils, J. R., & Aram, D. M. (1986). Handedness and sex of children with developmental language disorders. *Brain and Language, 28,* 53–65.

Nishizuka, M., & Arai, Y. (1981). Sexual dimorphism in synaptic organization in the amygdala and its dependence on neonatal hormone environment. *Brain Research, 211,* 31–38.

Nopolous, P., Flaum, M., O'Leary, D., & Andreasen, N. C. (2000). Sexual dimorphism in the human brain: Evaluation of tissue volume, tissue composition and surface anatomy using magnetic resonance imaging. *Psychiatry Research, 98,* 1–13.

Overman, W. H. (2004). Sex differences in early childhood, adolescence and adulthood on cognitive tasks that rely on orbital prefrontal cortex. *Brain and Cognition, 55,* 134–147.

Passe, T. J., Rajagopalan, P., Tupler, L. A., Byrum, C. E., MacFall, J. R., & Krishnan, K. R. R. (1997). Age and sex effects on brain morphology. *Progress in Neuropsychopharmacology and Biological Psychiatry, 21,* 1231–1237.

Pfefferbaum, A., Mathalon, D. H., Sullivan, E. V., Rawles, J. M., Zipursky, R. B., & Lim, K. O. (1994). A quantitative magnetic resonance imaging study of changes in brain morphology from infancy to late adulthood. *Archives of Neurology, 51,* 874–887.

Pipe, M. E. (1990). Mental retardation and left-handedness. Evidence and theories. In S. Coren (Ed.). *Left-handedness: Behavioral implications and anomalies* (pp. 293–318). Amsterdam: Elsevier.

Pugh, K. R., Shaywitz, B. A., Shaywitz, S. E., Constable, R. T., Skudlarski, P., Fulbright, R. K., et al. (1996). Cerebral organization of component processes in reading. *Brain, 119,* 1221–1238.

Rabinowicz, T., Dean, D. E., Petetot, J. M. C., & de Courten-Myers, G. M. (1999). Gender differences in the human cerebral cortex: More neurons in males; more processes in females. *Journal of Child Neurology, 14,* 98–107.

Reed, T. E., Vernon, P. A., & Johnson, A. M. (2004). Sex differences in brain nerve conduction velocity in normal humans. *Neuropsychologia, 42,* 1709–1714.

Reiss, A. L., Abrams, M. T., Singer, H. S., Ross, J. L., & Denckla, M. B. (1996). Brain development, gender and IQ in children: A volumetric imaging study. *Brain, 119,* 1763–1774.

Schlaepfer, T. E., Harris, G. J., Tien, A. Y., Peng, L., Lee, S., & Pearlson, G. D. (1995). Structural differences in the cerebral cortex of healthy female and male subjects: A magnetic resonance imaging study. *Psychiatry Research, 61*, 129–135.

Schultz, R. T., Cho, N. K., Staib, L. H., Kier, L. E., Fletcher, J. M., Shaywitz, S. E., et al. (1994). Brain morphology in normal and dyslexic children: The influence of sex and age. *Annals of Neurology, 35*, 732–742.

Shaywitz, B., Shaywitz, S., Pugh, K., Constable, R., & Skudlarski, P. (1995). Sex differences in the functional organization of the brain for language. *Nature, 373*, 607–609.

Sherwin, B. B. (1999). Can estrogen keep you smart? Evidence from clinical studies. *Journal of Psychiatry and Neuroscience, 24*, 315–321.

Sholl, S. A., & Kim., K. L. (1989). Estrogen receptors in the rhesus monkey brain during fetal development. *Brain Research: Developmental Brain Research, 50*, 189–196.

Spearman, C. (1923). *The nature of intelligence and principles of cognition.* London: Macmillan.

Springer, S. P., & Deutsch, G. (1998). *Left brain, right brain: Perspectives from Cognitive neuroscience* (5th ed.). New York: Freeman.

Stanley, J. C. (1993). Boys and girls who reason well mathematically. In G. R. Bock & K. Acrill (Eds.), *The origins and development of high ability* (pp. 119–138). New York: Wiley.

Stein, J. F. (1994). Developmental dyslexia, neural timing and hemispheric lateralization. *International Journal of Psychophysiology, 18*, 241–249.

Susman, E. J. (1997). Modeling developmental complexity in adolescence: Hormones and behavior in context. *Journal of Research on Adolescence, 7*, 283–306.

Swaab, D. F., & Fliers, E. (1985). A sexually dimorphic nucleus in the human brain. *Science, 228*, 1112–1115.

Tallal, P., Miller, S., & Fitch, R. H. (1993). Neurobiological basis of speech: A case for the preeminence of temporal processing. In P. Tallal, A. M. Galaburda, R. R. Llinas, and C. von Euler (Eds.), *Temporal information processing in the nervous system.* New York: New York Academy of Sciences.

Terman, L. M. (1916). *The measurement of intelligence.* Boston: Houghton Mifflin, p. 362.

Vogel, S. A. (1990). Gender differences in intelligence, language, visual-motor abilities, and academic achievement in students with learning disabilities: A review of the literature. *Journal of Learning Disabilities, 23*, 44–52.

Weiss, G., & Hechtman, L. (1979). The hyperactive child syndrome. *Science, 205*, 1348–1354.

Witelson, S. F. (1989). Hand and sex differences in the isthmus and genu of the human corpus callosum: A postmortem morphological study. *Brain, 112*, 799–835.

Witelson, S. F., Glezer, I. I., & Kigar, D. L. (1995). Women have greater density of neurons in posterior temporal cortex. *Journal of Neuroscience, 15*, 3418–3428.

Yakovlev, P. I., & Lecours, A. (1967). The myelogenetic cycles of regional brain maturation of the brain. In A. Minkowski (Ed.), *Regional brain development in early life* (pp. 3–70). Oxford: Blackwell Scientific.

Zhou, J. N., Hofman, M. A., Gooren, L. J. G., & Swaab, D. F. (1995). A sex difference in the human brain and its relation to transexuality. *Nature, 378,* 68–70.

CHAPTER **3**

The Concept of Atypical Brain Development (ABD) as Applied to Developmental Learning Disorders

JEFFREY W. GILGER and BONNIE J. KAPLAN

Contents

At the International Congress of Psychology in 2000, we presented a paper on the concept of atypical brain development (ABD) (Lyytinen, 2000) as part of a joint session on learning disabilities and neuropsychology. Subsequently, some of the papers from this conference were published in the journal *Developmental Neuropsychology* (Gilger & Kaplan, 2001), including a commentary by Utta Frith on theories of the etiology of developmental learning disorders (LD). Since that time, the ABD concept has been discussed, applied, and debated by ourselves and others (e.g., Gilger & Wise, 2004; Rice & Brooks, 2004; Kaplan, Dewey, Crawford, & Wilson, 2001; Fadjukoff, Ahonen, & Lyytinen, 2001; Frith, 2001; Bonifacci, 2004; Goldstein & Schwebach, 2004; Jeffries & Everatt, 2004; Sonuga-Barke, 2003; Valtonen, Ahonen, Lyytinen, & Lyytinen, 2004; Lyon, Fletcher, & Barnes, 2003; Davis, 2004; Gilger, Hynd, & Wilkins, in press).

Since the first publication in 2001, we have further developed our ideas and will present them here. Although we recognize that the ABD approach is controversial, we still hold to the belief that it is a reasonable and research-driven conceptualization of the causes of LD and that it has something important, and new, to say about mainstream approaches to LD classification and study, as well as clinical practice. Although originally conceptualized only in terms of children and their early development, the ABD concept applies equally throughout adulthood and hence pertains directly to adults with learning disorders.

In this chapter, we spend a little time repeating the essentials of the concept. We also attempt to better clarify how the ABD theory fits with other current approaches in the LD field. Our goal is to provide a summary of where the concept stands now, with greater elaboration of the implications of the 2001 paper. We also present some new thoughts about how ABD fits our observations of LD treatment and current trends in the diagnostic and treatment practices in the United States. Given the developmental perspective of the ABD formulation, we often speak of children but again, it is important to bear in mind that the ABD concept applies across the life span.

What Is the ABD Model?

As cited above, the ABD model has been described in several papers. We will highlight only the key aspects here, and the reader is referred to these other publications for more thorough discussions.

The ABD concept evolved primarily from thinking about the ecological validity of diagnostic categories, as well as the implications of ongoing genetic and neurological research, especially in the area of reading disabilities (RD). The original ABD conceptual framework reflected the belief systems of many researchers, clinicians, and educators who have extensive exposure to children with developmental problems.

There are three fundamental underlying assumptions of the ABD concept:

- The brain is the basis of behavior.
- Individual differences are due to variable brain structure and function.
- Ultimately, individual differences are the result of the complex interplay of genes and the environment.

It is important to realize that the concept of atypical brain development is a neurological or neuropsychological model, although it does not speak directly to how the brain is organized or how specific areas or functions of the brain explain specific abilities as do other theories or concepts (e.g., see Luria, 1973; Pennington, 1991; Lieberman, 1984; Eden & Zeffiro, 1998; Rice & Brooks, 2004; Ramus, 2001). As with other models, neuropsychological approaches are useful and can guide the direction of research, intervention, and prevention (Hynd & Orbrzut, 1986).

At the outset, it is important to distinguish ABD from the old MBD (minimal brain dysfunction) concept proposed 40 years ago (Gilger & Kaplan, 2001; Clements & Peters, 1962). The term *atypical* in ABD differs from the MBD concept of dysfunction or damage in that it can encompass phenomena at both ends of the continua related to abilities. The term *development* in ABD accurately describes our current understanding that developmental learning disorders are probably the result of prenatal, and to a lesser extent postnatal, brain growth and elaboration, including those processes due to genes and intrauterine environmental factors (Huttenlocher, 2002; Greenough, Black, & Wallace, 2002; Frith, 2001; Ramus, 2004). Moreover, the application of the ABD term clearly contrasts with that of MBD. MBD became an overly broad term employed to represent an ill-defined unitary syndrome for the categorization and diagnosis of a group of children (Satz & Fletcher, 1980). In contrast, ABD is meant to serve as a unifying concept regarding *etiology*, the expression of which is variable within and across individuals. As we expressed it then (Gilger & Kaplan, 2001),

> ABD does not itself represent a specific disorder or syndrome and ABD does not pertain to brain injury, trauma, or disease in the classic medical sense. Rather, ABD is a concept that describes the developmental variation of the brain and subsequent brain-based skills on either side of the real or hypothetical norm.

It is worth reiterating that final point: ABD pertains to *both sides* of the continuum of brain-based skills. ABD thereby emphasizes a need for the exploration and understanding of the etiology of superior abilities, an area seriously understudied (Kalbfleisch, 2004). ABD is also a reasonable formulation for explaining the co-occurrence of disorders and superior abilities in the same person (e.g., Geschwind & Galaburda, 1987). While some theorists have discussed the brain in relation to comorbidity and LD-giftedness co-occurrence (e.g., Newman & Sternberg, 2004; Geschwind & Galaburda, 1987), these hypotheses or explanations have tended to come from disease or medical models where giftedness is mentioned only briefly and secondarily.

Original ABD Concept Was Based on Three Facets of LD Research

Frequency of Overlapping Disorders

In 2001 we believed that one of the strongest arguments for considering children in terms of the ABD framework is the research that demonstrates the high frequency of comorbidity in individuals with developmental learning problems (Gilger & Kaplan, 2001; Kaplan et al., 2001; Shapiro, Church, & Lewis, 2002). Essentially we argued that the enormous amount of overlap found in people with LD suggests that the distinctions between disorders (e.g., RD, attention-deficit/hyperactivity disorder [ADHD], developmental coordination disorder, math disability, and so on) may, at times, be more artificial than real. However, we strongly advocate for continued research into the etiology and manifestations of each of these ostensibly separate LD-related categories. Such research continues to refine the nosology, symptomatology, and treatments for these disorders when considered independently (Fletcher, Shaywitz, & Shaywitz, 1999).

Yet it is our opinion that continued efforts to approach these disorders as if they were *completely* independent seems naive, particularly given their neurodevelopmental and genetic origins. Indeed, genetic and neurological research increasingly supports at least some degree of nonindependence, often showing indistinct and overlapping neurological substrates and genetic correlations for types of LD symptoms, brain morphology and function, and so forth (e.g., Ramus, 2001, in press; Rice & Brooks, 2004; Wood & Flowers, 1999; Voeller, 1999; Willcutt et al., 2002; Olson, Forsberg, & Wise, 1994; Sonuga-Barke, 2003). As discussed below, it is unlikely that there is a simple one-to-one mapping of genes to brain structures/areas or brain areas to cognitive abilities, and this is especially true when the concern is complex cognitive traits, the effects of developmental genes, neurodevelopment particularly of the cortex, and the evolution of cognitive abilities across the life span (Johnson, Munakata, & Gilmore, 2002; Hahn, van Ness, & Maxwell, 1978; Changeaux, 1985; Jones & Murray, 1991; Noctor, Flint, Weissman, Dammerman, & Kriegstein, 2001).

It is also possible that the very term *comorbid* poses a semantic problem, which could be alleviated if it were viewed in the context of ABD. Comorbid is a term borrowed from medicine, and its original meaning indicated the presence of at least two diseases. But what if the behaviors or phenotypes observed in LD individuals are not separate diseases or traits but rather correlated symptoms of an atypical brain? An individual with diabetes and asthma, who is said to be comorbid for two diseases derived from primarily distinct body systems, is in a different situation from an individual reporting frequent urination and unusual thirst. In the latter case, this person is not said to be comorbid for two diseases (frequent urination and thirstiness) because these are both symptoms arising from correlated body systems and their co-occurrence suggests morbidity for a single disease, diabetes. Similarly, we suggest that an individual with, say, RD, motor deficits, inattention, and so on may be expressing symptoms of an atypical brain affecting multiple areas of behavior simultaneously.

As we have argued elsewhere, the term *comorbidity* is misleading and should probably be abandoned when referring to developmental disorders (Kaplan et al., 2001). When the term *comorbidity* was transferred into the educational and mental health world, there was one element missing that has prevented its accurate application: the precise distinction between symptom and disease (or disorder). When an individual exhibits characteristics of ADHD and dyslexia, or memory problems, or motor skills deficits, we believe it is an open question as to whether that child is displaying comorbid disorders, variable manifestations of one underlying impairment, or several underlying impairments that may or may not be etiologically related. The co-occurrence of apparently disparate symptoms causes problems in both diagnosis and treatment, and at the same time, it raises questions about the etiology and mutual interdependence of various conditions (Gilger & Kaplan, 2001; Kaplan et al., 2001; Jeffries & Everatt, 2004; Sonuga-Barke, 2003; Bergman & Magnussen, 1997; Lyytinen, Leinonen, Nikula, Aro, & Leiwo, 1995; Narhi & Ahonen, 1995).

At this point of the discussion, we illustrate the ABD concept in Figures 3.1 and 3.2. Genes and environment affect brain growth and elaboration so that across individuals in the population there are differences in brain structure and function, sometimes subtle and unnoticed at the surface phenotype or behavior, and at other times more apparent. Also, within an individual there are variations in areas and circuits of the brain

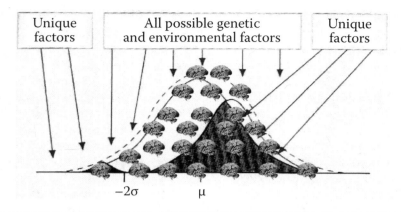

Figure 3.1 Overarching concept of ABD: Pre- and postnatal etiological factors contribute to brain morphology and functional variation in the population.

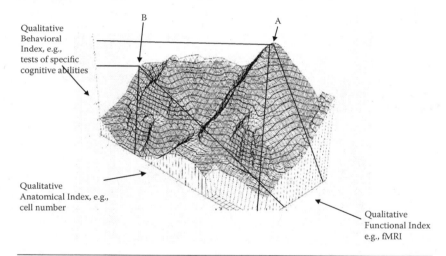

Figure 3.2 Hypothetical 3-D representation of ABD for a *single individual*; the correlated dimensions of structure, function, and behavior vary within individuals. A = Example peak cognitive ability culminating from relatively "special" neurological growth and function; B = Example low cognitive ability culminating from relatively less "elaborate" neurological growth and function.

(and therefore behavior) relative to some imaginary norm, resulting in profiles of neurological (and therefore behavioral) strengths and weaknesses, shown in Figure 3.2 as sort of a topographical map. As conceptualized by the ABD formulation, most of these between-people and within-person differences are a normal part of human development, while at the more extreme ends they may be more often due to unique experiential and biological factors. All of these variations in brain structures and systems can exist in the population as typical or atypical variants, which may or may not get identified at the behavioral level. In this manner, we conceptualize mild or developmental LD, giftedness, or any peak or valley in the profile of cognitive skills as the result of atypical deviations from the hypothetical, normal brain. Again, such variations occur all the time, and most go unnoticed, but some are identified through performance on psychometric or behavioral measures. For example, the atypical brain variant that results in RD would probably go unnoticed (and certainly does in illiterate societies) if reading were not emphasized in our culture.

In summary, the ABD concept suggests that variation occurs first at the neurological level and that this variation occurs within and between people in the population. Further, this variation can lead to correlated symptoms or traits, and the interpretation and identification of this variation will depend on the level of analysis applied (see Figures 3.1 and 3.2): from the level of the neuron or neurological structure, to the level of neurological function, and at the most removed level, that of behavior. Finally, brain variation and ABD often go unnoticed in the laboratory unless the "whole brain" is assessed appropriately and with sensitive enough instruments. Similarly, the consequences of atypical brain development may go unnoticed in a person's everyday life unless his or her experience or life demands tap into these peaks or valleys.

Genetic and Environmental Etiologic Variability in Learning Disorders

It is a virtual certainty that genes play a significant role in LD symptoms or phenotypes and therefore, logically, in the development of the brain that regulates the behaviors associated with LDs (Gayan et al., 1999; Pennington, 1997; Petryshen et al., 2001; Regehr & Kaplan, 1988; Smith, Gilger, & Pennington, 2002; Pennington, 2002). Tentative genes or "susceptibility alleles" have been identified as contributors to some forms of developmental LD (reviewed in Pennington, 2002; Gilger & Wise, 2004; Smith et al., 2002). Again using RD as a model, recent research points out that the genes putting individuals at risk for RD do not necessarily correspond to specific or independent cognitive aspects of reading ability (Fisher et al., 1999; Gayan et al., 1999; Grigorenko et al., 1997; Fisher et al., 2002; Olson et al., 1994; Smith et al., 2002). In other words, there are probably multiple heterogeneous effects of the RD-risk genes that act alone or together to give rise to multiple profiles of reading-related skills (Ramus, 2001; Frith, 2001). Thus, at this time, research suggests that genes may cause ABD, affecting multiple brain areas and contributing to the variance in learning in a complex manner rather than in a focused, singular, and direct manner as predicted by single-gene–single-disease models or by models of simple and complete neural modularity (e.g., Aaron, Joshi, & Ocker, 2004).*

Even if we consider the effects of a single gene variant for traits as complex as human learning, especially those involving cortical areas, such a gene may yield multiple typical and atypical behaviors, especially if this gene is influential during the early stages of neural development and brain organization (Luria, 1973; Huttenlocher, 2002; Greenough et al., 2002; Conn, 1992; Gerlai, 1996; Rondi-Reig, Caston, Delhaye-Bouchaud, & Mariani, 1999). It is far more likely that a developmental gene important to cortical cell migration or connection, for instance, affects multiple brain areas to varying degrees and thus most often influences multiple behavioral areas. Even if the discrimination of primary LD subtypes (RD versus math disability versus ADHD, etc.) were a function of several distinct major genes influencing a different primary brain area for each disorder, the enormous co-occurrence of these conditions argues for the multifocal actions of the pertinent gene or the multifocal developmental effects of single genes that originally operated on more specific brain areas (see also Marcus, 2004, with regard to genetic regulation of brain development).†

---

* It is worth mentioning that the research on language impairments suggests something similar to what we say here about RD. This makes some sense in that reading and language are intimately related (Stone et al., 2004). However, it is likely that research will ultimately reveal specific links between "language genes" and "language brain structures," given how language was selected for in evolution and the probable innate brain structures for spoken language acquisition. While a person with a language disorder may display atypicalities in the brain beyond the classic language areas, the genetic and neurological structure for language is probably more canalized (Waddington, 1975; Marcus, 2004) and prescribed than that for, say, reading. Thus, in the future it is more likely that specific key genes will be found that strongly determine the development of specific brain areas important to language acquisition.

† Readers familiar with the RD research are aware of the studies showing that certain areas of the brain are commonly activated during reading tasks and that anatomical reports suggest that similar brain areas may be atypical in structure (e.g., Galaburda, 1993; Mody, 2004; Shaywitz et al., 1998; Shaywitz et al. 2002) across individuals. Using the left angular gyrus as an example, this begs the question that if brains are *diffusely* atypical, why does this area of the brain repeatedly appear as a significant contributor to the risk for RD? First, these common findings do not a priori implicate a specific gene that modifies just the left angular gyrus. There are, of course, many genetic and environmental factors that modify the left angular gyrus. Second, part of the problem with the vast majority of the imaging studies of the angular gyrus is that they do not look at other areas and certainly not the whole brain performing a number of different types of tasks. Thus, it cannot be said that RD brains are specifically atypical only in this area because we really do not know that. It may be that they are *mostly* atypical in that area and that this gives rise to their primary disorder in reading, but it does not necessarily indicate that there are specific isolated brain areas that give rise to specific isolated LDs, and that these locations and aberrations are due to a very specific genetic or environmental event that does not also affect other aspects of neurodevelopment.

In summary, it is not likely that one common factor alone will explain a significant majority of developmental LD cases in the population. Many factors, genetic and environmental, interact to create a tendency toward or away from developmental LDs and also contribute to the variable expressivity of the underlying ABD of our model.

Variable Neuroanatomy of Developmental Disorders

As mentioned above, it is unlikely that there is a one-to-one correspondence between a single, finite brain area and type of developmental LD. More likely would be a collection of specific brain areas, circuits, or systems that act together to put an individual at risk for a certain type of LD, but these systems do not operate in isolation from the rest of the brain and other circuits. The structural or activational anomalies in the brain of an individual with a learning disability are probably numerous, although they may be more heavily focused in one region than another (e.g., Shaywitz et al., 1998; Shaywitz et al., 2002). Perhaps it is the area with the heavier focus that gives rise to a person's primary diagnosis, simply because it results in the most salient disability (see notes on page 62). Therefore, according to this perspective, the symptoms exhibited by people (e.g., deficits in reading, math, spelling, motor skills, attention, or some combination) depend on the relative amount of anomalous development in primary ability areas of the brain (e.g., language areas or connections in, around, to, or from the temporal lobe) and which of the many other brain areas are also affected. Moreover, a complete whole-brain study of an LD individual will show peaks and valleys in behaviors, where the peak skills may prove to have compensatory powers for the valleys. While it may be an oversimplification, the ABD concept reminds us that every individual is a product of the neurodevelopmental variations he or she carries, and that a person's integrated and fully functioning brain is kind of an average of these variations. Within the same person, certain daily experiences will at times call upon aspects of brain functioning that may tap his or her ABD at the low end of the continuum (e.g., RD when asked to read) or at the high end of the continuum (e.g., high spatial abilities when asked to solve a puzzle).

In summary, there are multiple pathways by which abilities such as reading, math, or intelligence can be affected, and irregularities in one or all of these pathways may yield similar symptoms at the surface behavioral level. Although not all areas of the brain are involved in all tasks, these sorts of results should be expected given what we know about the complexity of the brain, especially for higher order skills like academics.

The Case Against the ABD Model

Since 2001 we have received many comments, some formal and others informal, about the ABD concept (e.g., Rice & Brooks, 2004; Kaplan et al., 2001; Fadjukoff et al., 2001; Frith, 2001; Bonifacci, 2004; Goldstein & Schwebach, 2004; Jeffries & Everatt, 2004; Sonuga-Barke, 2003; Valtonen et al., 2004; Lyon et al., 2003; Davis, 2004). By and large, there is little research to refute our central tenet, albeit the ABD concept is post hoc. We have heard positive comments about how the concept draws attention back to the brain, how it argues for a more complete study of every individual's spectrum of strengths and weaknesses, how it brings together diverse disciplines toward a common understanding of how the brain develops through genetic and environmental influences, and how well the concept reminds us of natural brain variability in the population and the etiology of individual differences in behavior due to "normal" human variation. With regard to developmental or mild LD, and skills within and exceeding the average, we have also heard that ABD suggests new research agendas such as the neuroscience of giftedness, and a broader approach applied to nondisease-oriented models of brain development research. Some of these types of comments fit with the growing "positive psychology movement" in a neuroscience realm and, hopefully, new funding options through key governmental agencies ("Positive Psychology," 2001).

On the other hand, we have also heard negative comments about the ABD concept. The essential concern is best summarized in a very thorough and thoughtful paper by Lyon et al. (2003):

> Recent efforts to redefine the concept of MBD as "atypical brain development (ABD)" (Gilger & Kaplan, 2001) are not likely to prove useful as indicating that brain development is atypical in children with these "unexplained" learning and behavioral difficulties is hardly new and almost tautologous given the state of the evidence reviewed below. It is not much different than simply invoking "cerebral dysfunction" as an explanation of MBD or LD. History shows that such broad, overarching concepts lead to clumping together of behaviors and learning characteristics that need to be better differentiated in order to facilitate intervention. As we show below, this is becoming increasingly possible in the area of LD (and ADHD). (p. 530)

At the initial level, we do not disagree with this description of our original conceptualization of ABD. However, we hope that we are able to address this criticism with further elaboration of the ABD concept, discussed in the next section.

The ABD Concept Revisited

First, the ABD concept remains relevant to theory and practice and should not be summarily dismissed as "tautologous" or no better than the concept of "cerebral dysfunction" (Lyon et al., 2003). We have already pointed out how ABD is different from concepts of dysfunction and that the ABD concept, in our opinion, does more than state the obvious. Perhaps missing from our original presentation was a better statement about the fact that ABD is compatible with other approaches common today in the LD field. Recognition of the underlying tenets of the ABD concept and its value as an "overarching" concept does not require dispensing with efforts to differentiate LD categories. In fact, it is our hope that the implications of the ABD model will become part of the contemporary psychology of research and the practice zeitgeist of today, sharing space with (not replacing) the more molecular approaches to the study and treatment of LD. As part of our effort toward melding the ABD concept with more contemporary thinking, we list below seven related areas of consideration that flow logically from the ABD approach.

1. Whole-Brain Perspective

ABD as a concept strongly advocates for developmental and experimental studies of the whole brain. By this we mean that the commonplace methods of study that focus on distinct categories or on the specific and microanalytical cognitive processing approaches to a behavior should be supplemented with an explicit awareness of the brain as a whole organ. An illustration of this point can be found in the typical neurogenetic study of children with RD that assesses and then considers only verbal skills but not (for instance) motor coordination or attention; this approach has been common in the past, but investigators adhering to the ABD model would expand the assessment into realms other than verbal skills. Interestingly, when other, even nonlanguage, areas of the RD brain are examined, they are often found to be atypical as well (see Mody, 2004).

The call for a broader approach is important, especially with regard to the etiology and ultimate expression of behaviors being studied and our understanding of the whole person. For example, we have stated earlier that it is important to acknowledge that the search for the genes that influence learning abilities, disabilities, or specific cognitive processes is really a search for the genes that determine "atypical brain development" (Gilger & Kaplan, 2001; Gilger, 1995; Jones & Murray, 1991). In such behavior genetics research, we are not really looking for genes that affect the surface phenotype of learning ability as measured by standardized tests; instead, we are looking for genes that cause brain variation in the population, such that some people fare better than others when it comes to learning. Consequently, future dyslexia genetics research would be strengthened if it were to include multiple measures of brain integrity and function, including, but not limited to, tests of general reading, word recognition, math, processing speed, motoric processes, attention, visual-spatial abilities, and so forth. Research employing a more limited phenotype may miss much of the complexity of an individual's skills. This is said, of course, with the simultaneous recognition that fine-grained experimental studies of very specific abilities and neurogenetic processes are important but should not be the sole focus of a developmental disabilities research program.

A worst-case scenario illustrates our point. Suppose that researchers looking for dyslexia genes find a major predisposing gene that clearly influences phonological skills. It would be possible, given the limited assessments that are usually employed for phenotype definitions, for the researchers in question to assume that they had found a gene specific to reading-related skills when more in-depth assessments might reveal that the same gene affects other complex skills such as processing speed or attention as well. We suggest that a better scenario would be for researchers to include a broad spectrum approach to phenotypic assessment with careful brain-imaging and anatomical studies to permit the investigation of correlations among brain structure, genetics, and function.

2. Variation Can Be "Normal"

The ABD concept considers some "deficits" to be normal variation. It is one of the main tenets of the ABD approach that there is variation in brain structures resulting in functional variation that can be identified at the behavioral level—sometimes as apparently unitary disorders. But the compartmentalization of a collection of traits into independent categories of disorders may be misleading. Rather, the ABD concept suggests that such traits could be viewed simultaneously as simple symptoms of brain variation, and that the best method for understanding etiology and treatment approaches is to consider both the category as well as the broader presentation of traits as reflections of a variable brain or a diffusely atypical brain. Other theories on neurology and neuropsychology can be included to expand the ABD concept further. We recommend that with ABD as a sort of general perspective, more detailed and specific theories of brain-behavior relationships, networks, brain processing components, and so on (e.g., Ramus, in press; Mody, 2004; Eden & Zeffiro, 1998) can be tested and applied where valid, thus expanding our understanding even further. In the concluding section of this paper, we discuss the relationship between ABD and work with other neuropsychological models.

3. Redefinition of Behavioral Phenotypes in Terms of Neurological Basis

The concept of ABD helps us redefine behavioral phenotypes into terms dealing with their ultimate basis: the brain. In our opinion, in some ways study of LD has gradually taken us away from this central organ responsible for every behavior (Gilger & Kaplan, 2001). While this has been a natural evolution, and while the field is beginning to get back to its neurological roots, there is still a strong tendency to define individuals purely on the basis of behavior. Furthermore, behavioral phenotypes are currently driving brain research rather than allowing brain research to drive phenotypes. This is, perhaps, a necessary state-of-the-art phase, as our ability to view the brain in situ has only recently become possible (Kennedy, Haselgrove, & McInerney, 2003), and we are still very heavily reliant on psychometrics. However, along with the common methods of brain study, additional and unforeseen information may be obtained by approaching research from a bottom-up alongside a top-down methodology. These two approaches taken simultaneously may accelerate our understanding of brain-behavior relationships. It is noteworthy that some current efforts to form large, shared brain-imaging databases and to increase the number of common protocols in brain-imaging research may be a beginning in this endeavor (Kennedy et al., 2003). Specifically, we suggest the need for large-scale multivariate analyses where common brain areas are sought that show up in atypical and typical behavioral phenotypes *as well as* concomitant studies that begin with brain-imaging results and then look for their behavioral expression. Reconciliation of the findings from this sort of work is a first step toward a more fully developed and reliable picture of the brain, brain-behavior relationships, and individual variation in the population.

4. ABD Is Developmentally Reasonable

The ABD theory fits well with all of the available data on LD, genetics, and neurology. In this sense, we suggest that ABD be considered as a general conceptual starting place. Even if a researcher is focusing on, say, the cognitive processing components of reading, he or she must be aware that typical and atypical brain variation beyond the specific components pertinent to reading are really at the heart of the issue. ABD also makes a more general statement that a developmental perspective must be maintained when talking about genetic and neurologic effects on the learning or cognitive system.

As shown in Figure 3.3, at different points in time, the surface phenotype of, say, a reading test, may reflect genetic and environmental effects that occurred when the brain was just starting to form (e.g., G2 and G3), or it may be a manifestation of genetic and environmental effects on the

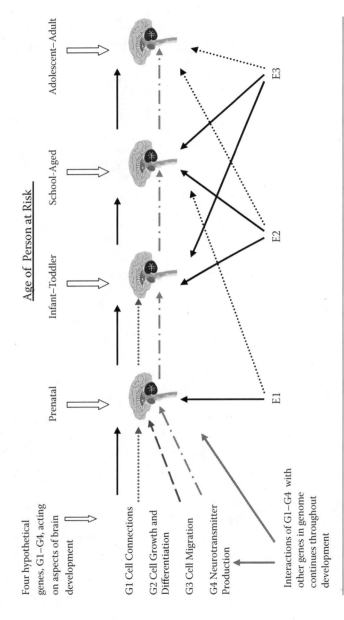

Figure 3.3 A simple hypothetical diagram of how genes and environments modify risk towards developing a reading disorder. E1–E3 are hypothetical environmental effects with different onset times in life, where dashed lines indicate weaker or no effect relative to solid lines where effects are stronger. G1–G4 represent a hypothetical four-gene model with each gene having unique effects on brain function or growth. Brain function is commonly assessed by a surface phenotype, say a reading test standard score. Note that genetic and environmental factors act differently at different points in time. See text for further explanation.

brain that continue throughout life (e.g., G1). Certain aspects of brain development, like cell migration and differentiation, occur very early and then more or less stop, and the key genes moderating these processes "turn off" as well or assume other functions (e.g., G2 and G3; see, e.g., Galaburda, 1992, 1993; Huttenlocher, 2002; Greenough et al., 2002). This fact has ramifications for research in that we are often looking for genes that have affected brain development during a specific window of time, such that when a 12-year-old person has RD, for example, we may be really looking for genes that are no longer active (Gilger, 1995).

The idea of ABD also reminds the clinician or teacher that remediation techniques will probably have limited effects on the major brain structures that are developmentally atypical and primarily responsible for the disorder. While intensive remediation may improve the interneuronal connections or communications within these developmental structures, improvement in reading skills is also achieved by changes in other, more intact systems that can help in some sort of compensatory process (Eden & Zeffiro, 1998; Eden & Moats, 2002). This assumption is based on what we know about brain development and the current understanding that certain developmental structures such as cell number, cell migration, and gyrification cannot be changed after birth. According to our present state of knowledge, the original developmental atypicalities responsible for reading problems can only be secondarily compensated for through other brain systems that work around the deficit areas or through modifications of connections across existing cells in and outside of these areas.

5. Avoidance of One-Size-Fits-All Way of Thinking

The ABD concept helps us avoid single etiology or one-size-fits-all schemes of thinking. This fact is somewhat paradoxical, given that the concept does, in fact, move toward a single overarching (as Lyon et al., 2003, labeled it) conceptual framework. It is again worth emphasizing that the ABD approach does not advocate against ongoing research or treatment approaches based on subtypes or diagnostic categories. Instead, we hope that the implications of ABD can be incorporated into these current models of study and treatment. The ABD concept should not be taken as anticategorization, antilabeling, or antinosological research. Perhaps the ABD concept can best be thought of as a thinking tool that, when used conjointly with other tools, will result in a broader and more accurate picture of the etiology of behavior.

Rather than employing one-size-fits-all ways of thinking, the ABD concept emphasizes the complexity of the brain and brain-behavior relationships. Simple diagnostic schemes or treatments that focus on only one aspect of the symptoms of the atypical brain do not do justice to the underlying causes of what is observed at the surface, and they increase the likelihood of treatment failure because of a limited focus on one behavioral category.

Appreciating the complexities of within-person abilities has value in the diagnostic and treatment domains and also has implications for prevention (see also Bergman & Magnussen, 1997; Shapiro et al., 2002). For example, there is currently a very welcome push toward early identification and prevention of learning disabilities (Stone, Silliman, Ehren, & Apel, 2004). There is, in fact, substantial research indicating that there are early behavioral or neurological signs that predict LDs (Stone et al., 2004). A developmental neuropsychological model, whatever its basis, suggests that the brains of at-risk individuals may manifest deficits at birth, and that preventative methods might be applied early in life to help ameliorate or reduce this risk (Lyytinen et al., 2004).

The ABD model suggests, again, that risk for disorders is only part of the picture, and that potentialities for strengths might also be present at birth. Furthermore, the ABD model in which a life-span developmental approach is highlighted tells us something about how we should think of therapies: namely, that we must approach therapies or preventative efforts with a full view of what systems we are operating on. In the future, with the likelihood of more molecular and chemical therapies, focusing on the whole brain or the entire person (at least in philosophy) will have great implications for the remediation of disorders. There will also be implications regarding how such interventions might affect the positive potentialities in the person with the risk for a disorder: When we treat one aspect of brain function, we likely affect other aspects as well, and at the behavioral level, such manipulations may significantly change the life course of the individual in directions we cannot know without some sort of time machine. This future ethical challenge is something to think about, but at this time must remain an unresolved point of discussion.

6. Treatment That Is Specific to Individual Profiles

The ABD conceptualization highlights the importance of formulating treatment and research plans around the idea of peaks and valleys within persons and between people. This approach pertains to the psychometrically assessed phenotypes such as cognitive processing skills, as well as correlating behavioral phenotypes with brain phenotypes. Peaks and valleys may include both ends of the continua of skills, as well as morphological differences and functional differences of the brain. Of course, practical constraints (time, money, local laws requiring labels, guarded clinical specialties and training, etc.) often preclude such thorough assessments in real-life settings. Certain theoretical and funding philosophies also limit (implicitly or explicitly) such an approach in the typical research setting.

7. Applicability to Adults With Learning Disabilities

The ABD concept may be especially useful in understanding the older child or adult who does not fit the usual or simple diagnostic schemes. At all ages, there are individuals who appear to have a variety of symptoms without clear etiology or coherence. These cases can be very confusing and frustrating to clinicians and educators, often requiring a huge amount of management effort, diagnostic tests, and failed treatments. Often such individuals do not receive appropriate treatments and, especially as children, can end up receiving placements in special programs better suited to other forms of LD when they have so many other issues ongoing—there is simply nowhere else to put them.

Such complexity is particularly likely in adults seeking assessments for the first time in their lives, as so many life experiences, skills, coping mechanisms, and learned behaviors can decrease the clarity with which deficits are manifest. We have seen such cases in both children and adults, and they often present with a diffuse clinical picture, with traits spanning nonverbal LD, reading and math problems, social skill deficits, anxiety, ADHD, and so on, while exhibiting basically normal IQs and an ability to function fairly well with guidance and practice. Applying the suggestions of the ABD concept does not require that such individuals be diagnosed per se but rather that they be recognized as having a diffusely atypical brain, of whatever etiology, that does not yield to simple classifications. Moreover, such individuals require broad-based assessments and treatments that focus on the many symptoms exhibited as well as the strengths displayed, which is very much in keeping with the ABD perspective. This type of approach would help avoid the expense and failures so often associated with such cases.

A second point of particular relevance to adults is that symptoms can change significantly with age. By the time children with learning problems become teenagers or adults, they often have had multiple shifting diagnostic labels, none of which alone has done justice to their individual profiles. Having multiple diagnostic labels that change over the years is due to more than diagnostic unreliability; it may reflect a real change in the profile of symptoms to life experiences and brain maturation (see Ehri & Snowling, 2004; Rice & Brooks, 2004). Again, ABD as an approach relieves the pressure to explain these changes and in fact predicts that they will occur.

Let us look at a hypothetical example of an adult to understand why the ABD concept is more compatible with understanding adult presentations of learning difficulties than our current methods of categorization and diagnosis. This particular hypothetical adult has significant problems in reading and also in developing social relationships. If a child presented with these difficulties, it is likely that the demands of the educational system, if nothing else, would result in the diagnoses of reading disability and perhaps a nonverbal learning disability. But our hypothetical adult does not need to be classified for funding purposes in an educational system and so need not be pigeonholed as "adult dyslexia" or "adult nonverbal LD." It would be far more flexible to view this person through the broader lens afforded by the ABD conceptualization: this adult presents with ABD, with particular symptoms and weaknesses clustered in two areas requiring careful assessment (reading and social interaction). A reading assessment might reveal problems in decoding, resulting in a recommended educational intervention. Evaluation of the social problems might reveal extreme shyness, resulting in a referral for psychological intervention.

In other words, one of the advantages of thinking about the ABD conceptualization in terms of adults is that some of the pressures present in our educational system for children are not present, although there is still some need for labels for adult attainment of services (e.g., Americans With Disabilities Act, PL 101-336, 1990). Therefore, treatments can be multifaceted at the start and flexible, dynamic, and addressing symptoms and profiles globally, without such a demand for individual subtyping or categorization.

Some Diagnostic Implications of ABD

Up to this point, the focus of this article has been on the description of ABD as a concept for research and the understanding of etiology. We have mentioned clinical applications throughout and we want to spend a little more time here, focusing on diagnoses.

We are certainly not the first to question the value of diagnostic categories. As Rapin (2002) pointed out in a discussion of "diagnostic dilemmas in developmental disabilities," developmental disorders "are not diseases that one does or does not have" (p. 49); rather, they are traits that are dimensional rather than categorical (Rapin, 2002). On the other hand, especially in what she refers to as prototypical cases of disorders such as dyslexia, assignment of diagnosis is not difficult.

Currently, there are many pressures to assign "pigeonhole" diagnoses to people, even while the concept of individual differences is acknowledged. It is possible that these pressures sometimes prevent thorough educational assessments of various skills. Recognition that children with ABD represent an enormously heterogeneous group at the neurological level can have important beneficial effects on educational assessment (and treatment) strategies. In our opinion, for educational purposes, children need to be assessed for their individual strengths and weaknesses, and treatment plans need to be developed to address both. Good treatment settings currently follow this strategy, of course. But financial, cultural, and other pressures often exist to distill a child's complex pattern of strengths and weaknesses into a few words describing a categorical diagnostic label.

In the ABD framework we are proposing, a thorough assessment might include a description of the person's strengths and weaknesses for treatment and tracking purposes *without the need for the diagnosis of a specific LD subtype*. Testing and diagnosis of weaknesses *and* strengths could be emphasized more than it is today. Calling children specifically language impaired or developmentally math disordered, for instance, is a good starting point, but it often does not do justice to the person's condition, and it does not fully describe all of the atypical symptoms seen in a large proportion of children with the same diagnosis. The ABD concept emphasizes a thorough, broad spectrum analysis of each individual with the explicit aim to identify irregularities on *both* ends of the continuum.

We recognize that the financially driven pressure to categorize for service funding is not likely to disappear quickly under any new conceptual framework. But there is good reason to believe that this pressure to categorize is more than financially driven. Our current approach to LD is guided in large part by the current culture of science; namely, long-standing theoretical biases and traditions have led us to our present "best practices" models. Only an open-minded reconsideration of the available data and approaches to research will allow a different perspective leading to different therapeutic and diagnostic techniques. But the cultural and political approach to LD is changing.

Today, for instance, there is a movement to initiate a multistep "three-tiered model" for remediation in the schools (e.g., Fletcher, Denton, Fuchs, & Vaughn, 2004). The focus of such models is not so much diagnosis but rather a careful assessment and tracking of a student with LD and a responsive and evolving research-based remediation plan. In fact, at the first two levels of "intervention," a child need not necessarily be diagnosed as a certain LD type to receive some sort of services in the regular education classroom. Instead, the teacher and other staff identify a student struggling with, say, reading in the regular curriculum, and then initiate a form of intervention with careful monitoring and testing. The teacher is supposed to modify his or her methods according to how well or poorly the student responds. This multilevel approach is just a beginning of what we foresee as some major changes in the LD field to come. For our purposes, it fits in well with the ABD concept, where diagnosis is less important and the focus on symptoms is key.

Finally, when discussing diagnostic implications, we would be remiss not to consider the ABD concept from the perspective of clients and their families. Those children or adults who fit fairly neatly into a single, current

LD category will not reap any particular benefit from the addition of an overarching ABD conceptual framework. But for the cases of children who are relatively complex, with deficits in multiple areas, there may be significant superiority in having a single diagnosis rather than several. Many clinicians and educators have heard the pain in a parent's voice when describing his or her child as having not just one but several diagnoses. We are not aware of studies looking at the emotional impact of multiple labels, but it is difficult to imagine any real personal benefit. The controversy over the past few decades about the potentially handicapping effects of being "labeled" more or less dissolved when it became clear that access to beneficial services would be dependent upon such labels. In the case of multiplex disorders, perhaps the single diagnostic term of ABD should be considered. A caveat here, however, is that in today's culture a label incorporating the term "brain" may, frankly, be worse than the now-popular diagnoses of dyslexia, ADHD, depression, and so on!

Conclusion

The history of the study of developmental disorders is replete with debates between "lumpers" and "splitters." Lumpers are people who develop large theories that tend to encompass many aspects of an issue; splitters are those who tend to be more concrete and who attempt to categorize and subtype a phenomenon into smaller parts. The criticism levied at our original exposition of the ABD concept by Lyon et al. (2003) essentially took a splitter's perspective and dismissed the value of a lumping approach such as the one we proposed. What we have tried to do in this chapter is to propose a somewhat novel solution to the lumper versus splitter tension: *We believe that in the area of learning disabilities, both approaches can live side-by-side harmoniously.*

It is true, as Lyon et al. (2003) claimed, that a broad concept can be "overarching" and consequently will not contribute to a field where diagnostic specificity is often the goal. But we question whether such diagnostic specificity should be the sole goal, given the fact that current diagnostic schemes seem to have failed to characterize the general population of people with learning disorders. We base this accusation of failure on the simple fact that at least 50% of all children are assigned multiple labels (the so-called "comorbidities"). As we have said elsewhere (e.g., Kaplan et al., 2001; Gilger & Kaplan, 2001), the very fact that "comorbidity is the rule rather than the exception" is a statement in need of a response, and it pertains directly to the adequacy of the diagnostic categories.

Our proposed approach of employing the concept of ABD does not presume to exclude the definition of a circumscribed phenotype; rather, it suggests there is value in more broadly characterizing the skill sets of

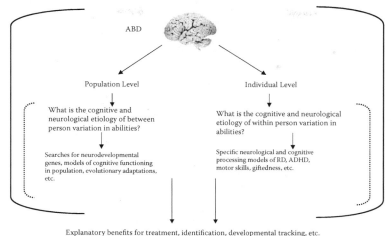

Figure 3.4 Typical and atypical brain development as an overarching concept.

the individuals being studied. The coexistence of the lumping and splitting approaches would likely offer an improved approach in both clinical and research applications, and particularly with adults.

In Figure 3.4 we show a possible way of thinking about ABD and how it might work alongside other theories. All neurological and neuropsychological research and modeling essentially deals with the atypical or typical brain, depending on its focus. Hence, for developmental disorders, we show in brackets that ABD can serve as the broader concept under which would fall the more specialized research. As the picture implies, the latter type of research is not isolated and it only takes place under the general umbrella of ABD. What this figure does is highlight the fact that as researchers we might do well to acknowledge the role of the whole brain, lest we lose sight of the forest for the trees.

References

Aaron, P. G., Joshi, M. R, & Ocker, E. S. (2004). Summoning up the spirits from the vast deep: LD and giftedness in historic persons. In T. Newman & R. Sternberg (Eds.), *Students with both gifts and learning disabilities* (pp. 199–234). New York: Kluwer Press.

Americans With Disabilities Act, PL 101–336, 1990.

Bergman, L. R., & Magnussen, D. (1997). A person-oriented approach in research on developmental psychopathology. *Development and Psychopathology, 9*, 291–319.

Bonifacci, P. (2004). Children with low motor ability have lower visual-motor integration ability but unaffected perceptual skills. *Human Movement Science, 23*, 57–68.

Changeaux, J.-P. (1985). *Neuronal man*. New York: Oxford.

Clements, S. G., & Peters, J. E. (1962). Minimal brain dysfunctions in the school-age child. *Archives of General Psychiatry, 6*, 185–197.

Conn, M. T. (Ed.). (1992). *Gene expression in neural tissue*. San Diego, CA: Academic.

Davis, A. (2004). The credentials of brain-based learning. *Journal of Philosophy of Education, 38*, 21–35.

Eden, G. F., & Moats, L. (2002). The role of neuroscience in the remediation of students with dyslexia. *Nature Neuroscience, 5*, 1080–1084.

Eden, G. F., & Zeffiro, T. A. (1998). Neural systems affected in developmental dyslexia revealed by functional neuroimaging. *Neuron, 21*, 279–282.

Ehri, L. C., & Snowling, M. J. (2004). Developmental variation in word recognition. In C. A. Stone, E. R. Silliman, B. J. Ehren, & K. Apel (Eds.), *Handbook of language and literacy* (pp. 433–460). New York: Guilford Press.

Fadjukoff, P., Ahonen, T., & Lyytinen, H. (Eds.). (2001). *Learning disabilities from research to practice*. Jyvaskyla, Finland: Niilo Mäki Institute.

Fisher, S. E., Francks, C., Marlow, A. J., MacPhie, I. L., Newbury, D. F., Cardon, L. R., et al. (2002). Independent genome-wide scans identify a chromosome 18 quantitative-trait locus influencing dyslexia. *Nature Genetics, 30*, 86–91.

Fisher, S. E., Marlow, A. J., Lamb, J., Maestrini, E., Williams, D. F., Richardson, A. J., et al. (1999). A quantitative-trait locus on chromosome 6p influences different aspects of developmental dyslexia. *American Journal of Human Genetics, 64*, 146–156.

Fletcher, J. M., Denton, C., Fuchs, L., & Vaughn, S. R. (2005). Multi-tiered reading instruction: Linking general education and special education. In S. Richardson & J. Gilger (Eds.). *Research-based education and intervention: What we need to know*. Baltimore, MD: International Dyslexia Association Press.

Fletcher J. M., Shaywitz, S. E., & Shaywitz, B. A. (1999). Comorbidity of learning and attention disorders: Separate but equal. *Pediatric Clinics of North America, 46*(5), 885–897.

Frith, U. (2001). What framework should we use for understanding developmental disorders? *Developmental Neuropsychology, 20*(2), 555–563.

Galaburda, A. M. (1992). Neurology of developmental dyslexia. *Current Opinion in Neurology and Neurosurgery, 5*, 71–76.

Galaburda, A. M. (1993). Neurology of developmental dyslexia. *Current Opinion in Neurobiology, 3*, 237–242.

Gayan, J., Smith, S. D., Cherny, S. S., Cardon, L. R., Fulker, D. W., Brower, A. M., et al. (1999). Quantitative-trait locus for specific language and reading deficits on chromosome 6p. *American Journal of Human Genetics, 64*, 157–164.

Gerlai, R. (1996). Gene-targeting studies of mammalian behavior: Is it the mutation or the background genotype? *Trends in Neuroscience, 19*, 177–181.

Geschwind, N., & Galaburda, A. M. (1987). *Cerebral lateralization*. Cambridge, MA: MIT Press.

Gilger, J. W. (1995). Behavioral genetics: Concepts for research in language and language disabilities. *Speech and Hearing Research, 38*, 1126–1142.

Gilger, J., Hynd, G., & Wilkins, M. (in press). Atypical natural neurodevelopmental variation as a basis for thinking about the gifted dyslexic. *Roeper Review*.

Gilger, J. W., & Kaplan, B. J. (2001). The neuropsychology of dyslexia: The concept of atypical brain development. *Developmental Neuropsychology, 20*, 469–486.

Gilger, J. W., & Wise, S. (2004). Genetic correlates of language and literacy. In C. Addison Stone, E. R. Silliman, B. J. Ehren, & K. Apel. (Eds.). *Handbook of language and literacy development and disorders.* New York: Guilford Press.

Goldstein, S., & Schwebach, A. J. (2004). The comorbidity of pervasive developmental disorder and attention deficit hyperactivity disorder: Results of a retrospective chart review. *Journal of Autism and Developmental Disorders, 34*(3), 329–339.

Greenough, W. T., Black, J. E., & Wallace, C. S. (2002). Experience and brain development. In M. H. Johnson, Y. Munakata, & R. O. Gilmore (Eds.), *Brain development and cognition: A reader* (pp. 186–216). Oxford: Blackwell.

Grigorenko, E. L., Wood, F. B., Meyer, M. S., Hart, L. A., Speed, W. C., Shuster, A., et al. (1997). Susceptibility loci for distinct components of developmental dyslexia on chromosomes 6 and 15. *American Journal of Human Genetics, 60,* 27–39.

Hahn, W. E., van Ness, J., & Maxwell, I. H. (1978). Complex population of mRNA sequences in large polydenylylated nuclear RNA molecules. *Proceedings of the National Academy of Science, 75,* 5544–5547.

Huttonlocher, P. R. (2002). *Neural plasticity: The effects of the environment on the development of the cerebral cortex.* Cambridge, MA: Harvard University Press.

Hynd, G. W., & Orbrzut, J. E. (1986). Exceptionality: Historical antecedents and present positions. In R. Brown & C. Reynolds (Eds.), *Psychological perspectives on childhood exceptionality: A handbook* (pp. 3–27). New York: John Wiley & Sons.

Jeffries, S., & Everatt, J. (2004). Working memory: Its role in dyslexia and other specific learning difficulties. *Dyslexia, 10,* 196–214.

Johnson, M. H., Munakata, Y., & Gilmore, R. O. (Eds.). (2002). *Brain development and cognition: A reader.* Oxford: Blackwell.

Jones, P., & Murray, R. M. (1991). The genetics of schizophrenia is the genetics of neurodevelopment. *British Journal of Psychiatry, 158,* 615–623.

Kalbfleisch, M. L. (2004). Functional neural anatomy of talent. *The Anatomical Record (Part B: New Anatomy) 277B,* 21–36.

Kaplan, B. J., Dewey, D. M., Crawford, S. G., & Wilson, B. N. (2001). The term comorbidity is of questionable value in reference to developmental disorders: Data and theory. *Journal of Learning Disabilities, 34,* 555–565.

Kennedy, D. N., Haselgrove, C., & McInerney, S. (2003). MRI-based morphometric analysis of typical and typical brain development. *Mental Retardation and Developmental Disabilities Research Reviews 9,* 155–160.

Lieberman, P. (1984). *The biology and evolution of language.* Cambridge, MA: Harvard College.

Luria, A. R. (1973). *The working brain.* Baltimore, MD: Penguin.

Lyon, G. R., Fletcher, J. M., & Barnes, M. C. (2003). Learning disabilities. In E. J. Mash & R. Barkley (Eds.), *Child psychopathology* (2nd ed., pp. 520–558). New York: Guilford.

Lyytinen, H., with Olson, R., Stein, J., Hynd, G., Gilger, J., Kaplan, B., et al. (2000). *The neuropsychology of dyslexia.* Paper presented at the 27th International Congress of Psychology, Stockholm, July, 2000.

Lyytinen, H., Aro, M., Eklund, K., Erskine, J., Guttorm, T., Laasko, M. L., et al. (2004). The development of children at familial risk for dyslexia: Birth to early school age. *Annals of Dyslexia, 54,* 184–220.

Lyytinen, H., Leinonen, M., Nikula, M., Aro, M., & Leiwo, M. (1995). In search of the core features of dyslexia: Observations concerning dyslexia in the highly orthographic regular Finnish language. In V. W. Berninger (Ed.), *The varieties of orthographic knowledge II: Relationships to phonology, reading, and writing.* Dordrecht: Kluwer.

Marcus, G. (2004). *The birth of the mind: How a tiny number of genes creates the complexities of human thought.* New York: Basic Books.

Mody, M. (2004). Neurobiological correlates of language and reading impairments. In C. Addison Stone, E. R. Silliman, B. J. Ehren, & K. Apel. (Eds.). *Handbook of language and literacy development and disorders* (pp. 49–72). New York: Guilford Press.

Narhi, V., & Ahonen, T. (1995). Reading disability with or without attention-deficit/hyperactivity disorder: Do attentional problems make a difference? *Developmental Neuropsychology, 11,* 337–350.

Newman, T. M., & Sternberg, R. J. (2004). *Students with both gifts and learning disabilities: Identification, assessment, and outcomes.* New York: Kluwer Academic/Plenum.

Noctor, S. C., Flint, A. C, Weissman, T. A., Dammerman, R. S., & Kriegstein, A. R. (2001). Neurons derived from radial glial cells establish radial units in neocortex. *Nature, 409,* 714–720.

Olson, R. K., Forsberg, H., & Wise, B. (1994). Genes, environment, and the development of orthographic skills. In V. W. Berninger (Ed.), *The varieties of orthographic knowledge I: Theoretical and developmental issues* (pp. 27–71). Dordrecht: Kluwer Academic.

Pennington, B. F. (1991). *Diagnosing learning disorders: A neuropsychological framework.* New York: Guilford Press.

Pennington, B. F. (1997). Using genetics to dissect cognition. *American Journal of Human Genetics, 60,* 13–16.

Pennington, B. F. (2002). Genes and brain: Individual differences and human universals. In M. H. Johnson, Y. Munakata, & R. O. Gilmore (Eds.), *Brain development and cognition: A reader* (pp. 494–508). Oxford: Blackwell.

Petryshen, T. L., Kaplan, B. J., Liu, M. F., Schmill de French, N., Tobias, R., Hughes, M. L., et al. (2001). Evidence for a susceptibility locus (DYX4) on chromosome 6q influencing phonological coding dyslexia. *American Journal of Human Genetics (Neuropsychiatric Genetcs), 105,* 507–517.

Positive psychology [Special issue]. (2001, March). *American Psychologist, 56*(3).

Ramus, F. (2001). Dyslexia: Talk of two theories. *Nature, 412,* 393–395.

Ramus, F. (2004). The neural basis of reading acquisition. In M. S. Gazzaniga (Ed.), *The new cognitive neurosciences* (3rd ed.). Cambridge, MA: MIT Press.

Rapin, I. (2002) Diagnostic dilemmas in developmental disabilities: Fuzzy margins at the edges of normality. An essay prompted by Thomas Sowell's new book: *The Einstein Syndrome. Journal of Autism and Developmental Disorders, 32,* 49–57.

Regehr, S., & Kaplan, B. J. (1988). Reading disability with motor problems may be an inherited subtype. *Pediatrics, 82,* 204–210.

Rice, M., & Brooks, G. (2004). *Developmental dyslexia in adults: A research review.* London: National Research and Development Centre for Adult Literacy and Numeracy.

Rondi-Reig, L., Caston, J., Delhaye-Bouchaud, N., & Mariani, J. (1999). Cerebellar functions: A behavioral neurogenetics perspective. In B. Jones & P. Mormede (Eds.), *Neurobehavioral genetics: Methods and applications* (pp. 201–216). New York: CRC Press.

Satz, P., & Fletcher, J. M. (1980). Minimal brain dysfunctions: An appraisal of research concepts and methods. In H. Rie & E. Rie (Eds.), *Handbook of minimal brain dysfunctions: A critical view* (pp. 669–715). New York: Wiley Interscience Series.

Shapiro, B., Church, R. P., & Lewis, M. E. B. (2002). Specific learning disabilities. In M. Batshaw (Ed.), *Children with disabilities* (pp. 417–442). Baltimore: Paul Brookes.

Shaywitz, B. A., Shaywitz, S. E., Pugh, K. R., Mencl, W. E. Fulbright, R. K., Skudlarski, P., et al. (2002). Disruption of posterior brain systems for reading in children with developmental dyslexia. *Biological Psychiatry, 52*(2), 101–110.

Shaywitz, S. E., Shaywitz, B. A., Pugh, K. R., Fulbright, R. K., Constable, R. T., Mencl, W. E., et al. (1998). Functional disruption in the organization of the brain for reading in dyslexia. *Proceedings of the National Academy of Science, 95*(5), 2636–2641.

Smith, S. D., Gilger, J. W., & Pennington, B. F. (2002). Dyslexia and other language/hearing disorders. In D. Rimoin, J. Connors, & R. Pyeritz (Eds.), *Emory and Rimoin's principles and practices in medical genetics* (5th ed., Vol. 3, pp. 2827–2865). New York: Livingstone Churchill.

Sonuga-Barke, E. J. S. (2003). On the intersection between ADHD and DCD: The DAMP Hypothesis. *Child and Adolescent Mental Health, 8*, 114–116.

Stone, C. A., Silliman, E. R., Ehren, B. J., & Apel, K. (Eds.). (2004). *Handbook of language and literacy.* New York: Guilford Press.

Valtonen, R., Ahonen, T., Lyytinen, P., & Lyytinen, H. (2004). Co-occurrence of developmental delays in a screening study of 4-year-old Finnish children. *Developmental Medicine and Child Neurology, 46*, 436–443.

Voeller, K. (1999). Neurological factors underlying the comorbidity of attentional dysfunction and dyslexia. In D. Duane (Ed.), *Reading and attention disorders: Neurobiological correlates* (pp. 185–211). Timonium, MD: York Press.

Waddington, C. H. (1975). *The evolution of an evolutionist.* Edinburgh: Edinburgh University Press.

Willcutt, E. G., Pennington, B. F., Smith, S. D., Cardon, L. R., Gayán, J., Knopik, V. S., et al. (2002). Quantitative trait locus for reading disability on chromosome 6p is pleiotropic for attention deficit hyperactivity disorder. *American Journal of Medical Genetics (Neuropsychiatric Genetics), 114*, 260–268.

Wood, F., & Flowers, L. (1999). Functional neuroanatomy of dyslexic subtypes. In D. Duane (Ed.), *Reading and attention disorders: Neurobiological correlates* (pp. 129–160). Timonium, MD: York Press.

PART 2

Neurobiology and Specific Learning Disorders

CHAPTER 4

Developmental Dyslexia in Adults
Implications for Studies of Its Etiology

ELENA L. GRIGORENKO

Contents

Conventionally, developmental dyslexia (DD) is viewed as a disorder of literacy acquisition (i.e., accurate and fluent word reading, spelling, and writing skills) that cannot be attributed to low intelligence, neurological abnormalities, or inadequate educational experiences. It is now an accepted fact that DD is a life-span disorder. When compared with the general population, adults with DD are characterized by lower profiles of indicators of educational background, employment status, and reading and writing activities at work and at home (Chapman, Tunmer, & Allen, 2003; Fawcett, 2003; Magajna, Kavkler, & Ortar-Krizaj, 2003; Taylor & Walter, 2003), as well as a raised profile of social maladaptation (Skaalvik, 2004; Winter, Holland, & Collins, 1997) and higher rates of emotional (McNulty, 2003) and mental health problems (Undheim, 2003).

However, as is often the case in development, trajectories of reading performance are not homogeneous across the life span in individuals with DD. Of importance for the discussion here is that, although the corner-stone of DD is substantial difficulty progressing through various steps of literacy formation, individuals with DD can achieve typical and even superior levels of reading performance in adulthood with proper education and remediation (Brunswick, McCrory, Price, Frith, & Frith, 1999; Gallagher, Laxon, Armstrong, & Frith, 1996).

Correspondingly, adults diagnosed with DD are typically referred to as either "compensated" or "non/uncompensated" readers. Compensated readers' reading skills reach average levels of functioning (as measured by standardized tests of reading and spelling), which allows them to continue formal academic studies and enter labor markers requiring adequate reading skills. Non/uncompensated readers' educational and employment opportunities remain limited in adulthood because of their depressed reading skills (Pennington et al., 1986).

There is a certain amount of ambiguity in the "compensated/uncompensated" distinction. First, many "compensated" adults continue to demonstrate profound differences on a number of reading-related tasks at both cognitive (Bruck, 1998; Brunswick et al., 1999; Elbro, Nielsen, & Petersen, 1994; Gottardo, Siegal, & Stanovich, 1997; Leong, 1999; Shaywitz et al., 1999; Snowling, Nation, Moxham, Gallagher, & Frith, 1997) and brain levels (Paulesu et al., 1996; Shaywitz et al., 2003). Second, the mechanisms of compensation are unclear. For example, it has been demonstrated that compensated adults with DD tend to rely more heavily on context when compared with typical readers (Ben-Dror, Pollatsek, & Scarpati, 1991). The researchers hypothesized that the slowness at word-level processing characteristic of adults with DD might be attributable to an activation of higher order, conscious metacognitive processes at the level that typical readers usually address with automatized unconscious processes. Other hypotheses suggest that better prognoses for adult outcomes of DD are related to better oral language and richer vocabulary (Bruck, 1990; Conners & Olson, 1990).

In sum, it appears that the presence and experience of the cognitive phenomenology of DD in childhood triggers a set of events that determines particular trajectories of cognitive development, whose resulting dynamic, distinct profiles of cognitive skills are detectable in adults, whether "compensated" or not. Yet the very fact that the manifestation of the deficit can change over the life span introduces a set of challenges for studying DD in adults. In this chapter, I briefly (a) summarize what is known about adult DD-related cognitive profiles and their components, (b) discuss the associations between these profiles and brains and genes, and (c) discuss the implications of what is currently known about these profiles and their components for studies of the etiology of DD.

Heterogeneity of Presentation of Developmental Dyslexia (DD) in Adults

The manifestation of DD in adults has been studied much less than has the manifestation of DD in children. Generally, the investigation has unfolded along the following two dimensions of inquiry: (1) which deficits in what modalities of information processing are characteristic of DD, and (2) are there general deficits that manifest themselves consistently across multiple modalities?

In What Domain Is the Signature DD Deficit?

With regard to "specific deficits" characteristic of DD, it would be an understatement to say that adult manifestations of reading deficiencies are variable; they are extremely heterogeneous. An illustration of such heterogeneity comes from a study conducted on 32 university students, half of whom had DD (Ramus et al., 2003). The participants in this study received a large battery of psychometric, phonological, auditory, visual, and motor tasks. The battery was compiled based on the field's understanding of the domains of cognitive functioning in which adult deficits in DD have been repeatedly registered in a number of studies. All participants in this research received all assessments. Of the assessed individuals with DD, all 16 demonstrated phonological deficits, 10 showed auditory deficits, 4 had motor deficits, and 2 showed visual deficits; in other words, all these adults with DD had phonological deficits and many had at least one or more deficits in other domains.

To exemplify a variety of procedural deficits registered in adults with DD in the domains assessed in the study above, here I summarize only the highlights of this work, referring the reader to chapters by Daniels and by Wolf and Kaplan.

As per the findings of Ramus and colleagues (2003), four domains of cognitive processing have been central to studies of the cognitive texture of DD in adults: visual, auditory, motor, and language.

A long-standing assumption in studies of DD is that visual impairment can form a foundation for difficulties processing printed letters and words

(Livingstone, Rosen, Drislane, & Galaburda, 1991; Lovegrove, Bowling, Badcock, & Blackwood, 1980). Correspondingly, some researchers have suggested that specific visual processing deficits contribute to DD in adults (Cornelissen, Richardson, Mason, Fowler, & Stein, 1995). These deficits were reported in a variety of manifestations, such as deficits in binocular fixation (Cornelissen, Munro, Fowler, & Stein, 1993) and sequential spatial frequency discrimination (Ben-Yehudah & Ahissar, 2003), among others. The mechanisms behind these deficits are not clear, but there is evidence that such deficits might arise in the lower levels of visual processing, for example, deficiencies in the magnocellular pathway of the visual system (Chase & Jenner, 1993; Livingstone et al., 1991; but see also Greatrex & Drasdo, 1995, for noncorroborative findings and hypotheses), as well as at the higher levels of visual processing, for example, visual attention (Facoetti, Paganoni, & Lorusso, 2000; Iles, Walsh, & Richardson, 2000) and visual memory (Ben-Yehudah & Ahissar, 2003).

Other researchers have pointed out auditory deficits in DD (Ahissar, Protopapas, Reid, & Merzenich, 2000; Amitay, Ahissar, & Nelken, 2002). Of interest here is that when individuals with DD perform tasks with single stimuli—for example, pure tones—DD readers do not differ from typical readers (Nicolson & Fawcett, 1993; Watson & Miller, 1993). It is the more complex tasks that appear to differentiate DD and typical readers clearly and substantially. Specifically, it has been shown that individuals with DD are impaired on a number of different psychoacoustic measures of auditory processing. For example, individuals with DD are characterized by a different performance profile than that of typical readers on tests of, among others, frequency acuity (Hill, Bailey, Griffiths, & Snowling, 1999), processing of natural phonemes or speechlike stimuli (Breier et al., 2001), auditory temporal-order judgments involving pure tone or syllable pairs with items presented for a short time and closely spaced in time (Helenius, Uutela, & Hari, 1999; Overy, Nicolson, Fawcett, & Clarke, 2003), binaural unmasking (McAnally & Stein, 1996), coding of voiced and voiceless consonant-vowel syllables in the presence of temporal cues (Giraud et al., 2005), and amplitude modulation (Hamalainen, Leppanen, Torppa, Muller, & Lyytinen, 2005). However, there is a body of literature that challenges a number of findings cited above (Breier, Gray, Fletcher, & Foorman, 2002; Chiappe, Stringer, Siegel, & Stanovich, 2002); this research indicates that the acceptance of the auditory processing deficit hypothesis is not unequivocal.

Yet another body of literature introduces a hypothesis that individuals with DD are characterized by deficits on a number of motor tasks (Nicolson et al., 1999). Once again, the mechanisms of these deficiencies are not clearly understood, but their presence and other supportive evidence from brain-function studies indicate the possible involvement of the cerebellum as the biological foundation for these deficits (Brown et al., 2001; Leonard et al., 2001; Nicolson et al., 1999). In appraising this hypothesis, it is important to note that a number of studies have failed to register any motor dysfunction in DD, at least in children (Kronbichler, Hutzler, & Wimmer, 2002; van Daal & van der Leij, 1999; Wimmer, Mayringer, & Landerl, 1998), or have registered some dysfunction only in a subgroup of individuals with DD, in particular the subgroup in which DD and attention-deficit/hyperactivity disorder (ADHD) are comorbid, with or without additional psychiatric disorders (Denckla, Rudel, Chapman, & Krieger, 1985; Ramus, Pidgeon, & Frith, 2003; Wimmer, Mayringer, & Raberger, 1999).

A number of studies of adults with DD resulted, collectively, in a widely accepted observation that adults with DD, like children with DD, have difficulties with a variety of aspects of language processing (Elbro et al., 1994; Felton, Naylor, & Wood, 1990; Kitz & Tarver, 1989; Wilson & Lesaux, 2001). First and foremost, adults with DD tend to demonstrate lower than average levels of literacy. These deficits are detectable at multiple levels, from text level (Ransby & Swanson, 2003) to word level (Bruck, 1990; Yap & van der Leij, 1993). Such deficits are demonstrated, specifically, by poor spelling and decreased indicators of reading speed and accuracy while reading single units of text, words, and pseudowords (Ramus et al., 2003). Second, many studies indicated the presence of deficits in performing phonological tasks (Snowling, 1995). Specifically, compared with typical adults, adults with DD are slower and less accurate while reading aloud familiar and unfamiliar single- and multisyllabic words (Bruck, 1992; Ben-Dror et al., 1991). In addition, they perform below average on tasks of phonemic awareness (Snowling, Nation, Moxham, Gallagher, & Frith, 1994; Wilson & Lesaux, 2001), omission (Bruck, 1992), phonemic fluency (Snowling et al., 1994; Wilson & Lesaux, 2001), rhyming (Nicolson & Fawcett, 1993), phonological disharmony (Levinthal & Hornung, 1992), and phonological memory (Wilson & Lesaux, 2001). Similarly, individuals with DD show less accurate spoonerism (Ramus et al., 2003; Wilson & Lesaux, 2001). Third, adults with DD tend to be characterized by a naming speed deficit, reflective of deficits in phonological retrieval and encoding (van der Leij & van Daal, 1999; Wolf & Katzir-Cohen, 2001). Yet the specificity of this deficit with regard to the nature of the stimuli to be named (e.g., graphological or nongraphological; Felton et al., 1990), the extent of the deficit in groups of compensated and noncompensated adults with DD (Kinsbourne, Rufo, Gamzu, Palmer, & Berliner, 1991), and its replicability in heterogeneous samples of adults is still under investigation (Everatt, 1997; Wolff, Michel, & Ovrut, 1990). Fourth, there appears to be a vocabulary deficit, demonstrated by challenged lexical access (Milne, Nicholson, & Corballis,

2003) and depleted vocabulary size (Ransby & Swanson, 2003). Finally, most adults with DD have difficulty with spelling (Brunswick et al., 1999; Elbro et al., 1994; Gallagher et al., 1996; Shaywitz et al., 1999).

Of particular importance are findings attesting to the presence of DD-related deficits in multiple information-processing systems simultaneously—for example, visual and linguistic (Slaghuis, Twell, & Kingston, 1996); visual and auditory (Breznitz & Meyler, 2003); auditory, visual, and linguistic (Cestnick, 2001; Meyler & Breznitz, 2005); and audiotactile, visuotactile, and audiovisual systems (Laasonen, Service, & Virsu, 2002). Different hypotheses attempting to explain the multidimensionality of DD-related deficits have been proposed (e.g., an extension of the magnocelluar theory [Stein & Walsh, 1997]), but the hypothesis of "combined deficits" has also been challenged (Birch & Chase, 2004).

In sum, this mosaic of findings makes it clear why Ramus and colleagues (2003) stressed the importance of administering such a comprehensive set of tasks to adults with DD—because the deficits in adults with DD are both pronounced and illusive, and depend on many factors, such as the type and severity of the deficits manifested in childhood and the amount of remediative efforts received.

Is DD Deficit Specific or General?

As mentioned earlier, another line of debate around the profile of cognitive deficits in DD has to do with whether these deficits are domain specific or domain general. One line of research posits the presence of more general problems in cognitive processing characteristic of individuals with DD. Indirectly, the hypothesis of a more generalized cognitive deficit is said to be supported by the above-cited literature, suggesting that DD might be related to information processing and production deficiencies in multiple domains.

For example, there is evidence, although controversial, that readers with DD demonstrate temporal processing impairment (Conlon, Sanders, & Zapart, 2004; Klein, 2002). Because reading requires convergence of multiple representations, if such a central timing deficiency exists, mismatches, miscoordination, and misintegration of different types of representation might occur (Breznitz, 2002). It has been argued that these timing deficits are especially pronounced at the linguistic as compared with the nonlinguistic level (Meyler & Breznitz, 2005).

Yet another "candidate" for such a central deficit is working memory (Swanson & Siegel, 2003). The assumption here is that the working memory capacity of individuals with DD is deficient, at least in processing linguistic stimuli (Gathercole & Baddeley, 1993).

An additional candidate for such a general deficit in DD is related to the idea that individuals with DD are unable to gain from experience or to integrate different types of representations at higher levels of processing. For example, in pursuing the old idea that DD is at least partially causally related to deficits in visual attention, researchers (Roach & Hogben, 2004) administered a set of tasks combining spatial cuing with a visual search task to measure psychophysical threshold in small groups of adults with and without DD. These experiments were designed to provide data that might differentiate what was deficient in individuals with DD compared with typical readers: (a) psychophysical threshold, (b) higher level integrated visual attention, (c) both, or (d) neither. The researchers reported that uncued search performance of typical readers was strongly associated with the number of elements in the stimulus array, but this association weakened substantially when the location of the target was cued; this change in the strength of association was interpreted as suggestive of an attention-based enhancement of task performance. In individuals with DD, however, there was no pronounced change in association in response to the introduction of cuing. In fact, although their performance on uncued search tasks was almost as good as that of typical readers, they did not benefit from cuing the same way typical readers did.

There are also research studies suggesting DD-related deficits at a metacognitive level, specifically, in executive functioning (Brosnan et al., 2002; Moores, Nicolson, & Fawcett, 2003).

Finally, it is important to mention that the literature contains evidence that the degree of DD-related deficits in adults is moderated by levels of general cognitive ability (Shaywitz et al., 2003), so that, for example, auditory deficits are expressed differently at different levels of cognitive ability (Ben-Yehudah, Banai, & Ahissar, 2004).

In summary, to close this section and return to the study of Ramus and colleagues (2003), it appears that a set of unquestionable deficits characterizing DD in adults is related to deficits in language processing. However, specific dimensions of these deficits have yet to be established unequivocally; it is possible that these deficits vary in heterogeneous subgroups of adults with DD. Yet there are many other nonlinguistic (i.e., visual, auditory, tactile, motor) deficits that also appear to be characteristic of individuals with DD. Given this mosaic of problems in individuals with DD, various theories suffer from their incapacity to explain either the presence or the absence of particular deficits (Ramus et al., 2003).

Developmental Transformations of DD Manifestations

The overwhelming majority of research on the cognitive texture of DD has been carried out with children. As mentioned earlier, the amount of work on adults with DD is considerably smaller. Lately, there has been growing interest in whether cognitive profiles of DD are similar in children and adults. The studies mentioned below do not comprise a comprehensive review of the literature, but they are representative of the findings in the field. Broadly, they can be classified into three categories: cross-sectional, prospective, and longitudinal.

The main thrust of the *cross-sectional studies* of DD is to compare "the same" DD-related deficits in children and adults. For example, Miller-Shaul (2005) compared four groups of readers—children with and without DD and adults with and without DD ($n = 25$ in each group)—on a large number of reading-related tasks. The readers with DD, regardless of their age group, differed significantly and substantially on the overwhelming majority of the studied indicators. Of special interest, however, are clear cross-sectional differences: the difference on orthographic tasks was much smaller between adults with and without DD than between children with and without DD, whereas group differences on phonological tasks in adults were comparable to those in children. Given the structure of the tasks used in this work, Miller-Shaul suggested that this "decreased" gap between adults with and without DD is attributable to the compensatory mechanisms of education—orthographical tasks require mostly visual recognition of words rather than articulating them anew. These findings are congruent with earlier results, indicating that phonological deficiencies improve little, if at all, with age and increased reading level (Bruck, 1992; Flowers, 1995; Snowling, 1980), whereas orthographical deficiencies appear to be minimized and compensated for as reading skills increase (Corcos & Willows, 1993).

In a different study, Breznitz and Misra (2003) investigated "asynchrony" in the speed of processing between the visual-orthographic and auditory-phonological modalities in 40 adults with a history of DD and 40 age/nonverbal IQ-matched typical readers. The researchers administered a set of experimental tasks designed to evaluate auditory and visual processing for nonlinguistic (tones and shapes) and linguistic (phonemes and graphemes) low-level stimuli as well as higher level orthographic and phonological processing (in a lexical decision task) to male university students. They also registered event-related potentials (ERPs) and reaction times (RTs) while the adults were engaged in these tasks. As expected based on substantial literature about children, adults with concurrent or historical DD demonstrated significantly slower RTs and longer P300 latencies* than did typical readers in most of the experimental tasks,

---

* The P300 component is a positive-going waveform that is assumed to index the distribution of resources (Kramer, 1991), mental effort (Wilson, Swain, & Ullsperger, 1998), and dynamic updating of information in working memory (Fitzgerald & Picton, 1983).

delayed P200 latencies* for the lexical decision task, and a systematic speed of processing gap in P300 latency between the auditory-phonological and visual-orthographic processing measures. Of special interest for the discussion here, however, is that their findings showed that the between-modalities asynchrony occurs at later processing stages in adults with DD compared with children with DD. These two illustrations, among many others, suggest that even when the domain and mechanism of the deficit are the same, substantive differences exist in the ways these deficits are manifested in adults.

The main objective of *prospective studies* of DD is to observe and quantify the development of literacy and reading-related skills in children of adults with DD (Carroll & Snowling, 2004; Gallagher, Frith, & Snowling, 2000; Lyytinen et al., 2004; Lyytinen & Lyytinen, 2004; Scarborough, 1990; Snowling, Gallagher, & Frith, 2003; van Alphen et al., 2004). The results of these studies provide an exciting quilt of findings, which are summarized here only in broad strokes. When compared with control groups of typical children, as a group, children of individuals with DD show a distinct pattern of differences in their linguistic developments, detectable at the levels of behavior and cognitive function. Among these detectable group differences are challenges in early motor development (Viholainen, Ahonen, Cantell, Lyytinen, & Lyytinen, 2002), early deficient patterns of ERPs to speech sounds (Lyytinen et al., 2005), a variety of difficulties in articulation and language-development difficulties (Elbro, Borstrom, & Petersen, 1998; Lyytinen & Lyytinen, 2004; Scarborough, 1990; van Alphen et al., 2004), substantial deficiencies in phonological skills (Carroll & Snowling, 2004; Gallagher et al., 2000; Pennington & Lefly, 2001), and relatively poor vocabulary (Gallagher et al., 2000). And, last but not least, the rate of DD among children of adults with DD is substantially higher than in the general population (Elbro et al., 1998). Thus, taken together, these studies indicate that children of individuals with DD are at substantially higher risk for the development of broadly defined language problems that are not limited to the domain of reading. These children, as a group, tend to demonstrate motor difficulties and early auditory deficiencies in processing speechlike sounds. Finally, it appears that children of individuals with DD are extremely heterogeneous in terms of their individual outcomes and prognoses; they do differ, as a group, from typically developing children, but the variability within them is remarkable. It is also important to know that this variability is present and impressive even when the parents

---

* The P200 component is a positive-going waveform that is assumed to reflect selective attention (Hackley, Woldorff, & Hillyard, 1990) and early sensory stages of item/feature detection (Luck & Hillyard, 1994) and encoding (Dunn, Dunn, Languis, & Andrews, 1998).

of these children are carefully selected to form as homogeneous a group of adults with DD as possible.

Finally, there is much interest in the field in *longitudinal* studies of children at risk for or diagnosed with DD. Such studies are still few and far between, given how time consuming and effortful it is to follow these children into adulthood. In addition, these studies are still in progress, permitting the field to gain insights into the adolescence but not (yet!) adulthood of the participants. But these studies have already produced interesting results. Once again, here I comment briefly on a selected set of findings from these studies that are relevant to our discussion. Generally speaking, results of these studies indicate that the development of reading and writing abilities in typical children and children with DD is closely related to the development of language in its multiple domains—vocabulary, grammar, and narration (Catts, Fey, & Proctor-Williams, 2000; Catts, Fey, Tomblin, & Zhang, 2002; Catts, Fey, Zhang, & Tomblin, 1999). Another important consideration is that, like prospective studies, longitudinal studies indicate that although between-group differences on different indices of language development are observed early, they appear to be even more pronounced as children acquire literacy in general and reading skills in particular. And, once again, researchers comment on the intergroup variability in outcomes for children at risk for DD: only a portion, although a substantial portion, of these children meet or continue to meet diagnostic criteria for DD, although many of them continue to demonstrate various process deficits in reading-related skills (Snowling, Bishop, & Stothard, 2000).

Summarizing these three lines of inquiry, three issues are ripe for discussion. First and foremost, across all types of studies, it seems that the best longitudinal predictors of reading outcomes in adulthood are general and specific aspects of language functioning in childhood. Yet it is important to note that there appear to be no direct connections between particular aspects of language functioning and particular aspects of reading—these indicators seem to form a complex network that both develops and is transmitted intergenerationally in a dynamic fashion. Second, it seems that DD-related deficits are not limited to the linguistic domain of functioning. Although most of the research literature is focused on these indicators, other indicators (e.g., motor and auditory) differentiate individuals at risk and diagnosed with DD both cross-sectionally and longitudinally. Third, the observed deficits appear to be of both a transient and continuous nature longitudinally. In other words, some deficits appear at a particular stage of development and then transform themselves into other deficits or normalize (e.g., although letter acquisition is difficult for children with DD, once the alphabet is acquired the deficiency is normalized). There are also other deficits that persist throughout the life span for the majority of individuals with DD.

The Brain With Respect to Typical and DD-Like Reading

Thus, as per the discussion above, the consensus is that DD—in both children and adults—is characterized by a failure (of various levels of severity) to develop a rapid, automatic, and accurate skill of processing (recognizing, identifying, reading aloud or silently) single words.* This failure is attributable to deficiencies in one or more types of representations of information required for this skill to emerge, develop, and crystallize adequately. In an attempt to reconstruct the mechanisms of this failure, researchers have considered deficiencies in the different types of systems involved in reading (e.g., visual, auditory, language) and different types of representations of information (e.g., phonological, orthographic, semantic). This general consideration is what has been targeted in an attempt to understand the brain correlates of DD.

It is important to mention that unlike behavioral studies of DD and typical reading, the majority of functional brain studies (e.g., position emission tomography, PET, and functional magnetic resonance imaging, fMRI) have been carried out on adults. These studies, summarized broadly, have identified and described neural structures involved in reading and reading-related processes in typical and atypical (specifically, DD) readers.

Broadly stated, a developed, automatized skill of reading single words engages a widespread, bilateral (but predominantly left hemispheric) network of brain areas, passing activation from the occipitotemporal regions through temporal (posterior) areas and toward the frontal (precentral and inferior frontal gyri) lobes (e.g., Brunswick et al., 1999; Elbro et al., 1994; Fiez & Petersen, 1998; Price & Mechelli, 2005; Shaywitz et al., 1999; Snyder & Downey, 1995; Turkeltaub, Gareau, Flowers, Zeffiro, & Eden, 2003). The process of reading is multifaceted and involves the activation of brain networks participating in visual, auditory, and conceptual processing (for a review, see Turkeltaub, Eden, Jones, & Zeffiro, 2002) that form the neural foundation for orthographical, phonological, and semantic representations (Fiez, 1997; Poldrack et al., 1999; Shaywitz et al., 1999; Tagamets, Novick, Chalmers, & Friedman, 2000). Correspondingly, it is expected that the areas of activation observed in reading studies serve as anatomic substrates

---

* Parts of this and the next section (Familiality, Heritability, and Molecular Bases of DD) of this chapter appeared in Grigorenko, E. L. (2007). "Triangulating Developmental Dyslexia: Behavior, Brain, and Genes," in D. Coch, G. Dawson, & K. Fischer (Eds.), *Human Behavior and the Developing Brain* (pp. 117–144) (New York: Guilford Press).

supporting all these types of representations and processing. However, possibly somewhat surprisingly, recent reviews indicate that there appear to be predominantly four areas of the brain of particular, specific interest with regard to reading (e.g., Brunswick et al., 1999; Shaywitz et al., 1999; Simos, Billingsley-Marshall, Sarkari, & Papanicolaou, 2008). These areas are: the fusiform gyrus (i.e., the occipitotemporal cortex in the ventral portion of Brodmann's area 37, BA 37); the posterior portion of the middle temporal gyrus (roughly BA 21, but possibly more specifically, the ventral border with BA 37 and the dorsal border of the superior temporal sulcus); the angular gyrus (BA 39); and the posterior portion of the superior temporal gyrus (BA 22). Of these areas, the left occipitotemporal and temporoparietal areas have emerged as those in which the absolute or relative patterns of activation distinguish individuals with and without DD most consistently (Agnew, Dorn, & Eden, 2004). It is also important to note that both developmental and remediation-induced changes in patterns of brain functioning occur with increased mastery of reading skill: progressive, behaviorally modulated development and increased engagement of left-hemispheric "versions" of these areas and progressive disengagement of homologous right-hemispheric areas (Eden et al., 2004; Gaillard, Balsamo, Ibrahim, Sachs, & Xu, 2003; Shaywitz et al., 1999; Turkeltaub et al., 2003).

Thus, similar to the behavior-related findings on DD in adults, it appears that the deficiencies of the brain systems involved in the manifestation of DD in adults, although descriptive of individuals with DD as a group, are complex and dynamic in nature. In fact, given the presence of the developmental shift in the dominant patterns of activation from the right to the left of the brain that parallels the acquisition of reading, the current trend in the field is not to look for particular anatomic differences that might implicate "faulty" anatomic structure in the brains of individuals with DD but rather to hypothesize explanations for the establishment of "faulty" connectivity networks between various brain structures that prohibit the realization of this shift during the developmentally appropriate period. Finally, it is important to note that the field's general knowledge of the brain "signature" of DD, at this point, is primarily correlational. Although there is an understanding of the general pathway of reading in the brain, researchers have not generated a clear understanding of the mechanisms underlying the formation of this pathway and its components. One possible avenue for discovering such mechanisms is in studying genes.

Familiality, Heritability, and Molecular Bases of DD

It is well established that DD is a familial disorder of genetic origin. There are multiple comprehensive reviews of the literature on the genetic bases of DD (e.g., Barr & Couto, 2008; Fisher & DeFries, 2002; Grigorenko, 2005). Though delivered in different words, voices, and often under different assumptions, three main conclusions can be drawn from this literature.

The first is that, even though the genetic basis of DD is extremely important, genes, at best, explain only a portion, although substantial, of the relevant variance (e.g., Grigorenko, 2004). Merely to provide an illustration, let me cite a few specific figures here. For example, the heritability estimates for word reading range from .19 (Stevenson, Graham, Fredman, & McLoughlin, 1987) to .55–.59 (Harlaar, Spinath, Dale, & Plomin, 2005). The estimates for phonemic awareness also leave a lot of room for environmental influences: .52 (Hohnen & Stevenson, 1999) and .83 (Gayan & Olson, 2003). In other words, even if the field fully understands the genetic machinery behind DD, it will be only halfway there; it will still need to identify to what factors the rest of the variance is attributable. Needless to say, researchers in the field have a great many guesses as to what these factors might be. Years of research into individual differences in reading skill point to the importance of three environmental (outside the individual) factors: an individual's (a) socioeconomic strata at large (e.g., an individual's country, community, and school, and his or her economic well-being); (b) teachers (e.g., amount of educational training and global pedagogical approach of teachers and teacher-specific pedagogical techniques); and (c) home environment (e.g., availability of relevant materials to practice the skill and motivate its further development).

The second conclusion refers to the realization that multiple genes appear to form the genetic bases for DD. Three lines of research are relevant here. The first line originates from quantitative genetics (Falconer & Mackay, 1996) and suggests that, to reach the appearance of uninterrupted, continuous distributions of a behavioral trait, many genes—each of which is responsible for a definable, discrete contribution—should form the genetic basis of this trait. This tradition has been very successful in contributing to the understanding of complex health-related continuous traits such as cholesterol concentration and bone density, and appears to be highly relevant to the literature on DD. The field has certainly enjoyed the quantitative nature of all reading-related traits, at least at some developmental periods (i.e., many phonemic awareness tasks trigger significant individual variability among preschoolers and show a ceiling effect after primary school), and no researcher will argue that reading-related traits are continuously distributed in the general population, although not everyone agrees on the nature of these distributions with regard to the number of modes and other characteristics of distributional moments. Thus, in looking at the behavioral traits of DD, it is only natural to assume that many genes are involved in forming these traits.

The second line of research is in the literature that attempts to fit different genetic models to behavioral data in an attempt to estimate the number of genes contributing to the manifestation of different reading-related skills (e.g., Marlow et al., 2003; Wijsman et al., 2000). The point of interest here is to model the observed familiality of reading-related componential processes by assuming various models of inheritance (e.g., dominant, recessive, additive), the number of genes involved, and the constellations of genes with regard to common and specific genes contributing to specific reading-related traits. Although there are disagreements about whether the genes contribute to *all* versus *some* reading-related processes, there is consensus that many genes, and likely genes of fairly small effects, contribute to DD-related processes.

Finally, the third line of research is traceable to the 1983 paper by Smith and colleagues that triggered the development of the molecular-genetic field of DD (Smith, Kimberling, Pennington, & Lubs, 1983). In that paper, the field got its first candidate region for DD, a region somewhere around the centromere on chromosome 15. The precision of genetic mapping was so low at that time that the boundaries of the region were huge, by genetic standards, and subsequent attempts to work with chromosome 15 resulted in both replications and nonreplications simply because researchers looked at various subregions of this initially flagged piece of the chromosome. Little did we know that it was only the beginning! The current state of affairs is quite remarkable: The field has nine candidate regions to entertain (Grigorenko, 2005). These regions are recognized as DD candidate regions; they are abbreviated as DYX1-9 and refer to the regions on chromosomes 15q, 6p, 2p, 6q, 3cen, 18p, 11p, 1p, and Xq, respectively. Each of these regions harbors dozens of genes so, clearly, the field offers empirical validation that multiple genes contribute to the manifestation of DD.

The third conclusion refers to the *putative function* of the contributing genes. A number of different research groups work on these loci in an attempt to identify plausible candidate genes. Four successful attempts have been announced in the literature: one for the 15q region, the candidate gene known as DYX1C1 (Taipale et al., 2003); two for the 6p region, the candidate gene known as KIAA0319 (Cope et al., 2005) and the candidate gene DCDC2 (Meng et al., 2005); and one for the 3cen region, ROB01 (Hannula-Jouppi et al., 2005). Yet, after the first presentation of the DYX1C1 gene, somewhat controversial evidence followed that challenged the association between DYX1C1 and dyslexia (Cope et al., 2004; Scerri et al., 2004). The association between KIAA0319 also awaits further confirmation, as there is at least one nonreplication (Barr, 2005); but there is some promising supporting evidence for DCDC2 (Schumacher et al., 2006). To my knowledge, no replications of ROB01 have yet been attempted.

Although the field has not yet converged on firm candidates, it is remarkable and of great scientific interest that all three current candidate genes for DD are involved with biological functions of neuronal migration and axonal crossing. It is possible that these genes are related to the establishment and dynamic development of the connectivity networks forming the brain bases for typical and atypical reading.

The three conclusions discussed above have been supported primarily by studies of families and units (e.g., pairs, trios, quadruples) of genetic relatives of various degrees (e.g., twins, siblings, and combinations of more distant genetic relatives) ascertained through children probands. In other words, when a child with DD has been identified, further assessment of his or her parents indicated the presence of higher than expected by chance accumulation of DD-related deficits. However, there is a set of studies in which families were ascertained through adults. Among these adults, three types of trajectories can be distinguished. First, there are adults who remained affected with DD throughout their lives. Second, there are adults who were identified with DD as children (i.e., had significant reading difficulties in childhood) but were remediated or compensated throughout their life span and do not meet criteria for DD in adulthood. Third, there are adults who were not diagnosed with DD as children but have had reading problems throughout their lives and then were recognized as having DD in adulthood. Most genetic studies of DD where families or units of relatives were identified through adults have been carried out with adults who meet the diagnostic criteria of DD in adulthood or in the presence of evidence of meeting these criteria in childhood, based on childhood records or retrospectively (e.g., Feldman et al., 1993; Gross-Glenn, Lewis, Smith, & Lubs, 1985).

Home Run: Implication of Studies of DD in Adults for Etiological Understanding

Having provided a brief overview of cognitive, brain, and genetic studies of DD in adults, I would like to close this chapter by discussing a number of issues.

The first issue relates to the overall importance of studies of DD in adults. Clearly, this research has a number of public health, education, and policy implications and is of great importance. With regard to the scientific significance of this research, the work with adults with DD permits the field to understand: (a) general developmental issues of life-span transformation of reading-related skills, in terms of understanding both abilities and disabilities; (b) group pathways for compensated and non/uncompensated adults and the overall role of remediation and education for ameliorating the impact of DD; and (c) general versus specific characteristics of DD-related cognitive deficits and their developmental transformations from childhood into adulthood.

Studies of DD in adulthood pose a number of difficult challenges, however. One of these challenges has to do with the definition of DD in adulthood. It is especially relevant to the discussion whether compensated adults can be referred to as adults with DD or should be viewed as "recovered." The issue here is the remaining cognitive deficits, which are detectable as demonstrated above, at both the cognitive and brain levels. And the corresponding question, as yet unanswered by the field, is whether DD in adulthood should be defined by strict clinical criteria or by the presence of residual cognitive-behavioral deficits or DD-specific signatures in the brain and the genes.

The second related challenge is qualifying and quantifying the deficits that segregate in families of probands with DD. If the family is ascertained through a child, the behavioral manifestation of DD in this child proband is typically fairly clear. But if the family is ascertained through an adult with DD, then the question is whether for such an ascertainment strategy the retrospective data on this adult in his or her childhood is enough to refer the adult as a proband, or whether this adult should be required to demonstrate deficits concurrent to the recruitment. The related issue pertains to the nature and severity of these deficits; clearly, there is an illusive border here with regard to the threshold between normative and deficit-like individual differences on reading-related traits, and collecting phenomenology for this threshold is important. Along the same line is the issue of the transient and continuous nature of DD-related deficits from childhood to adulthood. In the context of family studies, researchers need to define traits that are "the same" for children and adults to conduct quantitative or molecular genetic studies. The question here is whether, for example, orthographic deficits are the same in children and adults, indicating the same heritable "risk factor" for DD. Or should we take into account the transient developmental nature of this risk factor (see discussion above), and define it by, let's say, letter knowledge in children ages 5 to 6 and as comprehension deficit in adults older than 25? These are all issues that are currently under the scrutiny in the field.

Finally, the last issue of importance here is the comorbidity between DD and other childhood disorders as they continue into adulthood. For example, because there are only so many established links between DD and attention-deficit/hyperactivity disorder (ADHD) in childhood, it is reasonable to hypothesize that the links continue into adulthood. Unfortunately, only a very limited number of studies test this hypothesis empirically, and the results of these studies are rather surprising. For example, Biederman and colleagues (1994) administered the Arithmetic subtest of the Wide Range Achievement Test-Revised (WRAT-R) and either the Gilmore Oral Reading Test or the Reading Subtest of the WRAT-R to a group of 128 adults with ADHD and a comparable sample of control adults; no differences were found between the ADHD and control groups on either tests of arithmetic or reading achievement. Similarly, Seidman and colleagues (Seidman, Biederman, Weber, Hatch, & Faraone, 1998) compared performance on tests of arithmetic and reading in 64 unmedicated adults (19–59 years of age) with DSM-III-R ADHD of childhood onset who met criteria for ADHD when referred in adulthood and 73 non-ADHD controls of similar age and gender. The results of the comparison indicated no significant differences on the reading test, but the ADHD probands were significantly more impaired on the Arithmetic subtest. Samuelsson and colleagues (Samuelsson, Lundberg, & Herkner, 2004) commented on the fact that the WRAT-R achievement test of reading evaluated reading at a single-word processing level. To obtain a more complex representation of the reading skills in adults with ADHD, these researchers evaluated reading skills by administering four measures of word-decoding skills, three measures of phonological-processing skills, one measure of spelling, and one measure of reading comprehension. The participants of this study were 120 incarcerated and nonincarcerated male adults. ADHD diagnosis in this group was carried out with questionnaires used to assess (a) retrospective self-reports of childhood signs of ADHD, and (b) typical impairment associated with ADHD symptoms during the past 12 months. Twenty-four participants received an ADHD diagnosis and 21 of these individuals were in the incarcerated sample. The results indicate that there were no significant differences between the ADHD and the non-ADHD groups on tasks measuring phonological skills, word-decoding skills, and spelling, but there were significant group differences on the comprehension task. In addition to their analyses of componential skills of reading, the researchers investigated rates of categorically defined DD in the ADHD and non-ADHD samples using four different definitions of DD; these definitions were based on the discrepancy criteria between reading performance and verbal, nonverbal, and combined abilities, and the presence or absence of phonological core deficit. Like those discussed earlier, these results did not reveal any significant association between ADHD and DD. On the contrary, when comprehension deficit was dichotomized, there was a substantial association between this deficit and ADHD. Of interest in this context is the authors' observation that the four categorical schemes they used for establishing DD diagnoses overlapped with categorical comprehension deficit only minimally. Thus, studies of comorbidity between ADHD and DD in adulthood raise the issue of clear thresholds between different childhood diagnoses as they are expressed early in development versus later in the life span. One possible hypothesis here is that, because of the diffused nature of deficits characteristic of different developmental disorders and intensive remediational practices, at least in the developed world, developmental disorders of childhood "converge" in adulthood and form a more homogeneous "vulnerability" syndrome. The second possible hypothesis is driven by the concept of pleiotropy.* Specifically, given that both DD and ADHD appear to be controlled by multiple genes, it is possible that there is at least a partial overlap between the two groups of genes. This overlap establishes the basis for comorbidity between the two disorders. This hypothesis might be extended to propose that there are probably no exclusive dyslexia genes. Many genes contribute to the manifestation of typical reading (or attention) and, when one or several of these genes are challenged, atypical (dyslexic) reading can develop. Dyslexia is extremely heterogeneous etiologically; pleiotropy at multiple levels within the biological machinery of reading likely explains this.

In sum, studies of DD in adulthood have been instrumental in contributing to our understanding of the behavioral and cognitive manifestations of this disorder and its developmental transformations. Yet these studies posed a number of challenging issues that must be addressed in the future work.

Author's Note

Preparation of this chapter was supported by Grants No. REC-9979843 from the National Science Foundation, No. R206R00001 from the Javits Act Program administered by the Institute for Educational Sciences, U.S. Department of Education, and Nos. TW006764 and R21 DC07665 from the National Institutes of Health. Grantees undertaking such projects are encouraged to express freely their professional judgment. This article, therefore, does not necessarily represent the position or policies of the NSF, the IES, or the NIH, and no official endorsement should be inferred. The author expresses sincere gratitude to Ms. Robyn Rissman for her editorial assistance.

References

Agnew, J. A., Dorn, C., & Eden, G. F. (2004). Effect of intensive training on auditory processing and reading skills. *Brain and Language, 88*, 21–25.

---

* Pleiotropy, from the Greek *pleio*, or many, and *tropos*, manner, assumes "multiple impact," indicating diverse properties of a single agent, or that a single cause might have an impact on multiple outcomes.

Ahissar, M., Protopapas, A., Reid, M., & Merzenich, M. M. (2000). Auditory processing parallels reading abilities in adults. *Proceedings of the National Academy of Sciences, USA, 97*, 6832–6837.

Amitay, S., Ahissar, M., & Nelken, I. (2002). Auditory processing deficits in reading disabled adults. *Journal of the Association for Research in Otolaryngology, 3*, 302–320.

Barr, C. L. (2005). *Linkage studies of reading disabilities and ADHD in the chromosome 6p and 15q regions.* Paper presented at the Society for Scientific Studies of Reading: Annual Meeting, Toronto, CA.

Barr, C. L., & Couto, J. M. (2008). Molecular genetics of reading. In E. L. Grigorenko & A. Naples (Eds.), *Single-word reading: Cognitive, behavioral and biological perspectives.* (pp. 211–232) Mahwah, NJ: Lawrence Erlbaum.

Ben-Dror, I., Pollatsek, A., & Scarpati, S. (1991). Word identification in isolation and in context by college dyslexic students. *Brain and Language, 31*, 308–327.

Ben-Yehudah, G., & Ahissar, M. (2003). Sequential spatial frequency discrimination is consistently impaired among adult dyslexics. *Vision Research, 44*, 1047–1063.

Ben-Yehudah, G., Banai, K., & Ahissar, M. (2004). Patterns of deficit in auditory temporal processing among dyslexic adults. *Neuroreport: For Rapid Communication of Neuroscience Research, 15*, 627–631.

Biederman, J., Faraone, S. V., Spencer, T., Wilens, T. E., Mick, E., & Lapey, K. A. (1994). Gender differences in a sample of adults with attention deficit hyperactivity disorder. *Psychiatry Research, 53*, 13–29.

Birch, S., & Chase, C. H. (2004). Visual and language processing deficits in compensated and uncompensated college students with dyslexia. *Journal of Learning Disabilities, 37*, 389–410.

Breier, J. I., Gray, L., Fletcher, J. M., Diehl, R. L., Klaas, P., Foorman, B. R., et al. (2001). Perception of voice and tone onset time continua in children with dyslexia with and without attention deficit/hyperactivity disorder. *Journal of Experimental Child Psychology, 80*, 245–270.

Breier, J. I., Gray, L. C., Fletcher, J. M., Foorman, B. K., & Klaas, P. (2002). Perception of speech and nonspeech stimuli by children with and without reading disability and attention deficit disorder. *Journal of Experimental Child Psychology, 82*, 226–250.

Breznitz, Z. (2002). Asynchrony of visual–orthographic and auditory–phonological word recognition processes: An underlying factor in dyslexia. *Reading and Writing, 15*, 15–42.

Breznitz, Z., & Meyler, A. (2003). Speed of lower-level auditory and visual processing as a basic factor in dyslexia: Electrophysiological evidence. *Brain and Language, 16*, 785–803.

Breznitz, Z., & Misra, M. (2003). Speed of processing of the visual-orthographic and auditory-phonological systems in adult dyslexics: The contribution of "asynchrony" to word recognition deficits. *Brain and Language, 85*, 486–502.

Brosnan, M., Demetre, J., Hamill, S., Robson, K., Shepherd, H., & Cody, G. (2002). Executive functioning in adults and children with developmental dyslexia. *Neuropsychologia, 40*, 2144–2155.

Brown, W. E., Eliez, S., Menon, V., Rumsey, J. M., White, C. D., & Reiss, A. L. (2001). Preliminary evidence of widespread morphological variations of the brain in dyslexia. *Neurology, 56*, 781–783.

Bruck, M. (1990). Word recognition skills of adults with childhood diagnoses of dyslexia. *Developmental Psychology, 26*, 439–454.

Bruck, M. (1992). Persistence of dyslexics, phonological awareness deficits. *Developmental Psychology, 28*, 874–886.

Bruck, M. (1998). Outcomes of adults with childhood histories of dyslexia. In C. Hulme & J. R. Malatesha (Eds.), *Reading and spelling: Development and disorders* (pp. 179–200). Mahwah, NJ: Lawrence Erlbaum.

Brunswick, N., McCrory, E., Price, C. J., Frith, C. D., & Frith, U. (1999). Explicit and implicit processing of words and pseudowords by adult developmental dyslexics. *Brain, 122*, 1901–1917.

Carroll, J. M., & Snowling, M. J. (2004). Language and phonological skills in children at high risk of reading difficulties. *Journal of Child Psychology and Psychiatry, 45*, 631–640.

Catts, H. W., Fey, M. E., & Proctor-Williams, K. (2000). The relationship between language and reading. Preliminary results from a longitudinal investigation. *Logopedics, Phoniatrics, Vocology, 25*, 3–11.

Catts, H. W., Fey, M. E., Tomblin, J. B., & Zhang, X. (2002). A longitudinal investigation of reading outcomes in children with language impairments. *Journal of Speech, Language, and Hearing Research, 45*, 1142–1157.

Catts, H. W., Fey, M. E., Zhang, X., & Tomblin, J. B. (1999). Language basis of reading and reading disabilities: Evidence from a longitudinal investigation. *Scientific Studies of Reading, 3*, 331–361.

Cestnick, L. (2001). Cross-modality temporal processing deficits in developmental phonological dyslexics. *Brain and Cognition, 46*, 319–325.

Chapman, J. W., Tunmer, W. E., & Allen, R. (2003). Findings from the International Adult Literacy Survey on the incidence and correlates of learning disabilities in New Zealand: Is something rotten in the state of New Zealand? *Dyslexia: The Journal of the British Dyslexia Association, 9*, 75–98.

Chase, C. H., & Jenner, A. (1993). Magnocellular processing deficits affect temporal processing of dyslexics. *Annals of the New York Academy of Sciences, 682*, 326—329.

Chiappe, P., Stringer, R., Siegel, L. S., & Stanovich, K. (2002). Why the timing hypothesis does not explain reading disability in adults. *Reading and Writing: An Interdisciplinary Journal, 15*, 73–107.

Conlon, E., Sanders, M., & Zapart, S. (2004). Temporal processing in poor adult readers. *Neuropsychologia, 42*, 142–157.

Conners, F. A., & Olson, R. K. (1990). Reading comprehension in normal and dyslexic readers: A component-skills analysis. In D. Balota, G. F. d'Arcais & K. Rayner (Eds.), *Comprehension processes in reading* (pp. 557–579). Hillsdale, NJ: Lawrence Erlbaum.

Cope, N., Harold, D., Hill, G., Moskvina, V., Holmans, P., Owen, M. J., et al. (2005). Strong evidence that KIAA0319 on chromosome 6p is a susceptibility gene for developmental dyslexia. *American Journal of Human Genetics, 76*, 581–591.

Cope, N., Hill, G., van den Bree, M., Harold, D., Moskvina, V., Green, E. K., et al. (2004). No support for association between dyslexia susceptibility 1 candidate 1 and developmental dyslexia. *Molecular Psychiatry, 10*, 237–238.

Corcos, E., & Willows, D. M. (1993). The processing of orthographic information. In D. M. Willows, R. S. Kruk, & E. Corcos (Eds.), *Visual processes in reading and reading disabilities* (pp. 163–190). Hillsdale, NJ: Erlbaum.

Cornelissen, P., Munro, N., Fowler, S., & Stein, J. (1993). The stability of binocular fixation during reading in adults and children. *Developmental Medicine and Child Neurology, 35*, 777–787.

Cornelissen, P., Richardson, A., Mason, A., Fowler, S., & Stein, J. (1995). Contrast sensitivity measured at photopic luminance levels in dyslexics and controls. *Vision Research, 35*, 1483–1494.

Denckla, M. B., Rudel, R. G., Chapman, C., & Krieger, J. (1985). Motor proficiency in dyslexic children with and without attentional disorders. *Archives of Neurology, 42*, 228–231.

Dunn, B. R., Dunn, D. A., Languis, M., & Andrews, D. (1998). The relation of ERP components to complex memory processing. *Brain and Cognition, 36*, 355–376.

Eden, G. F., Jones, K. M., Cappell, K., Gareau, L., Wood, F. B., Zeffiro, T. A., et al. (2004). Neural changes following remediation in adult developmental dyslexia. *Neuron, 44*, 411–422.

Elbro, C., Borstrom, I., & Petersen, D. K. (1998). Predicting dyslexia from kindergarten: The importance of distinctness of phonological representations of lexical items. *Reading Research Quarterly, 33*, 36–60.

Elbro, C., Nielsen, I., & Petersen, D. K. (1994). Dyslexia in adults: Evidence for deficits in non-word reading and in the phonological representation of lexical items. *Annals of Dyslexia, 44*, 205–226.

Everatt, J. (1997). The abilities and disabilities associated with adult developmental dyslexia. *Journal of Research in Reading, 20*, 13–21.

Facoetti, A., Paganoni, P., & Lorusso, M. L. (2000). The spatial distribution of visual attention in developmental dyslexia. *Experimental Brain Research, 132*, 531–538.

Falconer, D. S., & Mackay, T. F. C. (1996). *Introduction to quantitative genetics* (4th ed.). New York: Longman.

Fawcett, A. J. (2003). The International Adult Literacy Survey in Britain: Impact on policy and practice. *Dyslexia: The Journal of the British Dyslexia Association, 9*, 99–121.

Feldman, E., Levin, B. E., Lubs, H., Rabin, M., Lubs, M. L., Jallad, B., et al. (1993). Adult familial dyslexia: A retrospective developmental and psychosocial profile. *Journal of Neuropsychiatry and Clinical Neurosciences, 5*, 195–199.

Felton, R. H., Naylor, C. E., & Wood, F. B. (1990). Neuropsychological profile of adult dyslexics. *Brain and Language, 39*, 485–497.

Fiez, J. A. (1997). Phonology, semantics, and the role of the left inferior prefrontal cortex. *Human Brain Mapping, 5*, 79–83.

Fiez, J. A., & Petersen, S. E. (1998). Neuroimaging studies of word reading. *Proceedings of the National Academy of Sciences of the United States of America, 95*, 914–921.

Fisher, S. E., & DeFries, J. C. (2002). Developmental dyslexia: Genetic dissection of a complex cognitive trait. *Nature Reviews: Neuroscience, 3*, 767–780.

Fitzgerald, P. G., & Picton, T. W. (1983). Event-related potentials recorded during the discrimination of improbable stimuli. *Biological Psychology, 17,* 241–276.

Flowers, D. L. (1995). Neuropsychological profiles of persistent reading disability and reading improvement. In C. K. Leong & R. M. Joshi (Eds.), *Developmental and acquired dyslexia* (pp. 61–77). Dordrecht: Kluwer.

Gaillard, W. D., Balsamo, L. M., Ibrahim, Z., Sachs, B. C., & Xu, B. (2003). fMRI identifies regional specialization of neural networks for reading in young children. *Neurology, 60,* 94–100.

Gallagher, A. M., Frith, U., & Snowling, M. J. (2000). Precursors of literacy delay among children at genetic risk of dyslexia. *Journal of Child Psychology and Psychiatry, 4,* 202–213.

Gallagher, A. M., Laxon, V., Armstrong, E., & Frith, U. (1996). Phonological difficulties in high-functioning dyslexics. *Reading and Writing: An Interdisciplinary Journal, 8,* 499–509.

Gathercole, S. E., & Baddeley, A. D. (1993). *Working memory and language.* Hillsdale, NJ: Lawrence Erlbaum.

Gayan, J., & Olson, R. K. (2003). Genetic and environmental influences on individual differences in printed word recognition. *Journal of Experimental Child Psychology, 84,* 97–123.

Giraud, K., Demonet, J. F., Habib, M., Marquis, P., Chauvel, P., & Liegeois-Chauvel, C. (2005). Auditory evoked potential patterns to voiced and voiceless speech sounds in adult developmental dyslexics with persistent deficits. *Cerebral Cortex, 15,* 1524–1534.

Gottardo, A., Siegal, L. S., & Stanovich, K. E. (1997). The assessment of adults with reading disabilities: What can we learn from experimental tasks? *Journal of Research in Reading, 20,* 42–54.

Greatrex, J. C., & Drasdo, N. (1995). The magnocellular deficit hypothesis in dyslexia: A review of reported evidence. *Ophthalmic and Physiological Optics, 15,* 501–506.

Grigorenko, E. L. (2004). Genetic bases of developmental dyslexia: A capsule review of heritability estimates. *Enfance, 3,* 273–287.

Grigorenko, E. L. (2005). A conservative meta-analysis of linkage and linkage-association studies of developmental dyslexia. *Scientific Studies of Reading, 9,* 285–316.

Grigorenko, E. L. (2007). Triangulating developmental dyslexia: Behavior, brain, and genes. In D. Coch, G. Dawson, & K. Fischer (Eds.), *Human behavior and the Developing Brain* (pp. 117–144). New York, NY: Guilford Press.

Gross-Glenn, K., Lewis, D. C., Smith, S. D., & Lubs, H. A. (1985). Phenotype of adult familial dyslexia: Reading of visually transformed texts and nonsense passages. *International Journal of Neuroscience, 28,* 49–59.

Hackley, S. A., Woldorff, M. G., & Hillyard, S. A. (1990). Cross-modal selective attention effects on retinal, myogenic, brain stem, and cerebral evoked potentials. *Psychophysiology, 27,* 195–208.

Hamalainen, J., Leppanen, P. H. T., Torppa, M., Muller, K., & Lyytinen, H. (2005). Detection of sound rise time by adults with dyslexia *Brain and Language, 94,* 32–42.

Hannula-Jouppi, K., Kaminen-Ahola, N., Taipale, M., Eklund, R., Nopola-Hemmi, J., Kääriäinen, H., et al. (2005). The axon guidance receptor gene ROB01 is a candidate gene for developmental dyslexia. *Public Library of Sciences, 1*, e50.

Harlaar, N., Spinath, F. M., Dale, P. S., & Plomin, R. (2005). Genetic influences on early word recognition abilities and disabilities: A study of 7-year-old twins. *Journal of Child Psychology and Psychiatry, 46*, 373–384.

Helenius, P., Uutela, K., & Hari, R. (1999). Auditory stream segregation in dyslexic adults. *Brain, 122*, 907–913.

Hill, N. I., Bailey, P. J., Griffiths, Y. M., & Snowling, M. J. (1999). Frequency acuity and binaural masking release in dyslexic listeners. *Journal of the Acoustical Society of America, 106*, L53–L58.

Hohnen, B., & Stevenson, J. (1999). The structure of genetic influences on general cognitive, language, phonological, and reading abilities. *Developmental Psychology, 35*, 590–603.

Iles, J., Walsh, V., & Richardson, A. (2000). Visual search performance in dyslexia. *Dyslexia, 6*, 163–177.

Kinsbourne, M., Rufo, D. T., Gamzu, E., Palmer, R. L., & Berliner, A. K. (1991). Neuropsychological deficits in adults with dyslexia. *Developmental Medicine and Child Neurology, 33*, 763–775.

Kitz, W. R., & Tarver, S. G. (1989). Comparison of dyslexic and nondyslexic adults on decoding and phonemic awareness tasks. *Annals of Dyslexia, 39*, 196–205.

Klein, R. M. (2002). Observations on the temporal correlates of reading failure. *Reading and Writing: An Interdisciplinary Journal, 15*, 207–232.

Kramer, A. (1991). Physiological metrics of mental workload: A review of recent progress. In D. Damos (Ed.), *Multiple task performance* (pp. 167–178). London: Taylor & Francis.

Kronbichler, M., Hutzler, F., & Wimmer, H. (2002). Dyslexia: Verbal impairments in the absence of magnocellular impairments. *Neuroreport, 13*, 617–620.

Laasonen, M., Service, E., & Virsu, V. (2002). Crossmodal temporal order and processing acuity in developmentally dyslexic young adults. *Brain and Language, 80*, 340–354.

Leonard, C. M., Eckert, M. A., Lombardino, L. J., Oakland, T., Kranzler, J., Mohr, C. M., et al. (2001). Anatomical risk factors for phonological dyslexia. *Cerebral Cortex, 11*, 148–157.

Leong, C. K. (1999). Phonological and morphological processing in adult students with learning/reading disabilities. *Journal of Learning Disabilities, 32*, 224–228.

Levinthal, C. F., & Hornung, M. (1992). Orthographic and phonological coding during visual word matching as related to reading and spelling abilities in college students. *Reading and Writing: An Interdisciplinary Journal, 4*, 231–243.

Livingstone, M. S., Rosen, G. D., Drislane, F. W., & Galaburda, A. M. (1991). Physiological and anatomical evidence for a magnocellular defect in developmental dyslexia. *Proceedings of the National Academy of Sciences of the United States of America, 88*, 7943–7947.

Lovegrove, W. J., Bowling, A., Badcock, B., & Blackwood, M. (1980). Specific reading disability: Differences in contrast sensitivity as a function of spatial frequency. *Science, 210*, 439–440.

Luck, S. J., & Hillyard, S. A. (1994). Electrophysiological correlates of feature analysis during visual search. *Psychophysiology, 31*, 291–308.

Lyytinen, H., Ahonen, T., Eklund, K., Guttorm, T., Kulju, P., Laakso, M.-L., et al. (2004). Early development of children at familial risk for dyslexia: Follow-up from birth to school age. *Dyslexia: An International Journal of Research and Practice, 10*, 146–178.

Lyytinen, H., Guttorm, T. K., Huttunen, T., Hamalainen, J., Leppanen, P. H. T., & Vesterinen, M. (2005). Psychophysiology of developmental dyslexia: A review of findings including studies of children at risk for dyslexia. *Journal of Neurolinguistics, 18*, 167–195.

Lyytinen, P., & Lyytinen, H. (2004). Growth and predictive relations of vocabulary and inflectional morphology in children with and without familial risk for dyslexia. *Applied Psycholinguistics, 25*, 397–411.

Magajna, L., Kavkler, M., & Ortar-Krizaj, M. (2003). Adults with self-reported learning disabilities in Slovenia: Findings from the international adult literacy survey on the incidence and correlates of learning disabilities in Slovenia. *Dyslexia: The Journal of the British Dyslexia Association, 9*, 229–251.

Marlow, A. J., Fisher, S. E., Francks, C., MacPhie, I. L., Cherny, S. S., Richardson, A. J., et al. (2003). Use of multivariate linkage analysis for dissection of a complex cognitive trait. *American Journal of Human Genetics, 72*, 561–570.

McAnally, K. I., & Stein, J. F. (1996). Auditory temporal coding in dyslexia. *Proceedings of the Biological Sciences/The Royal Society, 263*, 961–965.

McNulty, M. A. (2003). Dyslexia and the life course. *Journal of Learning Disabilities, 36*, 363–381.

Meng, H., Smith, S. D., Hager, K., Held, M., Liu, J., Olson, R. K., et al. (2005). DCDC2 is associated with reading disability and modulates neuronal development in the brain *Proceedings of the National Academy of Sciences of the United States of America, 102*, 17053–17058.

Meyler, A., & Breznitz, Z. (2005). Visual, auditory and cross-modal processing of linguistic and nonlinguistic temporal patterns among adult dyslexic readers. *Dyslexia: The Journal of the British Dyslexia Association, 11*, 93–115.

Miller-Shaul, S. (2005). The characteristics of young and adult dyslexic readers on reading and reading-related cognitive tasks as compared to normal readers. *Dyslexia, 11*, 132–151.

Milne, R. D., Nicholson, T., & Corballis, M. C. (2003). Lexical access and phonological decoding in adult dyslexic subtypes. *Neuropsychology, 17*, 362–368.

Moores, E., Nicolson, R. I., & Fawcett, A. J. (2003). Attention deficits in dyslexia: Evidence for an automatisation deficit? *European Journal of Cognitive Psychology, 15*, 321–348.

Nicolson, R. I., & Fawcett, A. J. (1993). Toward the origin of dyslexia. In S. F. Wright & R. Groner (Eds.), *Facets of dyslexia and its remediation* (pp. 371–391). Amsterdam: Elsevier Science.

Nicolson, R. I., Fawcett, A. J., Berry, E. L., Jenkins, I. H., Dean, P., & Brooks, D. J. (1999). Association of abnormal cerebellar activation with motor learning difficulties in dyslexic adults. *Lancet, 353*, 1662–1667.

Overy, K., Nicolson, R. I., Fawcett, A. J., & Clarke, E. F. (2003). Dyslexia and music: Measuring musical timing skills. *Dyslexia, 9*, 18–36.

Paulesu, E., Frith, U., Snowling, M. J., Gallagher, A., Morton, J., Frackowiak, R. S. J., et al. (1996). Is developmental dyslexia a disconnection syndrome? Evidence from PET scanning. *Brain, 119*, 143–157.

Pennington, B. F., & Lefly, D. L. (2001). Early reading development in children at family risk for dyslexia. *Child Development, 72*, 816–833.

Pennington, B. F., McCabe, L. L., Smith, S. D., Lefly, D. L., Bookman, M. D., Kimberling, W. J., et al. (1986). Spelling errors in adults with a form of familial dyslexia. *Child Development, 57*, 1001–1013.

Poldrack, R. A., Wagner, A. D., Prull, M. W., Desmond, J. E., Glover, G. H., & Gabrieli, J. D. (1999). Functional specialization for semantic and phonological processing in the left inferior prefrontal cortex. *Neuroimage, 10*, 15–35.

Price, C. J., & Mechelli, A. (2005). Reading and reading disturbance. *Current Opinion in Neurobiology, 15*, 231–238.

Ramus, F., Pidgeon, E., & Frith, U. (2003). The relationship between motor control and phonology in dyslexic children. *Journal of Child Psychology and Psychiatry and Allied Disciplines, 44*, 712–722.

Ramus, F., Rosen, S., Dakin, S. C., Day, B. L., Castellote, J. M., White, S., et al. (2003). Theories of developmental dyslexia: Insights from a multiple case study of dyslexic adults. *Brain, 126*, 841–865.

Ransby, M. J., & Swanson, H. L. (2003). Reading comprehension skills of young adults with childhood diagnoses of dyslexia. *Journal of Learning Disabilities, 36*, 538–555.

Roach, N. W., & Hogben, J. H. (2004). Attentional modulation of visual processing in adult dyslexia: A spatial-cuing deficit. *Psychological Science, 15*, 650–654.

Samuelsson, S., Lundberg, I., & Herkner, B. (2004). ADHD and reading disability in male adults: Is there a connection? *Journal of Learning Disabilities, 37*, 155–168.

Scarborough, H. S. (1990). Very early language deficits in dyslexic children. *Child Development, 61*, 1728–1743.

Scerri, T. S., Fisher, S. E., Francks, C., MacPhie, I. L., Paracchini, S., Richardson, A. J., et al. (2004). Putative functional alleles of DYX1C1 are not associated with dyslexia susceptibility in a large sample of sibling pairs from the UK. *Journal of Medical Genetics, 41*, 853–857.

Schumacher, J., Anthoni, H., Dahdouh, F., König, I. R., Hillmer, H. M., Kluck, N., et al. (2006). Strong genetic evidence of DCDC2 as a susceptibility gene for dyslexia. *American Journal of Human Genetics, 78*, 52–62.

Seidman, L. J., Biederman, J., Weber, W., Hatch, M., & Faraone, S. V. (1998). Neuropsychological function in adults with attention-deficit/hyperactivity disorder. *Biological Psychiatry, 44*, 260–268.

Shaywitz, S. E., Fletcher, J. M., Holahan, J. M., Shneider, A. E., Marchione, K. E., Stuebing, K. K., et al. (1999). Persistence of dyslexia: The Connecticut longitudinal study at adolescence. *Pediatrics, 104*, 1351–1359.

Shaywitz, S. E., Shaywitz, B. A., Fulbright, R. K., Skudlarski, P., Mencl, W. E., Constable, R. T., et al. (2003). Neural systems for compensation and persistence: Young adult outcome of childhood reading disability. *Biological Psychiatry, 54*, 25–33.

Simos, P. G., Billingsley-Marshall, B., Sarkari, S., & Papanicolaou, A. C. (2008). Single-word reading: Perspectives from magnetic source imaging. In E. L. Grigorenko & A. Naples (Eds.), *Single-word reading: Cognitive, behavioral and biological perspectives.* (pp. 255–281) Mahwah, NJ: Lawrence Erlbaum.

Skaalvik, S. (2004). Reading problems in school children and adults: Experiences, self-perceptions and strategies. *Social Psychology of Education, 7,* 105–125.

Slaghuis, W. L., Twell, A. J., & Kingston, K. R. (1996). Visual and language processing disorders are concurrent in dyslexia and continue into adulthood. *Cortex, 32,* 413–438.

Smith, S. D., Kimberling, W. J., Pennington, B. F., & Lubs, H. A. (1983). Specific reading disability: Identification of an inherited form through linkage analyses. *Science, 219,* 1345–1347.

Snowling, M. J. (1980). The development of grapheme-phoneme correspondence in normal and dyslexic readers. *Journal of Experimental Child Psychology, 29,* 294–305.

Snowling, M. J. (1995). Phonological processing and developmental dyslexia. *Journal of Research in Reading, 18,* 132–138.

Snowling, M. J., Bishop, D. V., & Stothard, S. E. (2000). Is preschool language impairment a risk factor for dyslexia in adolescence? *Journal of Child Psychology and Psychiatry and Allied Disciplines, 41,* 587–600.

Snowling, M. J., Gallagher, A. M., & Frith, U. (2003). Family risk of dyslexia is continuous: Individual differences in the precursors of reading skill. *Child Development, 74,* 358–373.

Snowling, M. J., Nation, K., Moxham, P., Gallagher, A., & Frith, U. (1997). Phonological processing skills of dyslexic students in higher education: A preliminary report. *Journal of Research in Reading, 20,* 31–41.

Snyder, L. S., & Downey, D. M. (1995). Serial rapid naming skills in children with reading disabilities. *Annals of Dyslexia, 45,* 31–49.

Stein, J., & Walsh, V. (1997). To see but not to read: The magnocellular theory of dyslexia. *Trends in Neurosciences, 20,* 147–152.

Stevenson, J., Graham, P., Fredman, G., & McLoughlin, V. (1987). A twin study of genetic influences on reading and spelling ability and disability. *Journal of Child Psychology and Psychiatry, 28,* 229–247.

Swanson, H. L., & Siegel, L. (2003). Learning disabilities as a working memory deficit. *Issues in Education: Contributions for Educational Psychology, 7,* 1–48.

Tagamets, M. A., Novick, J. M., Chalmers, M. L., & Friedman, R. B. (2000). A parametric approach to orthographic processing in the brain: An fMRI study. *Journal of Cognitive Neuroscience, 12,* 281–297.

Taipale, M., Kaminen, N., Nopola-Hemmi, J., Haltia, T., Myllyluoma, B., Lyytinen, H., et al. (2003). A candidate gene for developmental dyslexia encodes a nuclear tetratricopeptide repeat domain protein dynamically regulated in brain. *Proceedings of the National Academy of Sciences of the United States of America, 100,* 11553–11558.

Taylor, K. E., & Walter, J. (2003). Occupation choices of adults with and without symptoms of dyslexia. *Dyslexia: The Journal of the British Dyslexia Association, 9,* 177–185.

Turkeltaub, P. E., Eden, G. F., Jones, K. M., & Zeffiro, T. A. (2002). Meta-analysis of the functional neuroanatomy of single-word reading: Method and validation. *Neuroimage, 16*, 765–780.

Turkeltaub, P. E., Gareau, L., Flowers, D. L., Zeffiro, T. A., & Eden, G. F. (2003). Development of neural mechanisms for reading. *Nature Neuroscience, 6*, 767–773.

Undheim, A. M. (2003). Dyslexia and psychosocial factors: A follow-up study of young Norwegian adults with a history of dyslexia in childhood. *Nordic Journal of Psychiatry, 53*, 221–226.

van Alphen, P., de Bree, E., Gerrits, E., de Jong, J., Wilsenach, C., & Wijnen, F. (2004). Early language development in children with a genetic risk of dyslexia. *Dyslexia: An International Journal of Research & Practice, 10*, 265–288.

van Daal, V., & van der Leij, A. (1999). Developmental dyslexia: Related to specific or general deficits? *Annals of Dyslexia, 49*, 71–104.

van der Leij, A., & van Daal, V. H. P. (1999). Automatization aspects of dyslexia: Speed limitations in word identification, sensitivity to increasing task demands, and orthographic compensation. *Journal of Learning Disabilities, 32*, 417–428.

Viholainen, H., Ahonen, T., Cantell, M., Lyytinen, P., & Lyytinen, H. (2002). Development of early motor skills and language in children at risk for familial dyslexia. *Developmental Medicine & Child Neurology, 44*, 761–769.

Watson, B. U., & Miller, T. K. (1993). Auditory perception, phonological processing, and reading ability/disability. *Journal of Speech and Hearing Research, 36*, 850–863.

Wijsman, E. M., Peterson, D., Leutenegger, A. L., Thomson, J. B., Goddard, K. A. B., Hsu, L., et al. (2000). Segregation analysis of phenotypic components of learning disabilities. I. Nonword memory and digit span. *American Journal of Human Genetics, 67*, 631–646.

Wilson, A. M., & Lesaux, N. K. (2001). Persistence of phonological processing deficits in college students with dyslexia who have age-appropriate reading skills. *Journal of Learning Disabilities, 34*, 394–400.

Wilson, G. F., Swain, C. R., & Ullsperger, P. (1998). ERP components elicited in response to warning stimuli: The influence of task difficulty. *Biological Psychology, 47*, 137–158.

Wimmer, H., Mayringer, H., & Landerl, K. (1998). Poor reading: A deficit in skill-automatization or a phonological deficit? *Scientific Studies of Reading, 2*, 321–340.

Wimmer, H., Mayringer, H., & Raberger, T. (1999). Reading and dual-task balancing: Evidence against the automatization deficit explanation of developmental dyslexia. *Journal of Learning Disabilities, 32*, 473–478.

Winter, N., Holland, A. J., & Collins, S. (1997). Factors predisposing to suspected offending by adults with self-reported learning disabilities. *Psychological Medicine, 27*, 595–607.

Wolf, M., & Katzir-Cohen, T. (2001). Reading fluency and its intervention. *Scientific Studies of Reading, 5*, 211–238.

Wolff, P. H., Michel, G. F., & Ovrut, M. (1990). Rate variables and automatized naming in developmental dyslexia. *Brain and Language, 39*, 556–575.

Yap, R., & van der Leij, A. (1993). Word processing in dyslexics. *Reading and Writing, 5*, 261–279.

CHAPTER 5

Reading Fluency in Adults

ANNE DANIELS

Contents

Skilled readers read fluently, with accuracy and speed (Torgesen, 2000). The importance of fluent reading for text comprehension has recently been stressed by the National Reading Panel in its review of the scientific research literature on reading (U.S. Department of Health and Human Services, 2000). Yet fluent reading is a skill that eludes many adults, leading to hardship and frustration in career and educational pursuits. This chapter aims to explore some of the factors that might explain why some adults fail to become fluent readers, despite adequate instruction and years of schooling. Toward this end, I present a selective review of the literature that examines factors that appear to contribute to reading fluency. Next, to illustrate the impact of reading dysfluency on adults as well as some of the interventions and accommodations that can alleviate this impact, I present a case from a support program for graduate students at Harvard University. The final part of this chapter suggests directions for future research that might inform us about the causes, effects, and treatments for reading dysfluency in adults.

Definitions of reading fluency vary, with some conceptualizing fluency as oral reading that is quick and accurate (Torgesen, 2000; Torgesen, Rashotte, & Alexander, 2001) and others extending the definition to include the prosodic aspects of reading (Allington, 1983) or the ability to comprehend text (Torgesen et al. 2001). For the purpose of this chapter, reading fluency is defined as reading for understanding that is both quick and accurate (Lyon, Shaywitz, & Shaywitz, 2003; U.S. Department of Health and Human Services, 2000).

Dysfluent reading in adulthood is a descriptive term for a behavioral outcome that has many, often interrelated origins. Some dysfluent adults may have learned basic reading skills in school but lacked the reading practice necessary to build fluency due to environmental factors, such as disrupted schooling. Others may have learned basic decoding skills but encountered obstacles to fluency arising from neurocognitive-environmental interactions, such as a poor ability to sustain attention while reading, which can then lead to avoidance of the reading practice necessary to attain fluency. Still others may have had childhood reading disorders that were either never diagnosed or inadequately remediated. Adults in this latter group may have learned decoding skills but may also have lacked the consistent reading practice needed for fluency (Shaywitz et al., 2003). Yet another group may have had appropriate remediation as well as frequent reading practice to help them compensate for their childhood reading disorders but still have failed to develop adequate fluency (Fink, 1998). The focus here is on those adults with a childhood history of reading disability or dyslexia who learned to read but who continue to read dysfluently as adults.

Studies of adults with childhood histories of dyslexia or reading disability show that reading difficulties persist in some, but not all, of these individuals (Bruck, 1990, 1992; Felton, Naylor, & Wood, 1990; Fink, 1998; Helenius, Uutela, & Hari, 1999; Lefly & Pennington, 1991). Longitudinal research also notes the persistence of reading disabilities into adolescence, with the use of growth curve modeling allowing for prediction of these problems into the end of high school (Shaywitz et al., 1999). Although some of these adults continue to have decoding difficulties, many do not. What does characterize most of these adults is slow, dysfluent reading. Bruck (1990), for example, found that college students with a childhood diagnosis of dyslexia read single words and nonwords more slowly than both age-matched controls and sixth-grade children matched for reading level with the dyslexic adults. Using rate of oral paragraph reading to measure fluency, Lefly and Pennington (1991) found that even adults who had compensated for their childhood dyslexia read more slowly than nondyslexic adults. Similarly, in her study of 60 highly successful adults with childhood histories of dyslexia, Fink (1998) found that slow reading of text characterized many of these individuals, despite the fact that many had read widely in particular areas of interest during childhood.

An obvious question that arises from these studies is why some adults with a history of dyslexia are dysfluent readers and others are not. Some insights into the possible factors underlying dysfluency have emerged from the research on the relationship between the rapid naming of well-learned visual stimuli and reading. The idea that problems in automatizing, or learning to the level of automaticity, the names of visual stimuli might reflect processes that also contribute to the reading difficulties in dyslexics was in large part prompted by the research of Denckla and Rudel (1976). These researchers found that dyslexic children were significantly slower than both normal controls and nondyslexic learning-disabled children in rapidly naming letters, digits, colors, and pictured objects. Research that followed confirmed the association between the slow naming of well-learned visual stimuli and dyslexia (e.g., Wolf, 1984, 1991; Wolf, Bally, & Morris, 1986), and efforts to explain this association began, as well.

Studies examining the relative contributions of phonological skills and naming speed to specific reading skills have found that naming speed was more strongly related to reading rate or fluency, whereas phonological skill was more strongly related to nonword reading or decoding accuracy (e.g., Sunseth & Bowers, 2002; Wolf & Bowers, 1999). The hypothesized separability of naming speed and phonological processes (e.g., Manis, Doi, & Bhadha, 2000; Scarborough, 1998; Wolf & Bowers, 1999) has also led to the identification of subtypes of reading disability, including a rate-impaired group, on the basis of naming speed and phonological skill as well as to further evidence of an association between naming speed and reading fluency (Sunseth & Bowers, 2002; Wolf & Bowers, 1999; see also Lovett, 1987). Other studies have found evidence for slow reading rate in individuals with slow naming speed by using other techniques, such as cluster analysis (e.g., Morris et al., 1998). These findings of an association between slow naming speed and slow reading rate have not, however, explained *why* reading is slow for some individuals. To investigate causal factors in reading disability, some researchers have examined the processes involved in slow rapid naming, under the assumption that rapid naming performance taps lower level processes that are also used in reading (Wolf, 1991, 1999).

Consistent with research that points to phonological processing as a core deficit underlying dyslexia (Lyon et al., 2003; Manis et al., 2000; Shaywitz et. al., 1999; Torgesen et al., 1999), some researchers have suggested that slow naming speed and its correlate, slow word reading, reflect problems in this same phonological system, such as a difficulty in rapidly retrieving phonological information (e.g., Shaywitz, 2003; Stanovich, 1988) or a problem in phonological recoding (Zeffiro & Eden, 2000). Others have hypothesized that slow naming speed, and thus analogous reading processes, can result from a deficit in a process that is distinct from phonological processing (Bowers, 2001; Wolf & Bowers, 1999). Specifically, drawing on evidence of impaired rapid processing of auditory or visual stimuli in dyslexics (e.g., Bednarek & Grabowska, 2002; Helenius, Tarkiainen, Cornelissen, Hansen, & Salmelin, 1999; Helenius, Uutela, et al., 1999; Omtzigt, Hendriks, & Kolk, 2002; Stein, 2001; Wolf, Bowers, & Biddle, 2000; Wolff, Michel, & Ovrut, 1990; Zeffiro & Eden, 2000), these researchers have suggested that slow naming speed and thus slow word reading are manifestations of an underlying impairment in lower level temporal processing (e.g., Bowers, 2001; Wolf, 1991, 1999; Wolf & Bowers, 1999). Support for a timing deficit hypothesis has also been found through neuroanatomical research, which has documented abnormalities in those thalamic cellular layers involved in the processing of rapidly changing visual and auditory stimuli (Galaburda, Menard, & Rosen, 1994; Livingstone, Rosen, Drislane, & Galaburda, 1991).

The exact nature of this hypothesized temporal processing deficit, however, and the mechanism by which it could affect rapid naming and reading have been topics of debate. Some researchers have proposed, for example, that deficits in the rapid processing of visual stimuli may interfere with the development of orthographic, or letter string, representations, which are necessary for quick sight-word identification (e.g., Bowers, 2001; Levy, 2001; Stein, 2001; Wolf & Bowers, 1999). Others have suggested that deficits in the rapid processing of sequences of auditory stimuli could lead to impairment in the awareness of phonemes or phoneme order, which would then result in slow, laborious decoding and dysfluent reading (e.g. Helenius, Uutela, et al., 1999). Stressing the points that reading fluency depends on multiple processes and that processing-speed deficits have been found in a variety of domains (e.g., Wolff et al., 1990), still others have suggested that rate deficits in any number of lower level perceptual and motoric subprocesses or in their integration could occur (e.g., Berninger, Abbott, Billingsley, & Nagy, 2001; Wolf, 1999; Wolf & Bowers, 1999; Wolf & Katzir-Cohen, 2001). These deficits could then lead to slow naming speed— that is, slow lexical retrieval—that could then interfere with fluent reading.

Breznitz's work has investigated the timing hypothesis from the perspective of a possible asynchrony in neural integration (e.g., Breznitz, 2001; Breznitz & Misra, 2003). Noting, for example, that differences in processing speed between visual and auditory modalities might interfere with the integration of visual and auditory information required for fluent and accurate word recognition, Breznitz and Misra (2003) have investigated the time gap, or asynchrony, between these modalities in adult dyslexics and normal controls. Measuring reaction times and event-related potentials, they found not only slower processing of visual and auditory stimuli but also a longer time gap between the speed of processing for visual-orthographic stimuli and the speed of processing for auditory-phonological stimuli in the dyslexics compared to controls (see also Bowers, 2001; Breznitz, 2001; Breznitz & Berman, 2003; Poldrack, 2001; Wimmer & Mayringer, 2001).

Although a considerable body of research documents the correlation between timing deficits and reading disability, Waber and her colleagues (2000, 2001) caution against assigning a causal role to processing-speed deficits in dyslexia. In a series of studies, she and her colleagues have found deficits in processing speed on a variety of tasks, including rapid naming tasks, in both poor readers and normally achieving readers within a large sample of children referred for evaluation, compared to nonreferred children. Since rapid naming deficits were found in both poor and adequately reading referred children, Waber (2001) suggests that slow naming speed may reflect different underlying processes in different individuals. She proposes further that, rather than functioning as a causal mechanism, the rate of processing deficits observed in dyslexics may instead reflect problems in some underlying neurocognitive process, such as a disruption in the neural areas important for certain lower level processing. A disruption in lower level processing might then lead to behavior that is manifested as a slow information-processing rate, as well as, in some individuals, a reading disability.

Consistent with Waber's cautions, recent neuroimaging studies by Salmelin, Helenius, and Service (2000) provide evidence against a simple causal role for timing deficits in dyslexia. Using whole-head magneto-encephalographic imaging, they investigated the location and timing of cortical activations during reading tasks in dyslexic and fluently reading adults. They found no differences between dyslexics and fluent readers in the location and timing of cortical activations in response to tasks requiring mere visual feature analysis. At the level of processing that was specific to letter strings, however, weaker or missing activations in the left inferior occipitotemporal cortex and missing or abnormally early activations in the left superior temporal cortex were found in dyslexics compared to fluent readers. The dyslexics instead showed activations in the left inferior frontal cortex, possibly due to their use of this area to compensate for disrupted posterior areas. Salmelin et al. (2000) have also found slower responses at the level of lexical-semantic processing in dyslexics compared to fluent readers but suggest that this timing difference reflects the disruption at the presemantic, letter-string level of processing.

In addition to the phonological and timing hypotheses for dysfluent reading, some researchers have proposed that a general deficit in skill automatization underlies dysfluency (Fawcett & Nicolson, 2001; Nicolson & Fawcett, 2001). Noting the importance of the cerebellum for the automatization of motor and speech skills, for example, Nicolson and Fawcett undertook a positron emission tomography (PET) study in which adults performed both a prelearned and a novel motor sequence. Their findings of underactivation in cerebellar areas of dyslexics compared to controls led them to suggest that a general automatization deficit, resulting from cerebellar abnormalities, leads to dyslexia. Other researchers have cautioned, however, that the relationship between cerebellar abnormalities and dyslexia may be correlational in nature rather than causal (Bishop, 2002; Ivry, Justus, & Middleton, 2001). Raberger and Wimmer (2003) drew conclusions that differed from those of Nicolson and Fawcett, when they compared children with severely dysfluent reading to children with ADHD on cerebellar and rapid naming tasks. In contrast to Nicolson and Fawcett's findings, they found slow rapid naming but not cerebellar deficits in the dyslexic children, as well as cerebellar but not rapid naming deficits in the ADHD children. These results led Raberger and Wimmer to suggest that more specific automatization deficits—for example, for processes connecting visual with phonological information—rather than general automatization deficits, lead to reading dysfluency (also see van Daal & van der Leij, 1999; van der Leij & van Daal, 1999). A specific, rather than a general, deficit in skill automatization has also been proposed by Berninger et al. (2001) in their description of several subtypes of reading dysfluency. Specifically, they suggest that poor automaticity in lexical access can lead to a particular type of dysfluency that is characterized by slow, inaccurate reading with errors of false starts, hesitations, and repetitions.

Still other investigators have proposed that executive function problems play a role in slow naming speed or dysfluent reading. Conceptualizing processing speed as the ability to respond quickly and efficiently, and thus an aspect of the executive functions, Denckla and Cutting (1999) have found that rapid naming performance is partly explained by performance on processing-speed tasks. Berninger et al. (2001) have related executive function problems more directly to dysfluent reading. In describing several subtypes of dysfluency, they suggest that one type involves slow, inaccurate reading in which the errors reflect inattention to the orthographic and morphological features of words, word order in sentences, and prosodic aspects of text. They suggest further that these types of errors are due to poor self-monitoring and poor executive control of language processes.

Neuroimaging studies have contributed to our understanding of reading dysfluency by revealing some of the neuranatomical areas that are activated during word reading tasks. Recent studies indicate that a functional system consisting of three interrelated neural systems is involved in reading (Shaywitz et al., 2002; Shaywitz et al., 2003). In addition to a left inferior frontal area that is involved in phonemic articulatory processing, two posterior systems have been identified: a dorsal parietotemporal system involved in slow phonemic analysis of words and a ventral occipito-temporal area involved in the quick processing of word forms (e.g., Shaywitz et al., 2002). A number of studies have found evidence of disruption in these posterior systems in dyslexic adults during word reading tasks (e.g., Brunswick, McCroy, Price, Frith, & Frith, 1999; Horwitz, Rumsey, & Donohue, 1998; Paulesu et al., 2001; Salmelin et al., 2000; Shaywitz et al., 1998). There is also evidence indicating that adult dyslexics show increased activation in left inferior frontal areas in order to try to compensate for the dysfunctional posterior regions (Brunswick et al., 1999; Salmelin et al., 2000; Shaywitz et al., 2002). In addition, recent studies indicate that adult dyslexics who have learned to compensate for their dyslexia appear to rely on ancillary right frontal and temporal areas in order to do so (Shaywitz et al., 2003). Shaywitz et al. (2002) suggest that these compensatory areas allow adult dyslexics to read accurately but slowly. These neuroimaging studies must be interpreted cautiously, however, since evidence for activation of a region does not explain the function underlying that activation (Helenius, Salmelin, Service, & Connolly, 1999; Shaywitz et al., 2003). Activation of certain frontal areas, for example, may reflect effort or the attempt to use strategies to compensate for disrupted functioning in other neural areas.

Some have cautioned that reading is such a complex process that a single underlying deficit is likely insufficient to explain all cases of reading dysfluency (e.g., Wolf & Bowers, 2000; Wolf & Katzir-Cohen, 2001). Acknowledging the variability in the deficits associated with reading disability in different studies, a number of researchers have stressed the multidimensional nature of reading and suggested that disruption in different subprocesses could lead to the same behavioral outcome, reading dysfluency (Berninger et al., 2001; Morris et al., 1998; Wolf & Katzir-Cohen, 2001). The difficulty in untangling the possible sources of reading dysfluency increases further when the role of experience is considered. Considerable evidence indicates, for example, that reading practice improves fluency (e.g., Chard, Vaughn, & Tyler, 2002; Dowhower, 1987; Fink, 1998; U.S. Department of Health and Human Services, 2000; Meyer & Felton, 1999; Rashotte & Torgesen, 1985). Evidence also indicates that children who are dysfluent readers often find reading frustrating and thus avoid it, thereby reducing the amount of practice time, which in turn can compound the dysfluency (Meyer & Felton, 1999). In addition, though many dysfluent adults with a history of reading disability have had a great deal of reading practice by the time they graduate from high school or college, it is possible that much of this practice may have occurred after a point at which fluency can significantly improve (e.g., Abadzi, 1996). Different approaches to reading instruction could also variably facilitate the acquisition of decoding skills, delaying the time at which some children become independent readers, which might then affect later fluency.

To understand the impact of reading dysfluency in adulthood, it may be helpful to turn to evidence coming from clinical work. The Graduate Student Learning Support (GSLS) program at Harvard University provides learning support services for graduate students at five graduate schools. Not surprisingly, given the extensive reading assignments in these schools, students with a history of dyslexia or slow reading rate are frequently referred to the program. This very issue prompted Susan,* a master of theological studies student at Harvard Divinity School, to seek support from the program. Susan had repeated first grade because of her difficulty learning to read. She continued to have difficulty reading accurately and fluently throughout elementary and high school but was able to compensate for her difficulties by working extremely long hours. As an economics major, Susan was successful in undergraduate school, though she typically failed to finish standardized tests within the time limits. Susan also suffered from depression during her undergraduate and graduate school years. An evaluation at the end of undergraduate school found her pseudoword reading skills to be at the sixth-grade level, despite superior reasoning and problem-solving skills. A screening during the GSLS clinical interview found her reading speed for sentences to be at the 30th percentile, a level that was at an approximate mid-seventh-grade equivalent and far below her overall level of cognitive functioning (Woodcock-Johnson-III-Reading Fluency; Woodcock, McGrew, & Mather, 2001). As a result of her difficulty completing assigned readings and exams within the time limits, Susan experienced doubts about her ability to succeed in graduate school and in her chosen career path.

When asked to describe what the reading process was like for her, Susan noted that she had to read slowly in order to understand the text, adding that if she tried to read quickly, her comprehension suffered. (It is interesting that a number of dysfluent readers in the program state that it is not just the word reading that is slow but also the integration of concepts or elements needed for comprehension.) To be able to retain what she had read, she continued, she had to reread text and take notes on the material, a process that was extremely time consuming. Susan expressed frustration in trying to complete the reading assignments for her courses, stating that she thought her

---

* Susan is a pseudonym for this student, who consented to be used as a case example in this chapter. Important identifying information about her has been changed.

B-range grades were often "gifts" from her professors, because she was often so late in completing her assignments. Exams at the Divinity School were also challenging for her, particularly those that required her to read text and write analyses of the content within a time limit. Based on data from her earlier evaluation and the GSLS reading fluency screening, however, Susan was able to receive the accommodation of extended time on exams. This accommodation proved helpful in enabling her to demonstrate her sophisticated understanding of highly abstract content during exams. She also began working with a GSLS learning specialist in order to learn strategies to help her compensate for her slow reading rate. Although this instruction in reading strategies helped her to read somewhat more efficiently, her reading rate continued to be slow, particularly for complex, dense text. Given the limitations of strategy instruction in improving her reading rate, she is presently considering the use of assistive technology to compensate for her slow speed, such as software that enables a computer to read text aloud (e.g., Kurzweil 3000, 1996). Such assistive technology may be particularly important for Susan, since her plan is to work in a nonprofit organization after graduation, a career that will likely require considerable reading.

What conclusions can be drawn from this limited review of reading fluency research and insights from clinical work about the nature of reading dysfluency in adults? There is evidence to suggest that phonological processing deficits alone do not adequately explain reading dysfluency (e.g., Bowers, 2001; Torgesen, 2000; Wolf & Bowers, 1999).

Yet the hypothesis that timing deficits underlie dysfluency is also problematic. Several studies, for example, include in their samples individuals who perform slowly on rapid naming tasks but read with adequate fluency (e.g., Kinsbourne, Rufo, Gamzu, Palmer, & Berliner, 1991; Korhonen, 1995; Manis et al., 2000; Waber, 2001). In addition, some neuroimaging studies show evidence for reduced or absent, but not slowed, activation in certain cortical areas considered important for reading (e.g., Salmelin et al., 2000). There is also the possibility that purported causal factors such as magnocellular-related timing deficits or cerebellar-related automaticity deficits may be correlational rather than causal in nature, reflecting disruptions in more fundamental processes that may or may not be related (Bishop, 2002; Ivry et al., 2001; Waber, 2001). Caution in attributing dysfluency to a single underlying deficit also makes sense, given the evidence for variability in the deficits among dysfluent readers (Berninger et al., 2001; Morris et al., 1998; Wolf & Katzir-Cohen, 2001).

Evidence from neuroimaging studies also leaves some questions about dysfluency unanswered. Although there is evidence for disruption in the posterior neural pathways involved in reading in dysfluent adults (e.g., Shaywitz et al., 2002; Salmelin et al., 2000), it is unclear whether these regions are the only areas of disruption. Variability in the degree or locus of disrupted neural areas, for example, may result in some of the heterogeneous findings among dysfluent adults. In addition, it is possible that the use of less efficient, compensatory pathways for reading by dysfluent adults may lead not only to slow word reading but also to slowed processing at a later point in the reading process. Some studies, for example, have found slower, as well as weaker, activation in cortical areas involved in semantic processing in dysfluent adults compared to normal readers (Helenius, Salmelin, et al., 1999; Salmelin et al., 2000). The reports of dysfluent adults from clinical work support the notion that reading dysfluency may involve disruption in processes involved at later, as well as earlier, stages in the reading process, as they describe the time it takes to integrate the concepts or elements in a sentence or paragraph while reading. Disruption at the level of letter-string processing, for example, may lead to disrupted or slowed processing at later stages of lexical-semantic processing. Slow word reading might then require considerable use of working memory in order to integrate the elements in a sentence into a coherent thought, leaving little resource available for thinking about the text (e.g., Helenius, Salmelin, et al., 1999). There is also clinical evidence—for example, in the case of Susan, discussed above—that some adults can read fluently at the word level but not when comprehension of text is required. Findings such as this support the notion that differences in the degree or locus of neural disruption may underlie different types of reading dysfluency.

The present, limited review of reading fluency research indicates that there is much we do not know about dysfluency in adult readers. It is unclear, for example, why some adults who were dysfluent readers as children can read at an adequate rate in adulthood, while others cannot. Determining just what factors contribute to fluent outcomes in adulthood would require longitudinal studies that examine not only the cognitive processes involved in reading but also neuroanatomical areas activated during reading tasks and environmental factors, such as methods of reading instruction and amount of reading practice. Little is also known about how to help adults who read dysfluently. Research might tell us whether it is possible to increase the reading fluency in dyslexic adults through repeated reading techniques, for example, or through more comprehensive approaches aimed at improving fluency at the level of underlying component skills as well as reading per se (e.g., Chard et al., 2002; Rashotte & Torgesen, 1985; Sabatini, 2002; Wolf, Miller, & Donnelly, 2000). In addition, given the presence of assistive technology, it would also be important to investigate whether certain tools, such as computer readers, can actually improve fluency. This latter notion is particularly intriguing, given recent evidence that reading rate in dyslexic adults can be increased, if only temporarily, by increasing the rate of text presented on a computer (Breznitz, 2001; Breznitz & Leikin, 2001). Research into the causes and remediation of dysfluent reading in adulthood is particularly important, since adults who read slowly may experience not only a more limited range of educational and occupational choices but also more limited opportunities for occupational advancement, compared to those who read fluently.

References

Abadzi, H. (1996). Does age diminish the ability to learn fluent reading? *Educational Psychology Review, 8*, 373–96.

Allington, R. L. (1983). Fluency: The neglected reading goal. *The Reading Teacher, 36*, 556–560.

Bednarek, D. B., & Grabowska, A. (2002). Luminance and chromatic contrast sensitivity in dyslexia: The magnocellular deficit hypothesis revisited. *NeuroReport, 13*(18), 2521–2525.

Berninger, V. W., Abbott, R. D., Billingsley, F., & Nagy W. (2001). Processes underlying timing and fluency of reading: Efficiency, automaticity, coordination, and morphological awareness. In M. Wolf (Ed.), *Dyslexia, fluency, and the brain.* (pp. 383–414) Timonium, MD: York Press.

Bishop, D. V. M. (2002). Cerebellar abnormalities in developmental dyslexia: Cause, correlate or consequence? *Cortex, 38*, 491–498.

Bowers, P. G. (2001). Exploration of the basis for rapid naming's relationship to reading. In M. Wolf (Ed.), *Dyslexia, fluency and the brain.* (pp. 41–63) Timonium, MD: York Press.

Breznitz, Z. (2001). The determinants of reading fluency: A comparison of dyslexic and average readers. In M. Wolf (Ed.), *Dyslexia, fluency, and the brain.* (pp. 245–276) Timonium, MD: York Press.

Breznitz, Z., & Berman, L. (2003). The underlying factors of word reading rate. *Educational Psychology Review, 15*, 247–265.

Breznitz, Z., & Leikin, M. (2001). Effects of accelerated reading rate on processing words' syntactic functions by normal and dyslexic readers: Event-related potentials evidence. *Journal of Genetic Psychology, 162*, 276–296.

Breznitz, Z., & Misra, M. (2003). Speed of processing of the visual-orthographic and auditory-phonological systems in adult dyslexics: The contribution of "asynchrony" to word recognition deficits. *Brain and Language, 85*, 486–502.

Bruck, M. (1990). Word-recognition skills of adults with childhood diagnoses of dyslexia. *Developmental Psychology, 26*, 439–454.

Bruck, M. (1992). Persistence of dyslexics' phonological awareness deficits. *Developmental Psychology, 28*, 874–886.

Brunswick, N., McCroy, E., Price, C., Frith, C.D., & Frith, U. (1999). Explicit and implicit processing of words and pseudowords by adult developmental dyslexics. A search for Wernicke's Wortschatz? *Brain, 122*, 1901–1917.

Chard, D. J., Vaughn, S., & Tyler, B.-J. (2002). A synthesis of research on effective interventions for building reading fluency with elementary students with learning disabilities. *Journal of Learning Disabilities, 35*, 386–406.

Denckla, M. B., & Cutting, L. E. (1999). History and significance of rapid automatized naming. *Annals of Dyslexia, 49*, 29–42.

Denckla, M. B., & Rudel, R. G. (1976). Rapid automatized naming (RAN):
Dyslexia differentiated from other learning disabilities. *Neuropsychologia,
14*, 471–479.

Dowhower, S. (1987). Aspects of repeated reading on second-grade transitional
readers' fluency and comprehension. *Reading Research Quarterly, 22*,
389–406.

Fawcett, A. J., & Nicolson, R. I. (2001). Speed and temporal processing in dyslexia.
In M. Wolf (Ed.), *Dyslexia, fluency, and the brain.* (pp. 23–40) Timonium,
MD: York Press.

Felton, R., Naylor, C., & Wood, F. (1990). Neuropsychological profile of adult
dyslexics. *Brain and Language, 39*, 485–497.

Fink, R. P. (1998). Literacy development in successful men and women with
dyslexia. *Annals of Dyslexia, 48*, 311–346.

Galaburda, A. M., Menard, M. T., & Rosen, G. D. (1994). Evidence for aberrant
auditory anatomy in developmental dyslexia. *Proceedings of the National
Academy of Sciences, 91*, 8010–8013.

Helenius, P., Salmelin, R., Service, E., & Connolly, J. F. (1999). Semantic cortical
activation in dyslexic readers. *Journal of Cognitive Neuroscience, 11*,
535–550.

Helenius, P. Tarkianin, A., Cornelissen, P., Hansen, P. C., & Salmelin, R. (1999).
Dissociation of normal feature analysis and deficient processing of
letter-strings in dyslexic adults. *Cerebral Cortex, 4*, 476–483.

Helenius, P., Uutela, K., & Hari, R. (1999). Auditory stream segregation in dyslexic
adults. *Brain, 122*, 907–913.

Horwitz, B., Rumsey, J. M., & Donohue, B. C. (1998). Functional connectivity
of the angular gyrus in normal reading and dyslexia. *Proceedings of the
National Academy of Sciences USA, 95*, 8939–8944.

Ivry, R. B., Justus, T. C., & Middleton, C. (2001). The cerebellum, timing, and
language: Implications for the study of dyslexia. In M. Wolf (Ed.), *Dyslexia,
fluency, and the brain.* (pp. 189–211) Timonium, MD: York Press.

Kinsbourne, M., Rufo, D. T., Gamzu, E., Palmer, R. L., & Berliner, A. K. (1991).
Neuropsychological deficits in adults with dyslexia. *Developmental Medicine
and Child Neurology, 33*, 763–775.

Korhonen, T. T. (1995). The persistence of rapid naming problems in children with
reading disabilities: A 9-year follow-up. *Journal of Learning Disabilities, 28*,
232–9.

Kurzweil 3000. (1996). Bedford, MA: Kurzweil Educational Systems.

Lefly, D., & Pennington, B. (1991). Spelling errors and reading fluency in compensated dyslexics. *Annals of Dyslexia, 41*, 143–162.

Levy, B. A. (2001). Moving the bottom: Improving reading fluency. In M. Wolf (Ed.).
Dyslexia, fluency, and the brain. (pp. 257–279) Timonium, MD: York Press.

Livingstone, M. S., Rosen, G. D., Drislane, F. W., & Galaburda, A. M. (1991).
Physiological and anatomical evidence for a magnocellular deficit in developmental dyslexia. *Proceedings of the National Academy of Sciences USA,
88*, 7943–7947.

Lovett, M. W. (1987). A developmental approach to reading disability: Accuracy and speed criteria of normal and deficient reading skill. *Child Development, 58*, 234–260.

Lyon, G. R., Shaywitz, S. E., & Shaywitz, B. A. (2003). A definition of dyslexia. *Annals of Dyslexia, 53*, 1–14.

Manis, F. R., Doi, L. & Bhadha, B. (2000). Naming speed, phonological awareness and orthographic knowledge in second graders. *Journal of Learning Disabilities, 33*, 325–333.

Meyer, M. M., & Felton, R. H. (1999). Repeated reading to enhance fluency: Old approaches and new direction. *Annals of Dyslexia, 49*, 283–306.

Morris, R. D., Shaywitz, S. E., Shankweiler, D. P., Katz, L., Stuebing, K. K., Fletcher, J. M., et al. (1998). Subtypes of reading disability: Variability around a phonological core. *Journal of Educational Psychology, 90*, 347–373.

Nicolson, R. I., & Fawcett, A. J. (2001). Dyslexia, learning, and the cerebellum. In M. Wolf (Ed.), *Dyslexia, fluency, and the brain.* (pp. 159–187) Timonium, MD: York Press.

Omtzigt, D., Hendriks, A. W., & Kolk, H. H. J. (2002). Evidence for magnocellular involvement in the identification of flanked letters. *Neuropsychologia, 40*, 1881–1890.

Paulesu, E., Demonet, J.-F., Fazio, F., McCrory, V. C., Brunswick, N., Cappa, S. F., et al. (2001). Dyslexia: Cultural diversity and biological unity. *Science, 291*, 2165–2167.

Poldrack, R. A. (2001). A structural basis for developmental dyslexia: Evidence from diffusion tensor imaging. In M. Wolf (Ed.), *Dyslexia, fluency and the brain.* (pp. 213–233) Timonium, MD: York Press.

Raberger, T., & Wimmer, H. (2003). On the automaticity/cerebellar deficit hypothesis of dyslexia: Balancing and continuous rapid naming in dyslexic and ADHD children. *Neuropsychologia, 41*, 1493–1497.

Rashotte, C. A., & Torgesen, J. K. (1985). Repeated reading and reading fluency in learning disabled children. *Reading Research Quarterly, 20*, 180–202.

Sabatini, J. P. (2002). Efficiency in word reading of adults: Ability group comparisons. *Scientific Studies of Reading, 6*, 267–298.

Salmelin, R., Helenius, P., & Service, E. (2000). Neurophysiology of fluent and impaired reading: A magnetoencephalographic approach. *Journal of Clinical Neurophysiology, 17*, 163–174.

Scarborough, H. (1998). Predicting the future achievement of second graders with reading disabilities: Contributions of phonemic awareness, verbal memory, rapid naming, and IQ. *Annals of Dyslexia, 48*, 115–136.

Shaywitz, B. A., Shaywitz, S. E., Pugh, K. R., Mencl, W. E., Fulbright, R. K., Skudlarski, P., et al. (2002). Disruption of posterior brain systems for reading in children with developmental dyslexia. *Biological Psychiatry, 52*, 101–110.

Shaywitz, S. E., Fletcher, J. M., Holahan, J. M., Shneider, A. E., Marchione, K. E., Stuebing, K. K., et al. (1999). Persistence of dyslexia: The Connecticut longitudinal study at adolescence. *Pediatrics, 104*, 1351–1359.

Shaywitz, S. E., Shaywitz, B. A., Fulbright, R. K., Skudlarski, P., Mencl, W. E., Constable, R. T., et al. (2003). Neural systems for compensation and persistence: Young adult outcome of childhood reading disability. *Biological Psychiatry, 54*, 25–33.

Shaywitz, S. E., Shaywitz, B. A., Pugh, K. R., Fulbright, R. K., Constable, R. T., Menel, W. E., et al. (1998). Functional disruption in the organization of the brain for reading in dyslexia. *Proceedings in the National Academy of Science, 95*, 2636–2641 or 2535–2541.

Stanovich, K. E. (1988). The right and wrong places to look for the cognitive locus of reading disability. *Annals of Dyslexia, 38*, 154–177.

Stein, J. (2001). The neurobiology of reading difficulties. In M. Wolf (Ed.), *Dyslexia, fluency, and the brain.* (pp. 3–21) Timonium, MD: York Press.

Sunseth, K., & Bowers, P. G. (2002). Rapid naming and phonemic awareness: Contributions to reading, spelling, and orthographic knowledge. *Scientific Studies of Reading, 6*, 401–429.

Torgesen, J. K. (2000). Individual differences in response to early interventions in reading: The lingering problem of treatment resisters. *Learning Disabilities Research and Practice, 15*, 55–64.

Torgesen, J. K., Rashotte, C. A., & Alexander, A. W. (2001). Principles of fluency instruction in reading. In M. Wolf (Ed.), *Reading, fluency, and the brain.* (pp. 333–355) Timonium, MD: York Press.

Torgesen, J. K., Rashotte, C., Lindamood, P., Rose, E., Conway, T., & Garven, D. (1999). Preventing reading failure in young children with phonological processing disabilities: Group and individual responses to instruction. *Journal of Educational Psychology, 91*, 579–593.

U.S. Department of Health and Human Services. (2000). *Teaching children to read: An evidence based assessment on the scientific research literature on reading instruction* (NIH Publication No. 00–4769). Rockville, MD. National Reading Panel.

van Daal, V., & van der Leij, A. (1999). Developmental dyslexia: Related to specific or general deficits? *Annals of Dyslexia, 49*, 71–104.

van der Leij, A., & van Daal, V. H. P. (1999). Automatization aspects of dyslexia: Speed limitations in word identification, sensitivity to increasing task demands, and orthographic compensation. *Journal of Learning Disabilities, 32*, 417–428.

Waber, D. P. (2001). Aberrations in timing in children with impaired reading: Cause, effect, or correlate? In M. Wolf (Ed.), *Dyslexia, fluency, and the brain.* (pp. 103–125) Timonium, MD: York Press.

Waber, D. P., Weiler, M. D., Bellinger, D., Marcus, D. H., Forbes, P. I., Wypij, D., & Wolff, P. H. (2000). Diminished motor timing control in children referred for diagnosis of learning problems. *Developmental Neuropsychology, 17*, 181–197.

Wimmer, H., & Mayringer, H. (2001). Is the reading-rate problem of German dyslexic children caused by slow visual processes? In M. Wolf (Ed.), *Dyslexia, fluency, and the brain.* Timonium, MD: York Press.

Wolf, M. (1984). Naming, reading, and the dyslexias: A longitudinal overview. *Annals of Dyslexia, 34*, 34–115.

Wolf, M. (1991). Naming speed and reading: the contribution of the cognitive neurosciences. *Reading Research Quarterly, 2*, 123–40.

Wolf, M. (1999). What time may tell: Towards a new conceptualization of developmental dyslexia. *Annals of Dyslexia, 49*, 3–28.

Wolf, M., Bally, H., & Morris, R. (1986). Automaticity, retrieval processes, and reading: A longitudinal study in average and impaired readers. *Child Development, 57,* 988–1000.

Wolf, M., & Bowers, P. G. (1999). The double-deficit hypothesis for the developmental dyslexias. *Journal of Educational Psychology, 91,* 415–438.

Wolf, M., & Bowers, P. G. (2000). The question of naming-speed deficits in developmental reading disabilities: An introduction to the double-deficit hypothesis. *Journal of Learning Disabilities, 33,* 322–324.

Wolf, M., Bowers, P. G., & Biddle, K. (2000). Naming-speed processes, timing, and reading: A conceptual review. *Journal of Learning Disabilities, 33,* 387–407.

Wolf, M., & Katzir-Cohen, T. (2001). Reading fluency and its intervention. *Scientific Studies of Reading, 5,* 211–238.

Wolf, M., Miller, L., & Donnelly, K. (2000). Retrieval, automaticity, vocabulary elaboration, orthography (RAVE-O): A comprehensive, fluency-based reading intervention program. *Journal of Learning Disabilities, 33,* 375–386.

Wolff, P., Michel, G., & Ovrut, M. (1990). Rate variables and automatized naming in developmental dyslexia. *Brain and Language, 39,* 556–575.

Woodcock, R., McGrew, K., & Mather, N. (2001). *Woodcock-Johnson-III: Tests of Achievement.* Itasca, IL: Riverside.

Zeffiro, T., & Eden, G. (2000). The neural basis of developmental dyslexia. *Annals of Dyslexia, 50,* 3–30.

CHAPTER 6

Structural and Functional Imaging Research on Language Disorders

Specific Language Impairment and Autism Spectrum Disorders

HELEN TAGER-FLUSBERG, KRISTEN A. LINDGREN, and MARIA MODY

Contents

The cognitive neuroscience revolution has helped to redefine ways we can investigate the interplay between biological and behavioral processes in learning disabilities throughout the life span. Developmental language disorders encompass a wide range of disabilities in which delays and deficits in language acquisition are identified, including mental retardation syndromes, pervasive developmental disorders, and learning disorders. In some cases, language delays may be resolved by the time a child enters school; however, for most individuals, language impairments can persist into adolescence and adulthood. In this chapter, we focus on two specific disorders that include in their primary diagnostic criteria impairments in language and communication: specific language impairment (SLI) and autism spectrum disorders (ASD). Over the past decade, researchers have used a variety of imaging methodologies to investigate the neurobiological bases of language and related social communicative impairments in children and adults with these disorders. Our goal in this chapter is to provide an overview of this research, noting, however, that this field is still in its infancy and, to date, there is little consensus in identifying the neurobiological substrate of developmental language and social communicative impairments in either SLI or ASD.

Specific Language Impairment (SLI) and Autism Spectrum Disorders (ASD)

Specific Language Impairment

SLI has been defined as a failure to develop normal oral language abilities despite normal intelligence; no known hearing, emotional, or physical problems; and an adequate learning environment (Bishop, 1992). Children with SLI typically have nonverbal IQ scores within the normal range; however, their performance on standardized language tests is significantly below the level predicted by IQ or age. Despite apparently clear-cut criteria, there is little consensus about the IQ-discrepancy criterion (Plante, 1998). What further exacerbates the problem of identifying SLI is the considerable heterogeneity within language-impaired samples and the potential overlap between SLI and other learning disabilities such as dyslexia (Kamhi & Catts, 1989). Several studies have found that many children with SLI have reading problems (Aram & Nation, 1980; Catts, 1993; Tallal, Sainburg, & Jernigan, 1991). Similarly, many children with reading disability have impaired oral language skills (Fletcher & Satz, 1980; Lyon & Watson, 1981; Stanovich, 1986). According to Bailey and Snowling (2002), while some dyslexic children have concomitant language problems, SLI children have more extensive language problems encompassing phonological processing deficits, poor vocabulary, and grammatical deficits. Bishop and Snowling (2004) conclude that while these disorders have some overlapping phenotypic features, evidence from genetic, neuroimaging, and cognitive studies indicate that they do not simply fall along a continuum of severity but represent distinct neurodevelopmental learning disorders.

Current efforts in defining the core phenotypic features for SLI have focused on two behavioral markers for English-speaking children (Tager-Flusberg & Cooper, 1999): deficits on tests of nonword repetition (Bishop, North, & Donlan, 1996; Conti-Ramsden, 2003; Dollaghan & Campbell, 1998; Gathercole & Baddeley, 1990) and problems in the use in obligatory contexts of finite verb-related grammatical morphemes (Bedore & Leonard, 1998; Rice, 2003; Rice & Wexler, 1996). Impaired performance on tasks that tap these aspects of phonological and grammatical processing persists in adolescence (Conti-Ramsden, Botting, & Faragher, 2001), but no behavioral studies have extended beyond the school years into adulthood. Beyond these core features, however, SLI is a heterogeneous disorder that may include a range of other symptoms that vary within and across individuals at different developmental stages. Examples of these more variable symptoms include articulation problems, severe receptive language deficits, discourse impairments, motor problems, and difficulties on symbolic processing tasks (Leonard, 1998). Nevertheless, attempts to define specific subtypes within SLI that may inform genetic or neuro-imaging research have thus far failed to achieve significant results.

Autism Spectrum Disorders

ASD is an umbrella term that includes several psychiatric conditions that share core developmental impairments in reciprocal social interaction skills, communication, and the presence of stereotyped behavior or narrowly defined interests (American Psychiatric Association, 1994). These include classic autism, Asperger syndrome, and pervasive developmental disorder not otherwise specified (PDD-NOS). Although there is still some controversy regarding the boundaries between these diagnostic categories, the consensus is that these different types of ASD fall along a continuum but vary in overall severity in core symptoms, as well as in IQ and linguistic skills (Constantino et al., 2004; Macintosh & Dissanayake, 2004; Wing, 2004). As in other complex psychiatric disorders, ASD involves a number of variable characteristics that go beyond the core symptoms and that add to the heterogeneity of the population. Examples include sensory sensitivities, abnormalities in sleep or eating habits, behavior problems such as aggression or self-injury, and comorbid psychiatric conditions such as depression, anxiety, or attention-deficit/hyperactivity disorder. As with SLI, efforts at defining biologically meaningful subtypes within ASD have not yet met with much success, with the exception of defining different language subtypes among children with classic autism (Tager-Flusberg & Joseph, 2003). Although ASD is generally viewed as a lifelong disorder, symptoms often improve with age, and a minority of high-functioning individuals can achieve considerable success and independence when they reach adulthood.

Parallels Between SLI and ASD

SLI and ASD show a number of significant similarities. First, both are considered complex disorders that are diagnosed on the basis of core behavioral characteristics and with variable expression of secondary features. Second, in both ASD and SLI, symptoms are initially noticed in the toddler or early preschool years. Failure to acquire language is the most frequently presenting problem, and for both disorders, language delays and deficits are among the primary characteristics. Third, there is strong evidence that ASD and SLI are inherited disorders (for reviews, see Bespalova & Buxbaum, 2003; Fisher, Lai, & Monaco, 2003; Folstein & Rosen-Sheidley, 2001).

Family studies of children with ASD and SLI have found that although the majority of first-degree relatives do not share the same diagnosis, they may have some related features, referred to as the "broader phenotype"

(Piven, 1999; Tomblin, Freese, & Records, 1992). Of special interest are the findings that among family members of children with autism, there are significantly elevated rates of documented histories of language delay and language-based learning deficits (Bailey, Palferman, Heavey, & Le Couteur, 1998; Bolton et al., 1994; Fombonne, Bolton, Prior, Jordan, & Rutter, 1997; Piven, Palmer, et al., 1997). These studies suggest that SLI may occur significantly more frequently in families of autistic children than in the general population. There is also evidence that in families identified on the basis of having a child with SLI, there is a significantly elevated risk of autism among the siblings. Tomblin and colleagues (Tomblin, Hafeman, & O'Brien, 2003) found in a population-based sample of children diagnosed with SLI that about 1 out of every 100 siblings met criteria for classic autism. This rate is much higher than would be expected based on the current prevalence estimates of about 1 in 500 (Fombonne, 2003).

The findings from these family studies suggest that SLI and ASD may represent partially overlapping disorders (Bishop, 2003; Bishop & Norbury, 2002; Tager-Flusberg, 2003). In support of this view, a subgroup of children with autism has been identified with developmental language impairments that are identical to those that define SLI (Kjelgaard & Tager-Flusberg, 2001). At the same time, it is important to note key differences between SLI and ASD. In SLI, the core language problems involve difficulties with structural aspects of language, whereas in ASD, the most important diagnostic impairments are in the pragmatic uses of language. Moreover, in addition to impairments in language and communication, ASD is defined on the basis of deficits in social-affective abilities, which are not part of the phenotype for SLI. Based on these similarities and differences, we focus our review of the functional imaging studies of SLI on language-related tasks and for ASD on both language and aspects of social-affective information processing.

Brain-Imaging Methodologies

The introduction in the 1970s of a range of neuroimaging technologies provided a direct window on the potential abnormalities in structure and function that underlie behavioral symptoms in disorders such as SLI and ASD. We now have the ability to image brain anatomy and activity using a number of different methods, including computed tomography (CT), positron emission tomography (PET), single photon emission computed tomography (SPECT), structural magnetic resonance imaging (MRI), function MRI (fMRI), magnetoencephalography (MEG), and classic electrophysiological recordings including electroencephalography (EEG) and event-related potentials (ERPs).

These methods vary in their ability to provide high-quality information about brain structure, including volumetric and morphometric measures (e.g., MRI), information about the temporal dynamic of sensory and cognitive processing (ERP and MEG) or the spatial localization of cognitive processing (PET, SPECT, and especially fMRI). Each of these methods involves different kinds of challenges. For example, MRI and fMRI—which are now the most widely used for investigating the neural bases of neurodevelopmental disorders because, unlike PET or SPECT, they do not depend on the invasive introduction of radioactive tracers—require subjects to lie in a narrow bore and remain completely still for lengthy periods of time while hearing loud noises generated by the magnet. For these reasons, MRI and fMRI have more limited use with younger children or individuals with high levels of anxiety, hyperactivity, or hyperacusis. EEG and ERP methods require subjects to tolerate electrodes that are attached to the scalp and face, and movements need to be limited, though not to the same extent as for MRI or fMRI. The physiological source of the brain activity measured on the scalp remains poorly understood, especially when ERPs are used to investigate higher level cognitive processing. In general, these methods provide complementary information about brain structure and cognitive processing in children and adults. Studies of functional brain activity that include younger children primarily still depend on ERP and EEG methods, whereas fMRI tends to be employed in studies of adults and some older children and adolescents. Structural MRI scans can be acquired in children at all ages; however, in younger children, sedation is typically used to ensure the absence of movement during scan acquisition.

Challenges in the Design and Interpretation of Brain-Imaging Studies

Despite several years of investigation, there is still little agreement about the key abnormalities that define SLI and ASD at either a structural or a functional level. As illustrated in the following sections of this chapter, there are many conflicting findings that have yet to be reconciled. Before reviewing this literature, we note a number of key design issues that need to be considered in evaluating this program of research.

We have already noted the heterogeneity of SLI and ASD. This heterogeneity limits our ability to draw strong conclusions across different studies that may have included different subject populations. Other subject factors that are known to significantly influence findings from both structural and functional studies include age, gender, handedness, IQ, language level, attentional factors, other comorbid conditions, and the use of medications. A crucial factor in the design and interpretation of functional studies is the choice of a behavioral paradigm and the precise methods for implementing the paradigm in the imaging environment. Even small differences in task design can significantly influence results. Furthermore, numerous controversial issues continue to plague discussions about how to collect brain scans (e.g., thickness of slices; density of electrodes), what to measure (e.g., global or regional areas), how to conduct measurements, and how to analyze the data using different statistical approaches (Courchesne & Plante, 1996; Filipek, 1996)

Finally, it is important to be cautious about the interpretation of findings from brain-imaging studies. Neurodevelopmental disorders such as SLI and ASD are known to arise from disturbances in brain development, beginning, perhaps, during the early stages of embryonic development. At the same time, a brain image taken from either a child or adult with a disorder is the end product of abnormal brain development, and it is not clear whether observed abnormalities in the image are the cause of behavioral symptoms such as impaired language or the result of the atypical delayed developmental pathway that defines the disorder (Muller, 2004).

Specific Language Impairment

There have been surprisingly few imaging studies in SLI, in contrast to the extensive literature on brain dysfunction in dyslexia. This is probably because first, it is harder to diagnose SLI in older children and adults, and second, many researchers investigating dyslexia have included participants with SLI in their subject groups but have not separated out individuals with and without oral language deficits. Most of the studies that have been conducted focus on the neurobiological basis of language and auditory processing in SLI children and adults.

Structural Imaging Studies

Language Regions Postmortem studies of patients with developmental language disorders point to abnormalities in the perisylvian regions typically associated with language function (Cohen, Campbell, & Yaghmai, 1989; Landau, Goldstein, & Kleffner, 1960). With the availability of in vivo imaging tools, it has become evident that other language sites exist, extending beyond the perisylvian cortical regions of Broca's and Wernicke's areas. These additional language areas include the supramarginal gyrus, angular gyrus, and subcortical gray-matter regions such as the thalamus (Foundas, 2001), but their anatomy has been less extensively studied. The notion of left hemispheric asymmetry as related to language specialization comes from the fact that 90% of the population in all cultures is right-handed, and of these about 90% are also left-hemisphere dominant for language (Annett, 2002; Corballis, 1991; Rasmussen & Milner, 1975). As such, both structural and functional interhemispheric differences have been conceptualized as a dichotomy with a larger structure being related to "increased" function. However, as is well known, language functions are not completely dichotomous, with the distributions between the two cerebral hemispheres ranging from a complete left dominance to symmetry or, at the other extreme, to moderate right-hemispheric dominance (Foundas, 2001).

Anatomists have reported hemispheric asymmetries of language-related cortical areas for over 100 years, but their functional significance remained unclear until the groundbreaking work of Geschwind and Levitsky (1968), who proposed that the left-larger-than-right planum temporale found in 65% of their 100 postmortem brains was compatible with known functional asymmetries from studies of fluent aphasia following lesions to Wernicke's area. This left planar asymmetry was also found in fetuses, suggesting that the human brain may be biologically preprogrammed for asymmetric representation of speech and language (Geschwind & Levitsky, 1968). In keeping with postmortem brain studies, volumetric MRI scans have also found that asymmetries of the planum temporale differ by hand preference, with right-handers having an increased incidence and magnitude of leftward asymmetry in comparison with left-handers, who have a reduced leftward asymmetry (Steinmetz, Volkmann, Jancke, & Freund, 1991). Similar findings were obtained for the pars opercularis, the posterior portion of Broca's area (Foundas, Eure, Luevano, & Weinberger, 1998). In contrast, the more anterior pars triangularis, while showing a leftward asymmetry in right-handers, tended to be more anatomically variable in left-handers (Foundas, Leonard, & Heilman, 1995). Others have reported sex differences in planar asymmetry (Kulynych, Vladar, Jones, & Weinberger, 1994; Rossi et al., 1994), but the functional significance of this remains unknown. These findings clearly underscore the importance of controlling for handedness and gender in studies of brain-behavior relationships.

A natural question that arises is how the morphology of language-related brain structures as well as brain structure-function relationships are affected in SLI. The majority of studies have been conducted with children. The most consistent findings show that individuals with SLI frequently demonstrate reversed, weak, or absent asymmetry of the planum temporale. Using volumetric MRI measures, some investigators found that the right perisylvian regions were larger in some children with developmental language disorders than normal controls (Filipek et al., 1992; Plante, Swisher, Vance, & Rapcsak, 1991); in contrast, the left perisylvian regions have been either smaller (Herbert et al., 2002; Jernigan, Hesselink, Sowell, & Tallal, 1991) or similar in volume (Plante et al., 1991). In a quantitative study of anatomic differences in the brains of carefully diagnosed children with SLI and age-matched controls, Gauger, Lombardino, and Leonard (1997) found that children with SLI had significantly narrower right hemispheres, significantly smaller pars triangularis in the left hemispheres, and greater rightward asymmetry of the total planum, compared to normal controls. However, two more recent studies of boys with SLI carefully matched on age, handedness, and gender to normal controls found greater leftward asymmetry in the planum temporale region (De Fossé et al., 2004; Herbert et al., 2002).

Corpus Callosum Given that hemispheric asymmetry and interhemispheric connections are thought to be negatively correlated (Galaburda, Rosen, & Sherman, 1990), it is possible that the reduced cerebral asymmetry sometimes observed in language-impaired populations may imply stronger interhemispheric connectivity and hence a larger-sized corpus callosum or its subregions in language-disordered populations compared to normal controls. Gauger et al. (1997) mention normal total corpus callosum size, whereas Njiokiktjien, de Sonneville, and Vaal (1994) found that a subgroup of children who exhibited both familial SLI and dyslexia had a larger corpus callosum than nonfamilial subjects. In an elegant study that controlled for differences in brain size by relating corpus callosum area measure to forebrain volume, Preis, Steinmetz, Knorr, and Jäncke (2000) found no significant anatomical difference in corpus callosum or its subregions between a group of children with SLI and an age- and gender-matched control group, suggesting that a larger corpus callosum may be associated with dyslexia but not SLI.

KE Family As part of the ongoing studies of a unique multigenerational British family (known as the KE family), half of whom suffer severe language and oral motor impairments that have been linked to a mutation in the FOX2P gene (Lai, Fisher, Hurst, Vargha-Khadem, & Monaco, 2001), Vargha-Khadem and colleagues used MRI to explore brain structural differences between the affected and unaffected family members. The most significant findings were reduced gray matter bilaterally in the caudate nucleus, cerebellum, and inferior frontal gyrus in the affected individuals (Vargha-Khadem et al., 1998). Interestingly, Jernigan et al. (1991) also found reduced gray matter bilaterally in the caudate nuclei in children with SLI. The affected members of the KE family also had significantly more gray matter in the putamen bilaterally and in the superior temporal cortex, including the planum temporale (Vargha-Khadem et al., 1998; Watkins, Gadian, & Vargha-Khadem, 1999).

Summary The major areas in which abnormalities in brain structure have been found in SLI include language regions and structures, especially the basal ganglia, which are involved in motor functioning, although these latter findings may be limited to individuals with oral motor deficits.

Functional Imaging Studies

Auditory Processing   According to Tallal and colleagues (e.g., Tallal, Merzenich, Miller, & Jenkins, 1998), deficits in rapid auditory processing of both verbal and nonverbal stimuli are characteristic of language-learning disabilities such as SLI and dyslexia. Mody, Studdert-Kennedy, and Brady (1997), however, failed to find any significant difference between good and poor readers in discriminating acoustically matched nonspeech sine-wave analogues of /ba/ and /da/, despite significant group differences on the speech stimuli, /ba/-/da/. Uwer, Albrecht, and von Suchodoletz (2002) compared mismatch negativity (MMN) amplitudes, which are considered to be a preattentive ERP index of the brain's capacity to discriminate acoustic stimuli automatically, for speech and nonspeech stimuli. They found significantly attenuated MMN amplitudes to speech stimuli in children with SLI, whereas their processing of simple tone differences seemed unimpaired compared to normal controls, supporting the view that SLI impairments are restricted to the processing of speech stimuli. Evidence from animal studies (Kraus et al., 1994; Rauschecker, Tian, & Hauser, 1995) suggests that MMN generators are hierarchically organized such that pure tone contrasts elicit MMNs even at the thalamic level but rapid frequency change contrasts, including speech contrasts such as /ba/-/da/, require contributions from the auditory cortex. As such, abnormal development of these regions may lead to differential deficits seen in children with SLI. Nevertheless, Benasich, Thomas, Chaudhury, and Leppanen (2002) have found that rapid auditory processing skills differ in infants with a family history of language disorder and are predictive of later language outcome. This is somewhat surprising, given that the human auditory system does not fully mature until early adolescence (Ponton, Eggermont, Kwong, & Don, 2000). Clearly, the relationship between these behavioral manifestations and clinical categories within SLI is not straightforward (Mody, 2004).

Language Processing   Studies of children with SLI using SPECT revealed abnormal patterns of activation during language tasks (Tzourio, Heim, Zilbovicius, Gerard, & Mazoyer, 1994) or focal cerebral dysfunction (Lou, Henriksen, & Bruhn, 1990). Hugdahl and colleagues (2004) found significant brain activation differences in the middle temporal gyrus between SLI and normal controls in a listening task using isolated vowels, pseudowords, and real words. Using auditory ERPs, Neville and her colleagues (Neville,

Coffey, Holcomb, & Tallal, 1993) found that children with SLI who had the poorest grammatical skills failed to show the typical left-greater-than-right N400 amplitude asymmetry over anterior left hemisphere. More recently, Shafer and colleagues (2001) showed a similar reversal of functional asymmetry of an ERP response 200–400 ms poststimulus in a group of SLI children when examining their response to the grammatical marker "the" in a story-listening task.

In the first functional imaging study of the KE family, Vargha-Khadem and colleagues (1998) investigated two of the affected members using PET. Brain activation patterns to listening and repeating spoken words were compared to activation patterns related to listening to reversed speech and repeating a fixed word. These tasks have been shown to activate left hemisphere language-specific areas (Price et al., 1996). Compared to four control subjects, the two affected KE family subjects failed to activate a number of areas in the medial wall of the left hemisphere, including the cingulate cortex. However, they showed significantly greater activation in the left caudate nucleus and anterior Broca's area. In a more recent study using fMRI, Liégeois et al. (2003) compared brain activation patterns in affected and unaffected KE family members on two language tasks: one involved covert verb generations, and the other an overt word repetition task. Compared to the unaffected controls, the affected members showed significantly less left-hemisphere activation in Broca's area and a more posterior, bilateral pattern of activation. Taken together, these results suggest a poor lateralization of language function in SLI in keeping with the reduced or absent leftward asymmetry reported earlier, as well as heterogeneity in their neurobiological profiles.

Autism Spectrum Disorders

The brain-imaging literature on ASD is especially confusing and contradictory. As noted earlier, the heterogeneity of these disorders, and factors such as age and gender, may strongly influence findings in this paradigmatic neurodevelopmental disorder that affects significantly more males than females. Research is beginning to disentangle what is known and what is not known about the neurobiological bases of both the language and social communicative symptoms in ASD; however, until we are able to conduct studies with larger sample sizes, the findings summarized must still be considered quite provisional.

Structural Imaging Studies

Brain Volume Several imaging studies have investigated the presence of enlarged overall brain volume in individuals with autism. Early studies of adolescent and adult males with autism found overall increased brain volume after controlling for height and performance IQ (Piven, Arndt, Bailey, & Andreasen, 1996; Piven et al., 1995). Similar results have been reported for younger children with ASD (Hardan, Minshew, Mallikarjuhn, & Keshavan, 2001; Sparks et al., 2002). However, studies of older children (Herbert et al., 2003), adolescents, and adults with ASD (Aylward et al., 1999; Haznedar et al., 2000) found no significant differences in total brain volume. Recent findings suggest that this difference is only present in childhood and does not persist into adulthood (Aylward, Minshew, Field, Sparks, & Singh, 2002; Carper, Moses, Tigue, & Courchesne, 2002; Courchesne et al., 2001; Hardan et al., 2001), though the time of normalization is unclear. One study comparing head circumference in infancy and brain volume in early childhood found that a greater increase in head circumference at several points during the first year of life was correlated with greater whole-brain volume at age 2 to 5 (Courchesne, Carper, & Akshoomoff, 2003). These studies indicate that in autism accelerated brain growth occurs early but that increased brain volume is not present throughout life. It is unclear if these findings of enlarged brain volumes are consistent across gender in autism. One study of total brain volume in adolescents and adults with ASD reported an increase in males but not in females (Piven et al., 1996). However, in another study, enlarged brain volume was present in preschool girls with ASD (Sparks et al., 2002).

The presence of enlarged brain volume does not appear to be generalized but rather is due to specific regional increases. In a study of adolescent and adult males with autism, temporal, parietal, and occipital lobes, but not the frontal lobe, were significantly increased in size (Piven et al., 1996). Another study, using sulcal boundaries instead of relative distances, investigated regional gray and white matter in children with autism and found that frontal and parietal lobe white matter and frontal and temporal gray matter were significantly enlarged in the autism group, with the most significant differences found in the frontal lobe (Carper et al., 2002). However, these findings were only significant in children under 4 years of age, and no differences in gray- or white-matter volumes were observed in older children. However, we note that in this study measurements were not adjusted for overall brain or cerebrum volume.

A consistent finding across studies is that the observed increase in overall brain volume is due to greater white-matter volume (Carper et al., 2002; Courchesne et al., 2001; Herbert et al., 2003; Herbert et al., 2004). There are, however, conflicting results as to whether white-matter volume enlargement is localized to specific lobes. One study found increases in white matter localized to the frontal and parietal lobes in very young boys with ASD but not boys older than 4 years (Courchesne et al., 2001). Again, however, these measurements were not adjusted for total brain volume. Another study that did control for total brain volume found white matter increases in all lobes in high-functioning boys with ASD (Herbert et al., 2004). These increases were confined to the radiate compartment of white matter, which consists of mostly intrahemispheric and corticocortical connections and regions that take longer to fully myelinate or that myelinate later in development. No differences between the groups were observed in deep white matter, specifically the sagittal or bridging system components. In both of these studies, though, the white matter in the frontal lobe was the most significantly enlarged volume in autism, especially in the prefrontal cortex (Herbert et al., 2004). Interestingly, no differences in white-matter volume in any of these regions were found between children with ASD and children with SLI (Herbert et al., 2004).

Corpus Callosum Despite an overall increase in white-matter volume in autism, numerous studies have reported either no difference (Elia et al., 2000) or a decreased total area of the corpus callosum on midsagittal images (Egaas, Courchesne, & Saitoh, 1995; Manes et al., 1999). Studies into the area of white matter in specific regions of the corpus callosum have produced conflicting results. In adolescents and adults, reduced area has been found in the anterior regions of the corpus callosum (Chung, Dalton, Alexander, & Davidson, 2004; Hardan, Minshew, & Keshavan, 2000), the body (Manes et al., 1999; Piven, Bailey, Ranson, & Arndt, 1997), and posterior regions (Egaas et al., 1995; Piven, Bailey et al., 1997), including the splenium (Chung et al., 2004). However, other studies have reported no differences in anterior regions of the corpus callosum (Piven, Bailey et al., 1997), the rostrum (Manes et al., 1999), or splenium (Hardan et al., 2000; Manes et al., 1999). It has been suggested that the marked increase in total white-matter volume but the decreased size of the corpus callosum in autism may be attributed to decreased interhemispheric but increased intrahemispheric connectivity (Hardan et al., 2000).

Language Regions MRI studies have found structural abnormalities in language areas in autism. Using voxel-based morphometry, Abell and his colleagues found decreased gray-matter volume in the left inferior frontal gyrus in adults with ASD when compared to matched controls (Abell et al., 1999). Reversed asymmetry of regions associated with Broca's area has been reported in boys with ASD (De Fossé et al., 2004; Herbert et al., 2002). Herbert et al. (2002) found that the pars opercularis was 27% larger on the right in the ASD group versus 17% larger on the left in the control group. In a more recent study, the ASD sample was divided into those with and without language impairment. Only the boys with language impairment demonstrated a rightward asymmetry of the pars opercularis and pars triangularis (De Fossé et al., 2004).

Abnormal asymmetry has also been reported in the planum temporale in ASD. In one study the planum temporale in the left hemisphere was significantly smaller in adults with ASD when compared to a control group matched for age, gender, and handedness (Rojas, Bawn, Benkers, Reite, & Rogers, 2002). No differences were found in this structure in the right hemisphere, indicating a lack of asymmetry in the planum temporale in ASD. However, in another study of younger boys, Herbert et al. (2002) reported an exaggerated leftward asymmetry of the planum temporale when compared to age-, gender-, and handedness-matched controls. Again, this exaggerated asymmetry was later found only in boys with ASD and language impairment (De Fossé et al., 2004), so perhaps the participants in the study by Rojas and his colleagues (2002) were not language impaired.

Amygdala   Studies of the amygdala in ASD have reported reduced volume (Aylward et al., 1999), increased volume (Schumann et al., 2004; Sparks et al., 2002), and no differences in volume (Haznedar et al., 2000) when compared to control subjects. However, the discrepancies among these studies may be explained by differences in the age and clinical diagnoses of the subjects. Studies that found increased amygdala volume in ASD included children (Schumann et al., 2004; Sparks et al., 2002), while those that included adolescents, adults, or a mixture of age groups found either no difference (Haznedar et al., 2000) or smaller volume (Aylward et al., 1999). Additionally, clinical diagnosis affects amygdala volume. Children with Asperger syndrome showed a less significant increase in amygdala volume than children with autism (Schumann et al., 2004), while adults with Asperger syndrome possessed larger left amygdala volume (Haznedar et al., 2000). Furthermore, children with autism had significantly larger amygdala volume bilaterally than children with PDD-NOS (Sparks et al., 2002). However, it appears that amygdala volume is consistent across IQ levels in children with ASD (Schumann et al., 2004).

Cerebellum   There is a great deal of controversy about the presence of structural abnormalities of the cerebellum in ASD. The majority of the studies investigating the cerebellum in ASD have measured the area of the vermis and its lobules on mid-sagittal MRI images, but few have included volumetric measurements (Hardan, Minshew, Harenski, & Keshavan, 2001; Piven, Saliba, Bailey, & Arndt, 1997).

Several studies found no differences in the total area of the vermis or any of its lobules in children (Hashimoto, Murakawa, Miyazaki, Tayama, & Kuroda, 1992; Kleiman, Neff, & Rosman, 1992), adolescents (Holttum,

Minshew, Sanders, & Phillips, 1992; Piven, Saliba et al., 1997), or adults (Garber & Ritvo, 1992; Holttum et al., 1992; Piven, Saliba et al., 1997), even after controlling for brain size by comparing the ratio of the area of lobules VI–VII to that of lobules I–V between groups. Other studies, though, have found significant decreases in the total area of the vermis (Hashimoto et al., 1995), the area of lobules VI–VII (Courchesne, Yeung-Courchesne, Press, Hesselink, & Jernigan, 1988), and the area of lobules VIII–X (Hashimoto, Tayama, Miyazaki, Murakawa, & Kuroda, 1993; Levitt et al., 1999). It has been proposed that the findings of a lack of cerebellar abnormality in autism may be due to the presence of two subgroups of individuals with ASD, those with hypoplasia of cerebellar lobules VI–VII and those with hyperplasia (Courchesne, Townsend, & Saitoh, 1994), though these findings have not been replicated (Piven, Saliba et al., 1997).

Summary   The imaging literature on ASD is plagued with conflicting findings on structural brain abnormalities. One key variable appears to be the age of the participants included in studies. ASD involves abnormalities in the development and growth patterns of the brain that may be identified at different stages in the life span. Furthermore, subgroups within the population, divided on the basis of language functioning (which includes the distinction between classic autism and Asperger syndrome) may also account for some of the discrepancies between studies; in general, older children and adults with ASD but without language impairment show fewer abnormalities in studies of volumetric and morphometric brain analysis.

Functional Imaging Studies

Auditory Processing   There are several lines of evidence suggesting abnormal auditory processing in autistic individuals. Studies investigating short-latency auditory ERPs have found smaller amplitudes bilaterally in frontal sites (N1b; Bruneau, Roux, Adrien, & Barthelemy, 1999) and temporal sites (N1c; Bruneau, Bonnet-Brilhault, Gomot, Adrien, & Barthelemy, 2003; Bruneau et al., 1999) in low-functioning children with ASD when listening to tones. Although a longer latency was observed bilaterally at N1c, no latency shift was found at N1b (Bruneau et al., 1999). The authors hypothesized that the decreased amplitude may have been due to different orientation or abnormal activation of the signal generators, while differences in latency were due to slower propagation of signals along neuronal pathways or deficiencies in synaptic connections. In addition, the amplitude of the right N1c component of the ERP was positively correlated with verbal and nonverbal communication abilities (Bruneau et al., 2003).

Studies of auditory long-latency ERPs, more specifically P3b, have also found reduced amplitude but normal latency in autistic children and adults in response to such stimuli as clicks, tones, phonemes, and novel sounds (for review, see Bomba & Pang, 2004). Unlike the short-latency ERPs, long-latency ERPs are less modality specific and are involved in higher level cognitive processing, such as attributing meaningfulness and relevance to stimuli. Several explanations, including an inability to attach significance to the stimuli or deficits in attention, have been proposed for these differences. Interestingly, differences were not found in response to words, suggesting that the language deficits seen in autism are secondary to basic impairments in cortical auditory processing (Bomba & Pang, 2004).

Recently, an fMRI study of adult men with ASD also noted differences in the processing of voices versus nonvocal sounds from the environment when compared to age-matched healthy adults (Gervais et al., 2004). The ASD group exhibited decreased activation bilaterally in the upper bank of the superior temporal sulcus (an area previously identified as voice selective in normal adults) and in the right primary auditory cortex in response to vocal sounds. However, no significant differences were noted between the groups when presented with nonvocal sounds. Furthermore, unlike the healthy adults, the men with ASD did not demonstrate significantly more bilateral activation of the upper bank of the superior temporal sulcus when comparing vocal versus nonvocal sounds.

Reversed asymmetry has been described in autistic individuals with respect to auditory processing (Boddaert et al., 2003; Boddaert et al., 2004; Bruneau et al., 2003; Bruneau et al., 1999). ERP studies of low-functioning children with ASD found that while control children displayed a bilateral increase in intensity-related amplitude of N1c in response to tones, the children with ASD only showed this relationship in the right hemisphere (Bruneau et al., 2003; Bruneau et al., 1999). A PET study of adults with ASD compared to healthy adults found a reversed rightward asymmetry in the superior temporal gyrus in response to speechlike sounds (Boddaert et al., 2003). In addition, activation was greater in the right middle frontal gyrus in the ASD group but less in the left posterior middle and inferior temporal gyrus. The same study in children with ASD compared to mentally retarded children found a lack of leftward asymmetry in the superior temporal gyrus (Boddaert et al., 2004). Activation was significantly less in the ASD group in two left speech-related areas: the left middle temporal gyrus and the left precentral gyrus. Together, these findings suggest right-hemisphere dominance in auditory processing in ASD and a possible reorganization of right and left hemisphere function during early brain development (Bomba & Pang, 2004).

Studies using MEG have provided further insight into the auditory processing deficits found in ASD (Gage, Siegel, & Roberts, 2003; Tecchio et al., 2003). While the magnetic auditory evoked potential (M100) decreases linearly with age in both hemispheres in healthy children, the reverse was found to occur in the right hemisphere of high-functioning ASD children (Gage et al., 2003). In addition, the source of the M100 was located significantly deeper in low-functioning ASD individuals and did not become more superficial with age as was seen in healthy individuals matched for age and gender (Tecchio et al., 2003). Unlike in typically developing children, the latency of M100 in high-functioning boys with ASD was not proportional to the changes in the frequency of tones in the right hemisphere but was proportional in the left hemisphere (Gage, Siegel, Callen, & Roberts, 2003). These results implicate possible asymmetrical differences in the maturation of auditory areas in individuals with ASD.

Language Processing Few imaging studies have investigated language function in ASD. Two PET studies with very small sample sizes investigated regional cerebral blood flow in adults with ASD and matched controls while participants were listening to, repeating, and generating sentences (Muller et al., 1999; Muller et al., 1998). Abnormalities in the dentato-thalamo-cortical pathway were observed. While listening to sentences, activation in the right dentate nucleus was significantly lower in the ASD group. However, activation in this region and in the left Brodmann area (BA) 46 in dorsolateral prefrontal cortex was significantly greater when repeating sentences. Significantly decreased activation of the left BA 46 and the left thalamus was found while generating sentences. Reversed asymmetry was noted in BA 46 while listening to sentences (leftward in healthy adults, rightward in ASD adults) and in the thalamus while generating sentences (Muller et al., 1998). Reduced left dominance was also found in a composite region of interest composed of perisylvian language areas (Muller et al., 1999).

An fMRI study of sentence comprehension found increased activation of Wernicke's area (left laterosuperior temporal gyrus) and decreased activation of Broca's area (left inferior frontal gyrus) in high-functioning adults with ASD when compared to matched healthy adults (Just, Cherkassky, Keller, & Minshew, 2004). Differences between the groups were also noted in the distribution of activation in these areas. In addition, decreased synchronization was observed between cortical language areas in the autism group, thus suggesting underconnectivity between brain regions critical for complex language processing.

Face Processing   Face-processing deficits in ASD have been well established in the literature (e.g., Joseph & Tanaka, 2003), but their localization
to a particular region of the brain is still unclear. Several areas, including
the fusiform gyrus (FFA), have been implicated in face processing. Some
studies have concluded that, unlike in normal individuals, the FFA in
ASD is not specialized for face processing. One fMRI study compared face
and object discrimination in adult males with ASD and matched controls
(Schultz et al., 2000). As expected, the controls had greater activation of the
right FFA during the face discrimination task but not for objects. In contrast, the ASD group showed no FFA activation to faces. While activation
of the inferior temporal gyrus was greatest during object discrimination in
the control group, this area was also recruited during face discrimination
in the ASD group. The authors concluded that activation of the inferior
temporal gyrus during face discrimination in the ASD men suggested that
they were processing faces in the same manner as objects, perhaps to compensate for the lack of specialization of the FFA area in adults with ASD.
Decreased activation in FFA was found in a second fMRI study involving
adults with ASD and matched controls (Hubl et al., 2003). Participants
were asked to press a button whenever a female face appeared on the
screen. Activation of the right FFA was significantly higher in the control
group, whereas the ASD group demonstrated stronger activation of a more
object-related processing area, the medial occipital gyrus.

   In contrast, other fMRI studies have found normal activation of the
FFA in ASD adults during face discrimination tasks. Hadjikhani and colleagues (2004) found bilateral activation of FFA for faces compared to
nonfaces (objects and scrambled faces) in their ASD group that was not
significantly different from a matched control group. Similarly, activation in other face-specific areas, specifically the inferior occipital gyrus
and the superior temporal sulcus, was not significantly different between
the groups. FFA activation was specific to face discrimination in both
groups, and no areas implicated in object perception were associated with
face discrimination in the ASD subjects. These contradictory results were
attributed to differences in the stimuli, the behavioral tasks, and the use of
a fixation cross to increase attentiveness to the face stimuli. Another study
reporting normal FFA activation in adults with ASD compared activation
for personally meaningful faces (e.g., subject's mother) versus the faces
of strangers (Pierce, Haist, Sedaghat, & Courchesne, 2004). The ASD and
matched control adults demonstrated FFA activity in response to familiar
and unfamiliar faces, but greater activation was observed for familiar faces,
especially in the right hemisphere. The authors suggested that normal FFA
activation was due to increased attentiveness to the stimuli, as in the study
by Hadjikhani et al. (2004).

Several studies have also investigated the functional localization of the deficits in ASD individuals in recognition of facial expression of emotions. Studies in adults have suggested dysfunction of the fusiform gyrus, the inferior frontal gyrus, and the amygdala. Critchley and colleagues (2000) employed tasks tapping explicit and implicit processing of emotions from facial stimuli during functional MRI. In the explicit task, the participants judged whether a face was happy or angry; in the implicit task, they decided whether the same emotional faces were male or female. When compared to matched controls, adults with ASD demonstrated significantly less activation overall in the right FFA. For the explicit task, significantly less activation was observed in the left middle temporal gyrus in the ASD group, while activation in the left cerebellum and the left amygdalahippocampal region was reduced during the implicit task.

Decreased activation in FFA and the inferior frontal gyrus have also been reported during facial emotion recognition tasks (Hall, Szechtman, & Nahmias, 2003). When high-functioning adults with ASD were asked to concentrate on what emotion was being expressed on the presented face (disgust, fear, or happiness), activation in the left inferior frontal gyrus was significantly decreased for disgust and fear when compared to controls (Ogai et al., 2003). Significant decreases were also seen in the left insula and putamen in the ASD group when viewing disgusted faces. However, no significant differences were found between the groups when viewing happy faces. Similarly, a PET study in adults with ASD during an emotion recognition task enhanced by prosodic information when compared to a gender recognition task found decreased activation in the right FFA and the left inferior frontal gyrus (Hall et al., 2003). Similar findings have been obtained in studies that included children and adolescents with ASD (Piggot et al., 2004; Wang, Dapretto, Hariri, Sigman, & Bookheimer, 2004).

Theory of Mind　Children and adults with ASD have deficits in social intelligence, or theory of mind, which underlie their problems in social and communicative functioning (Baron-Cohen, Tager-Flusberg & Cohen, 1993, 2000). These deficits are evident on tasks that involve the attribution of mental states, including beliefs, emotions, and intentions in the interpretation of behavioral actions. Several studies have used functional imaging to address the neurobiological bases of this dysfunction. One proposed theory is dysfunction of the amygdala. Baron-Cohen and colleagues (Baron-Cohen, Ring et al., 1999) compared activation patterns among adults with ASD and controls in a task that required subjects to judge mental states from the eye region of the face. The ASD group showed significantly reduced activation of the left amygdala and decreases in activation were also seen in the left inferior frontal gyrus and the insula

(Baron-Cohen, Ring et al., 1999). The ASD group had significantly greater activation in the left superior temporal gyrus compared to controls, which may have been to compensate for amygdala dysfunction.

Other areas of the brain, including the left medial prefrontal cortex and the temporal poles, have also been implicated in theory of mind dysfunction in ASD (Frith, 2003). In a PET study, adults with ASD were found to have significantly less activation of the left angular gyrus and the temporal poles when asked to judge the mental state of story characters (Happe et al., 1996). Activation was seen in the left medial prefrontal cortex, but it was in a more ventral region (BAs 9/10) than was seen in normal adults (BA 8). Similarly, adults with ASD demonstrated significantly less activation of the medial prefrontal cortex, the right temporal pole, left fusiform gyrus, and bilateral superior temporal sulcus during a task that entailed the attribution of intentionality to animated shapes (Castelli, Frith, Happe, & Frith, 2002). Activation in the extrastriate cortex was not different between groups, but functional connectivity between this region and the superior temporal sulcus was reduced in the ASD group. Based on these findings, the authors suggested that dysfunction was not present in the lower order processing stream but rather in the connections between lower order areas and more specialized regions.

Future Directions

The future of brain-imaging research in the field of neurodevelopmental disorders holds much promise, yet it is clear from the review of the current state of the research in the previous sections that there is a great deal of work to be done to advance our understanding of the neurobiological substrate of the fundamental behavioral impairments in both SLI and ASD.

The existence of subtypes in both these complex heterogeneous disorders will necessitate a closer look for differences in brain activity to better operationalize the subgroups of SLI and ASD. Investigating brain abnormalities within different subtypes may yield more consistent findings within and across studies; in turn, neuroimaging studies may help to define different subtypes on the basis of neurobiological profiles rather than behavioral profiles (e.g., Tager-Flusberg & Joseph, 2003). Structural and functional studies of these learning disorders must adhere to state-of-the-art design and experimental control and ought to include sample sizes that are large enough to have the appropriate levels of statistical power.

A growing methodological trend is the effort made to combine EEG, MEG, and fMRI, which will allow for superior spatiotemporal characterization of the brain activity for these disorders and their subtypes. The recent addition of diffusion tension imaging methods (DTI), which allows one to investigate directly the connectivity between brain regions, will also enhance our understanding of brain pathology, especially since current studies highlight abnormalities in neural connectivity across different neurodevelopmental disorders. New methods that combine functional imaging methods with DTI are being developed. However, such an approach is not without problems. At the outset, a clearer specification of the behavioral variables along the lines of various subtypes will be essential. On the technical front, the development of accurate source localization from EEG and MEG, along with improved tools for dealing with eye blinks and motion-related artifacts, are currently underway. Finally, an examination of whether the different methods represent the same neural networks, referring to a common volume activity, appears necessary if they are to jointly clarify the functional connectivity of specific neural processes under investigation. It is important to note that while the mean correspondence of two or more methods over subjects may be significant, this may not be true at the individual level (Vitacco, Brandeis, Pascual-Marqui, & Martin, 2002), suggesting that one-to-one correspondence between fMRI activation patterns and MEG activity integrated over microstates cannot be assumed in all cases.

The ability to combine data across these different imaging methodologies will encourage the field to take a neural systems approach to neurodevelopmental disorders instead of continuing to limit investigations to localized brain areas. As we move forward in changing our conceptual frameworks for interpreting the neurobiology of SLI and ASD, it will become increasingly important to link in vivo brain-imaging findings to the neuropathological literature based on postmortem studies and to what is known about developmental neurobiology. In this way, we will begin to understand the developmental roots of these neurodevelopmental disorders and how specific genetic and other factors cause the basic impairments that define SLI and ASD.

Finally, we note the recent introduction of brain-imaging measures that can be used to chart effectiveness of different treatment or intervention programs. Within the field of learning disorders, this approach has been used, for example, to chart the effectiveness of a computer-based remediation program that targets auditory and language processing skills in children and adults with dyslexia (Temple et al., 2003). The subjects underwent fMRI and behavioral testing before and after the intervention. The fMRI paradigm focused on brain activation to phonological processing. The main findings of interest were that after the intervention the children and adults showed significant increases in brain activation in language-related and other brain regions, changes in brain function that were both normalizing (activation patterns similar to nondyslexic controls) and compensatory (increased activation in areas not typically activated during phonological processing tasks). It has been suggested that interventions that are capable of producing these kinds of changes in brain-activation patterns are "remapping" brain areas and that neuroplasticity in the brain is possible throughout the life span (Tallal, 2004). To date, using brain-imaging methods to chart the effectiveness of behavioral (or pharmacological) treatments for SLI or ASD have not been reported, but it is anticipated that this approach will begin to be implemented in the near future.

In conclusion, given the analysis tools available to us today, the field is wide open for new forays into studies investigating language impairment and social communicative deficits in SLI, ASD, and other neurodevelopmental disorders to improve our understanding of the relationship among various language-based learning disabilities and to design more effective interventions. Given the scant research to date in the neuroimaging of SLI and ASD, current advances in neuroimaging methodologies hold tremendous promise in moving the field forward, with the help of clinicians and researchers alike.

Acknowledgments

This chapter was written with support from the following grants to H. Tager-Flusberg: No. U19 DC 03610, which is part of the NICHD/NIDCD–funded CPEA; No. U54 MH 66398, which is part of the NIH-funded STAART Centers; and a grant from the Nancy Lurie Marks Family Foundation.

References

Abell, F., Krams, M., Ashburner, J., Passingham, R., Friston, K., Frackowiak, R., et al. (1999). The neuroanatomy of autism: A voxel-based whole brain analysis of structural scans. *NeuroReport*, 10, 1647–1651.

American Psychiatric Association. (1994). *Diagnostic and statistical manual of mental disorders* (4th ed.). Washington, DC: Author.

Annett, M. (2002). *Handedness and brain asymmetry: The right shift theory* (2nd ed.). Hove, UK: Psychology Press.

Aram, D. M., & Nation, J. E. (1980). Preschool language disorders and subsequent language and academic difficulties. *Journal of Communication Disorders*, 13, 159–170.

Aylward, E. H., Minshew, N. J., Field, K., Sparks, B. F., & Singh, N. (2002). Effects of age on brain volume and head circumference in autism. *Neurology*, 59, 175–183.

Aylward, E. H., Minshew, N. J., Goldstein, G., Honeycutt, N. A., Augustine, A. M., Yates, K. O., et al. (1999). MRI volumes of amygdala and hippocampus in non-mentally retarded autistic adolescents and adults. *Neurology*, 53, 2145–2150.

Bailey, A., Palferman, S., Heavey, L., & Le Couteur, A. (1998). Autism: The phenotype in relatives. *Journal of Autism and Developmental Disorders*, 28, 369–392.

Bailey, P. J., & Snowling, M. J. (2002). Auditory processing and the development of language and literacy. *British Medical Bulletin*, 63, 135–146.

Baron-Cohen, S., Ring, H. A., Bullmore, E. T., Wheelwright, S., Ashwin, C., & Williams, S. C. (2000). The amygdala theory of autism. *Neuroscience and Biobehavioral Reviews*, 24, 355–364.

Baron-Cohen, S., Ring, H. A., Wheelwright, S., Bullmore, E. T., Brammer, M. J., Simmons, A., et al. (1999). Social intelligence in the normal and autistic brain: An fMRI study. *European Journal of Neuroscience*, 11, 1891–1898.

Baron-Cohen, S., Tager-Flusberg, H., & Cohen, D. J. (Eds.). (1993). *Understanding other minds: Perspectives from autism*. Oxford: Oxford University Press.

Baron-Cohen, S., Tager-Flusberg, H., & Cohen, D. J. (Eds.). (2000). *Understanding other minds: Perspectives from Developmental Cognitive Neuroscience* (2nd ed.). Oxford: Oxford University Press.

Bedore, L. M., & Leonard, L. B. (1998). Specific language impairment and grammatical morphology: A discriminant function analysis. *Journal of Speech, Language, and Hearing Research*, 41, 1185–1192.

Benasich, A. A., Thomas, J. J., Choudhury, N., & Leppanen, P. H. (2002). The importance of rapid auditory processing abilities to early language development: Evidence from converging methodologies. *Developmental Psychobiology*, 40, 278–292.

Bespalova, I. N., & Buxbaum, J. D. (2003). Disease susceptibility genes for autism. *Annals of Medicine*, 35, 274–281.

Bishop, D. V. (1992). The underlying nature of specific language impairment. *Journal of Child Psychology and Psychiatry*, 33, 3–66.

Bishop, D. V. (2003). Autism and specific language impairment: Categorical distinction or continuum? *Novartis Foundation Symposium*, 251, 213–226; discussion 226–234, 281–297.

Bishop, D. V., & Norbury, C. F. (2002). Exploring the borderlands of autistic disorder and specific language impairment: A study using standardised diagnostic instruments. *Journal of Child Psychology and Psychiatry*, 43, 917–929.

Bishop, D. V., North, T., & Donlan, C. (1996). Nonword repetition as a behavioural marker for inherited language impairment: Evidence from a twin study. *Journal of Child Psychology and Psychiatry*, 37, 391–403.

Bishop, D. V., & Snowling, M. J. (2004). Developmental dyslexia and specific language impairment: Same or different? *Psychological Bulletin*, 130, 858–886.

Boddaert, N., Belin, P., Chabane, N., Poline, J. B., Barthelemy, C., Mouren-Simeoni, M. C., et al. (2003). Perception of complex sounds: Abnormal pattern of cortical activation in autism. *American Journal of Psychiatry*, 160, 2057–2060.

Boddaert, N., Chabane, N., Belin, P., Bourgeois, M., Royer, V., Barthelemy, C., et al. (2004). Perception of complex sounds in autism: Abnormal cortical processing in children. *American Journal of Psychiatry*, 161, 2117–2120.

Bolton, P., Macdonald, H., Pickles, A., Rios, P., Goode, S., Crowson, M., et al. (1994). A case-control family history study of autism. *Journal of Child Psychology and Psychiatry*, 35, 877–900.

Bomba, M. D., & Pang, E. W. (2004). Cortical auditory evoked potentials in autism: A review. *International Journal of Psychophysiology*, 53, 161–169.

Bruneau, N., Bonnet-Brilhault, F., Gomot, M., Adrien, J. L., & Barthelemy, C. (2003). Cortical auditory processing and communication in children with autism: Electrophysiological/behavioral relations. *International Journal of Psychophysiology*, 51, 17–25.

Bruneau, N., Roux, S., Adrien, J. L., & Barthelemy, C. (1999). Auditory associative cortex dysfunction in children with autism: Evidence from late auditory evoked potentials (N1 wave-T complex). *Clinical Neurophysiology*, 110, 1927–1934.

Carper, R. A., Moses, P., Tigue, Z. D., & Courchesne, E. (2002). Cerebral lobes in autism: Early hyperplasia and abnormal age effects. *Neuroimage*, 16, 1038–1051.

Castelli, F., Frith, C., Happe, F., & Frith, U. (2002). Autism, Asperger syndrome and brain mechanisms for the attribution of mental states to animated shapes. *Brain*, 125, 1839–1849.

Catts, H. W. (1993). The relationship between speech-language impairments and reading disabilities. *Journal of Speech and Hearing Research*, 36, 948–958.

Chung, M. K., Dalton, K. M., Alexander, A. L., & Davidson, R. J. (2004). Less white matter concentration in autism: 2d voxel-based morphometry. *Neuroimage*, 23, 242–251.

Cohen, M., Campbell, R., & Yaghmai, F. (1989). Neuropathological abnormalities in developmental dysphasia. *Annals of Neurology*, 25, 567–570.

Constantino, J. N., Gruber, C. P., Davis, S., Hayes, S., Passanante, N., & Przybeck, T. (2004). The factor structure of autistic traits. *Journal of Child Psychology and Psychiatry*, 45, 719–726.

Conti-Ramsden, G. (2003). Processing and linguistic markers in young children with specific language impairment (SLI). *Journal of Speech, Language, and Hearing Research*, 46, 1029–1037.

Conti-Ramsden, G., Botting, N., & Faragher, B. (2001). Psycholinguistic markers for specific language impairment (SLI). *Journal of Child Psychology and Psychiatry*, 42, 741–748.

Corballis, M. C. (1991). *The lopsided ape: Evolution of the generative mind*. New York: Oxford University Press.

Courchesne, E., Carper, R., & Akshoomoff, N. (2003). Evidence of brain overgrowth in the first year of life in autism. *JAMA: Journal of the American Medical Association*, 290, 337–344.

Courchesne, E., Karns, C. M., Davis, H. R., Ziccardi, R., Carper, R. A., Tigue, Z. D., et al. (2001). Unusual brain growth patterns in early life in patients with autistic disorder: An MRI study. *Neurology*, 57, 245–254.

Courchesne, E., & Plante, E. (1996). Measurement and analysis issues in neuro-developmental magnetic resonance imaging. In R. W. Thatcher, G. R. Lyon, J. Rumsey, & N. Krasnegor (Eds.), *Developmental imaging: Mapping the development of brain and behavior* (pp. 43–65). New York: Academic Press.

Courchesne, E., Townsend, J., & Saitoh, O. (1994). The brain in infantile autism: Posterior fossa structures are abnormal. *Neurology, 44*, 214–223.

Courchesne, E., Yeung-Courchesne, R., Press, G. A., Hesselink, J. R., & Jernigan, T. L. (1988). Hypoplasia of cerebellar vermal lobules VI and VII in autism. *New England Journal of Medicine, 318*, 1349–1354.

Critchley, H. D., Daly, E. M., Bullmore, E. T., Williams, S. C., Van Amelsvoort, T., Robertson, D. M., et al. (2000). The functional neuroanatomy of social behaviour: Changes in cerebral blood flow when people with autistic disorder process facial expressions. *Brain, 123*, 2203–2212.

De Fossé, L., Hodge, S. M., Makris, N., Kennedy, D. N., Caviness, V. S., Jr., McGrath, L., et al. (2004). Language-association cortex asymmetry in autism and specific language impairment. *Annals of Neurology, 56*, 757–766.

Dollaghan, C., & Campbell, T. F. (1998). Nonword repetition and child language impairment. *Journal of Speech, Language, and Hearing Research, 41*, 1136–1146.

Egaas, B., Courchesne, E., & Saitoh, O. (1995). Reduced size of corpus callosum in autism. *Archives of Neurology, 52*, 794–801.

Elia, M., Ferri, R., Musumeci, S. A., Panerai, S., Bottitta, M., & Scuderi, C. (2000). Clinical correlates of brain morphometric features of subjects with low-functioning autistic disorder. *Journal of Child Neurology, 15*, 504–508.

Filipek, P. A. (1996). Structural variations in measures in the developmental disorders. In R. W. Thatcher, G. R. Lyon, J. Rumsey, & N. Krasnegor (Eds.), *Developmental imaging: Mapping the development of brain and behavior* (pp. 169–186). New York: Academic Press.

Filipek, P. A., Richelme, C., Kennedy, D. N., Rademacher, J., Pitcher, D. A., Zidel, S., et al. (1992). Morphometric analysis of the brain in developmental language disorders and autism [abstract]. *Annals of Neurology, 32*, 475.

Fisher, S. E., Lai, C. S., & Monaco, A. P. (2003). Deciphering the genetic basis of speech and language disorders. *Annual Review of Neuroscience, 26*, 57–80.

Fletcher, J. M., & Satz, P. (1980). Developmental changes in the neuropsychological correlates of reading achievement: A 6-year longitudinal follow-up. *Journal of Clinical Neuropsychology, 2*, 23–27.

Folstein, S. E., & Rosen-Sheidley, B. (2001). Genetics of autism: Complex aetiology for a heterogeneous disorder. *Nature Reviews Genetics, 2*, 943–955.

Fombonne, E. (2003). Epidemiological surveys of autism and other pervasive developmental disorders: An update. *Journal of Autism and Developmental Disorders, 33*, 365–382.

Fombonne, E., Bolton, P., Prior, J., Jordan, H., & Rutter, M. (1997). A family study of autism: Cognitive patterns and levels in parents and siblings. *Journal of Child Psychology and Psychiatry, 38*, 667–683.

Foundas, A. L. (2001). The anatomical basis of language. *Topics in Language Disorders, 21*, 1–19.

Foundas, A. L., Eure, K. F., Luevano, L. F., & Weinberger, D. R. (1998). Mri asymmetries of broca's area: The pars triangularis and pars opercularis. *Brain and Language, 64*, 282–296.

Foundas, A. L., Leonard, C. M., & Heilman, K. M. (1995). Morphologic cerebral asymmetries and handedness. The pars triangularis and planum temporale. *Archives of Neurology*, 52, 501–508.

Frith, C. (2003). *What do imaging studies tell us about the neural basis of autism?* Novartis Foundation Symposium, 251, 149–166.

Gage, N. M., Siegel, B., Callen, M., & Roberts, T. P. (2003). Cortical sound processing in children with autism disorder: An MEG investigation. *NeuroReport*, 14, 2047–2051.

Gage, N. M., Siegel, B., & Roberts, T. P. (2003). Cortical auditory system maturational abnormalities in children with autism disorder: An MEG investigation. *Developmental Brain Research*, 144, 201–209.

Galaburda, A. M., Rosen, G. D., & Sherman, G. F. (1990). Individual variability in cortical organization: Its relationship to brain laterality and implications to function. *Neuropsychologia*, 28, 529–546.

Garber, H. J., & Ritvo, E. R. (1992). Magnetic resonance imaging of the posterior fossa in autistic adults. *American Journal of Psychiatry*, 149, 245–247.

Gathercole, S. E., & Baddeley, A. D. (1990). Phonological memory deficits in language disordered children: Is there a causal connection? *Journal of Memory and Language*, 29, 336–360.

Gauger, L. M., Lombardino, L. J., & Leonard, C. M. (1997). Brain morphology in children with specific language impairment. *Journal of Speech, Language, and Hearing Research*, 40, 1272–1284.

Gervais, H., Belin, P., Boddaert, N., Leboyer, M., Coez, A., Sfaello, I., et al. (2004). Abnormal cortical voice processing in autism. *Nature Neuroscience*, 7, 801–802.

Geschwind, N., & Levitsky, W. (1968). Human brain: Left-right asymmetries in temporal speech region. *Science*, 161, 186–187.

Hadjikhani, N., Joseph, R. M., Snyder, J., Chabris, C. F., Clark, J., Steele, S., et al. (2004). Activation of the fusiform gyrus when individuals with autism spectrum disorder view faces. *Neuroimage*, 22, 1141–1150.

Hall, G. B., Szechtman, H., & Nahmias, C. (2003). Enhanced salience and emotion recognition in autism: A PET study. *American Journal of Psychiatry*, 160, 1439–1441.

Happe, F., Ehlers, S., Fletcher, P., Frith, U., Johansson, M., Gillberg, C., et al. (1996). "Theory of mind" in the brain. Evidence from a PET scan study of Asperger syndrome. *NeuroReport*, 8, 197–201.

Hardan, A. Y., Minshew, N. J., Harenski, K., & Keshavan, M. S. (2001). Posterior fossa magnetic resonance imaging in autism. *Journal of the American Academy of Child and Adolescent Psychiatry*, 40, 666–672.

Hardan, A. Y., Minshew, N. J., & Keshavan, M. S. (2000). Corpus callosum size in autism. *Neurology*, 55, 1033–1036.

Hardan, A. Y., Minshew, N. J., Mallikarjuhn, M., & Keshavan, M. S. (2001). Brain volume in autism. *Journal of Child Neurology*, 16, 421–424.

Hashimoto, T., Murakawa, K., Miyazaki, M., Tayama, M., & Kuroda, Y. (1992). Magnetic resonance imaging of the brain structures in the posterior fossa in retarded autistic children. *Acta Paediatrica*, 81, 1030–1034.

Hashimoto, T., Tayama, M., Miyazaki, M., Murakawa, K., & Kuroda, Y. (1993). Brain stem and cerebellar vermis involvement in autistic children. *Journal of Child Neurology*, 8, 149–153.

Hashimoto, T., Tayama, M., Murakawa, K., Yoshimoto, T., Miyazaki, M., Harada, M., et al. (1995). Development of the brain stem and cerebellum in autistic patients. *Journal of Autism and Developmental Disorders*, 25, 1–18.

Haznedar, M. M., Buchsbaum, M. S., Wei, T. C., Hof, P. R., Cartwright, C., Bienstock, C. A., et al. (2000). Limbic circuitry in patients with autism spectrum disorders studied with positron emission tomography and magnetic resonance imaging. *American Journal of Psychiatry*, 157, 1994–2001.

Herbert, M. R., Harris, G. J., Adrien, K. T., Ziegler, D. A., Makris, N., Kennedy, D. N., et al. (2002). Abnormal asymmetry in language association cortex in autism. *Annals of Neurology*, 52, 588–596.

Herbert, M. R., Ziegler, D. A., Deutsch, C. K., O'Brien, L. M., Lange, N., Bakardjiev, A., et al. (2003). Dissociations of cerebral cortex, subcortical and cerebral white matter volumes in autistic boys. *Brain*, 126, 1182–1192.

Herbert, M. R., Ziegler, D. A., Makris, N., Filipek, P. A., Kemper, T. L., Normandin, J. J., et al. (2004). Localization of white matter volume increase in autism and developmental language disorder. *Annals of Neurology*, 55, 530–540.

Holttum, J. R., Minshew, N. J., Sanders, R. S., & Phillips, N. E. (1992). Magnetic resonance imaging of the posterior fossa in autism. *Biological Psychiatry*, 32, 1091–1101.

Hubl, D., Bolte, S., Feineis-Matthews, S., Lanfermann, H., Federspiel, A., Strik, W., et al. (2003). Functional imbalance of visual pathways indicates alternative face processing strategies in autism. *Neurology*, 61, 1232–1237.

Hugdahl, K., Gundersen, H., Brekke, C., Thomsen, T., Rimol, L. M., Ersland, L., et al. (2004). fMRI brain activation in a Finnish family with specific language impairment compared with a normal control group. *Journal of Speech, Language, and Hearing Research*, 47, 162–172.

Jernigan, T. L., Hesselink, J. R., Sowell, E., & Tallal, P. A. (1991). Cerebral structure on magnetic resonance imaging in language- and learning-impaired children. *Archives of Neurology*, 48, 539–545.

Joseph, R. M., & Tanaka, J. (2003). Holistic and part-based face recognition in children with autism. *Journal of Child Psychology and Psychiatry*, 44, 529–542.

Just, M. A., Cherkassky, V. L., Keller, T. A., & Minshew, N. J. (2004). Cortical activation and synchronization during sentence comprehension in high-functioning autism: Evidence of underconnectivity. *Brain*, 127, 1811–1821.

Kamhi, A. G., & Catts, H. W. (1989). Reading disabilities: Terminology, definitions, and subtype issues. In A. G. Kamhi & H. W. Catts (Eds.), *Reading disabilities: A developmental language perspective* (pp. 35–66). Boston: Little, Brown.

Kjelgaard, M., & Tager-Flusberg, H. (2001). An investigation of language impairment in autism: Implications for genetic subgroups. *Language and Cognitive Processes*, 16, 287–308.

Kleiman, M. D., Neff, S., & Rosman, N. P. (1992). The brain in infantile autism: Are posterior fossa structures abnormal? *Neurology*, 42, 753–760.

Kraus, N., McGee, T., Carrell, T., King, C., Littman, T., & Nicol, T. (1994). Discrimination of speech-like contrasts in the auditory thalamus and cortex. *Journal of the Acoustical Society of America*, 96, 2758–2768.

Kulynych, J. J., Vladar, K., Jones, D. W., & Weinberger, D. R. (1994). Gender differences in the normal lateralization of the supratemporal cortex: MRI surface-rendering morphometry of Heschl's gyrus and the planum temporale. *Cerebral Cortex*, 4, 107–118.

Lai, C. S., Fisher, S. E., Hurst, J. A., Vargha-Khadem, F., & Monaco, A. P. (2001). A forkhead-domain gene is mutated in a severe speech and language disorder. *Nature*, 413, 519–523.

Landau, W. M., Goldstein, R., & Kleffner, F. R. (1960). Congenital aphasia. A clinicopathologic study. *Neurology*, 10, 915–921.

Leonard, L. B. (1998). *Children with specific language impairment*. Cambridge, MA: MIT Press.

Levitt, J. G., Blanton, R., Capetillo-Cunliffe, L., Guthrie, D., Toga, A., & McCracken, J. T. (1999). Cerebellar vermis lobules VIII–X in autism. *Progress in Neuro-Psychopharmacology and Biological Psychiatry*, 23, 625–633.

Liégeois, F., Baldeweg, T., Connelly, A., Gadian, D. G., Mishkin, M., & Vargha-Khadem, F. (2003). Language fmri abnormalities associated with FOXP2 gene mutation. *Nature Neuroscience*, 6, 1230–1237.

Lou, H. C., Henriksen, L., & Bruhn, P. (1990). Focal cerebral dysfunction in developmental learning disabilities. *Lancet*, 335, 8–11.

Lyon, R., & Watson, B. (1981). Empirically derived subgroups of learning disabled readers: Diagnostic characteristics. *Journal of Learning Disabilities*, 14, 256–261.

Macintosh, K. E., & Dissanayake, C. (2004). Annotation: The similarities and differences between autistic disorder and Asperger's disorder: A review of the empirical evidence. *Journal of Child Psychology and Psychiatry*, 45, 421–434.

Manes, F., Piven, J., Vrancic, D., Nanclares, V., Plebst, C., & Starkstein, S. E. (1999). An MRI study of the corpus callosum and cerebellum in mentally retarded autistic individuals. *Journal of Neuropsychiatry and Clinical Neurosciences*, 11, 470–474.

Mody, M. (2004). Neurobiological correlates of language and literacy impairments. In C. Addison Stone, E. Silliman, B. Ehren, & K. Apel (Eds.), *Handbook of language and literacy: Development and disorders* (pp. 49–73). New York: Guilford Press.

Mody, M., Studdert-Kennedy, M., & Brady, S. (1997). Speech perception deficits in poor readers: Auditory processing or phonological coding? *Journal of Experimental Child Psychology*, 64, 199–231.

Muller, R. A. (2004). Genes, language disorders, and developmental archaeology: What role can neuroimaging play? In M. L. Rice & S. F. Warren (Eds.), *Developmental language disorders: From phenotypes to etiologies* (pp. 291–328). Mahwah, NJ: Lawrence Erlbaum.

Muller, R. A., Behen, M. E., Rothermel, R. D., Chugani, D. C., Muzik, O., Mangner, T. J., et al. (1999). Brain mapping of language and auditory perception in high-functioning autistic adults: A PET study. *Journal of Autism and Developmental Disorders*, 29, 19–31.

Muller, R. A., Chugani, D. C., Behen, M. E., Rothermel, R. D., Muzik, O., Chakraborty, P. K., et al. (1998). Impairment of dentato-thalamo-cortical pathway in autistic men: Language activation data from positron emission tomography. *Neuroscience Letters*, 245, 1–4.

Neville, H. J., Coffey, S. A., Holcomb, P. J., & Tallal, P. (1993). The neurobiology of sensory and language processing in language impaired children. *Journal of Cognitive Neuroscience*, 5, 235–253.

Njiokiktjien, C., de Sonneville, L., & Vaal, J. (1994). Callosal size in children with learning disabilities. *Behavioural Brain Research*, 64, 213–218.

Ogai, M., Matsumoto, H., Suzuki, K., Ozawa, F., Fukuda, R., Uchiyama, I., et al. (2003). Fmri study of recognition of facial expressions in high-functioning autistic patients. *NeuroReport*, 14, 559–563.

Pierce, K., Haist, F., Sedaghat, F., & Courchesne, E. (2004). The brain response to personally familiar faces in autism: Findings of fusiform activity and beyond. *Brain*, 127, 2703–2716.

Piggot, J., Kwon, H., Mobbs, D., Blasey, C., Lotspeich, L., Menon, V., et al. (2004). Emotional attribution in high-functioning individuals with autistic spectrum disorder: A functional imaging study. *Journal of the American Academy of Child and Adolescent Psychiatry*, 43, 473–480.

Plante, E. (1998). Criteria for SLI: The Stark and Tallal legacy and beyond. *Journal of Speech, Language, and Hearing Research*, 41, 951–957.

Piven, J. (1999). Genetic liability for autism: The behavioral expression in relatives. *International Review of Psychiatry*, 11, 299–308.

Piven, J., Arndt, S., Bailey, J., & Andreasen, N. (1996). Regional brain enlargement in autism: A magnetic resonance imaging study. *Journal of the American Academy of Child and Adolescent Psychiatry*, 35, 530–536.

Piven, J., Arndt, S., Bailey, J., Havercamp, S., Andreasen, N. C., & Palmer, P. (1995). An MRI study of brain size in autism. *American Journal of Psychiatry*, 152, 1145–1149.

Piven, J., Bailey, J., Ranson, B. J., & Arndt, S. (1997). An MRI study of the corpus callosum in autism. *American Journal of Psychiatry*, 154, 1051–1056.

Piven, J., Palmer, P., Landa, R., Santangelo, S., Jacobi, D., & Childress, D. (1997). Personality and language characteristics in parents from multiple-incidence autism families. *American Journal of Medical Genetics*, 74, 398–411.

Piven, J., Saliba, K., Bailey, J., & Arndt, S. (1997). An MRI study of autism: The cerebellum revisited. *Neurology*, 49, 546–551.

Plante, E., Swisher, L., Vance, R., & Rapcsak, S. (1991). MRI findings in boys with specific language impairment. *Brain and Language*, 41, 52–66.

Ponton, C. W., Eggermont, J. J., Kwong, B., & Don, M. (2000). Maturation of human central auditory system activity: Evidence from multi-channel evoked potentials. *Clinical Neurophysiology*, 111, 220–236.

Preis, S., Steinmetz, H., Knorr, U., & Jäncke, L. (2000). Corpus callosum size in children with developmental language disorder. *Cognitive Brain Research*, 10, 37–44.

Price, C. J., Wise, R. J., Warburton, E. A., Moore, C. J., Howard, D., Patterson, K., et al. (1996). Hearing and saying. The functional neuro-anatomy of auditory word processing. *Brain*, 119 (Pt 3), 919–931.

Rasmussen, K. J., & Milner, B. (1975). *Clinical and surgical studies of cerebral speech areas in man*. In K. J. Zulch, O. Creutzfeldt & G. Galbraith (Eds.), Otfried Förster symposium on cerebral localization (pp. 238–257). Heidelberg: Springer Verlag.

Rauschecker, J. P., Tian, B., & Hauser, M. (1995). Processing of complex sounds in the macaque nonprimary auditory cortex. *Science*, 268, 111–114.

Rice, M. L. (2003). A unified model of specific and general language delay: Grammatical tense as a clinical marker of unexpected variation. In: Y. Levy & J. Schaeffer (Eds.), *Language Competence across Populations: Towards a Definition of Specific Language Impairment* (pp. 63–95). Mahwah, NJ: Lawrence Erlbaum Associates.

Rice, M. L., & Wexler, K. (1996). Toward tense as a clinical marker of specific language impairment in English-speaking children. *Journal of Speech and Hearing Research*, 39, 1239–1257.

Rojas, D. C., Bawn, S. D., Benkers, T. L., Reite, M. L., & Rogers, S. J. (2002). Smaller left hemisphere planum temporale in adults with autistic disorder. *Neuroscience Letters*, 328, 237–240.

Rossi, A., Serio, A., Stratta, P., Petruzzi, C., Schiazza, G., Mattei, P., et al. (1994). Three-dimensional in vivo planum temporale reconstruction. *Brain and Language*, 47, 89–95.

Schultz, R. T., Gauthier, I., Klin, A., Fulbright, R. K., Anderson, A. W., Volkmar, F., et al. (2000). Abnormal ventral temporal cortical activity during face discrimination among individuals with autism and Asperger syndrome. *Archives of General Psychiatry*, 57, 331–340.

Schumann, C. M., Hamstra, J., Goodlin-Jones, B. L., Lotspeich, L. J., Kwon, H., Buonocore, M. H., et al. (2004). The amygdala is enlarged in children but not adolescents with autism; the hippocampus is enlarged at all ages. *Journal of Neuroscience*, 24, 6392–6401.

Shafer, V. L., Schwartz, R. G., Mor, M. L., Kessler, K. L., Kurtzberg, D., & Ruben, R. J. (2001). Neurophysiological indices of language impairment in children. *Acta Otolaryngologica*, 121, 297–300.

Sparks, B. F., Friedman, S. D., Shaw, D. W., Aylward, E. H., Echelard, D., Artru, A. A., et al. (2002). Brain structural abnormalities in young children with autism spectrum disorder. *Neurology*, 59, 184–192.

Stanovich, K. E. (1986). Cognitive processes and reading processes of reading disabled children: Evaluating the assumption of specificity. In J. K. Torgesen & B. Y. L. Wong (Eds.), *Psychology and educational perspectives in learning disabilities* (pp. 87–131). London: Academic Press.

Steinmetz, H., Volkmann, J., Jancke, L., & Freund, H. J. (1991). Anatomical left-right asymmetry of language-related temporal cortex is different in left- and right-handers. *Annals of Neurology*, 29, 315–319.

Tager-Flusberg, H. (2003). Language impairments in children with complex neurodevelopmental disorders: The case of autism. In Y. Levy & J. Schaeffer (Eds.), *Language competence across populations: Toward a definition of specific language impairment* (pp. 297–321). Mahwah, NJ: Lawrence Erlbaum.

Tager-Flusberg, H., & Cooper, J. (1999). Present and future possibilities for defining a phenotype for specific language impairment. *Journal of Speech, Language, and Hearing Research*, 42, 1275–1278.

Tager-Flusberg, H., & Joseph, R. M. (2003). Identifying neurocognitive phenotypes in autism. Philosophical Transactions of the Royal Society of London. Series B, *Biological Sciences*, 358, 303–314.

Tallal, P. (2004). Improving language and literacy is a matter of time. *Nature Reviews Neuroscience*, 5, 721–728.

Tallal, P., Merzenich, M. M., Miller, S., & Jenkins, W. (1998). Language learning impairments: Integrating basic science, technology and remediation. *Experimental Brain Research*, 123, 210–219.

Tallal, P., Sainburg, R. L., & Jernigan, T. L. (1991). The neuropathology of developmental dysphasia: Behavioral, morphological, and physiological evidence for a pervasive temporal processing disorder. *Reading and Writing*, 3, 363–377.

Tecchio, F., Benassi, F., Zappasodi, F., Gialloreti, L. E., Palermo, M., Seri, S., et al. (2003). Auditory sensory processing in autism: A magnetoencephalographic study. *Biological Psychiatry*, 54, 647–654.

Temple, E., Deutsch, G. K., Poldrack, R. A., Miller, S. L., Tallal, P., Merzenich, M. M., et al. (2003). *Neural deficits in children with dyslexia ameliorated by behavioral remediation: Evidence from functional MRI.* Proceedings of the National Academy of Sciences of the United States of America, 100, 2860–2865.

Tomblin, J. B., Freese, P. R., & Records, N. L. (1992). Diagnosing specific language impairment in adults for the purpose of pedigree analysis. *Journal of Speech and Hearing Research*, 35, 832–843.

Tomblin, J. B., Hafeman, L. L., & O'Brien, M. (2003). Autism and autism risk in siblings of children with specific language impairment. *International Journal of Language & Communication Disorders*, 38, 235–250.

Tzourio, N., Heim, A., Zilbovicius, M., Gerard, C., & Mazoyer, B. M. (1994). Abnormal regional CBF response in left hemisphere of dysphasic children during a language task. *Pediatric Neurology*, 10, 20–26.

Uwer, R., Albrecht, R., & von Suchodoletz, W. (2002). Automatic processing of tones and speech stimuli in children with specific language impairment. *Developmental Medicine and Child Neurology*, 44, 527–532.

Vargha-Khadem, F., Watkins, K. E., Price, C. J., Ashburner, J., Alcock, K. J., Connelly, A., et al. (1998). *Neural basis of an inherited speech and language disorder.* Proceedings of the National Academy of Sciences of the United States of America, 95, 12695–12700.

Vitacco, D., Brandeis, D., Pascual-Marqui, R., & Martin, E. (2002). Correspondence of event-related potential tomography and functional magnetic resonance imaging during language processing. *Human Brain Mapping*, 17, 4–12.

Wang, A. T., Dapretto, M., Hariri, A. R., Sigman, M., & Bookheimer, S. Y. (2004). Neural correlates of facial affect processing in children and adolescents with autism spectrum disorder. *Journal of the American Academy of Child and Adolescent Psychiatry*, 43, 481–490.

Watkins, K. E., Gadian, D. G., & Vargha-Khadem, F. (1999). Functional and structural brain abnormalities associated with a genetic disorder of speech and language. *American Journal of Human Genetics*, 65, 1215–1221.

Wing, L. (2004). The spectrum of autistic disorders. *Hospital Medicine*, 65, 542–545.

CHAPTER 7

Syndrome of Nonverbal
Learning Disabilities in Adults

KATHERINE D. TSATSANIS and BYRON P. ROURKE

Contents

To consider the manifestations and outcome of childhood learning disabilities (LD) in adulthood leads to a number of interesting questions, more so even than answers. While we know much about LD and subtypes of LD in children (though even here there continues to be debate about the very definition of LD), less is known about presentations in adults. Nonverbal learning disability (NLD) is a particularly interesting syndrome to examine both for the particular presentation of individuals with NLD and for the tenets of its model (Rourke, 1989). Specifically, in this model, there is an emphasis on a developmental neuropsychological approach to the study of LD. Underscored is the importance of a life-span or developmental approach, as well as *patterns* of performance and *models* of brain-behavior relationships. In all, what is eschewed is a static perspective that draws on structural and hierarchical definitions in favor of an approach that proposes a dynamic model that emphasizes not the things in themselves but the relations among them. It raises a question whether at least some adult psychopathology can be understood relative to the intersection of lifelong learning profiles, organization of the brain, and the environment or context for development. What follows is a description of the characteristics of NLD academic, vocational, and psychosocial dimensions, as well as a model of brain involvement, and finally a discussion of what future directions are needed.

Definition of Nonverbal Learning Disability (NLD): General and Specific

Background

An account of nonverbal learning disabilities was presented first by Johnson and Myklebust (1967; Myklebust, 1975) who identified groups of children impaired in their ability to make sense of the nonverbal aspects of day-to-day functioning. Other accounts followed that noted an association between a lack of ability to make sense of and navigate the social environment and deficits in visual spatial and mathematical skills in groups of clinic-referred children (Denkla, 1983; Gross-Tsur, Shalev, Manor, & Amir, 1995; Mykelbust, 1975; Tranel, Hall, Olson, & Tranel, 1987; Voeller, 1986; Weintraub & Mesulam, 1983). Terms included: "minimal brain dysfunction," "nonverbal learning disability," "developmental learning disability of the right hemisphere," "social and emotional learning disability," and "developmental right-hemisphere syndrome." Although basic features were held in common, the nomenclature was varied and different in emphasis. In addition, the works were comprised largely of clinical studies of groups of individuals with apparently similar learning difficulties selected out of a larger clinical population. There are striking parallels, but an understanding of why these particular difficulties should fall together is more limited. At minimum, this learning disability subtype has been commonly understood in the context of right hemisphere dysfunction.

We have tried to expand that view. The historical background for our research endeavors lies in Johnson and Myklebust's (1967) early work on LD. The authors advanced a notion (unfavorable at the time) that subtypes of LD were distinguishable and, more than this, that the identification of distinct patterns of asset and deficit in children's performance would inform learning approaches and intervention strategies. Myklebust's (1975) exposition on "nonverbal learning disabilities" further influenced the program of study at the University of Windsor to approach the identification of this type of learning disability in a systematic manner and to propose a coherent conceptual model by which to understand its manifestation. Research efforts in this laboratory were largely devoted to the delineation of subtypes of learning disability in children, though we and others have also presented clinical case reports as well as cross-sectional studies of neuropsychological profiles in adults with NLD.

We engaged in the intensive investigation of two subtypes of learning disability in particular (see Rourke 1975, 1978, 1982, 1987, 1988, 1989, 1993; Rourke & Finlayson, 1978; Rourke & Fisk, 1992; Rourke & Fuerst, 1992; Rourke & Strang, 1978, 1983; Strang & Rourke, 1983, 1985a, 1985b). As a result of our clinical observations and empirical investigations, we have been able to state with considerable confidence the characteristics of these two subtypes. One group of children, referred to as Group R–S (Reading–Spelling), demonstrated many relatively deficient psycholinguistic skills in conjunction with very well-developed visual–spatial–organizational, tactile-perceptual, psychomotor, and nonverbal problem-solving skills. These children also exhibited poor reading and spelling skills and significantly better, although still impaired, mechanical arithmetic competence. Their outstanding problem is in the area of phonological awareness and processing, and we have since referred to this subtype of learning disability as basic phonological processing disabilities (BPPD).

Children comprising the second subtype presented with a very different pattern of performance. These children exhibited outstanding neuropsychological deficits in visual-spatial-organizational, tactile-perceptual, psychomotor, and nonverbal problem-solving and concept-formation skills, within a context of clear neuropsychological assets in some psycholinguistic skills such as rote verbal learning, regular phoneme-grapheme matching, amount of verbal output, and verbal classification. On measures of achievement, major learning difficulties in mechanical arithmetic but advanced levels of word recognition and spelling were found. In addition, a particular pattern of psychosocial disturbance was identified, marked by a failure to appreciate the nonverbal aspects of communication. This subtype of LD was named *nonverbal learning disabilities* (NLD), the term originally coined by Myklebust (1975).

Clinical Features

We have endeavored to detail both the clinical characteristics of individuals with this disorder as well as devise a more formal definition derived empirically and based on neuropsychological test performance. The principal clinical manifestations (general content) of the NLD syndrome were identified through a process of intensive clinical examination. The following neuropsychological assets are typically exhibited:

1. Simple repetitive motor skills, such as finger tapping and static steadiness, that tend to normalize with increasing age.
2. Strong rote verbal capacities, including extremely well-developed rote verbal memory skills.
3. Little difficulty with the phonologic and syntactic aspects of language.
4. A well-developed vocabulary and varied store of rote verbal (factual) material as well as verbal associations.
5. An ability to benefit from repetitive acts and particularly repetitious input through the auditory modality.
6. An ability to deploy selective and sustained attention for straightforward, repetitive verbal material.
7. Simple visual discrimination, especially for material that can be verbalized, that usually approaches normal levels with age.
8. Much verbosity as well as intact receptive language skills.
9. Well-developed auditory perception, segmentation, and sound blending skills.
10. Proficiencies in reading (word recognition) and spelling.
11. Handwriting may reach age-appropriate levels with much practice.
12. A propensity for making use of language to problem solve and gather information.

The following neuropsychological deficits are identified in NLD:

1. Problems in dealing with complex tactile input; tactile-perceptual deficits are bilateral, but are usually more marked on the left side of the body.
2. Bilateral psychomotor coordination deficiencies, often more marked on the left side of the body; complex psychomotor skills, especially when required within a novel framework, tend to worsen relative to age-based norms.
3. Marked deficiencies in visual–spatial–organizational skills.

4. Notable difficulty in adapting to novel and otherwise complex situations.

5. Marked deficits in nonverbal problem-solving, concept-formation, and hypothesis-testing skills, as well as the capacity to benefit from positive and negative informational feedback in novel or otherwise complex situations.

6. Significant difficulties in dealing with cause-effect relationships and marked deficiencies in the appreciation of incongruities (e.g., as reflected in some aspects of humor).

7. A distorted sense of time, reflected in poor estimation of elapsed time during common activities, and poor estimation of time of day.

8. Difficulty with comprehension of more complex verbal material, including written text, usually because the material is novel, abstract, inferential, or requires an appreciation of relevant versus irrelevant detail.

9. Outstanding relative deficiencies in mechanical arithmetic as compared to advanced reading/decoding (word recognition) and spelling; misspellings that occur are almost exclusively of the phonetically accurate variety.

10. Language is relied on as the principal means for social relating, information gathering, and relief from anxiety but may be of a repetitive, straightforward, rote nature and not contextually appropriate.

11. Deficits in social perception, social judgment, and social interaction skills; of note, there is a marked tendency toward social withdrawal and even social isolation as age increases; the older child or adolescent with NLD is very much at risk for the development of psychosocial disturbance, especially "internalized" forms of psychopathology such as anxiety and depression.

As is characteristic of most disorders, including those identified in the *Diagnostic and Statistical Manual of Mental Disorders,* 4th ed.-Text Revision (*DSM-IV-TR;* American Psychiatric Association, 2000), there are varying degrees of expression of the NLD syndrome and there are individuals who exhibit many but not all of the neuropsychological assets and deficits outlined above. The vital aspect of expression is the *pattern of performance;* we are interested primarily in the gap between the individual's assets and deficits and in manifestations over time. As such, level of intellectual functioning is not a reason for diagnostic exclusion. An individual may perform in the range of mental retardation or in the superior range of psychometric intelligence and exhibit the NLD syndrome, which will be evident in his or her neuropsychological profile and adaptive behaviors. We also expect to find some modifications in manifestation depending on course. A person may manifest most but not all NLD features as a result of related early events; for example, chronic ear infections in a child may lead to auditory perceptual deficiencies, although the child may show many other critical aspects of NLD. Individuals who are affected with NLD since the earliest stages of development and those who demonstrate onset at older ages (e.g., acquired through head injury) may show differences in their performance. Relevant aspects of the individual's history should be taken into account when formulating a diagnosis. The other point to be made is that we generally expect to see an increasing discrepancy between assets and deficits over time (for which we have some preliminary evidence detailed below). One account for this finding is that persons with NLD will tend to overrely on their strengths, with learning primarily restricted to one modality, and show a concomitant decline in areas of weakness.

Rules for Classification of NLD

At present, there is no formal provision for NLD in the *DSM-IV-TR*; individuals with NLD as children may have been placed in inappropriate classroom environments because their behavior was misjudged to be a problem rather than to be a manifestation of a significant developmental disability. The reverse scenario is also encountered; the cognitive assets and verbal skills of individuals with NLD mask the degree of information processing difficulties they are experiencing. We have been working toward classification to aid the process of identification; this may also contribute to shared inclusion criteria for research in this area.

The principal or primary dimensions of NLD have been confirmed through a series of studies (Casey, Rourke, & Picard, 1991; Drummond, Ahmad, & Rourke, 2005; Harnadek & Rourke, 1994; Pelletier, Ahmad, & Rourke, 2001). In the two most recent papers, the rules for classification of NLD and BPPD were refined to improve their utility and increase ease of use. These criteria were based on data obtained from subjects who were initially classified as Definite or Probable NLD, and rules were developed for both younger children (7 to 8 years) (Drummond et al., 2005) and older children (9 to 15 years) (Pelletier et al., 2001). The criteria as defined by the empirical study of older children with NLD are presented below, with the numbers in brackets representing the percentages of children who met these criteria.

Revised Rules for Classifying Children With NLD (Ages 9 to 15 Years)

1. Fewer than two errors on simple tactile perception and suppression versus finger agnosia, finger dysgraphesthesia, and astereognosis composite greater than one standard deviation below the mean [90.9%].

2. WRAT/WRAT-R (Wide Range Achievement Test) standard score for Reading is at least 8 points greater than Arithmetic [85.7%].
3. Two of WISC/WISC-R (Wechsler Intelligence Scale for Children) Vocabulary, Similarities, and Information are the highest of the Verbal scale subtests [77.9%].
4. Two of WISC/WISC-R Block Design, Object Assembly, and Coding subtests are the lowest of the Performance scale [76.6%].
5. Target test performance is at least 1 standard deviation below the mean [63.6%].
6. Grip strength within 1 standard deviation of the mean or above versus Grooved Pegboard Test greater than 1 standard deviation below the mean [63.6%].
7. Tactual Performance Test Right, Left, and Both hand times become progressively worse vis-à-vis the norms [59.7%].
8. WISC/WISC-R Verbal IQ (VIQ) > Performance IQ (PIQ) by at least 10 points [27.3%].

Note: (1) It should be clear that not all of these are mutually exclusive. (2) For experimental purposes, we propose the following criteria:

- First 5 features: Definite NLD
- 7 or 8 of these features: Definite NLD
- 5 or 6 of these features: Probable NLD
- 3 or 4 of these features: Questionable NLD
- 1 or 2 of these features: Low probability of NLD

These criteria are neither mutually exclusive nor are they intended to replace the need for a thorough evaluation. These classification rules have been developed as a means to support diagnosis and research in this area as well as to highlight some important caveats in this process. For example, although a Verbal IQ-Performance IQ (VIQ-PIQ) discrepancy may serve as a red flag, it is not a *necessary* criterion for a diagnosis of NLD. In part, this reflects the fact that the Verbal and Performance dimensions of the Wechsler scales are not pure; IQ and Index scores represent composite numbers that may obscure individual subtest discrepancies. Thus, an adult who received the Wechsler Adult Intelligence Scale-Revised (WAIS-R) or who as a child was administered the WISC-III may have shown a solid or even superior base of verbal knowledge in the context of a poor performance on the Arithmetic subtest due to poor numerical skills or Comprehension subtest due to limited social knowledge, yet these discrepant scores both would factor into overall Verbal IQ. Additionally, many children with learning difficulties have received multiple evaluations. Subtests within the Performance scale of the WISC are especially sensitive to practice effects and certainly the novel element of these subtests (especially taxing for children with NLD) is reduced with each subsequent testing. Service provision also may impact performance when a child has received practice with some of the skills that are being measured. As is always true, test scores need to be interpreted within the broader context in order to achieve a more complete understanding. The rules distill a basic pattern of deficits in complex tactile, perceptual organizational, visual–spatial memory, and psychomotor functioning in the context of preserved verbal skills (e.g., phonological awareness and lexical knowledge).

Developmental Aspects of NLD

Academic, Vocational, and Psychosocial Dimensions

In this section, we describe clinical observations of the developmental course for NLD and in the following section we review the research literature on adults with NLD. Here, we examine the academic, vocational, and psychosocial dimensions of the disorder as they present over time.

Children with NLD encounter early challenges, but it is often the case that their behaviors are poorly understood at that time. In preschool and kindergarten, children with NLD are often diagnosed with ADHD or even early reading difficulties. In part, this is because the learning environment largely invites interaction with a world that is tactile, motor, and visual and thus does not as readily engage children with NLD who show a proclivity for talking. Parents may report that their children talk at a young age, even before acquiring motor skills such as walking. Concerns about reading difficulties arise in the primary grades when a visual or whole-word versus phonetic approach is applied to reading learning.

The gap between areas of asset and deficit, such as rote over learned types of knowledge or learning and visual spatial or novel problem-solving skills, typically increases over time (discussed below). Similarly, increasing discrepancies between reading/decoding and arithmetic skills are observed. In addition, activity levels change over time; apparent hyperactivity in the young child tends to turn to normoactivity in the school-age child and then to hypoactivity in the adolescent with NLD. We have observed that a phonetic approach is typically used when reading and words that are phonetically predictable are more easily read and spelled. In addition, over time, reading/decoding skills are superior to those required in reading/understanding. This finding is thought to reflect in part the difficulties inherent in reading for meaning (e.g., abstracting relevant versus irrelevant details). Reading comprehension measures that involve simple regurgitation of text (e.g., main points) are successfully completed.

However, shortcomings in reading comprehension are observed when the child with NLD is required to paraphrase what he or she has read, to apply the information read, or to draw out implications of the material read. Mechanical arithmetic skills are an area of relative deficiency; some children with NLD may excel at committing arithmetic facts or mathematical theorems to memory and reciting this information when asked to do so, thus relying on their verbal memory strength. The challenge lies in their capacity to reason through a problem, to know how to apply math facts or rules, or to problem solve adaptively. In advanced grades, geometry and physics are also problematic subjects. Written expression is an area of vulnerability with regard to organization and production of ideas, whereas graphomotor skills are generally poor in the primary school years but improve with age and practice.

Preadolescents and adolescents with NLD may be at risk for depression as well as anxiety. It remains to be seen whether and to what extent these comorbid conditions may be explained by neurobiological or family genetic factors. More commonly, an association is posited between increasingly negative experiences in adolescence and feelings of depression. Rates of peer isolation and victimization are high for the school-aged child with NLD (Little, 2001). It is not surprising, then, that varying degrees of depression are found as age and social pressures increase. The middle school years are often especially challenging as there is a shift in the social and academic environment; schools tend to be larger and require more transitions, and learning is increasingly abstract and less rote in nature.

Vulnerabilities in psychosocial functioning are an important aspect of the developmental picture for children with NLD. These children are socially interested and eager to please and to be liked. However, they encounter difficulty navigating the social world, particularly when interacting with peers and in the context of group situations. Information that is conveyed through nonverbal aspects of communication, such as facial expression, tone, gestures, is not as readily integrated (e.g., Petti, Voelker, Shore, & Hayman-Abello, 2003). This is especially true when the individual with NLD must sustain a natural to-and-fro conversation, analyzing and integrating the elements necessary for this exchange in real time. They are often more comfortable in the company of adults, who are more predictable in their behaviors and willing to scaffold or support the child's unconventional behaviors. A matter of significance for adolescents and adult relationships that is oft neglected is sexuality. Rourke and Fisk (1992) observed that intimate interactions in particular rely heavily on smooth, coordinated, sensorimotor functioning and spontaneous adaptation to changing social circumstances, which rely on skills that are often found to be inadequate in NLD.

Adults with NLD are expected to do reasonably well in academic courses and jobs that involve rote verbal skills, straight memorization, and patterns of responding that are highly predictable and straightforward. For the person with NLD, the principal dimensions are those that have to do with how courses are taught, what is expected on tests and examinations, and what is required in terms of essays, class participation, and the like. Programs and work environments that require on-the-spot flexible thinking and problem solving, or place an emphasis on fast visual-motor coordination or spatial analysis are less suited to persons with NLD. Time management, filling out visually detailed forms, social skills, commonsense judgment, and/or multitasking are other demands that may not be easily met. We are familiar with adults with NLD who have gone on to college (e.g., to major in history, law, and so forth) and those who have encountered job success in an academic setting or, for example, employment settings such as a travel agency.

Neuropsychological and Psychosocial Correlates of Adult NLD

Although there has been less in the way of a systematic examination of NLD in adults, there is research-based evidence for its manifestation. The studies include clinical accounts, as well as comparison studies of a cross-sectional nature. The results suggest (1) that NLD as described in children also presents in adults; (2) the discrepancy between assets and deficits may be more pronounced in adults with NLD; and (3) there may be associations with particular forms of psychosocial dysfunction.

In an early work to consider the developmental manifestations of NLD, a cross-sectional study was conducted comparing the performance of children with NLD and a group of clinic-referred adults with NLD (Rourke, Young, Strang, & Russell, 1986). Eight adults with NLD were identified who showed virtually identical patterns of neuropsychological assets and deficits as that observed in NLD children. Moreover, these adults were found to display deficient social skills, reported having few friends, exhibited low self-esteem, and demonstrated a tendency to become withdrawn and isolated. Two of the persons had previously received a diagnosis of schizophrenia. In addition to providing evidence for the presentation of NLD in adulthood, these findings also suggested that neuropsychological deficiencies may become exacerbated over time and accompanied by social and emotional disturbances.

The increasing gap between areas of asset and deficit may emerge in adolescence and continue into adulthood. When younger and older children (adolescents) are compared, verbal, reading, and spelling skills remain intact with increasing age, but there is a failure to make age-appropriate gains on measures of deficit areas, for example, visual–perceptual, complex tactile, psychomotor, problem-solving, and arithmetic skills (Casey et al., 1991). Notably also, whereas parents of the younger NLD children expressed concern about school performance, cognitive ability, and some degree of overactivity or distractibility, parents of the older NLD children expressed concerns regarding communication and social skills, as well as clumsy behavior and daydreaming. These results support an exacerbation of neuropsychological deficiencies over time and point to a dimension of the expression of this disorder that might be most salient to adult outcome.

In a more recent and extensive cross-sectional study of neuropsychological profiles in older children relative to adults with NLD ($n = 31$), there is additional evidence that the pattern of relative assets and deficits as predicted in children is found in adults (Ahmad, Rourke, & Drummond, 2007). Adults in this sample also showed more significant deficits in the areas of visual-spatial organization, tactile perception, and eye-hand coordination, and an especially marked weakness on a measure of concept formation. Verbal skills remained intact and an area of relative asset. These results provide further support for the notion that the NLD profile presents in adults, and also indicate a greater disparity between relative assets and deficits in clinic-referred samples of adults versus children with NLD.

Greiffenstein and Baker (2002) also found that this difference can eventuate in lower scores on measures of general intelligence. In their comparison of adults with arithmetic deficiencies (AD group) and those with reading deficiencies (RD group), the AD compared to RD group obtained significantly lower scores on the WAIS-R, due to their lower Performance IQ. The AD group also showed a higher Verbal Comprehension index score than the RD group, and a significantly greater frequency of VIQ relative to PIQ superiority. Moreover, it was found that the AD adults showed many of the same specific neuropsychological patterns as children and adolescents with arithmetic deficiencies, a profile that was consistent with NLD. Specifically, in addition to a poorer nonverbal performance on measured intelligence, they showed significantly lower scores on measures of visual-spatial, visual-constructional, and visual-motor tasks as well as greater impairment in switching mental sets on a measure involving conceptual reasoning.

In addition to deficits in the area of nonverbal problem solving, adults with NLD may be vulnerable in the use of organizational strategies that would result in better recall performance. When the performance of adolescents and adults with NLD and verbal learning disabilities (VLD) was compared on the California Verbal Learning Test (CVLT), the NLD group showed a preference for a serial versus semantic approach to list learning (Fisher & DeLuca, 1997). The mean performance of the NLD sample on the semantic clustering index fell 1 standard deviation below the normative mean, whereas the serial clustering score was within normal limits. Their serial score was also significantly greater than their semantic cluster score, whereas no difference in serial versus semantic cluster scores was observed in the VLD comparison group, who performed equally well and within normal limits on both indices. These results suggest that adults with NLD may be more likely to employ serial versus semantically driven learning strategies; they may show a preference for new learning and tasks that lend themselves to a sequential or step-by-step approach versus tasks that create demands for the organization, abstraction, or integration of information. Taken together, these three studies also raise the question whether adults with NLD are likely to perform poorly on a test battery designed to measure "executive function."

The results of the cross-sectional studies indicate whether LD exists in adulthood. They do not, of course, address whether the adults who currently manifest with LD also presented with the same LD in childhood. We hypothesize that NLD persists into adulthood, based both on retrospective reports, and the increasingly held view that LDs are not outgrown. In a large longitudinal study of LD, those with visual-spatial problems in childhood continued to demonstrate them in adulthood (Spreen & Haaf, 1986). A stable neuropsychological profile was also obtained in a follow-up study of five adults (aged 16–23 years) who had as children displayed markedly deficient arithmetic skills and presented with features of NLD (Del Dotto, Fisk, McFadden, & Rourke, 1991). These individuals scored above average in word recognition and spelling in the context of markedly deficient mechanical arithmetic skills. Their neuropsychological profile continued to be characterized by bilaterally impaired haptic perceptual abilities, left-sided tactually guided problem-solving deficits, bilaterally deficient fine finger-dexterity skills, poor nonverbal concept-formation capacities, and underdeveloped visual-spatial skills. Four of the five adults with NLD also displayed a significant degree of psychosocial dysfunction as indicated by clinically elevated scales on the Minnesota Multiphasic Personality Inventory (MMPI) as well as a significant number of maladaptive behaviors reported on the Vineland Adaptive Behavior Scales (Vineland) by their parents, although there was no consistent pattern of disturbance. The results of the Vineland scales also were notable for indicating disturbance in the children's abilities to function and maintain themselves independently and to meet demands of personal and social responsibility, as viewed by their parents.

We have observed that over time children with NLD are at risk for anxiety and depression. In a series of studies, we have shown that there are clear relationships between patterns of academic achievement and psychosocial outcome (Pelletier et al., 2001; Rourke & Fuerst, 1991; Tsatsanis, Fuerst, & Rourke, 1997). At least one third of children with NLD do not show significant psychosocial disturbance; another one-third show mild concerns, and the remaining one-third are at risk for severe psychopathology (Pelletier et al., 2001). Among the affected groups, internalized forms of psychopathology tend to predominate.

There has been some evidence to suggest that adolescents and adults with NLD are also at risk for an internalized form of psychopathology and, in turn, associated suicidal behavior. Support for this view is obtained from case studies (Bigler, 1989; Rourke, Young, & Leenaars, 1989), with consideration also given by Fletcher (1989) and Kowalchuk and King (1989). Weintraub and Mesulam (1983) report findings of major depression in a selected group of 14 adults with arithmetic disabilities (AD) as well as visual-spatial problems, and at least one study has shown in a larger young adult clinical group that depression is more frequent among those with poorest WRAT-R arithmetic scores (e.g., Cleaver & Whitman, 1998). However, two studies using the MMPI do not indicate a singular pattern in MMPI profiles of adult groups distinguished in terms of verbal or nonverbal, reading or arithmetic learning deficiencies (Greiffenstein & Baker, 2002; Waldo, McIntosh, & Koller, 1999), although elevations were found. Some variables that may account for differences in these kinds of studies include sample selection or referral source (e.g., in-patient subjects as in the study conducted by Cleaver and Whitman versus adults referred for work-adjustment difficulties following graduation from secondary school as in the study conducted by Greiffenstein and Baker) as well as use of clinical case studies versus a large-scale study. Although MMPI profiles were not unique to one LD group or another in the two reports cited above, for these kinds of studies it makes some sense to look at frequency data as well as mean scores based on group performance, given that significant elevations on the clinical scales of the MMPI (and similar instruments) have meaning in and of themselves. A related concern is whether differences are obtained when depression (or some other diagnostic construct) is measured based on clinical criteria obtained from interview versus from self-report on a questionnaire, and whether these differences may be group specific.

There is a need for more research on the manifestations of adult LD. The intriguing proposition of the NLD model is that some adult psychopathology could eventuate from a particular neuropsychological profile; this is understood not as an associated feature only but as a cause-and-effect outcome of the dynamics engendered by this particular set of strengths and weaknesses (see below). In addition to reconsidering how we view LD, this model raises the matter of another pathway to psychosocial disturbance. When such conditions present in adults, it is imperative to give consideration to and be able to recognize the manifestations of LD and entertain their contribution to forms of apparent psychopathology. From a research perspective, an interesting question arises as to whether certain groups defined in terms of a particular clinical presentation (e.g., depression, social anxiety, avoidant personality disorder, and so forth) show a subset of individuals presenting with NLD. This may represent yet another example of a final common pathway for which a varied source introduces the kind of heterogeneity that obscures research and treatment results.

Additionally, of course, prospective longitudinal studies of outcome in NLD would be a desirable area of research. Such studies would demonstrate whether NLD as hypothesized persists into adulthood. Longitudinal studies would also be helpful with regard to addressing changes in the manifestation of NLD over time. An outcome study also could be designed to evaluate the effectiveness of treatment and the nature of adult adjustment to this childhood disorder. The analysis should include both group and individual results because many follow-up studies obscure individual variation in favor of depicting group results. Mean scores are presented for the group at Time 1 and then Time 2. Such studies would be bolstered by stating whether the same individuals remain within the same subtype over time and demonstrate the same pattern of performance over time. Also, this kind of research would be well positioned to examine how and why some individuals show a more positive outcome and which protective factors, environmental or genetic variables, or strategies promoted a more successful adjustment. One challenge to such studies is whether a test is measuring the same ability or skill in the adult as in the child. The same test could be measuring quite different underlying abilities at different ages. Furthermore, the performance of adults may be confounded by the emergence of well-established compensatory strategies (e.g., encoding in verbal terms). One may wish to examine ability/disability relationships as well as neuropsychological test patterns in an effort to assess individual component processes in these broader neuropsychological constructs. Functional neuroimaging studies offer another avenue of research to support whether similar systems are recruited in children as in adults with NLD performing related tasks.

Dynamics

A distinguishing and salient feature of NLD relative to other learning disabilities is the extent of associated psychosocial and adaptive difficulties as well as the proposed account for why this particular constellation of difficulties should emerge over the course of development. As noted, the particular pattern of academic, psychosocial, and adaptive assets and deficits observed in NLD is considered to be the outcome of the pattern of neuropsychological assets and deficits displayed by persons with NLD (Rourke 1989, 1995).

In this model, the principal or primary dimensions of the NLD syndrome are deficits in tactile perception, visual-perceptual-organizational abilities, and complex psychomotor skills. The capacity to deal with novel material is further identified as a fundamental deficit and understood within a cognitive developmental perspective (see below). Primary assets include proficient rote verbal and some simple motor and psychomotor skills. In this section, we consider the NLD model in terms of the dynamic effects of this set of primary assets and deficits and the cause-and-effect relationships they engender. They are primary in the respect of their developmental importance and their basis in an interactive process of competing forces over time.

Piaget (1954; Piaget & Inhelder, 1969) emphasized sensorimotor functioning as one of the early developmental features upon which formal operational thought is founded (Casey & Rourke, 1992, 2002; Strang & Rourke, 1985a). From this perspective, development is characterized as an ongoing process of organization, integration, and consolidation of one's experiences that are engendered by newly emerging capacities. At the earliest stages, the interaction between self and environment is organized through the body (sensory processes) and action (Piaget, 1954). The external world is known to the young child principally through touch, vision, and movement. In addition, early learning takes place in the context of goal-directed behavior, which is outwardly manifested in action or active experimentation (Piaget, 1954). Motivated exploration and manipulation of the environment furnishes the child with the necessary information to begin forming mental schemata. This early activity is thought to yield the development of higher order mental processes, such as an understanding of cause-and-effect relationships, hypothesis testing, nonverbal concept formation, and reasoning abilities.

Piaget (1954) maintained that the adequacy of the child's sensorimotor experience is related in a direct way to his or her cognitive development. The primary deficits of NLD—tactile perception, psychomotor coordination, and visual perception—are precisely those domains identified as essential to early learning. These children are limited in their appreciation of the nonverbal aspects of their environment or perceptual experience with considerable difficulty adapting to novel stimuli; as such, they are unlikely to explore their environment or seek out stimulation. Because individuals with NLD show an early preference for learning about their environment through language and eschew physical exploration, their exposure to a large range of experiences and novel stimuli is more limited. It may be argued that, for children with NLD, there is little organized interaction between them and the external world, as well as a fundamental inability to make sense of the complex and novel stimuli. This constellation of difficulties conspires to render a smooth adaptation to the constantly changing milieu of social interactions all but impossible for the child or adult with NLD. Although some social rules may be learned, a formulaic descriptive system is not likely to eventuate in the spontaneous give-and-take of a social exchange. Despite an initial desire to interact with others, the totality of these problems may create an unrewarding social experience for the child with NLD.

Moreover, from early in development, individuals with NLD tend to display an overreliance on language for mediating behaviors and feelings; disparate events are related by making the connection in words, and experiences too may be encoded in words versus sensations. Language is structured to deal well with factual knowledge and categorical information but is less effective for conveying and apprehending direct experience, and is only one part of the context encoded in one's experience (e.g., a personal event may involve referenced facts but also the internal setting or subjective environment, such as sensations, personal significance of the time or place, as well as one's emotional state). Yet context is often the crucial factor in resolving meaning. Individuals with NLD may organize and make sense of their rational experience by using verbal language; they may be challenged to organize and integrate their internal experiences, which is important in the development of understanding self and other.

This observation is supported by preliminary evidence from an fMRI study reporting a difference in activation patterns in adolescents and adults with and without NLD when identifying emotion in faces (Vallabha, 2003). The results indicated relative hypoactivation in limbic areas responsible for processing emotion and in frontal regions that might be relevant to attention/emotional salience, and greater activation in structures that participate in language function for the subjects with NLD. The latter finding was interpreted to suggest that individuals with NLD relied on their linguistic assets to compensate for their nonverbal deficits. This is consistent both with clinical observations as well as expectations for vulnerable areas in brain development based on the white-matter model detailed below. There are no other reported MRI studies in the NLD literature, though they are needed to examine further the hypotheses generated by this model.

The precise dynamics of NLD have been discussed in detail elsewhere (Rourke, 1989, especially pp. 80–100 and 142–149) and have been presented here in brief. It is proposed that the patterns of academic and psychosocial deficits experienced by individuals who exhibit NLD are the direct result of the interaction of the primary, secondary, tertiary, and linguistic neuropsychological assets and deficits that are outlined schematically in Figure 7.1.

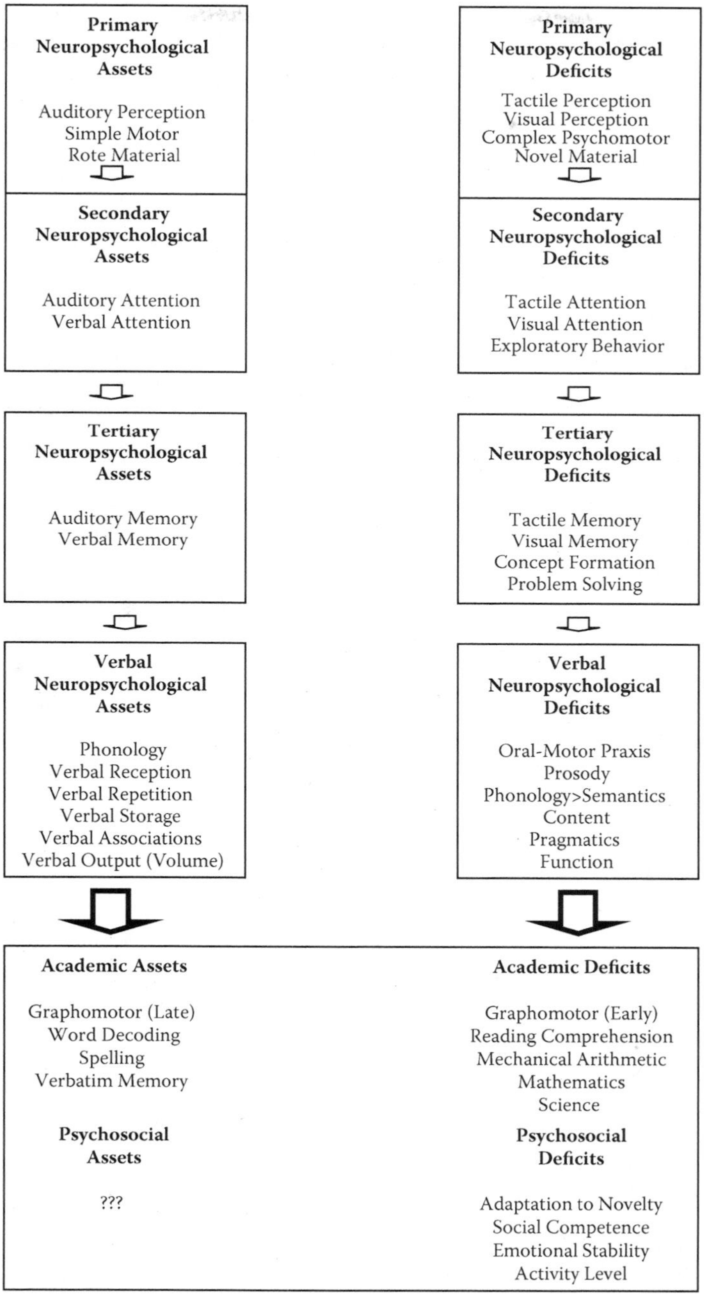

Primary Neuropsychological Assets	Primary Neuropsychological Deficits
Auditory Perception Simple Motor Rote Material ⊐⊏	Tactile Perception Visual Perception Complex Psychomotor Novel Material ⊐⊏
Secondary Neuropsychological Assets	**Secondary Neuropsychological Deficits**
Auditory Attention Verbal Attention	Tactile Attention Visual Attention Exploratory Behavior

⊐⊏   ⊐⊏

Tertiary Neuropsychological Assets	Tertiary Neuropsychological Deficits
Auditory Memory Verbal Memory	Tactile Memory Visual Memory Concept Formation Problem Solving

⊐⊏   ⊐⊏

Verbal Neuropsychological Assets	Verbal Neuropsychological Deficits
Phonology Verbal Reception Verbal Repetition Verbal Storage Verbal Associations Verbal Output (Volume)	Oral-Motor Praxis Prosody Phonology>Semantics Content Pragmatics Function

⬇   ⬇

Academic Assets	**Academic Deficits**
Graphomotor (Late) Word Decoding Spelling Verbatim Memory	Graphomotor (Early) Reading Comprehension Mechanical Arithmetic Mathematics Science
Psychosocial Assets	**Psychosocial Deficits**
???	Adaptation to Novelty Social Competence Emotional Stability Activity Level

Figure 7.1 Content and dynamics of NLD syndrome.

Considering the hypothesized "deficit" stream then, the primary neuro-psychological deficits experienced by the child with NLD are seen as having to do with aspects of tactile and visual perception, complex psychomotor skills, and the capacity to deal adaptively with novel material. Such deficits are expected to eventuate in disordered tactile and visual attention and stunted exploratory behavior; in turn, problems in memory for material delivered through the tactile and visual modalities as well as deficits in concept formation and problem solving would be expected to ensue. This set of deficits is considered to eventuate in the particular linguistic defi-ciencies outlined in Figure 7.1 (see Rourke & Tsatsanis, 1996, for a more extensive explanation of these linguistic deficits).

It is especially important to note that this set of neuropsychological deficits is expected to lead, in a necessary way, to a particular configuration of problems in psychosocial/adaptive behavior both within and without the academic situation (Rourke, 1988, 1989, 1995; Rourke & Fuerst, 1992). The notion that a particular pattern of *neuropsychological* assets and deficits (resulting in a particular subtype of learning disability) can lead to both a particular pattern of formal learning (e.g., *academic*) assets and deficits and a particular pattern of *psychosocial* disturbance is well illustrated by the NLD syndrome. In a series of investigations (Casey et al., 1991; Harnadek & Rourke, 1994; and Rourke & Fuerst, 1991, for a summary of several studies), we have been able to demonstrate the concurrent and pre-dictive validity of these formulations relating to the academic and psycho-social consequences of NLD. Also, it has been possible to demonstrate that particular patterns of academic assets and deficits are reliably related to particular patterns of psychosocial dysfunction across the age span of interest (Fuerst & Rourke, 1993; Tsatsanis et al., 1997).

White-Matter Model

A central theoretical hypothesis of the NLD model is that perturbations of white-matter (long myelinated fiber) development or damage to white matter are the cause of the phenotypical manifestations of NLD. From this perspective, the role of neural pathways (i.e., axonal or white-matter con-nections) in flexibly processing information and responding to changes in functional demands is seen as crucial. This can be contrasted to strict localizationist theory, which was until recently more strongly advanced. Rourke (1989) early on conceptualized outcome more broadly in terms of the functional organization of systems within the brain. In particular, three principal axes of neurodevelopment are considered for their role in the integrative action of the brain. A brief account is presented below. For a full description of the syndrome and the white-matter model designed to account for it, the interested reader is referred to Rourke (1989, 1995) and Tsatsanis and Rourke (1995).

Neurodevelopmental Factors

Critical events in the developing brain include neuronal proliferation and migration, cell differentiation, axon and dendrite growth, axon guidance and target recognition, and synaptic formation. The modification of cortical connections is further associated with processes such as nerve cell death and the formation and elimination of excess axonal connections and synapses. Cell proliferation and migration occur early in development and are complete at birth. However, relatively few fiber tracts are completely myelinated at birth; the most rapid period of myelination occurs within the first 2 years of life (Dietrich & Bradley, 1988). In addition, postnatal growth spurts in the brain are reported to occur without a concurrent increase in neuronal proliferation; rather, it is the growth of dendritic processes, synapses, and myelination that is thought to account for these postnatal increases in brain weight (Kolb & Fantie, 1989). As noted, an important event in postnatal development is also the excess production and eventual elimination of neurons, dendrites, and synapses (Huttenlocher, 1984, 1994). This is a process of dynamic organization that may begin with the sensory gateway. Studies of the developing brain provide evidence that the thalamus is involved in the functional differentiation of the cortex, with thalamic axons arriving early during fetal development, possibly representing the first afferent signals to the cortex, and showing a highly ordered topographical arrangement of connections with cortical regions in the mature brain (Blakemore, 1995; Ghosh, 1995; Molnár, Adams, Goffinet, & Blakemore 1998; O'Leary, 1989; O'Leary & Koester, 1993). The absence of thalamic input leads to poorly organized or less differentiated clusters of neurons (Bolz, Kossel, & Bagnard 1995; Katz & Shatz, 1996). As such, early coordinated patterns of thalamic activity may influence the organization of neural pathways by strengthening some synapses but not others (Steriade, McCormick, & Sejnowski, 1993), and serve as an intermediary mechanism by which precise patterns of connectivity are generated.

These findings indicate that the development of axonal connections (white-matter pathways) and the process of myelination are far from complete in the brain of the very young child. Moreover, the refinement of these systems is expected to bear upon the child's ability to adapt to increasing environmental demands. A description of these events underscores the notion that brain development involves a dynamic interplay between two main processes—differentiation and integration. The brain evolves to greater complexity through the integrative action of neuronal growth and differentiation and associated organization of these component parts to yield more refined neural systems (Majovski, 1989). Similarly, the mark of higher order processing is both the activation of specialized subsystems as well as the capacity to integrate them toward an identified goal.

The pattern of development displayed by children with NLD has been interpreted by Rourke (1982, 1987, 1989), on the basis of formulations of the Goldberg and Costa (1981) model, to involve right-hemisphere dysfunction. Through an analysis of differences in the neuroanatomical organization of the right and left hemispheres, Goldberg and Costa identified distinct roles for the cerebral hemispheres in the acquisition, integration, and application of descriptive systems. Their examination suggested that the right hemisphere has a crucial role in the initial stages of the acquisition of descriptive systems, whereas the left hemisphere is superior at deploying these codes in a routinized manner once they have been assembled. Hence, it is postulated that systems within the right hemisphere are highly efficient at processing novel information for which the individual has no preexisting code. In contrast, left-hemispheral systems are thought to be superior at processing that takes advantage of these fully formed codes—that is, the storage and application of multiple overlearned descriptive systems. The specific pattern of neuropsychological assets and deficits displayed by children with NLD is expected to develop under conditions that compromise the functioning or accessibility to right-hemispheral systems in particular.

This perspective is supported by findings using quantified electroencephalogram (EEG) or EEG coherence analyses obtained over the life span (Thatcher 1994, 1997). These studies reveal a left-right hemisphere pole of development, involving complementary sequences of predominantly left-hemisphere growth spurts followed by predominantly right-hemisphere growth spurts. Furthermore, cycles within the left hemisphere exhibit a developmental sequence involving a progressive lengthening or expansion of intracortical connections; that is, short-distance intracortical growth spurts followed by growth spurts in longer distance connection systems. In contrast, cycles in the right hemisphere consist of a sequential consolidation of intracortical connections; that is, a progression from growth spurts in long-distance connections to shorter distance subsystems over time. These results were interpreted to suggest a developmental sequence of functional integration of differentiated subsystems in the left hemisphere, and the convergence of distributed systems to form specialized subsystems in the right hemisphere. In brief, Thatcher (1997) described these developmental processes as "integrating differentiation" in the left hemisphere and "differentiating integration" in the right hemisphere. Consistent with Goldberg and Costa's (1981) formulation, the left hemisphere is found to predominate in the integration of systems that are fully formed, whereas the right hemisphere is involved in the assembly of new systems.

Thatcher's (1994, 1997) work also points to a frontal-to-caudal dominance of changes in intracortical connections. A role for frontal systems in higher level cognitive functioning has been well documented (Damasio & Anderson, 1993; Stuss, 1992). In particular, frontal systems are thought to play an integral role in (executive) control of novel responses (i.e., in directing, planning, and organizing lower level systems toward a selected goal). EEG coherence measures examining the development of intracortical connections offer support for this role. The results of these investigations indicate that postnatal cerebral maturation is characterized by the expansion of reciprocal connections between regions of the frontal lobes and posterior, central, and temporal cortical regions (Case, 1992; Thatcher, 1994, 1997). The finding of an anterior-posterior gradient of development in the formation of these connections has been interpreted to suggest a mechanism of integration by frontal systems of elemental sensorimotor units to form higher level abstractions and systems of abstraction (Thatcher, 1994). This is reminiscent of Piaget's developmental perspective of cognitive development, and again is suggestive that adults with NLD may show more pronounced deficits in executive function (e.g., planning, flexibility, capacity to shift set) upon neuropsychological assessment, which should not be confounded with broader patterns of asset and deficit.

Finally, the long fibers projecting from subcortical and limbic system structures to cortical areas, particularly frontal regions, are the third dimension of interest. There is evidence to suggest that reciprocal connections between these regions influence information processing at higher levels. Such roles include the assignment of affective meaning to external events, formation of novelty encoding networks, and synchronization and desynchronization of cortical activity (Barth & MacDonald, 1996; Damasio & Anderson, 1993; Mega, Cummings, Salloway, & Malloy, 1997; Steriade et al., 1993; Tulving, Markowitsch, Kapur, Habib, & Houle, 1994). Developmentally, a perturbation in these pathways would be expected to result in diminished subcortical-limbic influences on refinement and organization of the cortex, thereby affecting regulation and coordination of higher order mental activity.

Just as there is marked change in the early developing brain, the healthy adult brain is in a constant state of change. Periods of maturation continue into middle age; there is a progressive loss of myelin or decline in white-matter volume and structural integrity after this time that is widespread and includes the frontal lobes (Bartzokis et al., 2003; Fotenos, Snyder, Girton, Morris, & Buckner, 2005; Ge et al., 2002a, 2002b; Resnick, Pham, Kraut, Zonderman, & Davatzikos, 2003). In the current white-matter model, functions that involve inter- rather than intramodal processing are expected to be more likely affected by white-matter perturbations.

It follows that white-matter disturbances will have a more profound effect on neural systems that are characterized by a high degree of interregional connectivity and that these regions are especially affected in NLD (e.g., Njiokiktjien, de Rijke, & Jonkman, 2001). Notably also, when mathematically gifted adolescents (e.g., a group showing the opposite pattern of assets and deficits as those shown in NLD) are compared to normal-ability youth and college students on a global-local processing task, they show enhanced interhemispheric interaction as a unique functional characteristic (Harnam & O'Boyle, 2004).

In their capacity to deal with novel and complex information, it is expected that both the right hemisphere and frontal systems display greater interregional connectivity (e.g., Damasio, 1990; Tulving et al., 1994). Indeed, a comparison of prefrontal white-matter volume between human and other primates indicates that this area shows the largest difference in volume; no significant relative difference in gray-matter volume was obtained, further suggesting that refinement has occurred in the context of increased or more complex connectivity in the human brain (Schoenemann, Sheehan, & Glotzer, 2005). Additionally, as might be predicted by Thatcher's patterns of pathway development, age-related differences in *functional* connectivity must be considered. For example, when performing a recall task, older adults show stronger correlations between hippocampal activity and the dorsolateral prefrontal and parietal regions, and positive correlations between activity in these regions and better memory performance versus young adults who drew on more perceptually based processes (Grady, McIntosh, & Craik, 2003). The pattern of more pronounced deficits in adults with NLD may represent the intersection of vulnerabilities in white-matter development and aspects of the normal aging process.

Final Thoughts

Learning disabilities, including NLD, present and likely persist into adulthood. What follows from this is the need for a developmental or life-span framework within which to view LD. There is a developmental context within which to understand an individual's learning disability as well as a changing environmental context. Changes in age are accompanied by different developmental demands as well as varied situational experiences. In turn, these changing developmental demands and increasing complexities may affect the manifestation of an individual's learning disability.

In consideration of the developmental context then, a reevaluation of our definition of "learning" and, by extension, "learning disability" must be entertained. In the first instance, learning must be viewed as a lifelong developmental process. Second, our research, conception, and treatment of LD need to address the multidimensionality of the adult's life. The demands of adulthood are clearly wide ranging. Adult life includes working toward personal, social, and occupational competence in addition to achieving academic success. Major adult life demands include: employment, education, home and family, leisure pursuits, community involvement, emotional and physical health, and personal responsibility and relationships (e.g., Patton & Polloway, 1992).

However, LDs are most widely regarded in the context of childhood development and academic learning. Where performance on reading, spelling, or math tests represents measured *products*, the cognitive *processes* that affect academic learning conceivably have broader implications for learning in the world, and more important as in NLD, conception of oneself. Finally, "social learning" would appear to be an imperative consideration in the definition of LD.

NLD is considered a learning disability in the fullest sense. Early profiles of neuropsychological asset and deficit are understood in terms of their implications for how and what a child learns about self and others as well as adaptability, which is arguably the basis of brain-behavior development. The NLD syndrome was initially isolated in the context of research attempts aimed at the identification of reliable and valid subtypes of LD. However, the term *learning disability* also captures the fundamental challenge for individuals with NLD. In short, such persons are capable of learning virtually anything but need to learn almost everything. They must cope with core learning vulnerabilities that include: dealing with new learning, especially in complex or novel situations; an overreliance on previously learned rote information, such that overlearned procedures are used without regard for unique aspects of a new learning task; and a preference for processing information through one modality, namely, auditory-verbal, in the context of a limited capacity for intermodal integration.

From an educational standpoint, this raises the question of what form intervention should take, especially when the school program is set up to focus on academic improvement that is content based. Treating the specific referral problem (e.g., a learning difficulty in math or written expression) in this case may come at the expense of encouraging other aspects of development, such as strategies for learning in general, creating a success model, or promoting growth opportunities in the school environment. It is important to consider how personal strengths can be used to compensate for difficulties and to promote a positive motivation to learn and a positive view of the child by his or her peers. Academic learning is important, but other factors too may be relevant for long-term outcome with regard to vocational success, social interactions, interpersonal relationships, leisure pursuits, and so forth. This may include social skills development as well as helping individuals with NLD to recognize their personal strengths and weaknesses and to access environments where their assets can be emphasized and there is flexibility to meet their needs. From this perspective, early intervention is not just about supporting academic skills (i.e., formal learning) but addressing lifelong (informal learning) needs for better adjustment.

In addition to a developmental perspective, it is important to acknowledge that related changing "environmental" variables may also impact the expression of a learning disability in the long-term. This is an important consideration for NLD since it has been proposed to obtain in multiple neurodevelopmental manifestations (e.g., Rourke, 1995). Thus, an empirical question is how expression of the disorder compares when it is manifest on a developmental basis versus the product of a neurological/neuroendocrine disease, disorder, and dysfunction (e.g., hydrocephalus). Personal and social variables are also relevant, including family environment, support systems, past experiences, learning/socialization, socioeconomic status (SES), abuse history, and other psychosocial stressors. Additionally, because the adult with NLD has lived with his or her disability for an extended period of time, he or she may have experienced a pattern of particular academic and social failures. On the one hand, this learning history could yield pathological states of anxiety and depression. On the other, some adults with NLD have also presumably developed some compensatory strategies to manage the disability, and adults who generally have more control over their environment can be selective about playing to their strengths.

Although we often focus on disability and dysfunction, it would be worthwhile also to investigate positive sources of differences in outcome. Another context to be considered is the changing societal milieu; for example, what is the effect of the increase in the use of computers to connect socially, to be able to work from home, or as an occupational skill requirement? It would seem that for the person with particular difficulties in the nonverbal aspects of day-to-day life, computers could offer a helpful medium for connecting with others. Finally, a critical environment that has not been examined in NLD is the family; for example, what differences, if any, in presentation and outcome depend upon "goodness of fit" between parent and child? Of interest for adults with NLD who are parents too, what is the differential impact on their children's development?

The NLD model underscores the importance of examining patterns (i.e., profiles of performance) and context in development when framing our research questions. When we think about patterns (versus hierarchical levels of analysis), our outlook moves from the things themselves and the supremacy of one domain versus another to the relations among them and what this means for how both brain and behavior are organized. Moreover, it can be considered that such order or organization is maintained by communication. Sebeok (1991) defines this broadly as the transmission of any influence from one part of a living system to another part, thus producing change. From this, it becomes evident that context is crucial in its role for resolving the significance of a message. We can understand this at the level of social behavior; individuals with NLD tend to overvalue what is spoken—the words themselves—versus how they are spoken or in what circumstance when interpreting social meaning. We can also understand this at the level of the brain—for example, the neural context.

In lieu of a strict one-to-one correspondence of structure and function, the functional role of brain regions may depend in part on the neural context or the pattern of interactions among brain regions. McIntosh (1999) gives evidence that a region, such as the right prefrontal cortex, can play a different functional role in memory depending upon its interactions with anatomically related regions. Rather than being committed to specific functions, brain regions may play a role in a variety of cognitive and other operations and their interregional interactions will differ depending on the type of cognitive challenge. It may be argued also that our own interpretation of the functionality of a region of the brain is dependent on context. Some brain regions are activated by several different tasks; tasks that belong to different cognitive domains may share processing components and thus activate overlapping regions (e.g., the role of the fusiform gyrus in activation to faces versus objects as part of a perceptual expertise network or a component of the social brain; Schultz et al., 2003).

Finally, whereas a favorable area of research lies in "executive functions" and the role of the frontal lobe in the so-called executive brain, a consideration of the NLD model points to the importance of the somatosensory cortex and integration of sensory-perceptual networks in higher order thinking. Parietal regions in the right hemisphere are consistently activated during tasks involving attention, spatial perception and imagery, working memory, spatial episodic encoding, episodic retrieval, and skill learning (e.g., Cabeza & Nyberg, 2000, for a review). Moreover, neuroimaging studies reveal that mental imagery, important to many cognitive tasks such as perspective changes and problem solving as well as motor learning, may involve overlapping regions of the brain related to somatosensory perception and actual experience (e.g., Wolbers, Weiller, & Büchel, 2003). Perhaps a neural parallel to Piaget's developmental trajectories, attention to the spatial location of an object may engage overlapping regions responsible for tactile and guided visual motor (hand-arm) behavior. In their study, Wolbers et al. (2003) revealed that when mental rotation is combined with motor imagery of the hands, the superior parietal lobe is activated; this region is sensitive to signals arising from mental imagery in the absence of somatosensory input as well as to input in actual hand reaching and grasping. A task requiring a combination of visual spatial, tactile, and motor imagery is processed or integrated through activity in the parietal lobe; such functions can be expected to be impaired in NLD.

Similarly, a role for the right somatosensory cortex and emotion recognition is supported using lesion mapping (Adolphs, Damasio, Tranel, Cooper, & Damasio, 2000). The findings were significant for showing again that a seemingly visually based task, such as recognition of emotion from visually presented facial expressions, is significantly impaired by dysfunction in right-hemisphere regions processing somatosensory information. Moreover, distinct systems were critical for conceptual knowledge and knowledge of the name of an emotion versus knowledge based on one's ability to recognize another's emotional state by internally generating somatosensory representations that simulate how the other individual would feel when displaying a certain facial expression (e.g., based on one's own internal experience). Connections between frontal regions and the right postcentral gyrus (somatosensory cortex) and regions of (right inferior) parietal lobe as well as the amygdala may be central to processing perspective or self-other distinctions (Ruby & Decety, 2004).

Relative to other types of LD—such as deficiencies in reading, for example—NLD has not received the same kind of widespread research attention. Some challenges have been definitional and others diagnostic. Researchers have used disparate criteria for defining their NLD subject sample, which has reduced comparability between studies and perhaps deterred others. Further, NLD is not a recognized disorder in the *DSM* and thus may not attract a high level of attention and research resources. However, with the increase in private organizations centered on NLD, the demand for research and the funds to support it may be obtained. Historically, nonverbal learning disabilities have been understood in terms of a primary AD, a social disability, a right-hemisphere syndrome, and, here, in terms of a developmental neuropsychological profile. Myklebust's original conceptualization indicated subgroups within NLD and, indeed, so do research on arithmetic disabilities and impairment in social functioning. In our efforts, we have endeavored to examine one group of individuals presenting with a particular pattern of neuropsychological assets and deficits that we identified as NLD as well as consider the implications of these patterns on learning and connectivity in the brain. As revealed in this chapter, this is an interesting area of clinical investigation for which there is much systematic research to be done to test the hypotheses within the model proposed. Such investigations are likely to challenge our usual constructs for LD and open up new areas for question.

References

Adolphs, R., Damasio, H., Tranel, D., Cooper, G., & Damasio, A. R. (2000). A role for somatosensory cortices in the visual recognition of emotion as revealed by three-dimensional lesion mapping. *The Journal of Neuroscience, 20,* 2683–2690.

Ahmad, S. A., Rourke, B. P., & Drummond, C. R. (2007). *Comparison of older children and adults with basic phonological processing disabilities and nonverbal learning disabilities.* Manuscript submitted for publication.

American Psychiatric Association. (2000). *Diagnostic and statistical manual of mental disorders* (4th ed.)-Text Revision. Washington, DC: American Psychiatric Association.

Barth, D. S., & MacDonald, K. D. (1996). Thalamic modulation of high-frequency oscillating potentials in auditory cortex. *Nature, 383,* 78–81.

Bartzokis, G., Cummings, J. L., Sultzer, D., Henderson, V. W., Nuechterlein, K. H., & Mintz, J. (2003). White matter structural integrity in healthy aging adults and patients with Alzheimer disease: A magnetic resonance imaging study. *Archives of Neurology, 60,* 393–398.

Bigler, E. D. (1989). On the neuropsychology of suicide. *Journal of Learning Disabilities, 22,* 180–185.

Blakemore, C. (1995). Mysteries in the making of the cerebral cortex. *Ciba Foundation Symposia: The Development of the Cerebral Cortex, 193,* 1–19.

Bolz, J., Kossel, A., & Bagnard, D. (1995). The specificity of interactions between the cortex and the thalamus. *Ciba Foundation Symposia: The Development of the Cerebral Cortex, 193,*173–191.

Cabeza, R., & Nyberg, L. (2000). Imaging cognition II: An empirical review of 275 PET and fMRI studies. *Journal of Cognitive Neurosciences, 12,* 1–47.

Case, R. (1992). The role of the frontal lobes in regulation of cognitive development. *Brain and Cognition, 20,* 51–73.

Casey, J. E., & Rourke, B. P. (1992). Disorders of somatosensory perception in children. In I. Rapin & S. J. Segalowitz (Eds.), *Handbook of neuropsychology: Vol. 6. Child neuropsychology* (pp. 477–494). Amsterdam: Elsevier.

Casey, J. E., & Rourke, B. P., (2002). Somatosensory perception in children. In S. J. Segalowitz & I. Rapin (Eds.), *Handbook of neuropsychology: Vol. 8. Child neuropsychology* (2nd ed., pp. 385–403). Amsterdam: Elsevier.

Casey, J. E., Rourke, B. P., & Picard, E. M. (1991). Syndrome of nonverbal learning disabilities: Age differences in neuropsychological, academic, and socioemotional functioning. *Development and Psychopathology, 3,* 329–345.

Cleaver, R. L., & Whitman, R. D. (1998). Right hemisphere, white-matter learning disabilities associated with depression in adolescent and young adult psychiatric population. *Journal of Nervous and Mental Disease, 186,* 561–565.

Damasio, A. R. (1990). Synchronous activation in multiple cortical regions: a mechanism for recall. *Seminars in Neuroscience, 2,* 287–296.

Damasio, A. R., & Anderson, S. W. (1993). The frontal lobes. In K. M. Heilman & E. Valenstein (Eds.), *Clinical neuropsychology* (3rd ed., pp. 409–460). New York: Oxford University Press.

Del Dotto, J. E., Fisk, J. L., McFadden, G. T., & Rourke, B. P. (1991). Developmental analysis of children/adolescents with nonverbal learning disabilities: Long-term impact on personality adjustment and patterns of adaptive functioning. In B. P. Rourke (Ed.), *Neuropsychological validation of learning disability subtypes* (pp. 293–308). New York: Guilford Press.

Denckla, M. B. (1983). The neuropsychology of social-emotional learning disabilities. *Archives of Neurology, 40*, 461–462.

Dietrich, R. B., & Bradley, W. G. (1988). Normal and abnormal white matter maturation. *Seminars in Ultrasound, CT, and MR, 9*, 192–200.

Drummond, C. R., Ahmad, S. A., & Rourke, B. P. (2005). Rules for the classification of younger children with nonverbal learning disabilities and basic phonological processing disabilities. *Archives of Clinical Neuropsychology, 20*, 171–182.

Fisher, N. J., & DeLuca, J. W. (1997). Verbal learning strategies of adolescents and adults with the syndrome of nonverbal learning disabilities. *Child Neuropsychology, 3*, 192–198.

Fletcher, J. M. (1989). Nonverbal learning disabilities and suicide: Classification leads to prevention. *Journal of Learning Disabilities, 22*, 176, 179.

Fotenos, A. F., Snyder, A. Z., Girton, L. E., Morris, J. C., & Buckner, R. L. (2005). Normative estimates of cross-sectional and longitudinal brain volume decline in aging and AD. *Neurology, 64*, 1032–1039.

Fuerst, D. R., & Rourke, B. P. (1993). Psychosocial functioning of children: Relations between personality subtypes and academic achievement. *Journal of Abnormal Child Psychology, 21*, 597–607.

Ge, Y., Grossman, R. I., Babb, J. S., Rabin, M. L., Mannon L. J., & Kolson, D. L. (2002a). Age-related total gray matter and white matter changes in normal adult brain. Part I: Volumetric MR imaging analysis. *American Journal of Neuroradiology, 23*, 1327–1333.

Ge, Y., Grossman, R. I., Babb, J. S., Rabin, M. L., Mannon L. J., & Kolson, D. L. (2002b). Age-related total gray matter and white matter changes in normal adult brain. Part II: Quantitative magnetization transfer ratio histogram analysis. *American Journal of Neuroradiology, 23*, 1334–1341.

Ghosh, A. (1995). Subplate neurons and the patterning of thalamocortical connections. *Ciba Foundation Symposia: The Development of the Cerebral Cortex, 193*, 150–172.

Grady, C. L., McIntosh, A. R., & Craik, F. I. M. (2003). Related differences in the functional connectivity of the hippocampus during memory. *Hippocampus, 13*, 572–586.

Greiffenstein, M. F., & Baker, W. J. (2002). Neuropsychological and psychosocial correlates of adult arithmetic deficiency. *Neuropsychology, 16*, 451–458.

Goldberg, E., & Costa, L. D. (1981). Hemisphere differences in the acquisition and use of descriptive systems. *Brain and Language, 14*, 144–173.

Gross-Tsur, V., Shalev, R. S., Manor, O., & Amir, N. (1995). Developmental right-hemisphere syndrome: Clinical spectrum of the nonverbal learning disability. *Journal of Learning Disabilities, 28*, 80–86.

Harnadek, M. C. S., & Rourke, B. P. (1994). Principal identifying features of the syndrome of nonverbal learning disabilities in children. *Journal of Learning Disabilities, 27*, 144–154.

Harnam, S., & O'Boyle, M. W. (2004). Interhemispheric interaction during global-local processing in mathematically gifted adolescents, average-ability youth, and college students. *Neuropsychology, 18*, 371–377.

Huttenlocher, P. R. (1984). Synapse elimination and plasticity in developing human cerebral cortex. *American Journal of Mental Deficiency, 88*, 488–496.

Huttenlocher, P. R. (1994). Synaptogenesis in human cerebral cortex. In G. Dawson & K. W. Fischer (Eds.), *Human behavior and the developing brain* (pp. 137–152). New York: Guilford Press.

Johnson, D. J., & Myklebust, H. R. (1967). *Learning disabilities: Educational principles and remedial approaches.* New York: Grune & Stratton.

Katz, L. C., & Shatz, C. J. (1996). Synaptic activity and the construction of cortical circuits. *Science, 274*, 1133–1138.

Kolb, B., & Fantie, B. (1989). Development of the child's brain and behavior. In C. Reynolds & E. Fletcher-Janzen (Eds.), *Handbook of clinical child neuropsychology.* New York: Plenum Press, pp. 17–39.

Kowalchuk, B., & King, J. D. (1989). Adult suicide versus coping with nonverbal learning disorder. *Journal of Learning Disabilities, 22*, 177–179.

Little, L. (2001). Peer victimization of children with Asperger spectrum disorders. *Journal of the American Academy of Child and Adolescent Psychiatry, 40*, 995–996.

Majovski, L. V. (1989). Higher cortical functions in children: A developmental perspective. In C. Reynolds & E. Fletcher-Janzen (Eds.), *Handbook of clinical child neuropsychology.* New York: Plenum Press, pp. 41–67.

McIntosh, A. R. (1999). Mapping cognition to the brain through neural interactions. *Memory, 7*, 523–548.

Mega, M. S., Cummings, J. L., Salloway, S., & Malloy, P. (1997). The limbic system: An anatomic, phylogenetic, and clinical perspective. *The Journal of Neuropsychiatry and Clinical Neurosciences, 9*, 315–330.

Molnár Z., Adams R., Goffinet, A. M., & Blakemore, C. (1998). The role of the first postmitotic cortical cells in the development of thalamocortical innervation in the *Reeler* mouse. *Journal of Neuroscience, 18*, 5746–5765.

Myklebust, H. R. (1975). Nonverbal learning disabilities: Assessment and intervention. In H. R. Myklebust (Ed.), *Progress in learning disabilities* (Vol. 3, pp. 85–121). New York: Grune & Stratton.

Njiokiktjien, C., de Rijke, W., & Jonkman, E. J. (2001). Children with nonverbal learning disabilities (NLD): Coherence values in the resting state may reflect hypofunctional long distance connections in the right hemisphere. *Human Physiology, 27*, 523–528.

O'Leary, D. D. S. (1989). Do cortical areas emerge from a protocortex? *Trends in Neuroscience, 12*, 400–406.

O'Leary D. D. S., & Koester S. E. (1993). Development of projection neuron types, axon pathways, and patterned connections of the mammalian cortex. *Neuron, 10*, 991–1006.

Patton, J. R., & Polloway, E. A. (1992) Learning disabilities: The challenges of adulthood. *Journal of Learning Disabilities, 7*, 410–415.

Pelletier, P. M, Ahmad, S., & Rourke, B. P. (2001). Nonverbal learning disabilities and basic phonological processing disorder: Rules of classification and a comparison of psychosocial subtypes. *Child Neuropsychology, 7*(2), 84–98.

Petti, V. L., Voelker, S. L, Shore, D. L., & Hayman-Abello, S. E. (2003). Perception of nonverbal emotion cues by children with nonverbal learning disabilities. *Journal of Developmental and Physical Disabilities, 15*, 23–36.

Piaget, J. P. (1954). *The construction of reality in the child*. New York: Basic Books.

Piaget, J. P., & Inhelder, B. (1969). *The psychology of the child*. London: Routledge & Kegan Paul.

Resnick, S. M., Pham, D. L., Kraut, M. A., Zonderman, A. B., & Davatzikos, C. (2003). Longitudinal magnetic resonance imaging studies of older adults: A shrinking brain. *The Journal of Neuroscience, 23*, 3295

Rourke, B. P. (1975). Brain-behavior relationships in children with learning disabilities. *American Psychologist, 30*, 911–920.

Rourke, B. P. (1978) Reading, spelling, arithmetic disabilities: A neuropsychologic perspective. In H. R. Myklebust (Ed.), *Progress in learning disabilities* (Vol. 4, pp. 97–120). New York: Grune & Stratton.

Rourke, B. P. (1982). Central processing deficiencies in children: Toward a developmental neuropsychological model. *Journal of Clinical Neuropsychology, 4*, 1–18.

Rourke, B. P. (1987). Syndrome of nonverbal learning disabilities: The final common pathway of white-matter disease/dysfunction? *The Clinical Neuropsychologist, 1*, 209–234.

Rourke, B. P. (1988). Socio-emotional disturbances of learning-disabled children. *Journal of Consulting and Clinical Psychology, 56*, 801–810.

Rourke, B. P. (1989). *Nonverbal learning disabilities: The syndrome and the model*. New York: Guilford Press.

Rourke, B. P. (1993). Arithmetic disabilities, specific and otherwise: A neuropsychological perspective. *Journal of Learning Disabilities, 26*, 214–226.

Rourke, B. P. (Ed.). (1995). *Syndrome of nonverbal learning disabilities: Neurodevelopmental manifestations*. New York: Guilford Press.

Rourke, B. P., & Finlayson, M. A. J. (1978). Neuropsychological significance of variations in patterns of academic performance: Verbal and visual-spatial abilities. *Journal of Abnormal Child Psychology, 6*, 121–133.

Rourke, B. P., & Fisk, J. L. (1992). Adult presentations of learning disabilities. In R. F. White (Ed.), *Clinical syndromes in adult neuropsychology: The practitioner's handbook* (pp. 451–473) Amsterdam: Elsevier.

Rourke, B. P., & Fuerst, D. R. (1991). *Learning disabilities and psychosocial functioning*. New York: Guilford Press.

Rourke, B. P., & Fuerst, D. R. (1992). Psychosocial dimensions of learning disability subtypes: Neuropsychological studies in the Windsor Laboratory. *School Psychology Review, 21*, 360–373.

Rourke, B. P., & Strang, J. D. (1978). Neuropsychological significance of variations in patterns of academic performance: Motor, psychomotor, and tactile-perceptual abilities. *Journal of Pediatric Psychology, 3*, 62–66.

Rourke, B. P., & Strang, J. D. (1983). Subtypes of reading and arithmetical disabilities. A neuropsychological analysis. In M. Rutter (Ed.), *Developmental neuropsychiatry* (pp. 473–488). New York: Guilford Press.

Rourke, B. P., & Tsatsanis, K. D. (1996). Syndrome of nonverbal learning disabilities: Psycholinguistic assets and deficits. *Topics in Language Disorders, 16*, 30–44.

Rourke, B. P., Young, G. C., & Leenaars, A. (1989). A childhood learning disability that predisposes those afflicted to adolescent and adult depression and suicide risk. *Journal of Learning Disabilities, 21,* 169–175.

Rourke, B. P., Young, G. C., Strang, J. D., & Russell, D. L. (1986). Adult outcomes of childhood central processing deficiencies. In I. Grant & K. M. Adams (Eds.), *Neuropsychological assessment of neuropsychiatric disorders* (pp. 244–267). New York: Oxford University Press.

Ruby, P., & Decety, J. (2004). How would you feel versus how do you think she would feel? A neuroimaging study of perspective-taking with social emotions. *Journal of Cognitive Neuroscience, 16,* 988–999.

Schoenemann, P. T., Sheehan, M. J., & Glotzer, L. D. (2005). Prefrontal white matter volume is disproportionately larger in humans than in other primates. *Nature Neuroscience, 8,* 242–252.

Schultz, R. T., Grelotti, D. J., Klin, A., Kleinman, J., Van der Gaag, C., Marois, R., et al. (2003). The role of the fusiform face area in social cognition: Implications for the pathobiology of autism. *Philosophical Transactions of the Royal Society, Series B, 358,* 415–427.

Sebeok, T. A. (1991). *A sign is just a sign.* Bloomington: Indiana University Press.

Spreen, O., & Haaf, R. G. (1986). Empirically derived learning disability subtypes: A replication attempt and longitudinal patterns over 15 years. *Journal of Learning Disabilities, 19,* 170–180.

Steriade, M., McCormick, D. A., & Sejnowski, T. J. (1993). Thalamocortical oscillations in the sleeping and aroused brain. *Science, 262,* 679–685.

Strang, J. D., & Rourke, B. P. (1983). Concept-formation/non-verbal reasoning abilities of children who exhibit specific academic problems with arithmetic. *Journal of Clinical Child Psychology, 12,* 33–39.

Strang, J. D., & Rourke, B. P. (1985a). Adaptive behavior of children who exhibit specific arithmetic disabilities and associated neuropsychological abilities and deficits. In B. P. Rourke (Ed.), *Neuropsychology of learning disabilities: Essentials of subtype analysis* (pp. 302–328). New York: Guilford Press.

Strang, J. D., & Rourke, B. P. (1985b). Arithmetic disability subtypes: The neuropsychological significance of specific arithmetic impairment in childhood. In B. P. Rourke (Ed.), *Neuropsychology of learning disabilities: Essentials of subtype analysis* (pp. 167–183). New York: Guilford Press.

Stuss, D. T. (1992). Biological and psychological development of executive functions. *Brain and Cognition, 20,* 8–23.

Thatcher, R. W. (1994). Cyclic cortical reorganization: Origins of human cognitive development. In G. Dawson & K. W. Fischer (Eds.), *Human behavior and the developing brain* (pp. 232–266). New York: Guilford Press.

Thatcher, R. W. (1997). Neuroimaging of cyclic cortical reorganization during human development. In R. W. Thatcher (Ed.), *Developmental neuroimaging: Mapping the development of brain and behavior* (pp. 91–106). San Diego: Academic Press.

Tranel, D., Hall, L. E., Olson, S., & Tranel, N. N. (1987). Evidence for a right hemisphere developmental learning disability. *Developmental Neuropsychology, 3,* 113–120.

Tsatsanis, K. D., Fuerst, D. R., & Rourke, B. P. (1997). Psychosocial dimensions of learning disabilities: External validation and relationship with age and academic functioning. *Journal of Learning Disabilities, 30,* 490–502.

Tsatsanis, K. D., & Rourke, B. P. (1995). Conclusions and future directions. In B. P. Rourke (Ed.), *Syndrome of nonverbal learning disabilities: Neurodevelopmental manifestations* (pp. 476–496). New York: Guilford Press.

Tulving, E., Markowitsch, H. J., Kapur, S., Habib, R., & Houle, S. (1994). Novelty encoding networks in the human brain: Positron emission tomography data. *NeuroReport, 5*, 2525–2528.

Vallabha, T. L. (2003). Perception of facial affect: A functional magnetic resonance imaging study of adolescents and adults with and without nonverbal learning disabilities. *Dissertation Abstracts International: Section B: Sciences & Engineering.* Doctoral dissertation: Florida Atlantic University.

Voeller, K. K. S. (1986). Right-hemisphere deficit syndrome in children. American *Journal of Psychiatry, 143*, 1004–1009.

Waldo, S. L., McIntosh, D. E., & Koller, J. R. (1999). Personality profiles of adults with verbal and nonverbal learning disabilities. *Journal of Psychoeducational Assessment, 17*, 196–206.

Weintraub, S., & Mesulam, M.-M. (1983). Developmental learning disabilities of the right hemisphere: Emotional, interpersonal, and cognitive components. *Archives of Neurology, 40*, 463–469.

Wolbers, T., Weiller, C., & Büchel, C. (2003). Contralateral coding of imagined body parts in the superior parietal lobe. *Cerebral Cortex, 13*, 392–399.

CHAPTER **8**

Disorders of Mathematics
Implications for Adult Functioning

FRANK KRUEGER and JORDAN GRAFMAN

Contents

In the normal school-age population, about 3 to 6% of children are diagnosed with development dyscalculia (Kosc, 1974; Shalev, Manor, & Gross-Tsur, 1993). To date, no single definition for DD has been found (Badian, 1983; Cohn, 1968; Gordon, 1992; Gross-Tsur, Manor, & Shalev, 1993, 1996; Guttmann, 1937; Hennschen, 1919; Kosc, 1974; Shalev, Auerbach, & Gross-Tsur, 1995; Shalev, Manor, Amir, Wertman-Elad, & Gross-Tsur, 1995; Shalev, Manor, Auerbach, & Gross-Tsur, 1998; Slade & Russell, 1971; Temple, 1992, 1997a; von Aster, 2000). The *Diagnostic and Statistical Manual of Mental Disorders* (4th ed., *DSM-IV*; American Psychiatric Association, 1994) and the *International Classifications of Diseases*, 10th revision (*ICD-10*; World Health Organization, 1992) agree in their definition of disorders of arithmetic skills, requiring that an individual's arithmetical abilities are substantially age-derived norms, intelligence, and education. But neither the *ICD-10* classification ("Specific disorder of arithmetic skills") nor the *DSM-IV* classification ("Mathematics disorder") defines or uses the term "developmental." Recent research so far seems to indicate that DD is a brain-based learning disorder governed by genetic influences and occurring in children of normal intelligence (Kosc, 1974).

Compared to other learning disorders such as dyslexia, DD has been relatively neglected by the scientific community. Having poor numerical skills is socially more acceptable than having poor language or literacy skills (O'Hare, Brown, & Aitken, 1991). As the prevalence between DD and dyslexia is similar, there is a need for more interdisciplinary study, leading to a deeper understanding of the cognitive architecture of number processing and the cerebral basis of arithmetic abilities in children with DD. Moreover, studies have shown that arithmetical accomplishment has a direct impact on the individual's perception of his or her social and intellectual capabilities and future professional and academic success (Fogelman, 1983; Levine, Lindsay, & Reed, 1992).

In this chapter, the clinical characteristics of DD are described, and its impact on education, employment, and psychological well-being for adult functioning is discussed. This chapter is organized into four sections: In the opening section, the developmental changes in basic arithmetic skills from infancy to old age are explained. The second section describes the diagnosis, prevalence, incidence, and etiology of DD. In the third section, an overview about models of calculation, neuropsychological profiles, and the cerebral basis of DD is given. The final section discusses the treatment and prognosis of DD and its impact on the education, employment, and psychological health of affected individuals. The long-term prognosis of DD is unknown because of a lack of literature on adults with DD. Since there are no longitudinal studies that follow DD from childhood over adolescence to adulthood, this review focuses on data collected from children with DD and from neuroimaging studies in normal adults as well.

Development of Arithmetic Skills and Manifestation of Developmental Dyscalculia (DD)

Development of Arithmetic Skills

Research in developmental and cognitive psychology provides strong evidence that humans and many other species are born with an intrinsic set of basic quantitative competencies. Generally speaking, number sense has its roots in evolution (Dehaene, 1997; Rocha & Massad, 2002). Apart from the famous hoax of "clever Hans" (the horse that was able to perform calculations), many animal species such as salamanders (Uller, Jaeger, Guidry, & Martin, 2003), dolphins (Kilian, Yaman, von Fersen, & Gunturkun, 2003), lions (McComb, Packer, & Pusey, 1994), and macaques (Brannon & Terrace, 2000; Hauser, Carey, & Hauser, 2000) are able to discriminate stimuli that differ in numerosity or show spontaneously untrained behavior by selecting the more numerous of two sets (Hauser et al., 2000; Hauser, Dehaene, Dehaene-Lambertz, & Patalano, 2002; Hauser, Tsao, Garcia, & Spelke, 2003; McComb et al., 1994; Uller et al., 2003). Strictly speaking, adult arithmetic skills have their roots in development; children show evidence of a biologically based numerical capacity to acquire arithmetic skills (Ginsburg, 1997). Unlike reading skills, basic quantitative concepts with an implicit understanding of numerosity, counting, ordinality, and simple arithmetic develop naturally without formal teaching (Ackerman & Dykman, 1993; Geary, 1995; Ginsburg, 1997). These biologically primary abilities are present as early as infancy (Ackerman & Dykman, 1993; Geary, 1995; Ginsburg, 1997).

Several behavioral studies using the method of habituation provide evidence that 4-day-old to 7-month-old infants can discriminate, specifically on the basis of their numerosity, visual sets of three to four objects varying in shape and size as well as bisyllabic from trisyllabic words with controlled phonemic content, duration, and speech rate (Antell & Keating, 1983; Feigenson, Carey, & Hauser, 2002a; Feigenson, Carey, & Spelke, 2002; Starkey, 1992; Starkey, Spelke, & Gelman, 1990; Wechsler-Clearfield & Mix, 1999; Xu, 2003). Five-month-old infants appear to be sensitive to increases (addition) and decreases (subtraction) in the quantity of small sets in a display (Wynn, 1992; Wynn, Bloom, & Chiang, 2002). Within the first year, 10- to 12-month-old infants exhibit knowledge of ordinality ("greater than" or "lesser than"; Cooper, 1984). For example, they understand that a set of two toys is more than a set of one toy but less than a set of three toys (Brannon, 2002; Strauss & Curtis, 1984). By the age of about 6 months, infants still using a preverbal system can count a small series of discrete actions (e.g., two or three; Sharon & Wynn, 1998; Wynn, 1996), and by 18 months they manage to count up to three or four physical objects (Starkey, 1992).

The acquisition of these basic quantitative abilities leads to biologically secondary abilities (Geary, 1995, 1996, 2000). Much like language, the complexity of this system develops gradually during the preschool years (Gelman, 1990; Gelman & Gallistel, 1978) and provides the fundamental structure for the comprehension of more complex numbers, counting, magnitude, and number transcoding during the preschool years (Gelman, 1990; Gelman & Gallistel, 1978; Siegel, 1982; Siegler & Robinson, 1982). Between 4 and 7 years of age, children begin to learn the formal count-ing words (e.g., one, two, three) and enhance their ability in understand-ing ordinal relationships, adding, and subtracting (Bryant, 1995; Geary, 1994) Four-year-old children can count up to four items, and about 1 year later they already are able to count up to 15 (Bryant, 1995). By the end of the preschool years, children reach a good—but not yet fully mature—comprehension of the concept of counting, which allows them to enumerate relatively large sets of objects and to add or subtract objects from these sets (Geary, 1994).

In primary school, children learn to master the counting system, to understand the base-10 structure of the Arabic number system, to trans-code numbers from one representation to another (e.g., Arabic 105 to verbal one hundred five), and to memorize basic addition (e.g., 6 to 2 + 4), subtraction, and multiplication facts to memory (Geary, 2000). By the age of 8, children start to write down three-digit numbers and to carry out elementary addition and subtraction exercises, and between 9 and 12 years of age they improve their calculation abilities, mastering multipli-cation and division (Dehaene, 1997; O'Hare, 1999; Shalev, Manor, Amir, & Gross-Tsur, 1993).

Basic quantitative abilities in adults have not been so extensively stud-ied as in children and adolescents. The result of those studies suggest that the best predictors of algebraic skills in adulthood are the degree to which these skills were mastered, and the frequency to which these skills were practiced, in primary and secondary school (Bahrick, 1993; Bahrick & Hall, 1991; Geary, Frensch, & Wiley, 1993; Geary et al., 1997). Without both distributed and frequent practicing, basic quantitative competen-cies steadily decrease once the individual leaves school (Bahrick, 1993). For example, a study by Bahrick and Hall (1991) revealed that individuals who attended one or two algebra courses in secondary school lost more than 50% of their basic algebraic skills by the age of 45 years. Those who attended mathematics courses beyond calculus showed, even at age 75 years, little loss of algebraic skills independent of scores on standard mathematics achievement tests.

Manifestation of Developmental Dyscalculia

DD usually manifests during the period of elementary school education. Some children have trouble understanding the number concept; others are unable to identify, read, or write the correct word to numbers; some fail to receive arithmetic table knowledge; and others never will manage calculus algorithms in addition, subtraction, multiplication, and division (Shalev & Gross-Tsur, 2001). Studies found that children in first grade show more deficits in immature skills such as retrieving basic arithmetic facts or computation of arithmetic exercises, whereas 9- to 10-year-old children have problems in retrieving overlearned arithmetic tables (e.g., 12 − 8 or 8 × 4; Geary, 1994). For children with DD, deficits in number facts knowledge build up to problems in procedural arithmetic knowledge to solve arithmetic problems. Typical indicators are inattention to arithmetic signs, use of the wrong signs, forgetting the "carryover," or misplacement of digits, which all are necessary for complex calculation (Gross-Tsur et al., 1996; Shalev, Manor, & Gross-Tsur, 1997).

Diagnosis, Prevalence, Incidence, and Etiology of Developmental Dyscalculia

Diagnosis

The diagnosis of DD for a child is given if there exists a significant discrepancy between intellectual potential and arithmetic achievement or there is a discrepancy of at least 2 years between chronologic grade and level of achievement (Hammill, 1990; Shalev, Manor, Amir et al., 1993). Standardized arithmetic tests are used for the assessment of arithmetic skills in children. For clinical diagnostics, the following tests can be applied: timed tests that emphasize achievement such as the arithmetic subtests of the Wide Range Achievement Test-Revised (WRAT-R) (Jastak & Wilkinson, 1984) and the Young's Group Mathematics Test (Young, 1971), or tests that assess number concepts and arithmetic procedures such as the Neuropsychological Test Battery for Number Processing and Calculation (NUCALC) (Deloche et al., 1995; Services, 2000; von Aster, Deloche, Dellatolas, & Meier, 1997) and validated for Switzerland (von Aster, 2001; von Aster et al., 1997), France (Deloche et al., 1995), and Greece (Koumoula et al., 2004); the KeyMath-R Test (Connolly, 1988); the Test of Early Mathematics Ability (TEMA-3) (Ginsburg & Baroody, 2003);

and the arithmetic test by Shalev et al. (Shalev, Manor, Amir et al., 1993; Shalev et al., 1998; Shalev et al., 2001).

Prevalence

The *DSM-IV* defines DD as a rare learning disability with a prevalence of 1% in the normal school-age population (American Psychiatric Association, 1994). However, population studies in the United States (Badian, 1983), England (Lewis, Hitch, & Walker, 1994), Germany (Haeusser, 1995; Hein, 1999; Klauer, 1992), Switzerland (Temple & Carney, 1993), Israel (Gross-Tsur et al., 1996), and India (Ramaa & Gowramma, 2002) demonstrated that the prevalence of DD across countries is relatively uniform and ranges form 3 to 6% (Kosc, 1974; Shalev, Manor, & Gross-Tsur, 1993), similar to that of developmental dyslexia and attention-deficit/hyperactivity disorder (ADHD) (Shalev, Auerbach, Manor, & Gross-Tsur, 2000). Unlike dyslexia or ADHD, the majority of the studies have shown that DD tends to affect both sexes equally (Lewis et al., 1994).

Incidence

DD is common in many neurological disorders, and in some it is the most frequently encountered learning disability (Gross-Tsur et al., 1993). It is the most frequently encountered learning disability in epilepsy (Seidenberg et al., 1986), children treated with radiation and cytotoxic therapies (Ochs et al., 1991), children with phenylketonuria who have been appropriately treated by diet (Pennington, 1991), and children who have been born preterm with low and very low birth weights (Anderson, Doyle, & Group, 2003; Johnson & Breslau, 2000). In addition, some genetic disorders such as Williams syndrome, fragile X syndrome (Gross-Tsur et al., 1993; Hagerman et al., 1992; Temple & Carney, 1993), or Turner syndrome (Temple & Carney, 1993) are known to lead to DD (Reiss, Abrams, Greenlaw, Freund, & Denckla, 1995). DD is more prevalent in girls with Turner syndrome, aneuploidies, epilepsy, and sex-chromosome abnormalities (Gross-Tsur et al., 1993), and boys with sex-chromosome aneuploidies are at increased risk for reading disabilities but not arithmetic disorders (Pennington, 1991). In addition, DD occurs in the context of other developmental cognitive disorders such as developmental dyslexia (Manor, Shalev, Joseph, & Gross-Tsur, 2001), developmental right-hemisphere disorder (Weintraub & Mesulam, 1983), developmental language disorder (Shalev, 1998), ADHD (Faraone et al., 1993; Manor et al., 2001; Shaywitz & Shaywitz, 1984), and Gerstmann's syndrome (Shalev, 1998; Shalev & Gross-Tsur, 1993). For instance, 26% of kindergarten children with developmental language disorder will manifest significantly impaired arithmetic skills (Manor et al., 2001), and over

20% of males with ADHD have DD (Ackerman & Dykman, 1993; Faraone et al., 1993).

Etiology

No consensus has been reached about the etiology of DD. Genetic predisposition and environmental causes are discussed as possible contributing factors (Shalev, 2004). Using a twin-study paradigm, Alarcon, DeFries, Light, and Pennington (1997) investigated the role of the genetics in children with DD, and demonstrated that monozygotic (12 times) and dizygotic (8 times) co-twins were more likely to have dyscalculia compared to the normal population. In their family study, Shalev et al. (2001) found that approximately half of all siblings of children with DD were also dyscalculic with a 5 to 10 times greater risk than for the normal population, highlighting the role of heredity in dyscalculia (Kosc, 1974). Since most arithmetic skills are taught in school, other researchers have hypothesized that environmental factors such as environmental deprivation (Broman, Bien, & Shaughness, 1985; Fergusson, Horwood, & Lawton, 1990), inadequate teaching methods (Ginsburg, 1997; Cummig & Elkins, 1999; Miller & Mercer, 1997), classroom diversity (Miller & Mercer, 1997), untested curricula (Miller & Mercer, 1997), and mathematical anxiety (Ashcraft, 1995) may cause mathematic disorders. Studies indicate that children with math anxiety, for example, perform poorly even on the most basic arithmetic exercises (Ashcraft, 1995), but psychological intervention significantly improves competence in arithmetic (Faust, Ashcraft, & Fleck, 1996). Although environmental factors have been considered in the etiology of DD, evidence so far indicates that DD as a learning disability is a *brain-based* disorder with a familial-genetic predisposition (Broman et al., 1985; Fergusson et al., 1990; Shalev & Gross-Tsur, 2001). The neuroanatomic architecture of arithmetic still has to be precisely described, although the use of human neuroimaging and electrophysiology is providing compelling information.

Neuropsychological Models and the Neuroanatomic Basis of Developmental Dyscalculia

Neuropsychological Models

In 1925, Henschen (1925) established the term "acalculia," the loss of previously acquired arithmetic skills, to define a specific neurocognitive deficit in a distinct and autonomous cortical network for arithmetic. Moreover, it was Berger (1926), who demonstrated that acalculia could also appear within the context of a general cognitive decline. Several years later,

Hecanen, Angelergues, and Houilliers (1961) subdivided dyscalculia into an impairment with three distinct neurobehavioral syndromes—agraphia and alexia for numbers, spatial dyscalculia, and anarithmetia—to which Benson and Denckla (1969) added "number paraphasia" as a fourth syndrome. In addition, Rourke (1993) assumed that dyscalculia also may appear secondary to visuospatial or verbal and auditory-perceptual dysfunctions. These and other general neuropsychological deficits have been claimed as an underlying factors of DD: deficits in poor working memory (Koontz & Berch, 1996; McLean & Hitch, 1999), in processing speed (Bull & Johnston, 1997), in inhibitory mechanisms (Bull & Scerif, 2001), or in developing long-term memory representations (Geary & Wiley, 1991). But Temple and Sherwood (2002) demonstrated that arithmetic fact retrieval is a specialized function on its own and not linked to short-term memory or other cognitive domains. Thus the evidence from research in neuropsychology and in developmental and cognitive psychology all show that arithmetic skills are inherent and present from infancy (Antell & Keating, 1983; Wynn, 1998).

Above, we argued that arithmetic processing is dependent on a specialized cognitive mechanism rather than simply being a by-product of general neuropsychological processes (Temple & Sherwood, 2002). Neuropsychological models suggest representational and format-specific modules, located in different areas of the left and right cerebral hemisphere, that are relevant for both normal arithmetic processing and dyscalculia (Deloche & Willmes, 2000; Ernst et al., 1994; McCloskey, Caramazza, & Basili, 1985). The models of McCloskey et al. (McCloskey, 1992; McCloskey et al., 1985) and Dehaene et al. ("triple-code" model; Chochon, Cohen, van de Moortele, & Dehaene, 1999; Dehaene, 1992; Dehaene, Dehaene-Lambertz, & Cohen, 1998) are the two most influential models.

The model of McCloskey et al. (McCloskey, 1992; McCloskey et al., 1985) divides the cognitive architecture of arithmetic functions into three main subsystems: comprehension of number, production of numbers, and calculation processing. The comprehension of a number subsystem represents quantity processing (comprehension of quantities), lexical processing (symbolic nature of numbers), and syntactic processing (digit order). The number-production subsystem includes reading, writing, and counting numbers; and the calculation-processing system includes memorizing numerical facts, comprehending operation symbols, and executing arithmetic exercises.

Based on its cognitive architecture, this model can explain isolated impairment in a specific domain of arithmetic, when other facets of arithmetic function remain intact (McCloskey, Aliminosa, & Macaruso, 1991; McCloskey et al., 1985). An extensive literature exists in brain-damaged adults that provide dissociations and double-dissociations in number processing and calculation, but only a few cases have been described in children with DD. For example, Temple (1989) reported a dissociation in an 11-year-old boy with DD who demonstrated an isolated impairment in lexical number processing. Although the boy showed age-expected normal reading and spelling skills, he was impaired in reading Arabic numbers or writing dictated Arabic numbers correctly. This finding supports the existence of independent modules for syntactical and lexical processing of Arabic as well as written and spoken numbers. Additional case reports in children with DD support the model of McCloskey et al. (1992) by demonstrating isolated impairments in retrieving arithmetic facts from memory and an inability to execute arithmetic procedures (Temple, 1994).

Although case studies provide important theoretical inside views into cognitive structures, such dissociations are rare (Landerl, Bevan, & Butterworth, 2004). For example, the study of Ashcraft, Yamashita, and Aram (1992) in children with numerical processing difficulties revealed no dissociation between procedural ability and arithmetic fact ability, and another group of children with "mathematics difficulties" were impaired in both arithmetic fact retrieval and written calculation (Ginsburg, 1997).

The triple-code model of Dehaene et al. (Cohen & Dehaene, 2000; Cohen, Dehaene, Chochon, Lehericy, & Naccache, 2000; Dehaene, 1992; Dehaene & Cohen, 1995) describes the underlying architecture of arithmetic processing in both cognitive and neuroanatomical terms. They conceive that the arithmetic neural network is composed of three distinct codes for number processing and calculation: the visual-Arabic code, the analog-magnitude code, and the auditory-verbal code. Abilities such as verbal (spoken or written) numeral input and output, counting procedures in addition and subtraction, and arithmetical fact retrieval for simple addition and multiplication facts relay on the auditory–verbal code. The use of magnitude comparison and approximation depends on the analog-magnitude code, which represents numbers as an analog locus on an internal number line. The visual-Arabic code mediates Arabic numeral input and output, parity judgments, and multidigit operations. All three modules are autonomous but interconnected and differentially activated based on particular needs of a given task (Dehaene, Molko, Cohen, & Wilson, 2004).

On the neuroanatomic level, the triple-code model proposes that relatively simple arithmetic operations involve the verbal module within the left hemisphere (inferior parietal lobule, superolateral temporal lobe, and the frontal lobe), whereas more complex arithmetic procedures and manipulation of internal quantity engage the magnitude module and visual module within both hemispheres (intraparietal sulcus; Cohen & Dehaene, 2000). Experimental data from case reports of patients with focal brain lesions and from functional magnetic resonance imaging (fMRI) and event-related brain potentials (ERPs) studies in normal individuals performing arithmetic support this model (Dehaene, 1992; Dehaene, Spelke, Pinel, Stanescu, & Tsivkin, 1999; Iguchi & Hashimoto, 2000; Kong, Wang, Shang, Yang, & Zhuang, 1999; Skrandies, Reik, & Kunze, 1999). For example, a case study carried out by Grafman et al. (Grafman, Passafiume, Faglioni, & Boller, 1982) described a patient with a lesion in the left hemisphere. This patient was no longer able to remember overlearned arithmetic facts, but his number magnitude knowledge was still intact.

Neuroanatomic Architecture of Arithmetic

Recent developments in human neuroimaging have improved the understanding of the functional anatomy of the calculation processes (Shekim & Dekirmenjian, 1978; Sokoloff, Mangold, Wechsler, Kenney, & Kety, 1955) and indicated that a reproducible cerebral set of prefrontal, premotor, and parietal areas is systematically engaged whenever humans are involved in performing arithmetic procedures (Appolonio et al., 1994; Burbaud et al., 1999, 2000; Butterworth, 1999; Cappa & Wallesch, 1994; Chochon et al., 1999; Cohen et al., 2000; Dehaene & Cohen, 1997; Dehaene et al., 2004; Dehaene et al., 1999; Dehaene et al., 1996; Delazer et al., 2003; Dhamala, Pagnoni, Wiesenfeld, & Berns, 2002; Eger, Sterzer, Russ, Giraud, & Kleinschmidt, 2003; Fulbright et al., 2000; Gruber, Indefrey, Steinmetz, & Kleinschmidt, 2001; Hanakawa, Honda, Okada, Fukuyama, & Shibasaki, 2003; Jahanshahi, Dirnberger, Fuller, & Frith, 2000; Kawashima et al., 2004; Kazui, Kitagaki, & Mori, 2000; Lee, 2000; Menon, Rivera, White, Glover, & Reiss, 2000; Molko et al., 2003; Pesenti, Thioux, Seron, & De Volder, 2000; Pesenti et al., 2001; Pinel et al., 1999; Rickard et al., 2000; Rivera, Menon, White, Glaser, & Reiss, 2002; Rueckert et al., 1996; Sakurai, Momose, Iwata, Sasaki, & Kanazawa, 1996; Simon, Mangin, Cohen, Le Bihan, & Dehaene, 2002; Stanescu-Cosson et al., 2000; Zago et al., 2001; Zorzi, Priftis, & Umilta, 2002).

A meta-analysis by Dehaene, Piazza, Pinel, and Cohen (2003) revealed three parietal circuits—the horizontal segment of the bilateral intraparietal sulcus (HIPS), the left angular gyrus (AG), and the bilateral posterior superior parietal lobule (PSPL)—that play a dominant role in most neuroimaging studies of number processing besides the frequently activated areas of the precentral sulcus and inferior frontal gyrus. There exists a functional dissociation between these parietal regions. The PSPL is activated in several tasks requiring number manipulation: number comparison (Pesenti et al., 2000; Pinel, Dehaene, Riviere, & Le Bihan, 2001), approximation (Dehaene et al., 1999), subtraction of two digits (Lee, 2000), counting (Piazza, Mechelli, Butterworth, & Price, 2002), and carrying out two operations instead of one (Menon et al., 2000). However, the PSPL is not specific to the number domain; it rather supports attentional orientation on the mental number line, just like on any other spatial dimension (Dehaene et al., 2003). Language-dependent calculation showed activation in the left AG (Chochon et al., 1999; Dehaene et al., 1999; Fulbright et al., 2000; Gruber et al., 2001; Zago et al., 2001). Tasks such as nonrote quantity manipulation revealed activation in the HIPS (Dehaene & Cohen, 1997; Simon et al., 2002; Stanescu-Cosson et al., 2000). In more detailed fMRI studies, simply presenting numbers without explicit magnitude processing (Stanescu-Cosson et al., 2000) activated systematically the HIPS bilaterally (Chochon et al., 1999; Dehaene et al., 1999; Eger et al., 2003; Gruber et al., 2001; Naccache, Blandin, & Dehaene, 2002; Naccache & Dehaene, 2001; Pesenti et al., 2000; Pinel et al., 2001; Stanescu-Cosson et al., 2000). Another fMRI study investigated the effects of training on calculation problems (Delazer et al., 2004). Interestingly, the comparison between untrained and trained problems revealed a shift in activation from frontal to more parietal regions. This result is in accordance with the findings of an ERP study that investigated training effects in simple multiplication (Pauli et al., 1994), and also discovered a shift from frontocentral to centroparietal regions in the course of training. In addition, the study demonstrated a shift within the parietal lobe from the intraparietal sulcus in untrained problems to the AG in trained problems. Other regions such as the prefrontal cortex appear to take a more supportive role in the calculation process by sequential ordering of operations, control over their execution, inhibiting verbal responses, and so forth (Dehaene et al., 2004).

Cerebral Basis of Developmental Dyscalculia

Little is known about the neuropsychological profiles and the cerebral basis of DD. Recent neuroimaging studies using specific subpopulations of dyscalculic individuals have demonstrated both anatomical and functional deficits of parietal brain regions, particularly the intraparietal sulcus (IPS). In one study, a young adult with DD with no structural brain abnormalities underwent proton magnetic resonance spectroscopy (MRS) (Levy, Reis, & Grafman, 1999). The results pointed toward a focal wedge-shaped spectroscopic defect in the left parietotemporal brain region near the AG. These finding strengthen the assumption that DD is associated to subtle left parietal lobe architectural abnormalities. In another study, an adolescent with dyscalculia caused by a right temporal hemorrhage at infancy underwent neuropsychological evaluation and fMRI (Levin et al., 1996). Functional MRI activation during his impaired calculation performance was observed predominantly in the left intact hemisphere involving the frontal and posterior parietal regions at some distance from the IPS. The interhemispheric transfer of visuospatial skills normally committed to the right parietal area to the left parietal region probably caused the intra-hemispheric reorganization of the patient's calculation abilities by restricting their development.

Morocz et al. (2003) performed fMRI in four young adults with DD. While performing arithmetic exercises, activations were found in the right intra-parietal sulcus and the left middle frontal gyrus in comparison to bilateral activation in the IPS and minimal activation in the left frontal gyrus in controls. An fMRI study in two sets of twins (only one co-twin had dyscalculia) revealed larger areas of activations in the frontal, precentral, and dorsal parietal in the dyscalculic twins. However, their co-twins showed activation patterns predominantly in the left frontal and parietotemporal areas as seen in normal children (Kucian, Loenneker, Dietrich, et al., 2003).

Using voxel-based morphometry, Isaacs, Edmonds, Lucas, and Gadian (2001) studied differences in gray matter of two groups of adolescent children who had been born preterm at 30 weeks gestation or less and differed in the presence or absence of a dyscalculia. The authors demonstrated that children without dyscalculia had more gray matter in the left parietal lobe than children with dyscalculia. As reported above, the same area is activated when normal subjects perform arithmetic procedures. Finally, Molko et al. (2003) investigated the interaction between the abnormal development of numerical representation in Turner syndrome and the development of the IPS. Using structural imaging, the authors observed an abnormal length, depth, and sulcal geometry of the *right* intrapari-etal sulcus. In addition, fMRI during exact and approximate calculation revealed abnormally reduced activation in the right intraparietal sulcus as a function of number size. Two other fMRI studies with genetic conditions linked with dyscalculia, velocardiofacial syndrome (Eliez et al., 2001) and fragile X (Rivera et al., 2002), observed similar hypoactivation in a broader parieto-prefrontal network.

Case descriptions provide important neuroanatomic clues about the topography of DD, although generalizations from singular cases should be drawn with caution (Hartje, Dahmen, & Zeumer, 1982; Kiefer & Dehaene, 1997; Levin et al., 1996; Lucchelli & De Renzi, 1993; Ojemann, 1974; Takayama, Sugishita, Akiguchi, & Kimura, 1994; Weintraub & Mesulam, 1983). In addition, neuroimaging studies in DD are contaminated by the heterogeneity of arithmetic difficulties (e.g., long-term retrieval of arithmetic facts, slow processing speed, and poor working memory) and its frequent association with other developmental disorders (Dehaene & Cohen, 1995). But the data collected so far from normal individuals during arithmetic processing and the pathologic findings in patients with dyscalculia suggest that neuropsychological profile of DD favored a neural arithmetic network involving parietal lobes of both hemispheres of the brain. Children and young adults with dyscalculia are not able to activate regions that are normally engaged in arithmetic processing because of dysfunctions or lesions. When they perform arithmetic procedures, they tend to recruit other brain regions to compensate for these deficits and apply alternate, but usually inefficient, cognitive strategies. In turn, clinicians find different profiles of impairment in learning to manipulate numbers and in acquiring arithmetic procedures are caused by the extent and severity of the injury to the extended neural network dedicated to arithmetic and number processes (Hirohata & Taketani, 1987). Subtypes of DD have been defined to relate these specific cognitive impairments to maturational dysfunctions of distinct regions of the developmental brain (Geary, 1994; Kosc, 1974; Rourke, 1989; Temple, 1997b). Other subtypes of DD have been linked to either right-hemisphere or left-hemisphere dysfunctions (Geary, 1994).

Treatment and Prognosis of Developmental Dyscalculia

Treatment

Children with dyscalculia are exposed to the same risks as in other learning disorders (e.g., emotional instability, school dropout, and persistence of the disability; Shalev et al., 1998). For this reason, treatment of DD should include both improvement of general study skills ("classroom survival skills") and remediation of specific arithmetic problems (Lamminmaki et al., 1997; Snyder & Bambara, 1997). Intervention programs that ensure the acquisition of survival skills—preparation for school lessons, meeting arranged deadlines, demonstrating appropriate school behavior, following directions, and completing homework assignments—revealed long-term beneficial effects for all students, in particular for those with learning disabilities (Snyder & Bambara, 1997).

Several educational training programs have been developed to remediate specific arithmetic problems in children: a transcoding number program (Sullivan, Macaruso, & Sokol, 1996), a planning skills program (Naglieri & Gottling, 1997; Naglieri & Johnson, 2000), and a program to verbalize arithmetic concepts, procedures, and operations under teacher's feedback (Naglieri & Gottling, 1997). The interactive Mathematics Strategy Training for Educational Remediation (MASTER) program helps children with dyscalculia learn the concepts of multiplication and division by providing help with number concepts and problem-solving strategies (Naglieri & Gottling, 1997; Naglieri & Johnson, 2000). For children who understand number concepts but have difficulty in computation, the training of automatic recall for number facts is helpful (Bull & Scerif, 2001; Cummig &

Elkins, 1999). Since the intuitive knowledge of numbers and procedures is crucial in remediation of dyscalculia, children should be instructed in basic number concepts rather than rote memorization of number facts (Gersten & Chard, 1999; Neibert, 1985). For example, to teach and internalize the "number line" concept a thermometer as a representational system could be used.

Another way to help dyscalculic children is the application of assistive technology, such as mathematical software for learning number facts or interactive video programs for acquiring math concepts and problem-solving skills and for providing instructions about mathematical thinking (von Aster et al., 1997). In addition, other assistance tools such as calculators, talking clocks, calendars, or time-management programs can be implemented for daily life (Shalev, 2004). Under the assumption that a developmental change in comprehension of arithmetic concepts will occur, a "time-out" period as an alternative method can be also considered. If there is no improvement in basic arithmetic skills, as it is often observed in dyscalculic teenagers, theses interventions may help the child develop functional concepts such as reading calendars, dealing with money, and writing checks that are very important for daily life (Shalev et al., 2000).

Prognosis

There is basically nothing known about how DD manifests itself when the child develops into an adult. A priori, there is no reason to expect any dramatic change in the DD profile of childhood in the mature adult who had DD. Well-planned longitudinal studies would provide us with objective information about the natural history of DD (Faraone et al., 1993). Yet even short-term follow-up of children with DD is very limited, and strictly speaking, there are no longitudinal studies that follow DD from childhood over adolescence to adulthood. However, some knowledge can be extracted from the experience with other developmental disabilities such as dyslexia. Experimental data from longitudinal studies of dyslexia indicate that dyslexia is not merely an expression of a developmental lag but a long-lasting problem (Dahmen, Hartje, Bussing, & Sturm, 1982; Francis, Shaywitz, Stuebing, Shaywitz, & Fletscher, 1996; Rutter, Tizard, Yule, Graham, & Whitmore, 1976). For example, by applying a longitudinal paradigm, Shaywitz, Escobar, Shaywitz, Fletcher, and Makuch (1992) studied children in first, third, and fifth grades. There was a good outcome for 80% of children who were originally identified as being dyslexic in first grade. But children recognized as dyslexic in fifth grade did not improve in their reading abilities when reexamined in ninth grade (Schonhaut & Satz, 1983). Another study conducted by Satz, Taylor, Friel, and Fletscher (1978) supports the findings of the former study. Moreover, another dyslexia study investigated 9-year-old boys and provided evidence that more than half of the boys continued to be dyslexic over the next 5 years (Rutter et al., 1976). Only 6% of children that improved accomplished age-level reading abilities. Interestingly, boys demonstrated greater improvement for their arithmetic skills compared to their reading skills. Other longitudinal studies in dyslexia illustrated that the outcome might vary with the social-economic status of the child: from substantially poorer for a child from a low social-economic group to almost normal for a child from a high social-economic group (Rawson, 1968).

Children with DD will probably have a similar outcome (Shalev et al., 2000). They demonstrated considerable improvement in their counting ability between the first and second grades (Geary, 1994). In another study, kindergarten children with developmental language disorders and arithmetic disorders showed improvement over a similar 2-year period (Fazio, 1996). In a longitudinal study, Shalev et al. (2000) monitored 10- to 11-year-old male and female children diagnosed with DD and reexamined the same children 3 years later (Schonhaut & Satz, 1983; Shalev et al., 1998). While in eighth grade, the arithmetic performance of these children was still poor: 95% of them scored in the lowest quartile of their school class and almost half of them still met the criteria for DD (Shalev et al., 1998).

The long-term prognosis of DD is unknown. Current empirical data indicates that DD perseveres, at least for the short-term, in about half of affected children (Shalev & Gross-Tsur, 2001). In addition, the long-term consequences for children with DD are yet unknown, and the impact of DD on their education, employment, and psychological well-being has still to be determined (Shalev et al., 2000; Shalev & Gross-Tsur, 2001). However, studies in industrialized societies showed that quantitative competencies influence employability, productivity, and salary (Bahrick & Hall, 1991; Bishop, 1989; Rivera-Batiz, 1992). Paglin and Rufolo (1990) found a linear relation between quantitative demands for professions and salaries for theses same professions: the more math-intensive the profession, the higher the entry-level and subsequent salaries. Any psychological, neurological, or genetic impairment that withheld the comprehension of basic quantitative competencies results in both individual and social costs (Bishop, 1989; Rivera-Batiz, 1992).

Outlook

The evidence revealed in this chapter leads to the conclusion that DD is still a relatively underinvestigated learning disability. Empirical data indicates that arithmetic-related brain regions are under partial genetic control and play a significant role in early numerical development. Their disorganization or damage probably leads to a lifelong impairment in arithmetic.

Although evidence supports a biologically determined cerebral basis for DD, further research is necessary for more precise knowledge about how these regions mediate normal arithmetic processing.

Future investigations that focus on the neurobiological basis of DD would be helpful for its prognosis and treatment. For example, family genetic studies of DD could help to identify the genes that are associated with DD, eventually leading to corrective "replacement" therapies. The implementation of neuroimaging techniques has already enriched our understanding of the neurobiology of normal arithmetic function (Dehaene et al., 1999) and will be undoubtedly helpful in the future to study the cerebral development of individuals with DD from infancy to adolescence (Dehaene-Lambertz & Dehaene, 1994; Giedd et al., 1999). The challenge for the future is to understand the interactions of the pertinent brain regions and to use this knowledge to pave the way for brain-oriented intervention studies (Shalev, Manor, Amir et al., 1993), to guide rehabilitation attempts (Girelli & Seron, 2001), and to monitor progress with neuroimaging techniques in dyscalculia (Delazer et al., 2003).

The impact of the environment on DD needs further systematic investigation. Although the origin of DD might not be environmentally based, the environment might act as a moderator influencing the persistence and severity of DD, or children with DD might develop attendant behavior problems due their home and educational environment (Shalev et al., 2000). Future longitudinal studies from early childhood until adulthood will provide a powerful tool to study the organism-environmental transactions in the individual and general developmental course of dyscalculia. All these new approaches will encourage new ways of academic and social integration of affected individuals and contribute to improved terminology and a better outcome of DD in the future.

References

Ackerman, P. T., & Dykman, R. A. (1993). Gender and reading disability. *Journal of Learning Disabilities, 26*(8), 498.

Alarcon, M., DeFries, J. C., Light, J. G., & Pennington, B. F. (1997). A twin study of mathematics disability. *Journal of Learning Disabilities, 30*(6), 617–623.

American Psychiatric Association. (1994). *Diagnostic and statistical manual of mental disorders* (4th ed.). Washington, DC: Author.

Anderson, P., Doyle, L. W., & Group, V. I. C. S. (2003). Neurobehavioral outcome of school-age children born extremely low birth weight or preterm in the 1990s. *JAMA, Journal of the American Medical Association, 289*, 3264–3272.

Antell, S. E., & Keating, D. P. (1983). Perception of numerical invariance in neonates. *Child Development, 54*(3), 695–701.

Appolonio, I., Rueckert, L., Partiot, A., Litvan, I., Sorenson, J., Le Bihan, D., et al. (1994). Functional magnetic resonance imaging (fMRI) of calculation ability in normal volunteers. *Neurology, 44*(suppl.2), 262.

Ashcraft, M. H. (1995). Cognitive psychology and simple arithmetic: A review and summary of new directions. *Mathematical Cognition, 2*, 26–62.

Ashcraft, M. H., Yamashita, T. S., & Aram, D. M. (1992). Mathematics performance in left and right brain-lesioned children and adolescents. *Brain and Cognition, 19*(2), 208–252.

Badian, N. A. (1983). Dyscalculia and nonverbal disorders of learning. In H. R. Myklebust (Ed.), *Progress in learning disabilities* (pp. 235–264). New York: Grune & Stratton.

Bahrick, H. P. (1993). Extending the life span of knowledge. In L. A. Penner, G. M. Batsche, H. M. Knoff, & D. L. Nelson (Eds.), *The challenge in mathematics and science education: Psychology's response.* Washington, DC: American Psychological Association.

Bahrick, H. P., & Hall, L. K. (1991). Lifetime maintenance of high school mathematics content. *Journal of Experimental Psychology: General, 120*, 22–33.

Berger, H. (1926). Ueber Rechenstoerungen bei Herderkrankungen des Grosshirns. *Archiv fur Psychiatrie und Nervenkrankheiten, 78*, 238–263.

Beson, D. F., & Denckla, M. B. (1969). Verbal paraphasia as a source of calculation disturbance. *Archives of Neurology, 21*, 96–102.

Bishop, J. H. (1989). Is the test score decline responsible for the productivity growth decline? *American Economic Review, 79*, 178–197.

Brannon, E. M. (2002). The development of ordinal numerical knowledge in infancy. *Cognition, 83*(3), 223–240.

Brannon, E. M., & Terrace, H. S. (2000). Representation of the numerosities 1–9 by rhesus macaques (*Macaca mulatta*). *Journal of Experimental Psychology: Animal Behavioral Processes, 26*(1), 31–49.

Broman, S., Bien, E., & Shaughness, P. (1985). *Low-achieving children: The first seven years.* Hillsdale, NJ: Lawrence Erlbaum.

Bryant, P. (1995). Children and arithmetic. *Journal of Child Psychology and Psychiatry, 36*(1), 3–32.

Bull, R., & Johnston, R. S. (1997). Children's arithmetical difficulties: Contributions from processing speed, item identification, and short-term memory. *Journal of Experimental Child Psychology, 65*(1), 1–24.

Bull, R., & Scerif, G. (2001). Executive functioning as a predictor of children's mathematics ability: Inhibition, switching, and working memory. *Developmental Neuropsychology, 19*(3), 273–293.

Burbaud, P., Camus, O., Guehl, D., Bioulac, B., Caille, J. M., & Allard, M. (1999). A functional magnetic resonance imaging study of mental subtraction in human subjects. *Neuroscience Letters, 273*(3), 195–199.

Burbaud, P., Camus, O., Guehl, D., Bioulac, B., Caille, J., & Allard, M. (2000). Influence of cognitive strategies on the pattern of cortical activation during mental subtraction: A functional imaging study in human subjects. *Neuroscience Letters, 287*(1), 76–80.

Butterworth, B. (1999). A head for figures. *Science, 284*(5416), 928–929.

Cappa, S., & Wallesch, C. W. (1994). Subcortical lesions and cognitive deficits. In A. Kertesz (Ed.), *Localisation and neuroimaging in neuropsychology.* San Diego: Academic Press.

Chochon, F., Cohen, L., van de Moortele, P. F., & Dehaene, S. (1999). Differential contributions of the left and right inferior parietal lobules to number processing. *Journal of Cognitive Neuroscience, 11*(6), 617–630.

Cohen, L., & Dehaene, S. (2000). Calculating without reading: Unsuspected residual abilities in pure alexia. *Cognitive Neuropsychology, 17*(6), 563–583.

Cohen, L., Dehaene, S., Chochon, F., Lehericy, S., & Naccache, L. (2000). Language and calculation within the parietal lobe: A combined cognitive, anatomical and fMRI study. *Neuropsychologia, 38*(10), 1426–1440.

Cohn, R. (1968). Developmental dyscalculia. *Pediatric Clinics of North America, 15*(3), 651–668.

Connolly, A. J. (1988). *KeyMath-R.* Circle Pines, MN: American Guidance Service.

Cooper, R. G. (1984). Early number development: Discovering number space with addition and subtraction. In C. Sophian (Ed.), *Originals of cognitive skills* (pp. 157–192). Hillsdale, NJ: Lawrence Erlbaum.

Cummig, J. J., & Elkins, J. (1999). Lack of automaticity in the basic addition facts as a characteristic of arithmetic learning problems and instructional needs. *Mathematical Cognition, 1*, 3–34.

Dahmen, W., Hartje, W., Bussing, A., & Sturm, W. (1982). Disorders of calculation in aphasic patients—spatial and verbal components. *Neuropsychologia, 20*(2), 145–153.

Dehaene, S. (1992). Varieties of numerical abilities. *Cognition, 44*(1–2), 1–42.

Dehaene, S. (1997). *The number sense.* Oxford: Oxford University Press.

Dehaene, S., & Cohen, L. (1995). Towards an anatomical and functional model of number processing. *Mathematical Cognition, 1*(1), 83–120.

Dehaene, S., & Cohen, L. (1997). Cerebral pathways for calculation: Double dissociation between rote verbal and quantitative knowledge of arithmetic. *Cortex, 33*(2), 219–250.

Dehaene, S., Dehaene-Lambertz, G., & Cohen, L. (1998). Abstract representations of numbers in the animal and human brain. *Trends in Neuroscience, 21*(8), 355–361.

Dehaene, S., Molko, N., Cohen, L., & Wilson, A. J. (2004). Arithmetic and the brain. *Current Opinions in Neurobiology, 14*(2), 218–224.

Dehaene, S., Piazza, M., Pinel, P., & Cohen, L. (2003). Three parietal circuits for number processing. *Cognitive Neuropsychology, 20*(3/4/5/6), 487–506.

Dehaene, S., Spelke, E., Pinel, P., Stanescu, R., & Tsivkin, S. (1999). Sources of mathematical thinking: Behavioral and brain-imaging evidence. *Science, 284*(5416), 970–974.

Dehaene, S., Tzourio, N., Frak, V., Raynaud, L., Cohen, L., Mehler, J., et al. (1996). Cerebral activations during number multiplication and comparison: A PET study. *Neuropsychologia, 34*(11), 1097–1106.

Dehaene-Lambertz, G., & Dehaene, S. (1994). Speed and cerebral correlates of syllable discrimination in infants. *Nature, 370*(6487), 292–295.

Delazer, M., Domahs, F., Bartha, L., Brenneis, C., Lochy, A., Trieb, T., et al. (2003). Learning complex arithmetic—an fMRI study. *Brain Research Cognitive, 18*(1), 76–88.

Delazer, M., Domahs, F., Lochy, A., Bartha, L., Brenneis, C., & Trieb, T. (2004). The acquisition of arithmetic knowledge—an FMRI study. *Cortex, 40*(1), 166–167.

Deloche, G., von Aster, M., Dellatolas, G., Gaillard, F., Tieche, C., & Azema, D. (1995). Traitement des nombres et calcul en CE 1 et CE 2, quelques donneés et principes d'élaboration d'une batterie. *Approche Neuropsychologique Apprentissages chez l'Enfant, 230,* 42–51.

Deloche, G., & Willmes, K. (2000). Cognitive neuropsychological models of adult calculation and number processing: The role of the surface format of numbers. *European Child and Adolescent Psychiatry, 9*(suppl 2), II27–40.

Dhamala, M., Pagnoni, G., Wiesenfeld, K., & Berns, G. S. (2002). Measurements of brain activity complexity for varying mental loads. *Physical Review E, 65*(4, Pt 1), 041917.

Eger, E., Sterzer, P., Russ, M. O., Giraud, A. L., & Kleinschmidt, A. (2003). A supramodal number representation in human intraparietal cortex. *Neuron, 37*(4), 719–725.

Eliez, S., Blasey, C. M., Menon, V., White, C. D., Schmitt, J. E., & Reiss, A. L. (2001). Functional brain imaging study of mathematical reasoning abilities in velocardiofacial syndrome (de122q11.2). *Genetics Medicine, 3*(1), 49–55.

Ernst, M., Liebenauer, L. L., King, A. C., Fitzgerald, G. A., Cohen, R. M., & Zametkin, A. J. (1994). Reduced brain metabolism in hyperactive girls. *Journal of the American Academy of Child and Adolescent Psychiatry, 33*(6), 858–868.

Faraone, S. V., Biederman, J., Lehman, B. K., Spencer, T., Norman, D., Seidman, L. J., et al. (1993). Intellectual performance and school failure in children with attention-deficit/hyperactivity disorder and in their siblings. *Journal of Abnormal Psychology, 102*(4), 616–623.

Faust, M. W., Ashcraft, M. H., & Fleck, D. E. (1996). Mathematics anxiety effects in simple and complex addition. *Mathematical Cognition, 2,* 25–62.

Fazio, B. B. (1996). Mathematical abilities of children with specific language impairment: A 2-year follow-up. *Journal of Speech and Hearing Research, 39*(4), 839–849.

Feigenson, L., Carey, S., & Hauser, M. (2002a). The representations underlying infants' choice of more: Object files versus analog magnitudes. *Psychological Science, 13*(2), 150–156.

Feigenson, L., Carey, S., & Spelke, E. (2002b). Infant's discriminations of numbers vs. continuous extent. *Cognitive Psychology, 44,* 33–66.

Fergusson, D. M., Horwood, L. J., & Lawton, J. M. (1990). Vulnerability to childhood problems and family social background. *Journal of Child Psychology and Psychiatry, 31*(7), 1145–1160.

Fogelman, K. (1983). *Growing up in Great Britain.* London: Macmillan.

Francis, D. J., Shaywitz, S. E., Stuebing, K. K., Shaywitz, B. A., & Fletscher, J. M. (1996). Developmental lag versus deficit models of reading disability: A longitudinal and individual growth curves analysis. *Journal of Educational Psychology, 88,* 3–17.

Fulbright, R. K., Molfese, D. L., Stevens, A. A., Skudlarski, P., Lacadie, C. M., & Gore, J. C. (2000). Cerebral activation during multiplication: A functional MR imaging study of number processing. *American Journal of Neuroradiology, 21*(6), 1048–1054.

Geary, D. C. (1994). Mathematical disabilities. In D. C. Geary (Ed.), *Children's mathematical development* (pp. 155–187). Washington, DC: American Psychiatric Association.

Geary, D. C. (1995). Reflections of evolution and culture in children's cognition; Implications for mathematical development and instruction. *American Psychology, 50*(1), 24–37.

Geary, D. C. (1996). International differences in mathematical achievement: Their nature, causes, and consequences. *Current Directions in Psychological Science, 5,* 133–137.

Geary, D. C. (2000). From infancy to adulthood: The development of numerical abilities. *European Child and Adolescent Psychiatry, 9*(suppl 2), II11–16.

Geary, D. C., Frensch, P. A., & Wiley, J. G. (1993). Simple and complex mental subtraction: Strategy choice and speed-of-processing differences in younger and older adults. *Psychology of Aging, 8*(2), 242–256.

Geary, D. C., Hamson, C. O., Chen, G. P., Liu, F., Hoard, M. K., & Salthouse, T. A. (1997). Computational and reasoning abilities in arithmetic: Cross-generational change in China and the United States. *Psychonomic Bulletin & Review, 4,* 425–130.

Geary, D. C., & Wiley, J. G. (1991). Cognitive addition: Strategy choice and speed-of-processing differences in young and elderly adults. *Psychology of Aging, 6*(3), 474–483.

Gelman, R. (1990). First principles organize attention to and learning about relevant data: Number and animate-inanimate distinctions as examples. *Cognitive Science, 14,* 79–106.

Gelman, R., & Gallistel, C. R. (1978). *The Child's Understanding of Numbers.* Cambridge, MA: Harvard University Press.

Gersten, R., & Chard, D. (1999). Number sense: Rethinking arithmetic instruction for students with mathematical disabilities. *Journal of Special Education, 33,* 18–28.

Giedd, J. N., Blumenthal, J., Jefferies, N. O., Castellanos, F. X., Liu, H., Zijdenbos, A., et al. (1999). Cerebral cortical gray matter changes during childhood and adolescence: A longitudinal MRI study. *Nature Neuroscience, 10,* 861–863.

Ginsburg, H. P. (1997). Mathematics learning disabilities: A view from developmental psychology. *Journal of Learning Disabilities, 30*(1), 20–33.

Ginsburg, H. P., & Baroody, A. J. (2003). *Test of early mathematics ability (TEMA-3).* Austin, TX: Pro-Ed.

Girelli, L., & Seron, X. (2001). Rehabilitation of number processing and calculation skills. *Aphasiology, 15,* 695–712.

Gordon, N. (1992). Children with developmental dyscalculia. *Developmental Medicine and Child Neurology, 34*(5), 459–463.

Grafman, J., Passafiume, D., Faglioni, P., & Boller, F. (1982). Calculation disturbances in adults with focal hemispheric damage. *Cortex, 18*(1), 37–49.

Gross-Tsur, V., Manor, O., & Shalev, R. S. (1993). Developmental dyscalculia, gender, and the brain. *Archives of Diseases in Childhood, 68*(4), 510–512.

Gross-Tsur, V., Manor, O., & Shalev, R. S. (1996). Developmental dyscalculia: Prevalence and demographic features. *Developmental Medicine and Child Neurology, 38*(1), 25–33.

Gruber, O., Indefrey, P., Steinmetz, H., & Kleinschmidt, A. (2001). Dissociating neural correlates of cognitive components in mental calculation. *Cerebral Cortex, 11*(4), 350–359.

Guttmann, E. (1937). Congenital arithmetic disability and acalculia (Henschen). *British Journal of Medical Psychology, 16,* 16–35.

Haeusser, O. (1995). *Untersuchungen zur Haeufigkeit von isolierten und kombinierten Rechenstoerungen in einer repraesentierten Stichprobe von Schuelern 3. Klassen.* Dissertation thesis, Charite Medical School, Humboldt University Berlin.

Hagerman, R. J., Jackson, C., Amiri, K., Silverman, A. C., O'Connor, R., & Sobesky, W. (1992). Girls with fragile X syndrome: Physical and neuro-cognitive status and outcome. *Pediatrics, 89*(3), 395–400.

Hammill, D. D. (1990). On defining learning disabilities: An emerging consensus. *Journal of Learning Disabilities, 23*, 74–84.

Hanakawa, T., Honda, M., Okada, T., Fukuyama, H., & Shibasaki, H. (2003). Differential activity in the premotor cortex subdivisions in humans during mental calculation and verbal rehearsal tasks: A functional magnetic resonance imaging study. *Neuroscience Letters, 347*(3), 199–201.

Hartje, W., Dahmen, W., & Zeumer, H. (1982). Spezielle Schreib-und Rechenstoerungen bei drei Patienten nach Laesion im linken parieto-okzipitalen Uebergangsbereich. *Nervenarzt, 53*(3), 159–163.

Hauser, M. D., Carey, S., & Hauser, L. B. (2000). Spontaneous number representation in semi-free-ranging rhesus monkeys. *Proceedings of the Royal Society of London, Series B, Biological Sciences, 267*(1445), 829–833.

Hauser, M. D., Dehaene, S., Dehaene-Lambertz, G., & Patalano, A. L. (2002). Spontaneous number discrimination of multi-format auditory stimuli in cotton-top tamarins (*Saguinus oedipus*). *Cognition, 86*(2), B23–32.

Hauser, M. D., Tsao, F., Garcia, P., & Spelke, E. S. (2003). Evolutionary foundations of number: Spontaneous representation of numerical magnitudes by cotton-top tamarins. *Proceedings of the Royal Society of London, Series B, Biological Sciences, 270*(1523), 1441–1446.

Hecanen, H., Angelergues, R., & Houilliers, S. (1961). Les variétés cliniques des acalculies au cours des lésions rolandiques: Approche statistique du problème. *Revue Neurologique (Paris), 105*, 85–103.

Hein, J. (1999). *The specific disorder of arithmetical skills.* Dissertation thesis, Charite Medical School, Humboldt University, Berlin.

Hennschen, S. E. (1919). Ueber Sprach-, Musik- und Rechenmechanismen und ihre Lokalisationen im Grosshirn. *Zeitschrift fuer die Gesamte Neurologie und Psychatrie, 52*, 273–298.

Heuschen, S. E. (1925). Clinical and anatomical contributions in brain pathology. *Archives of Neurological Psychiatry, 13*, 226–249.

Hirohata, S., & Taketani, T. (1987). A serial study of changes in intrathecal immunoglobulin synthesis in a patient with central nervous system systemic lupus erythematosus. *Journal of Rheumatology, 14*(5), 1055–1057.

Iguchi, Y., & Hashimoto, I. (2000). Sequential information processing during a mental arithmetic is reflected in the time course of event-related brain potentials. *Clinical Neurophysiology, 111*(2), 204–213.

Isaacs, E. B., Edmonds, C. J., Lucas, A., & Gadian, D. G. (2001). Calculation difficulties in children of very low birth weight: A neural correlate. *Brain, 124*(Pt 9), 1701–1707.

Jahanshahi, M., Dirnberger, G., Fuller, R., & Frith, C. D. (2000). The role of the dorsolateral prefrontal cortex in random number generation: A study with positron emission tomography. *Neuroimage, 12*(6), 713–725.

Jastak, S., & Wilkinson, G. S. (1984). *Wide-range achievement test-revised: Administration manual*. Wilmington, DE: Jastak Associates.

Johnson, E. O., & Breslau, N. (2000). Increased risk of learning disabilities in low birth-weight boys at age 11 years. *Biological Psychiatry, 47*, 490–500.

Kawashima, R., Taira, M., Okita, K., Inoue, K., Tajima, N., Yoshida, H., et al. (2004). A functional MRI study of simple arithmetic: A comparison between children and adults. *Brain Research Cognitive, 18*(3), 227–233.

Kazui, H., Kitagaki, H., & Mori, E. (2000). Cortical activation during retrieval of arithmetical facts and actual calculation: A functional magnetic resonance imaging study. *Psychiatry and Clinical Neurosciences, 54*(4), 479–485.

Kiefer, M., & Dehaene, S. (1997). The time course of parietal activation in single-digit multiplication: Evidence from event-related potentials. *Mathematical Cognition, 3*, 1–30.

Kilian, A., Yaman, S., von Fersen, L., & Gunturkun, O. (2003). A bottlenose dolphin discriminates visual stimuli differing in numerosity. *Learning Behaviors, 31*(2), 133–142.

Klauer, K. J. (1992). In Mathematik mehr leistungsschwache Maedchen, im Lesen und Rechtschreiben mehr leistungsschwache Jungen? *Zeitschrift fur Entwicklungspsychologie und Paedagogische Psychologie, 26*, 48–65.

Kong, J., Wang, Y., Shang, H., Yang, X., & Zhuang, D. (1999). Brain potentials during mental arithmetic: Effects of problem difficulty on event-related brain potentials. *Neuroscience Letters, 260*(3), 169–172.

Koontz, K. L., & Berch, D. B. (1996). Identifying simple numerical stimuli: Processing inefficiencies exhibited by arithmetic learning disabled children. *Mathematical Cognition, 2*, 1–23.

Kosc, L. (1974). Developmental dyscalculia. *Journal of Learning Disabilities, 7*, 46–59.

Koumoula, A., Tsironi, V., Stamouli, V., Bardani, I., Siapati, S., Annika, G., et al. (2004). An epidemiological study of number processing and mental calculation in Greek schoolchildren. *Journal of Learning Disabilities, 37*(5), 377–388.

Kucian, K., Loenneker, T., Dietrich, T., et al. (2003). Development of cerebral pathways for calculations: A fMRI study in children and adults. *Neuroimage, 19*, 2.

Lamminmaki, T., Ahonen, T., Todd de Barra, H., Tolvanen, A., Michelsson, K., & Lyytinen, H. (1997). Two-year group treatment for children with learning difficulties: Assessing effects of treatment duration and pretreatment characteristics. *Journal of Learning Disabilities, 30*(4), 354–364.

Landerl, K., Bevan, A., & Butterworth, B. (2004). Developmental dyscalculia and basic numerical capacities: A study of 8–9-year-old students. *Cognition, 93*(2), 99–125.

Lee, K. M. (2000). Cortical areas differentially involved in multiplication and subtraction: A functional magnetic resonance imaging study and correlation with a case of selective acalculia. *Annals of Neurology, 48*(4), 657–661.

Levin, H. S., Scheller, J., Rickard, T., Grafman, J., Martinkowski, K., Winslow, M., et al. (1996). Dyscalculia and dyslexia after right hemisphere injury in infancy. *Archives of Neurology, 53*(1), 88–96.

Levine, M. D., Lindsay, R. L., & Reed, M. S. (1992). The wrath of math: Deficiencies of mathematical mastery in the school child. *Paediatric Clinics of North America, 39*, 525–536.

Levy, L. M., Reis, I. L., & Grafman, J. (1999). Metabolic abnormalities detected by 1H-MRS in dyscalculia and dysgraphia. *Neurology, 53*(3), 639–641.

Lewis, C., Hitch, G. J., & Walker, P. (1994). The prevalence of specific arithmetic difficulties and specific reading difficulties in 9- to 10-year-old boys and girls. *Journal of Child Psychology and Psychiatry, 35*(2), 283–292.

Lucchelli, F., & De Renzi, E. (1993). Primary dyscalculia after a medial frontal lesion of the left hemisphere. *Journal of Neurology and Neurosurgical Psychiatry, 56*(3), 304–307.

Manor, O., Shalev, R. S., Joseph, A., & Gross-Tsur, V. (2001). Arithmetic skills in kindergarten children with developmental language disorders. *European Journal of Paediatric Neurology, 5*(2), 71–77.

McCloskey, M. (1992). Cognitive mechanisms in numerical processing: Evidence from acquired dyscalculia. *Cognition, 44*(1–2), 107–157.

McCloskey, M., Aliminosa, D., & Macaruso, P. (1991). Theory-based assessment of acquired dyscalculia. *Brain and Cognition, 17*(2), 285–308.

McCloskey, M., Caramazza, A., & Basili, A. (1985). Cognitive mechanisms in number processing and calculation: Evidence from dyscalculia. *Brain and Cognition, 4*(2), 171–196.

McComb, K., Packer, C., & Pusey, A. (1994). Roaring and numerical assessment in contests between groups of female lions, *Panthera leo*. *Animal Behaviour, 47*, 379–387.

McLean, J. F., & Hitch, G. J. (1999). Working memory impairments in children with specific arithmetic learning difficulties. *Journal of Experimental Child Psychology, 74*(3), 240–260.

Menon, V., Rivera, S. M., White, C. D., Glover, G. H., & Reiss, A. L. (2000). Dissociating prefrontal and parietal cortex activation during arithmetic processing. *Neuroimage, 12*(4), 357–365.

Miller, S. P., & Mercer, C. D. (1997). Educational aspects of mathematics disabilities. *Journal of Learning Disabilities, 30*(1), 47–56.

Molko, N., Cachia, A., Riviere, D., Mangin, J. F., Bruandet, M., Le Bihan, D., et al. (2003). Functional and structural alterations of the intraparietal sulcus in a developmental dyscalculia of genetic origin. *Neuron, 40*(4), 847–858.

Morocz, I. A., Gross-Tsur, V., von Aster, M., et al. (2003). Functional magnetic resonance imaging in dyscalculia: Preliminary observations. *Annals of Neurology, 54*(7), 145.

Naccache, L., Blandin, E., & Dehaene, S. (2002). Unconscious masked priming depends on temporal attention. *Psychological Science, 13*(5), 416–424.

Naccache, L., & Dehaene, S. (2001). The priming method: Imaging unconscious repetition priming reveals an abstract representation of number in the parietal lobes. *Cerebral Cortex, 11*(10), 966–974.

Naglieri, J. A., & Gottling, S. H. (1997). Mathematics instruction and PASS cognitive processes: An intervention study. *Journal of Learning Disabilities, 30*(5), 513–520.

Naglieri, J. A., & Johnson, D. (2000). Effectiveness of a cognitive strategy intervention in improving arithmetic computation based on the PASS theory. *Journal of Learning Disabilities, 33*(6), 591–597.

Neibert, M. (1985). Ten is the key. *Academie des Ther, 20*, 593–598.

Ochs, J., Mulhern, R., Fairclough, D., Parvey, L., Whitaker, J., Ch'ien, L., et al. (1991). Comparison of neuropsychologic functioning and clinical indicators of neurotoxicity in long-term survivors of childhood leukemia given cranial radiation or parenteral methotrexate: A prospective study. *Journal of Clinical Oncology, 9*(1), 145–151.

O'Hare, A. E. (1999). Dysgraphia and dyscalculia. In K. Whitmore, H. Hart, & G. Willems (Eds.), *Clinics in developmental medicine* (Vol. 145, pp. 96–118). London: Mac Keith Press.

O'Hare, A. E., Brown, J. K., & Aitken, K. (1991). Dyscalculia in children. *Developmental Medicine and Child Neurology, 33*(4), 356–361.

Ojemann, G. A. (1974). Mental arithmetic during human thalamic stimulation. *Neuropsychologia, 12*(1), 1–10.

Paglin, M., & Rufolo, A. M. (1990). Heterogeneous human capital, occupational choice, and male-female earnings differences. *Journal of Labor Economics, 8*, 123–144.

Pauli, P., Lutzenberger, W., Rau, H., Birbaumer, N., Rickard, T. C., Yaroush, R. A., et al. (1994). Brain potentials during mental arithmetic: Effects of extensive practice and problem difficulty. *Brain Research Cognitive, 2*(1), 21–29.

Pennington, B. F. (1991). Genetics of learning disabilities. *Seminars in Neurology, 11*(1), 28–34.

Pesenti, M., Thioux, M., Seron, X., & De Volder, A. (2000). Neuroanatomical substrates of Arabic number processing, numerical comparison, and simple addition: A PET study. *Journal of Cognitive Neuroscience, 12*(3), 461–479.

Pesenti, M., Zago, L., Crivello, F., Mellet, E., Samson, D., Duroux, B., et al. (2001). Mental calculation in a prodigy is sustained by right prefrontal and medial temporal areas. *Nature Neuroscience, 4*(1), 103–107.

Piazza, M., Mechelli, A., Butterworth, B., & Price, C. J. (2002). Are substitution and counting implemented as separate or functionally overlapping processes? *Neuroimage, 15*, 435–446.

Pinel, P., Dehaene, S., Riviere, D., & Le Bihan, D. (2001). Modulation of parietal activation by semantic distance in a number comparison task. *Neuroimage, 14*(5), 1013–1026.

Pinel, P., Le Clec, H. G., van de Moortele, P. F., Naccache, L., Le Bihan, D., & Dehaene, S. (1999). Event-related fMRI analysis of the cerebral circuit for number comparison. *NeuroReport, 10*(7), 1473–1479.

Ramaa, S., & Gowramma, I. P. (2002). A systematic procedure for identifying and classifying children with dyscalculia among primary school children in India. *Dyslexia, 8*(2), 67–85.

Rawson, M. (1968). *Developmental language disability: Adult accomplishments of dyslexic boys.* Baltimore, MD: Johns Hopkins University Press.

Reiss, A. L., Abrams, M. T., Greenlaw, R., Freund, L., & Denckla, M. B. (1995). Neurodevelopmental effects of the FMR-1 full mutation in humans. *Nature Medicine, 1*(2), 159–167.

Rickard, T. C., Romero, S. G., Basso, G., Wharton, C., Flitman, S., & Grafman, J. (2000). The calculating brain: An fMRI study. *Neuropsychologia, 38*(3), 325–335.

Rivera, S. M., Menon, V., White, C. D., Glaser, B., & Reiss, A. L. (2002). Functional brain activation during arithmetic processing in females with fragile X syndrome is related to FMR1 protein expression. *Human Brain Mapping, 16*(4), 206–218.

Rivera-Batiz, F. L. (1992). Quantitative literacy and the likelihood of employment among young adults in the United States. *Journal of Human Resources, 27,* 313–328.

Rocha, A. F., & Massad, E. (2002). Evolving arithmetical knowledge in a distributed intelligent processing system. *Advances in Logic, Artificial Intelligence and Robotics, 85,* 68–74.

Rourke, B. P. (1989). *Nonverbal learning disabilities: The syndrome and the model.* London: Guilford Press.

Rourke, B. P. (1993). Arithmetic disabilities, specific and otherwise: A neuropsychological perspective. *Journal of Learning Disabilities, 26,* 214–226.

Rueckert, L., Lange, N., Partiot, A., Appollonio, I., Litvan, I., Le Bihan, D., et al. (1996). Visualizing cortical activation during mental calculation with functional MRI. *Neuroimage, 3*(2), 97–103.

Rutter, M., Tizard, J., Yule, W., Graham, P., & Whitmore, K. (1976). Research report: Isle of Wight Studies, 1964–1974. *Psychology and Medicine, 6*(2), 313–332.

Sakurai, Y., Momose, T., Iwata, M., Sasaki, Y., & Kanazawa, I. (1996). Activation of prefrontal and posterior superior temporal areas in visual calculation. *Journal of Neurological Science, 139*(1), 89–94.

Satz, P., Taylor, H. G., Friel, J., & Fletscher, J. M. (1978). Some developmental and predictive precursors of reading disabilities: A 6-year follow-up. In A. Beuton & D. Pearl (Eds.), *Dyslexia: An appraisal of current knowledge.* New York: Oxford University Press.

Schonhaut, S., & Satz, P. (1983). Prognosis for children with learning disability: A review of follow-up studies. In M. Rutter (Ed.), *Developmental neuropsychology* (pp. 542–563). New York: Guildford Press.

Seidenberg, M., Beck, N., Geisser, M., Giordani, B., Sackellares, J. C., Berent, S., et al. (1986). Academic achievement of children with epilepsy. *Epilepsia, 27*(6), 753–759.

Services, S. T. (2000). *Neuropsychological test battery for number processing and calculation in children.* Frankfurt: Swets & Zeitlinger B.V. Lisse.

Shalev, R. S. (1998). Developmental dyscalculia. In M. J. Perat (Ed.), *New developments in child neurology* (pp. 635–641). Bologna: Munduzzi Editore.

Shalev, R. S. (2004). Developmental dyscalculia. *Journal of Child Neurology, 19*(10), 765–771.

Shalev, R. S., Auerbach, J., & Gross-Tsur, V. (1995). Developmental dyscalculia behavioral and attentional aspects: A research note. *Journal of Child Psychology and Psychiatry, 36*(7), 1261–1268.

Shalev, R. S., Auerbach, J., Manor, O., & Gross-Tsur, V. (2000). Developmental dyscalculia: Prevalence and prognosis. *European Child and Adolescent Psychiatry, 9*(suppl 2), II58–64.

Shalev, R. S., & Gross-Tsur, V. (1993). Developmental dyscalculia and medical assessment. *Journal of Learning Disabilities, 26*(2), 134–137.

Shalev, R. S., & Gross-Tsur, V. (2001). Developmental dyscalculia. *Pediatric Neurology, 24*(5), 337–342.

216 • Frank Krueger and Jordan Grafman

Shalev, R. S., Manor, O., Amir, N., & Gross-Tsur, V. (1993). The acquisition of arithmetic in normal children: Assessment by a cognitive model of dyscalculia. *Developmental Medicine and Child Neurology, 35*(7), 593–601.

Shalev, R. S., Manor, O., Amir, N., Wertman-Elad, R., & Gross-Tsur, V. (1995). Developmental dyscalculia and brain laterality. *Cortex, 31*(2), 357–365.

Shalev, R. S., Manor, O., Auerbach, J., & Gross-Tsur, V. (1998). Persistence of developmental dyscalculia: What counts? Results from a 3-year prospective follow-up study. *Journal of Pediatrics, 133*(3), 358–362.

Shalev, R. S., Manor, O., & Gross-Tsur, V. (1993). Normal acquisition of arithmetic skills: Assessment by a cognitive model. *Developmental Medicine and Child Neurology, 35*, 593–601.

Shalev, R. S., Manor, O., & Gross-Tsur, V. (1997). Neuropsychological aspects of developmental dyscalculia. *Mathematical Cognition, 33*, 105–120.

Shalev, R. S., Manor, O., Kerem, B., Ayali, M., Badichi, N., Friedlander, Y., et al. (2001). Developmental dyscalculia is a familial learning disability. *Journal of Learning Disabilities, 34*(1), 59–65.

Sharon, T., & Wynn, K. (1998). Individuation of actions from continuous motion. *Psychological Science, 9*, 357–362.

Shaywitz, S. E., Escobar, M. D., Shaywitz, B. A., Fletcher, J. M., & Makuch, R. (1992). Evidence that dyslexia may represent the lower tail of a normal distribution of reading ability. *New England Journal of Medicine, 326*(3), 145–150.

Shaywitz, S. E., & Shaywitz, B. A. (1984). Diagnosis and management of attention deficit disorder: A pediatric perspective. *Pediatric Clinics of North America, 31*(2), 429–457.

Shekim, W. O., & Dekirmenjian, H. (1978). Catecholamine metabolites in non-hyperactive boys with arithmetic learning disability: A pilot study. *American Journal of Psychiatry, 135*(4), 490–491.

Siegel, L. S. (1982). The development of quantity concepts: perceptual and linguistic factors. In C. J. Brainerd (Ed.), *Children's logical and mathematic cognition: Progress in cognitive development research.* New York: Springer.

Siegler, R. S., & Robinson, M. (1982). The development of numerical understandings. In H. W. Reese & L. P. Lipsitt (Eds.), *Advances in child development and behavior.* New York: Academic Press.

Simon, O., Mangin, J. F., Cohen, L., Le Bihan, D., & Dehaene, S. (2002). Topographical layout of hand, eye, calculation, and language-related areas in the human parietal lobe. *Neuron, 33*(3), 475–487.

Skrandies, W., Reik, P., & Kunze, C. (1999). Topography of evoked brain activity during mental arithmetic and language tasks: Sex differences. *Neuropsychologia, 37*(4), 421–430.

Slade, P. D., & Russell, G. F. (1971). Developmental dyscalculia: A brief report on four cases. *Psychology and Medicine, 1*(4), 292–298.

Snyder, M. C., & Bambara, L. M. (1997). Teaching secondary students with learning disabilities to self-manage classroom survival skills. *Journal of Learning Disabilities, 30*(5), 534–543.

Sokoloff, L., Mangold, R., Wechsler, R. L., Kenney, C., & Kety, S. S. (1955). The effect of mental arithmetic on cerebral circulation and metabolism. *Journal of Clinical Investigation, 34*(7, Part 1), 1101–1108.

Stanescu-Cosson, R., Pinel, P., van De Moortele, P. F., Le Bihan, D., Cohen, L., & Dehaene, S. (2000). Understanding dissociations in dyscalculia: A brain imaging study of the impact of number size on the cerebral networks for exact and approximate calculation. *Brain, 123* (Pt 11), 2240–2255.

Starkey, P. (1992). The early development of numerical reasoning. *Cognition, 43*(93–126).

Starkey, P., Spelke, E. S., & Gelman, R. (1990). Numerical abstraction by human infants. *Cognition, 36*, 97–127.

Strauss, M., & Curtis, L. E. (1984). Development of numerical concepts in infancy. In C. Sophian (Ed.), *Origins of cognitive skills: The eighteenth Carnegie symposium on cognition.* Hillsdale, NJ: Lawrence Erlbaum.

Sullivan, K. S., Macaruso, P., & Sokol, S. M. (1996). Remediation of Arabic numeral processing in a case of developmental dyscalculia. *Neuropsychol Rehabilitation, 6*, 27–53.

Takayama, Y., Sugishita, M., Akiguchi, I., & Kimura, J. (1994). Isolated acalculia due to left parietal lesion. *Archives of Neurology, 51*(3), 286–291.

Temple, C. M. (1989). Digit dyslexia: A category-specific disorder in developmental dyscalculia. *Cognitive Neuropsychology, 6*, 93–116.

Temple, C. M. (1992). Developmental dyscalculia. In S. J. Segalowitz & I. Rapin (Eds.), *Handbook of Neuropsychology: Vol. 6. Child Psychology* (pp. 211–222). Amsterdam: Elsevier Science.

Temple, C. M. (1994). The cognitive neuropsychology of the development dyscalculia. *Current Psychology of Cognition (CPC), 13*, 351–370.

Temple, C. M. (1997a). Cognitive neuropsychology and its application to children. *Journal of Child Psychology and Psychiatry, 38*(1), 27–52.

Temple, C. M. (1997b). *Developmental cognitive neuropsychology.* East Sussex: Psychology Press.

Temple, C. M., & Carney, R. A. (1993). Intellectual functioning of children with Turner syndrome: A comparison of behavioural phenotypes. *Developmental Medicine and Child Neurology, 35*(8), 691–698.

Temple, C. M., & Sherwood, S. (2002). Representation and retrieval of arithmetical facts: Developmental difficulties. *Quarterly Journal of Experimental Psychology A, 55*(3), 733–752.

Uller, C., Jaeger, R., Guidry, G., & Martin, C. (2003). Salamanders (*Plethodon cinereus*) go for more: Rudiments of number in an amphibian. *Animal Cognition, 6*(2), 105–112.

von Aster, M. (2000). Developmental cognitive neuropsychology of number processing and calculation: Varieties of developmental dyscalculia. *European Child and Adolescent Psychiatry, 9*(suppl 2), II41–57.

von Aster, M. (2001). *ZAREKL—Neuropsychologische Testbatterie fuer Zahlenverarbeitung und Rechnen bei Kindern.* Lisse, Netherlands: Swets Test Service.

von Aster, M., Deloche, G., Dellatolas, G., & Meier, M. (1997). Zahlenverarbeitung und Rechnen bei Schulkindern der 2. und 3. Klassenstufe. Eine vergleichende Studie franzoesischsprachiger und deutschsprachiger Kinder. *Zeitschrift fur Entwicklungspsychol und Paedagogische Psychologie, 29*, 141–166.

Wechsler-Clearfield, M., & Mix, K. S. (1999). Number versus contour length in infants' discrimination of small visual sets. *Psychological Science, 10*, 408–411.

Weintraub, S., & Mesulam, M. M. (1983). Developmental learning disabilities of the right hemisphere: Emotional, interpersonal, and cognitive components. *Archives of Neurology, 40*(8), 463–468.

World Health Organization. (1992). *The ICD-10 classification of mental and behavioral disorders: Clinical description and diagnostic guideline.* Geneva: Author.

Wynn, K. (1992). Addition and subtraction by human infants. *Nature, 358*(6389), 749–750.

Wynn, K. (1996). Infants' individuation and enumeration of actions. *Psychological Science, 7,* 164–169.

Wynn, K. (1998). Psychological foundations of number: Numerical competence in human infants. *Trends in Cognitive Science, 2,* 296–303.

Wynn, K., Bloom, P., & Chiang, W. C. (2002). Enumeration of collective entities by 5-month-old infants. *Cognition, 83*(3), B55–62.

Xu, F. (2003). Numerosity discrimination in infants: Evidence for two systems of representations. *Cognition, 89*(1), B15–25.

Young, D. (1971). *Group mathematics test.* Sevenoaks, England: Hodder & Stoughton.

Zago, L., Pesenti, M., Mellet, E., Crivello, F., Mazoyer, B., & Tzourio-Mazoyer, N. (2001). Neural correlates of simple and complex mental calculation. *Neuroimage, 13*(2), 314–327.

Zorzi, M., Priftis, K., & Umilta, C. (2002). Brain damage: Neglect disrupts the mental number line. *Nature, 417*(6885), 138–139.

CHAPTER 9

Executive Functioning and Self-Regulation in Young Adults

Implications for Neurodevelopmental Learning Disorders

LORRAINE E. WOLF and EDITH KAPLAN

Contents

Self-determination and control of one's actions are perhaps *the* adult hallmarks of normal human development. Young children intuit this when they assert that "you are not the boss of me," as they yearn for greater autonomy. This attitude changes sequentially into the rebellion of the teenager and the independent stance of the young adult moving towards college and career, as they become the "chief executive officers" of their own lives. The biological and psychological mechanisms underlying these fundamental skills remain a central mystery of neuroscience and neuropsychology. The effort to define and identify the brain components and processes underlying this perhaps ultimate higher brain function is certainly one of the great challenges of these fields and thus generates great excitement and controversy.

The salient feature of this cognitive and behavioral control is the capacity to direct one's thinking and action towards achieving future goals. In the field of neuropsychology, definitions of control center usually relate in some fashion to the useful concept of "executive function" (EF). The *American Heritage Dictionary* (2000) defines executive as:

> 1. A person or group having administrative or managerial authority in an organization. 2. The chief officer of a government, state, or political division. 3. The branch of government charged with putting into effect a country's laws and the administering of its functions.

Thus, common synonymous terms invoked when discussing executive functioning include the "conductor" (Brown, 2006) or "supervisor" (Norman & Shallice, 1986; Shallice & Burgess, 1996). As we will explore later, these psychological entities are commonly believed to reside in the frontal lobes of the brain and represent the "command and control function of the prefrontal cortex" (Powell & Voeller, 2004).

The term "executive function" is broadly defined and often used as shorthand for a complex set of behaviors, thought to be unique to human cognition, that depend on the intact function of many centers of the brain. This construct of an overarching managing agent has a long tradition and much appeal from a scientific and commonsense perspective. Many models of this construct have emerged, each with its own terms but all attempting to describe the operation of an aspect of the brain that takes control over behavior under novel conditions and that monitors, detects, and corrects errors in ongoing behavior. Further, as these structural and functional systems mature over the life span, individuals come to rely on these processes to manage the complex tasks of adult life (see Wolf & Wasserstein, 2001). Clearly, the developmental disorders that compromise this system may have profound implications for the educational outcome and adaptive function of the individual.

Despite the large body of EF literature, there is one critical aspect that is almost entirely left out of the classical neuropsychological conceptualization of command and control. Although newer models discuss motivation and regulation of affect, the dimension of personal choice as a subcomponent of motivation is often overlooked. We believe this missing element is the key to understanding how executive dysfunction degrades the learning experience. We thus introduce the concept of "self-regulated learning" (SRL) as a model linking the classic definitions of EF with other regulatory functions critical to academic success.

In this chapter, we review some of the common relevant definitions and terminology and discuss alternative conceptual views. We discuss cognition and motivation as separable subcomponents of an overall regulatory system, and we briefly review the development and functional anatomy of cortical regions relevant to this dichotomy. As the focus of this book is on developmental learning disorders, we do not separately discuss acquired disorders but instead concentrate on understanding and assessing students who have difficulties in self-regulation as part of a neurodevelopmental disorder (see Rey-Casserly and Bernstein, Chapter 14, this volume, for a discussion of some acquired conditions). We therefore conclude that any assessment should always proceed with the understanding that executive dysfunction involves much more than problems with cognition.

Thus, we argue that clear distinctions must be drawn between the cognitive components of EF and the regulatory components of motivation and affect if we are to better understand how the system operates smoothly and how developmental disorders may affect overall self-regulation. We suggest that, in the academic learning environment in particular, an integrated self-regulatory system reflects the interaction of these two parallel systems. We shall argue below that we should keep these two systems distinct when discussing the overall regulatory framework. It has become clear that these separable functions indeed reside in different functional brain systems. In order to better understand this, we turn to a brief discussion of the neuroanatomical regions and the development of regulatory control.

Brain Regions

EF depends on the intact function of many centers of the brain, yet it is most closely associated with the frontal lobes. While the frontal lobes (particularly the prefrontal cortex) have traditionally been considered the "seat" of EF (Luria, 1966; Fuster, 1997), it is now well understood that a bilateral network of parallel, widely distributed cortical and subcortical circuits are involved (Alexander, DeLong, & Strick, 1986). A complete discussion of frontal cortical and subcortical brain anatomy and development is beyond the scope of this chapter. The interested reader is directed to the many excellent references for this topic (Miller & Cummings, 2007; Risberg & Grafman, 2006; Krasnegor, Lyon, & Goldman-Rakic, 1997; Bradshaw, 2001; Lichter & Cummings, 2001). Here, we review briefly the key concepts needed for further discussion. Although we may not state so explicitly, the reader is reminded that we are talking about a network of structures and circuitry.

Despite the caveat above, EF is tightly associated with the functions of the prefrontal cortical network. This area clearly must serve a principal integrative role in the brain, with its large white-matter tracts providing communication with posterior (sensory) systems, limbic (drive, affect, memory) systems, and anterior (motor) systems. Indeed, it has been stated that this brain region may be the only one capable of this integration between cognitive and sensory (internal and external) information, emotion, motivation, and goal direction (Royall et al., 2002). The prefrontal cortex can be further resolved into two major functional divisions that operate together in the regulation of information processing and emotional responses to control goal-directed behavior (Rule, Shimamura, & Knight, 2002). Again, it must be stressed that, despite its structural and neurofunctional differentiation and complexity, all parts of the executive brain work together in an integrated functional system (Luria, 1966).

One prefrontal subdivision is the dorsolateral prefrontal region (DLPFC), a critical area for the cognitive processing of information from the environment, memory (especially working memory), and the integration of sensory and cognitive information (Barbas, 2006; Grafman, 2006). The DLPFC is part of a circuit that includes the lateral convexity of the frontal lobe and associated subcortical structures and pathways to the caudate, globus pallidus, and thalamus. The DLPFC also contributes to the initiation and monitoring of movement patterns via its connection with the motor and premotor areas of the frontal lobe, as well as visual orientation via the frontal eye fields (Miller & Cummings, 2007). Massive connections between this region and other primary and secondary sensory and motor cortical areas as well as subcortical areas (thalamus, basal ganglia, and hippocampus) mediate its integrative role (Stuss, 1992). Classic definitions of EF (shifting, inhibition, working memory, etc.) refer to many of the cognitive functions associated with the DLPFC (Baddeley, 1986; Cummings, 1993; Lezak, 1983; Grafman, 2006). Lesions involving this area typically give rise to the so-called frontal lobe syndrome affecting movement, action, and initiation (Cummings, 1985). Features may include disorganization, perseveration, stimulus bound-ness, and deficits in working memory. Other symptoms include apathy and indifference (Cummings, 1985). This region therefore is thought to process information and to formulate rules about how the world works and to put these rules into action (Rule et al., 2002).

The other subdivision is the ventromedial prefrontal cortical region (VMPFC) comprised of the orbitofrontal cortex (OFC) and anterior cingulate cortex (ACC), including the more anterior parts of the prefrontal cortex as well as key ventral and medial structures (Rolls, 2004; Royall et al., 2002). These areas are connected via the lateral and ventral orbitofrontal and anterior cingulate circuits to limbic and thalamic areas, and to the brain stem (Royall et al., 2002; Rolls, 2004). Strong connections exist between the OFC and deeper limbic areas such as the ACC and the amydgala subserving emotional states and some aspects of memory (Rolls, 2001; Luu & Tucker, 2003). The OFC thus has a role in social cognition and social behavior, including theory of mind and empathy (Amodio & Frith, 2006; Stuss & Levine, 2004; Perry et al., 2001). Theory of mind has been described as the ability to have "flexible access to the mind of others" (Dennis, 2006, p. 143) and thus is a social construct closely related to empathy (or the recognition of feelings in others) (Becharra, Damasio, & Damasio, 2000; Eslinger, 1998). Ventral OFC regions are thought to be important in behavioral self-regulation and inhibition (Stuss & Levine, 2004; Stuss et al., 1983). The closely associated and more medial ACC has been shown to also mediate motivational behavior through its role in action planning, error detection, detecting novelty, and evaluating the potential reward benefit of actions (Rolls, 2001; Luu & Tucker, 2003; Rushworth, Walton, Kennerley, & Bannerman, 2004). The architectonics of the ACC parallel that of the PFC, with more dorsal parts responding to novel cognitive tasks and more ventral parts responding to emotion (Luu & Tucker, 2003; Amodio & Frith, 2006). Thus, together, the OFC and ACC are thought to regulate social-emotional behavior (Becharra, Damasio, Damasio, & Anderson, 1994), promote social and emotional appraisal of the environment (Eslinger & Damasio, 1985), mediate social behavior (Stuss & Levine, 2004), and measure the affective value of reward contingencies and thus maintain motivation (Rolls, 2001).

Damage to the VMPFC often results in derangements of personality (Cummings & Miller, 2007; Barbas, 2006; Grafman, 2006) and decision making (Barbas, 2006), while performance on cognitive neuropsychological tests may look entirely normal (Stuss & Levine, 2004: Becharra et al., 2000). A disinhibition syndrome may emerge (often called "acquired sociopathy" or pseudopsychopathic syndrome), which includes emotional outbursts, poor insight, risky behavior without regard for consequences, and violation of social conventions (Cummings, 1985; Miller & Cummings, 2007). Children with damage to these areas may show antisocial behavior and restricted empathy (Eslinger & Damasio, 1985). Injury to the ACC may result in disorders of volition and apathy, the so-called pseudodepressed state (Barbas, 2006; Cummings & Miller, 2007). These areas thus are believed to link our cognitive understanding of a situation with our affective responses (Becharra et al., 2000) and to shape future goals in keeping with their reward values.

Development of the Brain and Executive Functioning

The frontal lobes, and in particular the prefrontal cortex, are the last brain regions to develop in humans. Electrophysiological, neuroanatomical, neurochemical, and neuroendocrine changes continue from infancy through adolescence and adulthood. The protracted development of these regions and their associated functions (see Dennis, 2006, and Diamond, 2002, for reviews) reflects the importance and specificity of these functions for the life of an adult. In particular, the frontal white-matter connections develop slowly, continuing well into the adult years (Gogtay, Giedd, & Rapaport, 2002). While the basic architecture of the system is in place during infancy and early childhood, the period between ages 5 to 18 is characterized by reorganization and refinement, with emphasis on elaboration of the net of interconnecting tracts, of which the frontal connections represent a major portion (Giedd et al., 1996; Giedd et al., 1999). Brain development proceeds in sequential fashion by region, with the sensory and motor cortices maturing earlier than the parietal and frontal association cortices (Giedd et al., 1999; Gogtay et al., 2002). The delayed maturation of these regions follows a prolonged period of, first, early overproduction of gray matter and synaptic connections, peaking at puberty (Giedd et al., 1999), followed by extensive synaptic pruning (Huttenlocher & Dabholkar, 1997). These developmental anatomic changes may be related to hormonal influences, personal experience, and environmental milieu (Royall et al., 2002). Changes in synaptic density continue through adolescence and accompany increased white matter, decreased gray matter, and the corresponding increases in cerebrospinal fluid (CSF) in frontal areas (Jernigan, Trauner, Hesselink, & Tallal, 1991). Subcortical areas develop somewhat earlier than cortical regions; however, their full functional maturity awaits cortical development and the white-matter interconnections (Gogtay et al., 2002; Kinney, Brody, Kloman, & Gilles, 1988). White-matter density continues to increase in subcortical and frontal areas well into middle adulthood, with frontal lobe myelination occurring last (Jernigan et al., 1991; Yakovlev & Lecours, 1967; Fuster, 1997). Thus, later developing cognitive and regulatory processes reflect ongoing myelination, metabolic changes, hormonal influences, and environmental modifications (reviewed in Eslinger, Biddle, & Grattan, 1997).

In parallel with the structural changes described above, executive function develops well into adulthood, forming a critical scaffold for ongoing personal growth. Luria (1973) early on posited that frontal lobe functions matured between ages 4 and 7. By contrast, many neuropsychological studies find that children do not perform at adult levels until adolescence, leading to the belief that EF was a function of the mature brain, and that these cognitive control functions did not emerge until adolescence (Golden, 1981). We now understand that both views may be true depending on the nature of the task. Early emergence of cognitive EF is supported by evidence that some EF-like problem solving has been seen in infants when tested with appropriate measures (Diamond, 2002), and findings from developmental studies show that normal children achieve adult levels of performance on many cognitive tests of EF by about age 6 (see Romine & Reynolds, 2005, for a review and meta-analysis). The greatest period of development of these skills appears to be between ages 6 and 8 (reviewed in Romine & Reynolds, 2005) with continued, albeit apparently slower, development thereafter. However, many studies show that most tasks are mastered by age 12, depending on the task (Grattan & Eslinger, 1991; Welsh, Pennington, & Grossier, 1991; Levin et al., 1991; Chelune & Baer, 1986; also see Romine & Reynolds, 2005). This cognitive progression has its parallel in behavioral control. The rudiments of self-control and goal-directed behavior are evident in babies and toddlers, while the growing language skills of the young child permit more internal regulation of ongoing behavior, with increasing levels of flexibility, inhibition, and the ability to plan developing through mid-childhood (Vygotsky, 1962; Romine & Reynolds, 2005; also see Diaz & Berk, 1992). Finally, adolescence and early adulthood brings more sophistication and efficiency, increased organization, flexibility, and the capacity for self-monitoring in all cognitive and problem-solving domains (Passler, Isaac, & Hynd, 1985; Chelune & Baer, 1986; Stuss & Anderson, 2004; Romine & Reynolds, 2005).

The developmental trajectories of noncognitive (e.g., social-emotional) functions, those associated with the VMPFC, are much less well studied, but recent progress has been made (see review by Fernandez-Duque, Baird, & Posner, 2000). It appears that young children already possess the regulatory underpinnings of noncognitive control associated with the OFC and ACC, while the cognitive EFs, associated with the maturation of the DLPFC, develop through childhood and adolescence (Stuss & Anderson, 2004; Hongwanishkul, Happaney, Lee, & Zelazo, 2005). Case studies of children with brain damage inform us that early damage to these regions is associated with disruptions in social skills (including empathy), which may have greater implications for long-term functioning than cognitive changes (Eslinger 1996). Noncognitive functions also appear to have a protracted developmental course (Eslinger, 1996; Hongwanishkul et al., 2005). A recent study in young children highlighted that these functions also develop rapidly during the preschool years and that they may follow a somewhat different time course than the cognitive executive functions discussed above (Hongwanishkul et al., 2005; Kerr & Zelazo, 2004). Thus we see that the developmental course of the different regulatory functions is variable, with skills emerging sequentially through childhood, adolescence, and early adulthood. This progression reflects the continued development of the anterior cognitive systems (Denkla, 1996) and, in particular, the development of inhibitory controls (Barkley, 1997).

Having reviewed the development of the relevant structures and their function, we shall now examine the interplay of the components of control and regulation.

Executive Function and Self-Regulation

Unlike most traditional models of EF, which stress cognitive control, many newer models separate EF into cognitive and social-emotional subfunctions. Dennis (2006) outlines a multilevel system that includes traditional EF (working memory, inhibition) and social-emotional processing. Powell and Voeller (2004) describe three domains of self-regulation: cognitive, behavioral, and emotional regulation. Similarly, Gioia and colleagues (Gioia, Isquith, Guy, & Kenworthy, 2000) also define three dimensions for EF: (a) the *metacognitive* factor (working memory, initiate, plan/organize, task monitor), which reflects cognitive problem solving; (b) the *behavioral regulation* factor (inhibit, self-monitor), which captures inhibitory control of behavior; and (c) the *emotional regulation* factor (emotional control, shift), which encompasses emotional control of behavior. Their instrument—the BRIEF (Behavioral Rating Inventory of EF; Gioia et al., 2000)—rates the behavioral expression of EF (as distinct from the cognitive expression; Gioia, Isquith, Retzlaff, & Pratt, 2001; Gioia, Isquith, Retzlaff, & Espy, 2002). Eslinger and Grattan (1993) posit a "social executor" as a coordinated circuit operating with (as opposed to entirely independent) of EF. In this model, cognitive and metacognitive strategies are within the purview of the EF system, while an emotional regulation system controls affective responses between the person and the environment, social interactions, motivation, and empathy. In the context of attention-deficit disorders and development, Barkley (1997) has also argued that EF is inherently social and that the EF system is unique to humans because of the evolution of increased social complexity.

By contrast, Stuss has argued persuasively that, rather than contain the social-emotional dimension, EF lies within a hierarchy of self-organization that includes self-awareness (Stuss & Anderson, 2004). In this model, self-awareness includes the components motivation and metacognition (the capacity to reflect on one's mental processes or "flexible access to one's own mind" (Dennis, 2006, p. 142) and is mediated by the OFC (particularly in the right hemisphere). The OFC system is involved in the appreciation of humor, theory of mind, moral evaluation, and regulation of social behaviors, and deficits in these areas are borne out in both lesion and imaging studies (Stuss & Anderson, 2004). In Stuss' view, EF is at the middle level, receiving input from and, in turn, modulating more basic domain specific processes below, and receiving modulatory input from the OFC system above (Stuss, 1992, 2007). Thus, Stuss places EF in the middle between the basic processes and the "self," the latter being involved in motivation and values (Stuss, 2007). Nonetheless, this model emphasizes the important interplay between the cognitive and noncognitive elements in the regulatory scheme.

One additional recent dichotomy is that of "hot" versus "cool" executive functions. The cognitive components discussed above in association with the DLPFC have been termed "cool," as distinct from the "hot" EFs linked anatomically with the orbitofrontal and ventral aspects of the frontal lobes (Happaney, Zelazo, & Stuss, 2004; Kerr & Zelazo, 2004; Geurts, van der Oord, & Crone, 2006). Hot EFs subsume social rules of behavior, emotional saliency and reward processing, and emotional control (Rolls, 2004). Regulatory tasks would include self-determination, self-awareness, self-monitoring and flexibility, and choice of goals and prioritizing, with damage to the corresponding brain areas leading to difficulties in motivation and affective decision making (Rolls, 2004). This dichotomy underscores further the two separate properties of the regulatory system: the cognitive and the affective/motivational.

In summary, the concept of EF has evolved to either encompass or complement the growing understanding of the role of social, emotional, and self-oriented psychological processes in overall mental regulation. The details of this cognitive–noncognitive interface are the focus of ongoing research. Much research from structural and developmental studies has already pointed to the complex spatial and temporal interplay between these realms. Enough is known to encourage an integrated approach to academic learning. We now turn to a model from educational psychology that echoes these two regulatory domains, and brings noncognitive elements—and, in particular, motivation—into a framework for addressing the problems of challenged students.

Self-Regulated Learning (SRL): The Motivational Link

The theory of self-regulated learning (SRL) was introduced by educational psychologists to identify behaviors that distinguish proficient learners, to delineate processes that support effective classroom instruction, and as a framework for a program to promote educational success (Lienemann & Reid, 2006; Pintrich, 1989, 1999; Zimmerman, 2002). SRL involves self-generated processes that students use to guide, monitor, and direct the success of their performance and to manage and direct interaction with the learning environment (Pintrich, 1999; Bashir & Singer, 2006). SRL is clearly dependent on the interplay between cognitive and social-emotional processes, including affect regulation, motivation, and self-concept (Pintrich, 1999; Wolters, 2003). SRL processes work in parallel with EF, as conceived above, in the regulation of the learner's environment (Bashir & Singer, 2006). SRL theory delineates three main component processes that are used by a student to regulate behavior and control their learning environment in pursuit of (self-) identified goals. We focus on the two components most relevant to our discussion.

The first of these is a *cognitive* component that involves information processing (the what, when, and how of learning) (Pintrich & DeGroot, 1990). Students use a variety of techniques and strategies as they exercise the *cognitive* and *metacognitive* subprocesses. *Cognitive strategies* include rehearsal of information (supporting memory and working memory), followed by elaboration and organization (supporting further integration and synthesizing; Pintrich, 1999; Weinstein & Mayer, 1986). In this way, the effective student initially memorizes and learns terms and factual material from lectures, notes, and texts, then elaborates on and integrates this material with past knowledge, connects material from several sources, and formulates original beliefs and hypotheses based on this new knowledge. *Metacognitive strategies* operate on cognitive strategies in order to regulate cognitive operations and thereby direct learning. Reminiscent of the neuropsychological models reviewed above, these strategies include planning (setting goals), monitoring (comparing performance against goal), and evaluating operations and repairing as needed (adjusting behavior in line with goal; Pintrich 1999; Bashir & Singer, 2006; Boekaerts, 1999; Wolters, 2003). In this way, the student sets his or her own educational goals (for example, taking a particular course as a prerequisite for an interesting or satisfying major), monitors his or her schedule to allocate sufficient time and energy to the task (does not cram for an important exam or spend inordinate amounts of time on long-range projects when short-range deadlines are imminent), and continually evaluates and adjusts behavior according to goals (readjusts schedule to allow allocation of additional resources, locates and uses outside assistance as necessary to achieve mastery of information).

The second is an *affective* component, the most relevant aspect of which is motivation (the "why" of learning) (Bashir & Singer, 2006: Boekaerts, 1999; Zimmerman, 1986; Pintrich, 1999). This component, with its important "self" process, relates to the student's personal goals and provides the relevant emotional controls, and influences directly the cognitive and metacognitive components above. The affective component provides the sense of personal self-efficacy and the belief that the task is valuable. This has been shown to be key to maintaining academic motivation (Zimmerman, 1994; Bandura & Schunk, 1981; Bandura, 1997; Wolters, 1998, 2003). Indeed, regulating and maintaining motivation in the learning environment is a critical factor in student success (van Zile, 1999). Wolters (2003) breaks motivation down into components that include choice, effort, and persistence. In this schema, difficult or novel tasks demand a higher level of effort and a greater degree of motivation to sustain the increased effort (Wolters, 2003). Students use motivational strategies in the same way they use cognitive and metacognitive strategies. Such strategies might include self-talk (pep talks such as "I know you can do this" as well as negative performance appraisals such as "You are not going to pass this test"), environmental structuring (changing study location, eating or drinking), and self-rewards or punishments (see Wolters, 2003, for a detailed review).

In SRL, these processes integrate to allow the student to plan (set goals), self-monitor, self-evaluate, and change (Bashir & Singer, 2006; Pintrich, 1989). This ability is applied continually during task performance and is thought to be bound tightly to language (Bashir & Singer, 2006) and verbal self-mediation of behavior. Thus, SRL theory posits that cognitive and affective systems work reciprocally in language-based self-regulation of information processing and learning (Diaz & Berk, 1992; Vygotsky, 1962). The metacognitive component directs the use of cognitive strategies; however, this is mediated by the sense of personal choice, efficacy, and motivation that the student brings to the table, which is not central in most models of EF. Indeed, this option of choice is absent in all definitions of executive processes.

SRL and Higher Education

The integrated mental process we have described here is essential to optimal participation in higher education, especially for students with learning disorders (Reis, McGuire, & Neu, 2000; Ruban, McCoach, McGuire, & Reiss, 2003). The *self-regulated college student*, possessing this ability, uses cognitive strategies to promote deep learning of information (elaboration and organization). This student has learned how to use various meta-cognitive strategies (planning, evaluating, and monitoring) as an active process guided by inner speech (Singer & Bashir, 1999; Bashir & Singer, 2006; Iran-Nejad, 1990). He or she maintains intrinsic goals to support his or her investment of time and effort, and to sustain motivation in the face of difficulties. The student is aware of his or her goals and intents, and monitors and allocates available resources (internal and external) to support ongoing effort and engagement. This student knows how to direct his or her own learning process and does not rely on external support to provide structure and motivation; however, the student also knows how to access supports when needed. The student appreciates that he or she possesses the necessary abilities and skills to carry out the task success-fully. Finally, this student has exercised a high degree of personal choice in task selection, believes that the task at hand is important, and perceives that his or her personal goals are of value (Bandura & Schunk, 1981).

In contrast, the *dysregulated student* appears not to have an intrinsic ability to direct his or her own learning. This student may instead depend on external support (the "prosthetic frontal lobe" aptly termed by Denkla, 1989). He or she may present as a disorganized individual who fails to sustain energy and effort or follow through with tasks, may be rigid and inflexible, and has trouble using feedback to modify the task approach. This student may have difficulties managing and structuring time, materials, and space (Wolf, 2001). The student appears to lack motivation and does not set goals or plan ahead, may have weak academic skills and less well-developed cognitive strategies (e.g., uses rehearsal to memorize but not elaboration to integrate information) and metacognitive awareness (Trainin & Swanson, 2005). This student typically lacks insight and does not reflect on self and performance. Finally, this student's goals are imposed by others (teacher, parent, etc.) rather than reflecting his or her own desires.

Diagnostic Considerations

Deficits of SRL cut across the diagnostic landscape. In other words, the characteristics of academic dysregulation under review are more likely to be descriptive than diagnostic. Many neurodevelopmental and acquired disorders have been linked with executive dysfunction and learn-ing difficulties. One source (Powell & Voeller, 2004) listed 25 different neuropsychiatric conditions in children and adults that may be mediated by defects in frontal executive circuits. The struggling student with deficits in self-regulation might be diagnosed with a neurodevelopmental disorder such attention-deficit/hyperactivity disorder (ADHD), autism, or a classi-cal learning disability, a psychiatric disorder such as depression or bipolar illness, an acquired condition such as traumatic brain injury (TBI), or no diagnosable disability at all. The assessment of SRL deficits is not meant to substitute for a clinical diagnosis, where appropriate, but to better understand the nature of the executive problems that might accompany these conditions, in service of remediating or accommodating the suffering student.

Assessment of the Regulatory System

The definitions of EF are inextricably bound with its measurement, to the extent that it can be argued that, like IQ, EF is what tests of EF measure (although the utility of this approach has recently been challenged; see Alvarez & Emory, 2006). Available methodology always influences research, and this is seen in the study of executive function. Indeed, Stuss and Levine (2004) argue that the cognitive components are more readily captured by neuropsychological assessment than are affective or social regulatory functions. A discussion of the merits of individual tests of EF is beyond the scope of this chapter; however, the interested reader is referred to a recent comprehensive review and critique of many of the commonly used instruments associated with "frontal lobe" functions (Stuss & Levine, 2004). Because testing of cool EFs is better developed, studies have concentrated on this aspect of the regulatory system. Consequently, less is known about the development or assessment of motivational aspects of the regulatory systems (Stuss & Levine, 2004).

In keeping with our arguments above, the assessment of a student with apparent difficulties in academic self-regulation must be multimodal in nature, combining assessments of both cognitive and motivational components. We lay out a general game plan for conducting this assessment below, which is comprised of thorough history gathering and interview; a functional assessment of strengths, weaknesses, and environmental demands (Chaytor, Schmitter-Edgecombe, & Burr, 2006); and neuropsychological testing using both a psychometric and process approach.

History and Interview

A thorough interview and history will be important for assessing certain components of SRL reflecting the hot EFs that are not amenable to testing (see Mapou, Chapter 10, this volume, for more detail). This interview should include a functional assessment—for example, how is the student functioning currently and historically in the real world? This portion of the assessment forms the basis (and arguably the most important piece) of the clinical database in neurodevelopmental disorders as the clinician begins to identify symptoms, developmental difficulties, educational preparation, family history, and so forth.

The interview should also probe the cognitive component of SRL and inquire as to what cognitive strategies are available (what does the student know) and how the student uses them. The interview should pay particular attention to planning, time management, and organizational strategies. Data about the regulatory component of SRL and EF should also be sought, including the student's goals (e.g., are they internal or extrinsic?), modes of emotional regulation, sense of self-efficacy, and competence as a learner. Particular attention should be paid to probing the student's sense of personal efficacy, locus of control, values, and choices. This portion of the assessment might also include rating scales such as the BRIEF (Gioia et al., 2000) or the Dysexecutive Scale (Burgess, Alderman, Evans, Wilson, & Emslie, 1996). An experimental measure, the Motivated Strategies for Learning Questionnaire, has been developed to capture the learning strategies and motivation of college-age students (Pintrich, Smith, Garcia, & McKeachie, 1993); however, to the best of our knowledge, this is not available as a clinical instrument. Information about changes in patterns of strengths and weaknesses over time also provides important data about these functions.

Neuropsychological Testing

Decades of studies have delineated batteries for the assessment of frontal lobe function, incorporating many of the commonly used tests familiar to neuropsychologists. Most practicing neuropsychologists (and many researchers) adhere to a restricted number of tests that they believe capture the essence of EF as they understand the concept. We do not discuss or critique this approach but encourage the interested reader to see Stuss and Levine (2004) for an excellent discussion. We do endorse a flexible approach combining well-understood and standardized instruments with a qualitative and process-oriented analysis of strategy use.

This flexibility is most critical when we attempt to assemble batteries that might measure the social or affective component of regulatory disorders, in particular, motivation. One approach is to use instruments that present risky affective decision-making tasks, such as the Iowa Gambling Test (Bechara et al., 1994; also see Manes et al., 2002) and the Everyday Test of Attention (Shallice & Burgess, 1991). Another such test is the Strategies Application Test (Levine et al., 1998) in which subjects select among target stimuli with different reward contingencies. This instrument has been shown to be sensitive to damage in the ventral areas of the OFC (Levine et al., 1998).

An important recent methodological contribution is the Delis-Kaplan Executive Functioning System (D-KEFS) (Delis, Kaplan, & Kramer, 2001), a new instrument that includes nine different subtests of different aspects

Table 9.1 D-KEFS Subtests

Cognitive:
Sorting Test (problem solving and shifting)
Verbal and Design Fluency Tests (fluency in verbal and spatial domains)
Color Word Interference Test (verbal inhibition)
Tower Test (planning and impulse control)
Conceptual:
Sorting Test (verbal and spatial concept formation)
20 Questions Test (generating and testing hypotheses, abstract thinking)
Word Context Test (deductive reasoning)
Proverb Test (metaphorical thinking)

of EF and regulation. The D-KEFS is the first standardized battery designed for assessing multiple factors of executive and regulatory functioning in patients between ages 8 and 89. It has been conormed extensively on a large national sample, rectifying some of the interpretive problems inherent in informally selected batteries. The domains of assessment include inhibition, flexibility, planning, impulse control, conceptual and abstract thinking, concept formation, and creativity. The design of the instrument is faithful to the process approach (Kaplan, 1988) (see Table 9.1). It allows for evaluators to administer the entire battery or choose among nine carefully selected subtests as they generate and test hypotheses about performance for an individual patient. Examiners may pick and choose among tests of cognitive, inhibitory, and conceptual functions. In this way, a profile of different regulatory abilities may be elucidated, errors may be evaluated, and strategies employed in task solution may be analyzed. Because this instrument offers a choice of tests that have been conormed on the same population, the D-KEFS adds statistical rigor to the personally chosen clinical and research battery.

As discussed above, neuropsychological testing often is best suited to the cool EFs and to abstract concept formation. We stress that since so many different areas may be impacted by regulatory difficulties, testing should employ a number of different tests of the fractionated skills we have discussed, as no single test will capture all of the components. The examiner should also keep in mind that generating a score profile of strengths and weakness on a battery of EF tests alone will not be sufficient. Again, we want to emphasize that a score profile will not be diagnostic because of the lack of specificity of executive dysfunction for a particular neurodevelopmental disorder. However, the history and results of the interview, complete with a functional assessment of the subject's other strengths and weaknesses paired with the regulatory control demands of his or her environment, will serve to flesh out the profile.

It has been argued that neuropsychological testing of EFs is not valid ecologically because the structured test setting itself does not capture the real-world difficulties of patients with regulatory problems (Brown, 2006; Rabbit, 1997). For this reason, we stress that the neuropsychological assessment of such difficulties should include not only a flexible, wide battery of tests but also a qualitative or process interpretation of the cognitive testing. This approach (Kaplan, 1988) is based on the fundamental assumption that analysis of the underlying *processes* leading to a specific behavior is as important as the test data itself. Further, allowing subjects to employ different strategies to solve various problems and assessing the different ways they approach the task allows a less-structured view of the test situation itself and may increase the ecological validity of the test results.

Applying the Model

We now turn to the ways in which different defects in an integrated regulatory system give rise to the range of dysexecutive behavior seen in the different neurodevelopmental disorders.

Recent work in ADHD provides an excellent example of this reasoning. Sonuga-Barke (2003) has delineated two neuropsychological pathways in the dysfunction of ADHD. The "dysexecutive" circuit impacts effortful control and implicates anterior regions of the frontal lobe. The other "motivational" circuit involves reward processing and delay of gratification, and implicates limbic regions. Thus, two parallel pathways may underlie this one condition and may account for some of the variability in clinical presentation and in research findings (Sonuga-Barke et al., 2003; Castellanos, Sonuga-Barke, Milham, & Tannock, 2006). Castellanos and colleagues (2006) suggest that differential dysfunction in these two subsystems determines clinical subtype, with the "dysexecutive" correlating with the inattentive subtype, and the "motivational" correlating with the impulsive subtype.

Thus, one neurodevelopmental disorder may be classified according to both cognitive and motivational aspects of the disorder. These correspond to separate yet interacting neuroanatomy, related to different symptom profiles and (perhaps) different treatment needs. These systems operate reciprocally throughout development such that deficits in one may produce or modify expression of the functions of the other (e.g., motivational and reward deficits can constrain development of certain cognitive control processes and vice versa). Similarly, different disorders may be associated

Table 9.2 Executive and Regulatory Functions Relevant to College

Organize (space and materials)

Manage time (plan and prioritize)

Task initiation and follow-through

Sustain energy and effort

Flexible problem solving

Generate alternate solutions

Switch among tasks

Working memory

Monitor output (especially in relation to future goals)

Use feedback to adjust performance

Set goals and make choices

Evaluate social-emotional cues

Regulate emotions

Maintain motivation

with varying deficits of hot versus cool processing. For example, it has been suggested that autism may involve deficits in the hot areas of motivation and social emotion, while ADHD may be associated with cooler cognitive and attentional problems (Zelazo & Müller, 2002; Castellanos et al., 2006; Sonuga-Barke, 2003).

This sort of analysis helps explain how we can have so many different conditions (no fewer than 33 according to Eslinger, 1996) that have been reported to involve core deficits in EF. Rather than hunt for that defective EF core for each disorder, we can begin to conceptualize neurodevelopmental disorders of regulation along separable dimensions with concomitant cognitive and social-motivational symptoms in different combinations and at different points in development. In its dimensional approach, this parallels the theory of self-regulated learning. Together, this introduces the concept of an "academic regulatory system" comprised of traditional executive functions, social-emotional functions, metacognition, academic strategy use, and personal motivation and choice (see Table 9.2). We believe that these domains likely cut across many neurodevelopmental disorders and that they be applied as a descriptor and not as a diagnostic label. We assert that skills in this area are quite amenable to remediation and accommodation; addressing weak regulatory skills may alleviate considerable academic and personal distress in the struggling student and thus foster a successful academic outcome.

Table 9.3 Parallel Regulatory Systems

Dorsolateral System (Executive Functions)
Cognitive processing
Working memory
Set shifting
Perseveration
Integrates domain specific and sensory information with posterior cortical regions
Monitors output (with motor systems)
Ventromedial System (Self-Regulation)
Social and emotional processing
Motivation
Self awareness
Choice
Participates in goal setting and affective decision making
Processes saliency and rewards (with limbic systems)

Conclusions

The model we have outlined involves regulatory control through two inter-acting components: one cognitive, comprised of the familiar EF, and the other, motivational/self-regulatory (SR) (see Table 9.3). These EF and SR components may be traced to different brain regions that work together via the neuroanatomical connections between the cortical and limbic areas, which mediate interactions among cognitive, emotional, and moti-vational states. The broader concept of "regulatory disorders" that impact cognition, motivation, and self-awareness (as opposed to strictly cognitive "executive function disorders") is certainly not original (Stuss & Levine, 2004; also see Gioia et al., 2002). However, it has not been translated fully into a greater understanding of how deficits in cognitive EFs interact with social, emotional, and affective systems in neurodevelopmental disorders, particularly in young adults. We have discussed the dysregulated college student and have attempted to outline those regulatory functions that may be most relevant to college (see Table 9.3). As we wait for this relationship to be further elucidated, we believe that it is important to assess, remedi-ate (where feasible), and accommodate both systems in young adults with academic difficulties of regulatory origin.

Future Directions

The logical next step is the validation of the "academic regulatory system" in college students with and without disabilities. It will be important to assess the level of motivation, choice, strategy use, and executive skill in college students with a variety of disabilities to establish: (a) the validity of the academic regulatory deficit discussed above, and (b) whether there are perhaps different profiles in different disabilities. This would enable us to design intervention programs that might target these profiles in different ways.

Noncognitive domains of regulation such as motivation and choice have been attracting more attention from basic brain researchers. Assessing these functions in students with neurodevelopmental learning problems, as well as in normal college-aged students, will be critical for dissecting the complex interactions of these parallel systems.

In terms of assessment, we have outlined a battery that includes both a standardized and a process approach to executive function and other regulatory domains. The use of this sort of battery should be validated in a variety of students with nonspecific learning difficulties as well as in the assessment of students with known neurodevelopmental disorders.

Finally, further functional neuroimaging studies, using cognitive and noncognitive probe tasks in subjects with a range of neurodevelopmental disorders, would help elucidate the underlying brain mechanisms of regulatory dysfunction in this population. This approach should enhance the understanding of individual and group differences in this population and benefit the design of more effective interventions.

References

Alexander, G. E., DeLong, M. R., & Strick, P. L. (1986). Parallel organization of functionally segregated circuits linking basal ganglia to cortex. *Annual Review of Neuroscience, 9,* 357–381.

Alvarez, J. A., & Emory, E. (2006). Executive function and the frontal lobes: A meta-analytic review. *Neuropsychology Review, 16,* 17–42.

American Heritage dictionary (4th ed.). (2000). Retrieved September 26, 2007, from www.bartleby.com

Amodio, D. M., & Frith, C. D. (2006). Meeting of minds: The medial frontal cortex and social cognition. *Nature Reviews: Neuroscience, 7,* 268–277.

Baddeley, A. (1986). *Working memory.* Oxford: Clarendon.

Bandura, A. (1997). *Self-efficacy: The exercise of control.* New York: W. H. Freedman.

Bandura, A., & Schunk, D. (1981). Cultivating competence, self-efficacy, and intrinsic interest through proximal self-motivation. *Journal of Personality and Social Psychology, 41,* 586–598.

Barbas, H. (2006). Organization of the principal pathways of the prefrontal lateral, medial, and orbitofrontal cortices in primates and implications for their collaborative interaction in executive function. In J. R. Risberg & J. Grafman (Eds.), *The frontal lobes: Development, function, and pathology* (pp. 21–68). New York: Cambridge University Press.

Barkley, R. A. (1997). Behavioral inhibition, sustained attention, and executive functions: Constructing a unified theory of ADHD. *Psychological Bulletin*, *121*, 65–94.

Bashir, A. S., & Singer, B. D. (2006). Assisting students with becoming self-regulated writes. In T. Ukrainetz (Ed.), *Contextualized language interventions: Scaffolding K–12 literacy achievement* (pp. 123–136). Eau Claire, WI: Thinking Publications.

Becharra, A., Damasio, A. R., Damasio, H., & Anderson, S. W. (1994). Insensitivity to future consequences following damage to human prefrontal cortex. *Cognition*, *50*, 1–7.

Becharra, A., Damasio, H., & Damasio, A. R. (2000). Emotion, decision making, and the orbitofrontal cortex. *Cerebral Cortex*, *10*, 295–307.

Boekaerts, M. (1999). Self-regulated learning: Where are we today? *International Journal of Educational Research*, *31*, 445–457.

Bradshaw, J. L. (2001). *Developmental disorders of the frontostriatal system*. New York: Psychology Press.

Brown, T. E. (2006). Executive functions and attention-deficit/hyperactivity disorder: Implications of two conflicting views. *International Journal of Disability: Development and Education*, *53*, 35–46.

Burgess, P. W., Alderman, N., Evans, J. J., Wilson, B. A., & Emslie, H. (1996). The dysexecutive questionnaire. In B. A. Wilson, N. Alderman, P. W. Burgess, H. Emslie, & J. J. Evans (Eds.), *Behavioral assessment of the dysexecutive syndrome*. Bury St. Edmunds, UK: Thames Valley Test.

Castellanos, F. X., Sonuga-Barke, E. J. S., Milham, M. P., & Tannock, R. (2006). Characterizing cognition in ADHD: Beyond executive dysfunction. *Trends in Neuroscience*, *10*, 117–123.

Chaytor, N., Schmitter-Edgecombe, M., & Burr, R. (2006). Improving the ecological validity of executive functioning assessment. *Archives of Clinical Neuropsychology*, *21*, 217–227.

Chelune, C. J., & Baer, R. A. (1986). Developmental norms for the Wisconsin Card Sort Test. *Journal of Clinical and Experimental Neuropsychology*, *8*, 219–228.

Cummings, J. L. (1985). *Clinical neuropsychiatry*. New York: Grune & Stratton.

Cummings, J. L. (1993). Frontal-subcortical circuits and human behavior. *Archives of Neurology*, *50*, 873–880.

Cummings, J. L., & Miller, B. L. (2007). Conceptual and clinical aspects of the frontal lobes. In J. L. Cummings & B. L. Miller (Eds.), *The human frontal lobes: Functions and disorders* (pp. 12–24). New York: Guilford Press.

Delis, D. C., Kaplan, E., & Kramer, J. H. (2001). *The Delis-Kaplan executive function system*. San Antonio, TX: Psychological Corporation.

Denckla, M. B. (1989). Executive function: The overlap zone between attention-deficit/hyperactivity disorder and learning disabilities. *International Journal of Pediatrics*, *4*, 80–92.

Denckla, M. B. (1996). A theory and model of executive function: A neuropsychological perspective. In G. R. Lyon & N. A. Krasnegor (Eds.), *Attention, memory, and executive function* (pp. 263–276). Baltimore, MD: Paul H. Brookes.

Dennis, M. (2006). Prefrontal cortex: Typical and atypical development. In J. R. Risberg & J. Grafman (Eds.), *The frontal lobes: Development, function, and pathology* (pp. 128–162). New York: Cambridge University Press.

Diamond, A. (2002). Normal development of prefrontal cortex from birth to young adulthood: Cognitive functions, anatomy and biochemistry. In D. T. Stuss & R. T. Knight (Eds.), *Principles of frontal lobe function* (pp. 466–503). New York: Oxford University Press.

Diaz, R. M., & Berk, L. E. (1992). *Private speech: From social interaction to self-regulation.* Hillsdale, NJ: Lawrence Erlbaum.

Eslinger, P. J. (1996). Conceptualizing, describing, and measuring components of executive function: A summary. In G. R. Lyon & N. A. Krasnegor (Eds.), *Attention, memory, and executive function* (pp. 367–395). Baltimore, MD: Paul H. Brookes.

Eslinger, P. J. (1998). Neurological and neuropsychological bases of empathy. *European Neurology, 39,* 193–199.

Eslinger, P. J., Biddle, K. R., & Grattan, L. M. (1997). Cognitive and social development in children with prefrontal cortex lesions. In N. A. Krasnegor, G. Reid Lyon, & P. S. Goldman-Rakic (Eds.), *Development of the prefrontal cortex* (pp. 295–335). Baltimore, MD: Paul H. Brookes.

Eslinger, P. J., & Damasio, A. R. (1985). Severe disturbance of higher cognition after bilateral frontal lobe ablation: Patient EVR. *Neurology, 35,* 1731–1741.

Eslinger, P. J., & Grattan, L. M. (1993). Frontal lobe and frontal-striatal substrates for different forms of human cognitive flexibility. *Neuropsychologia, 31,* 17–28.

Fernandez-Duque, D., Baird, J. A., & Posner, M. I. (2000). Executive attention and metacognitive regulation. *Consciousness and Cognition, 9,* 288–307.

Fuster, J. M. (1997). *The prefrontal cortex: Anatomy, physiology and neuropsychology of the frontal lobe* (3rd ed.). New York: Raven Press.

Geurts, H. M., van der Oord, S., & Crone, E. A. (2006). Hot and cool aspects of cognitive control in children with ADHD: Decision-making and inhibition. *Journal of Abnormal Child Psychology, 34,* 813–824.

Giedd, J. N., Blumenthal, J., Jeffries, N. O., Castellanos, F. X., Lui, J., Zijdenbos, A., et al. (1999). Brain development during childhood and adolescence: A longitudinal MRI study. *Nature Neuroscience, 2,* 861–863.

Giedd, J. N., Snell, J. W., Lange, N., Rajapakse, J. C., Casey, B. J., Kozuch, P. L., et al. (1996). Quantitative magnetic resonance imaging and human brain development: Ages 4–18. *Cerebral Cortex, 6,* 551–560.

Gioia, G. A., Isquith, P. K., Guy, S. C., & Kenworthy, L. K. (2000). BRIEF: *Behavioral Rating Inventory of Executive Functions: Professional manual.* Odessa, FL: Psychological Assessment Resources.

Gioia, G. A., Isquith, P. K., Retzlaff, P. D., & Espy, K. A. (2002). A confirmatory factor analysis of the Behavioral Rating Inventory of Executive Function (BRIEF) in a clinical sample. *Child Neuropsychology, 8,* 249–257.

Gioia, G. A., Isquith, P. K., Retzlaff, P. D., & Pratt, B. M. (2001). Modeling executive functions with everyday behaviors: A unitary or fractionated system? *Brain and Cognition, 47,* 203–207.

Gogtay, N., Giedd, J., & Rapaport, J. (2002). Brain development in healthy, hyperactive, and psychotic children. *Archives of Neurology, 59,* 1244–1248.

Golden, C. G. (1981). The Luria-Nebraska Children's Battery: Theory and formulation. In G. W. Hynd & J. E. Obruzt (Eds.), *Neuropsychological assessment and the school-age child* (pp. 277–302). New York: Grune & Stratton.

Grafman, J. (2006). Human prefrontal cortex: processes and representations. In J. R. Risberg & J. Grafman (Eds.), *The frontal lobes: Development, function, and pathology* (pp. 69–91). New York: Cambridge University Press.

Grattan, L. M., & Eslinger, P. (1991). Frontal lobe damage in children and adults: A comparative review. *Developmental Neuropsychology, 7*, 283–326.

Happaney, K., Zelazo, P. D., & Stuss, D. T. (2004). Development of orbitofrontal functions: Current themes and future directions. *Brain and Cognition, 55*, 1–10.

Hongwanishkul, D., Happaney, K. R., Lee, W. S. C., & Zelazo, P. D. (2005). Assessment of hot and cool executive function in young children: Age related changes and individual differences. *Developmental Neuropsychology, 28*, 617–644.

Huttenlocher, P. R., & Dabholkar, A. S. (1997). Regional differences in synaptogenesis in human cerebral cortex. *The Journal of Comparative Neurology, 387*, 167–178.

Iran-Nejad, A. (1990). Active and dynamic self-regulation of learning processes. *Review of Educational Research, 60*, 573–602

Jernigan, T. L., Trauner, D. A., Hesselink, J. R., & Tallal, O. A. (1991). Maturation of human cerebrum observed in vivo during adolescence. *Brain, 114*, 2037–2049.

Kaplan, E. (1988). A process approach to neuropsychological assessment. In T. Boll & B. K. Bryant (Eds.), *Clinical neuropsychology and brain function: Research, measurement and practice* (pp. 129–67). Washington, DC: American Psychological Association.

Kerr, A., & Zelazo, P. D. (2004). Development of "hot" executive function: The children's gambling task. *Brain and Cognition, 55*, 148–157.

Kinney, H. C., Brody, B. A., Kloman, A. S., & Gilles, F. H. (1988). Sequence of central nervous system myelination in human infancy. *Journal of Neuropathology and Experimental Neurology, 47*, 217–234.

Krasnegor, N., Lyon, G. R., & Goldman-Rakic, P. S. (1997). *Development of the prefrontal cortex: Evolution, neurobiology, and behavior.* Baltimore, MD: Paul H. Brookes.

Levin, H. S., Culhane, K. A., Hartmann, J., Evankovich, K., Mattson, A. J., Harward, H., et al. (1991). Developmental changes in performance on tests of purported frontal lobe functioning. *Developmental Neuropsychology, 7*, 377–395.

Levine, B., Stuss, D. T., et al. (1998). The effects of focal and diffuse brain damage on strategy application: Evidence from focal lesions, traumatic brain injury and normal aging. *Journal of the International Neuropsychological Society, 4*, 247–264.

Lezak, M. (1983). *Neuropsychological assessment* (2nd ed.). New York: Oxford University Press.

Lichter, D. G., & Cummings, J. L. (Eds.). (2001). *Frontal-subcortical circuits in psychiatric and neurological disorders.* New York: Guilford Press.

Lienemann, T. O., & Reid, R. (2006). Self-regulated strategy development for students with learning disabilities. *Teacher Education and Special Education, 29*, 3–11.

Luria, A. R. (1966). *Higher cortical functions in man.* New York: Basic Books.

Luria, A. R. (1973). *The working brain,* New York: Basic Books.

Luu, P., & Tucker, D. M. (2003) Self-regulation and the executive functions: Electrophysiological clues. In A. Zani & A. M. Proverbio (Eds.), *The cognitive electrophysiology of mind and brain* (pp. 199–224). San Diego: Academic Press.

Manes, F., Sahakian, B., Clark, L., Rogers, R., Antoun, N., Aitken, M., et al. (2002). Decision making processes following damage to prefrontal cortex. *Brain, 125*, 624–639.

Miller, B. L., & Cummings, J. L. (Eds.). (2007) *The human frontal lobes: Functions and disorders* (2nd ed.). New York: Guilford Press.

Norman, D. A., & Shallice, T. (1986). Attention to action: Willed and automatic control of behavior. In R. J. Davidson, G. E. Schwartz, & D. Shapiro (Eds.), *Consciousness and self regulation: Advances in research* (pp. 1–17). New York: Plenum Press.

Passler, M., Isaac, W., & Hynd, G. W. (1985). Neuropsychological behavior attributed to frontal lobe functioning in children. *Developmental Neuropsychology, 1*, 349–370.

Perry, R. J., Rosen, H. R., Kramer, J. H., Beer, J. S., Levenson, R. L., & Miller, B. L. (2001). Hemispheric dominance for emotions, empathy, and social behavior: Evidence from right and left handers with frontotemporal dementia. *Neurocase, 7*, 145–160.

Pintrich, P. R. (1989). The dynamic interplay of student motivation and cognition in the college classroom. In C. Ames & M. Maehr (Eds.), *Advances in motivation and achievement: Motivation enhancing environments* (pp. 117–160). Greenwich, CT: JAI Press.

Pintrich, P. R. (1999). The role of motivation in promoting and sustaining self-regulated learning. *International Journal of Educational Research, 31*, 459–470.

Pintrich, P. R., & DeGroot, E. V. (1990). Motivational and self-regulated learning components of classroom academic performance. *Journal of Educational Psychology, 82*, 33–40.

Pintrich, P., Smith, D. A., Garcia, T., & McKeachie, W. (1993). Reliability and predictive validity of the Motivated Strategies for Learning Questionnaire (MSLQ). *Educational and Psychological Measurement, 53*, 801–813.

Powell, K. B., & Voeller, K. S. (2004). Prefrontal executive function syndromes in children. *Journal of Child Neurology, 19*, 785–797.

Rabbit, P. (1997). Methodologies and models in the study of executive function. In P. Rabbit (Ed.), *Methodology of frontal and executive function* (pp. 1–38). Hove, UK: Psychology Press.

Reis, S. M., McGuire, J. N., & Neu, T. W. (2000). Compensation strategies used by high ability students with learning disabilities who succeed in college. *Gifted Child Quarterly, 44*, 123–134.

Risberg, J. R., & Grafman, R. (Eds.). *The frontal lobes: Development, function, and pathology* (pp. 69–91). New York: Cambridge University Press.

Rolls, E. T. (2001). The orbitofrontal cortex and reward. *Cerebral Cortex, 10*, 284–294.

Rolls, E. T. (2004). The function of the orbitofrontal cortex. *Brain and Cognition, 55*, 11–29.

Romine, C. B., & Reynolds, C. R. (2005). A model of development of frontal lobe functioning: Findings from a meta-analysis. *Applied Neuropsychology, 12*, 190–201.

Royall, D. R., Lauterbach, E. C., Cummings, J. L., Reeve. A., Rummans, T. A., Kaufer, D. I., et al. (2002). Executive control function: A review of its promise and challenges for clinical research. *Journal of Neuropsychiatry and Clinical Neurosciences, 14,* 377–405.

Ruban, L. M., McCoach, D. B., McGuire, J., & Reiss, S. M. (2003). The differential impact of academic self-regulatory methods on academic achievement among university students with and without learning disabilities. *Journal of Learning Disabilities, 36,* 270–286.

Rule, R. R., Shimamura, A. P., & Knight, R. T. (2002). Orbitofrontal cortex and dynamic filtering of emotional stimuli. *Cognitive, Affective, and Behavioral Neuroscience, 2,* 264–270.

Rushworth, M. F., Walton, M. E., Kennerley, S. W., & Bannerman, D. M. (2004). Action sets and decisions in the medial frontal cortex. *Trends in Cognitive Science, 8,* 410–417.

Shallice, T., & Burgess, P. W. (1991). Higher-order cognitive impairments and frontal lobe lesions in man. In H. S. Levin, H. M. Eisenberg, & A. L. Benton (Eds.), *Frontal lobe function and dysfunction* (pp. 125–138). New York: Oxford University Press.

Shallice, T., & Burgess, P. W. (1996). The domain of supervisory processes and temporal organization of behaviour. *Philosophical Transactions of the Royal Society of London, Series B, 351,* 1405–1411.

Singer, B. D., & Bashir, A. S. (1999). What are executive functions and self-regulation and what do they have to do with language-learning disorder? *Language, Speech, and Hearing Services in Schools, 30,* 265–273.

Sonuga-Barke, E. J. S. (2003). The dual pathway model of ADHD: An elaboration of neurodevelopmental characteristics. *Neuroscience and Biobehavioral Review, 27,* 593–604.

Stuss, D. R. (1992). Biological and psychological development of executive functions. *Brain and Cognition, 20,* 8–23.

Stuss, D. R. (2007). New approaches to prefrontal lobe testing. In J. L. Cummings & B. L. Miller (Eds.), *The human frontal lobes: Functions and disorders* (pp. 292–305). New York: Guilford Press.

Stuss, D. T., & Anderson, V. (2004). The frontal lobes and theory of mind: Developmental concepts from adult focal lesion research. *Brain and Cognition, 55,* 69–83.

Stuss, D. T., Benson, D. F., Kaplan, E. F., Weir, W. S., Naeser, M. A., et al. (1983). The involvement of orbitofrontal cerebrum in cognitive tasks. *Neuropsychologia, 21,* 235–48.

Stuss, D. T., & Levine, B. (2004). Adult clinical neuropsychology: Lessons from studies of the frontal lobes. *Annual Review of Psychology, 53,* 401–433.

Trainin, G., & Swanson, H. L. (2005). Cognition, metacognition, and achievement of college students with learning disabilities. *Learning Disability Quarterly, 28,* 261–271.

van Zile-Tamsen, C. (1999). The differential impact of motivation on the self-regulated strategy use of high- and low-achieving college students. *Journal of College Student Development, 40,* 54–60.

Vygotsky, L. (1962). *Thought and language.* Cambridge, MA: MIT Press.

Weinstein, C. E., & Mayer, R. E. (1986). The teaching of learning strategies. In M. Wittrock (Ed.), *Handbook of research on teaching* (pp. 315–327). New York: Macmillan.

Welsh, M. C., Pennington, B. F., & Grossier, D. B. (1991). A normative-developmental study of executive functioning: A window on prefrontal function in children. *Developmental Neuropsychology, 7*, 131–149.

Wolf, L. E. (2001). College students with ADHD and other hidden disabilities. *Annals of the New York Academy of Sciences, 931*, 385–395.

Wolf, L. E., & Wasserstein, J. (2001). Adult ADHD: Concluding thoughts. *Annals of the New York Academy of Sciences, 931*, 396–408.

Wolters, C. A. (1998). Self-regulated learning and college students' regulation of motivation. *Journal of Educational Psychology, 90*, 224–235.

Wolters, C. A. (2003). Regulation of motivation: Evaluating an underemphasized aspect of self-regulated learning. *Educational Psychologist, 38*, 189–205.

Yakovlev, P. I., & Lecours, A. R. (1967). The myelinogentic cycles of regional maturation of the brain. In A. Minkowski (Ed), *Regional development of the brain in early life* (pp. 3–70). Oxford: Blackwell Scientific.

Zelazo, P. D., & Müller, U. (2002). Executive function in typical and atypical development. In U. Goswami (Ed). *Handbook of childhood cognitive development* (pp. 445–469). Oxford: Blackwell Scientific.

Zimmerman, B. J. (1986). Development of self-regulated learning: What are the key subprocesses? *Contemporary Educational Psychology, 16*, 307–313.

Zimmerman, B. J. (1994). Dimensions of academic self-regulation: A conceptual framework for education. In D. H. Schunk & B. J. Zimmerman (Eds.), *Self-regulation of learning and performance* (pp. 3–21). Hillsdale, NJ: Lawrence Erlbaum.

Zimmerman, B. J. (2002). Becoming a self-regulated learner: An overview. *Theory Into Practice, 41*, 64–70.

PART **3**
Diagnosis and Assessment

CHAPTER 10

Comprehensive Evaluation of Adults
With Learning Disabilities

ROBERT L. MAPOU

Contents

At the beginning of the 21st century, neuropsychological evaluation of the adult with a learning disability (LD) can now be guided by the results of research, much of which has been produced over the past 10 years. This is far cry from the "seat of the pants" approach to adult LD assessment, grounded in knowledge about LDs in children, which was the state of the field when I first became engaged in this work in the early 1990s. Interestingly, the evaluation of LDs and attention-deficit/hyperactivity disorder (ADHD) in adults is the only area of neuropsychological assessment that has been guided by extrapolating from what we know about children. In other areas of neuropsychological assessment and research, including the effects of specific neurological disorders and neuropsychological test development, it has usually been the case that children have been treated as "little adults." This assumption, of course, is almost always wrong and has been the source of much consternation to developmental neuropsychologists. However, there is now ample research on neurological disorders in children and burgeoning development of tests specifically for children.

In this chapter, I outline a comprehensive approach to neuropsychological evaluation of adult LDs (ALD). Before doing so, however, I discuss my rationale for comprehensive, as opposed to brief, evaluation. For the purpose of this chapter, the word *disorder* is sometimes used synonymously with the word *disability*. However, as noted later, it must be remembered that the legal definition of an LD applies a more rigorous standard than the traditional definition used in research and clinical work.

The Rationale for Comprehensive Assessment

In Parts 1 and 2 of this book, the authors have reviewed research on the neurological and cognitive basis for developmental written language (reading, writing) mathematics, nonverbal learning, and executive functioning disorders. Elsewhere (Mapou, 2004, 2008), I have summarized research relevant to ALD assessment. One can then apply this research to form hypotheses about the expected features of a specific LD, which, in turn, can be used to select measures included in a battery. For example, in Table 10.1, I have listed the typical features of language-based LDs, including disorders of spoken language, reading, and writing. As a second

Table 10.1 Typical Features of Verbal Learning Disorders, Including Reading and Writing Disorders

Verbal IQ/Verbal Comprehension Index < Performance IQ/Perceptual Organization Index

Strength in visual skills

Weaknesses in:

    Auditory phonemic awareness

    Span for auditory–verbal information

    Comprehension of oral language

    Word retrieval

    Decoding when reading and encoding when spelling

    Automaticity (speed) when decoding and reading single words

    Fluency (smoothness) when reading sentences

    Reading comprehension

May appear shy or withdrawn in social interactions because of communication difficulties

example, in Table 10.2, I have listed the typical features of nonverbal LDs. When evaluating for the presence of a mathematics disorder, one should include measures of all components of math (basic math fact knowledge, written calculation, math problem solving, higher level math knowledge), language skills, visuospatial skills, and executive functioning, as all have been found to be associated with mathematics problems (Cirino, Morris, & Morris, 2002; Greiffenstein & Baker, 2002).

Considering the research and the facts that (a) manifestations of ALD can be subtle, (b) the development of compensatory strategies can mask persisting deficits, (c) LDs frequently co-occur with ADHD, and (d) LDs often result in co-occurring psychiatric disorders, the neuropsychological evaluation must "cast a wide net." Clients may also come in with complaints unrelated to LDs, but review of their history and examination of test results leads to a new LD diagnosis. To assess these issues effectively, the clinician needs to take a thorough history, with particular attention to developmental and academic issues. The clinician must also use a broad group of tests, to be sure that difficulties are not missed. In addition, an assessment of the client's emotional state is very important, given the potential fallout of years of struggles due to an undiagnosed LD. Finally, detailed information, both behavioral and neuropsychological, can lead to more effective recommendations, including a rationale for accommodations when necessary, compensatory strategies, and direct intervention for skills such as reading. In summary, by taking a comprehensive approach,

Table 10.2 Typical Features of Nonverbal Learning Disorders

Performance IQ/Perceptual Organization Index < Verbal IQ/Verbal Comprehension Index

Strength in language skills and rote repetition/memory

Weaknesses in:

Interpersonal skills (socially awkward, fails to pick up on nonverbal cues, does not modulate voice tone and volume appropriately)

Visuospatial skills (may misperceive drawings and distort when copying)

Motor skills (poor coordination and fine motor dexterity, poor in sports)

Attention and processing speed

Mathematics, particularly if timed

Aspects of executive functioning and conceptual thinking

Feels pressured when required to perform under time constraints

Feels very anxious in social situations, more so as s/he gets older

Limited or nonexistent social circle

May meet criteria for Asperger's disorder, which is a behavioral/psychiatric diagnosis (nonverbal learning disorder is a cognitive diagnosis and can characterize features of different underlying conditions)

the clinician can make an accurate diagnosis, can differentiate between LDs and other conditions, can determine the presence of co-occurring conditions, and can make effective recommendations.

The Assessment Process

The components of a comprehensive assessment are listed in Table 10.3. Although these are the standard components of any good neuropsychological assessment, there is some difference in the emphasis placed on different aspects of each component. Historical information regarding early development and education is essential. For adults with an LD, there will always be evidence of a problem early in development, albeit sometimes subtle, even if the manifestations of the LD did not become obvious until

Table 10.3 Components of the Neuropsychological Evaluation

History interview

Record review

Behavioral rating scales for assessment of co-occurring ADHD (self and other report)

Intellectual/academic/cognitive evaluation, including behavioral observations

Personality/emotional assessment

Source: Mapou, 2008. (Reprinted with permission.)

the client faced the more complex and rigorous demands of postsecondary education. For example, there may have been early problems learning to read, with intervention in the first years of elementary school, followed by resolution of the problem but reemergence with the more complex demands of secondary or postsecondary education. Conversely, difficulties are far less likely to be due to an LD when an adult has shown consistently strong academic performance through high school and has no evidence of any previous developmental or academic difficulties.

Collecting Historical Information

Table 10.4 lists the key historical information that should be obtained (Mapou, in press-b). Again, all of this will be familiar to practicing neuropsychologists. I recommend obtaining records, to the extent possible, including report cards with teacher comments, routine academic testing from primary and secondary school (e.g., Comprehensive Tests of Basic Skills [CTBS], California Achievement Test [CAT], Comprehensive Testing Program [CTP], Otis-Lennon School Ability Test, Iowa Tests of Basic Skills, Stanford Achievement Test), any private school admissions testing (e.g., Secondary School Admission Test [SSAT]), college entrance examinations (e.g., SAT, SAT II, ACT), college transcripts, graduate or professional school entrance examinations (e.g., GRE, GMAT, LSAT, MCAT), and graduate or professional school transcripts. Especially for clients who attended school many years ago, these can be invaluable for obtaining detailed information on past problems. I have found some clients who have actually overestimated their grades in school and had more problems than they reported. Conversely, I have had clients who reported past difficulties but who turned out to have had a stellar early academic record. Prior standardized test scores can provide hints to the nature of client's LD (e.g., verbal scores on standardized academic tests that are far lower than spatial or quantitative scores can point toward a language-based learning disability). Interviewing a parent can be valuable, although not always practical.

I have previously recommended specific questions to target key characteristics that are common in adults with ALD (Mapou, 2004, 2006). These are listed in Table 10.5. Because ADHD commonly co-occurs with LDs, evaluating the client for the possibility of ADHD is also important (Katz, Goldstein, & Beers, 2001). A semistructured interview, based on the Utah Criteria for ADHD diagnosis (Ward, Wender, & Reimherr, 1993; Wender, 1995) can be used to cover the problems listed in Table 10.6. This should be supplemented by behavioral rating scales, also listed in Table 10.6, completed by the client and, whenever possible, by parents and a significant other (see Mapou, 2006) for a discussion of neuropsychological assessment of adults with ADHD.

Table 10.4 Historical Information

I. Reason for referral and current difficulty (perspective of client, significant other, and referral source)

II. Medical history

    A. Current medical, neurological, and psychiatric issues

    B. Past medical, neurological, and psychiatric issues

    C. Current and past substance use (alcohol, recreational drugs, cigarettes, caffeine)

    D. Current medications

III. Developmental history

    A. Pregnancy, labor, delivery, and problems immediately following birth

    B. Developmental milestones

    C. Serious illnesses or injuries as a young child

    D. Frequent ear infections and drainage tube placement

    E. Febrile or other types of seizures

    F. Primary language

IV. Educational history

    A. Early subject-specific difficulties (e.g., reading, spelling, handwriting, mathematics)

    B. Attentional problems and hyperactivity

    C. Diagnosed LD or ADHD

    D. Formal special education, accommodations, tutoring, and other assistance in primary and secondary education (e.g., IEP or 504 Plan)

    E. Private tutoring, speech-language therapy, or occupational therapy

    F. Repeated grades and reasons

    G. Results of testing

        1. Neuropsychological/psychological/psychoeducational testing

        2. Yearly testing (e.g., CTP III, CTBS, Iowa, Stanford, Otis-Lennon)

        3. Entrance examinations (e.g., SAT, GRE, LSAT, GMAT, MCAT)

    H. Total number of years in school

    I. Grades in high school, college, and beyond

    J. Specific problems in high school, college, and beyond

    K. Accommodations and support in postsecondary education

    L. Degrees received

Table 10.4 (continued) Historical Information

V.   Occupational history

    A.   Current job (e.g., length on it, responsibilities, salary, difficulties)

    B.   Past job history

        1.   Jobs held (e.g., length on it, responsibilities, salary, difficulties)

        2.   Periods of unemployment (e.g., reasons, length)

VI.   Social history

    A.   Marital or relationship status (e.g., length, children)

    B.   Social support outside the primary relationship

    C.   Recreational interests and activities (look for artistic, musical and athletic strengths)

VII.   Family history

    A.   Parents and siblings

        1.   Living (age) or deceased (age at and cause of death)

        2.   Relevant medical history

        3.   Educational attainment and academic difficulties

        4.   Occupation

    B.   Other family members

        1.   Relevant medical history

        2.   History of learning difficulties, LD, or ADHD

Source: Mapou, 2008. (Reprinted with permission.)

Having a complete history is crucial for documenting an LD in an adult, especially when accommodations or other supports are desired. Shaywitz (2003) recently made the same point in the context of dyslexia. As an example, I have worked with adults with very clear LDs who have initially been turned down for accommodations because a detailed history of their problems and interventions to address them were not included in the report. This is discussed further later in the chapter.

Neuropsychological Measures

My current battery for ALD assessment is shown in Table 10.7. This is based on a framework for cognitive functioning that I have presented previously (Mapou, 1995). The battery is constantly revised, based on new knowledge about ALD and development of new tests; two versions have been published previously (Mapou, 2004, 2008).

Table 10.5 Helpful Questions When Taking a History

Were there are any problems with your mother's pregnancy, labor, or delivery with you?

> Problems with pre- or postnatal development, especially anoxia, can suggest the presence of subtle brain damage, often associated with LDs.

Were you slow to develop speech, language, or motor skills?

> Hints to the presence of an LD can frequently be found in slowed development. Those with verbal LDs may report slow acquisition of speech and language, but normal or rapid acquisition of motor skills, while those with nonverbal LDs may report slow acquisition of motor skills, but normal or rapid development of speech and language.

Did you experience frequent ear infections as a young child? Were tubes placed for fluid drainage?

> These individuals may develop spoken language slowly, because they did not hear adequately during the critical period when phonological awareness developed. They are then at increased risk for spoken and written language LDs.

Did you ever suffer seizures or convulsions as a young child?

> Early seizures can be a sign of brain dysfunction and associated with the development of LDs, although one or a few febrile seizures may not be of much consequence.

When you first started school, did you have any trouble learning to read, spell, write, or do arithmetic?

Did you have problems paying attention or concentrating in class? Did you daydream frequently? Were you hyperactive? Did you get into trouble with your teachers for these behaviors? Did your teachers make comments about these behaviors to your parents or in your report cards?

Did you have problems completing your homework on time?

Were you in any special classes? Were you tutored? Did you receive special education services? Did you ever have an Individualized Education Program (IEP) or a 504 Plan?

Did you repeat any grades? If so, why?

Were you given any accommodations in school? What were they? Were they helpful?

For those completing or who have completed postsecondary education, the following questions are helpful:

> Do you have trouble paying attention or concentrating in large lectures?

> Is taking notes difficult for you? Do you get behind in what is being presented?

> Do you have difficulty completing tests in the allotted time?

> What types of tests are hardest for you—essays, short answer, or multiple choice? What makes these types of tests hard for you?

> Do you have problems with time management? Do you procrastinate? Do you have difficulty handing in your assignments on time? Do you complete work at the last minute? Do you pull all-nighters?

Table 10.5 (continued) Helpful Questions When Taking a History

Have you failed courses or taken incompletes? If so, which courses?

Have you received any accommodations in college? Were these helpful? On what basis did you receive the accommodations—informally, provisionally pending evaluation, or previous diagnosis of LD?

Source: Mapou, 2008. (Reprinted with permission.)

Table 10.6 Assessment of ADHD

Semistructured interview based on the Utah criteria:

Ask about past and/or current difficulties with:

Physical or cognitive restlessness, needing to be "on the go"

Attention and concentration when listening to others, reading, and/or doing cognitively demanding tasks

Remembering information heard and/or read

Forgetfulness

Physical organization at home and at school/work

Time management, time estimation, and associated procrastination

Initiating and following through on tasks

Impulsivity when speaking and acting

Taking unnecessary risks

Emotional expression, temper control, and handling stress

ADHD behavioral rating scales:

Wender Utah Rating Scale and Parents' Rating Scale (Ward, Wender, & Reimherr, 1993; Wender, 1995)

ADHD Rating Scale-IV–Retrospective and Current Forms (Barkley, Fischer, Smallish, & Fletcher, 2002; DuPaul, Power, Anastopoulos, & Reid, 1998; Murphy, 1996)

Conners' Adult ADHD Rating Scale (Conners, Ehrhardt, & Sparrow, 1998)

Note: See Mapou (2006) for additional details.

This is a comprehensive battery, covering the realms of intellectual skills; academic skills (reading, writing, mathematics); attention; executive functions, problem-solving skills, and reasoning abilities; language skills; visuospatial skills, and learning/memory. I use a core battery for all clients, with alternate measures used based on age. Core measures are marked with an asterisk (*). I include additional measures, based on the referral question, knowledge about the LD if diagnosed previously, and hypotheses generated from the history and presenting problems and during testing.

Table 10.7 Neuropsychological Test Battery

Skill level/component	Measures used
Global skills	
Intellectual functioning	Wechsler Adult Intelligence Scale-III*
Academic skills	
Reading	
Decoding	Woodcock-Johnson-III Tests of Achievement (WJ3ACH): Word Attack*
Recognition	WJ3ACH Letter Word Identification*
Automaticity	Test of Word Reading Efficiency (through age 24)
Comprehension	WJ3ACH Reading Fluency*
	Nelson-Denny Reading Test (Form G or H): Comprehension*
	Scholastic Abilities Test for Adults (SATA): Reading Comprehension
	Wechsler Individual Achievement Test-II (WIAT-II) Reading Comprehension
Writing	
Encoding	WJ3ACH Spelling of Sounds
Spelling and writing mechanics	WJ3ACH Spelling*
	SATA Writing Mechanics
Expressive writing	WJ3ACH Writing Fluency*
	WIAT-II Written Expression*
	SATA Writing Composition
	WJ3ACH Writing Samples
Mathematics	
Calculational skill	WJ3ACH Math Fluency*
	WJ3ACH Calculation*
	WRAT-3 Arithmetic
	SATA Math Calculation
Problem-solving	WJ3ACH Applied Problems
	SATA Math Application
Knowledge/concepts	WJ3ACH Quantitative Concepts

Table 10.7 (continued) Neuropsychological Test Battery

Skill level/component	Measures used
Foundation skills	
Attention	
Deployment	
Alertness	Observation
Focused attention	WAIS-III Digit Symbol-Coding*, Symbol Search*, and Processing Speed Index*
	WAIS-III Digit-Symbol-Copy
	Woodcock-Johnson-III Tests of Cognitive Abilities (WJ3COG): Visual Matching, Decision Speed, and Processing Speed cluster score (through age 19) or Trail Making Test and Digit Vigilance (age 20 and above)*
Sustained attention	Integrated Visual and Auditory (IVA) Continuous Performance Test or Test of Variables of Attention (TOVA)*
Encoding	
Span of attention	WAIS-III or Wechsler Memory Scale-III (WMS-III) Digit Span, Forwards*
	California Verbal Learning Test-II, Trial 1*
	WJ3COG: Memory for Sentences*
	WMS-III Logical Memory I 1st Recall*
Resistance to interference	Consonant Trigrams*
Mental manipulation/ divided attention	WAIS-III or WMS-III Digit Span, Backwards [a]
	WAIS-III Arithmetic,* Letter-Number Sequencing,* and Working Memory Index*
	Paced Auditory Serial Addition Test
Motor functions	
Strength	Grip Strength
Speed	Finger Tapping Test
Dexterity	Grooved Pegboard Test
Executive functions, problem-solving skills, and reasoning abilities	
Planning	Tower of London[DX]–2nd Edition*
	Delis-Kaplan Executive Functioning System (D-KEFS): Tower Test
	Porteus Maze Test

(continued)

Table 10.7 (continued) Neuropsychological Test Battery

Skill level/component	Measures used
Flexibility of thinking	Wisconsin Card Sorting Test*
Organization	California Verbal Learning Test-II, Semantic vs. Serial Clustering*
	Rey-Osterrieth Complex Figure Test, Copy*
Reasoning	WAIS-III Similarities, Comprehension, Picture Completion, Picture Arrangement, and Matrix Reasoning*
	D-KEFS: Twenty Questions Test*
	WJRCOG Verbal Analogies
	WJ3COG Concept Formation
Modality-specific skills	
Language	
Phonemic awareness	Lindamood Auditory Conceptualization Test-3
	Comprehensive Test of Phonological Processing (through age 24)
	WJ3ACH Sound Awareness
	WJ3COG Incomplete Words, Sound Blending and Phonemic Awareness
Comprehension	
Single word	WAIS-III Vocabulary*
	Peabody Picture Vocabulary Test-III
Complex	Oral and Written Language Scales (OWLS): Listening Comprehension (through age 21) or WJ3ACH Oral Comprehension and Listening Comprehension Cluster (age 22 and above)*
	WJ3ACH Understanding Directions*
Production	
Naming	WJ3ACH Picture Vocabulary (through age 19) or Boston Naming Test (age 20 and above)*
	WJ3COG Rapid Picture Naming
Single word	D-KEFS Verbal Fluency (through age 19) *or* Controlled Oral Word Association Test (COWAT; age 20 and above)*
Complex	Observation of speech and language production in conversation and in response to test items*
	OWLS: Oral Expression (through age 21)
Foreign language aptitude	Modern Language Aptitude Test

Table 10.7 (continued) Neuropsychological Test Battery

Skill level/component	Measures used
Visuospatial Skills	
Perception	Boston Naming Test*
	Rey-Osterrieth Complex Figure Test*
	WJ3COG Spatial Relations
	Benton Tests (Visual Form Discrimination, Judgement of Line Orientation, Facial Recognition)
Construction	WAIS-III Block Design*
	WAIS-III Object Assembly
	Rey-Osterrieth Complex Figure Test, Copy*
Integrated Skills	
Learning/memory	
Verbal	California Verbal Learning Test-II*
	WMS-III Logical Memory*
Visual	Rey-Osterrieth Complex Figure Test, Immediate and Delayed Recall*
	WMS-III Family Pictures or Faces*
	WAIS-III Digit Symbol-Incidental Learning*

* Core measures

I no longer routinely include sensory and motor tests because I have not found them very useful in either diagnosing ALD or for making recommendations for interventions. However, I include motor measures if there is question about fine motor skills or handwriting. I also include them if I am concerned about a neurological cause of the client's problems and want further data on possible lateralizing signs. In addition, sensory and motor measures can be used to support conclusions about a left- or right-hemisphere basis for the LD, which may be of interest. Because the listed tests are widely available through the major test publishers, I have not included references. It is also important to note that this is neither a definitive battery nor a comprehensive list of tests; other measures can be used, based on the clinician's preference. In the following sections, I discuss issues related to assessment of specific LDs. Please refer to Mapou (2004), where I have covered some of these issues in more depth, and to Mapou (2008) for additional thoughts.

Reading Disorders (Dyslexia) Research has found key skills that contribute to effective reading and that require the addition of several measures to the core battery. First, one must have information about auditory phonemic processing. The Comprehensive Test of Phonological Processing assesses several components of phonemic processing in clients up to age 24. For those over 24, measures from the Woodcock-Johnson-III Tests of Achievement (WJ3ACH) and Tests of Cognitive Abilities (WJ3COG) can be used. Another measure, the Lindamood Auditory Conceptualization Test-3 (LAC-3) is useful for all ages. In contrast with the other tests, on the LAC-3, the ability to work with phonemes is assessed by associating colored blocks with phonemes, without making associations between sounds and letters.

Naming and timed word-retrieval tests, which are included in the core battery, can help determine whether poor lexical access is contributing to slow reading. The WJ3COG Rapid Picture Naming subtest is a speeded measure of these skills and can be added, supplementing core naming and word-generation tasks. Assessment of span for auditory-verbal information, using several measures, is crucial. Adults with reading disorders frequently overload and miss verbal information when a large amount is presented to them at once. When span for verbal information is poor, especially at the sentence or paragraph level, one is likely to miss information when listening is required. This is further exacerbated by having to listen and take notes simultaneously. Overloading will also affect reading, since one may lose track of the beginning of a sentence or a paragraph by the time one reaches the end. This makes rereading necessary, which slows reading speed and can affect comprehension. This is a problem commonly experienced by adults with reading disorders (Shaywitz, 2003).

Decoding and single-word reading are often intact in adults with reading disorders when speed is not an issue. However, automaticity, or the ease with which one can read and sound out words, and fluency, or the smoothness with which one can read text, are more likely to be affected. Shaywitz (2003) has emphasized the need to use timed reading tests. The Test of Word Reading Efficiency is a measure of automaticity that assesses speeded oral reading of real words and decoding of pseudowords. It has normative data for adults up to age 24. Unfortunately, similar measures are not available for older adults. The WJ3ACH Reading Fluency subtest evaluates speeded comprehension at the sentence level; sentence difficulty level is the same throughout the test.

Reading skills in adults with reading disorders are much more likely to break down for longer passages and for books. Unfortunately, the comprehension measures that are available often do not adequately illustrate the problems that adults with reading disorders experience. This is because of the brevity of the passages and because passage complexity is frequently less than that of the material that adults in college, graduate school, or professional school must read. The Passage Comprehension subtest of the

WJ3ACH, although useful for adults with severe dyslexia, does not evaluate the skills needed for reading text at the high school level or above. Measures in which longer passages are presented, followed by multiple-choice questions that require data-based and inferential responses, are better, although scores can sometimes overestimate reading ability for more complex material. However, they are currently the best that we have. The Nelson-Denny Reading Test (NDRT) has standard (20-minute) and extended time (32-minute) versions. This is particularly useful, because the full extended time is a bit more than 50% longer than the standard time; 50% additional time is the most common extended-time accommodation. The test also has two forms, G and H. The manual describes using one version of the test or the other, with slight differences in administration (e.g., the Reading Rate is not administered with the extended time version), and with clear instructions about the length of time available to the client. However, for many years, I have administered the test by doing the standard version (20 minutes), asking the client to stop, marking where he or she is, and then telling the client to continue until finished or until I say stop again. I have also not told the client how much time was available. An informal survey conducted with colleagues locally and nationally in 2004 indicated that most administered the test in this way, although some reported doing each version separately, using the two alternate forms. At the time of this writing, I do not know the extent to which this approach compromises application of the normative data. However, testing agencies and organizations have never raised this as an issue. As an alternative, the SATA Reading Comprehension subtest can be used, if shorter passages are needed or if one needs a comparison between the longer passages of the NDRT and the shorter passages of this measure. However, there are no normative data for extended time with the SATA. For adults with more limited reading skills, one can use Level AR of the Gates-MacGinitie Reading Test, which has normative data for community college students.

In addition to formal assessment, the clinician should always ask the client about how he or she reads, to understand what may be contributing to slowness. It is important to know whether the client reads letter-by-letter or word-by-word, if that is the case, whether the client must reread frequently, and what compensatory strategies are used. Compensatory strategies may add to the time needed to read and should be documented. They do not, however, eliminate the problem. The clinician should also have the client read a passage aloud, to obtain a qualitative measure of his or her fluency, because the reading comprehension measures all use silent reading. Finally, the clinician should ask about functional reading problems to assess ways in which the reading disorder is interfering with everyday life. This can include difficulty reading labels when shopping, difficulty reading and filling out forms, difficulty reading and following signs simultaneously when driving, and avoiding recreational reading or limiting recreational reading to short pieces, such as newspaper and magazine articles.

Nonverbal Learning Disorders   Right-hemisphere difficulties are believed to be at the core of nonverbal LDs (Collins & Rourke, 2003; Katz et al., 2001). Therefore, the emphasis in assessment should be on visuospatial perceptual and constructional skills. Because of perceptual problems, individuals with nonverbal LDs often have great difficulty copying models. Unlike those whose constructional difficulties stem from purely organizational and planning weaknesses, individuals with nonverbal LDs may make visual errors on the Boston Naming Test, misperceive components of the Rey-Osterrieth Complex Figure, or struggle with nonmotor perceptual tasks, such as the Spatial Relations subtest of the WJ3COG. Problems with complex sensory and motor skills are also common, and so adding measures of sensory and motor skills can be helpful for this group. Mathematics difficulties were initially considered a key feature of nonverbal LDs (Rourke, 1995), although, in my own practice, I have not always found this to be the case. In fact, some of my clients with nonverbal LDs have been in technical positions that emphasize math, choosing these fields because they have to interact minimally with people. In my view, difficulty with the pragmatics of communication, including problems responding to nonverbal cues in interpersonal interactions, unusual modulation of voice tone and volume, and interpersonal awkwardness, which, in turn, lead to persisting problems with relationships, are key to diagnosing the disorder. In fact, I will not make a nonverbal LD diagnosis without evidence of these interpersonal problems. Finally, it is important to assess problem-solving and conceptual-thinking skills because recent research has indicated that deficits in these skills are prominent in adults with nonverbal LDs and that these skills decline over time (Ahmad, Rourke, & Drummond, 2002). Impairment in problem solving and conceptual thinking will also affect many aspects of everyday functioning.

Similar to reading disorders, it is helpful to ask clients about the functional problems that they experience. In addition to the interpersonal problems, this can include difficulty reading maps, following instructions provided as diagrams or flowcharts, working with computer programs that emphasize visual skills (e.g., spreadsheets, multiple windows), and driving. One client of mine reported that she preferred driving in heavy traffic that was moving slowly, as opposed to driving on the highway. Long-standing difficulties with complex motor skills and coordination are often common. These clients frequently report that they were poor at sports.

Mathematics Disorders Assessment of clients for the possibility of a mathematics disorder should include measures of visuospatial perceptual and constructional skills, attention, conceptual thinking, and problem-solving skills, as all are necessary for effective mathematics skills (Rourke & Conway, 1997). Because mathematics and reading disorders frequently co-occur (Katz et al., 2001), the possible contribution of language problems to difficulties with math should also be assessed. Furthermore, a recent study (Cirino et al., 2002) has indicated that language and executive functioning skills may be even more important to calculational abilities than visuospatial skills.

Like reading, several components of math skills should be assessed. One can evaluate speed when doing simple math problems using the Math Fluency subtest of the WJ3ACH, on which the difficulty level remains constant across the subtest. More complex written calculational skills can be evaluated with the Calculation subtest of the WJ3ACH and, if speed is thought to be an issue, results from this test can be compared with those from the Arithmetic subtest of the WRAT-3, which is timed. Finally, the ability to solve word problems and access to mathematical knowledge can be assessed, respectively, with the Applied Problems and Quantitative Concepts subtests of the WJ3ACH. However, the latter test is problematic as a pure measure of mathematical knowledge because it also includes a mathematical problem-solving section. Qualitatively, one can see if a client has more difficulty with WAIS-III Information questions that require numerical knowledge in comparison with those that do not.

Functionally, one should ask about math problems in everyday life, such as difficulty counting change, figuring out restaurant tips, balancing a checkbook, and managing money, in general. However, as a client recently pointed out, the best accommodation, a calculator, is widely used and can reduce or eliminate the functional impact of a math disorder in everyday life.

Spelling Disorders Most spelling disorders occur in the context of a reading disorder; if one has difficulty decoding and reading single words, then the same problem will occur when encoding sounds into letters. However, for some clients, spelling can be impaired in the absence of reading difficulties. The WJ3ACH Spelling of Sounds subtest is a spelling analog of the Word Attack subtest and measures the ability to convert phonemes (sound combinations) into graphemes (letter combinations). I also find this subtest very helpful when evaluating individuals for a reading disorder. The WJ3ACH Phoneme/Grapheme Knowledge cluster score, a composite formed by Word Attack and Spelling of Sounds, provides a measure of phonological awareness for written language. Unlike the Dictation subtest of the old Woodcock-Johnson-Revised tests, the WJ3ACH Spelling subtest measures spelling only, without contaminating the score with measures of writing mechanics. It is also important to examine language skills in detail, including measures of auditory phonological processing.

Like the calculator for mathematics disorders, the ubiquitous computer-based spell checker has limited the functional impact of spelling disorders. However, individuals who have underlying difficulties with phonological awareness and who have reading problems as well can have a hard time selecting the correct option when using a spell checker. Asking about this, then, is important.

Expressive Writing Disorders   Expressive writing disorders, which are a common reason why adults, particularly those in school, seek assessment, appear to stem from two factors. First, some adults have a long history of problems with fine motor skills, resulting in problems with handwriting. Typically, they had great difficulty learning to write in elementary school, may have started with a poor handwriting posture, had even more difficulty learning to write cursively, and, as a result, struggled to complete writing assignments from an early age. Many gave up on writing, which can be seen in comments from teachers. Those who did not grow up in the age of personal computers are likely to have never developed strong writing skills. Today, however, children with this type of problem often do well and can even come to enjoy writing by using a computer. For individuals with this type of difficulty, assessment of fine motor skills is important. They often do less well on measures of focused attention/processing speed that emphasize fine motor skills, such as the WAIS-III Digit Symbol subtest. Finally, their handwriting is typically difficult to read. All of these areas should be included in an assessment.

A second group of individuals struggles with writing because of difficulty with verbal organizational skills. Often able to express their ideas orally, albeit perhaps in not always the most organized and concise way, they struggle to express themselves on paper, reporting that they have a hard time knowing how to start when writing and how to put their thoughts on paper in a coherent, organized way. They often report a history of having been told that their ideas on paper were good but were not expressed clearly or were not elaborated. They sometimes have had problems with handwriting, as well, but this is not always the case. Although I have not seen any neuropsychological research on expressive writing disorders in adults, Mel Levine, a physician known for his work with children with LDs, has described this type of "output" disorder very well with children, noting that it is often seen in association with problems with motor skills, attention, and executive functioning (Levine, 2002). In my experience, adults with ADHD often struggle with expressive writing because of the impact of ADHD on initiation and organization.

Unfortunately, assessment of expressive writing in adults can be difficult. Simple writing speed can be assessed with the Writing Fluency subtest of the WJ3ACH, on which difficulty level, as on the other two fluency measures, remains constant across items. Individuals are marked off if they do not include one of the three specified words, if they change one of the specified words substantially, or if they write a very poorly constructed sentence. For adults with severe writing problems, the Writing Samples subtest of the WJ3ACH can be useful. However, because it does not require organizing sentences into a paragraph or paragraphs into a longer essay or paper, even adults with expressive writing difficulties can achieve a high score. A better choice, now that normative data are available across the life span, is the Written Expression subtest of the WIAT-II. This subtest includes three tasks: writing as many words from a specific category as quickly as possible (in essence, a written analog to the category portion of the COWAT), writing single sentences that combine several into one or that describe a picture within specific constraints, and writing an essay in the form of a letter to the editor. The essay test provides scoring based on a number of different criteria. However, only a single score is provided for the entire test, and so good performance on one section can mask poor performance on another. Also, having used this test now for over a year, I have still found it to be insensitive to writing problems in adults, particularly those in postgraduate study. Like the NDRT, it does not fully capture the complexity of the writing demands of college and postgraduate study. But, as with the NDRT, it is the best we have. When characterizing the results from the test, it is important to describe problems noted, because the total score does not capture this. Although I used the Writing Composition subtest of the SATA for many years, I found that its emphasis on creative writing, rather than expository writing, failed to capture the difficulties of adults with writing disorders.

Attention and Executive Functioning Disorders   Some adults have clear weaknesses in attention and executive functioning on testing. They also report problems with these skills in everyday life. Yet, based on their history and their symptoms, they do not meet the *DSM-IV* or the Utah diagnostic criteria for ADHD. To my knowledge, there is very limited research on individuals like this, apart from those with acquired disorders of attention and executive functioning, such as those with a history of traumatic brain injury, seizure disorders, or other neurological conditions. Assuming that I have ruled out a primary psychiatric disorder, such as an anxiety or affective disorder, as the cause of the attention and executive functioning problems, and assuming that the client's problems are not associated with some other type of learning disorder, I may diagnose an attention and/or executive functioning disorder. Although I recognize that this may be controversial, I believe that we need a category into which these individuals can be placed. Assessment, obviously, emphasizes attentional and executive functioning measures, which routinely form a large part of my core battery. As with the other disorders, it is also important to obtain information on the functional impact of these problems (see Wolf & Kaplan, Chapter 10, this volume, for a more detailed discussion of developmental dysexecutive disorders).

Learning and Memory Disorders   On rare occasions, I have evaluated individuals who have inordinate difficulty learning and memorizing information, both on testing and in everyday life. Although learning and memory problems are common in association with LDs and ADHD, these individuals show no signs of one of the described LDs or ADHD that appear to explain their difficulty. They also do not report a neurological disorder that could account for the problem. Again, assuming that I have ruled out a psychiatric cause as primary, I may diagnose a learning and memory disorder. However, we have no research on these types of pure problems from a developmental perspective, and this may be considered even more controversial than the prior category.

Personality and Emotional Assessment

Psychosocial and psychiatric problems are frequent in ALD. In fact, in my experience, it is a rare adult who has coped with a life of difficulty with academics who comes through totally unscathed. Anxiety related to academic tasks and depression over struggles and failure are common. For these reasons, personality and emotional assessment is an important component of the evaluation. In addition to providing information about how the client is coping with his or her LD, personality assessment can rule out psychiatric disorder as a primary cause of cognitive problems and can lead to recommendations for treating the emotional distress. For most clients, the Minnesota Multiphasic Personality Inventory-2 (MMPI-2) can be used. I have found the reading level of the MMPI-2 to be such that individuals with reading disorders, unless severely dyslexic, can complete the instrument reliably and validly, if allowed to do it at their own pace. However, they may have difficulty with double negatives and sometimes make erroneous responses because of this. Indices sensitive to variability may also be elevated. If this occurs, inquiry by the clinician can usually resolve any concerns. If, however, the clinician does not believe the client can complete the MMPI-2, then shorter self-report measures, supplemented by the clinical interview, can be used.

Some Further Considerations to Enhance the Testing Experience

Our practice, with a focus on LDs across the life span for more than 20 years, has always prided itself on making the testing experience a positive one. Adults with diagnosed LDs or who struggled in school without a formal diagnosis often associate any type of testing with failure. This can lead to considerable anxiety and apprehension about being evaluated, something that I have often observed. This is because the client is faced with his or her weaknesses throughout the testing process. To alleviate this response, I may give more feedback and encouragement than neuro-psychologists typically do. This is not to say that I give the answer away, but, rather, I may provide more frequent positive reinforcement about how the person is doing when this does not violate the standardized test administration. In addition, amending testing limits so that clients are allowed to complete a task successfully can also ease anxiety, even if this lengthens testing time. This is in addition to the value for documenting the problem more clearly, particularly when qualitative information is needed. This time is well spent, because with a reduction in anxiety, the clinician will obtain a far more accurate picture of the client's strengths and weaknesses. Most important, the client will have very positive response to the entire process, which, in turn, may increase the likelihood that he or she will follow up on recommendations made.

Final Diagnostic Considerations

There is no one accepted method used to diagnose an LD in adults. Methods that have been used have included aptitude/achievement discrepancies, regression models, and simple cutoff scores (Gregg, Hoy, & Gay, 1996; Katz et al., 2001). Although discrepancies between aptitude and achievement are important to consider, it is also necessary to show that the underlying cognitive weaknesses are consistent with research on the particular LD and that the weaknesses on testing are consistent with the person's difficulties in everyday life.

Making this type of diagnosis requires a client-centered approach to assessment, of the type described by Matarazzo (1990). When thinking about this approach, it is also helpful to consider the distinction that Matarazzo (1990) made between testing and assessment, which applies very well to the assessment of LDs in adults. Specifically, he wrote that

> the assessment of intelligence, personality, or type or level of impairment is a highly complex operation that involves extracting diagnostic meaning from an individual's personal history and objectively recorded test scores. Rather than being totally objective, assessment involves a subjective component. (Matarazzo, 1990, p. 1000)

This is very much in keeping with the approach to assessment outlined earlier. More recently, in a similar vein, Meyer et al. (2001) wrote,

> The use of test batteries is a final distinguishing feature of formal psychological assessment. In a battery, psychologists generally employ a range of methods to obtain information and cross-check hypotheses. These methods include self-reports, performance tasks, observations, and information derived from behavioral or functional assessments. ... By incorporating multiple methods, the assessment psychologist is able to efficiently gather a wide range of information to facilitate understanding the patient. (p. 144)

They went on to note that

> no clinical question can be answered solely by a test score, [as] many different conditions can lead to an identical score on a particular test. The assessment task is to use test-derived sources of information in combination with historical data, presenting complaints, observations, interview results, and information from third parties to disentangle the competing possibilities. ... The process is far from simple and requires a high degree of skill and sophistication to be implemented properly. (Meyer et al., 2001, p. 144)

The clinician, then, cannot rely solely on a simple discrepancy to make a diagnosis. Rather, the results must make sense in terms of our knowledge of brain functioning, our knowledge of LDs, and what is known about the client.

Finally, the clinician must always rule out other neurological, psychiatric, or medical disorders as a primary cause of a client's problems. This is not to say that these disorders cannot co-occur with LDs, only that they should not primarily account for the LD. Again, comprehensive assessment, including the outlined components, is necessary to do this. It is also important to remember that LDs are common in people with a history of traumatic brain injury, alcoholism, substance abuse, and other impulse-control disorders such as ADHD. This is because low self-esteem and impulsivity make it more likely that individuals with LDs will take risks or engage in behavior that is self-destructive. Of course, teasing out the contribution of the different disorders remains a considerable clinical challenge.

Concluding the Assessment With Feedback

Before writing the report—which should, in most cases, adhere to the testing guidelines described in the next section—the client should be given oral feedback on the test results. Thus, the interpretive conference, a 1- to 2-hour meeting with the client (and, if appropriate, with parents or significant others) is crucial. Given that many clients have problems with language, feedback should be provided in a clear and concise way, taking care not to overwhelm the client with details and scores. Although the client should always be provided with information on scores, because scores will be needed to advocate for services, he or she should understand the limitations of the test scores. This is most important when scores are low (or even average for some). Continuing from the positive approach established during the evaluation, the client needs to understand that low test scores do not take away from his or her accomplishments and that his or her strengths in everyday life may not have been assessed by the evaluation. It is, however, essential for the client to be aware of and have an understanding of the test scores, particularly when results are being used to document a disability for college, graduate school, professional school, a testing agency, or a licensing or certification authority. The interpretive conference is key to providing this information, for answering questions, and for preventing any misunderstandings; I have had a number of clients who were evaluated previously and who report that they were never given clear feedback by their prior examiner; as a result, the clients never really understood the nature of their problems and the associated diagnosis. The interpretive conference is especially important for clients with reading disorders, who may have a hard time reading and understanding the complex written report. To that end, clients with reading problems might be encouraged to tape-record the interpretive conference.

Recommendations

Any report is incomplete without recommendations. Elsewhere (Mapou, 2004, 2008), I have discussed the types of recommendations that are helpful for adults with LDs. These include interventions to improve weak skills (e.g., reading, writing), tutoring, compensatory strategies, accommodations, medical evaluation and/or treatment, psychotherapy, support groups, and books, among others. Our practice has emphasized detailed recommendations as an important part of the service provided to clients, and our reports typically include three to four pages of these. However, I have often found diagnostic LD reports to be sorely lacking in recommendations. Like the interpretive conference, the value of the evaluation for the client is what is provided at the end. Detailed recommendations are key for helping the client move on with his or her life and to achieve success in life.

Documentation Guidelines

Clinicians who are completing evaluations specifically to document the presence of an LD for higher education or "high-stakes" testing should adhere to established documentation guidelines, such as those of the Educational Testing Service (1998, revised in 2005 and 2007). This is because most universities and testing agencies use these guidelines, sometimes with slight modifications, when reviewing documentation. These can be obtained from the Web sites of these organizations (ETS: www.ets.org). Clinicians completing ALD evaluations must be familiar with these, especially if they are writing reports used to document the need for accommodations and academic support. Furthermore, since their inception, the ETS guidelines have been adopted by most postsecondary education institutions, testing agencies (e.g., GRE, MCAT, LSAT, GMAT), and licensing or certification organizations (e.g., state bar, National Board of Medical Examiners, specialty medical boards). However, because changes occur periodically, the clinician should stay up-to-date by checking the respective Web sites of these organizations (e.g., ETS, above; Law School Admission Council: lsac.org; National Board of Medical Examiners: www.nbme.org) before writing a report.

The guidelines established by these organizations typically require the following for documenting an LD:

- A professional experienced with LDs must conduct the evaluation, with the report printed on letterhead and the evaluator's licensing or certification information included.
- Documentation must be current (within 3 years, although more organizations are now accepting 5 years).
- A complete history relevant to the disability must be included, showing that the disability has been present since childhood, even if undiagnosed.
- The impact of the disorder on functioning must be demonstrated by neuropsychological or psychoeducational testing, the results of which must be consistent with the experienced difficulties. All tests must be listed and appropriate for the client's age. Qualitative results alone will not suffice. All scores must be reported in the form of standard scores or percentiles. The underlying neuropsychological difficulties must also be consistent with what is known about the disorder.
- An interpretive summary must be included that rules out alternative explanations, explains how the client's problems substantially limit functioning (i.e., a major life activity such as school or work), and must explain why accommodations are needed. If accommodations have not been provided previously, this should be explained.

- A diagnosis must be made, using the *DSM-IV-TR* or *ICD-9*, consistent with the client meeting criteria for diagnosis.
- Recommendations for accommodations and other interventions must be included, with a rationale for their use, based on evaluation findings.

Based on these guidelines, one can see that considerable detail must be included in a report. Over the past 10 years, I have found myself performing more detailed assessments and writing lengthier and more detailed reports, in order to meet the documentation requirements. However, if the clinician follows the assessment approach recommended in this chapter, the resulting report will be consistent with most published guidelines.

The 1990 Americans with Disabilities Act and Subsequent Legal Precedent

Legal issues relevant to ALD are covered in detail in several chapters in Part 4 of this volume. Clinicians completing evaluations for postsecondary education and high-stakes testing must keep in mind the legal definition of a disability, established by the Americans with Disabilities Act (ADA) (Americans with Disabilities Act, 1990). A recent court case, *Bartlett v. the New York State Bar* (Bartlett v. N.Y. State Bd. of Law Exam'rs 2001 U.S. Dist., 2001), has provided some additional guidelines to consider when completing an evaluation, based on interpretation of the ADA and other legal precedents. The following is a brief discussion of these issues.

The ADA established a definition of disability that applies to LDs, as well as to physical disabilities. Specifically, the ADA defines a disability as "a physical or mental impairment that substantially limits one or more of the major life activities of [an] individual" (Americans with Disabilities Act, 1990). Furthermore, Title II goes on to state that "a person is considered an individual with a disability ... when the individual's important life activities are restricted as to the conditions, manner, or duration under which they can be performed in comparison to most people."

Because of this definition, a cognitive weakness or a learning disorder does not always meet the legal definition of a disability. Moreover, the terminology developed in the LD field emerged before applicable law. Thus, many LDs that fit with research knowledge are not necessarily disabilities in the legal sense. In that regard, much has been made of the "average person standard" as applied to neuropsychological assessment (Gordon & Keiser, 1998). Specifically, these authors (and others) have argued that based on the ADA, anyone with average scores on testing, even relative to far higher skills in other areas, is not legally disabled. This, however, works against the gifted person with an LD, since the deficit is usually relative to high intelligence. From a clinical standpoint, bright individuals with LDs typically do not read, learn, or analyze information at the same level at which they can think (see, for example, Weinstein & Schreiber, Chapter 17, this volume). Although most clinicians recognize the validity of the problems experienced by such individuals, legally there is considerable disagreement regarding whether to accommodate the gifted individual with an LD.

Court precedent has provided some additional guidelines when completing a neuropsychological evaluation that can be used to document the presence of an LD as a disabling condition. Specifically, the court, in *Bartlett v. the New York State Board of Law Examiners* (Bartlett v. N.Y. State Bd. of Law Exam'rs 2001 U.S. Dist., 2001) found that (a) average scores on testing do not necessarily equate with average skills in everyday life, because most academic tests were designed to assess basic competence in children and not the skills required of most adults, and (b) qualitative information must be used to demonstrate the presence of the disability. Thus, according to the court in *Bartlett*, the evaluator must demonstrate that the person does not complete a life skill "in the way that most people do." This statement actually provides a legal rationale for collecting information beyond the test scores, as outlined by Kaplan (1988) in the Boston Process Approach and by others (Lezak, Howieson, & Loring, 2004). This also means that the evaluator should ask the client how he or she performs tasks in everyday life and in school.

New Directions

We are, to quote an often used phrase, "not there yet." As much as we strive to base our assessments on science, neuropsychological assessment of ALD is still part art. Furthermore, I am not sure whether we will ever reach the point of having "evidence-based guidelines" for any form of psychological assessment, for the reasons eloquently stated by Matarazzo (1990) and by Meyer et al. (2001). However, in looking toward the future, answering the following questions could help us do our job more accurately and effectively:

What are the profiles of LDs in adults? How do they differ from those of children?
Knowing this, what are the most sensitive measures for assessment of different LDs?
Can we use more targeted batteries based on empirical knowledge and reduce the time needed for assessment?
How can we more effectively capture the qualitative features of ALD?

What is the role of computerized assessment and functional neuro-imaging in LD diagnosis?

Can we develop better and more realistic measures of reading comprehension and expressive writing skills in adults?

How can we better assess and diagnose adults with disorders of attention, executive functioning, learning, and memory that do not fit into the current nosology?

Can we find more effective ways to link accommodations and interventions to neuropsychological data?

References

Ahmad, S. A., Rourke, B. P., & Drummond, C. (2002). A comparison of older children and adults with BPPD and NLD. *Journal of the International Neuropsychological* Society, *8*, 298.

Americans with Disabilities Act of 1990, 42 U.S.C.A. §12101 et seq.

Barkley, R. A., Fischer, M., Smallish, L., & Fletcher, K. (2002). The persistence of attention-deficit/hyperactivity disorder into young adulthood as a function of reporting source and definition of disorder. *Journal of Abnormal Psychology*, *111*, 279–289.

Bartlett v. New York State Board of Law Examiners. (2001). U. S. District Court for the Southern District of New York.

Cirino, P. T., Morris, M. K., & Morris, R. D. (2002). Neuropsychological concomitants of calculation skills in college students referred for learning difficulties. *Developmental Neuropsychology*, *21*, 201–218.

Collins, D. W., & Rourke, B. P. (2003). Learning-disabled brains: A review of the literature. *Journal of Clinical and Experimental Neuropsychology*, *25*, 1011–1034.

Conners, C. K., Ehrhardt, D., & Sparrow, E. S. (1998). *Conners' Adult ADHD Rating Scales (CAARS).* North Tonawanda, NY: Multi-Health Systems.

DuPaul, G. J., Power, T. J., Anastopoulos, A. D., & Reid, R. (1998). *ADHD Rating Scale—IV: Checklists, norms, and clinical interpretation.* New York: Guilford.

Educational Testing Service. (1998). *Policy statement for documentation of a learning disability in adolescents and adults.* Princeton, NJ: Author.

Gordon, M., & Keiser, S. (1998). *Accommodations in higher education under the Americans With Disabilities Act: A no-nonsense guide for clinicians, educators, administrators, and lawyers.* New York: Guilford Press.

Gregg, N., Hoy, C., & Gay, A. F. (Eds.). (1996). *Adults with learning disabilities.* New York: Guilford Press.

Greiffenstein, M. F., & Baker, W. J. (2002). Neuropsychological and psychosocial correlates of adult arithmetic deficiency. *Neuropsychology*, *16*, 451–458.

Kaplan, E. (1988). A process approach to neuropsychological assessment. In T. Boll & B. K. Bryant (Eds.), *Clinical neuropsychology and brain function: Research, measurement, and practice* (pp. 129–167). Washington, DC: American Psychological Association.

Katz, L. J., Goldstein, G., & Beers, S. R. (2001). *Learning disabilities in older adolescents and adults.* New York: Kluwer Academic/Plenum.

Levine, M. (2002). *A mind at a time*. New York: Simon & Schuster.

Lezak, M. D., Howieson, D. B., & Loring, D. W. (2004). *Neuropsychological assessment* (4th ed.). New York: Oxford University Press.

Mapou, R. L. (1995). A cognitive framework for neuropsychological assessment. In R. L. Mapou & J. Spector (Eds.), *Clinical neuropsychological assessment: A cognitive approach* (pp. 295–337). New York: Plenum Press.

Mapou, R. L. (2004). Assessment of learning disabilities. In J. Ricker (Ed.), *Differential diagnosis in adult neuropsychological assessment* (pp. 370–420). New York: Springer.

Mapou, R. L. (2006). Adult attention-deficit/hyperactivity disorder. In P. J. Snyder, P. D. Nussbaum, & D. Robins (Eds.), *Clinical neuropsychology: A pocket handbook for assessment* (2nd ed.). Washington, DC: American Psychological Association, pp. 626–648.

Mapou, R. L. (2008). Learning disabilities in adults. In J. E. Morgan & J. H. Ricker (Eds.), *Comprehensive textbook of clinical neuropsychology*. New York: Psychology Press, pp. 696–728.

Matarazzo, J. (1990). Psychological assessment versus psychological testing: Validation from Binet to the school, clinic, and courtroom. *American Psychologist, 45*, 999–1017.

Meyer, G. J., Finn, S. E., Eyde, L. D., Kay, G. G., Moreland, K. L., Dies, R. R., et al. (2001). Psychological testing and psychological assessment: A review of evidence and issues. *American Psychologist, 56*, 128–165.

Murphy, K. (1996). Adults with attention deficit hyperactivity disorder: Assessment and treatment considerations. *Seminars in Speech and Language, 17*, 245–253.

Rourke, B. P. (Ed.). (1995). *Syndrome of nonverbal learning disabilities*. New York: Guilford Press.

Rourke, B. P., & Conway, J. A. (1997). Disabilities of arithmetic and mathematical reasoning: Perspectives from neurology and neuropsychology. *Journal of Learning Disabilities, 30*, 34–36.

Shaywitz, S. (2003). *Overcoming dyslexia*. New York: Alfred A. Knopf.

Ward, M. F., Wender, P. H., & Reimherr, F. W. (1993). The Wender Utah Rating Scale: An aid in the retrospective diagnosis of childhood attention deficit hyperactivity disorder. *American Journal of Psychiatry, 150*, 885–890.

Wender, P. H. (1995). *Adult attention deficit disorder*. New York: Oxford University Press.

CHAPTER 11

The Importance of Phonological Processing Rather Than IQ Discrepancy in Understanding Adults With Reading Disorders

LINDA S. SIEGEL and IAN S. SMYTHE

Contents

The assessment of college or university students to determine whether or not they have a specific learning disability has become an important part of the landscape of higher education in many parts of the world. Most colleges and test agencies have specified strict assessment guidelines specifying the type and amount of required testing to demonstrate that one is disabled by a reading disorder. Access to accommodations and services hinges on a comprehensive assessment that includes a standard measure of intelligence and comprehensive tests of information processing (see Mapou, Chapter 10, this volume). Ostensibly, the purpose of IQ testing is to allow the calculation of the so-called aptitude-achievement discrepancy. The aptitude-achievement discrepancy, which is the cornerstone of the discrepancy definition of dyslexia, specifies that the score on an achievement test must be significantly lower than the score on an IQ test in order for the individual to be considered learning disabled. The history of the development and use of this discrepancy definition is reviewed in detail in Meyer (2000).

Obviously, this type of definition requires that an achievement test (or tests) and an IQ test be administered to the individual who is seeking a classification for having a learning disability. There are several crucial questions to ask about this process. These questions include, but are not limited to, the following: Is the inclusion of this type and amount of testing necessary to provide a diagnosis of reading disability in an adult? Has the assessment become unnecessarily complex to the point of becoming burdensome to the individual seeking services for his or her disorder? Are documentation guidelines well grounded in empirical data and do they provide important data relevant to the provision of accommodations and services in the university setting?

In this chapter, we demonstrate the logical flaws in the use of this discrepancy definition of learning disabilities in adults. We provide evidence from a review of the relevant psychological and educational research, and our own empirical evidence. Challenges to long-held beliefs about the measurement of LD in adults may lead to improvement in the operational definition of LD in adults.

What Are the Types of Learning Disabilities?

Before beginning our discussion, we need an understanding of the terminology. Specific learning disabilities fall broadly into two categories. Our focus is on the first category—the reading disorders or dyslexia. The terms *reading disability* and *dyslexia* can be used interchangeably. One definition of dyslexia (Siegel & Smythe, 2005) attempts to synthesize the latest debates about the way to conceptualize dyslexia and defines it as a "difficulty in the acquisition of literacy skills that is neurological in origin. It is evident when accurate and fluent reading, spelling and writing develop very slowly and incompletely." The other category involves difficulties with computational arithmetic and/or mathematical problem solving (e.g., Mazzocco, 2001; Morrison & Siegel, 1991; Siegel & Feldman, 1983; Siegel & Ryan, 1988). These two subtypes have been identified in adults in Shafrir and Siegel (1994). It is important to note that although these definitions have been developed in research with children, the manifestations and difficulties appear to be very similar in children and adults.

Who Is the Individual Who Has a Reading Disability?

First, let us consider the issue of who has a reading disability for the purposes of accommodations and services in colleges and universities. Typically, there is an assessment to determine whether or not an individual has a specific learning disability and to determine that individual's specific educational needs. This assessment is often required to follow specific guidelines (for an example, see ETS.org, "Guidelines for the Assessment of Learning Disability in an Adolescent and Adult"). These guidelines typically require measures of aptitude, academic achievement, and information processing. Obviously, measures of academic achievement are critical to the diagnosis of a learning disability. However, we assert there is no justification for including measures of aptitude and information processing in an assessment to determine whether or not there is a learning disability and what should be done to help the individual in terms of remediation and accommodations. We will substantiate these assertions by examining the relevant underlying logic and the empirical evidence.

According to the discrepancy model, scores on an intelligence test define aptitude. Over the past decades, there has been much controversy over what is meant by "intelligence." Any measure of intelligence, a poorly defined concept to begin with, is dependent on a particular culture and set of beliefs about what is important. Because there is a lack of consensus as to what intelligence is, it is difficult to imagine what a valid measure of it might be. Therefore, it is necessary to note that any reference to "IQ" here is really a shorthand term for "results of a test that is referred to as an intelligence test." Put another way, the test may be said to measure what the tester constructor determines as intelligence.

For historic reasons, the IQ has gained a primary role in assessment of the individual with learning disabilities. Although there may have been some rationale for the use of the IQ test in the early days of the development of the concept of specific learning disabilities to distinguish then from mental retardation, three decades of research have shown it to be irrelevant in both the categorization of specific learning disabilities and the understanding of strengths and weaknesses of those with literacy difficulties (e.g., Siegel, 1989a,b). However, simple logic can succinctly explain why the IQ is not required in the assessment of the dyslexic individual (Smythe & Siegel, 2004). The use of this discrepancy definition means that *only* individuals whose reading is significantly below the level expected from their *IQ score* are called reading disabled.

It is this definition of a learning disability that is severely flawed for a variety of reasons. The IQ-reading discrepancy definition requires that there be a significant discrepancy between measured intelligence and achievement. If the definition of dyslexia that we have used above is accepted, then only reading measures are relevant to the definition of dyslexia.

If one is to adopt a definition similar to that given above—that is, neurologically based difficulty in the acquisition of literacy skills evidenced by slow or incomplete development of accurate and fluent reading, spelling, and writing—then the assessment needs to demonstrate (a) the presence of problems with fluency and accuracy, and (b) that the problems are in the acquisition of these skills.

Empirical Evidence Concerning the Discrepancy Definition

It is not only logic that is a problem for the discrepancy definition. We present data concerning the discrepancy between IQ and achievement as a measure of a reading problem. There has been much debate about the use of the IQ score (e.g., Fletcher, 1992; Fletcher, Francis, Rourke, Shaywitz, & Shaywitz, 1992; Francis, Espy, Rourke, & Fletcher, 1990; Siegel, 1988a, 1988b, 1989a, 1989b, 1990a, 1990b; Stanovich, 1991; Valtin, 1978–1979). To summarize across studies, the logic of the use of IQ assumes that IQ measures some kind of "potential," and that the cognitive deficits of individuals with reading disabilities in memory, expressive language, fine motor skills, factual knowledge, and so forth, do *not* interfere with their performance on an IQ test. Furthermore, the assumption of the discrepancy definition is that individuals with low IQ scores should, of necessity, be poor readers. Siegel (1989a, 1989b), Stanovich (1991), and Rispens and van Yperen (1990), among others, have questioned these assumptions. In addition, the calculation of this discrepancy is difficult because there are a number of statistical decisions that need to be made without a precise or consistent way of knowing which method is the best one (e.g., Francis et al., 1990). There are also issues involving how much discrepancy constitutes a meaningful discrepancy and how the discrepancy score should be calculated—that is, whether the discrepancy should be measured with a regression formula in which the correlation between IQ and reading scores is taken into account or, instead, with an absolute IQ–reading-level difference score.

One of the arguments in defense of the IQ test is that patterns of performance on the IQ test are useful in understanding learning disabilities. There is little empirical evidence to support this contention. For example, Watkins (1966) found that the Wechsler Discrimination Index (the difference between a group of subtests that are relatively insensitive to decline, e.g., "Vocabulary" versus those that are sensitive, such as "Digit Span") did not show a difference between learning-disabled and nonlearning-disabled children. D'Angiulli and Siegel (2003) found that patterns of scores on the IQ test did not distinguish between reading disabled and normally achieving children. Neither Verbal-Performance discrepancies *nor* significantly low scores on Digit Span Arithmetic and Coding were uniquely characteristic of children with reading disabilities.

Another argument that has been offered is that IQ scores are useful because they predict reading achievement. In a detailed analysis of this relationship, Gough and Tunmer (1989) concludes that IQ and achievement are correlated and the correlation ranges between .4 and .6, depending on the study. He also notes that the correlation between parental income and reading is in the same range and suggests, not entirely facetiously, that perhaps we should use the discrepancy between parental income and reading to decide who is reading disabled.

There are other arguments against the discrepancy definition. Dyslexics and poor readers do not differ in the degree of genetic determination of the reading disorder. For example, Pennington, Gilger, Olson, and DeFries

280 • Linda S. Siegel and Ian S. Smythe

(1992) have shown that dyslexics (defined by the discrepancy definition) and poor readers (defined by low achievement) do not differ in the heritability of reading disorders. In other words, the genetic component of a reading disability seems to be equivalent in these two subtypes.

Flowers, Meyer, Lovato, and Wood (2000) have shown that the discrepancy definition applied in third grade does not predict the course of reading development in fifth, eighth, and twelfth grades. Scarborough (1989) has shown that IQ scores do not predict the course of reading acquisition.

In studies with children, Vellutino et al. (1996) (Vellutino et al., 2000) have shown that IQ scores do not predict the ability to benefit from remediation.

In addition to these issues, there is the empirical question of whether or not there is actually a difference between individuals whose reading is significantly lower than that predicted by their IQ (dyslexics) and those whose reading is below the level expected for their chronological age but at the level predicted by their IQ, called poor readers. The dyslexics are those with unexpected reading failure whose difficulties with reading are presumably not a function of low IQ. The poor readers, also called "garden variety" poor readers (e.g., Gough & Tunmer, 1986) are reading at the level that would be predicted by their IQ, and their reading failure is not unexpected.

The answer to the question of whether or not there are differences between dyslexics and poor readers in basic cognitive processes is a complex one. All the studies of this issue have been conducted with children. In tasks directly related to the reading process, such as pseudoword reading, reading accuracy, reading comprehension, and spelling, poor readers and dyslexics did not differ although both had scores that were significantly lower than normally achieving readers (e.g., Ellis & Large, 1987; Felton & Wood, 1991; Fletcher et al., 1992; Fredman & Stevenson, 1988; Jiménez-Glez & Rodrigo-López, 1994; Johnston, Rugg, & Scott, 1987a, 1987b; Jorm, Share, Matthews, & Maclean, 1986; Share, McGee, McKenzie, Williams, & Silva, 1987; Siegel, 1992; Silva, McGee, & Williams, 1985; Stanovich & Siegel, 1994). However, on some, but not all, tasks that are not directly related to reading or its component phonological processes such as arithmetic or visual-spatial tasks, there is evidence that children with dyslexia perform better than poor readers (e.g., Das, Mensink, & Mishra, 1990; Ellis & Large, 1987; Siegel, 1992; Stanovich & Siegel, 1994). For simple memory tasks, for example, the type of rote memory measured by Digit Span, dyslexics achieve higher scores than poor readers. Little is known, however, about the differences and similarities between adults with dyslexia and adults with lower IQ scores who are merely poor readers.

We examined the question of possible differences between dyslexics and poor readers in the context of a cognitive approach to understanding a reading disability. A consensus is emerging that one of the core deficits in a reading disability is a deficit in phonological processing (e.g., Rack, Snowling, & Olson, 1992; Siegel, 1993; Stanovich, 1988a, 1988b). Most of this evidence about the nature of this cognitive deficit in dyslexia has been accumulated from research in children, although there have been some studies of adults with reading disability or those who have been diagnosed as dyslexic as children (e.g., Felton, Naylor, & Wood, 1990; Scarborough, 1984). Deficits in phonological processing and pseudoword reading in adult dyslexics have been found (Pennington, Van Orden, Smith, Green, & Haith, 1990; Read & Ruyter, 1985; Russell, 1982). Bruck (1992) found evidence of persistent deficits of phonological awareness in adults who had been diagnosed as dyslexic in childhood, and Greenberg, Ehri, and Perin (1987) and Pratt and Brady (1988) found similar deficits in adults with poor levels of literacy skills. A number of studies have documented word-recognition deficits in adults with childhood diagnoses of dyslexia (Bruck, 1990; Felton et al., 1990; Scarborough, 1984) or dyslexic adults (Russell, 1982).

The purpose of the present study was to examine in detail the question of the nature of the cognitive processing deficits in adults with a reading disability. Tasks measuring a number of aspects of reading, phonological processing, spelling, language, and memory were administered to adults with reading problems and to normally achieving readers. Specifically, it was predicted that adults with a reading disability will experience a deficit in phonological processing and that this deficit will be a pervasive one. In addition, comparisons were made among the groups as a function of reading level. This type of comparison allows insights into the severity of the deficit because the adults are compared with younger, normally achieving readers who are reading at the same level. If the older reading-disabled individuals still show poorer performance than the normally achieving readers, it indicates a very severe deficit. If the performance of the reading-disabled individuals and reading-level-matched normal readers is merely the same under these conditions, it indicates a delay.

On the basis of the studies conducted with children with a reading disability, it is predicted that there will be no differences between adults with dyslexia and adult poor readers on a variety of phonological tasks that represent a critical aspect of the reading process, and both will have lower scores than normally achieving readers, although there may be differences between the adults with dyslexia and the poor readers on tasks such as arithmetic, vocabulary, and visual-spatial functioning that are further removed from the reading process.

In addition, we compared dyslexics and poor readers matched on reading age. Reading age is frequently used in studies of dyslexia to compare normally achieving readers and dyslexics matched not on chronological age but on reading age—that is, how well they read words. The rationale for the use of this design is that it provides a match for experience with reading. If dyslexics perform more poorly on a particular task than normal readers of the same reading age who are, of course, much younger, then this indicates a fundamental cognitive deficit in the dyslexics. We tested the assumption that the phonological deficit is the core deficit in dyslexia.

Method

The participants in this study were 626 individuals, ages 17 to 59. They were divided into three groups based on their estimated IQ scores (Silverstein, 1982) on the Wechsler Adult Intelligence Scale-Revised (WAIS-R; Wechsler, 1981) and the Wide Range Achievement Test-Revised (WRAT-R, Jastak & Wilkinson, 1984). These groups were: *Poor Readers* were individuals whose Reading subtest scores on the WRAT were at or below a standard score of 90 and whose reading scores were not more than 15 points lower than their WAIS-R IQ scores; *Dyslexics* were individuals whose Reading subtest scores on the WRAT were at or below a standard score of 90 and whose Reading scores were at least 15 standard score points below their IQ scores; and *Normally Achieving Readers* were individuals whose WRAT Reading standard scores were above 90. There were 144 Dyslexics, 82 Poor Readers, and 400 Normally Achieving Readers. The mean ages of the groups (in years) were as follows: Dyslexics, 27.7; Poor Readers, 29.0; and Normally Achieving Readers, 28.9. There were no significant differences among the groups in terms of chronological age ($F < 1$). The percentage of females in each group was as follows: Dyslexics, 38.9%; Poor Readers, 62.2%;, and Normally Achieving Readers, 54. 5%. The mean number of years of education for the three groups was as follows: Dyslexics, 12.8 years; Poor Readers, 12.4 years, and Normally Achieving Readers, 14.1 years. The Dyslexics and the Poor Readers did not differ in the average number of years of education; however, the Normally Achieving Readers did complete significantly more years of education than either of the groups with a reading disability.

The participants in this study were volunteers who were referred to the project by community agencies, physicians, and staff from community colleges and universities. They were a very diverse group in educational background and occupational status. The majority was Caucasian; however, approximately 1 to 2% were Afro-Canadian and of West Indian origin, and 1 to 2% were of Asian origin. Individuals who had not received most of their education in English, individuals who were reported to have psychiatric or severe emotional difficulties, and individuals with histories of substance abuse or neurological problems were excluded from the study. This information was collected at an intake interview.

Tests and Tasks

The participants were divided into groups based on their WRAT-R Reading and WAIS-R IQ estimated scores, based on Vocabulary and Block Design as indicated above. In addition to these tests, the participants were administered a variety of standardized tests and experimental tasks that are described in detail below. As some of the data were collected for several published and unpublished studies (e.g., Shafrir & Siegel, 1994; Siegel, 1994; Siegel, Share, & Geva, 1995) and combined for the purposes of these analyses, not all the subjects had scores on all of the tests and tasks, except, of course, the WRAT-R and the WAIS-R. It should be noted that the data on tasks as a function of IQ have never been published before. However, each data point represents at least 30 subjects and many had substantially more.

General Cognitive Functioning

The Vocabulary, Block Design, and Digit Symbol subtests of the WAIS-R were administered. The Space Relations subtest of the Differential Abilities Test (DAT) was also administered (Bennett, Seashore, & Wesman, 1973). This test involves spatial rotation and visualization. The Block Design as well as the Digit Symbol and Space Relations subtests of the DAT were considered visual-spatial tests.

Reading, Spelling, and Arithmetic Tests

The participants in the study were administered several achievement tests, including the reading, spelling, and arithmetic subtests of Wide Range Achievement Test-Revised, the Word Identification and Word Attack subtests of the Woodcock Reading Mastery Test-Revised (Woodcock, 1987), and one of two reading comprehension tests, either the Nelson-Denny Reading Test (Brown, Bennett, & Hanna, 1981) or the Canadian Achievement Test (1981). An experimental Word Reading test was also administered. In this task, 40 exception (e.g., have, does) and regular (e.g., came, five) high-frequency words (20 of each type) were presented individually to the subject, who was required to read them aloud.

Phonological Tasks

The following phonological tasks were used in the study.

Woodcock Word Attack The Word Attack subtest of the Woodcock Reading Mastery Tests, which involves naming pronounceable pseudo-words, was administered.

Pseudowords   The stimuli in this set were the following 32 pseudowords: dite, mive, nowl, vake, gove, bave, fote, gick, vone, yate, bome, sice, tace, koes, hant, zale, cint, hode, woth, tood, jope, pame, gead, zool, kear, lipe, voal, tays, kade, bage, pute, yaid. Some of the pseudowords were derived from word bodies that had one pronunciation (the "ake" in "vake") and some of the pseudowords were derived from word bodies that had alternative pronunciations (the "ave" in "bave"). For the purposes of this analysis, both the regular and exception pronunciations of the pseudowords were scored as correct.

Analogy Pseudowords   The stimuli in this set were the following 18 pseudowords: fody, dastle, sinth, buide, inswer, honot, sugan, womat, galace, risten, domach, lagon, puscle, farage, tepherd, meart, leopark, pongue. The pseudowords were derived from words that had irregular pronunciations (e.g., sugar, answer) and had been used in a study by Manis, Szeszulski, Howell, and Horn (1986). For the purposes of this analysis, both the regular and exception pronunciations of the pseudowords were scored as correct.

Phonological-Lexical Task   This task was adapted from the work of Olson, Kliegl, Davidson, and Foltz (1985). The subject viewed pairs of pseudowords (e.g., kake-dake, joak-joap) and indicated which pseudoword sounded like a real word when pronounced. Thus, there is some lexical involvement in the task. However, because the stimulus pairs are both nonwords and the only way to respond correctly is to recode the stimuli phonologically, the task taps phonologically recoding skill—but without the overt pronunciation required in pseudoword naming. There were 26 trials (chance performance is 13 correct) and the raw number correct was used in the analysis.

Visual Task   This task was adapted from the work of Olson et al. (1985). The subject viewed pairs of letter strings that sounded alike (e.g., rain-rane, boal-bowl) and indicated which one was spelled correctly. There were 26 trials (chance performance was 13 correct) was used in the analysis.

Orthographic Awareness Task   In this task (Siegel et al., 1995), the subject was shown two pronounceable nonword strings (e.g., filv-filk). They are told that neither string looks or sounds like an actual word but that one letter string is more *like* a word. One member of each pair contains an orthographic sequence that never occurs in English in that particular position in a word (e.g., filv). The score is the number of times that the nonword with the legal letter string was chosen. There were 17 trials and the number correct was used in the analysis.

Memory and Language Tasks

Digit Span   The Digit Span subtest of the WAIS-R was administered. The individual is required to repeat an increasing number of digits forward and backward. Standardized scores are available for the total score and raw scores were used for the forward and backward scores.

Short-Term Memory (STM) Letter Span   The STM Letter-Span task (Siegel & Linder, 1984) was similar to that used by Shankweiler, Liberman, Mark, Fowler, and Fischer (1979), with some minor procedural differences. The individuals were shown cards with five letters on them. Half of the letter sets were composed of letters from the rhyming group B, C, D, G, P, T, V, and half of the stimulus sets were composed of letters from the nonrhyming group H, K, L, Q, R, S, W. There were seven trials of each type (rhyming versus nonrhyming), and the order of trial type was intermixed and determined randomly. The stimuli were presented for 3 seconds and the subject was required to write down the letters that had been on the card. Only letters recalled in the correct serial position were scored as correct. The subjects were given separate scores for performance on the rhyming and nonrhyming sets (the maximum score for each was 35).

Working Memory Words   This working memory task was modeled on the procedure developed by Daneman and Carpenter (1980) and similar to that used by Siegel and Ryan (1989). The participants were orally presented sentences that were missing their final words (e.g., "In summer it is very ____" or "People go to see monkeys in a ____"). The participants were instructed to supply the final word of the sentences and to remember the words that they supplied. After responding to each of the sentences in a set, the subject was then required to repeat the words that he or she selected in the same order that the sentences had been presented (scoring without regard to order produced virtually identical results). There were three trials at each of four set sizes (2, 3, 4, and 5); thus the maximum score on the task was 12. Task administration was stopped when the individual failed all the items at one level. To minimize word-finding problems, the sentences were chosen so that the word was virtually predetermined. None of the participants experienced any difficulty in supplying the missing word.

Durrell Listening Comprehension   The Durrell Listening Comprehension subtest of the Durrell Analysis of Reading Difficulty (Durrell & Catterson, 1980) was administered. As it is not designed for this age group, there were no standardized scores available. Instead, raw scores were calculated on the basis of the number of questions answered correctly after the passages were read orally to the participant.

Oral Cloze Task   In the Oral Cloze Task (Siegel & Ryan, 1988), 20 sentences with one word missing were read aloud and the individual was asked to supply the missing word in each sentence. The class (i.e., noun, verb, preposition, adjective, or conjunction) of the missing word varied across each sentence. The subjects were instructed to listen while the experimenter read aloud each sentence and were then to supply a word that would fit in that sentence. The experimenter said "blank" in place of the missing word. The sentence could be repeated several times if necessary. Few repetitions were requested. The number of sentences that were completed with semantically and syntactically acceptable words was used as a criterion variable in the analyses.

Results

General Cognitive Functioning

The scores of the Dyslexics, Poor Readers, and Normally Achieving Readers on the Vocabulary, Block Design, and Digit Symbol Subtests of the WAIS-R and the Space Relations subtest of the DAT are shown in Table 11.1. There were significant overall group effects for each variable: Estimated IQ, $F(2, 623) = 101.2, p < .00001$; Vocabulary, $F(2, 623) = 98.1, p < .00001$; Block Design, $F(2, 623) = 46.7, p < .0001$; Digit Symbol, $F(2, 623) = 12.0$, ns; and DAT-Space Relations, $F(2, 623) = 47.3, p < .00001$.

The Scheffe was used for all group comparisons; differences were considered significant if p was < .05. The Normally Achieving Readers obtained higher scores than both the Poor Readers and Dyslexics on the Estimated IQ and the WAIS Vocabulary subtest. The Dyslexics and the Normally Achieving Readers did not differ on the three visual-spatial tasks, specifically WAIS-R Block Design and Digit Symbol and DAT-Space Relations. The Dyslexics had higher scores than the Poor Readers on Estimated IQ, Vocabulary, Block Design, Digit Symbol, and DAT-Space relations.

Reading, Spelling, and Arithmetic Tests

Table 11.2 shows the scores of the three groups on the standardized test of reading, spelling, arithmetic, and reading comprehension. There were significant overall effects on all the variables: WRAT Reading, $F(2, 623) = 917.5, p < .00001$; Woodcock Word Identification, $F(2, 441) = 320.3, p < .00001$; Word Reading, $F(2, 382) = 19.3, p < .00001$; Nelson-Denny Reading Comprehension, $F(2, 425) = 30.4, p < .00001$; Reading Comprehension,

Table 11.1 Mean Scores (and Standard Deviations) on General Cognitive Functioning for the Three Groups

	Dyslexics	Poor Readers	Normally Achieving Readers
n	144	82	400
WAIS			
Vocabulary[a]	8.8 (2.2)	7.9 (1.6)	11.3 (2.6)
Block Design[b]	10.8 (2.7)	7.7 (1.9)	10.6 (2.6)
Digit Symbol	9.5 (4.3)	9.1 (2.9)	9.9 (2.8)
Estimated IQ[a]	101.6 (12.2)	88.6 (6.3)	108.6 (12.6)
DAT-Space Relations[b]	52.1 (30.5)	33.1 (24.6)	55.0 (28.9)

[a] Dyslexics had significantly higher scores than Poor Readers and significantly lower scores than Normally Achieving Readers.
[b] Dyslexics and Normally Achieving Readers did not differ; both groups had significantly higher scores than the Poor Readers.

Table 11.2 Mean Percentile Scores (and Standard Deviations) on the Reading, Spelling, and Arithmetic Tasks as a Function of a Group

	Dyslexics	Poor Readers	Normally Achieving Readers
n	144	82	400
WRAT Reading[a]	8.2 (7.5)	11.6 (7.4)	63.5 (20.1)
Woodcock Word Ident[a]	12.8 (13.5)	18.3 (14.2)	57.3 (20.0)
Word Reading[a] (% correct)	95.2 (7.4)	97.1 (5.5)	99.7 (1.0)
Woodcock Word Attack[c]	14.5 (15.2)	26.3 (21.1)	59.7 (23.7)
Reading Comprehension			
Nelson-Denny[a]	21.3 (24.9)	19.6 (20.6)	39.5 (28.1)
CAT[a]	20.4 (24.2)	14.2 (17.9)	49.8 (33.4)
WRAT			
Spelling[a]	10.8 (14.4)	15.9 (17.4)	52.1 (24.7)
Arithmetic[b]	21.3 (22.9)	14.1 (14.7)	38.2 (25.7)

[a] Dyslexics and Poor Readers did not differ and both had significantly lower scores than the Normally Achieving Readers.
[b] Dyslexics had significantly higher scores than the Poor Readers and significantly lower scores than the Normal Readers.
[c] Poor Readers and Dyslexics had significantly lower scores than Normally Achieving Readers; Dyslexics had significantly lower scores than Poor Readers.

$F(2, 223) = 37.0$, $p < .00001$; WRAT Spelling, $F(2,673) = 283.5$, $p < .00001$; and WRAT Arithmetic, $F(2, 623) = 78.5$, $p < .00001$. On the WRAT Reading, Woodcock Word Identification, Experimental Word Reading, CAT, and Nelson-Denny Reading Comprehension Tests, the Dyslexics and Poor Readers did not differ and both groups had significantly lower scores than the Normally Achieving Readers. On the Woodcock Word Attack, the Poor Readers and the Dyslexics both had significantly lower scores than the Normally Achieving Readers; however, the Poor Readers had significantly *higher* scores than the Dyslexics.

Phonological and Orthographic Processing

The performance of the three groups on the four phonological tasks include: Woodcock Word Attack, Pseudoword Reading, Analogy/Rule Pseudoword Reading, and Phonological Lexical, was compared. On all these four tasks, the univariate analyses of variance were significant: Woodcock Word Attack, $F(2, 623) = 305.0$, $p < .00001$; Pseudoword Reading, $F(2,556) = 116.2$, $p < .00001$; Analogy/Rule, $F(2, 559) = 152.1$, $p < .00001$; and Phonological Lexical, $F(2, 623) = 158.0$, $p < .00001$.

On the Pseudoword Reading, Analogy/Rule, and Phonological Lexical tasks, the Normally Achieving Readers had higher scores than both the Dyslexics and Poor Readers, who did not differ significantly from each other. On the Woodcock Word Attack, the Dyslexics and Poor Readers had significantly lower scores than the Normally Achieving Group; however, the scores of the Dyslexics were significantly lower than those of the Poor Readers.

The scores of the three groups on the Orthographic Awareness and the Visual Tasks are also shown in Table 11.3. The univariate analyses were significant for both variables (Orthographic Awareness, $F(2, 623) = 8.9$, $p < .0002$; Visual Task, $F(2, 623) = 33. 4$, $p < .00001$) and on both tasks the Normally Achieving Readers had significantly higher scores than the Dyslexics and Poor Readers but the latter two groups did not differ significantly in their performance.

Memory and Language Tasks

The scores of the three groups in the Memory and Language tasks are shown in Table 11.4. There were significant differences among the three groups on the Rhyming, $F(2, 623) = 59.44$, $p < .00001$; Nonrhyming Letters, $F(2, 623) = 76.00$, $p < .00001$; Working Memory, $F(2, 443) = 36.9$, $p < .00001$; Durrell Listening Comprehension, $F(2, 419) = 12.7$, $p < .00001$; WAIS-R Digit Span, $F(2, 623) = 49.70$, $p < .00001$; Digits Forward, $F(2, 413) = 37.90$, $p < .00001$;

Table 11.3 Mean Percent Correct (and Standard Deviations) on the Phonological and Orthographic Skills as a Function of a Group

	Dyslexics	Poor Readers	Normally Achieving Readers
Woodcock Word Attack[b]	51.8 (21.1)	64.1 (19.0)	85.0 (10.4)
Pseudoword Reading[a]	76.4 (19.4)	84.5 (15.9)	95.7 (5.9)
Analogy/Pseudoword Reading[a]	65.5 (20.2)	73.9 (21.1)	91.3 (9.9)
Phonological Lexical[a]	73.5 (18.2)	77.2 (17.2)	93.2 (10.6)
Orthographic Awareness[a]	82.5 (16.4)	86.4 (9.7)	89.1 (10.5)
Visual Task[a]	94.9 (10.2)	96.9 (.8)	99.0 (2.3)

[a] The Poor Readers and Dyslexics were not significantly different from each other and both these groups had significantly lower scores than the Normally Achieving Readers.

[b] The Dyslexics and Poor Readers had significantly lower scores than the Normally Achieving Readers; the scores of the Dyslexics were significantly lower than those of Poor readers.

Table 11.4 Means and (Standard Deviations) on the Memory and Language Tasks as a Function of a Group

	Dyslexics	Poor Readers	Normally Achieving Readers
Short-Term Memory			
Rhyming Letters[b]	25.0 (5.9)	25.0 (4.7)	28.9 (4.4)
Nonrhyming Letters[b]	28.1 (5.0)	29.0 (5.1)	32.1 (3.5)
Working Memory[c]	44.6 (16.3)	43.6 (14.4)	55.4 (18.0)
Listening Comprehension			
Durrell	5.3 (1.0)	5.1 (1.0)	5.5 (1.0)
WAIS-R			
Digit Span[a,b]	7.6 (2.1)	7.6 (2.2)	9.8 (2.7)
Forward[b]	6.4 (1.8)	6.5 (1.7)	8.2 (2.1)
Backward[b]	5.3 (1.9)	5.4 (1.7)	7.1 (2.3)
Oral Cloze[c]	77.4 (15.3)	77.7 (13.3)	88.0 (10.1)

[a] This score is standardized; the Forward and Backward Digit Span are raw scores. The remaining scores are percent correct.

[b] The Dyslexics and the Poor Readers did not differ significantly; both groups had significantly lower scores than the Normally Achieving group.

[c] The Dyslexics had significantly higher scores than the Poor Readers; the Normally Achieving Readers had higher scores than the Dyslexics and Poor Readers.

Digits Backward, $F(2, 413) = 28.70$, $p < .00001$; Oral Cloze, $F(2, 442) = 63.6$, $p < .00001$.

The Normally Achieving readers had significantly higher scores than both reading disabled groups who did not differ significantly from each other on the following tasks: Digits Forward, Digits Backward, WAIS-R Digit Span, Short-Term Memory Rhyming, and Nonrhyming. The reading disabled groups *did* differ significantly from each other on the Working Memory and Oral Cloze tasks.

Reading-Level Comparisons

Phonological Tasks Comparisons among the three groups on the phonological tasks for two reading grade levels are shown in Table 11.5. These were the only reading grade levels where there were sufficient numbers of subjects to make these comparisons. The Normally Achieving group includes a number of normally achieving children and adolescents who were reading

Table 11.5 Mean Percent Correct (and Standard Deviations) on the Phonological Processing Tasks for Reading Level (Matched Groups)

WRAT Reading Grade Level 7			
	Dyslexics	Poor Readers	Normally Achieving Readers
n	21	13	242
IQ	106.6 (13.0)	87.5 (3.0)	107.9 (13.0)
Woodcock Word Attack[a]	51.9 (19.5)	57.7 (16.5)	83.4 (10.6)
Pseudoword[a]	78.1(16.5)	82.8 (16.0)	94.1 (7.0)
Analogy/Rule[a]	65.1(17.7)	72.2 (14.0)	93.2 (10.2)
Phonological/Lexical[a]	72.5 (17.8)	74.0 (17.7)	92.4 (10.7)

WRAT Reading Grade Level 8			
	Dyslexics	Poor Readers	Normally Achieving Readers
n	24	20	141
IQ	106.6 (10.8)	89.1 (6.4)	109.2 (12.8)
Woodcock Word Attack[a]	63.1 (15.1)	67.2 (10.6)	89.7 (10.5)
Pseudoword[a]	85.2 (11.9)	85.7 (11.4)	96.7 (4.3)
Analogy/Rule[a]	69.0 (19.7)	76.8 (13.1)	95.5 (7.4)
Phonological/Lexical[a]	80.3 (18.2)	76.7 (16.6)	89.3 (11.5)

[a] On all of the phonological processing tasks, the scores of the Dyslexics and the Poor Readers were not significantly different; however, both groups had significantly lower scores than the Normally Achieving Readers.

at reading grade level 7 or 8. The univariate ANOVAs were significant for all of these tasks, reading grade level 7 and 8, respectively: Woodcock Word Attack, $F(2, 171) = 74.6$, $p < .00001$, $F(2, 229) = 87.5$, $p < .00001$; Pseudo-word Reading, $F(2, 78) = 15.4$, $p < .00001$, $F(2, 140) = 35.9$, $p < .00001$; Analogy/Rule, $F(2, 66) = 32.1$, $p < .00001$, $F(2, 128) = 60.6$, $p < .00001$; Phonological Lexical, $F(2, 71) = 16.6$, $p < .00001$, $F(2, 75) = 5.0$, $p < .009$).

At reading grade levels 7 and 8, the Dyslexics and the Poor Readers had significantly lower scores than the Normally Achieving Readers but did not differ from each other on the Woodcock Word Attack Test, Pseudo-word Reading, Analogy/Rule Task, and the Phonological Lexical Task. Therefore, the performance of the Dyslexics and the Poor Readers did not differ on any of the tasks directly measuring phonological processing, but both these reading disabled groups had significantly *lower* scores than reading-level-matched normally achieving readers.

The performance of the Dyslexics, Poor Readers, and Normally Achieving Readers, matched on reading grade level were compared on the language and memory tasks. The results are shown in Table 11.6. In contrast to the results of the phonological processing tasks, none of these differences was significant.

Table 11.6 Means (and Standard Deviations) on the Memory and Language Tasks as a Function of a Group

	Dyslexics	Poor Readers	Normally Achieving Readers
Reading Grade Level 7			
Short-Term Memory			
Rhyming	71.3 (15.3)	66.2 (16.9)	75.0 (15.5)
Nonrhyming	83.6 (14.6)	76.0 (20.9)	85.8 (13.5)
Working Memory	40.9 (17.6)	41.7 (12.4)	43.2 (17.7)
Oral Cloze	80.0 (13.0)	78.6 (15.5)	81.5 (13.1)
Reading Grade Level 8			
Short-Term Memory			
Rhyming	75.4 (18.5)	76.9 (10.1)	78.5 (12.5)
Nonrhyming	84.1 (14.2)	86.6 (9.9)	89.5 (9.8)
Working Memory	52.6 (16.8)	49.0 (10.9)	48.9 (18.4)
Oral Cloze	86.2 (8.9)	75.6 (10.3)	81.7 (13.5)

Conclusions

These data suggest that the IQ–reading-discrepancy definition of dyslexia is not relevant to understanding the problems of adults with reading disabilities. The IQ score does not have significant consequences for the development of any reading skills; individuals with a reading disability do not differ in their reading skills as a function of their IQ score. Individuals whose IQ score is discrepant from their reading score have similar reading skills to individuals without a discrepancy between their reading and their IQ scores.

There were some differences between the dyslexics and poor readers in certain visual-spatial, language, and memory skills. The higher IQ scores of the Dyslexics, as opposed to the Poor Readers, are an indication of more developed expressive language (Vocabulary, Oral Cloze) and memory skills than the Poor Readers. The Dyslexics also had significantly higher scores on the experimental Working Memory and Oral Cloze tasks. However, these skills do *not* allow the Dyslexics to compensate for their basic deficit in phonological processing. These cognitive skills do not even provide sufficient compensation to increase reading comprehension scores, as the Dyslexics did not have significantly higher scores than the Poor Readers on two reading comprehension tests, the Nelson-Denny and the Canadian Achievement Tests.

The higher IQ scores and better memory, language, and visual-spatial skills of the adults with dyslexia did not allow them to achieve higher levels of education than the Poor Readers. The cognitive strengths of the Dyslexics in the areas of general cognitive functioning, language, memory, visual-spatial, and listening comprehension skills do not allow them to compensate for their severe deficits in phonological skills. Although the Dyslexics had higher scores than the Poor Readers on the Vocabulary subtest of the WAIS-R, the Dyslexics had lower scores than the Normally Achieving Readers on the Vocabulary subtest, so their cognitive resources cannot compensate for the lack of exposure to vocabulary through reading. This lower Vocabulary score may be an illustration of the Matthew effect described by Stanovich (1986) in that the Dyslexics who, because of their reading problems, read less than the Normal Achieving Readers and, consequently, miss opportunities to develop their vocabulary skills. It should be noted that, based on cross-sectional data, Dyslexics as children did have similar vocabulary scores to Normally Achieving Readers (Siegel, 1992), perhaps a reflection of the fact that the Matthew effects were not yet operating.

The Dyslexics and the Normally Achieving Readers did not differ in their scores on a Listening Comprehension task. Although this task is called Listening Comprehension, it places demands on working memory because the questions can only be answered correctly if the individual *remembers* the details of the passage. On both this task and the experimental Working Memory task, the Dyslexics had significantly higher scores than the Poor Readers. In spite of these superior memory skills, the Dyslexics did not have higher scores on any reading task, including reading comprehension.

One fundamental cognitive deficit in adults with reading disabilities involves severe problems with phonological processing. This deficit is independent of general cognitive functioning, as measured by IQ. This phonological deficit is an arrest, not merely a delay, because even when a reading-level match of younger, normally achieving readers was used, the phonological differences remained, even though the differences in language and memory did not.

A question arises as to whether or not there are subtypes within the reading-disabled population. For subtypes to be a viable concept, they must be distinctive; overlapping scores on cognitive measures suggest that subtypes are not really a viable concept. On both Block Design and the DAT, both measures of visual-spatial functioning, there were significant differences between the Poor Readers and the Dyslexics but no significant difference between the Dyslexics and the Normally Achieving Readers. These results may indicate two distinctive subtypes within the reading-disabled population, one with intact or above-average visual-spatial skills and the other with poor skills in this area. Even if this is a viable subtype (a broad range of tasks would be needed to provide definitive evidence for this possibility), there do not appear to be any consequences for reading; these groups did not differ on reading tasks.

This finding adds additional evidence to the significance of the phonological deficit in a reading disability. This result also suggests that the use of listening comprehension rather than IQ as the basis to measure the discrepancy between reading and IQ does not really solve the problem (e.g., Stanovich, 1991). The results of this study are clear—whether or not the individual with reading disability has a high IQ or good listening comprehension skills, he or she has a serious deficit in phonological processing, and cognitive strengths in other areas do not provide significant opportunities for compensation.

These data clearly indicate that both the Dyslexics and the Poor Readers had severe deficits in phonological processing. Adults with a reading disability, whatever their measured IQ score is, have great difficulties with phonological processing and do not catch up to normally achieving readers, even in adulthood.

Information Processing

Although this chapter is primarily about the use of intelligence testing, there are also some other issues to discuss with regard to the role of tests of information processing in the assessment of RD. Most test agencies and many universities require that documentation include tests of information processing such as memory, attention, and so forth (see ETS.org). However, the assessment of "information processing" in this context is problematic for a variety of reasons. First of all, there are an almost infinite number of cognitive processes that could be assessed. How does the assessor know which one to choose? Even an apparently simple concept such as short-term memory is complex and multidimensional. To even begin to do justice to the concept, one would have to assess memory for sounds, words, numbers, visual patterns, orthographic features of the language, sentences, and so on. The list is almost endless.

Second, suppose an individual has poor short-term memory for digits. What impact does that have on his or her reading? The answer is that we do not know, but there is evidence that many good readers have relatively poor Digit Span scores (D'Angiulli & Siegel, 2003) and some poor readers have good scores, as we showed earlier in this chapter. There is no indication that the score on Digit Span (or any of the other information processing tasks) is related in any causal way to reading difficulties.

Furthermore, if an individual has very low scores on reading and spelling tasks but high scores on Digit Span or some other measure of short-term memory, does that mean her or she does not have dyslexia? Of course it does not; the reading difficulties are still the same. What do we gain by testing information processing in terms of its direct impact on the diagnosis or remediation or accommodations provided? Insofar as possible, all aspects of the assessment should be related to possible remedial programs and accommodations. For example, if there is the possibility for extra time on examinations, a reading comprehension test should be given in timed and untimed conditions and the difference in performance noted. If an individual performs better in the untimed condition, then that provides evidence for the need for extra time on examinations. We have shown that extra time on a reading comprehension task benefits adults with reading difficulties but not those adults who do not have a reading problem (Lesaux, Lipka, & Siegel, 2006).

Future Research and New Directions

The assessment of the adult to determine possible learning disabilities has become quite, and perhaps unnecessarily, complex. Although it is obvious that comprehensive testing should include measures of achievement that are necessary for the diagnosis of a learning disability, often this is not the case. For example, McGuire, Madaus, Litt, and Ramirez (1996) have reviewed documentation reports written on behalf of students seeking a Learning Disabilities classification in a postsecondary institution and found that only about 20% of the reports had any achievement measures. This figure is astonishing, as measures of achievement are crucial to the definition of a learning disability.

We assert that measures of aptitude (IQ) and information processing are not crucial in assessing adults for the purposes of accommodations and services. We believe they add little to the understanding of the reading process in the adult dyslexic and may be an impediment to needed services for many students.

Some important new directions in research are suggested by our analyses. For example, a reading disability (dyslexia) should be defined as a low score on a reading test. Assessing reading should include measures of word recognition, pseudoword reading, and reading comprehension. Speed and accuracy should be measured in each of these domains. Spelling of words and pseudowords should be measured. Although assessing the skill of writing is complex, the Woodcock-Johnson has two subtests that are helpful, Writing Fluency and Writing Samples. These tests are standardized and may provide a clue to the composition and handwriting of the individual.

Assessment should emphasize testing of achievement, including detailed analyses of errors that may help with remediation. For example Greenberg et al. (2002) have shown that adults with reading difficulties show a different pattern of errors from children who are normally achieving and were matched on reading level. They found that the reading errors of adults were more often real words that resembled the target word while the errors of the good readers were decoding errors. The spelling errors of the adults were less phonetic. These reading and spelling errors of adults indicate significant problems with phonological processing that need to be addressed in any remediation program.

Assessment should address the definition of specific learning disabilities, clearly address accommodations, and provide evidence for accommodations. For example, if extended time for examinations is recommended, there should be some evidence for it. That is, a reading comprehension test should be given in the time allotted for the test according to the standardized procedures, and then the person should have extra time (for example, double time) to do the test. If the score with extra time is higher than the score in the standardized condition, then this suggests that extra time for examinations is appropriate and justified. We have shown that extra time given to adults with reading disabilities helps them achieve higher scores on a reading comprehension test, but that extra time does not benefit normally achieving readers and in some cases results in lower scores for them.

An analysis of the errors that people make in spelling can be very enlightening. For example, do they spell nature as *natur* or *nachure*? The latter indicates good phonological skills because we can recognize the word if we pronounce it as it is spelled but indicates poor visual memory. The former indicates good visual memory because the word looks like the correct spelling and is missing only one letter. However, if one were to pronounce what is written, it would not be pronounced as nature because the *e* is necessary to change the pronunciation of the vowel *u*.

The point is that these types of analyses should be part of an assessment, not the IQ test, which is time consuming and does not provide any specific information to help decide what remediation and accommodations to provide for the person.

We need to carefully rethink assessment and decide what is necessary to diagnose the difficulties in academic skills. We need to provide insights into what are appropriate remedial techniques and necessary accommodations. Assessment has become too time consuming and expensive and not really helpful to the educational program of the students. Future research should be designed to develop meaningful and appropriate assessments that help the student.

Author Note

This research was supported by a grant from the Natural Sciences and Engineering Research Council of Canada to L. S. Siegel. The authors wish to thank Keith Stanovich for his comments on earlier drafts and Norman Himel for help with the data collection and analysis.

References

Bennett, G. K., Seashore, H. G., & Wesman, A. G. (1973). *Differential aptitude tests*. San Antonio, TX: Psychological Corp.

Brown, J. I., Bennett, J. M., & Hanna, G. (1981). *The Nelson-Denny Reading Test*. Lombard, IL: Riverside.

Bruck, M. (1990). Word-recognition skills of adults with childhood diagnoses of dyslexia. *Developmental Psychology, 26*, 439–454.

Bruck, M. (1992). Persistence of dyslexics' phonological awareness deficit. *Developmental Psychology, 28*, 874–886.

Canadian Achievement Tests. (1981). Scarborough, ON.: McGraw Hill Ryerson.

Daneman, M., & Carpenter, P. A. (1980). Individual differences in working memory and reading. *Journal of Verbal Learning and Verbal Behavior, 19,* 450–466.

D'Angiulli, A., & Siegel, L. S. (2003). Cognitive functioning as measured by the WISC-R: Do children with LD have distinctive patterns of performance? *Journal of Learning Disabilities, 36,* 48–58.

Das, J. P., Mensink, D., & Mishra, R. K. (1990). Cognitive processes separating good and poor readers when IQ is covaried. *Learning and Individual Differences, 2,* 423–436.

Durrell, D. D., & Catterson, J. H. (1980). *Durrell analysis of reading difficulty* (3rd ed.). New York: Harcourt Brace Jovanovich.

Ellis, N., & Large, B. (1987). The development of reading: As you seek so shall you find. *British Journal of Psychology, 78,* 1–28.

Felton, R. H., Naylor, C. E., & Wood, F. B. (1990). Neuropsychological profile of adult dyslexics. *Brain and Language, 39,* 485–497.

Felton, R., & Wood, F. (1991). A reading level match study of nonword reading skills in poor readers with varying IQ. *Journal of Learning Disabilities, 25,* 318–326.

Fletcher, J. M. (1992). The validity of distinguishing children with language and learning disabilities according to discrepancies with IQ: Introduction to the special series. *Journal of Learning Disabilities, 25,* 546–548.

Fletcher, J., Francis, D., Rourke, B., Shaywitz, S., & Shaywitz B. (1992). The validity of discrepancy-based definitions of reading disabilities. *Journal of Learning Disabilities, 25,* 555–561.

Flowers, L., Meyer, M., Lovato, J., Felton, R., & Wood, F. (2001). Does third grade discrepancy status predict the course of reading development? *Annals of Dyslexia, 50,* 1–23.

Francis, D. J., Espy, K. A., Rourke, B. A., & Fletcher, J. M. (1990). Validity of intelligence scores in the definition of learning disability: A critical analysis. In B. P. Rourke (Ed.), *Neuropsychological validation of learning disability subtypes* (pp. 15–44). New York: Guilford Press.

Fredman, G., & Stevenson, J. (1988). Reading processes in specific reading retarded and reading backward 13 year olds. *British Journal of Developmental Psychology, 6,* 97–108.

Gough, P. B., & Tunmer, W. E. (1986). Decoding, reading, and reading disability. *Remedial and Special Education, 7,* 6–10.

Greenberg, D., Ehri, L. C., & Perin, D. (1987). Are word-reading processes the same or different in adult literacy students and third–fifth graders matched for reading level? *Journal of Educational Psychology, 89,* 262–275.

Jastak, S., & Wilkinson, G. S. (1984). *Wide Range Achievement Test-Revised.* Wilmington, DE: Jastak.

Jiménez-Glez, J. E., & Rodrigo-López, M. R. (1994). Is it true that differences in reading performance between students with and without LD cannot be explained by IQ? *Journal of Learning Disabilities, 27,* 155–163.

Johnston, R. S., Rugg, M. D., & Scott, T. (1987a). The influence of phonology on good and poor readers when reading for meaning. *Journal of Memory and Language, 26,* 57–68.

Johnston, R. S., Rugg, M. D., & Scott, T. (1987b). Phonological similarity effects, memory span and developmental reading disorders: The nature of the relationship. *British Journal of Psychology*, *78*, 205–211.

Jorm, A., Share, D., Matthews, R., & Maclean, R. (1986). Cognitive factors at school entry predictive of specific reading retardation and general reading backwardness: A research note. *Journal of Child Psychology and Psychiatry*, *27*, 45–54.

Lesaux, N. K., Lipka, O., & Siegel, L. S. (2006). Investigating cognitive and linguistic abilities that influence the reading comprehension skills of children from diverse linguistic backgrounds. *Reading and Writing*, *19*, 99–131.

Manis, F. R., Szeszulski, P., Howell, M., & Horn, C. (1986). A comparison of analogy- and rule-based decoding strategies in normal and dyslexic children. *Journal of Reading Behavior*, *18*, 203–218.

Mazzocco, M. M. M. (2001). Math learning disability and math LD subtypes: Evidence from studies of Turner syndrome, fragile X syndrome and neuro-gibromatosis type 1. *Journal of Learning Disabilities 34*, 520–533.

McGuire, J. M., Madaus, J. W., Litt, A. V., & Ramirez, M. O. (1996). An investigation of documentation submitted by university students to verify their learning disabilities, *Journal of Learning Disabilities*, *20*, 297–304.

Meyer, M. S. (2000). The ability-achievement discrepancy: Does it contribute to an understanding of learning disabilities? *Educational Psychology Review*, *12*, 315–335.

Morrison, S. R., & Siegel, L. S. (1991). Learning disabilities: A critical review of definitional and assessment issues. In J. E. Obrzut & G. W. Hynd (Eds.), *Neuropsychological foundations of learning disabilities: A handbook of issues, methods, and practice* (pp. 79–97). San Diego: Academic Press.

Olson, R., Kliegl, R., Davidson, B. J., & Foltz, G. (1985). Individual and developmental differences in reading disability. In T. G. Waller (Ed.), *Reading research: Advances in theory and practice* (Vol. 4, pp. 1–64). New York: Academic Press.

Pennington, B., Gilger, J. W., Olson, R., & DeFries, J. (1992). The external validity of age- versus IQ-discrepancy definitions of reading disability: Lessons from a twin study. *Journal of Learning Disabilities 25*, 9 562–573.

Pennington, B. F., Van Orden, G. C., Smith, S. D., Green, P. A., & Haith, M. M. (1990). Phonological processing skills and deficits in adult dyslexics. *Child Development*, *61*, 1753–1778.

Pratt, A. C., & Brady, S. (1988). Relation of phonological awareness to reading disability in children and adults. *Journal of Psychology*, *80*, 319–323.

Rack, J. P., Snowling, M., & Olson, R. (1992). The nonword reading deficit in developmental dyslexia: A review. *Reading Research Quarterly*, *27*, 28–53.

Read, C., & Ruyter, L. (1985). Reading and spelling skills in adults of low literacy. *Remedial and Special Education*, *6*, 43–52.

Rispens, J., & van Yperen, T. A. (1990). The identification of specific reading disorders: Measuring a severe discrepancy. In G. T. Pavlidis (Ed.), *Perspectives on dyslexia*, (Vol. 2, pp. 17–42). New York: Wiley.

Russell, G. (1982). Impairment of phonetic reading in dyslexia and its persistence beyond childhood: Research note. *Journal of Child Psychology and Psychiatry*, *23*, 459–475.

Scarborough, H. S. (1984). Continuity between childhood dyslexia and adult reading. *British Journal of Psychology, 75*, 329–348.

Scarborough, H. S. (1989). Prediction of reading disability from familial and individual differences. *Journal of Educational Psychology* 81,1, 101–108.

Shafrir, U., & Siegel, L. S. (1994). Subtypes of learning disabilities in adolescents and adults. *Journal of Learning Disabilities, 27*, 123–134.

Shankweiler, D., Liberman, I. Y., Mark, L. S., Fowler, C. A., & Fischer, F. W. (1979). The speech code and learning to read. *Journal of Experimental Psychology: Human Learning and Memory, 5*, 531–545.

Share, D. L., McGee, R., McKenzie, D., Williams, S., & Silva, P. A. (1987). Further evidence relating to the distinction between specific reading retardation and general reading backwardness. *British Journal of Developmental Psychology, 5*, 35–44.

Siegel, L. S. (1988a). Evidence that IQ scores are irrelevant to the definition and analysis of reading disability. *Canadian Journal of Psychology, 42*, 202–215.

Siegel, L. S. (1988b). Definitional and theoretical issues and research on learning disabilities. *Journal of Learning Disabilities, 21*, 264–266.

Siegel, L. S. (1989a). IQ is irrelevant to the definition of learning disabilities. *Journal of Learning Disabilities, 22*, 469–478.

Siegel, L. S. (1989b). Why we do not need IQ test scores in the definition and analyses of learning disability. *Journal of Learning Disabilities, 22*, 514–518.

Siegel, L. S. (1990a). IQ and learning disabilities: R.I.P. In H. L. Swanson & B. Keogh (Eds.), *Learning disabilities: Theoretical and research issues* (pp. 111–128). Hillsdale, NJ: Lawrence Erlbaum.

Siegel, L. S. (1990b). Siegel's reply. [Letter to the editor]. *Journal of Learning Disabilities, 23*, 268–269.

Siegel, L. S. (1992). An evaluation of the discrepancy definition of dyslexia. *Journal of Learning Disabilities, 25*, 618–629.

Siegel, L. S. (1993). Phonological processing deficits as the basis of a reading disability. *Developmental Review, 13*, 246–257.

Siegel, L. S. (1994). Working memory and reading: A life-span perspective. *International Journal of Behavioral Development, 17*, 109–124

Siegel, L. S., & Feldman, W. (1983). Non-dyslexic children with combined writing and arithmetic difficulties. *Clinical Pediatrics, 22*, 241–244.

Siegel, L. S., & Linder, B. A. (1984). Short-term memory processes in children with reading and arithmetic learning disabilities. *Developmental Psychology, 20*, 200–207.

Siegel, L. S., & Ryan, E. B. (1988). Development of grammatical sensitivity, phonological, and short-term memory skills in normally achieving and learning disabled children. *Developmental Psychology, 24*, 28–37.

Siegel, L. S., & Ryan, E. B. (1989). The development of working memory in normally achieving and subtypes of learning disabled children. *Child Development, 60*, 973–980.

Siegel, L.S., Share, D., & Geva, E. (1995). Evidence for superior orthographic skills in dyslexic readers. *Psychological Science, 6*, 250–254.

Siegel, L. S., & Smythe, I. (2004). Dyslexia and English as an additional language (EAL): Towards a greater understanding. In G. Reid & A. Fawcett (Eds.), *Dyslexia in context: Research, policy and practice* (pp 132–146). London: Whurr.

Siegel, L. S., & Smythe, I. S. (2005). Reflections on research on reading disability with special attention to gender issues. *Journal of Learning Disabilities 5*, 473–477.

Silva, P. A., McGee, R., & Williams, S. (1985). Some characteristics of 9-year-old boys with general reading backwardness or specific reading retardation. *Journal of Child Psychology and Psychiatry, 26*, 407–421.

Silverstein, A. B. (1982). Two- and four-subset short forms of the Wechsler Adult Intelligence Scale-Revised. *Journal of Counseling and Clinical Psychology, 50*, 415–418.

Stanovich, K. E. (1986). Matthew effects in reading: Some consequences of individual differences in the acquisition of literacy. *Reading Research Quarterly, 21*, 360–406.

Stanovich, K. E. (1988a). Explaining the differences between the dyslexic and garden variety poor reader: The phonological-core variance-difference model. *Journal of Learning Disabilities, 21*, 590–604.

Stanovich, K. E. (1988b). The right and wrong places to look for the cognitive locus of reading disability. *Annals of Dyslexia, 38*, 154–177.

Stanovich, K. E. (1991). Discrepancy definitions of reading disability: Has intelligence led us astray? *Reading Research Quarterly, 26*, 7–29.

Stanovich, K. E., & Siegel, L. S. (1994). The phenotypic performance profile of reading-disabled children: A regression-based test of the phonological-core variable-difference model. *Journal of Educational Psychology, 86*, 24–53.

Turner, W. (1989). Mental test differences as Matthew effects in literacy: The rich get richer and the poor get poorer. *New Zealand Sociology, 4*, 64–84.

Valtin, R. (1978–1979). Dyslexia: Deficit in reading or deficit in research? *Reading Research Quarterly, 14*, 201–221.

Vellutino, F. R., Scanlon, D. M., Sipay, E. R., Small, S. G., Pratt, A., Chen, R. S., & Denckla, M. B. (1996). Cognitive profiles of difficult to remediate and readily remediated poor readers: Early intervention as a vehicle for distinguishing between cognitive and experiential deficits as basic causes of specific reading disability. *Journal of Educational Psychology, 88*, 601–638.

Vellutino, F. R., Scanlon, D. M., et al. (2000). Differentiating between difficult-to-remediate and readily remediated poor readers: More evidence against the IQ-achievement discrepancy definition of reading disability. *Journal of Learning Disabilities, 33*, 233–238.

Watkins, M. W. (1966). Diagnostic utility of the WISC-111 developmental index as a predictor of learning disabilities *Journal of Learning Disabilities, 29(3)*, 305–312.

Wechsler, D. (1981). *Wechsler Adult Intelligence Scale-Revised*. San Antonio, TX: Psychological Corp.

Woodcock, R. W. (1987). *Woodcock Reading Mastery Tests-Revised*. Circle Pines, MN: American Guidance Service.

CHAPTER 12

Assessment of Written Expression in the Adult Population

NOEL GREGG, CHRIS COLEMAN, and JENNIFER LINDSTROM

Contents

Written language disorders are symptomatic for a large percentage of adults with learning disabilities. As the demands of literacy are increasing daily, an understanding of the processes that influence written language production becomes not only a theoretical interest but also a pragmatic necessity. Mastery of basic written expression skills is a requirement for graduation from high school, entry into and exit from postsecondary institutions (technical schools, universities), and success on the job. For instance, the majority of states have graduation exit examinations requiring essay writing. The College Board recently added an essay section to the Scholastic Achievement Test I (SAT), a change that underscores the importance of written expression skills in higher education.

For adolescents and adults who struggle to express themselves well in writing, this increased emphasis on written composition constitutes a significant obstacle. Yet difficulty obtaining competence with written discourse is not always due to a developmental or acquired learning disorder. Underachievement on writing tasks may be the result of poor instruction, learning English as a second language, or an overall intellectual or emotional consideration. The purpose of this chapter is to provide professionals with an overview of written language, as well as to explore different tools that provide information for the purpose of diagnosis for the adult population. Six areas of written expression are discussed: motor, spelling, syntax, text structure, sense of audience, and fluency. Our model of written expression based on research from the fields of sociolinguistics, cognitive psychology, and neurolinguistics provides the framework for a better understanding of written language disorders among the adult population.

Multidimensional Model of Written Expression

Neurolinguistic Models

Throughout each area of written language covered in this chapter, we discuss the influence of cognitive and linguistic processes on specific areas of written expression (e.g., spelling, syntax). In the neuropsychological literature, written expression disorders have often been referred to as *agraphia* or *dysgraphia*. However, the validity of the subgroups associated with many neuropsychological models of agraphia or dysgraphia has been challenged (see Gregg, 1992, 1995, for in-depth discussions). A great deal of the attention in these models has primarily focused on spelling. Therefore, professionals should be careful how they interpret, generalize, or use the word *dysgraphia*. The serial hierarchical processing models initially used to define dysgraphia have been replaced by theories proposing neural networking. Neural networking models imply that different networks of neuroanatomical entities are configured in response to different functional demands, and a given neuroanatomical entity may contribute to several functions (Berninger, 1996). The difficulties an adult with learning disabilities might demonstrate with written expression often extend beyond spelling.

Cognitive psychologists have contributed to a better understanding of the strategic aspects of learning so vital for the ability to write. Strategic learning relies more on the executive processing abilities of a writer. *Intentional learning,* an active attempt to acquire new information or skills, is an important construct to consider in our attempts to better understand why adults with learning disabilities struggle with written expression (Bereiter & Scardamalia, 1985). Mastery of written expression skills obviously requires a great deal of intentional learning. Some scholars term this the problem-solving aspect of writing (Flower & Hayes, 1979).

The role of cognitive processes such as working memory or executive functioning to writing competency has been documented by researchers investigating the learning skills and strategies of children (Brown, Bransford, Ferrara, & Campione, 1983; Englert, 1990; Graham & Harris, 1999). However, it is important to keep in mind that research results from child literature cannot be directly interpreted as applicable to the adult population since cognition, language functioning, and experiences vary across the life span. Therefore, we have attempted to reference mainly research that is specific to the adult population. We identify specific cognitive and linguistic processes (e.g., working memory, orthographic awareness, and executive functioning) that influence different aspects of written expression performance that are important for evaluators to consider during the assessment process.

Sociolinguistic Models

Under the rubric of sociolinguistic models, we include a discussion of affective, situational, and social variables influencing performance on written expression tasks. The study of written expression in broad or specific contexts requires an examination of how an adult constructs knowledge. The boundaries between cognitive, linguistic, affective, and social processes are often ambiguous. Sociolinguistic models of written expression reflect that social relationships and culture influence writing performance. Luria (1981) eloquently identified the relevance of social linguistic models: "One must seek the origins of conscious activity and 'categorical' behavior not in the recesses of the human brain or in the depths of the spirit, but in the external conditions of life" (p. 25).

The affective reaction to a writing task or the adult writer's social-emotional state will contribute to writing performance. Anxiety, attributions,

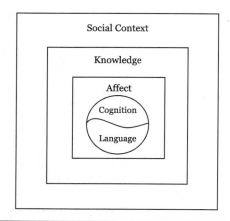

Figure 12.1 Model of written expression.

and motivation are three affective variables that obviously influence success on a writing task. Writing anxiety is a term that has been applied rather loosely across disciplines. The significance of anxiety to performance on specific writing tasks cannot be understated, since generalized anxiety disorders often co-occur with learning disabilities in adults (Gregg, Hoy, King, Moreland, & Jagota, 1992; Manglitz, Hoy, Gregg, Wisenbaker, King, & Moreland, 1995). Even in the absence of a clinical anxiety disorder, adults with dyslexia may experience emotional distress when asked to perform tasks such as spelling, composition, or oral reading. Writers' anxiety has been argued from neurologically based and psychologically based perspectives. Some researchers suggest that it is both organic and psychological in etiology (Lebrun, Devreux, & Leleux, 1991). Whatever future research is able to support, clinically one can predict that if a writing disorder is present, situations requiring writing will likely produce anxiety—particularly as the stakes increase.

Figure 12.1 provides our model of written expression, a multidimensional model that incorporates cognitive, linguistic, social, and affective factors as well as the situational context of learning. The center of the model represents the interaction between *thought and language*. Vygotsky (1962) referred to this interdependence of thought and language by using the term "verbal thought" (p. 65). Models of written expression and writing disorders require the integration of several theoretical perspectives, each informed by a variety of experimental procedures.

What Are You Measuring?

The assessment of writing requires consideration of the task demands, the tools used for responding, and the topic. Discrepant performance across measures purporting to evaluate a specific writing skill (e.g., spelling) is not always the result of an adult's motivation or the validity of a measure. The task, the topic demands, and the tool may vary greatly across alternative measures of a single academic skill.

Task

The modality and degree of structure required by a writing task is important to consider when evaluating the capabilities of an adult. An examiner should note the input and output modalities of a given task. For instance, a spelling task might be dictated to a writer (auditory-verbal), but the output may require writing the correct word (visual-motor/verbal). Alternatively, the output modality for a dictated spelling task may minimize motor and verbal demands (e.g., a multiple-choice recognition format). In addition, the information presented to an examinee could be either verbal (spoken or written) or nonverbal (pictures or environmental sounds).

Understanding task structure requires examination of the writing prompt as well as the response requirements. Prompts are cues provided in the presentation of a task. For instance, a writer could be asked to generate a composition in response to a single picture, a series of pictures, a story starter, or an essay topic. Writing from a series of pictures is the most structured of the above prompts, while an essay would provide the least structure. Adults with differing cognitive profiles may find one task more difficult than another. Knowledge of these differences should influence both interpretation of test scores and determination of appropriate accommodations.

Luria and Task Format

Luria (1980) described three essential task formats for assessing writing: *copying, dictation,* and *spontaneous.* He proposed that any professional who evaluates writing should utilize each of these formats in order to observe how different cognitive and linguistic processes impact performance in different situations. First, he suggested that a writer be given different types of copying tasks (e.g., letters, single words, sentences, paragraphs). Spelling, sentence structure, and organizational deficits can be noted as the task demands increase the need for integration of cognitive and linguistic processes. More taxing than copying tasks, dictation tasks require an individual to integrate phonological awareness (sound awareness), orthographic awareness (sound/symbol awareness), and word/sentence structure. Again, varying the type of task demands, such as dictating individual letters, words, sentences, and then paragraphs, is important. To distinguish between linguistic and motor disorders, the evaluator might vary the response tool by using scrabble tiles or blocks bearing single letters. Spontaneous writing, the most demanding format, requires that an adult write a sentence, paragraph, story, or essay on a specific topic. Ideally, the evaluator should collect writing samples of an adult's written expression across different audiences, genre, and topics in both timed and untimed situations.

Topic

An evaluator should always give careful consideration to the background knowledge and motivation an adult brings to the writing task. The more knowledge a writer possesses about a topic, the better the individual's writing quality and fluency. Also, a writer can produce more elaborate and better organized text when he or she is familiar or comfortable with the audience and the register (e.g., narrative, technical). Unfortunately, most writing experiences adults face focus on writing to the evaluator (e.g., instructor, high-stakes test, employer).

One of the many functions of writing is test taking (e.g., fill-in-the blank, short answer, copying, dictation, and translation). Planning and organization demands are minimized with such tasks. Informational tasks, such as note taking, reports, and summaries, represent another function of writing. Within this function, more emphasis is placed on planning, organizing, and transcribing abilities. An evaluator should examine samples of work across different functions of writing to determine whether detected error types are generalized or if they seem to be specific to a particular task, format, or topic demand.

Tool

Whatever the area of writing under examination, an evaluator should compare situations in which an adult is allowed to use different writing tools (e.g., pencil or pen, computer, voice-activated software). Motor-related deficits, for example, may be factors in some learning-disabilities profiles but not in others. Across a variety of profiles, the use of computers for enhancing writing competencies has increased dramatically over the past decade (Becker, 1999). Research findings indicate that composing with a computer improves writing fluency, editing, and quality of writing for a majority of students (Goldberg, Russell, & Cook, 2003).

Areas of Written Expression

Motor

The comorbidity of motor deficits with many developmental and acquired learning disorders is supported by the literature (see Gregg, 1995, for an in-depth discussion). Motor execution is controlled by highly specialized neural associative processes. Networking theories suggest that a breakdown in motor functions might occur during a specific stage of motor execution or when an adult is faced with certain task demands (Deuel, 1992; Kinsbourne & Cook, 1971; Luria, 1981). Interestingly, recent studies provide evidence of greater cerebellar involvement with activities such as handwriting, decoding, and encoding than has been reflected in previous research (Fawcett & Nicholson, 1999; Fawcett, Nicholson, & Dean, 1996; Justus & Ivry, 2001). Throughout this section, we focus only on those motor disorders associated with learning disabilities. We remind the reader that learning disabilities often co-occur with other developmental disorders. Three specific types of motor problems commonly identified in the adult population with learning disabilities are characterized by (a) symbolic deficits, (b) motor speed deficits, and (c) dyspraxia. Quite often, an adult with learning disabilities will demonstrate problems in more than one of these areas (e.g., motor speed and symbolic deficits).

Symbolic motor pattern deficits are consequences of phonological and orthographic deficits. Luria (1980) and Myklebust (1965) described dysgraphia as symbolic in nature, thus distinguishing it from ataxia and paralytic disorders. Accordingly, they proposed that the breakdown in writing occurs between the mental image of a word and the motor system. Characteristics of symbolic motor disorders include distortions and inversions of graphemes (letters and numbers), an inability to copy, intact oral language, difficulty with word finding, and rapid automatized naming difficulties (Marcie & Hecaen, 1979). Historically, some neuropsychologists referred to this profile as Gertsmann syndrome (Benton & Meyers, 1956). This syndrome included deficits in spelling, calculation, finger agnosia, and right-left disorientation (Critchly, 1970). However, the validity of Gertsmann syndrome has been challenged over the years (Deuel, 1992). Recent research with children provides support for the direct relationship of orthographic awareness rather than fine motor abilities to handwriting. Abbot and Berninger (1993) found that the path between orthographic coding and handwriting was significant but that fine motor skills contributed only indirectly through orthography. In addition, an adult with symbol-based motor problems often can draw, create, or integrate nonverbal designs (e.g., cartoons) with great skill. Yet when asked to form visual-verbal symbols, he or she performs below expectations in creating letters. Visual-verbal production requires very different neurological processing than visual-nonverbal. It is always important to observe adult construction of single letters and words as opposed to their production of nonverbal symbols.

Adults demonstrating *motor speed* deficits usually perform writing tasks in the correct sequence; however, their speed is extremely slow. In their purest form, motor speed deficits occur in the absence of spelling deficits. Historically, motor speed problems have been described as clumsiness or limbkinetic apraxia (Liepmann, 1900). The significant behavior for an examiner to observe is a slowness in the formation of letters and words (Deuel, 1992). Motor speed deficits are noted across simple neuropsychological tasks (finger tapping), complex fine motor tasks (handwriting, typing, buttoning), and gross motor tasks (riding a bike).While they can co-occur with symbolic or dyspraxia disorders, they constitute a separate motor disorder.

Dyspraxia is most often noted with adults demonstrating nonverbal learning disabilities. Dyspraxia is the "inability to learn and perform age-appropriate sequences of voluntary movements in the face of preserved coordination, strength, and sensation" (Deuel, 1992, p. 264). This type of motor deficit results in difficulty mastering the motor patterns required to form letters and numbers. Observing an adult with this problem, one would note inversions and distortions not specific to the writing task (e.g., copy, dictation, spontaneous). For an adult identified with dyspraxia, both motor performance and motor learning are compromised with verbal or nonverbal symbols (Cermak, 1985). Unlike an individual with motor speed deficits, an individual with dyspraxia may form letters and words quickly; however, the letters are often distorted, inverted, and out of order. It is also common for oral and facial dyspraxia to accompany this disorder (Ferry, Hall, & Hicks, 1975). One of the most distinguishing aspects of dyspraxia is the unusual formation of letters and words. An adult with this disorder will often print in distinct block-like symbols, usually in all capitals. Inaccurate space between letters and words as well as difficulty with letter formation are noted. Upon observing such problems, an examiner might consider asking an individual to spell orally, or use Scrabble-like blocks to help distinguish between motor and symbolic deficits.

Spelling

Simply defined, *spelling* refers to a person's skill at representing words in print. As many researchers have shown, underachievement in this area is one of the earliest and most persistent symptoms of dyslexia (Bruck, 1993; Gregg et al., 2001; Hatcher, Snowling, & Griffiths, 2002; Treiman, 1997). Due to the prescriptive nature of spelling (within a culture there is typically only one accepted representation for a given lexical item), it is commonly assessed with standardized measures that use real words and a dichotomous (0/1) scoring system. However, recent research on dyslexia subtypes suggests that spelling development, and the various processes that affect it, are considerably more complex than was once supposed. From an assessment perspective, obtaining a standard score for real-word spelling is no longer sufficient "coverage." An evaluator should use multiple measures of spelling (and related cognitive/linguistic processes), varied formats, and qualitative analyses.

Spelling can be thought of as a form of *word knowledge*. It seems clear that for each word a person acquires, a cognitive network of associated information gradually develops: how the word is pronounced, what it means, what connotations it seems to have, how it should be used grammatically, and (once literacy begins) how it is spelled. Among individuals with dyslexia or other language-based learning disabilities, aspects of this network do not develop as they should. Depending on the nature and severity of a particular disability, symptoms may be more noticeable (e.g., early language delays and persisting problems with most forms of word knowledge and verbal expression) or more subtle (e.g., intact oral language skills but difficulty with decoding and spelling). A thorough evaluation should include assessment of the various branches of the word knowledge network and a determination of which branches function well and which do not. The list of cognitive, linguistic, and social factors in Table 12.1 can help an evaluator investigate spelling performance (as well as performance with other forms of word knowledge).

Table 12.1 is not intended to be entirely comprehensive—there is no reference, for example, to vision or hearing acuity, both of which are clearly important to spelling acquisition. Similarly, the right-hand column includes *examples* of tests designed to measure particular abilities. It is hoped that Table 12.1 provides evaluators with both a guideline for assessment of possible dyslexia and an appreciation for the complex array of processes pertinent to spelling skills. It seems clear that in addition to environmental factors (e.g., instruction, exposure to print) and what might be described as secondary cognitive influences (e.g., attention), there are several primary cognitive/linguistic areas that play a role.

First and foremost, a wealth of research on phonological dyslexia underscores the importance of assessing cognitive and linguistic processes such as sound discrimination (rhyming included), auditory/phonological working memory (sometimes called the *phonological loop*), phonemic awareness (appreciation of discrete sounds or *phonemes* within spoken words), and morphological awareness (appreciation and use of affixes such as "-ing" or "-ed"). Depending on their severity, deficits in these areas can affect a person's spoken language (e.g., semantic errors, word-finding problems) as well as literacy skills. More recently, research has revealed the possibility of (neurologically) separate deficits in orthographic processing (Foorman, 1994; Holmes & Castles, 2001; Roberts & Mather, 1997). That is, some poor spellers demonstrate intact phonological abilities but struggle with the visual/symbolic aspects of spelling (including, in some cases,

Table 12.1 Spelling

Cognitive/Linguistic/ Social Variable	Relationship to Spelling Skill	Standardized Tests (Adult Population)
Spelling	achievement	−WJ III Spelling, Spelling of Sounds, Editing[a] −WIAT[b] −WRAT-3[c]
Graphomotor functioning	letter formation; legibility	−WJ III Writing Samples[d] (Handwriting Analysis)
Auditory discrimination	accurate recognition of spoken sounds/words/pseudowords	−WJ III Auditory Attention[d] −Speech Sounds Perception Test[j]
Auditory (phonological) working memory	retention/analysis of spoken words in the phonological loop during execution of spelling attempt	−WAIS-III/WMS-III Digit Span,[e] Letter–Number Sequencing −WJ III Numbers Reversed, Auditory Working Memory
Phonemic awareness	appreciation of the concept that words contain phonemes; accurate identification of phonemes; accurate identification of slightly distorted words	−WJ III Sound Blending, Incomplete Words, Sound Awareness[d]
Morphological awareness	appreciation of prefixes, affixes, and other morphological forms/patterns	−CASL[f]
Orthographic awareness	knowledge of phoneme-grapheme correspondences; accurate perception/encoding of symbols; sensitivity to implicit spelling rules	−WJ III Word Attack, Spelling of Sounds[a] −WIAT-II Spelling[b]
Word knowledge/retrieval	appreciation and on-demand recall of various aspects of words (pronunciation, spelling, primary/secondary meanings, semantic/syntactic constraints)	−WJ III Verbal Comprehension, Rapid Picture Naming[d] −WAIS-III Vocabulary[e] −Boston Naming Test[g]
Print exposure/instruction	experience with/exposure to printed words and general patterns related to their spelling and use	−Adult Reading History Questionnaire[h] −Author Recognition Test[i]

Table 12.1 (continued) Spelling

[a] Woodcock, McGrew, & Mather (2001b)
[b] Wechsler, D. (2001)
[c] Jasktak & Wilkinson (1993)
[d] Woodock, McGrew, & Mather (2001a)
[e] Wechsler (1997a)
[f] Carrow-Woolfolk (1996)
[g] Kaplan, Goodglass, Weintraub, & Segal (1983)
[h] Lefly & Pennington (2000)
[i] Cunningham & Stanovich (1997)

graphomotor skills). Finally, the relationship between rapid automatized naming (RAN) and spelling is unclear; it is worth noting, however, that RAN—the ability to quickly retrieve familiar words in response to visual prompts or symbols—has been linked to decoding, a skill closely related to spelling (Wolf, Bowers, & Biddle, 2000). Recent discoveries about the neural basis of reading can inform our conceptualization of "how the brain spells" (e.g., Palmer, Brown, Petersen, & Schlaggar, 2004; Sandak, Mencl, Frost, & Pugh, 2004).

As noted above, the most widely used format for assessing spelling itself involves free recall of real-word spellings (e.g., *Spell "candy" as in "The children asked for candy." "Candy."*) and a scoring system that distinguishes between correct responses (1 point) and incorrect ones (0 points). This format is used on many test batteries. In some cases (e.g., with adults whose motor functioning is compromised), a multiple-choice recognition format may be more appropriate; in general, though, the free recall format is preferable because it provides examiners with more qualitative information. A clever and useful variation on the traditional free-recall spelling test, *Spelling of Sounds* (Woodcock, McGrew, & Mather, 2001a) features pseudowords. According to the administrative manual, the test "is a measure of spelling ability, particularly phonological and orthographic coding skills" (p. 15). The reference to spelling *ability* is a distinction worth making, since examinees must create accurate spelling representations rather than simply retrieving overlearned patterns from memory. The manual encourages analysis of errors, which "can help the examiner determine if the subject is able to sequence sounds correctly, but has difficulty assimilating or recalling common orthographic patterns" (p. 66). Finally, early items on *Spelling of Sounds* use an expanded scoring rubric (0 to 2 or 0 to 3 points) that helps ease somewhat the limitations of a dichotomous system. Evaluators are encouraged to administer at least two standardized measures of spelling (e.g., one with real words and one with pseudowords). It is also advisable to analyze and describe the errors on those tests.

Further evidence can often be gleaned from other writing samples, such as spontaneous essays or case history form responses.

Consider two examinees of similar age, educational level, and general ability who obtain similarly low scores on a traditional 0/1 spelling test. An evaluator who interprets and reports only standard scores may overlook information that is vital to (a) the nature of the examinees' underachievement, and (b) remediation or accommodation of their problems. Certainly, distinctions can be made between incorrect attempts such as *gullable, guliball,* and *glubl.* The first attempt, *gullable,* is both phonetically plausible (i.e., it accurately captures the sequence of sounds in the spoken word) and sophisticated in its orthographic/morphological features (particularly since the suffix *-able* is more common than *-ible*). The second attempt, *guliball,* is phonetically plausible but unsophisticated in terms of orthographic/morphological conventions (i.e., gemination problems and the absence of an adjectival suffix). The third attempt, *glubl,* lacks both phonetic and orthographic plausibility. For a more detailed approach to qualitative analysis, see the flowchart in Figure 12.2 and the accompanying examples in Table 12.2. In addition to describing trends in error types, an evaluator should consider the *kinds* of words that have been misspelled. For example, plausible but incorrect attempts to spell irregular, low-frequency words (e.g., *yacht*) may be developmentally normal; frequent misspellings of words that are overlearned or highly predictable may suggest deficits in aspects of orthographic processing.

While most adults (particularly English speakers) are likely to make a spelling mistake now and then, individuals with learning disorders exhibit higher error rates and lower plausibility rates. In a recent study, we counted and categorized spelling mistakes in the impromptu essays composed by 263 university students. The students without disabilities ($n = 90$) averaged two to three errors per 1,000 words, and about 80% of their incorrect attempts were judged to be plausible (e.g., *airate* for *aerate*). Students with attention-deficit/hyperactivity disorder (ADHD) ($n = 44$), though they made more errors (about four per 1,000 words), achieved a similar plausibility rate. The errors of students with dyslexia ($n = 77$) were considerably more frequent (seven per 1,000 words) and less plausible (65%). Similarly, students with both dyslexia and ADHD demonstrated significant problems (eight errors, 71% plausibility). It should be noted that many adults will demonstrate more severe error rates than the university students described here.

Syntax

The term *syntax* refers to sentence-level language, or the manner in which words are assembled to form sentences. Within this section we also

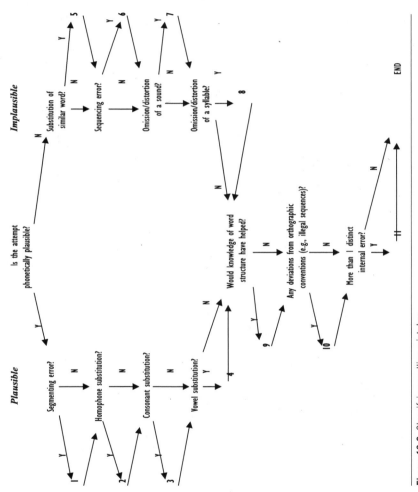

Figure 12.2 Classifying spelling mistakes.

Table 12.2 Examples of Spelling Mistake Types

Error Type	Description	Examples
1	Segmenting problem	*my self, police man, alot, landmass*
2	Homophone substitution	*witch [which], to [too], bear [bare]*
3	Consonant substitution	*repheree, electrick, elefant, majic*
4	Vowel substitution	*gullable, leef, ful [fuel], weard [weird]*
5	Substitution of similar word	*casual [causal], cord [court], dabble [double]*
6	Sequencing problem	*edcuation, impotrant, thier, neice, revelant*
7	Sound omission/distortion	*libary, redeption, industral, sester [sister]*
8	Syllable omission/distortion	*permiscuous, illustion [illustration], corpation*
9	Morphological problem	*gullibal, buildig, direcshun, eksplode*
10	Orthographic problem	*livd [lived], rabit, qestion, brig [bridge]*
11	Multiple problems	*redicullus, cairfull, efichancy, inprisond*

Note: See also Figure 12.2.

cover *semantics* (word usage in context), *grammar* (e.g., agreement), and *mechanics* (e.g., application of punctuation and capitalization rules), since execution of these skills occurs within, and has an effect upon, sentences. In contrast to spelling, which lends itself to a dichotomous scoring system, syntax is exponentially more nebulous and complex.

There is, in fact, no limit to the number of legal (i.e., grammatically acceptable) sentence structures that are possible; and for each structure, word choices allow for infinite variations (Pinker, 1994). This is true whether you write (or speak) in Spanish, English, Tagalog, or any other human language. Perhaps because of its daunting complexity—does the prospect of diagramming sentences inspire horror in you?—written syntax has received only limited attention from researchers and test developers.

As summarized in Table 12.3, development of age-appropriate written syntax skills depends on a number of variables. Foremost among these is oral language development (i.e., receptive and expressive syntax); after all, writing systems were invented as a means of recording what people say. Thus, an adult with an expressive (or receptive–expressive) language disorder will struggle to construct written sentences, just as he or she struggles to construct spoken ones. Of course, this is not to imply that intact oral syntax abilities automatically transfer to the written arena; they are necessary but not sufficient for writing proficiency. Mastery of a formal writing system also requires adequate functioning in other cognitive and

Table 12.3 Written Expression: Commonly Used Accommodations

	Description
Low-Tech	
Dictionary	use of a regular dictionary during written tests
Spelling dictionary	use of a specialized spelling dictionary during written tests
Proofreading assistance	once the initial draft of an essay test is completed, access to a service provider or other professional who can help identify and correct errors in spelling
Special allowances	amnesty from penalties related to spelling mistakes
High-Tech	
Computer spellcheck	use of the spellchecking program with a word-processor
Hand-held spelling tools	use of a spelling pen or other hand-held electronic device designed to provide spelling assistance
Dictation software	use of computer technology that essentially transcribes what is spoken into the microphone

social areas as well as extensive instruction in grammar, punctuation, word usage, and other conventions. Print exposure is also important, since familiarity and proficiency with different styles and registers (e.g., expository, narrative, and technical) depend on it.

How can an evaluator assess an area as nebulous as syntax? The challenge is difficult enough with regard to the child population; for the adult population, it is complicated further by an increase in the variety and sophistication of language structures typically used and a decrease in the standardized assessment tools available. There are, however, several useful tests that are normed beyond age 17 (for examples, see Table 12.4). These measures require the generation of individual sentences in response to specific prompts (e.g., composing a sentence that contains the words *would*, *time*, and *if*). Such a "constrained" format often yields important information about an examinee's mastery of different kinds of sentence structures (e.g., conditionals). Some standardized tests include time constraints (e.g., *Writing Fluency*, Woodcock, McGrew, & Mather, 2001a), while others do not (e.g., *Written Expression*: Carrow-Woolfolk, 1996). Use of both task types is advised since, as Mather and Woodcock (2001) note, the evaluator wants to determine "whether the subject work[s] (a) slowly but inaccurately, (b) slowly and accurately, (c) rapidly but inaccurately, or (d) rapidly and accurately" (p. 86). Beyond standard scores, error patterns can help an evaluator determine which subskills within syntax (e.g., punctuation, grammar, word usage) merit more thorough/narrow assessment.

Table 12.4 Syntax (Including Semantics, Grammar, and Mechanics)

Cognitive/Linguistic/ Social Variable	Relationship to Sentence Construction Skill	Standardized Tests (Adult Population)
Sentence construction	achievement	–WJ III Writing Fluency, Writing Samples[a] –OWLS Written Expression Scale[b]
Auditory (phonological) working memory	being able to "compose" (mentally) and write at the same time without making errors (e.g., word omissions/ duplications)	–WAIS-III/WMS-III Digit Span, Letter-Number Sequencing[c] –WJ III Numbers Reversed, Auditory Working Memory[d]
Morphological awareness	grammatical agreement between subjects and verbs, pronouns and referents, etc.	–CASL[e]
Word knowledge/retrieval	use of varied/age-appropriate vocabulary choices; avoidance of semantic errors	–WJ III Verbal Comprehension[a] –WAIS-III Vocabulary[c] –Boston Naming Test
Receptive syntax/ syntactic sensitivity	understanding of spoken sentences; appreciation of their structural and internal details	–WJ III Oral Comprehension, Memory for Sentences[d] –CASL[e]
Expressive syntax	use of varied/age-appropriate sentence structures; avoidance of grammar/structural errors	–CASL[e] –OWLS Oral Expression[b]
Executive functions	organization of ideas; time management; monitoring	–D-KEFS[f] –WJ III Exec. Processes Cluster[d]
Knowledge of conventions/ mechanics	application of rules related to punctuation, capitalization, indentation, etc.	–WJ III Editing[d] –OWLS Written Expression Scale[b]
Print exposure/ instruction/language variety	experience with/exposure to different registers/genres (e.g., formal academic writing)	–Adult Rdg. History Questionnaire[g] –Author Recognition Test[g]

[a] Woodcock, McGrew, & Mather (2001b).
[b] Carrow-Woolfolk (1996)
[c] Wechsler (1997a,b)
[d] Woodcock, McGrew, & Mather (2000a)
[e] Carrow-Woolfolk (1999)
[f] Delis, Kaplan, & Kramer (2001)
[g] LeFly & Pennington (2000)
[h] Cunningham & Stanovich (1997)

Impromptu writing tasks also provide invaluable qualitative information about syntax (among other skills and abilities). For example, individuals with intact language abilities but poor executive functions may generate competent sentences within a constrained (i.e., highly structured) format like that of *Writing Samples* (Woodcock, McGrew, & Mather, 2001a) but make monitoring errors (e.g., leaving out words) when faced with the more taxing demands of planning and composing an entire essay. The unconstrained prose of adults with dyslexia or other language-related learning disorders may vary considerably depending on the nature and severity of the disorder, the task approach, and affective factors. Some adults with dyslexia actually make less frequent errors in essays—when they can control or "dumb down" sentence structures and word choices—than on constrained tasks. Others may make more frequent errors because higher level task demands (e.g., organization, idea development) draw critical cognitive resources away from the execution of already-weak basic skills (e.g., grammar). In reviewing qualitative writing samples, an evaluator should consider several aspects of syntax: number of words, clauses, or T-units per sentence; diversity of sentence structures; variety of word choices; frequency of changes or corrections; and frequency and severity of errors in subskill areas (capitalization, comma usage, apostrophe usage, word usage, agreement, sentence structure). A thorough analysis will include not only numbers of errors (e.g., two omitted apostrophes) but error *rates* as well (e.g., errors in two of six situations where an apostrophe was required). Such information is critical to diagnostic and remediation decisions.

Text Structure

Text structure refers to the means by which individuals organize their ideas in writing. According to Bruner (1985), adults utilize two main frameworks when systematizing their ideas. These means of organizing thoughts include narrative or paradigmatic modes. Paradigmatic discourse is one that is objective and logical-scientific in nature. Narrative discourse is context sensitive and focuses on human intention. Bruner notes, "The significance of constituent processes lies in the role they play in narrative construction and paradigmatic reasoning respectively" (p. 103). Word and sentence structures, as well as function, can be very different depending on the chosen mode of writing. Therefore, the language one uses in discourse comprises a structure just as words in a sentence determine a syntactic structure. When evaluating an adult's text structure, one must consider the relationship between the microstructure (sentence level) and the macrostructure (total text; Kintsch, 1998; Van Dijk & Kintsch, 1983). We have chosen to focus only on the paradigmatic forms of writing—in particular, expository writing—since this is the genre of writing most often required of adults across instructional and work situations.

The interaction of the oral language, attention, executive functioning, and working memory processes necessary to construct written text has received little attention in the adult learning disorders literature. Researchers examining the written text of children with learning disabilities note that these writers often demonstrate difficulty with executive functions, such as planning, monitoring, evaluating, and revising (Englert, 1990; Graham & Harris, 1999). The role of working memory in text construction is controversial. Perfetti (1985) and Stanovich (1980) suggested that word decoding and encoding contribute to an overload in working memory, leading to text-structure difficulties on reading and writing tasks. However, Kintsch (1998) suggests that long-term memory plays a greater role in text structure. Whatever the etiologies of problems that led to difficulty producing written text, an examiner should review the attentional, working memory, executive processing, and oral-language functioning of any adult participating in an evaluation.

Cohesion   Cohesive ties provide the meaningful connections within and between sentences (Halliday & Hasan, 1976). Functionally, they operate to require text to be more than a mere collection of statements no matter how syntactically mature or grammatically correct such sentences appear. We suggest an evaluator observe a writer's use of three basic types of cohesive ties: grammatical ties (e.g., pronominals, demonstratives); transitional ties (i.e., ties between phrases and clauses); and word ties (e.g., synonyms, superordinates). The number of ties is not as relevant as the accuracy of ties used or the absence of needed ties in a writing sample. Again, the content of an essay or paragraph will determine the appropriateness of including specific ties.

Adults with learning disabilities often demonstrate difficulty utilizing cohesive ties in written language. For instance, such writers will fail to identify to whom a pronoun or demonstrative is referencing, or they will overuse specific nouns, providing very little word variety. Incorrect use or absence of cohesive ties leads to writing samples that appear disorganized or lack a sense of audience. Gregg (1985) was one of the first researchers to document that the adult population with learning disabilities appears to use fewer demonstratives in their written language than adult writers without disabilities. Noting that many of these adults demonstrate significant word-finding and spelling problems, Gregg also suggested that this could be one reason for those writers' lack of flexibility with word choice (e.g., synonyms or superordinate ties). Several other researchers noted the difficulty adult writers with learning disabilities demonstrate with ties that

Cohesive Tie Checklist

Name:_____   Time:_____

Topic:_____   Fluency Index:_____

Type of Tie	Definition	Frequent Use	Accurate Use
Grammar Ties	- *Pronouns that refer to a noun* - *Word deletions*		
pronominals	he, she, it	_____	_____
demonstratives	this, these	_____	_____
definite article	then, the	_____	_____
comparatives	similarly, other	_____	_____
ellipsis	some, in his opinion (word deletion)	_____	_____
Lexical Ties	- *Vocabulary Selection*		
same items	boy/boy		_____
synonyms	huge/big	_____	_____
superordinates	sports/baseball	_____	_____
Transitional Ties	- *Words or phrases that show relationships between statements*		
consequence	therefore, then, as a result	_____	_____
likeness	likewise, similar	_____	_____
contrast	but, however	_____	_____
amplification	and, again, also	_____	_____
example	for instance	_____	_____
sequence	first, second, finally	_____	_____
restatement	in other words, that is	_____	_____
recapitalization	in conclusion, to summarize	_____	_____
time or place	later, here, there	_____	_____

Figure 12.3 Cohesive Tie Checklist.

connect phrases and clauses (Herbert & Czerniejewski, 1976; Johnson & Blalock, 1987; Wiig & Semel, 1984). Gregg (1985) found that in her sample of adult writers, those with learning disabilities tended to use a greater percentage of "and" and "but" transitional ties (rather than more sophisticated ties or structures). Such a pattern is more typical of the writing of young children or inexperienced writers.

Difficulty accurately using cohesive ties in writing can be the result of different cognitive or linguistic deficits (see Figure 12.3). An evaluator might begin by exploring the word-knowledge competency of an adult writer, since use of cohesive ties is dependent on a writer's sophistication with words. However, an extensive vocabulary may be obscured or compromised by problems related to decoding and encoding, organizational functioning, self-regulatory skills, or reasoning. As noted previously, word-finding problems can lead to inaccurate use of lexical ties. Gregg (1985) found that among adult writers, a significant number of apparent cohesive tie errors resulted from difficulty with morphological endings and inadvertent omission of entire words. Therefore, one might infer that word and word knowledge will influence the production of text.

Coherence   Coherence refers to the macrostructure of text. It is the wholeness or structural blueprint of an essay, article, or other composition. However, each genre of writing (e.g., narrative, expository, persuasive, descriptive) uses somewhat different frameworks to build or develop ideas. In addition, the fluidity and clarity of written texts are dependent on appropriate use of cohesion. Without cohesion, a writer cannot produce coherent text. Research has supported the idea that utilization and formulation of coherent text are dependent on right-frontal hemispheric functioning (Engel-Ortlieb, 1981; Cannito, Jarecki, & Pierce, 1986; Huber, 1989). Interestingly, other researchers suggest that individuals with right-hemispheric disorders have less trouble creating linguistic and informational structures than they do maintaining self-regulatory processes in order to sustain ambiguity and inferential information (Brownell, Carroll, Rehak, & Wingfield, 1992). Therefore, adults with verbal or nonverbal learning disabilities are likely to demonstrate difficulty with text structure.

Chapman et al. (1992) proposed a model of discourse processing that provides several aspects that would be useful to an evaluator trying to understand why an adult is having trouble producing written text. They suggested that one observe the linguistic structures (word knowledge, syntax, cohesion), informational structures (macrostructure), and information-handling structures an individual brings to language production. It is the last of these areas that we suggest be incorporated into the evaluation of text coherence (see Figure 12.4). Chapman's information-handling processes include such abilities as retrieving, selecting, isolating, sorting, reducing, and sequencing information. These abilities depend on such processes as metalinguistics, executive functioning, working memory, and long-term memory.

Sense of Audience

Adults demonstrating underachievement in writing often differ from their higher achieving cohorts in the degree and manner in which they consider their audiences (Rubin & Looney, 1990). They seldom view writing as a means of communication or persuasion; rather, they tend to think infrequently of potential readers and fail to use information about their readers even when it is available to them. According to Rubin (1984),

Observational Checklist
for
Paradigmatic Text Structure

Name: _____   Date: _____

Time: _____hours _____minutes   Topic: _____

Genre: Prompts: _____
___expository   ___argumentative
___descriptive   ___rewrite | Fluency Index
                                     | Number of words   ____
                                     | Number of different words ____
                                     | Words ÷ Different Words   ____

Performance	Deficit	Commensurate with Ability	Strength
Word usage			
fluency	← — — — — →		
word ties	← — — — — →		
content appropriate	← — — — — →		
Cohesion			
grammatical ties	← — — — — →		
transitional ties	← — — — — →		
Topic Development			
introduced topic	← — — — — →		
maintained topic	← — — — — →		
concluded topic	← — — — — →		
Idea Development			
retrieved ideas	← — — — — →		
selected ideas	← — — — — →		
reduced ideas	← — — — — →		
supported ideas	← — — — — →		
organized ideas	← — — — — →		
Sense of Audience	← — — — — →		

Figure 12.4 Observational Checklist for Paradigmatic Text Structure.

underachieving writers experience particular problems in "processual role-taking—considering the information-processing needs of their readers. Consequently, they neglect to disambiguate pronoun references, leave predicates afloat without subjects, and omit critical supporting details" (Rubin & Looney, 1990, p. 281). The problems underachieving writers experience in revision and audience awareness are interdependent. Rubin (1984) has argued that audience awareness is fundamental to revision; to revise is to step back from the writer's own subjective understanding of a text and experience it with naïve eyes (Murray, 1978).

The assessment of audience awareness via standardized measurement tools alone is not only challenging but also untenable (considering the lack of such tools). To investigate a writer's sense of audience requires evaluation of the writer's voice, the writer's perceptions of the audience, and the context in which the writing occurred (Gregg, Sigalas, Hoy, Weisenbaker, & McKinley, 1996). In the past, audience awareness has been treated as a "monolithic" rather than "multidimensional" construct (Rubin, 1984). However, writer, audience, and context are all involved in the dynamic creation of text and lead to choices regarding concepts, vocabulary, style, and text organization. Sense of audience is a fluid construct that should be conceived as a set of interacting variables rather than a separate entity from the process of text creation (Gregg et al., 1996).

In an effort to evaluate such variables, researchers have identified a number of subskills involved in producing text sensitive to audience needs. These subskills include: content knowledge, execution (spelling/mechanics), perspective taking, differentiation of voice, and organization of text (Gregg & McAlexander, 1989; Gregg et al., 1996; Napierkowski, 2001). By and large, holistic scoring measures have been (and continue to be) used most frequently, as this method allows evaluators to study text as a whole and not merely as collections of isolated parts (Gregg et al., 1996). It also yields valuable qualitative information about an individual's writing skills, including sensitivity to audience.

Certain social cognition subskills can be evaluated with formal measures, allowing the examiner to perform an atomistic, in-depth analysis of specific aspects of written expression using standardized instruments. Table 12.5 provides (a) a detailed description of five primary social cognition subskills required in developing sensitivity to audience in written language, (b) the related cognitive, linguistic, and social processes, and (c) examples of standardized measurement tools that can be used with adults to assess these latent traits.

Deficits in any one (or more) of these areas have been shown to impact a writer's ability to identify and remain sensitive to a specific audience. For example, confusing predication (e.g., verb tense inconsistency) and ambiguous pronoun-referent schemes—both of which are captured under the broader social cognition subskill "execution"—are often the result of a writer's inability to take the reader's perspective (Gregg & McAlexander, 1996). In a study exploring the relationship between sense of audience and specific learning disabilities, Gregg and McAlexander (1996) emphasized that certain learning disabilities are more likely to cause problems with sense of audience skills in addition to execution; for example, organization deficits are found to be highly detrimental to a sense of audience. Rubin (1984) identified a connection between audience awareness and self-concept: "Developing a sense of the generalized other is a prerequisite to developing a stable self-concept, for self-concept is our understanding of how we are

Table 12.5 Sense of Audience

Area	Cognitive, Linguistic, and Social Processes	Measurement Tools
Content *actual knowledge of topic and writer's confidence with this knowledge*	Comprehension-knowledge	*WAIS-III: Information[c]; WJ III Cog: Comprehension-Knowledge Cluster[d]*
	Fluid reasoning	*WJ III Cog: Fluid Reasoning Cluster[d]*
	Processing speed	*WAIS-III: PSI; WJ III Cog: Processing Speed Cluster[c]; WJ III Ach: Academic Fluency Cluster[a]*
	Long-term retrieval	*WJ III Cog: Long-Term Retrieval Cluster[d]*
	Executive processes	*Stroop; WJ III Cog: Planning; D-KEFS[d,f]*
Execution *actual linguistic resources, including mechanical ability, grammar, and vocabulary*	Processing speed	*WAIS-III: PSI; WJ III Cog: Processing Speed Cluster[c]; WJ III Ach: Academic Fluency Cluster[a]*
	Long-term retrieval	*WJ III Cog: Long-Term Retrieval Cluster[d]*
	Short-term memory	*WAIS-III: Digit Span, Arithmetic[c]; WJ III: Short-Term Memory Cluster[d]; WMS-III: Immed Mem Index[c]*
	Attention	*WAIS-III: Picture Completion[c]; WJ III Ach: Editing[a]*
	Mechanics	*TOWL-3: Contextual Conventions, Story Construction[1]; WIAT-II: Wr Exp; WJ III Ach: Editing, Wr Samples[a]*
	Grammar	*TOWL-3: Contextual Conventions, Story Construction; WIAT-II: Wr Exp; WJ III Ach: Editing, Wr Samples[a]*
	Syntax	*WJ III Ach: Oral Comprehension; TOWL-3: Logical Sent, OWLS: Conventions, Content[b]*

(continued)

Table 12.5 (continued) Sense of Audience

Area	Cognitive, Linguistic, and Social Processes	Measurement Tools
	Vocabulary knowledge	*WAIS-IIII: Vocabulary*[c]; *PPVT-III; WJ III Cog: Verbal Comprehension*[d]
Perspective taking *awareness that the reader has a different point of view*	Self-concept	*Adult Self-Concept Scale*[2]
	Attribution	
	Pragmatic communication	
	Comprehension	*WAIS-III: Comprehension*[c]; *WJ III Ach: Oral Expression, Listening Comprehension*[a]
	Social inferencing	
	Executive processes	*Stroop; WJ III Cog: Planning; D-KEFS*[f]
Differentiation of voice *the transfer of the mental image of the audience into communication strategies aiding message delivery*	Vocabulary knowledge	*WAIS-IIII: Vocabulary*[c]; *PPVT-III*[3]; *WJ III Cog: Verbal Comprehension*
	Long-Term Retrieval	*WJ III Cog: Long-Term Retrieval Cluster*[d]
	Social Cognitive Complexity	*Crockett Role Category Questionnaire*
	Social Inferencing	
	Logical Inferencing	*WAIS-III: Comprehension; Similarities; D-KEFS: Proverbs*[f]
	Executive Processes	*Stroop; WJ III Cog: Planning; D-KEFS*[f]
Organization of Text *ability to follow the text structure of the genre requested for the task*	Cohesion	*TOWL-3: Log Sent, Contextual Lang, Story Construction; WIAT-II: Wr Exp; WJ III Ach: Wr Samples*[c]
	Understanding directions	*WJ III Ach: Understanding Directions; OWLS: Content*[b]
	Sentence Structure	*TOWL-3: Style, Logical Sent, Contextual Conventions, Story Construction; WJ III Ach: Wr Samples*[a]
	Executive Processes	*Stroop; WJ III Cog: Planning; D-KEFS*[f]
	Coherence	*OWLS: Content*[b]

Table 12.5 (continued) Sense of Audience

[a] Wechsler (1997)
[b] Woodcock, McGrew, & Mather (2001)
[c] Golden (1998)
[d] Delis, Kaplan, & Kramer (2001)
[e] Hammill & Larsen (1996)
[f] Wechsler (2001)

generally perceived" (p. 230). Deficits in perspective taking, which requires the writer to engage in social inference and perceive or express various traits in others, are often characteristic of developing writers as well.

Fluency

Fluency is a critical construct to address in the evaluation of writing. However, the terms *fluency* and *speed* are often defined differently or interchangeably depending on the discipline. In the area of reading disorders, for example, fluency refers to "high-speed word recognition" as well as "comprehension processes" (National Reading Panel, 2000, p. 6). In other disciplines (e.g., linguistics), fluency may be referred to as "verbosity" and measured by the length or number of words in a composition. Gregg, Coleman, Stennett, and Davis (2002) investigated the written discourse complexity of college writers with and without learning disabilities. They found that verbosity, quality, and lexical complexity (as measured by type/token ratios) were significantly correlated. In particular, verbosity and quality could not be viewed as separate constructs but were statistically co-occurring functions. A critical finding from this study was that vocabulary and fluency proxies—number of words (tokens), number of different words (types), and number of words with more than two syllables—were the best discriminators between college writers with and without dyslexia. It should be noted that for the above study, in order to minimize bias, raters were given versions of student essays that had been (a) converted to a word-processed format, and (b) edited for spelling and mechanical errors.

In this chapter, we have chosen to define writing fluency as "the ability to produce words or larger language units in a limited time interval" (Harris & Hodges, 1995). While there are many psychometric measures (in both cognitive and achievement areas) whose names include terms such as "fluency" or "processing speed," research has not been conclusive as to the predictive value of these measures in the area of written expression. In interpreting the significance of a fluency index or score, it is suggested that an examiner take into account task requirements as well as the average performance of an examinee's peer group on a similar task. For noncollege adult writers or graduate students, different expectations might

326 • Noel Gregg, Chris Coleman, and Jennifer Lindstrom

be appropriate. Any interpretation of an adult writer's fluency requires knowledge of a comparable group of peers with a similar level of writing instruction and experience.

Conclusions

Theorists over the centuries have contended that written expression is a tool for promoting cognitive growth (Bruner, 1968; Vygotsky, 1962; Wertsch, 1991). As Bruner (1968) stated, "The shape or style of mind is, in some measure, the outcome of internalizing the functions inherent in the language we use" (p. 107). The importance of utilizing both neuro-linguistic and sociolinguistic research to better understand the underlying cognitive, linguistic, and social processes influencing written expression is central to our thinking and expressed in our model of written expression (Figure 12.1).

Three consistent themes are identified throughout this chapter as crucial to the evaluation of written expression in the adult population. First, although there are standardized instruments available to professionals for some areas of written expression, the majority of these tests screen general aspects of writing. Therefore, systematic means of collecting observations and informal scores are crucial to interpreting when a writing sample truly reflects a disability. Second, we suggest that only through comparison of written product(s) with other data collected during a psychological evaluation (e.g., cognitive and linguistic processing) can identification of a disorder or difference be determined. Writing underachievement alone should not constitute a written expression disorder. Third, we propose that an adult's writing sample(s) must be evaluated in light of task demands, his or her individual profile, the situational context, and the writing samples of adults with similar writing experience/instruction.

It is imperative that future researchers explore the cognitive, linguistic, and social processes used in text production by adult writers with and without developmental disorders. Further investigation of adult writers across a multitude of task demands, with and without accommodations, will lead to a better determination of strategies and modifications appropriate for enhancing the writing of adults with learning disabilities. A wide range of methodologies such as single-subject, statistical (structural equation modeling, item-level response), phenomenological-ethnographic, think-aloud, retrospective accounts, and collaborative writing designs will improve our ability to assess and determine appropriate accommodations for the adult population (Smagorinsky, 1994). Understanding written expression at the adult level requires the integration of many perspectives and methodologies.

References

Abbott, R. D., & Berninger, V. W. (1993). Structural equation modeling of relationships among developmental skills and writing skills in primary and intermediate grade writers. *Journal of Educational Psychology, 85*, 478–508.

Becker, H. J. (1999). *Internet use by teachers: Conditions of professional use and teacher-directed student use.* Irvine, CA: Center for Research on Information Technology and Organizations.

Benton, A. L., & Meyers, R. (1956). An early description of the Gerstmann syndrome. *Neurology, 6*,838–842.

Bereiter, C., & Scardamalia, M. (1985). Cognitive copying strategies and the problem of "inert knowledge." In S. F. Chipmon, J. W. Segal, & R. Glaser (Eds.), *Thinking and learning skills: Research and open questions* (pp. 65–80). Hillsdale, NJ: Lawrence Erlbaum.

Berninger, V. (1996). *Reading and writing acquisition: A developmental neuropsychological perspective.* Oxford: Westview Press.

Brown, A. L., Bransford, J. D., Ferrara, R. A., & Campione, J. C. (1983). Learning, remembering, and understanding. In J. H. Flavell & E. M. Markman (Eds.) *Handbook of child psychology: Vol. 3. Cognitive development* (4th ed., pp. 77–166). New York: Wiley.

Brownell, H. H., Carroll, J. J., Rehak, A., & Wingfield, A. (1992). The use of pronoun anaphora and speaker mood in the interpretation of conversational utterances by right hemisphere brain-damaged patients. *Brain and Language, 42*, 121–147.

Bruck, M. (1993). Component spelling skills of college students with childhood diagnoses of dyslexia. *Learning Disability Quarterly, 16*, 171–184.

Bruner, J. (1968). *Towards a theory of instruction* (2nd ed.). New York: Norton.

Bruner, J. (1985). Narrative and paradigmatic modes of thought. In E. Eisner (Ed). *Learning and teaching the ways of knowing: 84th yearbook of the National Society for the Study of Education* (pp. 97–115). Chicago: National Society for the Study of Education.

Cannito, M., Jarecki, J., & Pierce, R. S. (1986). Effects of thematic structure on syntactic comprehension in aphasia. *Brain and Language, 27*, 310–321.

Carrow-Woolfolk, E. (1996). *Oral and Written Language Scales (OWLS).* Circle Pines, MN: American Guidance Service.

Carrow-Woolfolk, E. (1999). *Comprehensive Assessment of Spoken Language (CASL).* Circle Pines, MN: American Guidance Service.

Cermak, S. (1985). Developmental dyspraxia. *Advances in Psychology, 23*, 225–243.

Chapman, S. B., Culhane, K. A., Levin, H. S., Harwood, H. Mendelsohn, D., Ewing-Cobbs, L., et al. (1992). Narrative discourse after closed head injury in children and adolescents. *Brain and Language, 43*, 42–65.

Critchly, M. (1970). *The dyslexic child.* London: Heinenmann Medical Books.

Cunningham, A. E., & Stanovich, K. E. (1997). Early reading acquisition and its relation to reading experience and ability 10 years later. *Developmental Psychology, 33*(6), 934–945.

Delis, D. C., Kaplan, E., & Kramer, J. H. (2001). *Delis-Kaplan Executive Function System (D-KEFS).* San Antonio, TX: Psychological Corporation.

Deuel, R. K. (1992). Motor skill disorders. In S. R. Hooper, G. W. Hynd & R. E. Mattison (Eds.), *Developmental disorders: Diagnostic criteria and clinical assessment* (pp. 239–282). Hillsdale, N.J.: Lawrence Erlbaum.

Engel-Ortlieb, D. (1981). Discourse processing in aphasics. *Text, 1*, 361–383.

Englert, C. S. (1990). Unraveling the mysteries of writing through strategy instruction. In T. E. Scruggs & B. Y. L. Wong (Eds.), *Intervention research in learning disabilities* (pp. 186–223). New York: Springer-Verlag.

Fawcett, A. J., & Nicholson, R. I. (1999). Performance of dyslexic children on cerebellar and cognitive tests. *Journal of Motor Behavior, 31*, 68–78.

Fawcett, A. J., Nicholson, R. I., & Dean, P. (1996). Impaired performance of children with dyslexia on a range of cerebellar tasks. *Annals of Dyslexia, 46*, 259–283.

Ferry, P., Hall, S., & Hicks, J. (1975). Dilapidated speech: Developmental verbal dyspraxia. *Developmental Medicine and Child Neurology, 17*, 749–756.

Flower, L. S., & Hayes, J. R. (1979). Problem solving strategies and the writing process. *College English, 39*, 449–461.

Foorman, B. R. (1994). Phonological and orthographic processing of words: Separate but equal? In V. W. Berninger (Ed.), *The varieties of orthographic knowledge I: Theoretical and developmental issues* (pp. 319–355). Dordrecht, The Netherlands: Kluwer Academic Publishers.

Goldberg, A., Russell, M., & Cook, A. (2003). The effect of computers on student writing: A meta-analysis of studies from 1992–2002. *The Journal of Technology, Learning and Assessment 2*(1), 1–51.

Golden, C. J. (1978). *Stroop Color and Word Test*. Los Angeles, CA: Western Psychological Services.

Graham, S., & Harris, K. (1994). The role of self-regulation in the writing process. In D. Schunk & B. J. Zimmerman (Eds.), *Self-regulation of learning and performance: issues and educational applications* (pp. 203–228). Hillsdale, NJ: Lawrence Erlbaum.

Graham, S., & Harris, K. (1999). Assessment and intervention in overcoming writing difficulties: An illustration from the self-regulated strategy development model. *Language, Speech and Hearing Services in Schools, 30*, 255–264.

Gregg, N. (1985). College learning disabled, normal, and basic writers: A comparison of frequency and accuracy of cohesive ties. *Journal of Psychoeducational Assessment, 3*, 223–231.

Gregg, N. (1992). Expressive writing disorders. In S. Hooper, G. Hynd, & R. Mattison (Eds.). *Assessment and diagnosis of child and adolescent psychiatric disorders: Current issues and procedures* (pp. 127–167). Hillsdale, NJ: Lawrence Erlbaum.

Gregg, N. (1995). *Written expression disorders, neuropsychology and cognition*. Boston, MA: Kluwer.

Gregg, N., Coleman, C., Stennett, R., & Davis, M. (2002). Discourse complexity of college writers with and without disabilities: A multidimensional analysis. *Journal of Learning Disabilities, 35*(1), 23–38.

Gregg, N., Coleman, C., Stennett, R., Davis, M., Nielsen, K., Knight, D., et al. (2001). Sublexical and lexical processing of young adults with learning disabilities and attention deficit/ hyperactivity disorder. In E. Witruk (Ed.), *Basic functions of language and language disorders* (pp. 1–31). Dordrecht: Kluwer Academic.

Gregg, N., Hoy, C., King, M., Moreland, C., & Jagota, M. (1992). The MMPI-2 profile of adults with learning disabilities at a rehabilitation setting. *The Journal of Applied Rehabilitation Counseling, 23*, 52–59.

Gregg, N., & McAlexander, P. (1989). The relation between sense of audience and specific learning disabilities: An exploration. *Annals of Dyslexia, 39*, 206–226.

Gregg, N., Sigalas, S., Hoy, C., Weisenbaker, J., & McKinley, C. (1996). Sense of audience and the adult writer: A study across competence levels. *Reading and Writing: An Interdisciplinary Journal, 8*, 121–137.

Halliday, M. A. K., & Hasan, R. (1976). *Cohesion in English.* London: Longman Group.

Harris, T. L., & Hodges, R. E. (1995). *The literacy dictionary: The vocabulary of reading and writing.* Newark, DE: IRA.

Hatcher, J., Snowling, M. J., & Griffiths, Y. M. (2002). Cognitive assessment of dyslexic students in higher education. *British Journal of Educational Psychology, 72*, 119–133.

Herbert, M. A., & Czerniejewski, D. (1976). Language and learning therapy in a community college. *Bulletin of the Orton Society, 26*, 96–106.

Holmes, V. M., & Castles, A. E. (2001). Unexpectedly poor spelling in university students. *Scientific Studies of Reading, 5*, 319–350.

Huber, W. (1989). Text comprehension and production in aphasia: Analysis in terms of micro and macro processing. In Y. Joanette & H. Brownell (Eds.). *Discourse ability and brain damage: Theoretical and empirical perspectives* (pp. 154–179). New York: Springer-Verlag.

Jastak, S., & Wilkinson, G.(1993). *Wide Range Achievement Test-Revision 3.* Wilmington, DE: Jastak.

Johnson, D. J., & Blalock, J. N. (1987). *Adults with learning disabilities: Clinical studies.* New York: Grune & Stratton.

Justus, T. C., & Ivry, R. B. (2001). The cognitive neuropsychology of the cerebellum. *International Review of Psychiatry, 13*, 276–282.

Kaplan, E., Goodglass, H., Weintraub, S., & Segal, O. (1983). *The Boston Naming Test.* Media, PA: Lippincott Williams & Wilkins.

Kinsbourne, M., & Cook, J. (1971). Generalized and internalized effects of concurrent verbalization on a unimanual skill. *Journal of Experimental Psychology, 23*, 341—345.

Kintsch, W. (1998).*Comprehension: A paradigm for cognition.* Cambridge: Cambridge University Press.

Lebrun, Y., Devreux, F., & Leleux, C. (1991). Writer's cramp. In R. M. Joshi (Ed.), *Written language disorders* (pp. 127–142). Dordrecht: Kluwer Academic Press.

LeFly, D. L., & Pennington, B. F. (2000). Reliability and validity of the Adult Reading History Questionnaire. *Journal of Learning Disabilities, 33*, 286–296.

Liepmann, H. (1900). *Drie Aufsätze aus dem Apraxiegebrief* [Three Essays on Apraxia]. Berlin: Karger.

Luria, A. R. (1980). *Higher cortical functions in man.* New York: Basic Books.

Luria, A. R. (1981). *Language and cognition* (J. V. Wertsch, Trans.). New York: Wiley Intersciences.

Manglitz, E., Hoy, C., Gregg, N., Wisenbaker, J., King, M., & Moreland, C. (1995). The relationship of depression and anxiety to ability and achievement in adults with learning disabilities at university and rehabilitation settings. *Assessment in Rehabilitation and Exceptionality 2*(3), 163–178.

Marcie, P., & Hecaen, H. (1979). Agraphia. In K. M. Heilman & E. Valenstein (Eds.), *Clinical neuropsychology* (pp. 105–131). New York: Oxford University Press.

Mather, N., & Woodcock, R. W. (2001). Examiner's Manual. *Woodcock-Johnson III Tests of Achievement.* Itasca, IL: Riverside.

Murray, D. (1978). Internal revision: A process of discovery. In C. Cooper & L. Oddell (Eds.), *Research on composing: Points of departure* (pp. 85–103). Urbana, IL: NCTE.

Myklebust, H. R. (1965). *Development and disorders of written language: Picture Story Language Test.* New York: Grune & Stratton.

Napierkowski, H. (2001, March). *Collaborative learning and sense of audience in two computer-mediated discourse communities.* Paper presented at the annual meeting of the Conference on College Composition and Communication, Denver, CO.

National Reading Panel. (2000). *Teaching children to read: An evidence based assessment of the scientific research literature on reading and its implications for reading instruction.* Bethesda, MD: National Reading Board, National Institute of Child Health and Human Development.

Palmer, E. D., Brown, T. T., Petersen, S. E., & Schlaggar, B. L. (2004). Investigation of the functional neuroanatomy of single word reading and its development. *Scientific Studies of Reading, 8*, 203–224.

Perfetti, C. A. (1985). *Reading ability.* New York: Oxford University Press.

Pinker, S. (1994). *The language instinct.* New York: William Morrow.

Roberts, R., & Mather, N. (1997). Orthographic dyslexia: The neglected subtype. *Learning Disabilities Research and Practice, 12*, 236–25.

Rubin, D. (1984). Social cognition and written communication. *Written Communication, 1*(2): 211–245.

Rubin, D., & Looney, J. (1990). Facilitation of audience awareness: Revision processes of basic writers. In G. Kirsch & D. Roen (Eds.), *A sense of audience in written communication* (pp. 280–292). CA: Sage.

Sandak, R., Mencl, W. E., Frost, S. J., & Pugh, K. R. (2004). The neurobiological basis of skilled and impaired reading: Recent findings and new directions. *Scientific Studies of Reading, 8*, 273–292.

Smagorinsky, P. (1994). *Speaking about writing: Reflections on research methodology.* London: Sage

Stanovich, K. (1980). Toward an interactive compensatory model of individual differences in the development of reading fluency. *Reading Research Quarterly, 16*, 32–71.

Treiman, R. (1997). Spelling in normal children and dyslexics. In B. A. Blanchman (Ed.), *Foundations of reading acquisition and dyslexia: Implications for early intervention* (pp. 191–218). Mahwah, NJ: Lawrence Erlbaum.

Van Dijk, T. A., & Kintsch, W. (1983). *Strategies of discourse comprehension.* New York: Academic Press.

Vygotsky, L. S. (1962). *Thought and language.* Cambridge, MA: MIT Press.

Wechsler, D. (1997a). *Wechsler Adult Intelligence Scale* (3rd ed.). San Antonio, TX: Psychological Corporation.

Wechsler, D. (1997b). *Wechsler Memory Scale* (3rd ed.). San Antonio, TX: Psychological Corporation.

Wechsler, D. (2001). *Wechsler Individual Achievement Test* (2nd ed.). San Antonio, TX: Psychological Corporation.

Wertsch, J. V. (1991). *Voices of the mind: A sociocultural approach to mediated action*. Cambridge, MA: Harvard University Press.

Wiig, E. H., & Semel, E. M. (1984). *Language assessment and intervention for the learning disabled* (2nd ed.). Columbus, OH: Merrill.

Wolf, M., Bowers, P. G., & Biddle, K. (2000). Naming-speed processes, timing, and reading: A conceptual review. *Journal of Learning Disabilities, 33*, 387–407.

Woodcock, R. W., McGrew, K. S., & Mather, N. (2001a). *Woodcock-Johnson III, Achievement Ability Tests*. Itasca, IL: Riverside.

Woodcock, R. W., McGrew, K. S., & Mather, N. (2001b). *Woodcock-Johnson III, Cognitive Ability Tests*. Itasca, IL: Riverside.

CHAPTER **13**

Coexisting Psychiatric Disorders in Postsecondary Students Referred for Neuropsychological Evaluation for Learning Disorder (LD) or Attention Deficit/Hyperactivity Disorder (ADHD)

HOPE SCHREIBER

Contents

The National Comorbidity Survey Replication (NCS-R) has indicated that 46.4% of their 9282-member sample reported a lifetime history of a mental disorder (Kessler, Berglund, Demler, Jin, & Walters, 2005a). The NCS-R showed a 12-month prevalence of 26.2% for anxiety, mood, impulse control and substance abuse disorders; 45% of these individuals met *Diagnostic and Statistical Manual of Mental Disorders* (4th ed., *DSM-IV*; American Psychiatric Association, 1994) criteria for two or more disorders (Kessler, Berglund, Demler, Jin, & Walters, 2005b). Furthermore, half of those individuals who said they had a mental disorder over a 12-month period reported an onset by age 14; three quarters of the individuals said their onset occurred by age 24 (Kessler et al., 2005b). The high prevalence of many psychiatric disorders, as well as their relatively early age of onset, suggests that attention to the well-being of the postsecondary student population is of paramount importance.

In fact, the coexistence of psychiatric and learning disorders in postsecondary students and other young adults has long been recognized. Noel Gregg et al. (Gregg, Hoy, King, Moreland, & Jagota, 1992) noted that university students evaluated by the University of Georgia's Learning Disabilities Adult Clinic showed "feelings of fear, obsessive thoughts, lack of self-confidence, self-doubt and extreme self-criticism" (p. 394) in Minnesota Multiphasic Personality Inventory-2 (MMPI-2) profiles. Both university students with learning disorders (LD) and those individuals in a rehabilitation setting showed MMPI-2 profiles consistent with extreme short- and long-term stress, leading to anxiety. Anxiety proved to be problematic for college students with learning disorders, both in general settings and in testing situations (Hoy et al., 1997). Students who had an early diagnosis of LD and supportive families (Nielsen, 2001) experienced lower levels of distress.

Students who are referred for neuropsychological evaluation for potential learning disorders (LD) or attention-deficit/hyperactivity disorder (ADHD) often do not have simple, well-defined deficits in a discrete academic area; rather, many experience complex psychiatric concerns of some significance. Although it is quite apparent that some psychiatric disorders are derived effects of the long-term struggles and frustrations experienced by young adults with LD and ADHD in academic settings (Gregg et al., 1992; Hoy et al., 1997), information from a variety of contexts suggest that some disorders may co-occur frequently. Marks, Newcorn, and Halperin (2001) and Newcorn et al. (2001) raise concerns about the appropriateness of the study of "comorbidities" in their consideration of a neurodevelopmental disorder such as ADHD. They question whether such comorbid disorders represent independent clinical "entities" or whether they are related to similar genetic or environmental factors. They further question whether subtypes can be derived from characteristic clusters of comorbidities or whether the presence of one disorder heightens the risk for others.

Frequently co-occurring disorders may be the result of atypical development, suggest Gilger and Kaplan (2001, and this volume). This view is buttressed by research findings showing that the etiology of learning disorders is variable. Learning disorders appear to involve multiple genes or genes that affect multiple brain areas, in varying degrees. Research to date suggests that multiple neural systems are involved in learning disorders such as dyslexia, rather than a single brain area being associated with a single cognitive deficit (Grigorenko, 2001, and this volume; Tager-Flusberg, this volume; Pugh et al., 2002; Shaywitz et al., 2002; Shaywitz et al., 2003). Numerous feedback mechanisms from educational and psychosocial environments may modify the outcome of educational and vocational competence and emotional integrity over time. The critical developmental time period that postsecondary education often captures may represent the age of onset of a number of disorders that co-occur with LD or ADHD, a possibility underlined by the recent NCS-R. Despite the advancement in knowledge provided by such large epidemiological studies, we are only just beginning to delineate the problems and even understand the right questions to ask about this complex population.

This chapter describes the Tufts–New England Medical Center (Tufts–NEMC) College Learning Disorders/ADHD Program and discusses some of the findings in an ongoing pilot project that demonstrates multiple problem areas and complex neurodevelopmental and family histories are highly prevalent in college, medical, law, and graduate students referred for neuropsychological evaluation. Addressing the coexisting psychiatric concerns of the students with LD and ADHD, and their families, these findings raise questions about the nature of the association between LD and psychiatric disorders. The chapter describes some of the NCS-R epidemiological findings that may be relevant to the studied group. In addition, the chapter reviews a selection of the literature addressing psychiatric complications that may coexist with LD in postsecondary students. Such disorders may present differential diagnostic challenges when it is unclear whether a learning disorder, the cognitive effects of the psychiatric disorder, or the effects of the medications to treat it interfere with academic, personal, and social functioning. Cases demonstrating the complexity and interplay of LD, ADHD, and coexisting psychiatric disorders are presented. Discussion of directions for future research conclude the chapter.

College LD/ADHD Program Pilot Study

The College LD/ADHD Program and its associated ADHD Clinic are based at the Tufts–NEMC and specialize in the neuropsychological, psychiatric, educational, and medical treatment of postsecondary students with academic struggles. Students were referred by university counseling centers or academic support services for evaluation of potential learning disorders or attention-deficit/hyperactivity disorder. Alternatively, they sought reevaluation for confirmation of the need for academic accommodations at a postsecondary level after diagnosis earlier in their academic career.

Tufts-NEMC is a tertiary-care teaching hospital that often receives complex referrals of all sorts. Consequently, while it is tempting to assume that the study of postsecondary students referred to the College LD/ADHD Program would lead to ascertainment bias and a particularly complex student population, it was not clear that this was the case, given most studied samples also have found significant numbers of coexisting disorders in their students. Certainly, over the period of 10 years of the program's existence, it did become clear that many of the students were not referred for single learning disorders; complexity in clinical presentation was more frequent. Furthermore, many students also experienced psychiatric concerns of some significance. Such observations prompted the exploration of the types and prevalences of such psychiatric disorders coexisting with learning disorders or ADHD in these students, as well as relevant neurodevelopmental and family history.

The pilot project focused on chart review of 115 recent consecutive referrals to the program. Family, academic, and neurodevelopmental histories were acquired through a questionnaire mailed to the student prior to evaluation, with the instructions for their parents to complete some sections. In addition, in most cases a parent was directly contacted by telephone or direct interview to confirm and expand upon the contents of the questionnaire. This information, along with diagnostic and testing data, was entered into a database by a research assistant; each entry was confirmed for accuracy and completeness by this writer. All testing was completed by this writer.

Diagnosis of ADHD was made if the student met *DSM-IV* criteria, if there was a consistent history with this disorder reported by a parent or early school documentation, and if academic history or neuropsychological testing appeared to be consistent with the disorder. LD diagnoses were made through examination of the history of specific academic difficulty, review of prior documentation, parent and school reports, and neuropsychological testing results consistent with the disorder. In addition, a general psychiatric interview was a part of the evaluation. Most students also received a Beck Depression Inventory and the Symptom Checklist 90-R (SCL-90-R). Some students also received an MMPI-2 or Personality Assessment Inventory (PAI), but this data was not entered in to the database due to the comparatively smaller number of individuals in the sample who received these tests.

Sample

Of the 115 recent consecutive referrals, the mean age of the group was 23.5; mean years of education were 15. Gender distribution was relatively balanced, with 48.7% female and 51.3% male. Ninety-one percent of the group was Caucasian. While the mean Wechsler Adult Intelligence Scale (3rd ed.) (WAIS-III) Full Scale IQ was 114, students showed a broad range of IQ scores, between 90 and 143. The most frequent diagnoses included ADHD predominantly inattentive type (40.87%), language-based learning disorder (40.87%) and/or reading disorder (27.83%), and ADHD combined type (26.96%). Other types of learning disorders, including nonverbal learning disorder (NVLD), constituted only 6.08% of the group, possibly due to different referral patterns for those individuals who show primarily social and organizational concerns or who may be diagnosed with Asperger disorder. In fact, these individuals have tended to be referred for neuropsychological evaluation to the general outpatient psychiatry service at Tufts–NEMC. Disorders of mathematics and visuoconstruction often appeared in conjunction with other disorders such as ADHD or a reading disorder. Only 32% of the referred individuals had one diagnosis, most commonly ADHD. Of those students who met *DSM-IV* criteria for ADHD, 19% also reported that they were depressed when asked on questionnaire and in interview.

Psychiatric and Family History Findings

The Beck Depression Inventory (BDI) was administered to 106 students; the group mean was 11.6, with a standard deviation (SD) of 9.10. This figure is slightly higher than Lightfoot and Oliver's mean from a sample of 204 college students (mean = 7.28, *SD* = 6.8; 1985) using the same 1978 version of the BDI. Perhaps of more interest was that 29% of the Tufts-NEMC referred sample had a BDI score of 16 or higher (16 to 23 indicated moderate depression in Beck's original scoring schema for a normal population; Oliver & Simmons, 1984). Twenty of these students had a BDI score of 24 or higher (11% of the referred students), indicating severe depression. To a lesser degree, anxiety was of concern in our sample; 8.69% reported significant anxiety symptoms. In the SCL-90-R, completed at the end of the evaluation, however, students often acknowledged more anxiety symptoms than they had initially reported (see cases below).

Review of family histories of the 115 referrals to the college's LD/ADHD program showed that 30.4% of the students reported one or more parent with a lifetime incidence of significant depression. When all first-degree relatives were considered (addition of siblings), 42% had one or more family member with a significant depression. Such figures are significantly higher than those observed in the general population, as will be discussed below. Thus, the referred postsecondary student group showed a higher incidence of depression in themselves and in their parents (or first-degree relatives) than expected. Anxiety disorders were also highly prevalent in students' first-degree relatives; 29% said they had a family member with a significant anxiety disorder.

National Comorbidity Survey

Findings from the Tufts–NEMC College LD/ADHD pilot project raise questions about the nature of the association between LD/ADHD and mood and anxiety disorders in postsecondary students. These findings are of interest when compared to systematically collected family histories from the NCS-R. Family data was collected in house-to-house surveys from February 2001 to December 2002 using the World Health Organization Composite International Diagnostic Interview, a structured, lay-administered, diagnostic interview that provided both *ICD-10* and *DSM-IV* diagnoses (Kessler et al., 2005b). Lifetime prevalence of major depression was 16.2% (Kessler et al., 2003), similar to the lifetime prevalence figure obtained in the National Comorbidity Survey of 17% (Kessler et al., 1994). Prevalence of any mood disorder was 20.8%, lifetime prevalence of anxiety disorders was 28.8%, substance abuse disorders 14.6%, and impulse control disorder 24.8%. In the latter group, 8.1% of their population reported having ADHD (Kessler et al., 2005b).

Kendler, Davis, and Kessler (1997) conducted a family history study, finding that of those individuals with a lifetime history of major depression, 34.4% also had a parent who experienced the disorder. Individuals without depression showed a significantly lower rate (16.1%) of parents with major depression. Furthermore, 34.4% of those individuals who had generalized anxiety disorder had a parent with the disorder, compared to 14.2% in the general population. Although data collection about family history in the Tufts-NEMC pilot project took place in a clinical context rather than being derived from structured interview, college LD/ADHD program students resembled Kendler's depressed population with respect to family frequency of depression.

Given the apparently high prevalence of psychiatric disorders among postsecondary students with LD and ADHD, a selective review of literature relevant to the psychiatric disorders in this group may move us toward a better understanding of the mechanisms of association between psychiatric disorders and LD /ADHD.

Depression and Anxiety Disorders

Caution has been suggested in interpreting relatively high BDI scores in the college population. Gotlib (1984) reported difficulty differentiating specific disorders from such scores, and Tanaka-Matsumi and Kameoka (1986) found BDI results related to the overlapping issues of depression, anxiety, and social desirability. Nevertheless, one must presume some discomfort was present in the studied students. Caution has also been suggested when interpreting undergraduate SCL-90-R responses, given that nonpatient undergraduates were characteristically more symptomatic than a general adult population, although they were less symptomatic than the undergraduate counseling center population (Todd, Deane, & McKenna, 1997). Johnson, Ellison, and Heikkinen (1989) noted that SCL-90-R mean scores in all client subgroups in their counseling center dropped by more than 1 standard deviation when compared to adolescents instead of adults. Despite such adjustments, 30.3% of male students and 26.5% of female students showing psychiatric disturbance (cutoff scores of $\geq T = 63$, as suggested by Derogatis, c1994). Certainly, there are many possible reasons why such disturbance may be present.

A high frequency of depression and anxiety symptoms in apparent reaction to academic failure can be observed in clinical practice. Such symptoms may be circumscribed, as in the student who experiences autonomic symptoms of anxiety, such as rapid heartbeat, sweaty palms, and "blanking out" during examinations. Other individuals may slowly become demoralized, frustrated, and depressed over a long period of time, as it becomes clear that the student cannot live up to his or her own or others' standards in an academic context. Some individuals may become avoidant about completing their work, even going to the library, feeling shame at perceived lack of effectiveness in studying. Yet in other situations, associations among LD, ADHD, depression, anxiety, and behavioral disorders may be of a different nature.

Children and adolescents with reading disorders have been shown to exhibit significantly higher rates of internalizing and externalizing disorders than individuals without reading disorders (Willcut & Pennington, 2000a). A relationship between psychiatric referral, externalizing pathology and receptive language disorders in children ages 4 to 12 was described by Cohen, Barwick, Horodezky, and Isaacson (1996).

In a similar fashion, nonverbal learning disabilities have been described as associated with depression in an inpatient adolescent and young adult population (Cleaver, Whitman, & Douglas, 1998), who found an arithmetic-disabled group showed more depression than a reading-disabled group. These authors speculate that as an older child with NVLD enters more complex social situations, his or her cluster of deficits (including difficulty appreciating social nuance and cues, and difficulty with novel situations) may lead to increased confusion and social and academic failure. Others have shown that individuals with NVLD and right-hemisphere disorders may be more susceptible to depression as well (Weintraub & Mesulam, 1983; Rourke, 1987, 1989). Developmental considerations in the evolution of psychiatric disorders in children and adults with NVLD are discussed further by Tsatsanis and Rourke (this volume); certainly, the developmental transition as students enter college is significant. New social demands and pressures, as well as the lack of externally imposed structure, could transform a susceptibility to depression into a major depression. Social skill deficits appear to be part of the general experience of a substantial number of students with all sorts of LD, demonstrated in meta-analysis (Kavale & Forness, 1996).

Thus, comprehensive assessment of postsecondary students referred for neuropsychological evaluation is complicated by the potential presence of a coexisting psychiatric disorder. In addition, the cognitive deficits that accompany the disorders themselves add further complexity. Cognitive deficits associated with major depression are well studied in older patients, who show impairments in psychomotor speed, memory, working memory, attention, and executive functioning (Landro, Stiles, & Sletvold, 2001; Ravnkilde et al., 2002; Den Hartog, Derix, Van Bemmel, Kremer, & Jolles, 2003). Younger, unmedicated, outpatients with major depression (mean age 41.6; $SD = 12.4$) showed slowed information processing in automatic tasks; functioning in more effortful tasks appeared stronger in this group than in controls (Den Hartog et al., 2003). Deficits in attention set shifting and the ability to sustain motor responses were found in 20 young patients (mean age 37.5; range 18 to 52), with unipolar depression compared to age-, education-, and IQ-matched controls (Purcell, Maruff, Kyrios, & Pantelis, 1997); 12 of these patients were taking medication and 7 had a history of inpatient hospitalization. Less spontaneous use of appropriate strategies in test performance was noted in another study group in their early 40s (Channon & Green, 1999). Among the college-age population, poorer performance in the Wisconsin Card Sorting Test has been reported in dysphoric undergraduates (Channon, 1996). In particular, difficulty using feedback to match cards and shift set to a new matching rule was noted. More severe depression may lead to a higher level of impairment of academic productivity and interpersonal problems in college students, although feelings of inadequacy, distress, and disinterest in school were more prevalent than academic impairment (Heilgenstein, Guenther, Hsu, & Herman, 1996).

ADHD and Coexisting Psychiatric Disorders

Significant symptoms associated with ADHD persist into adulthood (Weiss, Hechtman, Milroy, & Perlman, 1985; Mannuzza, Klein, Bessler, Malloy, & Lapadula, 1993); as many as 60% of individuals diagnosed in childhood continue to have significant symptoms in adulthood (reviewed by Kessler, Adler, Barkley, Biederman, Connors, Faraone, et al., 2005). The NCS-R found 36.3% of subjects who were classified as having ADHD in childhood continued to meet full criteria for the disorder in adulthood; childhood severity predicted persistence (Kessler, Adler, et al., 2005). The estimated clinician-assessed prevalence of ADHD in adults was 4.4%. The authors acknowledged this is a conservative estimate, given the current limitations in applicability of *DSM-IV* criteria for ADHD in adults (Kessler et al., 2006).

It is also well documented that ADHD in children and adults is frequently accompanied by other psychiatric disorders (Marks et al., 2001). Biederman et al. (1993) suggested that the psychiatric disorders observed in adults with ADHD were similar to those seen in children and included antisocial personality disorder, conduct disorder, oppositional defiant disorder, substance use, anxiety disorders, enuresis, and speech and language disorders, regardless of gender. Mood disorders have been described in 10–75% of children with ADHD (Biederman, Faraone, Keenan, & Tsuang, 1991), and 31% of referred adults with ADHD have been reported to have major depression (Biederman et al., 1993). Individuals who have ADHD and bipolar disorder (as well as ADHD and conduct disorder) may represent familial subtypes (Doyle & Faraone, 2002). Coexisting anxiety has been reported in varying degrees by Shekim, Asarnow, Hess, and Zaucha (1990), as well as Biederman et al. (1994). Internalizing (anxiety or depression) and externalizing (oppositional defiant disorder or conduct disorder) comorbid disorders were reported by Jenson et al. (2001). Kessler et al. (2006) reported frequent comorbidity of mood, anxiety, substance abuse, and intermittent explosive disorder in their sample of adults with ADHD. Murphy, Barkley, and Bush (2002) reported that young adults with the combined and inattentive type of ADHD showed greater likelihood of dysthymia, alcohol dependence or abuse, cannabis dependence or abuse, and learning disorders than did the control subjects. In addition, they noted greater distress than controls in all scales of the SCL-90-R. Concerns have been raised about whether such "comorbidities" represent independent clinical entities (Marks et al., 2001) or whether new integrative models of study (Newcorn et al., 2001) are more appropriate in studying character-istically associated disorders. The frequency with which children (ages 8 to 18) with ADHD showed coexisting disorders suggested to Willcutt et al. (Willcutt, Pennington, Chhabildas, Friedman, & Alexander, 1999) that evaluations for ADHD must be comprehensive.

LD and ADHD

Studies of frequency of coexisting LD with ADHD vary widely, in part due to differences in diagnostic patterns of ADHD and LD over time and due to methodological differences between studies. Estimates of coexisting LD and ADHD range from 11–92% (Schulte, Conners, & Osborne, 1999), but these findings are often based on reading disorders or nonspecific LD. There is little known about the association of ADHD and disorders in mathematics or handwriting in adults (Marks et al., 2001). In addition, at times it may be as difficult to ascertain the coexistence of reading disorders with ADHD in adults as it is to ascertain the presence of the reading disorder itself, because limited automaticity alone can be the hallmark of such a disorder in young adults (see Chapter 5, this volume).

Nevertheless, a strong link between reading disorders and ADHD has been noted by Willcutt and Pennington (2000b), who recount a number of studies to date that note a higher coexistence than chance between these dis-orders and describe it as "phenotypic overlay" (p. 179). Willcut et al. (2002) reported that the quantitative trait locus on chromosome 6p, a susceptibility locus for ADHD, is a quantitative trait locus for reading disability as well. While the nature of this association remains under discussion, Friedman et al. (Friedman, Chhabildas, Budhiraja, Willcutt, & Pennington, 2003) conducted a study as part of the Colorado Learning Disabilities Research Center. Studying twins and their parents, the researchers found that data did not support nonrandom mating as an explanation of the coexistence of reading disorders and ADHD. Results appeared most consistent with shared genetic influences on both disorders. Doyle et al. (Doyle, Faraone, DuPre, & Biederman, 2001) suggested that in girls the relationship between ADHD and learning disorders showed independent conditions and may represent a familial subtype. Such findings were not consistent with this group's prior work with boys that suggested assortive mating (Faraone et al., 1993; Seidman et al., 1995). Faraone has noted recently, with regard to ADHD and LD, that "although there is some evidence for assortive mating, it is weak" (personal communication, August 2, 2005). Willcut et al. (2001) hypothesized multiple possible connections between ADHD and reading disorders, including pleiotropic effects where the same genetic influences may affect more than one phenotype; further study at the molecular genetic level will be necessary to elucidate this relationship. In their review paper addressing the use of executive functions to define endophenotypes of ADHD, Doyle et al. (2005) underscored the importance of the neurocognitive heterogeneity of ADHD, marked by varied neuropsychological test performance, observed in individuals in ADHD. Such variability in the disorder itself makes the task of defining the relationship of a coexisting disorder all the more difficult. Other psychiatric disorders have also been associated with executive dysfunction, as will be described below.

Obsessive-Compulsive Disorder and Tourette's

Confounding factors of medication effect, severity of illness, choice of tests administered, and coexisting disorders were noted in a review of the neuropsychological concomitants of obsessive–compulsive disorder (Kuelz, Hohagan, & Voderholzer, 2004). Although nondepressed, never-medicated children with obsessive-compulsive disorder (OCD) performed as well as healthy children on neuropsychological tests (Beers et al., 1999), the effects of development and later treatment remain unclear, given inconsistent findings across studies (Kuelz et al., 2004). Nevertheless, impaired organizational and encoding strategies appeared to be consistent with abnormalities in orbital frontal-subcortical pathways, and caudate (Saxena, Bota, & Brody, 2001; Anderson & Savage, 2004) in such patients. OCD has been associated with ADHD, Tourette's, and other tic disorders, although the exact nature of this association remains in discussion (Peterson, Pine, Cohen, & Brook, 2001; Geller et al., 2002; Gadow, Nolan, Sprafkin, & Schwartz, 2003; Hoekstra et al., 2004). Channon, Pratt, and Robertson (2002) hypothesize that cognitive impairment in Tourette's is confined to the inhibitory aspects of executive functioning, in a fashion consistent with the involvement of the dopaminergic basal ganglia circuitry.

Bipolar Disorder and Schizophrenia

Bipolar disorder affects 0.4% to 1.6% of community samples. Approximately 10–15% of adolescents with recurrent major depressive episodes will go on to develop Bipolar I Disorder. Mixed episodes are reported to be more frequent in adolescents and young adults (college age) than in older adults (American Psychiatric Association, 1994). One of the most complicated differential diagnostic evaluations may involve the question about whether observed cognitive deficits are due to LD, ADHD, or bipolar disorder.

Verbal encoding and retrieval dysfunction has been reported in bipolar patients, even in a euthymic state (Cavanagh, Van Beck, Muir, & Blackwood, 2002) when compared to matched controls. The authors proposed an association between number of affective episodes and neurocognitive impairment. Deficits in verbal working memory, verbal fluency, and sustained attention were found to be associated with enlargement of the right hippocampus in patients with bipolar disorder (Ali et al., 2000). Quraishi and Frangou (2002), in reviewing a number of studies, also suggest that sustained attention and verbal memory appear to be affected in most bipolar patients, even those who appear recovered. They, as do most authors addressing bipolar disorder, acknowledge the challenge of separating out the effects of medications from the effects of the illness itself. Zubieta, Huguelet, O'Neil, and Giordani (2001) studied euthymic Bipolar I patients, who showed poorer performance on tests of verbal learning, executive function, and motor coordination than did the controls. Executive function was negatively correlated with the number of episodes of mania and depression. The potential effects of medication, particularly lithium, were noted. In addition, adolescents with Bipolar I in remission had significantly poorer mathematics scores on standardized testing and poorer math functioning in school than adolescents with major depression and with no diagnosis (Lagace, Kutcher, & Robertson, 2003). The authors speculated that executive functioning could be involved in such deficits. It remains clear that further evaluation of a number of parameters of this illness, its neurobiological substrate, and the effects of its treatment must be further investigated before a definitive cognitive profile can be derived. Bipolar disorder itself frequently has other disorders coexisting besides ADHD, including major depression, dysthymia, social phobia and fears, substance abuse, anxiety disorders, and eating disorders (Kessler et al., 1994; Krishnan, 2005; Boylan et al., 2004).

While psychotic processes can be a part of bipolar disorder and contribute to cognitive disruption, more cognitive deficits have been associated with thought disorders such as schizophrenia, including global impairment, memory, verbal fluency, executive functioning, and psychomotor speed (Aleman, Hijman, de Haan, & Kahn, 1999; Fitzgerald et al., 2004; Heydebrand et al., 2004) The impact of medication remains a concern for many authors (Bilder et al., 2000). Yet neuropsychological impairment in first-episode schizophrenics includes deficits in verbal memory (Saykin et al., 1994), and no difference in any neuropsychological variable between first episode schizophrenics who were medication free and those who were not was described by Riley et al. (2000).

Review of case studies can elucidate the complex interplay between a neurodevelopmental and psychiatric disorder. At times, the effects of each appear inextricably intertwined. At other times, the clarification of all factors leading to academic distress is necessary for adequate intervention.

Case Studies

Several students referred for neuropsychological evaluation due to suspected learning disorders are discussed below. (Demographic information has been substantially changed to protect the identity of each student.) Each student's concerns were complex from a diagnostic and psychosocial perspective. The academic environment in which each student struggled provided specific challenges to his or her particular profile of strengths and weaknesses. Furthermore, the developmental moment of entering a new and more challenging academic environment—that is, beginning college—accentuated each of their learning and psychiatric vulnerabilities. Each of these individuals was also troubled by a significant mood or anxiety disorder requiring treatment.

Case 1: Sarah

Sarah was recruited to play basketball, a sport that she had played since middle school, by a large urban university. She worked very hard academically and was a C+ student in high school despite difficulty sustaining attention to classroom activity and a very slow reading rate. She characteristically had difficulty with math and foreign language courses. Sarah showed a WAIS-III Full Scale IQ of 102, with Verbal and Performance IQ scores also 102, in the average range. Working Memory and Processing Speed Index scores were slightly below the mean. While most WAIS-III subtest scores were in the average range or higher, Letter–Number Sequencing (scaled score 7, mean 10) and Block Design (scaled score 7) were significantly below the mean. In contrast, Sarah's Vocabulary (14) and Matrix Reasoning (14) were significantly above the mean.

In the Woodcock-Johnson-III Tests of Achievement, all subtests were below the mean. Sarah showed particularly weak phonemic decoding and syllable blending, as well as limited reading and arithmetic automaticity. In the Nelson-Denny Reading Test, Sarah was able to complete only five of seven passages in the allotted 20 minutes, leading to a score at the 34th percentile, again suggesting less than optimal reading automaticity.

Tests of executive functioning tended to be below the mean, as well. In particular, she showed limited Inhibition (scaled score 6, mean 10) in the Delis-Kaplan Executive Function System (D-KEFS) Color Word Interference Test, measuring her ability to inhibit the most automatic response of word reading. Inhibition Switching, measuring her ability to shift back and forth between two conditions (word reading and color naming), was also well below the mean (scaled score 5). The D-KEFS Tower Test, measuring spatial planning, learning patterns of successful completion of items and inhibiting trial-and-error responses, was also below the mean (scaled score 8). Sarah was slow to utilize feedback from the examiner to shift set in the Wisconsin Card Sorting Test. She did not easily apply active organizational strategies to tests of complex learning such as the California Verbal Learning Test-II and the Rey-Osterrieth Complex Figure.

Sarah completed an ADHD Rating Scale based on DSM-IV criteria for this disorder, easily fulfilling criteria for the combined type of ADHD. Her father acknowledged that she and other family members shared a tendency to "fidget" in childhood. While Sarah's father, a successful businessman, characteristically pushed Sarah to perform better academically, in a joint interview it became clear that both family members not only shared a reading disorder but also depression. Her father had difficulty learning to read, leading to his repeating the first grade; depression had been an intermittent feature of his life. Sarah reported that she had felt increasingly demoralized at school and had begun treatment for depression with an selective serotonin reuptake inhibitor (SSRI) and counseling.

At the time of testing, Sarah's Beck Depression Inventory was 19 (moderate). The SCL-90-R (Table 13.1) showed very high elevations on most clinical scales when she was compared to nonpatient adults, with a Global Severity Scale score of $T = 74$ (clinical significance = 63). In this context, adolescent norms were most appropriate, given her relatively recent entry into college and her relationship with her father. Even under these conditions, most clinical scales were elevated (see Table 13.1). Several months after the completion of this evaluation, her adviser reported that Sarah's father had been more supportive of her efforts in school, and Sarah's depression had mitigated. Her grades were improving with additional academic support, and she had become more interested in considering use of stimulant mediation. For the first time, she had begun to consider a number of options for her vocational future.

Case 2: Jason

Jason had attended a prestigious liberal arts college, where most of his courses required papers rather than exams. Jason was always aware that he worked more slowly than his peers. He also had great difficulty mastering mathematical concepts and operations; he chose a college where he

Table 13.1 SCL-90-R: Case 1 T-Scores

	SOM	O-C	I-S	DEP	ANX	HOS	PHOB	PAR	PSY	GSI	PS
Adult nonpt	76	>80	>80	>80	>80	77	>80	79	79	74	69
Outpt psych	63	59	59	62	61	61	64	64	58	52	53
Adol nonpt	67	68	70	75	71	62	69	68	64	61	63

Som = somatization; O–C = obsessive–compulsive; I–S = interpersonal sensitivity; DEP = depression; ANX = anxiety; HOS = hostility; PHOB = phobic anxiety; PAR = paranoid ideation; PSY = psychoticism; GSI = Global Severity Index; PD = Positive Symptom Distress Index.

was not required to take math courses. Jason graduated college with a GPA of 3.6, but his GRE scores were Verbal 605, Math 365. Once in graduate school, biostatistics and epidemiology proved to be daunting for him and he repeated each course. He noted that all his courses required examinations, which he sometimes could not finish. He "froze" under the pressure of such exams, at times.

Jason's birth and early development were unremarkable, but he was a shy boy and stuttered occasionally. He had mild difficulty paying attention in the classroom but excelled in reading and in those courses requiring conceptual thinking. Jason did not meet criteria for ADHD by either his or his mother's report. Rather, a long-standing history of slow processing was most problematic for him. Jason's maternal family showed a history of mood disorders and volatility in some paternal family members. His early life was replete with volatility and trauma. Jason was directed toward treatment of depression when he was in college, and was taking an SSRI at the time of testing. His Beck was 15 (mild), but in the SCL-90-R a number of scales reached clinical significance when compared to nonpatients, consistent with his reported symptoms of depression and anxiety (Table 13.2). His prior therapist had suspected that depression, anxiety, and a dissociative quality to his responses, at times, might have been associated with his early history of traumatic events; he had repeated suicidal thoughts, although with no prior attempts. He also experienced anxiety symptoms specifically when he took tests, noting he had difficulty thinking clearly at such times.

Jason had a WAIS-III Verbal IQ of 122 and a Performance IQ of 98. Many Verbal subtests were significantly above the mean, and Vocabulary was particularly strong, at scaled score 17. Several Performance subtests were at the mean or below. WAIS-III Index scores ranged from superior to low average (Verbal Comprehension 124; Perceptual Reasoning 101; Working Memory 113; Processing Speed 88). In the Nelson-Denny Reading Test, Jason completed 23 of a possible 38 items in 20 minutes, leading to a Comprehension score at the 10th percentile. When allowed to complete the test, he required 31 minutes and 40 seconds. His score was then at the 52nd percentile (four errors). While Jason's Woodcock-Johnson-III Passage Comprehension score was superior, his Reading Fluency was below the mean, supporting his report of a slow reading rate.

In Jason's approach to both the WAIS-III Block Design subtest and the Rey-Osterrieth Complex Figure, difficulty with visuoconstruction was suggested. In the Block Design subtest, Jason was able to complete only the easiest of the three block-by-three-block designs. When copying the Rey-Osterrieth Complex Figure, Jason's final product was accurate (90th percentile, 36 point system). However, fragmentation in his strategy

Table 13.2 SCL-90-R: Case 2 T-Scores

	SOM	O-C	I-S	DEP	ANX	HOS	PHOB	PAR	PSY	GSI	PD
Adult nonpt	62	67	64	65	67	66	43	67	45	72	52
Outpt psych	52	52	50	44	48	50	38	52	30	56	35

Som = somatization; O–C = obsessive–compulsive; I–S = interpersonal sensitivity; DEP = depression; ANX = anxiety; HOS = hostility; PHOB = phobic anxiety; PAR = paranoid ideation; PSY = psychoticism; GSI = Global Severity Index; PD = Positive Symptom Distress Index.

to completion was notable and appeared to lead to poor immediate and delayed recall; scores were at the < 10th and 13th percentiles, respectively. In contrast, Jason had little difficulty applying an active organizational strategy when asked to learn a 16-item word list in the California Verbal Learning Test-II.

Jason appeared to show a nonverbal learning disorder with an early history of shyness, and a long-standing difficulty with processing speed, mastery of nonverbal and math concepts, and visuoconstruction. Extended time on examinations and use of a tutor in math courses as accommodations led to an improvement in his grades. In addition, Jason considered taking a reduced course load as he completed his work for his graduate degree, given his very slow reading rate. He aspired to continue to use his facility with research ideas and design and to work with a statistician after graduation. The specific demands of Jason's graduate school program challenged his areas of weakness. Nevertheless, with increased awareness of this "fit" problem, he began to find ways to navigate through his program; he remained committed to its completion. He continued to receive treatment for depression with both medication and psychotherapy, being aware that during those times he was "stressed out," such as during exams, he was more inclined to feel symptoms of depression and anxiety. In addition, his psychiatrist reported that the addition of a mood stabilizer to his SSRI enhanced its effectiveness and reduced his suicidal thinking considerably, underlining the importance of identifying and treating coexisting disorders.

Case 3: Max

Max reported that he had been treated for ADHD for several years with a stimulant medication, and met *DSM-IV* criteria for the combined type of ADHD at the time of testing. He noted that he had several periods of depression, one of which was treated with Wellbutrin. During that time, his friends described him as very difficult and irritable; he subsequently lost his job. When he stopped taking Wellbutrin, he continued to feel the benefits of a stimulant, and others noted the improvement in his behavior. Neuropsychological testing was requested because he had withdrawn from business school and wished to return. Understanding the nature and type of his difficulty was important to him; he believed ADHD did not explain all of his school problems.

Max reported characteristic difficulty with time management, planning, and task prioritization. He reported difficulty listening well, frequently interrupted others, and acknowledged difficult reading social cues, a difficulty that had been observed in early childhood. He described himself as having periods when he was able to successfully complete complex and multiple projects and other periods where he had difficulty completing just one. Family history was positive for bipolar disorder, substance abuse, dyslexia, and ADHD.

Max's Full Scale IQ was in the very superior range, with all Index scores superior or very superior except Processing Speed, which was average. All academic testing was high average or superior with the exception of reading and math fluency, which were average. His timed Nelson-Denny Reading Test performance (Comprehension) was completed earlier than the 20-minute time limit and at the 80th percentile. Tests of executive functioning were only mildly variable. His copy of the Rey-Osterrieth Complex Figure was square rather than rectangular in shape, but otherwise accurate. However, his retention of the figure upon immediate and delayed recall was quite limited, at the less than 10th percentile.

Max showed a marked elevation on the "mania" scale in the Personality Assessment Inventory ($T = 86$, mean $= 50$). Inspection of subscale scores showed particular elevations on grandiosity ($T = 78$) and irritability ($T = 84$). On the SCL-90-R, he noted that volatility and irritability were factors in his life, in addition to difficulty concentrating. His Beck was only a 3; Max did not experience himself as depressed currently but was having difficulty finding a job. The possibility of bipolar disorder was evident to Max at the end of the evaluation. In addition, specific difficulty with effective management of visuoconstructive material and a long-standing history of difficulty understanding social information were interesting; it remained unclear if they were related to bipolar disorder, ADHD, or an additional learning disorder component.

Conclusions and Future Directions

There is considerable room for further research addressing coexisting psychiatric and learning disorders on many different levels of analysis: epidemiological, familial, genetic linkage, and molecular biological. From an epidemiological perspective, the NCS-R did not address the prevalence of LD or frequently occurring coexisting disorders in a large sample. The prevalence of such disorders in special populations, defined by age, education, and work function would certainly be of interest as well. One such a special population consists of postsecondary students. The significance of the high frequency of coexisting psychiatric disorders in the clinically referred postsecondary student population with LD or ADHD in the Tufts-NEMC College LD/ADHD Program is multifold. First, it raises questions about who is referred. It may be that the criteria for referral is not the presence of LD or ADHD per se or the need for accommodation, so much as it is the student's subjectively experienced distress and academic jeopardy. Such referrals may reflect risk factors for distress in the academic setting, providing information about the interaction of neurodevelopmental vulnerabilities and environment. If this is the case, it has implications for what constitutes an appropriately comprehensive evaluation (see Chapter 10, this volume).

The review of family history in the Tufts-NEMC group suggests that a wide range of disorders can be found in various family members of LD students. As suggested by studies reviewed above, the means of transmission to the student may well be complex. While assortive mating may be questionable between ADHD and LD, a moderate degree of assortive mating has been suggested both within and across psychiatric diagnoses (Maes et al., 1998). The degree of assortive mating may be higher for bipolar disorder than major depression (Mathews & Rues, 2001). Furthermore, as described above, the NCS-R showed greater incidence of some disorders in first-degree relatives of individuals who had the disorders, as well as frequent possession of two or more disorders; 45% had two or more diagnoses (Kessler et al., 2005b). Certainly further investigation is warranted to explore the relationship of ADHD, mood, anxiety, and thought disorders to learning disorders.

In addition, prospective studies comparing the type and frequency of coexisting learning and psychiatric disorders in postsecondary students with the psychiatric disorders in students with no history of academic jeopardy or use of academic support services would be helpful in clarifying the nature of the relationship between the two kinds of disorders. To address the effects of utilization of a clinically referred sample in such research, study of nonreferred students with known LD would also be of interest. The exploration of the frequency of psychiatric and neurodevelopmental disorders in the families of such students may also clarify the differences between these populations, and the mechanisms for the transmission of these disorders.

The multiple phenotypes of reading and other learning disorders, as well as their relationship to coexisting psychiatric disorders, may become better understood through continued molecular genetic and neuroimaging studies (Doyle et al., 2005; Gilger & Kaplan, 2001; see Grigorenko, this volume). Reading disorders, perhaps the most easily operationalized, and thus most studied, learning disorders, appear to be related to multiple susceptibility genes, suggesting reading disorders, like ADHD, may be of heterogeneous origin or may be disorders in which different genes have partial and overlapping process-specific function (Grigorenko, 2001). Regardless of mechanism, focusing on only one manifestation of a reading disorder in an evaluation could result in missing a genetically linked behavior. In some cases it may be unclear whether two or more disorders in the same individual, such as a learning disorder and depression, have been inherited independently, or if they co-occur in an individual who has developed atypically over time. Such atypical development may result in impairment in academic, behavioral, and emotional domains (Kaplan, Dewey, Crawford, & Wilson, 2001; Gilger & Kaplan, 2001). Through this interpretive lens, the phenotypic expression of learning disorders in young adults, and in other groups, may begin to look far more varied than we have expected in the past.

The presumption of the possible presence of coexisting disorders in the postsecondary context, and perhaps other clinical contexts, could alter or expand the provision of service, especially given the current concern about college-age suicide and apparent prevalence of emotional distress in the student population with learning disorders. Finally, self-knowledge can only be helpful in facilitating a successful academic and vocational outcome in the postsecondary students with neurodevelopmental disorders. Such self-knowledge may enhance students' resilience in the academic context (Miller, 2002) and lead to more successful accomplishment of the student's goals.

Author Note

The author wishes to express gratitude to Hocine Tighiouart of the Biostatistics Research Center, Institute of Clinical Research and Health Policy Studies, Tufts-New England Medical Center, for assistance with the descriptive statistics used in this chapter.

References

Aleman, A., Hijman, R., de Haan, E., & Kahn, R. (1999). Memory impairment in schizophrenia: A meta-analysis. *American Journal of Psychiatry, 156*, 1358–1366.

Ali, S. O., Denicoff, M. D., Altshuler, L. L., Hauser, P., Li, X., Conrad, A. J., et al. (2000). A preliminary study of the relation of neuropsychological performance to neuroanatomic structure in bipolar disorder. *Neuropsychiatry, Neuropsychology, and Behavioral Neurology, 13*, 20–28.

American Psychiatric Association. (1994). *Diagnostic and statistical manual of mental disorders* (4th ed.). Washington, DC: Author.

Anderson, K., & Savage, C. (2004). Cognitive and neurobiological findings in obsessive-compulsive disorder. *Psychiatry Clinics of North America, 27*, 37–47.

Beers, S., Rosenberg, D., Dick, E., Williams, T., O'Hearn, K., Birmaher, B., et al. (1999). Neuropsychological study of frontal lobe function in psychotropic-naïve children with obsessive-compulsive disorder. *American Journal of Psychiatry, 156*, 777–779.

Biederman, J., Faraone, S. V., Keenan, K., & Tsuang, M. (1991). Evidence of familial association between attention deficit disorder and major affective disorders. *Archives of General Psychiatry, 48*, 633–642.

Biederman, J., Faraone, S. V., Spencer, T., Wilens T., Mick, E., & Lapey, K. A. (1994). Gender differences in a sample of adults with attention deficit hyperactivity disorder. *Psychiatry Research, 53*, 13–29.

Biederman, J., Faraone, S. V., Spencer, T., Wilens, T., Norman, D., Lapey, K. A., et al. (1993). Patterns of psychiatric comorbidity, cognition, and psychosocial functioning in adults with attention deficit hyperactivity disorder. *American Journal of Psychiatry, 150*, 1792–1798.

Bilder, R., Goldman, R., Robinson, D., Reiter, G., Bell, L., Bates, J., et al. (2000). Neuropsychology of first-episode schizophrenia: Initial characterization and clinical correlates. *American Journal of Psychiatry, 157*, 549–559.

Boylan, K., Bieling, P., Marriot, M., Begin, H., Young, L., & MacQueen, G. (2004). Impact of comorbid anxiety disorder on outcome in a cohort of patients with bipolar disorder. *Journal of Clinical Psychiatry, 65*, 1106–1113.

Cavanagh, J. T. O., Van Beck, M., Muir, W., & Blackwood, D. H. R. (2002). Case-control study of neurocognitive function in euthymic patients with bipolar disorder: An association with mania. *The British Journal of Psychiatry, 180*, 320–326.

Channon, S. (1996). Executive dysfunction in depression: The Wisconsin Card Sorting Test. *Journal of Affective Disorders, 39*, 107–114.

Channon, S., Pratt, P., & Robertson, M. (2003). Executive function, memory and learning in Tourette's syndrome. *Neuropsychology, 17*, 247–254.

Channon, S., & Green P. S. S. (1999). Executive function in depression: The role of performance strategies in aiding depressed and non-depressed participants. *Neurology, Neurosurgery, and Psychiatry, 66*, 162–171.

Cleaver, R. L., Whitman, R. D., & Douglas, R. (1998). Right hemisphere, white-matter learning disabilities associated with depression in an adolescent and young adult psychiatric population. *The Journal of Nervous and Mental Disease, 186*, 561–565.

Cohen, N., Barwick, M. A., Horodezky, N., & Isaacson, L. (1996). Comorbidity of language and social-emotional disorders: Comparison of psychiatric outpatients and their siblings. *Journal of Clinical Child Psychology, 25*, 192–200.

Den Hartog, H. M., Derix, M., Van Bemmel, A., Kremer, B., & Jolles, J. (2003). Cognitive functioning in young and middle-aged unmedicated out-patients with major depression: Testing the effort and cognitive speed hypothesis. *Psychological Medicine, 33*, 1443–1451.

Derogatis, L. (c1994). *SCL-90-R: Administration, scoring and procedures manual* (3rd ed.). Minneapolis, MN: National Computer Systems.

Doyle, A., & Faraone, S. (2002). Familial links between ADHD, conduct disorder and bipolar disorder. *Current Psychiatry Reports, 4*, 146–152.

Doyle, A., Faraone, S. DuPre, E., & Biederman, J. (2001). Separating attention deficit hyperactivity disorder and learning disabilities in girls: A familial risk analysis. *American Journal of Psychiatry, 158*, 1666–1672.

Doyle, A., Faraone, S., Seidman, L., Willcutt, E., Nigg, J., Waldman, I., et al. (2005). Are endophenotypes based on measures of executive functions useful for molecular genetic studies of ADHD? *Journal of Child Psychology and Psychiatry, 46*, 774–803.

Faraone, S., Biederman, J., Lehman, B. K., Keenan, K., Norman, D., Deidman, L., et al. (1993). Evidence for the independent familial transmission of attention deficit hyperactivity disorder and learning disabilities: Results from a family genetic study. *American Journal of Psychiatry, 150*, 891–895.

Fitzgerald, D., Lucas, S., Redoblado, M. A., Winter, V., Brennan, J., Anderson, J., et al. (2004). Cognitive functioning in young people with first episode psychosis: Relationship to diagnosis and clinical characteristics. *Australian and New Zealand Journal of Psychiatry, 38*, 501–510.

Friedman, M., Chhabildas, N., Budhiraja, N., Willcutt, E., & Pennington, B. (2003). Etiology of the comorbidity between RD and ADHD: Exploration of the non-random mating hypothesis. *American Journal of Medical Genetics, Part B (Neuropsychaitric Genetics), 120B*, 109–115.

Gadow, K., Nolan, E., Sprafkin, J., & Schwartz, J. (2002). Tics and psychiatric comorbidity in children and adolescents. *Developmental Medicine and Child Neurology, 44*, 330–338.

Geller, D., Biederman, J., Faraone, S., Cradock, K., Hagermoser, L., Zaman, N., et al. (2002). Attention-deficit/hyperactivity disorder in children and adolescents with obsessive-compulsive disorder: Fact or artifact? *Journal of the American Academy of Child and Adolescent Psychiatry, 41*, 52–58.

Gilger, J. W., & Kaplan, B. J. (2001). Atypical brain development: A conceptual framework for understanding developmental learning disabilities. *Developmental Neuropsychology, 20*, 465–481.

Gotlib, I. H. (1984). Depression and general psychopathology in university students. *Journal of Abnormal Psychology, 93*, 19–30.

Gregg, N., Hoy, C., King, M., Moreland, C., & Jagota, M. (1992). The MMPI-2 profile of adults with learning disabilities in university and rehabilitation settings. *Journal of Learning Disabilities, 25*, 386–395.

Grigorenko, E. L. (2001). Developmental dyslexia: An update on genes, brains, and environments. *Journal of Child Psychiatry, 42*, 91–125.

Heiligenstein, E., Guenther, G., Hsu, K., & Herman, K. (1996). Depression and academic impairment in college students. *Journal of American College Health, 45*, 59–64.

Heydebrand, G., Weiser, M., Rabinowitz, J., Hoff, A., DeLisi, L., & Csernansky, J. (2004) Correlates of cognitive deficits in first episode schizophrenia. *Schizophrenia Research, 68*, 1–9.

Hoekstra, P. J., Steenhuis, M., Troost, P., Korf, J., Kallenberg, C., & Minderaa, R. (2004). Relative contribution of attention-deficit hyperactivity disorder, obsessive-compulsive disorder, and tic severity to social and behavioral problems in tic disorders. *Journal of Developmental and Behavioral Pediatrics, 25*, 272–279.

Hoy, C., Gregg, N., Wisenbaker, J., Manglitz, E., King, M., & Moreland, C. (1997). Depression and anxiety in two groups of adults with learning disabilities. *Learning Disability Quarterly, 20*, 280–291.

Jenson, P. S., Hinshaw, S., Kraemer, H., Lenora, N., Newcorn, J., Abikoff, H., et al. (2001). ADHD comorbidity findings from the MTA study: Comparing comorbid groups. *Journal of the American Academy of Child and Adolescent Psychiatry, 40*, 147–158.

Johnson, R., Ellison, R., & Heikkinen, C. (1989). Psychological symptoms of counseling center clients. *Journal of Counseling Psychology, 36*, 110–114.

Kaplan, B. J., Dewey, D. M., Crawford, S. G., & Wilson, B. N. (2001). The term *comorbidity* is of questionable value in reference to developmental disorders: Data and theory. *Journal of Learning Disabilities, 34,* 555–565.

Kavale, K. A., & Forness, S. R. (1996). Social skill deficits and learning disabilities: A meta-analysis. *Journal of Learning Disabilities, 29,* 226–237.

Kendler, K. S., Davis, C. G., & Kessler, R. C. (1997). The familial aggregation of common psychiatric and substance use disorders in the national comorbidity survey: A family history study. *The British Journal of Psychiatry, 170,* 541–548.

Kessler, R., Adler, L., Barkley, R., Biederman, J., Conners, K., Demler, O., et al. (2006). The prevalence and correlates of adult ADHD in the United States: Results from the National Cormorbidity Survey Replication. *American Journal of Psychiatry, 163,* 716–723.

Kessler, R., Adler, L., Barkley, R., Biederman, J., Connors, C. K., Faraone, S., et al. (2005). Patterns and predictors of attention-deficit/hyperactivity disorder persistence into adulthood: Results from the National Comorbidity Survey Replication. *Biological Psychiatry, 57,* 1442–1451.

Kessler, R., Berglund, P., Demler, O., Jin, R., & Walters, E. (2005a). Lifetime prevalence and age-of-onset distributions of DSM-IV disorders in the National Comorbidity Survey Replication. *Archives of General Psychiatry, 62,* 593–602.

Kessler, R., Berglund, P., Demler, O., Jin, R., & Walters, E. (2005b). Prevalence, severity, and comorbidity on 12-month DSM-IV disorders in the National Comorbidity Survey Replication. *Archives of General Psychiatry, 62,* 617–627.

Kessler, R. C., Berglund, P., Demler, O., Robert, J., Korentz, D., Merikangas, K., et al. (2003). The epidemiology of major depressive disorder: Results from the National Comorbidity Survey Replication (NCS-R). *Journal of the American Medical Association, 289,* 3095–3105.

Kessler, R. C., McGonagle, K. A., Zhao, S., Nelson, C. B., Hughes, M., Eshleman, S., et al. (1994). Lifetime and 12-month prevalence of DSM-III-R psychiatric disorders in the United States: Results from the national co-morbidity survey. *Archives of General Psychiatry, 51,* 8–19.

Krishnan, K. (2005). Psychiatric and medical comorbidities of bipolar disorder. *Psychosomatic Medicine, 67,* 1–8.

Kuelz, A., Hohagan, F., & Voderholzer, U. (2004). Neuropsychological performance in obsessive-compulsive disorder: A critical review. *Biological Psychiatry, 65,* 185–236.

Lagace, D. C., Kutcher, S. P., & Robertson, H. A. (2003). Mathematics deficits in adolescents with Bipolar I disorder. *American Journal of Psychiatry, 160,* 100–104.

Landro, N. I., Stiles, T. C., & Sletvold, H. (2001). Neuropsychological function in nonpsychotic unipolar major depression. *Neuropsychiatry, Neuropsychology, and Behavioral Neurology, 14,* 233–240.

Lightfoot, S. L., & Oliver, J. M. (1985). The Beck Inventory: Psychometric properties in university students. *Journal of Personality Assessment, 49,* 434–436.

Maes, H., Neale, M. C., Kendler, K. S., Hewitt, J. K., Silberg, J. L., Foley, D. L., et al. (1998). Assortive mating for major psychiatric diagnoses in two population-based samples. *Psychological Medicine, 28,* 1389–1401.

Mannuzza, S., Klein, R., Bessler, A., Malloy, P., & Lapadula, M. (1993). Adult outcome of hyperactive boys: Educational achievement, occupational rank, and psychiatric status. *Archives of General Psychiatry, 50,* 565–576.

Marks, D. J., Newcorn, J. H., & Halperin, J. M. (2001). Comorbidity in adults with attention deficit/hyperactivity disorder. In J. Wasserstein, L. Wolf, & F. F. LeFever (Eds.), *Adult Attention Deficit Disorder* (pp. 216–238). New York: Annals of the New York Academy of Sciences.

Mathews, C. A., & Rues, V. (2001). Assortive mating in the affective disorders: A systematic review and meta-analysis. *Comprehensive Psychiatry, 42,* 257–262.

Miller, M. (2002). Resilience elements in students with learning disabilities. *Journal of Clinical Psychology, 58,* 291–298.

Murphy, K., Barkley, R. & Bush, T. (2002). Young adults with attention deficit hyperactivity disorder: Subtype differences in comorbidity, education and clinical history. *Journal of Nervous and Mental Disease, 190,* 147–157.

Newcorn, J. H., Halperin, J. M., Jenson, P. S., Abikoff, H. B., Arnold, L. E., Cantwell, D. P., et al. (2001). Symptom profiles in children with ADHD: Effects of comorbidity and gender. *Journal of the American Academy of Child and Adolescent Psychiatry, 40,* 137–146.

Nielsen, J. (2001). Successful university students with learning disabilities. *Journal of College Student Psychotherapy, 15,* 37–48.

Oliver, J., & Simmons, M. (1984). Depression as measured by the DSM-III and the Beck Depression Inventory in an unselected adult population. *Journal of Consulting and Clinical Psychology, 52,* 892–898.

Peterson, B., Pine, D., Cohen, P., & Brook, J. (2001). Prospective, longitudinal study of tic, obsessive-compulsive, and attention-deficit/hyperactivity disorders in an epidemiological sample. *Journal of the American Academy of Child and Adolescent Psychiatry, 40,* 685–695.

Pugh, K., Mencl, W. E., Jenner, A., Katz, L., Frost, S., Lee, J. R., et al. (2000). Functional neuroimaging studies of reading and reading disability (developmental dyslexia). *Mental Retardation and Developmental Disabilities Research Reviews, 6,* 207–213.

Purcell, R., Maruff, P., Kyrios, M., & Pantelis, C. (1997). Neuropsychological function in young patients with unipolar depression. *Psychological Medicine, 27,* 1277–1285.

Quraishi, S., & Frangou, S. (2002). Neuropsychology of bipolar disorder: A review. *Journal of Affective Disorders, 72,* 209–226.

Ravnkilde, B., Videbech, P., Clemmensen, K., Egander, A., Rassmussen, N. A., & Rosenberg, R. (2002). Cognitive deficits in major depression. *Scandinavian Journal of Psychology, 43,* 239–251.

Riley, E., McGovern, D., Mockler, D., Doku, V., O'Ceallaigh, S., Fannon, D., et al. (2000). Neuropsychological functioning is first-episode psychosis-evidence of specific deficits. *Schizophrenia Research, 43,* 47–55.

Rourke, B. P. (1987). Syndrome of nonverbal learning disabilities: The final common pathway of white matter disease/dysfunction. *The Clinical Neuropsychologist, 1,* 209–234.

Rourke, B. P. (1989). A childhood learning disability that predisposes those afflicted to adolescent and adult depression and suicide risk. *Journal of Learning Disabilities, 22,* 169–175.

Saxena, B., Bota, R., & Brody, A. (2001). Brain-behavior relationships in obsessive-compulsive disorder. *Seminars in Clinical Neuropsychiatry, 6*, 82–101.

Saykin, A., Shtasel, D., Gur, R., Kester, D., Brian, D., Mozley, L., et al. (1994). Neuropsychological deficits in neurolepteic naïve patients with first-episode schizophrenia. *Archives of General Psychiatry, 51*, 124–131.

Schulte, A. C., Conners, C. K., & Osborne, S. S. (1999). Linkages between attention deficit disorders and reading disability. In D. Duane (Ed.), *Reading and attention disorders* (pp. 161–184). Baltimore, MD: York Press.

Seidman, L., Biederman, J., Faraone, S., Milberger, S., Norman, D., Seiverd, K., et al. (1995). Effects of family history and comorbidity on the neuropsychological performance of children with ADHD: Preliminary findings. *Journal of the American Academy of Child and Adolescent Psychiatry, 34*, 1015–1024.

Shaywitz, S., Shaywitz, B., Fulbright, R., Skudlarski, P., Mencl, W. E., Constable, R. T., et al. (2003). Neural systems for compensation and persistence: young adult outcome of childhood reading disability. *Biological Psychiatry, 54*, 25–33.

Shaywitz, B., Shaywitz, S., Pugh, K., Mencl, W. E., Fulbright, R., Skudlarski, P., et al. (2002). Disruption of posterior brain systems for reading in children with developmental dyslexia. *Biological Psychiatry, 52*, 101–110.

Shekim, W., Asarnow, R., Hess, E., & Zaucha, K. (1990). A clinical and demographic profile of a sample of adults with attention deficit hyperactivity disorder. *Comprehensive Psychiatry, 31*, 416–425.

Tanaka-Matsumi, J., & Kameoka, V. A. (1986). Reliabilities and concurrent validities of popular self-report measures of depression, anxiety and social desirability. *Journal of Consulting and Clinical Psychology, 54*, 328–333.

Todd, D., Deane, F., & McKenna, P. (1997). Appropriateness of SCL-90-R adolescent and adult norms for outpatient and nonpatient college students. *Journal of Counseling Psychology, 44*, 294–301.

Weintraub, S., & Mesulam, M.-M. (1983). Developmental learning disabilities of the right hemisphere: Emotional, interpersonal and cognitive components. *Archives of Neurology, 40*, 463–468.

Weiss, G., Hechtman, L., Milroy, T., & Perlman, T. (1985). Psychiatric status of hyperactives as adults: A controlled prospective 115-year follow-up of 63 hyperactive children. *Journal of the American Academy of Child Psychiatry, 24*, 211–220.

Willcutt, E. G., & Pennington, B. F. (2000a). Psychiatric comorbidity in children and adolescents with reading disability. *Journal of Child Psychology & Psychiatry & Allied Disciplines, 41*, 1039–1048.

Willcutt, E. G., & Pennington, B. F. (2000b). Comorbidity of reading disability and attention deficit/hyperactivity disorder: Differences by gender and subtype. *Journal of Learning Disabilities, 33*, 179–191.

Willcutt, E. G., Pennington, B. F., Boada, R., Ogline, J., Tunick, R., Chhabildas, N., et al. (2001). A comparison of the cognitive deficits in reading disability and attention deficit/hyperactivity disorder. *Journal of Abnormal Psychology, 110*, 157–172.

Willcutt, E. G., Pennington, B. F., Chhabildas, N. A., Friedman, M. C., & Alexander, J. (1999). Psychiatry comorbidity associated with DSM-IV ADHD in a nonreferred sample of twins. *Journal of the American Academy of Child and Adolescent Psychiatry, 38*, 1355–1362.

Willcutt, E. G., Pennington, B., Smith, S., Cardon, L., Gayan, J., Knopik, V., et al. (2002). Quantitative trait locus for reading disability on chromosome 6p is pleiotropic for attention-deficit/hyperactivity disorder. *American Journal of Medical Genetics, 114,* 260–268.

Zubieta, J.-K., Huguelet, P., O'Neil, R. L., & Giordani, B. J. (2001). Cognitive function in euthymic Bipolar I disorder. *Psychiatry Research, 102,* 9–20.

PART **4**
Life Outcomes

CHAPTER **14**
Making the Transition to Adulthood for Individuals With Learning Disorders

CELIANE REY-CASSERLY and JANE HOLMES BERNSTEIN

Contents

Our perspective on learning disorders in adulthood is that of clinicians who are asked to help prepare young adults for the transition from the highly structured academic setting of high school to the notably less-structured environment of the college or workplace—and the responsibilities and pleasures of adult life. As clinicians, we provide a comprehensive clinical assessment, the primary goal of which is to promote the individual's ongoing progress at the optimal level for him or her. The assessment is comprised of a detailed evaluation of the individual's competencies that leads to a diagnostic formulation and a structured management plan. The latter includes counseling and education about the individual's potential match—or mismatch—with both the general expectations of these life stages and the particular goals of the individual in question, along with specific guidance and assistance in managing the various challenges—administrative, intellectual, and socioemotional—of the transition from one context to the next.

Transition Issues

Successful progression through the developmental stages of adolescence into early adulthood is contingent upon a young person's ability to successfully negotiate numerous physical, psychosocial, and personal transitions (i.e., puberty, independence, establishing intimate relationships outside of the family, developing a sense of one's self, moving from high school into college or a chosen vocation). The developmental stage between the ages of 19 and 25 is a particularly vulnerable period. Society typically recognizes the individual as an adult when he or she reaches the age of majority (18 years of age). From that point forward, they obtain the right to make independent medical and legal decisions and to participate in society (e.g., voting, military service). Yet few have reached full adult developmental status (completion of education, independent living, full-time employment, and involvement in intimate relationships) by this age. Entry into adulthood is no longer seen as marked by a specific age and is described as a more gradual and ambiguous process (Furstenberg, Rumbaut, & Settersten, 2005). Arnett (2000) has put forward an eloquent argument for two stages between 19 to 25 and 26 to 35, arguing that developmentally speaking, the term "young adulthood" better suits 26- to 35-year-olds, and that a more apt term to describe the 19- to 25-year-old population is "emerging adulthood." He presents compelling evidence that this is a distinct period demographically, subjectively, and in terms of identity explorations.

Health care and survivorship issues faced by individuals in the 19 to 25 year age range support Arnett's argument. Medical professionals and society as a whole have generally neglected this age group (Bleyer, 2002; Pentheroudakis & Pavlidis, 2005). This transition population frequently "falls through the cracks" between pediatric and adult primary- and tertiary-care medicine. Frequently, they are "too old" to be followed by a pediatrician but have not yet established themselves with an internist. Likewise, emerging adults are more likely to be underinsured. They no longer qualify for insurance coverage under their parents' policies, but few have obtained the type of full-time employment that provides full insurance benefits. It is not often recognized that "emerging adults" need to negotiate systemic changes in the programs and supports that have organized their lives. These systems changes are quite salient for young people leaving public systems such as foster care, juvenile justice, and special education as well as specialized health care (Foster & Gifford, 2005). These are just a few of the challenges that highlight this transitional period and distinguish emerging adulthood from young adulthood.

Negotiation of these developmental stages and transitions can be demanding for all individuals. However, it often presents all but insurmountable obstacles for young people experiencing physical, cognitive, or psychosocial stressors or sequelae associated with a life-threatening chronic illness. The degree of difficulty posed by such life-stage negotiations for emerging and young adults with special health care needs has been recently recognized; the issues associated with the "health care transition" have been addressed by the combined expertise of the American Academy of Pediatrics, the American Academy of Family Physicians, and the American College of Physicians–American Society of Internal Medicine in 2002 (Consensus Statement on Health Care Transitions, 2002). The factors involved in the development of self-efficacy skills in adolescents with special health-care needs is a critical area for specialized research (see Anie & Telfair, 2005, for an analysis of the issues associated with sickle cell disease). The skills required by emerging adults with learning disabilities to successfully transition into adulthood have also been identified (Blalock & Patton, 1996). Relevant studies examining the issues faced by emerging adults with health care needs and learning disorders associated with a wide range of neurodevelopmental and acquired disorders of childhood are badly needed to address their needs as they progress through adolescence and transition into adulthood.

Neuropsychological Assessment

Pediatric neuropsychologists play a critical role in contributing to the over-all management of the transition to adulthood of adolescents with the learning disorders associated with neurodevelopmental and acquired disorders. The focus is on understanding neurobehavioral functioning from a developmental perspective as well as appreciating the multiple influences that have affected the individual's development (Baron, 2004). This promotes a longer-range view of outcome and of the skills needed to negotiate expected developmental challenges. In assessing the functioning of the developing child in a neuropsychological framework, our approach not only emphasizes the longer-term developmentally referenced perspective but also the brain-context interactions in which observed behavior is embedded and which changes dynamically over the course of development from infancy to adulthood. This theoretical matrix—brain-context-development—shapes the clinical analysis of behavior (Bernstein, 2000). The goal of the clinical analysis is not diagnosis per se, although a diagnostic formulation of the presenting difficulty is a necessary component of the assessment. The clinician's mandate is to intervene to maximize, to the extent possible, the individual's adult outcome—that is, to help the child become the most comfortable, most competent, and most independent individual he or she can be as an adult member of society. This developmental focus makes consideration of the transition from adolescence to adulthood a critical element in our thinking and intervention strategy, and one that is inherent in our clinical thinking from early in the child's developmental journey.

This discussion focuses on the needs and challenges of individuals with "learning disorders" as contrasted with learning disabilities. For us, the term *learning disorders* responds to a clinical analysis that is *neuro*psychological in that it encompasses the compromise of the full range of behavioral competencies (behavioral/emotional regulation, cognition, motor/sensory capacity, social skills) supported by the brain—in contrast to learning disabilities, which is typically understood as referring to deficits in specific academic skills (reading, math, writing). Our practice centers on individuals for whom expectable developmental trajectories are threatened by medical/neurological disease and whose problems in learning go beyond difficulties in acquiring the academic skills that are typically subsumed under the rubric of "learning disability." The contribution of neuropsychology, providing insights from knowledge of the biology of the organism, is critical to our work in that it is the biology that is threatened by disease and the biological substrate for behavior that is changed. Our experience with this broader population has enriched our understanding of the nature of the challenges facing individuals with more specific learning disabilities. We organize our discussion in terms of the three components of the theoretical matrix that frames our clinical work: brain, context, and development (Bernstein, 2000).

Brain

The disorders of brain that we deal with include the full range of neuropathologies of childhood. These range from the so-called simple genetic syndromes including Down, Turner, Prader-Willi, fragile X, Williams, and so forth, to complex genetic syndromes such as autism, specific language impairment, and dyslexia, to structural brain abnormalities such as congenital hydrocephalus, agenesis of the corpus callosum, Dandy-Walker, Sturge-Weber, and Arnold-Chiari, to acquired insults including cerebrovascular accidents, missile injury, traumatic brain injury, toxic exposures, prematurity, and also including "other disease" insults secondary to compromised functioning of other organ systems (such as organ transplantation, metabolic disorders, etc.) as well as iatrogenic insult secondary to life-preserving treatment as occurs in the context of radiation, chemotherapy, steroids, and other medical and pharmaceutical agents (Tager-Flusberg, 1999). What all of these neurodevelopmental disorders have in common, however, is that they all occur in the context of the dynamic change that is the hallmark of development. Thus, they all have potential for derailing behavioral development and changing behavioral outcomes. Genetic and structural disorders set up conditions for alternative developmental trajectories from the beginning; later acquired derailments have potential for resulting in so-called late effects. Notwithstanding the source or timing of the insult in question, the pathology is or becomes part of the developmental course of each individual with the disorder.

Contextual Demands

The expression of behavioral change across development (resulting in alternative trajectories, sudden breakdown, or late effects) is variable, both between disorders and individuals and within individuals. The sources of this variability are many. Possibly the most important, however, is that of contextual demands. Like Fischer (Fischer, Rotenberg, Bullock, & Raya, 1993), we understand competence not as a unitary, static concept or fixed capacity; rather, an individual's competence is linked to the context in which the competence is elicited. There are contextual (social, cultural) as well as individual (biological, experiential) constraints on the expression of competence that lead to multiple pathways for development. Fischer's dynamic developmental pathways model integrates multiple systems and accounts for the variability seen across development. In addressing the issue of the emergence of reflective thinking in young adulthood, he notes that this capacity is not only dependent on the increasing sophistication and maturation of neural networks that subserve these capacities but also on the individual's experiences with this level of thinking (Fischer & Pruyne, 2003).

This model can also be applied to the concept of "late effects." Late effects refer to complications, disabilities, or adverse outcomes that develop over time as a result of a physical or psychological insult, or of a disease process, including its treatment. Late effects have been an active area of research in pediatric cancer survivors as the focus has moved from not only developing curative treatments but also to fostering optimal quality of life (National Cancer Policy Board, 2003). Late effects can be physical, cognitive, or psychological and may have an interactive and interdependent impact on all of these areas of functioning (Patenaude & Kupst, 2005). Late effects can emerge as children are expected to master increasingly complex tasks and behaviors. The critical role of development, both the stage at which the disorder was diagnosed as well as the current contextual demands, contributes to the "developmental pathway" or trajectory that is observed. Understanding the principles underlying the "late effects" phenomenon is also critical for the development of a coherent management plan for each individual.

Development

Development involves dynamic change. It is not a sequence of discrete steps or increments in skills or knowledge; it is an ongoing process whereby interaction with the environment promotes increasing differentiation of brain networks that are then mobilized to support more and more complex behaviors. Developmental outcomes reflect this interaction of brain competencies with contextual demands over time.

Current findings in neurology and neuroscience emphasize this interplay of biological status and developmental context with respect to the impact of insult from prenatal environment through development. For example, it is the developmental context of the premature infant's brain that determines the response to insult and the type of brain injury experienced (Ferriero, 2004; Volpe, 1998). Developmentally referenced models of assessment in pediatric neuropsychology are essential in order to incorporate current rapid developments in neuroscience (Bernstein, 2000; Bernstein & Weiler, 2000; Rey-Casserly, 1999). Such models are critical for understanding the impact of a range of neurodevelopmental and acquired disorders on the developing brain. The developmental trajectory of children with neurological disorders can vary significantly. Some can be derailed by multiple complications and neurological dysfunction and thus be set "off developmental track" (Bernstein, Prather, & Rey-Casserly, 1995), whereas others may experience failures in adaptation to specific environmental or developmental demands at different stages

(Holmes, 1987). Investigators studying neuropsychological outcomes of a range of disorders are increasingly focusing on developmentally based models that emphasize the impact of disease or insult on the child's overall developmental trajectory (Anderson, Northam, Hendy, & Wrennall, 2001; Armstrong, 2002; Mulhern, 2002). These models imply that we must incorporate an understanding of expectable developmental demands in our evaluation of outcome.

A major challenge for researchers in neurodevelopmental disorders is the heterogeneity of outcomes. This is well illustrated in the case of brain tumor and its treatment. Here, behavioral development is changed as a function of the medical disorder and its treatment—and the subsequent cognitive and neurobehavioral impact. The child faces the expectations of ongoing development with an altered set of skills and competencies. In this population, functional outcomes reflect three major patient-centered variables that are interrelated: medical, cognitive, and neuropsychological/neurobehavioral. Medical variables range from minor to major effects on physical and sensory functions (endocrinopathies, hemiparesis, visual loss, etc.); cognitive variables include general intelligence/cognitive reserve (ability to adapt and problem solve; constraints thereon); and neurobehavioral factors include compromise of fundamental processing capacities (attention, memory, executive functions, social cognition and skills). The individual's ability to resist the potentially damaging effects of these factors is influenced by · socioeconomic status, family values, family adjustment, patient psychological adjustment, availability of resources, and societal attitudes (Yeates et al., 2004). The interactions among these variables can have major impact on the individual's ability to acquire adaptive skills and functional independence. These factors also play a significant role in how developmental transitions will be effected.

Transitions throughout an individual's developmental trajectory are typically relatively gradual as well as discontinuous and, generally speaking, this is true of a child's progress through grade school. This is in marked contrast to the transition from high school to college or high school to work that is imposed by societal structures; this transition is typically very abrupt and, as such, can pose enormous challenges to the young person who is on a "different" developmental trajectory.

Neuropsychological Assessment

Measurement and Prediction

Providing neuropsychological services to the transitional population requires a broad range of relevant information. The traditional focus of psychological testing models and assumptions in the measurement of children's abilities in the educational setting is, however, narrowly defined, setting notable limits on effective clinical work when the goal is to understand the impact of change in the underlying biological substrate on observed behavioral outcomes. Traditional measurement models typically assume a linear, incremental increase in competence with age, and an often unexamined assumption is that development of competencies in all areas will proceed at a more or less equal rate. In typically developing individuals, formal psychometric measures such as IQ and academic achievement have some predictive value with respect to adult outcomes. However, these predictions are typically based on the assumption—not usually formally recognized—of the normal expectable context or environment. In individuals whose changed developmental trajectory (secondary to biological insult) entails a changed experience of the environment, the predictive value of the measures, if any, is not well understood. Typically, there is a discrepancy between skills and knowledge on the one side and the self-regulatory capacities that are critical to using these skills and knowledge independently in the environment, on the other.* In our experience, self-regulatory capacity can vary independently of psychometric IQ level. Indeed, it is these populations of youngsters who serve to demonstrate the independence of measured abilities and functional competencies. We see many youngsters with adequate psychometric IQ levels who cannot manage even simple activities of daily living and independent function. We also see youngsters whose psychometric IQ levels are low but who do well in "real life" as a result of well-developed commonsense reasoning skills, supportive families, appropriate self-regulatory capacity, and good matches between skills and goals. We also see youngsters with formally

---

* The concept of "executive functions" was derived from the study of behavioral breakdown in adults. As is the case with many adult-derived neuropsychological concepts, application of the construct to children's behavior requires a developmentally framed theoretical reanalysis (Bernstein & Waber, 2007). In the developmental context, we take executive functions (characterized dimensionally in terms such as working memory, set shifting/cognitive flexibility and inhibition; e.g., Pennington, 1997) to be a subset of the broader category of regulatory capacities. The developing child not only acquires problem-solving skills but also learns to manage him- or herself, that is, to acquire self-regulatory skills that modulate both emotional and cognitive behavior. Clinicians regularly see youngsters in whom self-regulatory and executive skills are separable—in both directions: the socially appropriate child with executive function deficits that primarily affect academic work as contrasted with the child who functions well in the classroom with its regular rules and expectations but who is intrusive, overexcitable, and so forth in social situations with peers and family. The increasing prominence of the field of developmental affective neuroscience highlights the importance of the distinction between cognitive and affective development and their respective neural foundations. See Wolf, this volume, for further discussion.

grade-appropriate academic skills who cannot use these effectively in the world and youngsters who rely on "survival" reading and math capacities—and a host of compensatory strategies—to manage the requirements of daily interactions with considerable success.

Ecological Validity

An important consideration for the clinician is the artificiality of the measurement situation with respect to its relevance to the real-world context. Recognizing and managing this discrepancy is central to managing the transition from the supportive environment of grade school to the markedly less-constrained and less-structured environments of college or the workplace. The artificiality of the measurement situation may not need to be factored in to the evaluation of skills of the typically developing individual. However, failure to recognize it has significant potential for obscuring the very real deficits and limitations of the individual developing on an alternative trajectory: for these individuals, the evaluation context may be so supportive of regulatory skills that a false picture of the availability of these skills in an ecologically valid setting is created—to the detriment of the individual's outcome. For an individual with a learning disorder progressing through school, the educational setting provides similar support, with the all-too-frequent result that the individual's limited capacity for independent functioning outside of the school environment is obscured.

The critical abilities of independent adjustment are the regulatory capacities of judgment, behavioral modulation, inhibitory control, and novel problem-solving. These capacities are also critical for resilience and ability to cope with adverse circumstances (Buckner, Mezzacappa, & Beardslee, 2003). These are, however, precisely what is shaped and supported by the inherent structure of both the psychological test setting and school-based special-education support services. The presence of this support all too frequently disguises the lack of these critical regulatory capacities—with the result that all too often students are advanced through the grades and graduated at the end of high school without the basic skills required for independent success.

Managing Transitions

There are several transition points that are important for the developing child in school. Kindergarten to first grade, third to fourth grade, elementary school to middle school, and middle school to high school, as well as the post-high school adjustment, all involve significant changes in both content and contextual support that pose a range of potential challenges to the child with learning issues (Bernstein, 2000; Holmes, 1987).

The perturbations of developmental course and the changed trajectories with which they are associated result in different needs and demands for the child. Clinicians working in any of these transition zones need to incorporate an understanding of five important variables that have a bearing on optimal outcomes for young adults: psychometric IQ, skills achievement, regulatory and metacognitive capacity, adaptive function, and life adjustment (both skills and psychological/emotional status).

To illustrate the challenges faced by the clinician trying to help and by the individual and family in trying to manage the transition period and the impact of neurological and learning disorders, we present three cases that highlight the interaction of brain, context, and development.

Case Illustrations

Case 1

John is an 18-year-old young man who was diagnosed with a brain tumor in the hypothalamic/optic chiasm region at the age of 12 years. He was treated with surgery and subsequently with radiation due to tumor progression. He developed visual field, vascular, and endocrine abnormalities that required ongoing follow-up and treatment. He developed learning difficulties in school and received special educational services, including support of an aide, extended time, and occupational therapy for fine motor and writing difficulties. He underwent periodic neuropsychological evaluations that revealed average to low-average general cognitive abilities. When seen at age 17, Full Scale IQ was 87, Verbal IQ was 96, and Performance IQ was 77. Speed of output was significantly compromised. Basic academic skills were scored in the average range. Neuropsychological findings were consistent with poor regulation of attention, difficulty integrating information, problems with multitasking, and a passive approach to learning. At school, John was reportedly succeeding with respect to grades received, though assignments and tasks were substantially modified for him. Similarly, at home he relied on his parents to initiate activities and to structure his daily life. Socially, he maintained good relationships with adults but was fairly isolated from his peer group. The school had planned for him to graduate from high school, though he had not been able to complete his senior-year project. As this plan emerged, his parents came to the realization that their son was not equipped to manage this transition. He had not developed any vocational skills, and he was not capable of organizing himself independently. A transition plan had not been developed within the context of his educational plan. Follow-up neuropsychological evaluation documented significant problems with ability to organize and integrate information.

Independent problem solving was particularly compromised, and he was vulnerable to becoming confused and overwhelmed in less-structured contexts. He did not have the skills to function independently in vocational, educational, or home arenas. His educational plan was reorganized to provide him with an integrated program that would provide interventions and experiences to help him develop academic, social, self-advocacy, and independence skills. Graduation was deferred so that these services could be provided. Although this young man demonstrated low-average to average intellectual ability, appropriately developed language skills, and average basic academic performance on tests, his inability to manage less-structured environments independently compromised his transition to young adulthood.

Case 2

Mary suffered a traumatic brain injury affecting the left frontal brain region at the age of 14. She had previously been an honors-level student with excellent verbal and academic skills. Following her injury, she developed memory and learning difficulties, as well as frustration and anxiety around these issues. She required a modified course load and needed to transfer out of her honors courses. She was seen for neuropsychological evaluation at the age of 16. The assessment revealed a persistent and highly motivated adolescent. Overall intellectual ability was in the average range with verbal ability in the high-average range and nonverbal skills in the low-average to average range. Significant difficulty in learning novel and unrelated information was seen as well as problems holding on to multiple dimensions of information simultaneously. Mary was maintaining good grades at school but noted that she needed to expend more effort and required more time to maintain this level of performance. Specific recommendations were made for course-load accommodations, specific supports, and learning strategies to deal with her vulnerability to overload. Planning for college and the need for student disability services were also discussed with Mary and her family. Mary was seen in consultation 3 years later. In the interim, she had enrolled in a competitive college, taking a somewhat reduced course load. She was able to maintain good grades in her classes but became unable to manage the demands for independent decision making required of the college setting with respect to establishing priorities, attending to her health, multitasking, and following through with daily living expectations. Her problems with managing anxiety increased as she became unable to follow multistep instructions to attain specific goals. She subsequently dropped out of college and returned to live at home. Her plan was revised to include gradual reentry into college taking a community college course, living at home, and participating in psychotherapy and rehabilitation services.

Case 3

Billy is a 17-year-old young man who was referred for follow-up neuro-psychological assessment due to his experience of increasing difficulty keeping up with his academic work as a junior in high school. Billy had been treated for leukemia at a young age with cranial radiation and chemotherapy. He developed learning difficulties in elementary school and needed to transfer out of a demanding private school environment to the public school. He received special educational support in the areas of language arts and writing through the seventh grade and services were discontinued in high school. He did well his first year of high school and took honors-level classes. In the 11th grade, he encountered increasing difficulty with these courses and noted that his success in a class often depended on how the material was presented. He had trouble multitasking and could become overwhelmed if too much material was presented at one time. His parents expressed concern about his inconsistent performance and felt that he was not putting forth maximal effort. Socially, he was well integrated into his peer group and identified with the students in his honors-level classes. He had been evaluated by a neuropsychologist at the age of 12 years and was noted to have average general cognitive abilities and weaknesses in organization. He had been evaluated subsequently by the school system, and weaknesses in written language and short-term memory had been identified. Follow-up neuropsychological evaluation at age 17 again noted average general cognitive abilities and average basic achievement scores. Insecurities in executive functions were salient, however; Billy was susceptible to overload, had difficulty retrieving information effectively, struggled when required to attend to multiple streams of information simultaneously, and was inflexible and inefficient in his problem solving. The neuropsychologist spent a considerable amount of time in the feedback discussing issues of self-advocacy and making choices to manage multiple demands, and recommended specific accommodations needed at the high school level for Billy. Problem-solving and learning strategies were outlined with him and his parents, as well as needs in the college setting. Initially, Billy had trouble incorporating an understanding of his learning issues into his overall self-concept. His parents also assumed that because he could function at a high level in some contexts, he would be able to do so in all settings. Ultimately, Billy and his parents were engaged as members of his "treatment team" and were able to make adjustments that maintained Billy's positive motivation and investment in the process. He was able to make choices that would balance his course load yet maintain his involvement with his peer group. With realistic and focused assistance from the student disability services program at his college, he graduated from college, though acknowledged that it was a struggle for him. When last seen in the clinic, we were informed that he had gotten a job and was planning his wedding.

Retrospective review of these young people's experiences raised the following questions. Why did some of these emerging adults end in a such compromised state with respect to the transition to the adult world even with neuropsychological follow-up and management? Where in the clinical management did the breakdown occur so that they lacked critical skills needed for the transition to adulthood? To address this question, we examined each individual's clinical management history and from four vantage points: the respective roles of the individual, his or her parents, the school team, and the neuropsychological assessment.

Contribution of Neuropsychology

Each individual had three or more neuropsychological assessments at approximately 3-year intervals. We reviewed the neuropsychological evaluation reports and were able to document that the neuropsychologist had specifically discussed two issues: (a) impact of development and changing demands, and (b) implications for independence. In the reports, the degree to which this was emphasized varied but clearly increased with the increasing age of the child. We were, however, not privy to the emphasis and extent of discussion of these issues in the feedback sessions.

Contribution of the School

In the first two cases, two regularly recurring themes were that the school team was strongly focused on the child's psychometric IQ and scores on achievement tests and that they failed to fully appreciate the implications of the amount of support being provided within the sheltered environment of the school context. The neuropsychologist did mention independence with more emphasis as these individuals approached transition. In the third case, issues with metacognitive and organizational skills had been identified, but the interaction of these vulnerabilities with the specific contextual demands the young man was facing had not been addressed. The assumption was made that normal scores on tests and good performance in some contexts justified withdrawal of supports. In these cases, these students' learning difficulties needed to be understood with reference to both context and content of demands (Pardes, 1988).

Contribution of the Parents

In these cases, the parents also lacked an understanding of the role of the context in supporting or not supporting their child's performance and ability to manage the transition to adulthood. The expectation was that adequate performance in one context would necessarily generalize to multiple situations without difficulty.

Contribution of the Individual

The young persons in these case illustrations all encountered deficits in executive or "how to" skills, not in psychometric intelligence or specific academic abilities. Unfortunately, it is just these skills that are required to weather the transition to adulthood effectively. In addition, they had not developed the self-advocacy and self-awareness skills needed to manage the transition from the more-structured educational support system of the public school to the more independent postsecondary setting. In general, these skills are not well addressed at the high school level for a range of students (Janiga & Costenbader, 2002).

Comparing Alternative Trajectories

As we discussed the experiences of the foregoing young people and considered the challenges for the clinician in providing optimal management services for them, we found ourselves comparing their experiences with those of other individuals who had sought neuropsychological services over the years. The contrasts were striking—and informative! Fortuitously, three young men who had been followed as children and adolescents had very recently reappeared seeking follow-up neuropsychological assessment as young adults. The young men were all in their mid-twenties, were planning to go to graduate school (two for doctoral degrees, one for a master's degree), and were seeking the assessment to document the ongoing need for time accommodations for the GREs. As in the previous illustrative case examples, all three had had comparable neuropsychological follow-up and management over their school careers, with either three or four prior assessments. All three individuals had experienced difficulty in the academic context from the start of formal education. School-based evaluations had been completed prior to the provision of special education services. Neuropsychological assessment was first sought at fourth, sixth, and seventh grades respectively.

The first young man could be described as "classically dyslexic": he had experienced significant difficulties in learning to read at the very early decoding level, with effortful written language skills thereafter. Intensive one-on-one reading instruction had been provided from the first grade. Neuropsychological assessment consistently documented language and language-related processing deficits in a youngster with strong spatial reasoning skills. Progress resulted from hard work, intensive academic supports, and accommodations to allow knowledge to be demonstrated effectively (waiving of time constraints, shortening of assignments where practicable, and use of technology). Outside of school, early opportunities for learning to sail revealed sailing talent leading to a passion for boats and ship construction and subsequent career goals focusing on naval architecture.

The second young man also demonstrated language and language-related processing problems on neuropsychological evaluation. He learned to decode—albeit very effortfully—but struggled thereafter with lack of fluency that made reading both very slow and very unrewarding. He was, however, a good thinker who enjoyed ideas and problem solving. Again, the written output demands of the junior high and high school grades were a major challenge that was met with the use of technology, the modifications of assignments to their "bare bones," and a resigned acceptance of the need simply to "put in the time." This young man was physically coordinated and enjoyed sports activities, but the rapid moment-to-moment verbal instructions of team sports proved challenging. In contrast, an intense interest and considerable success in a "single person" sport in the secondary school years not only provided a strong sense of efficacy and pleasure but also encouraged reading—of technical manuals related to his sport. He eventually became skilled at computer-based activities and sought a career in technically sophisticated medical computing.

The third fellow's learning issues were centered on organizational deficits. These had a significant impact on his ability to learn in the standard classroom setting and led to a private school placement at the fourth grade, transferring to a second private school for the high school years. He also struggled with the written language demands of the curriculum as he proceeded to the middle and high school grades. Again, his success was built on very hard work and effective use of computer technology. His family's strong commitment to public service was something he readily adopted and he found great pleasure and success in his teenage years in helping disadvantaged individuals. He completed his undergraduate degree with his hard-earned mix of hard work, long hours, technology, and appropriate accommodations, continuing to work in the public sector with disadvantaged individuals. With increasing experience, he appreciated the role of documenting social needs in a formal fashion as the basis for effective intervention. His educational goals at the graduate level were to provide himself with the necessary skills to contribute to his chosen career path in the human service sector.

What did these three young men have in common? Neuropsychologically, they had constitutionally based learning disabilities rather than acquired neuropsychological deficits. They had all grown up with and developed their sense of self in the context of their particular thinking and learning styles. None of them defined themselves by their learning disability/disorder; while they might have seen themselves as "different," they saw any limitations secondary to their unique learning styles as a challenge to be overcome or circumvented in order to achieve their goals. A major contribution of the neuropsychological intervention was the education provided by the clinician around the issue of "difference": this offered a reframing of their situations that supported and encouraged a positive view of themselves and thus of their ongoing adjustment.

In these cases, the neuropsychological assessment not only documented the nature of the learning problem and "normalized" it for the boy and his family but also documented the integrity of regulatory capacities. For these young men, behavioral modulation was not an issue, social skills were adequately developed, and they had built and could use effectively independent thinking skills.

Psychometric IQ was above average for all three boys (although not dramatically so) and, in terms of overall scores, continued to be so over time. Inter-subtest variability was present, however, with very high-level knowledge in some areas. Of note was the change in the pattern of inter-subtest variability at different points in their careers. Typically, they lost ground on tasks whose scores depended on time bonuses but gained points for increasing sophistication with respect to knowledge and conceptual thinking.

Most important, we believe, were the difficult-to-quantify psychological variables that promoted the boys' progress. They all had very supportive parents who recognized their difficulties immediately and obtained help from an early age. Of note in each family dynamic was the mutual respect among family members that led to the boys being taken very seriously and given credit for their effort even when the product was limited. All three boys proved to have an impressive capacity for hard work that had got them through grade school. And—at different points in their academic careers—all three boys had found a passion for a particular topic that had fired their imaginations and created goals to work for (see Fink, 1995, 1998, for the importance of a "passionate interest" in the successful outcomes of early learning disability).

In the case of these three individuals, the contribution of the neuropsychologist was not only to document the nature of the learning problem and, at each new level of demand, provide guidance, strategies, and interventions to address the impact of the learning issues on current developmental expectations. The neuropsychologist also identified strengths and skills and helped the youngster and his family understand how these worked to his advantage. The clinician also participated in the growth and development of both child and family by providing education on a continuing (if intermittent) basis around neuropsychological capacities, normalizing perceived deficits, and empowering the individual to problem solve and advocate for himself.

The individuals with acquired learning disorders also had supportive parents and school team, a capacity for hard work, and at least average scores on a standardized intelligence test. They differed from the constitutionally learning disordered young men in at least two important ways. They were not learning to match a "different," but coherent, package of neuropsychological strengths and weaknesses to the demands of the academic and social worlds but had to deal with both the neuropsychological and the psychological impact of significant change affecting both skills and their sense of self. The medical condition had resulted in neuropsychological deficits with wide-ranging impact on basic processing skills and regulatory capacities that affected their educational adjustment in major ways. In addition, they had sustained a threat to their already developing/developed sense of self both as a person and as a learner (Palombo, 2001) via the potentially life-threatening medical disorder. This has the potential for changing the development of the personality. It also involves an experience of loss—of current skills and of expectations for the future, both for the individual him- or herself and for the families. (This "loss of the future" is, in our experience, not always appreciated in the management of individuals with acquired neuropsychological disorders, with the frequent result that appropriate grief work is not facilitated. For many families, this can be a serious lack in overall clinical care and one that can limit the availability of psychological resources toward optimal developmental progress.)

Given the salience of the educational system in children's lives, it is not surprising that the impact of the acquired neuropsychological disorder is most readily appreciated in that setting, and typically, the educational team mobilizes a range of special educational services to support the child's acquisition of academic skills and knowledge. This was true in the case of the individuals with acquired neuropsychological disorders described above. Over the course of their childhood and adolescence, they obtained a range of educational and psychological services to develop skills in the academic or vocational domains. Unfortunately, however, the educational services by their very nature provided a high degree of support, organization, and structure; over time, this served to mask the lack of development—on the part of the individual—of the "nonacademic" skills of self-regulation, judgment, and independence that are the crucial foundation for taking advantage of the expectations and possibilities of the adult world. Although the neuropsychologists recognized the complementary roles of cognitive and regulatory capacities (as indicated in their reports), either they were unable to make adequate meaning of this for the child, family, and educators, or the latter were unable to "hear" the message, or both.

For the individuals with constitutionally based learning disorders, then, it was not just the technical skills that allowed them to find a place for themselves in the adult world. They also had crucial "self" skills that allowed themselves to buy into the expectations and possibilities of the adult world. In contrast, two of the individuals with acquired learning disorders were never able to engage "with the program" of independent adult functioning; they were defeated by the same expectations and possibilities. For cases 1 and 2, the impact of the acquired problems with behavioral regulation was overwhelming: they could not access all of the processes needed for effective functioning on an independent basis. Case 3 was vulnerable to overload but did not have a major problem with regulatory capacities per se. However, it required a major effort on his part and of his team for him to gain a comprehensive and realistic view of his capabilities and needs as the basis for making progress.

Our conclusion is that the most important difference between the individuals described above is the availability—or otherwise—of adequate self-regulatory capacities as these are expressed in behavioral flexibility and modulation, in self-control, in appropriate social comportment, and in independence in thinking and reasoning—and lead to a realistic sense of self and emotional stability. These are the capacities that are critical to successful adjustment in the adult world—not just for getting and holding a job but also for the healthy development of the individual as a social being: making friends, pursuing intimate relationships, and developing social networks as a member of the wider community. It is the necessity to develop the skills to pursue these latter goals that must be appreciated by the members of a developing child's treatment team. We recognize that these skills are not usually taught but rather are typically "osmosed" in the transactions over time between an individual and his or her peers, family, and community. We also recognize that it is not easy to provide instruction, examples, and explicit modeling of regulatory skills in the formats of the academic setting and the curriculum. Nonetheless, we feel strongly that clinicians and educators must address these issues directly for the students who need help in these areas and must work with the child and family to foster the necessary life skills.

The problem for the child, family, educators, and clinicians is, as we have noted above, that deficits in regulatory and executive skills are inherently shaped and supported by the school context and the nature of special education provision—to the extent that the student's need for intensive instruction and education in this area is obscured. The responsibility for clinicians is to educate the educators and then the individual and the family about the full range of neuropsychological competencies and the need to develop them all. It is the individuals with better developed regulatory processing capacities who are likely to be more successful in negotiating the challenges and opportunities of the adult world. A major goal for clinicians, families, and educators is to identify and provide the educational scaffolding required to promote such skill development. The educational experience of a child who has sustained injury that can be expected to derail behavioral development needs to incorporate—from very early on— comprehensive instruction and support designed to develop self-control and self-awareness in terms of thinking skills and limitations, social comportment, and emotional well-being with the goal of self-acceptance and the capacity for engagement in active problem solving and social relationships. These will be crucial to the independence in both thinking and social skills needed for effective participation in adult life (Palombo, 2001).

The Challenges for the Clinician

The foregoing less-than-optimal outcomes in some individuals with acquired neuropsychological disorders demand serious consideration by the responsible clinician. A basic tenet of our approach is that it is the responsibility of the clinician to make a difference in the lives of the individuals who seek care. Individuals seek care because something is "wrong"; it is thus the clinician's job to change outcomes to the extent possible using the best available evidence and rigorously applied clinical expertise in the context of the client's values (National Institute of Medicine, 2001). In the foregoing situations, the question is: Could the clinician have changed the outcome in some way? And on what evidence? How can (should?) the clinician advise the client and family about the potential risks that are likely to severely constrain the achievement of post-high school goals?

There are three possible approaches. In the first, the clinician describes the findings of the neuropsychological assessment and outlines interventions and recommendations that follow therefrom. In the second, the clinician challenges the client's goals as inappropriate and unrealistic and insists that the individual must not proceed to college. In the third, the clinician describes the client's strengths and weaknesses, explains how these interact with external demands (both academic and in everyday life situations), clearly expresses reservations about the client's likelihood for success or otherwise—and educates as to why this is the case, offers recommendations for optimal management of the experience should the client decide to go ahead, and makes it clear that the clinician will be available for help as needed in the future.

In discussion with colleagues at various times, we find that the first option is one that many clinicians believe to be acceptable. The clinician provides relevant information and steps back respectfully to allow the client and family to make their own decisions. We find this unacceptable in at least two ways: (a) it lacks imaginative engagement with the client's future development in supporting his or her specific goals and aspirations (the client and family values), and (b) it fails to make use of the full range of evidence and expertise that is available to the clinician. The second option is one that few, if any, clinicians would endorse—although, having a strong sense of what this young person will have to go through in the face of failure, many of us wish that we could! The third option is preferred; it provides evidence-based education about the role of "brain" in "context" (Bernstein, 2000), it outlines both risks and protective factors, it shows respect for the client's own goals and values, it offers specific recommendations to help the client meet those goals (to the extent possible), and—importantly—it provides a "safety net" should the clinician's fears be realized.

As highlighted in the previous discussion, the foregoing cases and discussion highlight the critical role of context in both supporting and constraining a child's developmental progress (Hoagwood, Burns, Kiser, Ringeisen, & Schoenwald, 2001). Contextual support is a critical element in the management of brain-based learning disorders in young people. It is equally critical, however, that the treatment team for any individual with a learning disorder be educated about the impact of context and the need for principles underlying that support to be transferred from the adults (teachers, family members) to the individual him- or herself as an integral part of instruction in school and out. The provision of support and accommodations must be accompanied by a systematic weaning of the learning-disordered individual from the support of adults in order that he or she should be independently capable of managing specific tasks and situations in the future.

The need to wean the child, adolescent, or young adult from adult support is, in our view, one of the most underappreciated components in a child's education, both in the classroom and out. By and large, the development of independence in skills happens "naturally" in the typically developing child in their moment-by-moment transactions with society, family, and peers. In contrast, independence needs to be explicitly and systematically taught and fostered in the child on an alternate developmental trajectory or with a learning disorder. As such youngsters progress through school, instructional strategies should include: challenge of intellectual abilities and curiosity; direct instruction in strategic and critical thinking behaviors; support for the mechanics of production by means of the powerful tools of technology, modifications, and accommodations; and—last, but not least—systematic and explicit weaning of the young person to independence.

This latter is the goal of the weaning process. All too often, fostering independence is interpreted to mean the removal of supports. This is both inappropriate and unrealistic. Fostering independence is a systematic process that requires the introduction, practice, and transfer of the "how-to" (Bernstein, 1998) or executive skills that allow knowledge to be used effectively, as well as instruction and practice of the knowledge skills themselves.

There are four critical elements of independence: (a) mastery of the skills and strategies to solve academic and everyday tasks effectively; (b) ability to recognize where and when one needs support, and (c) how to advocate for and access needed resources. These resources may be external or internal, such as strategies that the individual has mastered. Of equal importance to these skill variables, however, are (d) the young person's psychological and emotional resources, his or her understanding and acceptance of learning issues, and his or her sense of efficacy as learners (Palombo, 2001).

The four components of instructional strategies noted above must apply not only to academic skills but also to the activities of daily living and the social world in which a given individual will participate. At a minimum, the responsibility of the clinician—at every stage in a child's development—is to address the following: practical skills/adaptive functioning, social skills, intimate relationships, judgment/insight, emotional status, personality development, and academic skills—and the degree to which the child (adolescent, emerging adult) is independent in each of these domains at the age-expected level. When exploring with the client post–high school academic options, the postsecondary academic settings include not only the traditional 4-year college but also the 2-year college, the community college, and the special education/vocational college programs. When exploring employment possibilities post–high school, the clinician will need to review issues such as: the amount and intensity of supervision to support the client in doing the job; the need for a job coach, rehabilitation counselor, or therapist; the client's social comportment, social skills, and ability to work with other people; and his or her emotional status, motivation to succeed, and self-regulatory capacities. For many individuals, social skills and the behaviors appropriate to the search for intimate relationships can also be expected to need direct instruction and support. Different individuals will be able to participate at different levels, but all individuals should be educated, supported, and encouraged to be as independent as they can be, both vocationally and socially.

Clinical Management Considerations

The primary requirement for effective transition planning from school to life is a management plan that is comprehensive with respect to both the individual's competencies and the demands he or she can expect to face in the pursuit of chosen goals. The clinician must therefore consider the following:

- The developmental status of the individual—including mastery of the developmental goals of separation, individuation, independent functioning; the sense of self and efficacy as a person and as a learner in the larger context of the development of personhood.
- The cognitive and regulatory capacity for self-management—as manifest in the capacity for judgment and insight, and awareness of limitations and needs.
- Awareness of medical needs and of physical and mental limitations secondary to sensory, motor, and cognitive deficits—including the skills required for mobility and navigation and for manipulation of daily objects (vision, hearing, motor, spatial awareness/processing).
- The degree of independence in skills (appropriate to the individual's capabilities and realistic in that context).
- The capacity for maintaining safety—including self-preservation and safety knowledge and skills (ability to get help, first aid, sexuality).
- The capacity for self-advocacy and ability to access assistance— ranging from knowing when and who to ask for help to information about the availability of social, medical, educational, and rehabilitation services.

Specific issues to be addressed in transition planning are highlighted in Table 14.1.

For the individual who wants to go to college, development of self-advocacy skills and self-awareness needs to be addressed. The student's ability to manage a range of settings needs to be evaluated to understand the degree of contextual support required for optimal performance. In our experience, individuals who have problems integrating skills in active and challenging environments, who are easily overwhelmed by multiple demands, and who struggle to adapt flexibly to change are at high risk for failing to manage the demands of the college setting.

One cannot rely on IQ level as an index of successful adaptive functioning at an age-expected level for individuals with unique developmental trajectories. The neuropsychological assessment is a "complex clinical activity" (Vanderploeg, 1994), wherein the clinician's job is to review the individual's competencies, integrate these at the level that the individual is functioning; make a systematic, detailed analysis of the challenges the individual can be expected to face; and then—in close collaboration with the individual, the parents, and the mental health and educational teams— develop a comprehensive management plan that incorporates recommendations to promote both academic/vocational and psychosocial progress.

Table 14.1 Basic Functional–Adaptive Skills

Daily living skills	Self-care/grooming (hygiene, bathing, continence; dressing)
Nutrition	Nutritional choices, grocery shopping, food preparation
Household chores	Laundry, room maintenance
Financial management	Money, purchases, banking
Health	Understanding of medical history and specific medical issues; follow-up for late effects; access to care
Sexuality/intimate relationships	The right to, and responsibilities of, a sexual life; counseling around safety issues; skills required for initiating and fostering potentially intimate relationships; support for parents
Services/resources	Identification and access of available services, maintaining documentation for continued eligibility
Access/use of community-based services	Public transportation, recreational activities
Social integration	Identification of opportunities for social relationships/networks (individuals of different ages): social groups, volunteer activities
Practical academics	Math → checking, shopping; reading → getting around the world, reading instructions/warnings (to support vocational choices and workplace expectations)

Future Research Directions

What factors predict successful outcomes when a developmental course has been changed? What variables—social, academic, vocational, adaptive—support resilience (Bonanno, 2004)? What are the implications of changes in the nature and duration of adolescence and young adulthood for individuals with changed developmental trajectories? Arguably the most pressing research needs in this area are that of a developmentally framed and more ecologically valid investigative methodology as well as an integrated, multifaceted conceptualization of factors that contribute to diverse outcomes. Research strategies and diagnostic categories that are framed in terms of the "atomization" of isolated skills are extremely limited when the clinical goal is for better integration of the individual into his or her particular and unique societal niche.

The development of ecologically valid methodologies will require a more rigorous analysis of the nature of the assessment process itself—as a description of the individual who actually "behaves" in the ecological niche. It will also require a more detailed examination of the predictive validity of the measurement tools. How well does performance on a given task predict how an individual functions in the normally expectable range of different contexts throughout the day? The necessary paradigms must incorporate and analyze the interactions among the multiple complex capacities—emotional, cognitive, regulatory, social, adaptive, and academic—of the individual, and systematically explore and integrate the critical role of context in supporting and constraining ongoing behaving in the real world. This will require sophisticated research designs that evaluate clinical and functional outcomes with an appreciation of those variables that are related to contextual, as well as individual, risk factors. Such models will also incorporate a detailed analysis of the range of protective factors that contribute to resilience. Such factors will be indispensable in guiding future intervention strategies and promoting optimal outcomes.

References

Anderson, V., Northam, E., Hendy, J., & Wrennall, J. (2001). *Developmental neuropsychology: A clinical approach*. Philadelphia: Taylor & Francis.

Anie, K. A., & Telfair, J. (2005). Multi-site study of transition in adolescents with sickle cell disease in the United Kingdom and the United States. *International Journal of Adolescent Medicine and Health, 17*(2), 169–178.

Armstrong, D. (2002). *Developmental late effects of brain tumor treatment in children: Measurement and treatment issues that affect the quality of life.* Paper presented at the Effects of Radiotherapy on Brain and Behavior Through the Lifespan, Rio Grande, PR.

Arnett, J. J. (2000). Emerging adulthood. A theory of development from the late teens through the twenties. *The American Psychologist, 55*(5), 469–480.

Baron, I. S. (2004). *Neuropsychological evaluation of the child*. New York: Oxford University Press.

Bernstein, J. H. (1998). Supporting the "how-to" of learning: Intervention for executive functioning. *The Educational Therapist, 19*, 3–5.

Bernstein, J. (2000). Developmental neuropsychological assessment. In K. Yeates, M. D. Ris, & H. Taylor (Eds.), *Pediatric neuropsychology: Research, theory, and practice* (pp. 405–438). New York: Guilford Press.

Bernstein, J. H., Prather, P. A., & Rey-Casserly, C. (1995). Neuropsychological assessment in preoperative and postoperative evaluation. *Neurosurgical Clinics of North America, 6*(3), 443–454.

Bernstein, J. H., & Waber, D. P. (2003). Pediatric neuropsychological assessment. In T. E. Feinberg & M. J. Farah (Eds.), *Behavioral neurology and neuropsychology* (2nd ed., pp. 773–781). New York: McGraw-Hill.

Bernstein, J. H., & Waber, D. P. (2007). Executive capacities from a developmental perspective. In L. Meltzer (Ed.), *Understanding executive function: Implications and opportunities for the classroom* (pp. 39–54). New York: Guilford Press.

Bernstein, J., & Weiler, M. (2000). Pediatric neuropsychological assessment examined. In G. Goldstein & M. Hersen (Eds.), *Handbook of psychological assessment*. New York: Pergamon Press.

Blalock, G., & Patton, J. R. (1996). Transition and students with learning disabilities: creating sound futures. *Journal of Learning Disabilities, 29*(1), 7–16.

Bleyer, A. (2002). Older adolescents with cancer in North America deficits in outcome and research. *Pediatric Clinics of North America, 49*(5), 1027–1042.

Bonanno, G. A. (2004). Loss, trauma, and human resilience: Have we underestimated the human capacity to thrive after extremely aversive events? *American Psychologist, 59*(1), 20–28.

Buckner, J. C., Mezzacappa, E., & Beardslee, W. R. (2003). Characteristics of resilient youths living in poverty: The role of self-regulatory processes. *Development and Psychopathology, 15*(1), 139–162.

Consensus statement on health care transitions for young adults with special health care needs. (2002). *Pediatrics, 110*(6 Pt 2), 1304–1306.

Ferriero, D. M. (2004). Neonatal brain injury. *The New England Journal of Medicine, 351*(19), 1985–1995.

Fink, R. P. (1995). Successful dyslexics: A constructivist study of passionate interest reading. *Journal of Adolescent and Adult Literacy, 39*(4), 268–280.

Fink, R. P. (1998). Literacy development in successful men and women with dyslexia. *Annals of Dyslexia, 68*, 311–346.

Fischer, K. W., & Pruyne, E. (2003). Reflective thinking in adulthood: Emergence, development, and variation. In J. Demick & C. Andreoletti (Eds.), *Handbook of adult development* (pp. 169–198). New York: Kluwer Academic/Plenum.

Fischer, K. W., Rotenberg, E. J., Bullock, D. H., & Raya, P. (1993). The dynamics of competence: How context contributes directly to skill. In R. H. Wozniak & K. W. Fischer (Eds.), *Development in context: Acting and thinking in specific environments* (pp. 93–117). New York: Lawrence Erlbaum.

Foster, E. M., & Gifford, E. J. (2005). The transition to adulthood for youth leaving public systems: Challenges to policies and research. In R. A. J. Settersten, F. F. J. Furstenberg, & R. N. G. Rumbaut (Eds.), *On the frontier of adulthood: Theory, research, and public policy* (pp. 501–533). Chicago: University of Chicago Press.

Furstenberg, F. F. J., Rumbaut, R. N. C., & Settersten, R. A. J. (2005). On the frontier of adulthood: Emerging themes and new directions. In R. A. J. Settersten, F. F. J. Furstenberg, & R. N. G. Rumbaut (Eds.), *On the frontier of adulthood: Theory, research, and public policy* (pp. 3–25). Chicago: University of Chicago Press.

Hoagwood, K., Burns, B. J., Kiser, L., Ringeisen, H., & Schoenwald, S. K. (2001). Evidence-based practice in child and adolescent health services. *Psychiatric Services, 52*(9).

Holmes, J. (1987). Natural histories in learning disabilities: neuropsychological/environmental demand. In S. Ceci (Ed.), *Handbook of cognitive, social, and neuropsychological aspects of learning disabilities* (Vol. 2, pp. 303–319). Hillsdale, NJ: Lawrence Erlbaum.

Janiga, S. J., & Costenbader, V. (2002). The transition from high school to postsecondary education for students with learning disabilities: A survey of college service coordinators. *Journal of Learning Disabilities, 35*(5), 462–468.

Mulhern, R. (2002, December). *Risk factors for cognitive deficits in children treated for leukemia and brain tumors.* Paper presented at the Effects of Radiotherapy on Brain and Behavior Through the Lifespan, Rio Grande, PR.

National Cancer Policy Board. (2003). *Childhood cancer survivorship: Improving care and quality of life.* Washington, DC: National Academies Press.

National Institute of Medicine. (2001). *Crossing the quality chasm: A new health system for the 21st century.* Washington, DC: National Academy Press.

Palombo, J. (2001). *Learning disorders and disorders of the self in children and adolescents.* New York: W. W. Norton.

Pardes, J. R. (1988). Beyond the diagnosis. In R. G. Rudel, J. M. Holmes, & J. R. Pardes (Eds.), *Assessment of developmental learning disorders.* New York: Basic Books.

Patenaude, A. F., & Kupst, M. J. (2005). Psychosocial functioning in pediatric cancer. *Journal of Pediatric Psychology, 30*(1), 9–27.

Pennington, B. F. (1997). Dimensions of executive functions in normal and abnormal development. In N. A. Krasnegor, G. R. Lyon, & P. Goldman-Rakic (Eds.), *Development of the prefrontal cortex: Evolution, neurobiology and behavior* (pp. 265–281). Baltimore: P. H. Brookes.

Pentheroudakis, G., & Pavlidis, N. (2005). Juvenile cancer: Improving care for adolescents and young adults within the frame of medical oncology. *Annals Of Oncology: Official Journal of the European Society for Medical Oncology/ ESMO, 16*(2), 181–188.

Rey-Casserly, C. (1999). Neuropsychological assessment of preschool children. In E. Nuttal, I. Romero, & J. Kalesnik (Eds.), *Assessing and screening preschoolers: Psychological and educational dimensions* (2nd ed., pp. 281–295). Boston: Allyn & Bacon.

Tager-Flusberg, H. (Ed.). (1999). *Neurodevelopmental disorders.* Cambridge, MA: MIT Press.

Vanderploeg, R. D. (1994). Interview and testing: The data collection phase of neuropsychological evaluation. In R. D. Vanderploeg (Ed.), *Clinician's guide to neuropsychological assessment.* Hillsdale, NJ: Lawrence Erlbaum.

Volpe, J. (1998). Brain injury in the premature infant: Overview of clinical aspects, neuropathology, and pathogenesis. *Seminars in Pediatric Neurology, 5*(3), 135–151.

Yeates, K. O., Swift, E., Taylor, H. G., Wade, S. L., Drotar, D., Stancin, T., et al. (2004). Short- and long-term social outcomes following pediatric traumatic brain injury. *Journal of the International Neuropsychological Society, 10*(3), 412–426.

CHAPTER 15

Accommodations

Research to Practice

NOEL GREGG, DEANNA MORGAN,
JENNIFER LINDSTROM, and CHRIS COLEMAN

Contents

Understanding the issues surrounding accommodations begins with recognition of the consequences for an adult who is not provided equal opportunities to demonstrate knowledge. Dropout rates from secondary educational institutions for students with learning disabilities continue to be disproportionately high compared to their peers (Scanlon & Mellard, 2002). With the ongoing focus on high-stakes testing throughout public education, dropout rates for students with learning disabilities have the potential to grow. In addition, the percentage of these students going on to postsecondary education and later to professional schools is significantly lower than the parallel percentage for students without documented disabilities (Vogel & Reeder, 1999). Lack of access to professional studies has an unsettling effect on both career development and adult income (Bowen & Bok, 1998; Vogel & Reeder, 1999).

The fact that many adults with learning disabilities do not receive adequate accommodations in educational or work situations is a contributing factor to the depressing employment statistics reported by Vogel and Reeder (1999). Their data provides evidence that 43% of adults with learning disabilities are living at or below the poverty level, compared to 18% of the general population. In the section below, we describe the situation of an adult named John who demonstrates severe dyslexia. John currently works for a large landscaping firm that would like him to advance to a supervisory role. However, without the accommodations listed below, John will continue to be underemployed and underpaid. The accommodations selected will be effective because they were matched to his learning profile and work demands. In relation to accommodations, one shoe does not fit all sizes. It is critical for clinicians to remember that accommodations are necessary for instruction (schooling and vocational training) and work, not just testing situations.

John, Landscaper

John, a 32-year-old male, has worked for a large landscaping firm for the past 3 years. The firm's largest division focuses on specialized gardens. John would like to advance to a supervisory role in this division, which would require the management of several teams. The company is very impressed with his extraordinary creativity, leadership skills, and ability to please customers. They envision him becoming one of their key supervisors. John has explained his disability and the need for accommodations, both in any classroom training required as well as on the job. Recognizing his talents, the company has agreed to the low- and high-technology accommodations recommended in the report from a recent evaluation completed by vocational rehabilitation.

John was diagnosed with dyslexia at the age of 8. He received special education services in the public school through 10th grade. In 10th grade, he dropped out of school due to his frustrations with academics. He reports that he tried going back to adult basic education classes to get his GED, but he felt he was not advancing enough in the classes so again he dropped out. During his K–12 and adult education experiences, John was provided no type of alternative technology or media to help modify his learning environment. Past school records document severe deficits in phonological awareness, orthographic awareness, working memory, and distinguishing left and right. Math, listening, and speaking are his strengths.

Work Accommodations for John

Key accommodations are: assistive technologies to help in the reading of on-site, office, and training materials. In addition, accommodations will be required to enable John to write down information (e.g., tasks, orders, directions, phone numbers, addresses), as well as to produce any reports necessary in his new role as supervisor.

Assistive Technologies Required for Work and Training
1. Lightweight laptop with speech recognition
2. Scanner and conversion electronic software
3. Speech recognition software
4. Screen reader software to access and read digital texts
5. Recorder, sized to fit in his pocket, to use in lieu of a notepad
6. Cell phone that is voice-activated and has programmable speed-dial features
7. Scanning and reading pen to read small-print text on site (e.g., names and prices of plants)
8. Wristwatch organizer with personal data application and laptop-synchronized features to help with time-management issues
9. GPS navigation technology installed in his work vehicle
10. Blackberry with origination software for calendar, voice-activated notes, and connection to the Internet
11. Talking calculator for office budget-related issues
12. Web-reading software

Professionals who understand the importance of individual differences (cognitive and language processes), task formats (e.g., structured, auditory modality, visual modality), and response choices (e.g., written, oral, read) recognize the many factors that must be considered when recommending specific accommodations for an adult with learning disabilities. Critical to the success of any accommodation is the information obtained from a psychological evaluation. Matching an adult's profile to specific types of accommodations enhances the probability of effectiveness. Context is equally important to consider when determining accommodations. An accommodation might be appropriate in one setting or situation but not at another time or place. Situations that might necessitate an accommodation include testing, instruction, and work. Depending again on the vocational and technical standards of a particular setting, a professional might recommend similar or different accommodations. See Tables 15.1 and 15.2 for suggested learning, work, and testing accommodations.

Before we explore different types of accommodations, it is important to remember that equity for adults with learning disabilities requires more than just accommodations.

Individual Threat to Identity

Some adults with learning disabilities maintain preconceived perceptions that others view them as unsuccessful learners. Steele and Aronson (1995), speaking about black students, use the term *stereotype threat*, which they define as a person believing he or she is viewed through the lens of negative stereotypes, or the fear that he or she will do something that would inadvertently confirm that stereotype (p. 797). Stereotype threats have the potential of negatively influencing performance.

A stereotype threat is a situational peril causing intense and acute pressure in a person's life (Allport, 1954; Steele, 1999). Steele refers to Allport's use of the term "obsessive concern" to describe the anxiety that a person in this situation undergoes at the prospect of being seen and treated stereotypically. A great deal of cognitive and emotional energy is expended to guard oneself against a perceived untrusting environment (e.g., testing situation). It is critical to keep in mind that the stereotype threat occurs "not because of reduced self-expectancies, but because the salience of the stereotype fosters a mistrust of the situation" (Steele, 1999, p. 5). Many adults with learning disabilities believe that their performance will be judged through the negative stereotypes others may have about their disabilities. The threat to self-esteem is not global but rather specific to the situation (Crocker & Major, 1989). Many of the African American university students that Steele observed taking tests appeared to try too hard, by

Table 15.1 Learning and Work Accommodations

Accommodations	Underachievement/Deficit Areas								
	Reading			Writing			Math		Organization
	Decoding	Rate	Comprehension	Spelling	Rate	Expression and Motor	Calculation	High Level	
Alternative media	×	×	×						×
e-text									
audio									
tape									
CD									
Digital voice recorder			×	×	×	×			×
Reader	×	×	×						
Magnification	×								
Screen reader	×	×	×	×		×			
Scanner	×	×	×	×	×	×			
Voice to text			×						
Headset	×								
Word processor				×	×	×			
Modified keyboard						×			
Proofreader				×		×			
Modified mouse						×			

• Noel Gregg, Deanna Morgan, Jennifer Lindstrom, and Chris Coleman

Table 15.1 (continued) Learning and Work Accommodations

| | Underachievement/Deficit Areas | | | | | | | | |
| | Reading | | | Writing | | | Math | | |
Accommodations	Decoding	Rate	Comprehension	Spelling	Rate	Expression and Motor	Calculation	High Level	Organization
Hand-held spell checker									
Personal data organizer				×					×
Written instructions									×
Electronic organizer									×
Print or computer thesaurus	×		×	×					×
Grammar check						×			
Note-taking assistance				×	×		×		×
Reduced course work	×		×		×	×			×
Appeal for course substitution	×								
Job restructuring	×		×			×	×		
Modify training	×		×			×	×		
Modify work schedule									
Voice auto dialer									×

Table 15.2 Testing Accommodations

Accommodations	Academic Deficit Areas								
	Reading			Writing			Math		
	Decoding	Rate	Comprehension	Spelling	Rate	Expression and Motor	Calculation	Rate	Higher Level Math
Quiet testing room	×		×						
Private testing room	×		×						
Extended time		×			×			×	
Speech to text				×					
Magnification						×			
Text to speech	×	×	×	×		×			
Word processor				×	×	×			
Scheduled breaks not counted as test time		×			×			×	
Calculator							×		
Scribe to record oral responses				×	×	×	×		
Proofreader				×		×			
Hand spell checker				×		×			
Reader	×		×						
Modified keyboard					×	×			
Word bank			×	×					

(continued)

Table 15.2 (continued) Testing Accommodations

Accommodations	Academic Deficit Areas								
	Reading			Writing			Math		
	Decoding	Rate	Comprehension	Spelling	Rate	Expression and Motor	Calculation	Rate	Higher Level Math
Formula sheet									×
Print or computer thesaurus			×	×					
Permission to write directly on test						×			
Proctor to transfer information to scan form						×			

rereading and rechecking too many times: "Stereotype-threatened participants spent more time doing fewer items more inaccurately—probably as a result of alternating their attention between trying to answer the items and trying to assess the self-significance of their frustration" (Steele & Aronson, 1995, p. 809). The interference of stereotype threats on the test performance of adults with learning disabilities should not be ignored or underestimated by professionals.

High-Achieving Adults With Learning Disabilities

Access to accommodations among high-functioning adults with learning disabilities has recently become a topic of controversy. Some professionals appear to have difficulty understanding how a bright and high-achieving person can also demonstrate learning disabilities. Legally, to access an accommodation, an adult must demonstrate a "substantial limitation" as compared to "the general population" (see Macurdy & Geetter, this volume, for an in-depth discussion of the Americans with Disabilities Act [ADA]). The term "substantial limitation" has been interpreted differently in several recent court cases (see, e.g., Bartlett, 2001; Wong, 2004). One perspective stresses that substantial limitation literally means achievement below the statistical average, based on scores derived from a bell-curve metric (i.e., below the 16th percentile). Within this perspective, therefore, underachievement is synonymous with learning disabilities. However, the Supreme Court has never relied on a cutoff eligibility criteria to define disability (Mather, Gregg, & Simon, 2005). The ADA does not indicate that low performance or poor outcomes should determine whether or not a person has a disability. Rather, the ADA requires "a highly individualized assessment of the effect the impairment has on that person's life—the *condition, manner or duration* in which one performs a major life activity—not whether or not one can perform it, but how one performs it" (Mather et al., in press).

Intertwined with the debate over defining substantial limitations are concerns as to the comparison (i.e., nondisabled) group to use as the standard for "typical" functioning. For instance, should a doctor taking his or her medical boards be compared to all adults in the population—some having never graduated from high school—or his or her peers in medical school? If the proper comparison group under ADA is to be "most people," then one could argue that individuals with learning disabilities might never have the opportunity to access accommodations in professional schools since their scores would not appear significantly discrepant from the general population of nonmedical students. We suggest that one should not "conflate the comparison group with what is being compared—what is being compared is the *condition, manner, and duration* in which one performs an activity, not the actual resulting achievement itself" (Mather et al., 2004, p. 140).

The following section presents a description of Maria, a high-functioning adult requesting accommodations to take the bar exam. The law board denied her request based on its interpretation of the terms "substantial limitations" and "general population." In this case study, it is important to appreciate the role of accommodations in Maria's daily work world, as well as the types of accommodations requested for a testing situation.

Maria, Attorney

Maria is a 25-year-old law school graduate who is currently working as a clerk while studying for her bar examination. Her supervisor reports that she is a hard worker, persistent, very organized, reliable, and efficient. Maria enjoys problem solving, particularly surrounding issues that will help others. Due to documented learning disabilities that interfere with reading and written expression productivity, she requested extra time on all sections of the bar examination. The law board refused to allow this accommodation. The reason for the denial was that Maria's untimed reading of isolated, regular words (20th percentile), her reading rate (23rd percentile), and her spelling (18th percentile) were all above the 16th percentile and thus "within normal limits." Maria obtained a verbal intelligence standard score of 136.

Maria reports a long history of literacy problems, beginning in the first grade (e.g., difficulty learning the sounds of letters and writing in cursive). However, her parents did not want her tested or given any type of special education services. She did work harder than her peers and received extra tutoring after school from professionals trained in reading disorders. Maria reports being very anxious about "looking normal," how long it takes her to read traditional print-based materials, and going to great lengths to hide her poor spelling.

Maria was evaluated in college when preparing for the LSAT because she knew her ability to finish the exam in the allotted time would be compromised. As with the bar exam, she was denied accommodations. She completed only 70% of the examination. Despite this disadvantage, she scored high enough to gain admission to a second-tier law school.

Maria's Accommodations at Work

Key   In order for Maria to demonstrate her superior abilities and to complete work on time, she relies heavily on assistive technology. She is very comfortable with the technology, recognizing that it allows her to access print and demonstrate her excellent analytical thinking. To succeed in her profession, it is essential that she have multiple programs running together, allowing her to move seamlessly from program to program. Maria is a master at multitasking—if she is able to access technology.

Work Environment   E-mail, telephone contacts, notes on telephone conversations, and appointments should all go through one system. In addition, in order for Maria to keep up with the vast amount of reading as a lawyer must do, she uses a text reader and scanner. Because spelling is her primary written-expression problem, she prefers not to use voice-activated writing software and is content with access to spell-checking devices.

Technologies Used in the Workplace

1. Laptop
2. Scanner with PDF conversion software and screen reader
3. Microsoft Office Suite software with spell-check, auto text, and auto summarize
4. Word prediction software such as WordQ
5. Blackberry with origination software for calendar, voice-activated notes, and connection to the Internet
6. Digital voice-recorder system that downloads text onto laptop
7. Text-to-audio software system, which helps to create an electronic library for audio feedback reading
8. Calendar
9. A scanning and reading pen

Test Accommodations

Test taking has been the main focus of discussion within the topic of accommodating adults. The purpose of a test accommodation is to adjust conditions with the goal of equalizing the opportunity for an individual to demonstrate knowledge. Equalizing also requires preservation of construct validity to allow for score comparability across individuals. Accommodations are assumed to have a beneficial impact on the test scores of students receiving them but not to provide accommodated students with an advantage (Zuriff, 2000). An accommodation, in other words, must not change the nature of the construct being measured (Sireci, 2005). The concept of differential boost (Fuchs, Fuchs, Eaton, Hamlett, & Karns, 2000; Thompson, Blount, & Thurlow, 2002) likewise has as its premise that an accommodation will lead to greater score improvements for students with disabilities than for those without disabilities. However, Cohen and Gregg (2004) found that a test taker's status (accommodated or nonaccommodated) provides little information related to outcome performance (test scores). What we are certain about is that accommodating tests and testing situations for students with learning disabilities and other disorders has led to the widespread use of measurement modifications (Thurlow, Lazarus, Thompson, & Robey, 2002; Sireci, Li, & Scarpati, 2003).

The empirical research pertaining to test accommodations provides professionals with inconsistent findings due to the variety of accommodations used and implemented, as well as the heterogeneity of students investigated (see Sireci et al., 2003, for an in-depth review of the adult literature). In the Sireci et al. review, it is noted that only 41% of the studies investigated were published in peer-reviewed journals, and quasi- or nonexperimental designs were the most frequently used methodology. Even more disturbing was the fact that no published experimental designs were found at the secondary level, and only one involving postsecondary students. Therefore, a great many generalizations about the effectiveness of accommodations have been made based on either quasi/nonexperimental designs or research with students at the elementary level.

Recent reviews of the K through 12 literature on test accommodations for students with disabilities and English-language learners (ELL) identify *read-aloud* and *extended time* as the most frequently used and investigated accommodations (Chi & Pearson, 1999; Sireci et al., 2003; Thompson et al., 2002; Tindal & Fuchs, 2000). Chi and Pearson investigated the magnitude of score gain due to test accommodations. They concluded that students with disabilities demonstrate significant score gains under accommodated conditions but that the gains are very small. According to Sireci et al., a limitation of much of the current accommodation research is that effect sizes are often not even reported. Before discussing some exciting new research investigating accommodations in greater depth, we would like to address some of the issues surrounding the application of extended time and read-alouds for the adult population in testing, instructional, and work settings.

The reason that extended time and read-aloud accommodations are the most frequently suggested modifications for adults with learning disabilities pertains to the issue of reading fluency. At the adult level, reading fluency is the strongest discriminator between individuals who do and do not demonstrate dyslexia (McGrew, Woodcock, & Ford, 2002). We know that among the adult population, individuals identified with dyslexia represent the largest subgroup of learning disabilities (Shaywitz et al., 1998). Due to significant deficits in underlying phonological and orthographic awareness abilities, adults with dyslexia do not automatically recall or recognize the words they read. Therefore, their reading speed is significantly slowed down. In addition, they can easily omit or substitute incorrect words while reading, distorting their comprehension of text. Depending on the severity of the dyslexia, extended time or read-aloud accommodations are often recommended.

Read-Alouds

The findings from outcome studies related to the effectiveness of read-aloud accommodations (i.e., proctor reading, individual reading, screen-reading software) remain unclear (Sireci et al., 2003). Alternative media (e.g., readers, e-text, books on tape) and the alternative technologies used to access text (text-to-speech software, screen readers, large print, scanners) are the accommodations most frequently referenced in the literature as appropriate for individuals with learning disabilities (Sireci et al., 2003).

Learning is fluid and dynamic—and it begins at a point of entry for knowledge and information. Print is still the primary mode of delivering and acquiring knowledge for the majority of nondisabled adults. However, for those adults who are print disabled (learning disabled or blind), reading with one's ears is equally as valid as—and more effective than—reading with one's eyes. Alternative format options and technologies are improving by the moment. It is essential that this technology for accessing and expressing knowledge be made available as an accommodation for adults with learning disabilities to facilitate access to professional and personal reading.

The decision to allow or not allow read-aloud accommodations depends partly on how one defines reading (i.e., with eyes alone, with ears alone, or with eyes and ears). Currently, the increasing popularity of audio text over print text among the adult population without disabilities is challenging old definitions of reading (Harmon, 2005). Understanding the complex issues surrounding reasonable accommodations requires us to revisit the terminology used to describe familiar constructs. A dialogue is needed to review what we mean by reading at the adult level in this highly technological world. If the purpose of a test is to measure knowledge of content, does reading with one's ears result in any different measurable construct?

Extended Time

Support for providing extended time as an accommodation during test taking rests with research documenting that many adults with learning disabilities demonstrate deficits in quickly accessing symbols (letters, words, numbers) despite strong comprehension and reasoning abilities. In the area of reading, researchers have been able to identify specific functional neural systems responsible for reading fluency performance (Shaywitz & Fletcher, 1999; Shaywitz et al., 1998; Shaywitz, Shaywitz, Pugh, Fulbright, & Skudlarski, 2002). Accuracy scores for adults demonstrating dyslexia often improve over their fluency scores. For adults with learning disabilities, automaticity problems are often not restricted to reading performance but observed as well in written expression (Gregg, Coleman, Stennett, & Davis, 2002) and mathematics (Badian, 1983).

The professional faced with determining if extended time is an appropriate accommodation should review an adult's accuracy and fluency performance. In the area of reading, for instance, it is necessary to compare the reading of single words in timed and untimed situations. Due to repeated exposure to words through reading experiences, an adult might perform in the low-average or even-average range on the reading of single words (accuracy) but take an extraordinary amount of time to recognize these same words in text. In addition, the use of nonsense words in reading and spelling tasks helps one to identify the influence of phonological and orthographic awareness skills on reading (see Chapter 12) and spelling performance (see Chapter 12). On reading comprehension tests, an evaluator must be careful to look at the task demands (e.g., cloze, multiple choice, recall) and conditions (oral versus silent, timed versus untimed). As these tests measure significantly different aspects of reading comprehension, fluency demands will vary.

Identifying measures that might indicate the source of an adult's slow speed in accessing symbols requires knowledge of the literature as well as astute clinical thinking. Terms such as *cognitive fluency, processing speed,* and *cognitive efficiency* are, unfortunately, often used interchangeably by many professionals. Therefore, one must be sure to note how a term is defined by a test author or publisher. In addition, average performance on general processing speed tasks using nonverbal items (e.g., Wechsler Adult Intelligence Scales–III, Processing Speed Index) does not mean that an adult will not have difficulty with reading or writing fluency tasks (i.e., orthographic fluency). It is imperative that a clinician keep in mind the complexity of literacy tasks and the fact that there is no single source for all fluency and rate deficits.

Assistive Technology

The value of specific assistive technologies as accommodations for the adult population cannot be stressed enough. The first legislation that directly addressed assistive technology was the Technology Related Assistance for Individuals With Disabilities Act of 1988 (the Tech Act), which was amended in 1994. In 1990, the Americans with Disabilities Act (ADA) reinforced the provisions of the Rehabilitation Act of 1973 and extended civil rights protection to students with disabilities attending institutions that do not receive federal assistance (Day & Edwards, 1996). The ADA did not specifically define or address assistive technology, but its definition of "auxiliary aids and services" includes assistive technology as a form of support (§ 12101; Mull & Sitlington, 2003).

Assistive technology is defined by the Tech Act as "any technology used to increase, maintain, or improve the functional capabilities of individuals with disabilities" (Day & Edwards, 1996, p. 486). Although assistive technology is recognized in the area of rehabilitation as a means to improve quality of life for persons with physical disabilities, it has received little attention as a tool for helping adults with learning disabilities to compensate for specific cognitive deficits. In the field of education, reports addressing the benefits of using assistive technology to compensate for specific learning disabilities have been generated primarily by professionals at the postsecondary level attempting to meet the needs of increasing numbers of students with learning disabilities attending college (Raskind, 1994).

For adults with learning disabilities across postsecondary settings, the most common technologies available include word processors with spell checking, proofreading assistance, abbreviation expanders (programs that allow students to type abbreviations for frequently used words or phrases and press the space bar or mouse to produce the complete word or phrase), and outlining software programs (Day & Edwards, 1996). Additional assistive technologies often used among the adult population with learning disabilities include variable-speed-control tape recorders, optical character recognition systems (reading machines), listening aids (systems that use a microphone and headset designed for students with auditory deficits), speech-synthesis/screen reader programs (voice output systems that read back text displayed on the computer screen), speech-recognition systems (systems that allow the user to operate the computer by speaking to it), data managers (technologies that store personal information for students with organization and memory difficulties), and talking calculators (Day & Edwards, 1996).

Unfortunately, a significant number of adults with learning disabilities still reach the postsecondary level without being exposed to assistive technologies. For this reason, it is important for professionals working with the adult population to be familiar with selection criteria and training guidelines concerning assistive technology. Raskind and Scott (1993) emphasized the importance of choosing technologies relative to the individual, the functions to be performed, and the contexts in which the technologies will be used. Constraints limiting the use of technology across the contexts of home, school, workplace, and social settings may be physical (e.g., insufficient lighting, excessive noise, or a lack of space) or psychosocial (e.g., reactions of others to use of the device) and should be considered in selecting technology.

Looking at Differences in Greater Depth

The increase in the identification of adults with learning disabilities over the past decade has led to a greater need to study both the conditions and the accommodations that are in place to address the needs of individuals with disabilities. While many researchers have made comparisons between individuals within different disability subgroups and within different subgroups by accommodation type, much of this work has focused on mean scores for each group as measured by a specified instrument. Studies of the mean scale score differences and standard deviations for various subgroups can be meaningful and provide good preliminary information about subgroup differences. However, to begin to more fully unravel and understand the complexities of subgroup differences for types of disabilities and types of accommodations, it is necessary to go beyond descriptive statistics. The field of psychometrics offers many methodologies that enable professionals to look at group differences in more depth. Among those available, three seem particularly relevant to the study of adults with learning disabilities: *differential item functioning* (DIF), *generalizability theory* (G-theory), and *factor analysis* (FA). It is essential that psychologists have at least a cursory background in these methodologies to interpret test scores across new and advanced measurement tools, as well as critique the findings from research focused on effective accommodations for adults with learning disabilities. Scientifically based decisions as to the most valid instruments to use and the effectiveness of accommodations have changed with advancements in test methodologies. Psychologists must keep current with these advances and make adjustments to their past practices as needed.

Differential Item Functioning (DIF)

Topics related to item bias and fairness have been the source of many debates in the educational measurement community. DIF is a generic term indicating that some effort has been made to match examinees on total test score or proficiency before examining subgroup differences in item or test performance. For dichotomously scored items, an item is said to be functioning differentially when the probability of a correct response to the item is different for examinees at the same ability level but from different groups.

The presence of DIF items on a test poses a serious threat to the validity of the test use. In this regard, Standard 7.3 in the *Standards for Educational and Psychological Testing* (AERA, APA, & NCME, 1999) specifies that

> When credible research reports that differential item functioning exists across age, gender, racial/ethnic, cultural, disability, and/or linguistic groups in the population of test takers in the content domain measured by the test, test developers should conduct appropriate

studies when feasible. Such research should seek to detect and eliminate aspects of test design, content, and format that might bias test scores for particular groups. (p. 81)

In order to make a fair test, test developers should investigate the performance of examinees of different subgroups empirically. In addition, users of test information should have the opportunity to evaluate the extent of the inappropriate characteristics of the test and the differences in test performance. A DIF analysis for a test, therefore, can be seen as an essential step to protect the rights of test takers and the general public.

Cohen and Gregg (2004), using a Mixed DIF Model, investigated the performance of examinees (with and without learning disabilities) administered a statewide mathematics test. All individuals with learning disabilities were given only extended time as an accommodation. The purpose of the research was to identify the influence of extended time on item difficulty. Using the mixed model, the groups were identified based on the pattern of responses given by accommodated (extended time only) and nonaccommodated examinees rather than group membership (learning disabilities/extended time versus normally achieving). Cohen and Gregg (2004) found that the cause of DIF across items on the mathematics test was less related to use of extended time than to item content (e.g., word problems, algebra). This mixed-model approach provided more information concerning the causes of DIF. The findings of these studies have significant implications for issues surrounding construct validity.

Further studies of the types described above should be performed to investigate differences in performance for adults with learning disabilities using various accommodations. This goal should be to determine the influence of specific learning disability profiles and accommodations on scores. Additionally, by more closely inspecting items that do exhibit DIF for adults with learning disabilities across different accommodations, we can provide a better understanding of the many factors influencing test performance.

Generalizability Theory (G-Theory)

Multivariate generalizability analyses can go beyond the estimation of variance due to disability or accommodation type and provide more detailed information by measurement condition to inform research. The current thrust for accountability and the use of test scores as indicators of teacher and school effectiveness occur based on the assumption that these facets, teacher and school, are major contributors to the observed differences in student performance on standardized assessments. To accurately gauge the contribution of each facet on the resulting test scores, a more complicated design is needed that takes these facets into account.

Generalizability theory provides an avenue to investigate these effects (Brennan, 1992, 2001; Shavelson & Webb, 1991).

In the current age of accountability for all students, generalizability theory can yield valuable information on generalizability of test scores to the population. Often studies are conducted on a sample of students with very few, if any, students with disabilities. As federal mandates push for the inclusion of students with disabilities in assessment programs, the ability to use the power of generalizability theory to estimate generalizability coefficients on diverse samples of students while varying the sample size of the accompanying measurement conditions (e.g., number of items, number of raters, and so forth) can greatly facilitate decision making. Pilot tests, which perform generalizability analyses early in the process of test development, can benefit from using generalizability results from decision studies to determine the optimal conditions for measurement to achieve acceptable generalizability of results. As the population of students becomes more diverse, it is expected that the number of items, raters, or other measurement conditions will need to increase.

Comparisons of generalizability coefficients on diverse samples with and without the inclusion of students with disabilities or specific accommodation types can be informative in decisions of test and accommodation appropriateness for general testing conditions. Comparisons of generalizability coefficients estimated separately for each disability type or accommodation type can also be informative as to the appropriateness of the test for a specific disability type and the appropriateness of a particular accommodation on the assessment in question. The application of generalizability theory to investigate the effects of disability or accommodation on score variance is a relatively new field of study.

In education or work settings, adults are nested within programs or businesses and then further nested within institutions, states, and similar organizational levels. The result is that adults within each setting or cluster are linked by common experiences and exposure to information (Guion, 1995). No attempt is made by many researchers to account for the reality that adults are incorporated within institutions or that test items may be representative of different subcategories within the larger construct being measured and, therefore, nested within a category. As a result, the variance attributable to factors extraneous to the adult's ability or the item itself are aggregated into the separate "student" and "item" variance components or confounded with the interaction between student and item as undifferentiated error. Therefore, a cluster effect may be observed with clusters formed by the institutional membership of the individual (Cronbach, Linn, Brennan, & Haertel, 1997). This cluster effect may be defined as bias in adults' scores that are caused by dependencies among adults due, in this example, to the grouping or clustering of individuals within institutions with a common instructor or supervisor. These clusters result in shared experiences and interactions within the cluster that are shared by group or class members but unique from other institutional units that may in a typical analysis be viewed as equivalent. How these institutional or cluster effects influence the variance of examinee scores should be investigated further (Linn & Burton, 1994).

The current thrust for accountability and the use of test scores as indicators of instructor and institutional effectiveness occur based on the assumption that these facets, instructor and institution, are major contributors to the observed differences in examinee performance on standardized assessments. To accurately gauge the contribution of each facet on the resulting test scores, we require a more complicated design that takes these facets into account. Generalizability theory provides an avenue to investigate these effects (Brennan, 1992, 2001; Shavelson & Webb, 1991).

Factor Analysis (FA) and Structural Equation Modeling (SEM)

One fundamental component of construct validity is to ensure that the test measures the same construct across various groups of examinees. If evidence indicates that the test is not measuring the same construct across the groups of interest, then scores for the groups may not be comparable. Internal consistency reliability estimates and dimensionality analyses may be used to compare the latent structure of assessments between examinees tested with accommodations (e.g., extended time conditions) and examinees who received no accommodations (e.g., standard timing conditions). Due to the high-stakes use of test scores for graduation, promotion, or retention decisions, admissions and placement decisions, and scholarship awards, it is important to ensure that scores from students testing with varying degrees and types of accommodations are comparable to scores from students testing without accommodations.

Principal factor analysis (PFA) is one of the conventional methods of exploring test dimensionality. PFA is a powerful method for identifying the underlying latent structure of assessments. Score validity requires the latent structure of an assessment to remain similar across varying groups of examinees. Studies have compared the latent structure of assessments when administered to examinees with differing characteristics. Similar studies should be conducted to compare the latent structure of assessments for groups of different disability types or to compare different accommodation groups. However, numerous studies have shown that factor analytic methods can overestimate the number of factors when binary data (such as dichotomously scored test data) are analyzed.

Confirmatory factor analyses (CFA) also provide a detailed picture of test dimensionality. Other, more complex studies that could be performed include cross-validation of confirmatory factor analyses in cohorts of students within different disability groups or who used different accommodations types, and comparison of the underlying factor structure in different disability or accommodation groups via multiple-group methodology.

Willingham et al. (1988) provide a comprehensive view of issues related to testing examinees with disabilities on the SAT I. Typically, individuals who request extended time accommodations on the SAT I have a physical, learning, or emotional disability. An investigation of the dimensionality of the SAT for examinees with disabilities was conducted in the 1980s. Dorans and Lawrence (1987) used SAT I data to investigate the dimensionality of the SAT I, but they did not compare test structure for those testing under standard timing conditions versus those receiving extended time. The techniques used in these studies should be further explored and extended to other populations of examinees who have disabilities or use accommodations.

Morgan and Huff (2002) used PFA and multidimensional scaling (MDS) to determine whether the latent structure of test data on the verbal and math sections of the SAT I differed substantially for those testing under standard time versus those testing with extended time. Results from the factor analysis indicated some differences in latent structure at the item level. Preliminary results from weighted MDS indicated similar structure on most of the fitted dimensions. Thus, there is no real evidence to suggest that the scores on the SAT I have different interpretations when examinees have an extended time administration as opposed to the standard time administration.

Structural equation modeling (SEM) techniques can be powerful tools for investigating the structural validity of an assessment. SEM employs techniques of path analysis, conceptual synthesis of latent variable and measurement models, and general estimation procedures (Bollen, 1989). Path analysis provides a pictorial representation of equations detailing the relationship between each variable and any disturbances or errors that may exist. This allows the direct, indirect, and total effects of one variable on another to be investigated. SEM techniques allow investigation of not only the relationship between variables but also the effects and causations associated with the relationships. Using SEM to research the relationships between variables such as accommodations, disability types, education, gender, and test scores may result in a better understanding of the underlying causes and effects surrounding issues of disability, accommodations, and performance in a variety of settings.

Summary

Equality, according to our Roman ancestors, meant being able to live *ex aequo et bono*, literally according to "what is just and good." Justice becomes integral to providing accommodation solutions for adults with learning disabilities. However, justice goes beyond simply following the laws of a country. Informed decisions based on research across disciplines such as measurement, psychology, sociology, linguistics, and education are necessary to provide the foundation for determining appropriate accommodations for the adult population with learning disabilities. Knowledge is the first step toward equity.

Professionals might reflect upon their own perspectives related to the meanings of constructs such as reading, writing, merit, equality, or fairness in relation to modifying standardized approaches to accessing and demonstrating knowledge. Change is dependent upon the willingness of individuals and systems to consider new constructs.

Allport (1924) defined personality as the "dynamic organization within the individual of those psychophysical systems that determine his unique adjustments to his environment" (p. 48). Therefore, personality is really a creative accommodation to environmental circumstances. The reaction adults with learning disabilities receive from individuals and systems pertaining to a belief in their potential will partially influence the success of any accommodations they are granted.

Allport's (1968) main premise is that the thoughts, feelings, and behavior of individuals are influenced by other people. The possibility of being negatively stereotyped by a community (academic, vocational) is a serious threat to success. For adults with learning disabilities, the fear of being perceived by others as different can mask their potential by causing them not to request accommodations. Many adults with learning disabilities are well aware of their potential but fear that a person in power (e.g., employer, instructor, licensing agency) will compromise their efforts through negative perceptions and treatment. Greater power and control over learning by these adults—through accommodations—enables them to gain command of their role as learners, hopefully leading to reduced stereotype threats (Lather, 1991).

One of the most significant barriers facing the population of adults with learning disabilities is the fact that many professionals involved in the assessment process lack critical knowledge related to identifying appropriate accommodations. Knowledge of current research pertinent to accommodation decision-making moves professionals away from the mentality of "one shoe fits all sizes" toward a more informed and effective selection of appropriate assessment measures and accommodations.

Table 15.3 Steps to Follow When Making Accommodation Decisions

1. Consult available validation research that has systematically investigated the effects of different accommodations on the performance of students with disabilities.
2. Determine the skills and knowledge an assessment is intended to evaluate (target skills).
3. Identify cognitive/linguistic processing deficits and their impact on the individual's ability to demonstrate proficiency with target skills (e.g., academic skills).
4. Identify the additional (ancillary) skills and knowledge/experience an individual needs to demonstrate his or her proficiency with the target skills.
5. Consult with the individual for whom the accommodation will be provided (e.g., determine if he or she has used a particular accommodation in the past; consider his or her past experience with computers, assistive technology, etc.).
6. Determine the accommodations that would be appropriate, given the particular target and ancillary skills called for in a given assessment and the particular disability or language-development profile that characterizes a given test taker.

Table 15.3 provides suggested steps for those involved in determining accommodations needs for adults with learning disabilities.

Greater dialogue and sharing of knowledge across disciplines pertaining to assessment and accommodations is critical. Unfortunately, the old Indian fable of the blind men trying to describe the elephant appears an appropriate analogy for the issues surrounding accommodating adults with learning disabilities; it all depends on where one stands, often in isolation of the bigger picture (Wertsch, 1998). In addition, equity for the adult population requires professionals to remind themselves of the importance of context. There is a critical need for refocusing solutions (e.g., legal, measurement, educational) to fit what Bruner (1996) identified as the "narrative construal of reality" (p. 32). In using this term, he encouraged all of us to recognize the role of context in understanding and challenging doctrine and theory.

References

Allport, G. W. (1924). *Social psychology*. Boston: Houghton Mifflin.

Allport, G. W. (1954). *The nature of prejudice*. Reading, MA: Addison-Wesley.

Allport, G. W. (1968). History of modern social psychology. In G. Lindzey & E. Aronson (Eds.), *Handbook of social psychology* (Vol. I, pp. 1–80). Reading, MA: Addison-Wesley.

American Educational Research Association, American Psychological Association, & National Council on Measurement in Education. (1999). *Standards for educational and psychological testing*. Washington, DC: American Psychological Association.

Americans With Disabilities Act of 1990, 42 U.S.C. § 12101.

Badian, N. A. (1983). Arithmetic and nonverbal learning. In H. R. Myklebust (Ed.), *Progress in learning disabilities* (Vol. V, pp. 235–264). New York: Grunt & Stratton.

Bartlett v. New York State Board of Law Examiners, 970 F. Supp. 1094 (S.D.N.Y.) (Bartlett I); aff'd 2 F. Supp. 2d 388 (S.D.N.Y. 19) (Bartlett II); aff'd in part, rev'd and remanded in part, 156 F. 3d 321 (2d Cir. 1998) (Bartlett III); vacated and remanded, 119 S. Ct. 2388 (1999) (Bartlett IV); aff'd in part and remanded, 226 F. 3d 69 (2d Cir. 2000) (Bartlett V); 2001 WL 930792 (S.D.N.Y. Aug. 15, 2001) (Bartlett VI).

Bollen, K. A. (1989). *Structural equations with latent variables.* New York: Wiley-Interscience.

Bowen, W. G., & Bok, D. (1998). *The shape of the river.* Princeton, NJ: Princeton University Press.

Brennan, R. L. (1992). Generalizability theory. *Educational Measurement: Issues and Practice, 11*(4), 27–34.

Brennan, R. L. (2001). *Generalizability theory.* New York: Springer-Verlag.

Bruner, J. (1996). *The culture of education.* Cambridge, MA: Harvard University Press.

Chi, C. W. T., & Pearson, P. D. (1999, June). *Synthesizing the effects of test accommodations for special education and limited English proficient students.* Paper presented at the National Conference on Large Scale Assessment, Snowbird, UT.

Cohen, A. S., & Gregg, N. (2004). *A mixture model analysis of the item-level impact of testing accommodations on examinees' responses to achievement test items.* Paper presented at the annual meeting of the International Testing Conference, College of William and Mary.

Crocker, J., & Major, B. (1989). Social stigma and self-esteem: The self-protective properties of stigma. *Psychological Review, 96,* 608–630.

Cronbach, L. J., Linn, R. L., Brennan, R. L., & Haertel, E. H. (1997). Generalizability analysis for performance assessments of student achievement or school effectiveness. *Educational and Psychological Measurement, 57*(3), 373–399.

Day, S. L., & Edwards, B. J. (1996). Assistive technology for postsecondary students with learning disabilities. *Journal of Learning Disabilities, 29*(5): 486–492.

Dorans, N. J., & Lawrence, I. M. (1987). *The internal construct validity of the SAT (RR-87-35).* Princeton, NJ: Educational Testing Service.

Fuchs, L. S., Fuchs, D., Eaton, S. B., Hamlet, C. L., & Karns, K. M. (2000). Supplementing teacher judgments of mathematics test accommodations with objective data. *School Psychology Review, 29,* 65–85.

Gregg, N., Coleman, C., Stennett, R., & Davis, M., (2002). Discourse complexity of college writers with and without learning disabilities. *Journal of Learning Disabilities, 35,* 23–38.

Guion, R. M. (1995). Commentary on values and standards in performance assessments. *Educational Measurement: Issues and Practice, 14*(4), 25–27.

Harmon, A. (2005, May 26). Loud, proud, unabridged: It is too reading. *New York Times,* p. 11.

Lather, P. (1991). *Getting smart: Feminist research and pedagogy with/in the postmodern.* New York: Routledge.

Linn, R. L., & Burton, E. (1994). Performance-based assessment: Implications of task specificity. *Educational measurement: Issues and practice, 13,* 5–8, 15.

Mather, N., Gregg, N., & Simon, J. (2005). The curse of high stakes tests and high abilities: Reaction to *Wong v. Regents of the University of California. Learning Disabilities: A Multidisciplinary Journal 13*, 139–144.

McGrew, K. S., Woodcock, R., & Ford, L. (2002). The Woodcock-Johnson Battery (3rd ed.). In A. S. Kaufman & E. O. Lictenberger (Eds.), *Assessing adolescent and adult intelligence* (2nd ed.). Needham Heights, MA: Allyn & Bacon.

Morgan, D. L., & Huff, K. (2002). *Reliability and dimensionality of the SAT for examinees tested under standard timing conditions and examinees tested with extended time.* Unpublished research report at the Educational Testing Service.

Mull, C., & Sitlington, P. (2003). The role of technology in the transition to postsecondary education of students with learning disabilities. *Journal of Special Education, 37*(1), 26–33.

Raskind, M. H. (1994). Assistive technology for adults with learning disabilities: A rationale for use. In P. J. Gerber & H. B. Reiff (Eds.), *Learning disabilities in adulthood: Persisting problems and evolving issues* (pp. 152–162). Stoneham, MA: Andover Medical.

Raskind, M. H., & Scott, N. (1993). Technology for postsecondary students with learning disabilities. In S. A. Vogel & P. B. Adelman (Eds.), *Success for college students with learning disabilities* (pp. 240–280). New York: Springer-Verlag.

Scanlon, D., & Mellard, D. F. (2002). Academic and participation profiles of school-age dropouts with and without disabilities. *Exceptional Children, 68*, 239–258.

Shavelson, R. J., & Webb, N. M. (1991). *Generalizability theory: A primer.* Newbury Park, CA: Sage.

Shaywitz, S., & Fletcher, J. M. (1999). Persistence of dyslexia: The Connecticut longitudinal study at adolescence. *Pediatrics, 104*, 1351–1260.

Shaywitz, S. E., Shaywitz, B. A., Pugh, K. R., Fulbright, R. K., Constable, R. T., Mencl, W. E., et al. (1998). Functional disruption in the organization of the brain for reading in dyslexia. *Proceedings of the National Academy of Science, USA, 95*, 2636–2641.

Shaywitz, B. A., Shaywitz, S. E., Pugh, K. R., Mencl, W. E., Fulbright, R. K., & Skudlarski, P. (2002). Disruption of posterior brain systems for reading in children with developmental dyslexia. *Society of Biological Psychiatry, 52*, 101–110.

Sireci, S., Li, S., & Scarpati, S. (2003, October). *The effects of test accommodation on test performance: A review of the literature.* Symposium on the Effect of Accommodations on Accountability. Abstract reviewed January 4, 2004, from http://www.eprri.org/sumposia_10_03.html.

Sireci, S. (2005). Unlabeling the disabled: A perspective on flagging scores from accommodated test administrations. *Educational Researcher 34*(1), 3–12.

Steele, C. (1999). *Thin ice: "Stereotype threat" and black college students.* Retrieved January 4, 2004, from www.theatlantic.com/issues/99aug/9908stereotype.htm

Steele, C. M., & Aronson, J. (1995). Stereotype threat and the intellectual test performance of African Americans. *Journal of Personality and Social Psychology, 69*, 797–811.

Thompson, S., Blount, A., & Thurlow, M. (2002). *A summary of research on the effects of test accommodations: 1999 through 2001* (Technical Report 34). Minneapolis: University of Minnesota, National Center on Educational Outcomes, Retrieved January 4, 2004, from www.education.umn.edu/ NCEO/OnlinePubs/ Technica134.htm.

Thurlow, M. L., Lazarus, S., Thompson, S., & Robey, J. (2002). *2001 state policies on assessment participation and accommodations.* Retrieved January 4, 2004, from www.education.umn.edu/NCEO/OnlinePubs/Technica146.htm.

Tindal, G., & Fuchs, L. (2000). *A summary of research on test changes: An empirical basis for defining accommodations.* Lexington, KY: Mid-South Regional Resource Center.

Vogel, S., & Reeder, S. (1999). *Learning disabilities, literacy, and adult education.* Baltimore, MD: Brookes.

Wechsler, D. (1997). *Wechsler Adult Intelligence Scale* (3rd ed.). San Antonio, TX: Psychological Corporation.

Wertsch, J. V. (1998). *Mind as action.* New York: Oxford University Press.

Willingham, W. W., Ragosta, M., Bennett, R. E., Braun, H., Rock, D. A., & Powers, D. E. (1988). *Testing handicapped people.* Needham Heights, MA: Allyn & Bacon.

Wong v. Regents of the University of California, WL 1837752 (9th Cir. 2004).

Zuriff, G. E. (2000). Extra accommodation time for students with learning disabilities: An examination of the maximum potential thesis. *Applied Measurement in Education, 13*(1), 99–117.

CHAPTER **16**

Legal Issues for Adults With Learning Disabilities in Higher Education and Employment

ALLAN H. MACURDY and ERIKA GEETTER

Contents

When an adult with a learning disability seeks reasonable accommodations under antidiscrimination statutes such as the Americans with Disabilities Act of 1990 (ADA) or the Rehabilitation Act of 1973 (Section 504) the clinician's role is a limited one. Although the clinician provides the employer or educational institution with medical documentation of the client's physical or mental impairment and the client's resulting functional limitations, the clinician does not determine whether the client is disabled or whether accommodations should be provided. That determination is in the hands of school officials or the client's employer, who must base his or her decision not only on clinical information, but also on the requirements of the job or program, specific statutory definitions, and—in difficult cases—a review of the way courts have ruled when presented with similar fact patterns.

Despite his or her limited role, a clinician who understands the entirety of the decision-making process relating to reasonable accommodations can assist the student or employee in formulating and justifying accommodation requests so that they are more likely to be granted. In this chapter, we hope to further that understanding, first by setting out the basic framework of the Americans with Disabilities Act (ADA) in both the higher education and employment contexts, including the documentation, eligibility and accommodation processes. We then examine in greater detail two particular areas where legal requirements can cause difficulties, particularly for individuals with learning disabilities, as they seek to obtain the services or accommodations they believe are necessary for their success.

The Basic Framework of the ADA

Disability

The ADA, drawing upon the Rehabilitation Act, defines disability, with respect to an individual, as "(A) a physical or mental impairment that substantially limits one or more of the major life activities of such individual; (B) a record of such an impairment; or (C) being regarded as having such an impairment" (ADA, 1990, 42 U.S.C.A. §12102). An individual with a learning disability is entitled to the protections of Section 504 and the ADA only when he can demonstrate that he falls under this very particularized definition of "disability." Moreover, terms embedded within the definition of disability, such as "substantially limits," and "major life activity" are defined in ways that end up further narrowing the number of individuals with learning disabilities who have legal protection. For instance, to prove one is "substantially limited" by a learning disability, one must show a significant restriction not in comparison to what one could personally achieve without the disability but when compared to what the general population achieves (Regulations, 1999, 29 C.F.R. 1630.2[j][1]).

To fall under the ADA, the "substantial limitation" must be to a "major life activity." Although there has been much disagreement over what constitutes a major life activity, the Supreme Court held in 2002 that major life activities are those that are of central importance to most people's daily lives (Toyota Motor Mfg., Inc. v. Williams, 2002, p. 195). While "learning" will generally qualify as a major life activity, a college student's well-documented and unchallenged diagnosis of a "learning disability" does not mean that the student has a substantially limiting impairment within the meaning of the ADA or Section 504 (*Guckenberger v. Boston University*, 1997, p. 133; holding that analysis of legal claims under Section 504 is similar to that under the ADA). This is because the degree of the student's impairment is to be determined not in comparison to other similarly situated individuals attending the student's institution but rather in comparison to the "average person." This has led many courts to find that college students with learning disabilities are not substantially limited because, even with their impairments, they have a history of scholastic achievement and are able to read and write at least as well as the average person in the population.

One notable exception to these findings is the case of *Bartlett v. New York State Board of Law Examiners* (2001), which went all the way to the U.S. Supreme Court and then back to the trial court on the issue of whether Ms. Bartlett, who was requesting accommodations in connection with the New York State Bar Examination, had a substantial limitation in the major life activity of reading. When the case was finally resolved (after 8 years of litigation and six court opinions), the trial judge held that Ms. Bartlett was substantially limited when compared to the average reader "by her slow reading rate and by the fatigue caused by her inability to read with automaticity" (*Bartlett v. New York State Board of Law Examiners*, 2001, p. 3). The final opinion by the trial court provides an excellent overview of the law in this area as well as the type of expert testimony relevant to such determinations.

Much more typical are the recent cases involving medical students, who have been unable to show substantial limitations so as to qualify for accommodations under the ADA. In *Wong v. University of California* (2005), for example, a medical student claimed that, due to a learning disability limiting his ability to process and communicate information, he was substantially limited in learning and reading. In finding that he was not disabled under the ADA or Section 504, the court held that his claim "was contradicted by his ability to achieve academic success" (*Wong v. University of California*, 2005, p. 1065), including completion of the first 2 years of medical school without accommodations and with a B average and passing the required national boards. In light of this, the Court found irrelevant his contention "that his learning impairment makes it impossible for him to keep up with a rigorous medical school curriculum" (p. 1065). Likewise, in two recent cases brought by former medical students who were dismissed from George Washington University School of Medicine due to poor academic performance, the court found that the students' previous academic achievements and successes demonstrated that their impairments, which included dyslexia and ADHD, were not a substantial limitation (*Singh v. George Washington University School of Medicine and Health Sciences*, 2006; *Steere v. George Washington University School of Medicine and Health Sciences*, 2006).

This restrictive understanding of "substantially limited" is what *courts* will use when deciding whether a student plaintiff deserves ADA protection. Most institutions of higher education, however, will provide accommodations to students who present legitimate documentation of a "learning disability" as that term is understood clinically. The clinical definition of the term looks at discrepancies between ability and achievement with regard to the particular individual and not in comparison with the rest of the population. The result is that many college or graduate students receive accommodations for a learning disability not because it is legally mandated but because schools have decided that students who have a legitimate clinical diagnosis of a learning disability should qualify for accommodations, without comparison to the general population.

One commentator has opined that schools may be willing to offer accommodations even when not legally required because "doing so is consistent with their academic mission of enabling students to realize their full academic potential" (Levy, 2001, p. 117). The practical result of this broader interpretation of "disability" by educational institutions is that individuals who received accommodations for a learning disability throughout their education may not meet the statutory definition of disabled in order to qualify for accommodations in the workplace. Employers, who are generally more interested in the success of their enterprise than in helping an employee reach his potential, may insist upon a stronger showing of an employee's "substantial limitation" before agreeing that the employee is entitled to protection under the ADA.

In the workplace, individuals with learning disabilities often point to working as the major life activity that is substantially limited by their impairment. In such cases, the individual must demonstrate that he or she is precluded from performing an entire class of jobs or a wide range of jobs in various classes. In the Bartlett case mentioned above, for example, the court found that Ms. Bartlett was also substantially limited in the life activity of working because her disability made it impossible for her to pass the employment test of the bar exam, thus preventing her from engaging in an entire class of jobs for which she was otherwise qualified (*Bartlett v.*

New York State Board of Law Examiners, 2001, p. 44). If the individual is simply struggling with one particular job or his job of choice, then under the ADA, he is not "substantially limited" in his ability to work (*Sutton v. United Airlines*, 1999, p. 491).

Further, under federal law, mitigating measures can be taken into account in determining whether someone has a disability (*Sutton v. United Airlines*, 1999, pp. 482–483). For instance, if an individual with severe ADD can control it through use of medication and counseling, his level of impairment will be reviewed in its "corrected" state and he may not be found to be disabled. In *Hess v. Rochester School District* (2005), for instance, the court found that a middle school teacher with ADHD could not establish that he was disabled because his difficulties occurred only when he was taking medications that were not entirely effective. The court held that the teacher "has not shown that when he is properly medicated for ADD or ADHD he nevertheless is substantially limited in a major life function such as working or learning" (*Hess v. Rochester School District*, 2005, p. 74).

Otherwise Qualified

Once an individual is deemed to be disabled, the employer or higher education institution will examine the impact of that disability and of possible accommodations for the disability on that individual's qualifications for enrollment or employment. This part of the process addresses not whether the individual is disabled but whether the individual is capable of meaningful participation in the academic program or appropriate employment in the position. The focus of the analysis is on the capabilities of the individual instead of his medical conditions. Thus, the statute requires that an individual with a learning disability demonstrate that he is "otherwise qualified." In the workplace, an individual is otherwise qualified if he satisfies the skill, education, experience, and other requirements of an employment position and can perform the essential functions of that position with or without accommodation (Regulations, 1999, 29 C.F.R. §1630.2[m]). In the educational context, an individual is otherwise qualified if he or she is able to meet the program's admission, academic, and technical standards with or without accommodation (Nondiscrimination, 1991, 34 C.F.R. §104.3[1][3]).

Accommodations

If an individual has passed the twin hurdles of demonstrating "disability" and "otherwise qualified," then he or she is entitled to request accommodations either from the institution of higher education where the individual is enrolled as a student or from his or her employer.

Academic Accommodations The legal requirements governing accommodations for students with disabilities at the postsecondary level differ from the special education requirements that pertain to elementary and secondary schools, in that postsecondary schools have much more flexibility in how they structure their accommodations process to ensure nondiscrimination on the basis of disability. Unlike primary and secondary education where the rights of disabled students are governed largely by the IDEA (Individuals with Disabilities Education Act, 2005), legal obligations under federal law toward students with disabilities in postsecondary education fall solely under the ADA or Section 504. That being said, while the accommodations process for students varies somewhat among different postsecondary institutions, the basic framework is the same. Prior to admission, an institution may not ask an applicant if he or she has a disability, except where accommodations might be necessary for the application process itself, such as a sign language interpreter for an admissions interview with a deaf applicant. Applicants are certainly under no obligation to inform the institution that they have a disability—learning or otherwise—although an applicant may choose to do so in order to explain a deficit in grades or standardized test scores. If self-disclosure is made, the university can consider whether the disability merits giving the individual special consideration for admission. However, unless the student's disability clearly shows that he or she is unqualified for admission because he or she cannot meet technical standards of the program, it cannot be used a basis for rejecting the student. After admission, institutions of higher education, including colleges and universities, are not obligated to consider a student to have a disability or to provide accommodations, unless and until a student reveals that he has a disability. Thus, for example, an institution has no obligation to readmit a previously dismissed student who subsequently learns that his problems with his courses were a result of a disability. In *Ferrell v. Howard University* (1999), a medical student who was diagnosed with ADHD only after she had been dismissed from medical school for failure to pass required examinations claimed that the school's failure to readmit her was discriminatory. The court dismissed her claim, holding that

> defendants had no notice of her alleged disability prior to her dismissal, and the defendants cannot now be forced to re-admit plaintiff as a post hoc accommodation for an alleged disability discovered only after she was dismissed pursuant to a school policy based on academic requirements. (*Ferrell v. Howard University*, 1999, p. 6)

The process of revealing a disability, known as "self-identification," must include notice to the university not only of the disability but also of the nature of accommodations the student is requesting. Once self-identification has occurred, most institutions require the student to provide current medical documentation in order to enable the institution to determine the student's eligibility for accommodations and, if the student is eligible, to determine appropriate academic accommodations. For students with learning disabilities, that documentation often takes the form of a report of a neuropsychological evaluation conducted or supervised by a qualified evaluator. The policies of different schools vary significantly regarding the expected qualifications of evaluators, but the clinician at least needs to be trained in an appropriate discipline. For example, policy at our institution requires that an evaluator be

> a physician, licensed clinical psychologist, or one who holds a doctorate in neuropsychology, clinical psychology, educational psychology, or other appropriate specialty. Such evaluators are required to have been 1) trained in psychiatric, psychological, neuropsychological and/or psychoeducational assessment; and 2) have at least three years experience in the evaluation of students with learning disabilities, ADHD/ADD, or psychiatric disabilities. (Boston University, 2004)

The clinician's report needs to clearly identify the diagnosis of the student's condition, establish the basis for that diagnosis, and describe the functional limitations created by the diagnosis. Ideally, the evaluation should include the results—including raw and standard test scores—of widely recognized IQ tests, such as the Wechsler Adult Intelligence Scale, and psychoeducational testing such as the Woodcock-Johnson Psychoeducational Battery. It should also include *DSM* or *ICD* diagnoses (along with their specific code designations), and should recommend specific academic accommodations (Boston University, 2004).

In reviewing the specific accommodation requested by the student or recommended by the evaluator, an institution may find that, while a recommendation is clinically supported, it may not be the most appropriate accommodation given the requirements of a particular student's academic program. Such accommodations may be inconsistent with fundamental requirements of the student's program, or may, in the experience of the institution, simply not be effective in that setting. Students, clinicians, and institutions should bear in mind that the accommodations process is expected to be individualized and collaborative, as both sides work towards effective solutions. Some accommodations may be effective for many students but not for a specific student; unanticipated academic and course requirements may call for unexpected approaches; a student's condition may change; or new technology may become available. Students are always free, and probably should be encouraged, to request other accommodations as their academic situation warrants. In addition, an institution, drawing upon that experience in evaluating and implementing accommodations, may also propose clinically supported accommodations that would be appropriate and useful for the student but which neither the student nor the evaluator has requested.

Accommodations in the Workplace A student with a disability who received accommodations in college or graduate school is certainly under no obligation to inform his employer about his impairment. In fact, the same individual who struggled with mandatory course or degree requirements that were made exceedingly difficult by his disability may be able to choose a profession in which his disability is not an impediment. Often, the need to disclose a learning disability arises only when the employee begins to struggle with some aspect of the job and realizes that, in order to successfully perform his duties, he will need some type of accommodation from his employer. Once the employee discloses a disability and the need for accommodations, the employer is legally required to engage in an interactive process with the employee regarding provision of accommodations. Many, though not all, employers have developed specific forms or protocols for accommodation requests whereby employees are led through a series of questions designed to assist the employer in assessing the validity of the request.

For an employer, the first step in this process is to determine whether the employee has a disability within the meaning of the ADA. In the case of a learning disability, it would not be unusual for the employer to require the employee to provide documentation of his or her disability from a qualified clinician. The employee should anticipate this request and, before beginning the accommodations process, should obtain necessary documentation. The clinician must not only establish that the employee suffers from a particular impairment but should also specifically describe the limitations this impairment poses on the employee's life activities, as well as the accommodations that would help the employee succeed in the workplace. A report that was written to support a request for accommodations in an academic setting will not necessarily be appropriate for workplace accommodations, as these must be determined in reference to the duties of a particular job.

Accommodations that may assist an individual with a learning disability to succeed in the workplace include reducing distractions, providing extra clerical support, providing frequent evaluations, and setting forth clear employment expectations. In deciding what accommodations to request, clinicians must keep in mind that requests that are deemed to be unreasonable are not likely to be granted. For example, in *Robertson v. Neuromedical Center*, the court found that the proposed accommodation of a neurologist with ADHD—working part time, no call duty, hiring additional staff to help him with his administrative work, all without a reduction of pay—were unreasonable as a matter of law (*Robertson v. Neuromedical Center*, 1997, p. 674). The clinician should also be prepared to answer follow-up questions from the employer either about the limitations posed by the employee's impairment or the suggested accommodations. An employee who works with his clinician to carefully document his disability and his requested accommodations will be in a much better position should he be forced to bring legal action against his employer for failure to accommodate (see Brown, 1997, pp. 13–17).

Special Areas of Concern for Individuals With Learning Disabilities

Although the ADA was designed to assist individuals with disabilities to fully participate in education and employment, there are a number of ways in which its framework operates to prevent an individual with a learning disability from obtaining accommodations the individual feels are necessary to his or her academic and vocational success. In the workplace, this difficulty comes in demonstrating that one's learning disability is a "disability" as that term is defined by federal law. In the educational setting, the difficulty is in determining when the accommodations requested or required by a student are inconsistent with fundamental academic requirements, such that a student who can succeed only with those accomodations is not otherwise qualified as required by the ADA.

The Difficulty in Qualifying as Disabled in Order to Receive Workplace Accommodations

During a successful employment relationship with a valued employee, employers may be willing to overlook the question of whether an employee with a learning disability falls under the statutory definition of disabled and simply make the workplace accommodations necessary to help the employee succeed. If the work relationship sours, however, and that same individual brings suit for disability discrimination, employers will make every effort to defend the claim by arguing that the employee did not fall within the statute's protections in the first place. A review of the case law in this area demonstrates that very few employees have successfully secured protection under the ADA when the basis for their disability discrimination claim is a learning disability.

The majority of the court cases under the ADA dealing with learning disabilities and employment discrimination never even make it to a jury because the judge decides, as a matter of law, that the individual bringing the claim does not meet the statutory definition of disability. Typically, the claim is dismissed because the plaintiff fails to show that his or her impairment "substantially limits a major life activity." The major life activities generally relied on by plaintiffs with learning disabilities are "learning" and "working," though employees have also pointed to "reading," "thinking," "speaking," and "concentrating" as major life activities that are limited by their impairment.

Employees who have pointed to "learning" as the major life activity that is substantially limited have had trouble showing that their ability to learn is substantially restricted in comparison to the average person in the general population. Because most individuals who are successfully employed have made it through some level of schooling and have had to learn skills at their job, it is difficult, if not impossible, for them to show that their present learning skills are substantially below average, particularly because courts may take into account the employee's own ability to mitigate the effects of his disability (see *Price v. National Board of Medical Examiners*, 1997, p. 427; *Betts v. Rector and Visitors of University of Virginia*, 2000, p. 977). In *Calef v. Gillette Co.* (1983), for example, the court held that the plaintiff's claim failed because his

> life experience shows no substantial limitation on learning. ... [He] has a high school GED, has taken other courses, and has received on-the-job training where he learned new job skills. His history both before and after Gillette shows no limitation in his learning ability. (*Calef v. Gillette Co.*, 1983, p. 84)

Employees who have pointed to "working" as the major life activity that is substantially limited by their learning disability are generally unable to show that their disability precludes them from a class of jobs or a broad range of jobs in various classes. The Supreme Court has held that if jobs are available that utilize an individual's skills in some capacity, the individual is not precluded from working, even if he cannot perform jobs that utilize his unique talents (*Sutton v. United Airlines*, 1999, p. 492). In other words, the ADA does not entitle an employee to the job of his choice. Therefore, the inability to obtain or retain a particular job is insufficient to demonstrate a substantial impairment in working. In *Whitlock v. Mac-Gray, Inc.* (2003), for instance, the court found that an employee diagnosed with ADHD failed to show a substantial limitation in working, even though he required partitions around him to block visual distractions and a radio to block noise. Because these requirements did not preclude him from performing a broad class of jobs, he was not disabled under ADA.

A review of the cases makes clear that if an individual has successfully held other jobs, either before or after the job that forms the basis of the discrimination claim, the court will find that he or she is not substantially limited in the major life activity of working. This is so, even if other employers voluntarily offered accommodations that allowed the individual to succeed in the workplace. In *Barker v. Martin Marietta Materials, Inc.* (2001), a quality control engineer argued that his "inability to multi-process" resulted in substantial limitations to the major life activity of working. The court rejected this claim, finding that "the fact that the jobs [he] is qualified for require less multi-processing or are not as difficult or demanding as his job at Martin Marietta does not make [him] disabled" when there were still a wide range of jobs open to him (*Barker v. Martin Marietta Materials, Inc.*, 2001, p. 1254).

In a few cases, claimants have been able to establish that their learning disability constituted an ADA-defined disability or that there was at least sufficient evidence to allow the claim to go forward for decision by a jury. Sometimes employees can meet the disability requirement by showing that their supervisors viewed them as unable to work due to their mental impairments and thus "regarded them" as disabled. In *Mattice v. Memorial Hospital of South Bend, Inc.* (2001), for instance, an anesthesiologist was allowed to go forward with his claims because he showed that the hospital where he worked "regarded him as having a substantial impairment in the major life activity of cognitive thinking" (p. 684). In addition, individuals with dyslexia may be better able to show that they are substantially impaired than those with ADHD. In a few cases, for example, plaintiffs with dyslexia were able to proceed to trial because they were able to produce evidence that their impairments substantially limited the major life activities of seeing, learning, and reading as compared to an average person in the general population (*Merry v. A. Sulka & Co.*, 1997, p. 926; *Vinson v. Thomas*, 2002, p. 1153). In *Merry v. A. Sulka & Co.* (1997), for example, a salesperson in a luxury men's apparel store disclosed his dyslexia to the store manager when he was interviewing for the job and at several points during his employment. He also made requests for specific accommodations, such as a credit card imprinter. The court found that his learning disability presented sufficient limitations to his numerical, reading, and writing skills to allow him to go forward to trial (Merry, 1997, p. 922).

Employees who have gotten over the hurdle of showing disability may still find their cases dismissed by the court if they fail to show that they are "otherwise qualified." This happens when an employee fails to meet legitimate performance or behavioral expectations on the job. Even if the failure is clearly due to the disability, courts have held that, unless the employee's deficiencies are due to the employer's failure to provide reasonable accommodations, employees with disabilities may be held to the same workplace standard as all others in the workplace. The law is also clear that an employer is under no obligation to grant an accommodation that would negate an essential job function. In *Hess v. Rochester School District* (2005), for instance, the court held that an employer is under no obligation to relieve a teacher with ADD from supervising disruptive students or shield that teacher from disruptions in the classroom. Further, if the teacher's ADD causes him to react inappropriately to such disruptions, he may be disciplined or terminated. Because supervision of disruptive children is an essential job function that cannot be eliminated as an accommodation, a teacher who cannot perform that supervision is not "otherwise qualified" and is therefore not entitled to protection under the ADA (Hess, 2005, pp. 76–77).

In the workplace, the concept of "otherwise qualified" is determined by looking at essential functions of a particular job, which are often either clearly set forth in a job description or understood by an employer. In the education context, however, deciding whether a disabled individual is "otherwise qualified" is often a more complex undertaking.

The Interaction of "Otherwise Qualified" and "Accommodations" in Higher Education

The ADA or Section 504 only provide legal protection for a student with a learning disability who is otherwise able to meet the admissions, academic, and technical standards of a particular program. In other words, the student must be "otherwise qualified," despite the learning disability. The question of whether a student with a learning disability is otherwise qualified necessarily requires a determination of what can reasonably be required of a student to successfully complete a particular course of study and whether certain requested accommodations are inconsistent with those requirements. Each such determination occurs against the backdrop of a perception held by many in our society that the dramatic increase in the number of students with disabilities in public schools and higher education is a result of policies that inappropriately raise the expectations of unqualified students, the hijacking of education programs by affluent parents, or even a genetic decline of the population (see Shalit, 1997; Henderson, 2001; Kelman & Lester, 1997).

The American Council on Education (Henderson, 2001) reported that approximately 1 in 11 college freshmen self-identified as having a disability, triple the number who did so in 1978, resulting in a dramatic increase in the number of students with disabilities seeking and gaining admission and requiring accommodations. Given these perceptions, colleges have become sensitive to the need to show that granting accommodations to students with learning disabilities does not compromise the rigor and integrity of their programs. This concern focuses not only on academic standards and degree obligations, often known as "fundamental requirements," but also encompasses the prevention of academic misconduct, fairness to other students, methodologies of instruction, and necessary vehicles for measuring student learning.

The federal regulations state that educational institutions "shall make such modifications to [their] academic requirements as are necessary to ensure that such requirements do not discriminate" (Nondiscrimination, 1991, 34 C.F.R. §104.44[a]). Although modification of academic policies and procedures is mandated, there are limits to that obligation. Where the institution can demonstrate that the requirement is "essential to the instruction being pursued by such student or to any directly related licensing requirement," modification is not required. In *Southeastern Community College v. Davis* (1979), the Supreme Court was asked to consider whether Section 504 required a college to make changes to its nursing program for a student with a hearing loss. The college, in denying admission to the student, claimed "[the] modifications that would be necessary to enable safe participation would prevent her from realizing the benefits of the program" (*Southeastern Community College v. Davis*, 1979, pp. 401–402). Justice Powell, writing for the majority, concluded that Section 504 "does not compel educational institutions to disregard the disabilities of handicapped individuals or to make substantial modifications in their programs to allow disabled persons to participate" (p. 405). Although the student argued that the college was obligated to provide individual supervision or an exemption from clinical course work to ensure that she could participate, the Court found that "such a fundamental alteration in the nature of a program is far more than the 'modification' regulation requires" (p. 410). Justice Powell noted that the student "could not participate in Southeastern's nursing program unless the standards were substantially lowered [and that the statute] imposes no requirement upon an education institution to lower or effect substantial modifications to accommodate a handicapped person" (p. 413).

Simply put, the institution may determine that certain academic requirements are fundamental and refuse to modify or substitute. The courts, however, will usually impose requirements on that decision-making process. In *Wynne v. Tufts University School of Medicine*, a student challenged as discriminatory the medical school's failure to offer an alternative to multiple-choice examinations (*Wynne v. Tufts University School of Medicine*, 1991 [hereinafter *Wynne I*]; *Wynne v. Tufts University School of Medicine*, 1992 [hereinafter *Wynne II*]). The First Circuit Court of Appeals noted that while deference needed to be given to the institution's decision makers, "there is a real obligation on the academic institution to seek suitable means of reasonably accommodating a handicapped person" (*Wynne I*, 1991, p. 25).

But if the institution comes "to a rationally justifiable conclusion that the available alternatives would result either in lowering academic standards or requiring substantial program alteration ... [it has] met its duty of seeking reasonable accommodation" (p. 26). Finding that the decision was "a reasoned, professional academic judgment," the court concluded that Tufts had successfully "demythologized the institutional thought processes leading to its determination that it could not deviate from its wonted format to accommodate Wynne's professed disability" (*Wynne I*, 1991, p. 27; *Wynne II*, 1992, p. 795).

A substantive academic requirement can be deemed to be fundamental utilizing the same deliberative process. Thus, colleges and universities have sometimes denied a request to waive or substantially modify foreign language, writing, or clinical requirements on the basis that these requirements are fundamental. In the *Davis* case, described above, the student sought an exemption from clinical course work. In *Guckenberger v. Boston University* (1997), a group of students challenged, among other things, the university's refusal to waive or permit substitution of its foreign language requirement. The Federal District Court began by noting that the degree requirements at issue went to the heart of academic freedom, to the university's prerogative to determine "what may be taught [and] how it shall be taught" (*Guckengerger v. Boston University*, 1997, p. 148). In the court's view, so long as the institution, following *Wynne*, "undertake[s] a diligent assessment of the available options, and makes a professional, academic judgment that reasonable accommodation is simply not available," a university can refuse to modify academic degree requirements, including requirements that students with learning disabilities cannot satisfy (*Guckenberger v. Boston University*, 1997, p. 149). Federal law does not "require a university to provide course substitutions that the university rationally concludes would alter an essential part of its academic program" (*Guckenberger v. Boston University*, 1997, p. 149). The court ordered the university to undertake a "deliberative process" to consider whether the foreign language requirement was fundamental to the degree program. On completion of that process, the court ruled that the university had complied with its order and that the requirement was fundamental and could not, therefore, be substituted for or waived (*Guckenberger v. Boston University*, 1998). Once a requirement is found to be fundamental to a degree program, a student who, because of a learning disability, is unable to meet such requirements with available accommodations is not otherwise qualified.

Reasonable accommodation is a dynamic concept. Rather than creating a regulatory "laundry list" of changes, services, or devices, the statute requires an individualized and collaborative determination of what students would need to ensure their full participation in, and enable them to meet the requirements of, their academic program. So, for example, an institution may be asked to modify existing requirements, policies, and procedures that have the effect of excluding students with disabilities. These might include substantive but nonfundamental academic components such as a particular course, procedural rules such as the length of time permitted for the completion of degree requirements, and classroom regulations such as use of a tape recorder or the presence of animals (for students using guide dogs). Likewise, adjustment of testing methods or conditions might be called for, as the regulations require use of testing methods that "will best ensure that the results of the evaluation represents the student's achievement in the course, rather than reflecting the student's impaired sensory, manual, or speaking skills (except where such skills are the factors that the test purports to measure)" (Nondiscrimination, 1991, 34 C.F.R. §104.44[c]). Auxiliary aids such as sign language interpreting, a reader or scribe for examinations, a laboratory assistant, or equipment including magnification devices, adaptive computer technology, or even a special desk are required if necessary "to ensure that no handicapped student is denied the benefits of, excluded from participation in, or otherwise subjected to discrimination because of the absence of educational auxiliary aids" (Nondiscrimination, 1991, 34 C.F.R. §104.44[d][1]).

Academic accommodations that do not modify degree requirements rarely implicate the institutions' fundamental requirements, but they clearly can. The most common academic accommodations are extended time on examinations, use of a note taker in class, use of a computer sometimes with spell checker, and for many students with learning and attention disabilities, a distraction-reduced environment. These accommodations require the institution to undertake the same analysis as for modification. For example, extended time for in-class examinations is intended to remedy a variety of functional limitations such as information processing or physical difficulty in writing. But in certain medically related science courses such as gross anatomy, for example, students have *clinical* examinations where they might be asked to make a visual identification of a series of tissue samples. Those skills do not require extended time to test, and application of such an accommodation would clearly conflict with fundamental academic requirements. Similarly, a student in a CPR class might be entitled to extended time on the written portion of the examination, but obviously would not be entitled to the accommodation for the demonstration of CPR skills. Time is clearly at issue. Finally, teacher-training programs at higher education institutions might refuse to permit use of spell checker or calculator in teacher-training courses where teachers would be expected to be able to spell or do math.

All these examples presuppose and require a deliberate inquiry on the part of the institution as to whether a particular accommodation is consistent with fundamental requirements or, stated otherwise, whether a student who can meet academic requirements only with that particular accommodation is "otherwise qualified." The subtlety of the interaction between the question of what can be required of a student to be "otherwise qualified" and the accommodation obligations of the institution can be clearly seen in the regulatory limitation upon auxiliary aids, which notes that "[institutions] need not provide attendants, individually prescribed devices, readers for personal use or study, or other devices or services of a personal nature" (Nondiscrimination, 1991, 34 C.F.R. §104.44 [d][2]). Such items are certainly necessary and many students could not participate without such services or devices, but providing them is not the institution's obligation because they are not directly related to participation in the program.

Conclusion

In order to assist their patients in obtaining recognition and reasonable accommodations, clinicians need to understand the disability determination process and the accommodations process under the ADA and Section 504. Because it is useful for clinicians to understand the limits of an entity's duty to provide reasonable accommodations, even where such accommodations may be clinically supported, we also discussed in some detail the problem of demonstrating "disability" in the workplace, fundamental academic requirements, and the concept of "otherwise qualified." By introducing clinicians to the individualized and collaborative process of determining eligibility and providing accommodations, we hope to enable them to better educate employers and institutions of higher education about particular learning disabilities, their functional implications, and possible accommodation solutions. Employers and institutions of higher education, in turn, can assist clinicians as well as individuals with disabilities in formulating accommodation requests that fulfill their functional needs as well as the job or academic requirements. Our hope is that by providing a common base of knowledge about the process and its difficulties, clinicians, patients, and the employers and institutions that provide accommodations will be better positioned to ensure that adults with learning disabilities have an equal opportunity to succeed.

Author Note

Thanks to Lorre Wolf for her input, and for including us. For research assistance, thanks to Boston University School of Law students Melissa Kubit, Elizabeth Gaskell, and Sean Gavin.

References

Americans With Disabilities Act of 1990, 42 U.S.C.A. §12101–213.

Barker v. Martin Marietta Materials, Inc., 130 F. Supp. 2d 1249 (D. Kansas 2001).

Bartlett v. New York State Board of Law Examiners, No. 93 Civ. 4986(22) 2001 WL 930792 (S.D.N.Y. 2001).

Betts v. Rector and Visitors of University of Virginia, 113 F. Supp. 2d 970 (W.D.Va. 2000).

Boston University Office of Disability Services. (2004). Evaluators of students with learning and attentional disabilities. Retrieved September 30, 2007, from http://www.bu.edu/disability/policies/eval-learning.html

Brown, D. S. (1997, Fall). Tips for self-advocacy in the workplace. *Linkages*, 13–17. Retrieved September 30, 2007, from www.ldonline.org/ article/6011

Calef v. Gillette Co., 322 F.3d 75 (1st Cir. 1983).

Ferrell v. Howard University, No. Civ.A. 98–1009, 1999 WL 1581759 (D.D.C. 1999).

Guckenberger v. Boston University, 8 F. Supp. 2d 82 (1998).

Guckenberger v. Boston University, 974 F. Supp. 106 (1997).

Henderson, C. (2001). *College freshmen with disabilities: A biennial statistical profile*. Washington, DC: American Council on Education.

Hess v. Rochester School District, 396 F. Supp. 2d 65 (D.N.H. 2005).

Individuals with Disabilities Education Act, 20 U.S.C.A. §1400 et seq. (2005).

Kelman, M., & Lester, G. (1997). *Jumping the queue: An inquiry into the legal treatment of students with learning disabilities*. Cambridge, MA: Harvard University Press.

Levy, T. I. (2001). Legal obligations and workplace implications for institutions of higher education accommodating learning disabled students. *Journal of Law and Education*, 85, 117.

Mattice v. Memorial Hospital of South Bend, Inc., 249 F.3d 682 (7th Cir. 2001).

Merry v. A. Sulka & Co., 953 F. Supp. 922 (N.D. Ill. 1997).

Nondiscrimination on the basis of handicap in programs or activities receiving federal financial assistance, 34 C.F.R. 104 et. seq. (1991).

Price v. National Board of Medical Examiners, 966 F. Supp. 419 (S.D.W.Va. 1997).

Regulations to implement the equal employment provisions of the Americans with Disabilities Act, 29 C.F.R. 1630.2 (1999).

Robertson v. Neuromedical Center, 983 F. Supp. 669 (M.D. La. 1997).

Section 504 of the Rehabilitation Act of 1973, 29 U.S.C. §701–96(i) (2001).

Shalit, R. (1997). Defining disability down: Why Johnny can't read, write, or sit still. *The New Republic*, 217(8), 16–22.

Singh v. George Washington University School of Medicine and Health Sciences, No. 13–1681, 2006 WL 1897220 (D.D.C. 2006).

Southeastern Community College v. Davis, 442 U.S. 397 (1979).

Steere v. George Washington University School of Medicine and Health Sciences, No. 03–1900, 2006 WL 1897223 (D.D.C. 2006).

Sutton v. United Airlines, 527 U.S. 471 (1999).

Toyota Motor Manufacturing, Inc. v. Williams, 534 U.S. 184 (2002).

Vinson v. Thomas, 288 F.3d 1145 (9th Cir. 2002).

Whitlock v. MacGray, Inc., 345 F.3d 44 (1st Cir. 2003).

Wong v. University of California, 410 F.3d 1052 (9th Cir. 2005).

Wynne v. Tufts University School of Medicine [Wynne I], 932 F.2d 19 (1st Cir. 1991).

Wynne v. Tufts University School of Medicine [Wynne II], 976 F.2d 791 (1st Cir. 1992).

CHAPTER 17

The Professional Student With a Learning Disorder
Focus on Medicine and Law

CHERYL WEINSTEIN, LORRAINE E. WOLF, and
HOPE SCHREIBER

Contents

Students with learning disabilities are advancing through college in increasing numbers and with remarkable success (Perreira & Richards, 2000). Educators and administrators now understand that learning disorders are not outgrown in childhood (Hechtman, 1996) and that high school students with learning disabilities (LD) go to college (Wolf, 2001). A result of this awareness, increased academic support is now available at the undergraduate level. As one would predict, successful college students with LD are pursuing advanced and professional degrees. This is evidenced by an increase in requests for accommodations for professional school entrance examinations such as the Medical College Aptitude Test (MCAT) (see Rosebrough, 2003), Graduate Record Examination, Graduate Management Aptitude Test, and Law School Admissions Test (GRE, GMAT, and LSAT) (see Burgoyne & Mew, 2001). Recent lawsuits brought by students with learning disabilities have focused attention on professional certification exams, as well as calling attention to a number of issues faced by successful students with LD seeking to practice law (Eichorn, 1997; Duhl & Duhl, 2004) and medicine (see Burgoyne & Mew, 2001, for more case details).

The appearance of students with disabilities into these venues raises concerns in some quarters, mostly centered around who is disabled, to what standard should they be compared, what sorts of accommodations would be reasonable, and the less commonly voiced concern about whether these students are competent to function as major professionals. The medical community, with its special responsibility for patient safety, has been active in raising this concern in press (e.g., Hafferty & Gibson, 2001, 2003; Julien, Ingersoll, Etienne, & Hilger, 2004; Scotti, 1997). Recent lawsuits against the Law School Admissions Counsel, which administers the LSAT and the New York State Bar (*Bartlett v. the New York State Board of Bar Examiners*, 1998; see also Eichorn, 1997) attest to the importance of this debate in legal communities as well. A detailed discussion of this debate, while fascinating, is beyond the scope of this chapter. The interested reader is further directed to Macurdy and Geetter (this volume, Chapter 16), Keiser and Gordon (2000), and Ranseen and Parks (2005).

Many factors contribute to success for the student with LD in a professional program. As a student decides to pursue advanced training, he or she optimally moves into an area that provides a good fit in terms of individual cognitive strengths and interests (Gerber, Ginsberg, & Reiff, 1992). While "goodness of fit" is important for all students to sustain the enormous effort and sacrifice required to complete professional training, it is particularly crucial for the student who also has to overcome limitations imposed by a disability. It is not difficult to speculate that law school, with its very high demand on critical reading, research writing, and verbal argument, might pose a challenge for a student with a language-based learning disability, slow reading, and/or effortful writing. This student could expect to spend an inordinate amount of time digesting case books or writing briefs. Should this student secure accommodations, complete law school, and pass the bar examination, the volume of work required in a law firm with billable hours might compromise earning potential. Similarly, the business student whose disability compromises visual scanning (think accounting, statistics, and spreadsheets) or the medical student with very slow information processing (think rapid clinical formulation) must realistically confront the match between the fundamental competencies and demands of their chosen field and their natural strengths and weaknesses.

Students with disabilities who do well in professional schools thus need to feel comfortable with themselves and with their disability and also must be prepared to make personal sacrifices. This may mean working longer hours and limiting social and recreational activities as they work overtime to circumvent neurodevelopmental learning problems. It may mean delaying paid employment, marriage, or child rearing by progressing through training at slower rate. Certain critical behaviors, including high energy and stamina, a resilient personality style, a strong social network, solid problem-solving skills (Perreira & Richards, 2000), and excellent executive skills (Wolf, 2001; also see Wolf & Kaplan, this volume) contribute to good *academic* performance. However, less is known about the critical factors underlying good employment outcome.

This chapter explores some of the ways in which the neuropsychologist and the neuropsychological assessment can inform choices and decisions about pursuing a graduate or professional career for the student with LD. We have chosen medicine and law as our focus, due to the often lively, sometimes contentious, debate within those communities about this issue, as well our combined experience with a great number of prospective lawyers and doctors with LD. We present several illustrative case examples of students who met with varying degrees of success in pursuit of their career goals. Neuropsychological and historical data are presented in a somewhat informal manner, as our aim is to illustrate how qualitative factors are as important as numbers in the formulation of these cases. We use this case material to illustrate how assessment data informs goodness of fit and eventual outcome. Finally, we suggest future areas of research that will enhance our understanding of these issues.

What Can Assessment Offer the LD Professional Student?

A comprehensive and current neuropsychological assessment can play an undeniably important role in a student's ability to access accommodations and services within his or her program, from extended time on entrance exams to use of adaptive technology for note taking on rounds. Overall, accommodations are intended to level the playing field so that the student may demonstrate what he or she knows (Shaywitz, 2003). The interested reader is referred to Mapou (this volume, Chapter 10) for more information about the structure of the assessment; to Gregg, Coleman, & Hartwig (this volume, Chapter 12) for more information on the accommodation process; and to Macurdy and Geetter (this volume, Chapter 16) for a discussion of the legal issues at stake.

Most neuropsychologists understand the role of assessment in securing services; however, an equally valuable (though less well-articulated) role of assessment is to assist students in planning their graduate or professional careers and to evaluate the reality of their choices in light of their cognitive functioning. In helping students and their families to appreciate their unique neurocognitive profile, the neuropsychologist can facilitate realistic decision making. Specifically, a comprehensive evaluation delineates neurocognitive strengths and weaknesses, addresses the meaning of learning abilities, and gauges the impact of weaknesses on an individual's life and future plans. The neuropsychologist may provide guidance by supplying information and insights regarding the match between cognitive functions and professional demands or by highlighting potential barriers that the student may encounter should he or she pursue a particular path. Understanding this process may enhance later decision making for students as they approach vocational and other life goals.

Gaining a solid understanding of the disability will also be critical for students in accessing accommodations and securing services (Wolf, 2001) in order to make the most of their abilities and efficiently circumvent their cognitive deficits (Sohlberg & Mateer, 2001). Moreover, while academic supports may have been available at the undergraduate level, a high degree of support is unlikely at the professional school level (Ganschow, Coyne, Parks, & Antonoff, 1999). Consequently, the possibility of success is enhanced when the student possesses considerable skill and knowledge, including excellent interpersonal and negotiation skills, a solid understanding of

Table 17.1 Attention Strategies for Individuals With LD and Attention-Deficit/Hyperactivity (ADHD)

Talk to yourself to focus attention.
Write down essential information.
Ask for repetition of instructions.
Ask speakers to present information more slowly.
Break down tasks into small, simple steps.
Learn to identify and avoid overload.
Take rest periods.
Work on detailed tasks when maximally alert.
Avoid lengthy monotonous tasks.
Work in a quiet space.
Try to do one thing at a time.
Practice learning to divide attention.

Table 17.2 Memory Strategies

Establish clear expectations in advance about what is to be learned.
Outline the sequence of a task.
Organize/categorize/chunk information.
Increase attention to material that is to be learned.
Repeat instructions to make certain messages are understood.
Rehearse material to be learned.
Establish a routine doing the same task in the same order and on the same schedule.
Develop cues to aid recall.
Use a memory notebook.

how accommodations work, and a broad set of effective recommendations based on comprehensive neuropsychological testing.

The informed neuropsychologist assists students in being realistic, whether it is about their chances of academic success, their chances of being approved for accommodations, or their present and future vocational comfort level in light of their unique profiles. In addition to knowledge of their own cognitive strengths, professional students benefit from learning adaptive strategies (Tables 17.1 and 17.2) that facilitate their negotiation of the complexities of professional training (Weinstein, 1994). Thus, those students who are well aware of their cognitive strengths and weaknesses, and who accept them, appear to have the greatest chance of making positive and adaptive career decisions.

The Law Student With LD

Law School Curricular Challenges

Law school is a logical choice for students with superior verbal abilities. Prospective law students must also have solid reading skills, good public speaking ability, strong writing skills, interpersonal and negotiation skills, and excellent verbal reasoning ability. Gaining admission to law school is perhaps a more strenuous endeavor for some students than the curriculum itself. After completing law school, the job market is highly competitive as well. Yet more and more students with LD choose to enter this fray.

Many learning-disordered students struggle with the demands of the heavy reading load, which can be particularly daunting for individuals with word retrieval difficulties. This becomes most apparent when called upon in class in the Socratic method typical of law school or when in court clinics or moot court. In addition, the law student with deficits in executive skills may do well within the structure of law school yet struggle in the practice of law, where time management and organization become critical. Deficits may become unmasked once the learning-disabled law student passes his or her state bar examination and enters the professional arena.

Access to law school for a student with LD may well begin with securing and utilizing accommodations in college so that his or her grade point average may be competitive. The next hurdle may be the law school entrance exam. Requests for accommodations on the LSAT increased 100% between 1990 and 1993 (Law School Admissions Council, data cited in Mosier, n.d.). Once in law school, many students find that schools will provide accommodations to qualified students with disabilities. However, not all LD students will meet the increasingly rigorous standards for determining who is eligible to receive disability accommodations (Ranseen & Parks, 2005). Even if approved, many will find the accommodations to be more limited than what they enjoyed as undergraduates. Finally, many requirements of law school (such as mandatory class attendance and examination in the Socratic method) are fundamental to the mission of training lawyers, and as such are not subject to accommodation. Given the difficulties and uncertainties in navigating the system, the prospective student must assess whether law school is a realistic goal. The following case illustrates how neuropsychological assessments assisted one young student make the decision and persevere to good outcome.

Case 1

This case study demonstrates how the fit between a student's cognitive strengths and career choice is critical to the student's comfort and success. We discuss a law student who recognized his own cognitive strengths and pursued a career path that highlighted his verbal skills rather than one that taxed his nonverbal liabilities.

Background and History   FB was seen as a senior in college. He reportedly was a shy child, and his teachers noted that he had trouble finishing work within the allotted time. Early report cards indicated that he was a good reader with verbal strengths. He was, however, diagnosed with a mathematic learning disorder and attention-deficit disorder (ADD) in primary grades. Because inattentive symptoms occurred primarily in reading group and because family history was positive for reading disability, the family had always wondered whether he might have a primary reading disorder rather than ADD.

Reading tutoring was provided for FB in grade school, with resulting improvement in grades. With increased academic support, the attention symptoms noted on reading tasks abated, although FB's reading rate remained slow and vulnerabilities in mathematics persisted. His Preliminary SAT (PSAT) verbal score was at the 47th percentile and mathematics performance was at the 28th percentile.*

On the SAT, FB scored in the 74th percentile in the verbal area and the 59th percentile in mathematics. He entered college with a government major, determined at all costs to avoid mathematics courses. At the same time, he was "always the last person to finish examinations" and accepted that he read slowly. Assessment in his freshman year of college indicated that "he had a pattern of weaker perceptual motor skills and relatively stronger language abilities." This led to accommodations through his college learning-disability service.

Neuropsychological Testing Highlights   When FB was preparing to go to law school (a presumably good choice given his verbal strengths), he self-referred for an extensive neuropsychological evaluation. The results indicated that verbal and visual reasoning skills were both well above average; however, there was a significant split in his IQ scores (Verbal IQ [VIQ] 95th percentile, Performance IQ [PIQ] 34th percentile). Very significant problems were seen in dealing with visual details, with three instances of broken configurations on the Block Design subtest of the Wechsler Adult Intelligence Scale (3rd ed.) (WAIS-III). The copy trial of the Rey-Osterrieth Complex Figure (ROCF) revealed visual-spatial planning and organization problems. His recall was significantly flawed and he again broke configuration of the design. Even when he was taught to copy the ROCF in specific steps to

---

* The PSAT provides valuable insight regarding a student's performance on timed tests. Students are less likely to attend special courses preparing them for this examination. Thus it may provide a more accurate indication of performance under timed conditions.

teach organized encoding of the design (Waber & Isquith, 1996), his performance did not improve. FB was also prone to sequencing errors, and when he had to arrange pictures into a logical sequence he spoiled three picture arrangements with one sequencing error. It was hypothesized that visual sequencing difficulties contributed, in part, to poorly developed mathematical abilities. In addition, his slower visual processing led to slower reading under timed conditions (Nelson-Denny Reading Test time conditions 17th percentile rank [PR]; extended time 46th PR).

Formulation and Outcome FB's slow and effortful reading and his visual-spatial deficits resulted in diagnoses of a reading disorder and learning disorder not otherwise specified (NOS). Reading disorders secondary to visual processing deficits are less commonly seen than those that are linguistically driven (Drummond, Ahmad, & Rourke, 2005; also see Sherman, this volume, Chapter 1). This may have contributed to the confusion regarding FB's earlier diagnoses. FB was commended for focusing on his relatively stronger verbal conceptualization abilities throughout his education. Recommendations were made to help him to achieve in law school, including extended time for exams with significant reading demand and access to books on tape. He mastered outlining skills so that he could write in an efficient, well-organized manner. He worked on developing oral presentations so that he could highlight his verbal abilities, and he had advanced access to course syllabi so that he could begin prereading assignments during semester breaks. FB graduated from law school with success. He was granted extended time accommodations on the bar exam, and he currently works as an entertainment attorney (an excellent choice given his profile of strengths and weaknesses).

Students With LD and Medical School

The lawyer above sought an updated evaluation in preparation for his legal studies, and used the information to guide his career choice. However, other students with learning disorders may successfully work around difficulties in college and only encounter difficulties after they have entered graduate school. We see this commonly in medical students. Indeed, a survey by the Association of American Medical Colleges (AAMC) in 1994 found that medical students typically seek assessment (self-referral or by their program) following failure after their first year (Hafferty & Gibson, 2003). Notably, the number of medical students with learning disorders is increasing (Guyer & Guyer, 2000). A 1994 survey of 126 U.S. medical schools found that the frequency of medical students with LD had more than doubled over a 5-year period between 1988 and 1994, such that it is now estimated that 3% of U.S. medical students are learning disabled (Rosebrough, 2000).

Medical School Curricular Challenges

Important questions emerge regarding medical students with learning disorders, including ethical and professional issues. One key question is whether learning disabled students belong in medical school. A discussion of this sensitive issue is beyond the scope of this chapter; however, interested readers should see Hafferty and Gibson (2003) and Guyer (2000) for both sides of this debate. A second question is whether medical students with LD are frankly disabled or whether they reflect a group of average students asking for accommodations to keep up with an increasingly demanding work load. Again, interested readers should see Julien et al. (2004) for more detail. We address a third question, namely whether learning disorders are becoming more apparent in medical school because the processing demands of medical school are greater than the student's learning capacity and, relatedly, whether learning problems differ as the student progresses through medical school. The answers to these questions are as difficult as medical education is complex.

Medical education is a biphasic process. The first phase is academic and curricular, while the later phase includes clinical training and professional development as physicians-in-training learn to synthesize and integrate large amounts of information rapidly. Studies have shown that medical students with LD are typically strong in simultaneous learning (hands-on, concrete, direct) and weaker in sequential learning (learning random lists, lectures, imposing structure). Slow reading, poor spelling, and poor written language are also common (Accardo, Haake, & Whitman, 1989).

The first 2 years include the expansion of the students' vocabulary as they are inundated with a new lexicon of polysyllabic words that must often be memorized out of context. Under such conditions, students who had difficulty with automatic decoding (reading fluency) as they first learned to read, write, and spell can expect a recurrence of such difficulties. There are multiple cumulative exams, often in a complicated multiple-choice format unique to clinical examinations. Compared to nondisabled peers, the academic load may seem denser, the hours longer, and the time constraints even greater when academic fluency and reading are not automatic. Students may now be required to register for 20 credit hours per semester plus clinics, whereas they may have been used to reduced course loads as undergraduates to compensate for cognitive deficits (Guyer & Guyer, 2000).

In the third and fourth years of school, students move from the academic phase of medical education to the professional phase of their training. Clinical rotations and clerkships become central. In this setting, the student with reading disorders or other language-based deficits may perform better because application of medical knowledge and social skills are now stressed, and interaction with others can help the learning process. In contrast, a nonverbal LD student or an individual with ADHD may have more difficulties as report writing, time management, sequencing, organization, and prioritization functions are stressed. The extensive use of online medical records may also tax individuals with visual processing disorders. Further, as the nature of the curriculum changes, accommodations may need to shift to reflect both clinical demands as well as preparation for future licensing examinations. Common characteristics of medical students with LD have been summarized in Table 17.3 (adapted from Brinckerhoff, 1996). Despite the difficulties they face, many professionals advocate for physicians with high intellect and specific learning disabilities, arguing that such students have much to offer the medical profession (Shaywitz, 1998).

Case 2

The residua of phonological deficits during childhood may make reading slower, more effortful, and automatic even for the brightest LD young adult (Shaywitz, 1998). Case 2 illustrates the impact of slow reading on medical school performance.

Background and History   LK self-referred for evaluation in his first year of medical school to assess whether his long-standing reading problems would interfere with his medical school performance. Reading was first evaluated when he was in the second grade and he received tutoring in the public school system. While his intellect was above average, very mild problems were seen in auditory attention word span. The school system did not find that he was learning disabled, but concluded that his difficulties were best explained by emotional immaturity. It was hoped that his performance would improve with emotional support. His parents were, however, concerned about the quality of public school evaluations and sought private tutoring in grades 4 through 12. In addition, his parents helped with writing and proofing skills.*

---

* It is not uncommon for parents to elect to not have their child receive academic support in school. They do not want their child to be placed in the special education system or placed in a noncollege preparatory track. This leads them to tutor their child when academic difficulties emerge. While parental involvement in a child's education is an important strategy, there are potential problems later in the student's academic career. Specifically, when dealing with advanced professional licensure boards, there is no "paper trail" of diagnostic reports and special academic support beginning in the early grades. This may lead the professional boards to conclude that the student's current difficulties are due to lower aptitude or overachievement.

Table 17.3 Characteristics of Medical Students With Learning Disabilities

Cognitive and Academic Areas

    IQ scores above average to gifted range

    MCAT scores are good in science; reading skills low

    Verbal skills are very high; relates well to others in clinical settings

    Reading comprehension is poor

    Spelling is consistently inconsistent

    Handwriting is illegible

Affective Domains

    Highly anxious about disclosure; fear of exposure as a "marginal student"

    Loss of self-confidence; feeling of shame and humiliation

    Seldom asks for help; doesn't want to appear "stupid"

    Often feels isolated not realizing that other classmates may also be struggling

    Depression

Nature of Learning Disability

    History of difficulty with standardized tests

    LD becomes more of a problem as the demands of medical curriculum increase

    Performance drops under time pressure, time management

    Loss of control; techniques which used to work are no longer effective

    Attention deficit disorder is often present

Source: Brinckerhoff, 1966. (Reprinted with permission.)

LK ultimately graduated high school with honors without school-system support or accommodation. As he graduated in the top 10% of a demanding high school, his poor SAT performance (Verbal 550, Mathematics 620, and English Achievement 490) was a surprise. LK entered an Ivy League college, but he quickly experienced academic difficulties. He subsequently underwent an educational evaluation that resulted in a diagnosis of a "language-based learning disability involving a weak auditory short-term memory." He was provided extended time on all examinations as well as extended time for the MCAT.

Neuropsychological Testing Highlights   LK did not contact the disability office for accommodations when he first entered medical school, as he thought that he could manage the work load without being identified as having a learning disability. There was also concern that such a label might negatively influence his chances for a good residency training program. It became apparent, however, that extended time was needed for examinations.

Prior to approving accommodations, the medical school requested that he submit the results of a more comprehensive and updated assessment of his learning disorder.

The results of the testing indicated that superior verbal functions (VIQ 94th PR) and visual-spatial functions at the upper end of the average range (PIQ 73rd PR). Notably, the processing speed index was markedly reduced (18th PR). Deficits consistent with the problems identified in second grade were found, including poor attention span (25th PR), poor initial intake of information on the California Verbal Learning Test, low auditory span (WAIS Digit Span 25th PR), poor phonological analysis (Woodcock-Johnson Reading Battery Incomplete Words 19th PR), and poor reading comprehension (further complicated by somewhat slow reading rate; Nelson-Denny Reading Test Timed Comprehension Conditions 28th PR).

Formulation and Outcome   LK was diagnosed with both a language-based learning disorder and reading disorder due to deficits in speed of information processing, auditory processing, and reading. He presented this information to his medical school, was granted academic accommodations, and did very well. However, when he applied for extended time for the medical licensing exam, he was denied accommodations because his record of continued disability and academic need were inconsistent through high school. It was suggested that he was an overachiever rather than a student with a disability. Fortunately, LK's parents had maintained records of the extensive outside support that they had provided for their son. Based on this, LK challenged this decision and was ultimately granted the accommodation of extended time. He entered a strong residency training program and has continued to perform successfully. Notably, the program he entered was not particularly fast paced, permitting him the time needed to complete his required reading.

Some medical students with LD have historically managed their academic requirements and struggled silently. Their learning issues may have been attributed to emotional or environmental problems, and the significance of their difficulties are undiagnosed. Increased challenges, however, confront them when beginning advanced training, and personal sacrifices become more significant. When faced with steeply increasing academic demands, professional responsibility, stress, and possibly sleep deprivation, students may find that previously manageable problems have become more problematic. While patient LK received accommodations in medical school and for the medical boards, accommodations are less likely in an individual with a newly diagnosed learning disorder.

Case 3

In the case of LK, the meticulous records of his prior services eventually convinced the medical licensing board that he was in fact disabled for purposes of accommodations. This highlights the importance of a "paper trail" for students with LD who are pursing professional or graduate training. This means that students must have the finances for evaluations in childhood and/or attend a school with funds for neuropsychological assessments. The case below illustrates the difficulty encountered when this trail is absent.

Background and History   RS was always a good student although she was aware that she was a slow reader. After graduation from college, she excelled in the culinary profession. She always dreamed, however, of being a physician and began the daunting task of medical school education in her early thirties. She sought accommodations for the MCAT; however, her request was denied because she did not have comprehensive documentation demonstrating an ongoing learning disability from childhood. She was accepted into medical school; however, her professor evaluations noted that her exam performance was poor despite her understanding of the materials.

Neuropsychological Testing Highlights   A comprehensive neuropsychological evaluation was completed. Overall, RS's intellectual functions were solidly in the average range, with a significant discrepancy between verbal and performance-based abilities (Verbal Comprehension Index [VCI] 91st PR; Perceptual Organizational Index [POI] 42nd PR). Reading comprehension under timed conditions was at the 1st PR, which increased to 34th PR with extended time. She endorsed a number of symptoms on the Brown ADD scale, suggestive of attention deficits, including "being excessively forgetful," "procrastinating," "spacing out," "running out of steam," "feeling distractible," and "getting lost in day dreams."

Formulation and Outcome   RS was diagnosed with a reading disorder and attention-deficit disorder, which led to a wide range of supports. She was found eligible for extended time for examinations at medical school, which resulted in improvement in her grades. She also pursued tutoring to improve her test-taking strategies and used adaptive reading technology to compensate for her very slow reading (see www. Kurzweil.com for more information). Finally, she had an excellent response to medications for attention deficits. She ultimately graduated from medical school and passed the national licensing board examinations, although she was denied accommodations because of the lack of good childhood track record of disability. Notably, her board scores were low due to her deficits and she was accepted to a second-tier residency training program. According to reports received from her medical school, RS was an excellent resident who became involved in research and traveled extensively to complete special projects.

Case 4

While RS benefited from interventions, including medications to enhance attention, technology, and tutoring, some students may ultimately need more specialized support. The case discussed below provides another example of a medical student who did not receive accommodations in medical school because her learning deficits remained silent (Hoffschmidt & Weinstein, 2003). While she was distraught by her difficulties, the significance of her problems emerged in residency training. The Medical Higher Education for Learning Problems (Medical H.E.L.P.) program (see below) also proved beneficial to address her problems.

Background and History   TG was a 41-year-old resident who was referred by her program for evaluation of significant organization problems. It was hard for her to keep records in order as she moved through different treatment sites and clinics. She had a history of childhood depression that increased as she experienced organizational problems. TG also had a history of bulimia and anorexia, and when she was told that she "was not working up to her potential," symptoms of her eating disorder reemerged as well.

TG attended a prominent college and majored in foreign languages. While a strong student, TG was aware that she never really understood grammatical rules. TG worked as a translator before returning to school to take prerequisites for medical school. She ultimately was accepted to a solid medical college where she performed relatively well. She did acknowledge that she got by with cramming. She passed the first steps of the medical licensing examinations without accommodation. She was aware, however, that she needed more time to study than her peers and arranged her schedule so that there was ample study time.

TG initially began residency training in medicine. Concerns about her organization skills, however, led her to seek a better match for her interests and strengths. She transferred to a psychiatry training program but again became overwhelmed by the demands of completing patient reports and records. She took a medical leave, but there was considerable controversy among faculty and administration regarding her return to the program. Some felt that her clinical skills were superior, whereas other staff were concerned about poor time management, disorganization, and "scattered" behavior that compromised patient care. Because of the concern about TG's work performance, she was referred for monitoring, treatment of depression, and neuropsychological evaluation.

Neuropsychological Testing On the formal assessment, TG's overall intellect was in the superior range. Memory functions, language skills, and attention functions were consistent with her intellect and visual-spatial planning and organization skills were intact. In contrast, her reading speed (39th PR) and writing fluency (35th PR) were relatively low compared to her intellect. Finally, higher level planning was impaired. Specifically, she struggled on both the Tower of London test as well as Porteus Mazes performance (both below the 20th PR).

Formulation and Outcome Based on the neuropsychological evaluation, TG received a diagnosis of ADHD-predominantly inattentive subtype, with executive dysfunction and dysthymia. Recommendations were made for medications for attention, environmental manipulation to improve sleep hygiene, and continued psychotherapy. Modifications were introduced to help TG complete medical records, including use of a dictation service, a voice-activated computer, and a computer template to help her write organized chart notes. Her residency was cooperative in setting aside a specific time each day to write notes as well as a specific time at the end of week to complete all charts. She also had a coach to review work that needed completion. Extended time for the final step of the licensing exam was denied (again due to the lack of documentation of childhood learning disorder and history of prior accommodation). TG was referred to the Medical H.E.L.P. to address her test-taking skills. She ultimately passed the licensing exam but special tutoring was required to pass the oral Psychiatry Boards. Practice was needed to quickly organize extensive patient records and make an appropriate formulation.

Discussion

Neuropsychologists play a critical role in clarifying neurocognitive functions, anticipating potential difficulties in academic and postgraduation realms, building appropriate supports, and working with academic institutions to develop an accommodation plan that optimizes the student's success. Feedback from postsecondary institutions can inform neuropsychologists about the ecological validity of tests administered, the accuracy of predictions, and the utility of recommendations.

Fine tuning and adjusting a plan over time is a frequent occurrence, as a student may have different needs as he or she moves from academic training to law internships or medical rotations. In addition, helping the student develop good cerebral hygiene is important. This includes learning how to protect one's attention with good sleep (Brown & McMullen, 2001), stress management, and relaxation techniques (Arnold, 2001), weight control (Altfas, 2002) and implementation of cognitive remediation strategies (Weinstein, 1994).

Some specialized support programs have been developed to address these needs. One highly regarded program to assist medical students with LD is the Medical H.E.L.P. program at Marshall University (Guyer & Guyer, 2000). Begun in 1986, this unique program is designed to help medical students and physicians succeed in their medical careers. During a 5-week intensive program, students address reading comprehension, reading automaticity, note taking, organization of time and space, mapping strategies (including color-coding and imagery), improving memory with verbalization and visualization, test-taking strategies (concentrating on multiple-choice tests), analyzing errors on test questions, and learning to deal more effectively with frustration and stress. Addressing lowered self-esteem is also a goal of Medical H.E.L.P., as individuals are obviously saddened as they confront failure. Student 4 in our vignettes above participated in this program with good results.

When looking at the association between neurocognitive functioning and employment status, (1) executive functioning, (2) intellectual functioning, and (3) memory proved to be the strongest in a recent meta-analysis (Kalechstein, Newton, & van Gorp, 2003). The authors note, "The association between the capacity to organize, process and remember information and the capacity to remain employed has substantial face validity." Other studies have looked at clusters of tests to seek ecological validity reported executive dysfunction and memory as critical variables (Kibby, Schmitter-Edge-Combe, & Long, 1998; Burgess, Alderman, Evans, Emslie, & Wilson, 1998; Higgenson, Arnett, & Voss, 2000; Ready, Stierman, & Paulsen, 2001).

Certainly, the ability to adapt to changing circumstances must also be a factor in the outcome of the first three cases presented in this chapter. In contrast, Case 4, with executive dysfunction and concomitant poor flexibility, continued to struggle professionally. However, a battery of neuropsychological tests alone may not be as useful in detecting this aspect of presumed prefrontal cortical functioning. Overall, it appears more fruitful to combine psychosocial variables with neuropsychological data to increase accuracy in employment outcome (Guilmette & Kastner, 1998). Specifically, impaired performance in the cognitive and social realm may more accurately predict work failure than a normal performance predicts work success (Guilmette & Kastner, 1998). The latter statement, however, is not without problems, as there are reports that physicians with average intellect are more likely to be referred to a state medical board for making significant medical errors (Perry & Crean, 2005).

The most useful neuropsychological assessment delineates attention, memory, and language; visual-spatial functions; sustained and selective attention; planning, organization, and prioritization; and efficient integration of information. For appropriate measures refer to Mapou, this volume). Clarification of academic functions, reading, spelling, mathematical skills, and writing functions is essential. Notably, assessment of complex writing skills is often neglected in the neuropsychological battery, and yet this is a crucial skill for students in professional programs. The evaluation is also incomplete without addressing motivation, personality style, coping strategies, and personal support systems. Some students may progress with sheer determination, as seen in the case studies above. Personality measures might include the Minnesota Multiphasic Personality Inventory (MMPI), the Personality Assessment Inventory, the Coping Skill Inventory, and the NEO Five-Factor Inventory.

Directions for Future Research

Much research on learning disorders in adults has focused on college students, with relatively less attention paid to professional adults. Despite continued advances in our knowledge, much remains to investigate. For example, there are increasing guidelines for diagnosing learning disorders in younger and older children (Drummond et al., 2005), but there is little agreement regarding diagnosing learning disorders in adulthood. We question if professional students who have high intellect, good motivation, and the ability to benefit from adaptive strategies have different neuropsychological profiles compared to less successful adults with similar disabilities. Do different patterns of comorbidity contribute to outcome? Does higher education or professional training impart strategies that change the underlying pattern of strengths and weaknesses? Are we simply dealing with a selection bias in the student who pursues advanced training versus the one who does not? Finally we must question if we are even using appropriately normed tests, particularly when assessing the bilingual and multilingual learning-disabled professional student.

At this point, we know little about why one individual with LD may succeed while another may not be successful. Certainly a student may perform well academically and flounder in the work environment. Anecdotally, a working physician who had little difficulty in medical school may come to the attention of neuropsychologists because he or she is behind in record keeping, cannot keep track of multiple time demands, struggles in the fast pace of a managed care environment, or makes a medical error.

Similarly, an excellent law student with a nonverbal learning disorder may find that social or conversational difficulties ultimately compromise the practice of law. Individuals who are labored readers may not be able to keep up with the medical literature or current case law as they prepare legal briefs, teach classes, or engage in scholarly writing. Or the business student with visual processing deficits may make errors dealing with complex computer spreadsheets. While accommodations can be enormously helpful in the workplace (see Macurdy & Geetter, this volume), many core professional skills are not amenable to accommodation. Thus, while goodness of fit between vocational choice and cognitive strengths and weaknesses is critical for the success of professional students over time (Gerber, Ginsburg, & Reiff, 1992), we have little hard data to support this concept.

As noted above, less is known about the ecological validity of neuropsychological tests in predicting employment success after school is successfully negotiated. Much of the research on ecological validity has involved brain-injured and forensic populations (Sweet, 1999). Frequently, ecological validity studies have reported low to moderate correlations between neuropsychological testing and everyday skills (Williams, 1996), providing an argument for gathering information from a number of sources in the course of the evaluation. Seidman, Biederman, Weber, Hatch, and Faraone (1998) did, however, find that when ADHD subjects and controls with comparable intellect were compared, the controls had higher level occupational attainment. Limited data are available comparing vocational outcomes of professional students to their earlier neuropsychological evaluations. Nor is there any research on what learning disorder subtypes succeed as a professional and what subtypes are at greater risk for poor outcome (Pennington, 1991).

Minimal research is available on the developmental progression of individuals with learning disabilities across the adult life span. For example, what is the relationship between developmental learning disorders and normal aging in the general LD population and specifically in the population of professionals with LD? Does the synergy between neurodevelopmental deficits and cognitive changes associated with normal aging lead to a relatively different pattern of decline, once demographic and lifestyle conditions are held constant (Miner, 1994)? One might also speculate that if an individual has a neurodevelopmental vulnerability/deficit he or she would be less able to accommodate age-related stress, medical illness, or neurological assaults (Hoffschmidt & Weinstein, 2003; Spencer, 2005). We attempt to illustrate this interaction in Figure 17.1 with several routes leading to neurocognitive deficits in the adult with LD. In addition, the issue of cognitive reserve (Satz, 1997) in individuals with neurodevelopmental

Learning Disorder

↓

Aging→   **Neurocognitive Deficits** ← Medical Illness

↑

Stress

Figure 17.1 Influences on brain functions in professionals with LD. A proposed model that accounts for a number of interacting variables impinging on a core neurocognitive deficit. Influences presumably change as the individual ages, confronts increasingly stressful career and life demands (managed care, increased workload, family demands, etc.), medical issues (neurological insults, hypertension, cardiovascular disease, diabetes, poor sleep, limited time for exercise and good health practices etc.), as well as impinging in different ways on different LDs (reading, writing, nonverbal learning disorder [NLD], ADHD, etc.).

disorders remains a very important and totally underinvestigated avenue for future research.

Sally Shaywitz (1998) provides an interesting perspective:

Society in general, has acknowledged the great need for diversity within the community of physicians. Just as it has been important historically to open the circle of physicians to include individuals representing all religions, races, and both sexes, it is now time to allow other capable groups to be incorporated into the tapestry of medicine. By including individuals who are bright, compassionate, and also LD, LD medical students have much to teach their fellow students and future physicians about chronic disability, adversity, and resilience, and much to contribute to the care and well-being of their future patients. (p. 308)

Clearly, we have much to learn. However, the neuropsychologist plays an essential role in helping learning disabled students progress through professional schools and move into the work environment. It is highly rewarding as we assess and consult with highly motivated and resilient individuals.

References

Accardo, P., Haake, C., & Whitman, B. (1989). The learning disabled medical student. *Developmental and Behavioral Pediatrics, 10*, 253–257.

Altfas, J. R. (2002). Prevalence of attention-deficit/hyperactivity disorder among adults in obesity treatment. *Biomedical Psychiatry, 2*, 1–14.

Arnold, L. E. (2001). Alternative treatments for adults with attention-deficit/hyperactivity disorder (ADHD). In J. Wasserstein, L. E. Wolf, & F. F. LeFever (Eds.), *Adult attention deficit disorder: Brain mechanisms and life outcomes* (pp. 310–341). New York: Annals of the New York Academy of Sciences.

Bartlett v. New York State Board of Law Examiners 970 F. Suppl. 1094 (S.D.N.Y. 1997).

Brinckerhoff, L. (1996). *Learning disabilities and accommodations for the learning disabled.* Paper presented at management education program by American Medical Colleges, San Diego, CA, January 18–20.

Brown, T. E., & McMullen, W. J., Jr. (2001). Attention deficit disorder and sleep/arousal disturbance. In J. Wasserstein, L. E. Wolf, & F. F. LeFever (Eds.), *Adult attention deficit disorder: Brain mechanisms and life outcomes* (pp. 271–286). New York: Annals of the New York Academy of Sciences.

Burgess, P. W., Alderman, N., Evans, J., Emslie, H., & Wilson, B. (1998). The ecological validity of tests. *Journal of the International Neuropsychology, 25,* 1186–1191.

Burgoyne, R. A., & Mew, C. (2001). ADA update: Bartlett V, Gonzales, Garrett, Buckhannon, and Edwards. *Bar Examiner, 70,* 31–18.

Drummond, C. R., Ahmad, S. A., & Rourke, B. P. (2005). Rules for the classification of younger children with nonverbal learning disabilities and basic phonological processing disabilities. *Archives of Clinical Neuropsychology, 20,* 171–182.

Duhl, S., & Duhl, G. (2004). Testing applicants with disabilities. *The Bar Examiner, 73*(1).

Eichorn, L. (1997). Reasonable accommodations and awkward compromises: Issues concerning learning disabled students and professional schools in the law school context. *Journal of Law and Education, 26,* 31–63.

Ganschow, L., Coyne, J., Parks, A. W., & Antonoff, S. J. (1999). A 10-year follow-up survey of programs and services for students with learning disabilities in graduate and professional schools. *Journal of Learning Disabilities, 32,* 72–84.

Gerber, P. J., Ginsberg, R. J., & Reiff, H. B. (1992). Identifying alterable patterns in employment success for highly successful adults with learning disabilities. *Journal of Learning Disabilities, 25,* 475–487.

Guilmette T. J., & Kastner, M. P. (1998). The prediction of vocational functioning from neuropsychological data. In R. J. Sbordone & C. J. Long (Eds.), *Ecological validity of neuropsychological testing* (pp. 387–411). Boca Raton, FL: St. Lucie Press.

Guyer, B. P., & Guyer, K. E. (2000). Doctors with learning disabilities: Prescription for success. *Learning Disabilities: A Multidisciplinary Journal, 10,* 65–72.

Hafferty, F. W, & Gibson, G. G. (2001). Learning disabilities and the meaning of medical education. *Academic Medicine, 76*(10), 1027–1031.

Hafferty, F. W., & Gibson, G. G. (2003). Learning disabilities, professionalism, and the practice of medical education. *Academic Medicine, 78,* 189–201.

Hechtman, L. (Ed.). (1996). *Do they grow out of it? Long-term outcomes of childhood disorders.* Washington. DC: American Psychiatric Press.

Higgenson, C. I., Arnett, P. A., & Voss, W. D. (2000). The ecological validity of clinical tests of memory and attention in multiple sclerosis. *Archives of Clinical Neuropsychology, 15,* 185–204.

Hoffschmidt, S. J., & Weinstein, C. S. (2003). The influence of silent learning disorders on the lives of women. In M. E. Banks & E. Kaschak (Eds.), *Women with visible and invisible disabilities* (pp. 81–94). New York: Halworth Press.

Julien, E. R., Ingersoll, D. J., Etienne, P. M., & Hilger, A. (2004). The impact of testing accommodations on MCAT scores: Descriptive results. *Academic Medicine, 79,* 360–364.

Kalechstein, A. D., Newton, T. F., & van Gorp, E. G. (2003). Neurocognitive functioning associated with employment status: A quantitative review. *Journal of Clinical and Experimental Neuropsychology, 25,* 1186–1191.

Keiser, S., & Gordon, M. (2000). *Accommodations in higher education under the American With Disabilities Act: A no-nonsense guide for clinicians, educators, administrators, and lawyers.* New York: Guilford Press.

Kibby, M. Y., Schmitter-Edgecombe, M., & Long, C. (1998). Ecological validity of neuropsychological tests: Focus on California Verbal Learning Test and the Wisconsin Card Sorting Test. *Archives of Clinical Neuropsychology, 13,* 523–534.

Miner, J. (1994). Normal cognitive aging. In J. Ellison, C. Weinstein, & T. Hodel-Malinofsky (Eds.), *The psychotherapist's guide to neuropsychiatry: Diagnostic and treatment issues* (pp. 465–485). Washington, DC: American Psychiatric Association.

Mosier, T. L. (n.d.). *Employment discrimination against the disabled in the legal profession.* Retrieved September 30, 2007, from www.tlmosier.4t.com/discrimination.html.

Pennington, E. F. (1991). *Diagnosing learning disorders.* New York: Guilford Press.

Perreira, D. C., & Richards, A. M. (2000). The role of undergraduate programs in preparing students with learning disabilities for professional school enrollment. *Learning Disabilities: A Multidisciplinary Journal, 10,* 57–64.

Perry, W., & Crean, R. D. (2005). A retrospective review of the neuropsychological test performance of physicians referred for medical infractions. *Archives of Clinical Neuropsychology, 20,* 161–170.

Ranseen, J. D., & Parks, G. S. (2005). Test accommodations for postsecondary students: The quandary resulting from the ADA's disability definition. *Psychology, public policy and law.* Washington, DC: American Psychological Association.

Ready, R. E., Stierman, L., & Paulsen, J. S. (2001). Ecological validity of neuropsychological and personality measures of executive functions. *Clinical Neuropsychologist, 15,* 314–323.

Rosebrough, C. J. (2003). Learning disabilities and medical schools. *Medical Education, 34,* 994–1000.

Satz, P. (1997). *Behavior-brain relationships in children with developmental disabilities: Concepts and methods.* Paper presented at the 105th annual convention of the American Psychological Association, Chicago, August 17.

Scotti, M. J. (1997). Medical school admission criteria: The needs of patients matter. *Journal of the American Medical Association, 278,* 1196–1197.

Seidman L. J., Biederman, J., Weber, W., Hatch, M., & Faraone S. V. (1998). Neuropsychological function in adults with ADHD. *Biological Psychiatry, 44,* 260–268.

Shaywitz, S. E. (1998). Dyslexia. *The New England Journal of Medicine, 338,* 307–312.

Shaywitz, S. E. (2003). *Overcoming dyslexia.* New York: Random House.

Sohlberg, M. M., & Mateer, C. A. (2001). Improving attention and managing attentional problems. In J. Wasserstein, L. E. Wolf, & F. F. LeFever (Eds.), *Adult attention deficit disorder: Brain mechanisms and life outcomes* (pp. 357–375). New York: Annals of the New York Academy of Sciences.

Spencer, T. J. (2005). *Adult ADHD.* Paper presented at the Attention Deficit Hyperactivity Disorder Across the Life Span conference, Boston, MA, March 20, 2005.

Sweet, J. (1999). Malingering: Differential diagnosis. In J. Sweet (Ed.), *Forensic neuropsychology: Fundamentals and practice.* Lisse: Swets & Zeitlinger.

Waber, D. P., Isqith, P. K., & Kahn, C. M. (1994). Metacognitive factors in visuospatial skills of long-term survivors of acute lymphoblastic leukemia: An experimental approach to the Rey-Ossterrieth Complex Figure Test. *Developmental Neuropsychology 10,* 349–367.

Weinstein, C. (1994). Cognitive remediation strategies: An adjunct to the psychotherapy of adults with attention-deficit/hyperactivity disorder. *The Journal of Psychotherapy Research and Practice, 3,* 44–57.

Williams, J. M. (1996). A practical model of everyday assessment. In R. Sbordone & C. Long (Eds.), *Ecological validity of neuropsychological testing.* Delray Beach, FL: St. Lucie Press.

Wolf, L. (2001). College students with ADHD and other hidden disabilities. In J. Wasserstein, L. E. Wolf, & F. F. LeFever (Eds.), *Adult attention deficit disorder: Brain mechanisms and life outcomes* (pp. 385–395). New York: Annals of the New York Academy of Sciences.

CHAPTER 18

Outcomes in Probable Nonverbal Learning Disabled (NLD) Adults

A Naturalistic Study

JEANETTE WASSERSTEIN, NEHAL P. VADHAN,
KATHERINE BARBOZA, and GERRY A. STEFANATOS

Contents

Historical Evolution of the Construct

In the normal course of child development, the capacity to interpret subtle nonverbal cues in social interaction unfolds effortlessly and without much formal instruction. The successful acquisition of these skills is dependent on the normal elaboration and function of complex brain systems dedicated to processing of information in the social domain (Frith & Frith, 2001). Perturbations in the neurodevelopment of these or related systems can result in "inborn" or biologically based difficulties that particularly affect social development and adjustment.

Clinical evidence in support of this conceptualization began to emerge approximately 40 years ago when Johnson and Myklebust (1967) distinguished a subtype of "psychoneurological learning disability" in which children demonstrated specific problems in social perception and adjustment. This "social perception disability" was reflected in limitations in the capacity to interpret subtle nonverbal cues as conveyed through hand and arm gestures, posture, facial expression, or eye gaze, and prosodic features of speech such as intonation stress, voice quality, and speaking style. Johnson and Myklebust conceived of this constellation of difficulties as fundamentally based in distortions of perceptual experience stemming from subtle impairments in perception and imagery. These deficiencies also negatively impacted the individual's ability to interpret human states, feelings, and attitudes. Johnson and Myklebust later noted that math difficulties were commonly, but not invariably, seen in children with this primarily social learning disorder (1971). They further observed that the disorder was frequently associated with abnormal findings on neurological exams, supporting a neurobiological basis to these problems.

Myklebust later (1975) coined the term "nonverbal learning disabilities" (NLD) to collectively refer to this subtype of learning disorder and linked NLD specifically with dysfunction of the right cerebral hemisphere. He highlighted delays in adaptive functioning in NLD and argued that the disorder was more debilitating than verbal learning disabilities because it impeded "the development and acquisition of meaning, of *inner* experience" (p. 87). A critical aspect of the social disability, he further postulated, related to the child's "lack of ability to understand his social environment, especially in terms of his own behavior" (p. 86). This was reflected in immature behavior and difficulties making many routine judgments required in everyday life. Modifying the previous conceptualization, Myklebust here considered that the functional locus was not based in perceptual problems per se but in basic deficiencies in memory storage and imagery. Importantly, while social perception problems were explicitly linked with global right-hemisphere dysfunction, a consistent relationship between NLD and dyscalculia was never articulated.

Subsequent studies in the medical literature examined the relationship between the NLD symptoms (both cognitive and socioemotional) and neurological signs of right-hemisphere dysfunction. Denckla (1978) observed that children with deficits in social functioning and visual-spatial perception also exhibited left-sided motor system problems suggestive of right-hemisphere dysfunction. This left "hemisyndrome" was manifested by at least three of the following lateralized symptoms: weakness, poor tone, gait disturbance, abnormal reflexes, tremors, incoordination, nystagmus, and strabismus. Weintraub and Mesulam (1983) later described 14 mostly adult clients selected for both socioemotional problems and nondyslexic learning disabilities (LD) who showed "neurologic and neuropsychological signs consistent with right-hemisphere dysfunction" (p. 463). The neuropsychological signs included visuospatial disturbances, attention dysfunction, and inadequate paralinguistic abilities (e.g., lack of eye contact, gesture, and prosody). Almost all (13 of 14) of the cases showed significantly higher Verbal IQ (VIQ) scores on the Wechsler Adult Intelligence Scale (WAIS). Academically, reading was a relative strength for most of these individuals (11 of 14), while poor calculation and spelling problems were common but not universal. Two individuals were exceptionally strong in abstract mathematics (e.g., calculus), although their mastery of simple calculations was sometimes slow.

Similarly, Voeller (1986) described the socioemotional and neuropsychological profiles of 15 children referred for evaluation of behavior or learning problems who also showed right-brain dysfunction on the basis of neurologic exam or structural neuroimaging. As a group, these children exhibited poor social perception and/or expression, as well as attention-deficit disorder. Most, but not all, had significant Verbal IQ–Performance IQ (PIQ) differences and performed significantly better on word decoding than arithmetic. These findings were used to argue for the existence of a neurological substrate for some forms of psychopathology (especially depression, anxiety, and attention disorders) and that differential compromise of right anterior or posterior brain regions resulted in different forms of social dysfunction.

Together, these findings from neuropsychiatric populations provided convergent evidence for an association between right-brain dysfunction and social problems, internalizing psychopathology, and nonlanguage-based learning problems (i.e., math and handwriting problems). However, the deficits in social functioning were not uniform in presentation and their association with problems in other domains of function was variable. For example, observed social problems sometimes appear to reflect poor self-regulation or poor self-expression, and at other times seemed related to poor reading of social cues. As a group, these disabilities were thought of as right-hemisphere LD or syndromes.

In parallel with these clinical reports, Rourke and colleagues observed similar associations in the course of a series of studies directed to identifying subtypes of learning disabilities in children (Rourke, 1975; Rourke & Finlayson, 1978; Rourke & Strang, 1978; Strang & Rourke, 1983). Examining children initially selected for having academic difficulties of some sort, they identified two principle LD clusters: (a) children with relatively weaker reading and writing skills, and (b) children with primary difficulties in mechanical arithmetic, and at least age-appropriate levels of reading (word recognition) and spelling. The latter group demonstrated characteristic neuropsychological profiles, including impaired visual-spatial organization, poor nonverbal problem solving, anomalies of tactile perception and psychomotor function (usually left side worse than right side), and socioemotional problems. Labeled "nonverbal perceptual-organizational output disabled" (Rourke & Finlayson, 1978) or NLD in later papers, their difficulties with mechanical arithmetic were related to spatial disorganization, misreading visual details such as signs (e.g., + or −), visual motor difficulties, procedural errors, and poor judgment or reasoning (Strang & Rourke, 1983, 1985). The cluster of problems was evident in the context of relatively strong rote verbal and psycholinguistic skills. The overall constellation of strengths and weaknesses stood in marked contrast to a second subtype of children who demonstrated relatively good function in these nonverbal domains but demonstrated poor psycholinguistic skills.

Integrating the education and medical findings, Rourke (1988, 1989, 1995) subsequently developed the most well-known developmental neuropsychological model of NLD. Like earlier conceptualizations, this model inferred core dysfunction in right-hemisphere processes, and hypothesized a novel underlying neuropathological mechanism involving white-matter abnormalities for many cases (Rourke, 1987; also Tsatsanis & Rourke, this volume, for an elaboration). In contrast to previous descriptions of this syndrome, however, this model drew explicit cause-and-effect relationships between basic neuropsychological deficits (and assets) and the academic and psychosocial aspects of the syndrome. In essence, the model suggests that the symptoms are linked in an "NLD triad": (a) *neuropsychological dysfunction* in visual and tactile perception and complex psychomotor output; and adaptive processing of novel material result in secondary (attention, exploratory behavior) and tertiary (memory, concept formation, problem solving) neuropsychological deficits; (b) *academic dysfunction* in mechanical arithmetic, graphomotor skills, and reading comprehension; and (c) *psychosocial/adaptational deficits* in pragmatics, social competence, adapting to new situations, emotional stability, time sense, and in processing language prosody.

Given that the clinical samples that Rourke's model was based on were originally selected for some form of academic dysfunction, this linkage between specific academic skill deficits and the neuropsychological and social deficits seems biased. As discussed above, basic academic skill deficits were not universal in the original studies about NLD and may therefore not be present in a proportion of individuals with the syndrome. By focusing on symptom linkage, a critical diagnostic ambiguity may have been created, particularly with respect to the math deficits. In addition, the neuropsychological profile of NLD has more recently been linked with the psychiatric diagnosis of Asperger's syndrome (Klin, Volkmar, Sparrow, Cicchetti, & Rourke, 1995), a pervasive developmental disorder wherein social deficits are also central. The authors did not specify whether they considered the two entities synonymous or distinct, or if they considered Asperger's syndrome to be a subset of NLD. Thus, ambiguity about the meaning and boundaries of the NLD diagnosis continued to exist.

A useful by-product of Rourke's assiduous and systematic approach to studying NLD has been the development of explicit algorithms for identifying NLD (see Tsatsanis & Rourke, this volume, Chapter 7, for a most current presentation) to facilitate consistency of diagnosis among researchers. However, the criteria for these algorithms rely heavily on administration of the Halstead-Reitan neuropsychological test battery, limiting their utility for clinicians who do not use these instruments (see Lezak, Loring, Howieson, Hannay, & Fischer, 2004, for a discussion). Thus, absent a full administration of this specific battery, it is not uncommon for clinicians to rely on data derived from more widely used instruments. In this context, relative deficiencies in nonverbal aspects of cognition are most commonly inferred from the presence of a significant discrepancy between VIQ and PIQ and, despite its limitations, this has often been regarded as prima facie evidence of likely NLD.

There is currently no consensus about the necessary diagnostic features of NLD. Some have argued that deficits in math or handwriting sometimes exist separately from deficits in social cognition, and all should therefore be examined independently (Pennington, 1991). Others have suggested that there may be subtypes of NLD (Semrud-Clikeman & Hynd, 1990; Grodzinsky, 2003) and that these may reflect different underlying neural substrates. For example, to the extent that dyscalculia, dysgraphia, and spatial confusion constitute NLD, there is a distinctly *left*-hemisphere type of NLD, exemplified in a developmental variant of Gerstmann's syndrome (Strub & Geschwind, 1974). Even within the right-hemisphere NLD cluster, there may be differences along an anterior to posterior gradient. For example, attention-deficit/hyperactivity disorder (ADHD) has been related to dysfunction in right frontocortical circuits (see Stefanatos & Wasserstein, 2001) and is often associated with social deficits growing out of impulsivity and poor self-monitoring. In contrast, Weinberg and McLean (1986) identified two different types of LD in children, arithmetic and social-emotional difficulties, which they attributed to right parietal-lobe syndrome. These children were found to misperceive social situations and to have overly emotional gestures and poor expressive prosody. Last, dyscalculia and social deficits may be highly correlated because they are both often associated with right-hemisphere dysfunction, but each may still be subserved by different functional regions within the right brain (Wasserstein, Zappulla, Rosen, & Gerstman, 1984) and thus actually be independent.

However, as reviewed by Tsatsanis and Rourke, this volume, there is a consensus that the neuropsychological deficit constellations seen in children with NLD continue in adults, and that these deficits may be associated with particular forms of psychopathology (e.g., depression, schizoid personality disorder) and adaptive dysfunction (e.g., isolation and occupational problems). There are a handful of studies addressing adult NLD, although the use of different selection criteria across different studies has complicated the synthesis of study findings. For example, elevated frequencies of depression, episodic behavioral dyscontrol, and psychosis were seen in adult psychiatric clients selected for NLD by a Verbal–Performance IQ discrepancy greater than 15 (Grace & Malloy, 1992), as well as in NLD adults selected via weakness in arithmetic relative to IQ (Cleaver, & Whitman, 1998). However, emotional dysfunction was not observed in another NLD sample selected for "arithmetic deficiency" (Greiffenstein & Baker, 2002). There are also suggestions that the discrepancy between weaknesses and other intact abilities may widen by adulthood (reviewed by Tsatsanis & Rourke, this volume), and that executive dysfunction may become more apparent (e.g., Fisher & DeLuca, 1997). But, again, selection criteria vary widely. Together, evidence-based understanding of adult presentations and outcomes in NLD are even more limited than for children.

Statement of Purpose

The child literature implies the existence of a right-hemisphere neuro-developmental syndrome that impacts social functioning, arithmetic skills, and visual, spatial, or motor functions to varying degrees. However, the nature of the social disorder and associated symptom clusters vary, and the boundaries of the NLD diagnosis are ambiguous.

Arguably, at this stage of our understanding of NLD, an excessive reliance on any given criterion may artificially accentuate the relationship between that criterion and the rest of the syndrome (e.g., math and social/adaptive deficits). Use of broader descriptors (such as significant differences between verbal and nonverbal aptitudes) may permit a more flexible examination of the interrelationships among the target symptoms. In so doing, it may ultimately permit creation of diagnostic paradigms that do not rely upon a specific test battery and reflect the diversity of possible presentations. Furthermore, similar to child studies, NLD is inconsistently diagnosed in the existing adult literature, and samples are often limited to populations. Thus, the range of known outcomes may be negatively skewed.

This descriptive study attempts to address some of the above concerns. We provide data, both cross-sectional and longitudinal, collected from intellectually higher functioning adults seen in a private practice setting. Given questions about the boundaries that define the syndrome, we take as a starting point all cases that would be considered as possibly NLD due to their relative weakness in nonverbal aptitude. We initially present group data from the sample of adults, using measures widely used by practicing clinicians. In order to examine the developmental course of NLD, we next present several adult case studies for which childhood results were available.

Group Study

Method

Study participants were selected from a computerized data bank of all adult clients ($N = 239$) evaluated in the private practice setting of the first author between 1995 and 2006 who were administered an adult version of the Wechsler IQ scale as well as academic achievement and neuropsychological tests.

Clients were classified as possible NLD if *either* their Verbal IQ was greater than Performance IQ or their Verbal Comprehension Index (VCI) was greater than their Perceptual Organization Index (POI) by at least 15 points. Not all people had been given the same version of the Wechsler IQ scale over the 11 years of the study. Yet while algorithms have been proposed to adjust for small differences in absolute scores between different versions of the Wechsler Intelligence Scale for Children (WISC), no special accommodations were made when the field transitioned from the WISC-R to the WAIS-III due to small (~2.9 points) differences in IQ estimates. Instead, the pattern of Wechsler scores has been seen as important for the diagnosis of NLD. We therefore assumed gross equivalency in the adult tests and collapsed across the two Wechsler versions to select participants.

Seventy-eight clients initially met these criteria, but 30 of these were excluded because they had histories of neurological insult or disorder acquired during adulthood (e.g., dementia, stroke, head injury, or Lyme disease). The final probable NLD sample consisted of 48 adults who were evaluated for a variety of clinical complaints that typically dated back to their childhoods (Tables 18.1 and 18.2, discussed below). Notably, as a group, the clients also met Rourke's criteria (e.g., Drummond, Ahmad, & Rourke, 2005) for NLD to the extent that it was possible to assess this using our test battery. That is, in addition to significant differences between VIQ and PIQ or between VCI and POI, on average the group exhibited the following characteristics: (a) Vocabulary/Similarities/Information subtest scores greater than Block Design/Digit Symbol/Object Assembly subtest scores, (b) reading ability at least 8 points greater than math computation (Table 18.3, discussed below), (c) weak visual-motor skills, and (d) weak visual-memory skills (Table 18.4, discussed below).

Most of the final set of clients had been administered the WAIS-III, and only a small number had been administered the WAIS-R ($n = 5$). As discussed above, all IQ, index, and subtest scores were collapsed across the two Wechsler versions. Similarly, clients had not been administered the same achievement and neuropsychological tests over the lengthy study (e.g., WRAT-R, WRAT-III, WJ-III, Scholastic Achievement Test for Adults [SATA]). We again assumed significant overlap between measures designed to assess the same abilities and integrated results by skill type. Finally, archival test data were stored at different levels of detail, such as standard scores, percentiles, or verbal descriptions (e.g., "within normal limits" [WNL], "borderline" [BL]). Thus, in the current study, all ability data were presented by category of test (e.g., reading decoding, math computation), as were some of the neuropsychological measures (e.g., motor skills). Scores were presented in metrics that allowed us to include the most data from the most participants. For example, IQ and achievement scores

Table 18.1 Demographic Characteristics (N = 48)

	Mean	SD	Range
Age (years)	28.6	13.0	16–59
Education (years)	15.0	2.7	11–20
	%		**N**
Gender			
Male	50		24
Female	50		24
Race			
White	92		44
Black	4		2
South Asian	4		2
Handedness			
Right	82		37
Left	18		8
Employment (Hollingshead)			
Students	60		28
Managers	15		7
Professionals	13		6
Administrative	6		3
Homemakers	4		2
Skilled manual	2		1

were presented in interval scaling (standard scores) and neuropsychological data were presented in ordinal scaling (e.g., "WNL," "BL," "Impaired"). Details of tests used, as well as methodology for clustering and scaling are provided in the tables.

Results

Demographic Characteristics Demographic characteristics are presented in Table 18.1. As seen, the average client in the sample was generally in his or her late twenties with 1 year postbaccalaureate education. The sample was evenly mixed with respect to gender, but was generally white, right-handed, and in school or working at the professional or managerial level. Hence, this NLD population represented predominantly educated or relatively high-functioning young adults, although their global adaptive functioning was problematic enough to trigger a neuropsychological evaluation.

Table 18.2 Clinical Characteristics

	%	N
Reasons for Referral[a]		
Diagnostic clarification	54	26
Academic/educational planning	52	25
Seeking accommodations	21	10
Vocational dysfunction	2	1
Reported lifetime math problem	60	27
Reported lifetime reading problem	36	17
Psychiatric Characteristics		
Depressive symptoms[b]		
Normal	64	16
Mild	12	3
Moderate	4	1
Severe	20	5
Anxiety symptoms[c]		
Normal	56	14
Mild	16	4
Moderate	12	3
Severe	16	4
Social functioning[d]		
3–4	21	10
2	51	24
1	23	11
0	4	2
Diagnoses Assigned After Evaluation[e]		
Learning disability (educational definition)	75	36
DSM-IV		
ADHD inattentive	69	33
ADHD combined	17	8
Other mood disorder	17	8
Depression/dysthymia	15	7
Generalized anxiety disorder	6	3
Oppositional defiant disorder	2	1

Table 18.2 (continued) Clinical Characteristics

a Cumulative percentage is > 100 because many clients had more than one reason for referral.
b Ratings based on classifications of a subsample of clients from either the Beck Depression Inventory (BDI-II; n = 18) or the Symptom Checklist 90-Depression Subscale (SCL-90-DS; n = 7).
c Based on classifications of a subsample of clients from either the Beck Anxiety Inventory (BAI-II; n = 17) or the Symptom Checklist 90-Anxiety Subscale (SCL-90-AS; n = 7).
d Refers to the number of social environments that the client reported maintaining good relations with (significant other, family, friends, or coworkers).
e Cumulative percentage is > 100 because many clients received multiple diagnoses.

Clinical Characteristics   Clinical characteristics of this sample are presented in Table 18.2. Clients primarily presented needing assistance with diagnostic clarification or academic/educational planning.* Notably, more than half of the sample reported a lifetime problem with math, consistent with the selection for probable NLD. However, the remainder did not complain of math dysfunction and more than a third of the sample reported a lifetime problem with reading, perhaps reflecting the high level of educational planning needs in this group. Those with reading problems complained of decoding and comprehension difficulties, with or without coexisting math deficits.

Psychiatric characteristics were formally assessed in about half of the sample, using standardized scales such as the Beck Depression and Beck Anxiety Inventories (BDI-II, BAI-II) and the Symptom Checklist-90-R (SCL-90-R). In this group, mood and anxiety symptoms were frequent (36 to 44%, respectively) but spanned a broad range of severity. About 20% of the sample reported serious symptom levels of depression, and about 16% reported serious levels of anxiety. Another 16% reported symptoms of mild to moderate depression and 28% reported similar levels of anxiety. Yet more than half of the sample fell in the normal range for levels of depression and anxiety symptoms.

Since no formal measures of social functioning had been collected, social functioning was assessed via the clients' reports during the clinical interview of good relationships with the following four social clusters: significant other, family, friends, and coworkers (a score of 1 to 4 was assigned based on these reports). Similar to the findings for their psychiatric functioning, a noteworthy percentage of these NLD adults reported reasonably intact

---

* Most of these people were not in therapy

social functioning in at least one domain. Although it was rare for these individuals to report good functioning in all four domains, about 21% reported adequate or better relationships with most groups of people in their lives (i.e., 3 out of 4). Thus, a sizable percentage of these adults exhibit adequate social adaptation. The remaining 78%, however, reported some degree of social concern, consistent with the prevailing beliefs about their primary deficits. Of these, the majority (i.e., 51%) described a narrow range of social success (i.e., in only two out of four clusters) and 27% reported severe problems (i.e., social isolation, with adequate relationships with no or one group).

Taken together, mood, anxiety, and social problems were common among these probable NLD adults but were not universal. Moreover, a sizable percentage of these individuals reported that they functioned adequately in one or more socioemotional realms.

Regarding final diagnoses, consistent with the high rate of educational planning requests in this sample, we diagnosed the majority of clients as having a learning disability of some type (75%). Depression/dysthymia or other mood disorder was diagnosed in only about one-third. However, an even larger majority was diagnosed as ADHD (85%), mostly inattentive type (69%), which is consistent with many other observations of high rates of inattention in the NLD population (discussed previously). Thus, and importantly, attention disorder was the predominant diagnosis in this probable NLD sample.

Intellectual and Academic Functioning   Scores from the Wechsler Adult Scale of Intelligence and academic achievement domain scores derived from either the Woodcock-Johnson-III or the Wide Range Achievement Test-3 are presented in Table 18.3.

As seen, the sample's global intellectual functioning, as estimated by WAIS Full Scale IQ, were in the high average range ($M = 113.3$, $SD = 14.9$), consistent with the high educational and vocational levels of the sample. There was, however, a wide range of scores, with the minimum score in the low-average range (83) and the maximum score in the very superior range (140). Performance Scale IQ was about 21 points lower than Verbal Scale IQ ($t_{47} = 15.70$, $p < 0.001$). This discrepancy between the two scales (in either direction) was seen in only 8.5% of the original standardization sample of the WAIS-III at this level Full Scale IQ (i.e., 110 to 119). Thus, consistent with the intent of the selection criteria, the uneven pattern of cognitive ability in this sample, exemplified by unusual degree of relative weakness in visual-spatial reasoning abilities, is uncommon in the typical population (estimated at about 4%).

Table 18.3 Intellectual and Academic Testing Results

Wechsler Adult Intelligence Scale	%		N
WAIS-III	90		43
WAIS-R	10		5
IQs and Subtests	**Mean**	**SD**	**Range**
Full scale IQ	113	14.9	83–140
Verbal scale IQ	121	14.4	94–144
Performance scale IQ	100	13.6	70–128
VIQ–PIQ difference	21	9.3	2–47
VCI–POI difference	22	10.4	6–52
Verbal Scale Subtests			
Vocabulary	16	2.5	
Similarities	15	3.3	
Comprehension	14	3.2	
Information	14	2.2	
Digit span	12	2.9	
Arithmetic	12	2.9	
Letter–number sequencing	11	3.7	
Performance Scale Subtests			
Matrix reasoning	12	3.0	
Picture arrangement	11	2.7	
Block design	10	2.5	
Picture completion	10	2.8	
Symbol search	9	2.6	
Digit symbol-coding	9	2.6	
Object assembly	9	3.9	
Academic achievement[a]			
Decoding ability[b]	111	10.4	85–129
Spelling ability[c]	109	9.8	80–124
Math ability[d]	102	11.8	70–122

[a] Achievement domain scores were derived from subtest standard scores from either the Woodcock-Johnson Tests of Academic Achievement-Third Edition (WJ-III; n = 26) or the Wide Range Achievement Test (WRAT; n = 22) subtests.
[b] Either WRAT Reading or WJ-III Letter-Word Identification.
[c] Either WRAT Spelling or WJ-III Spelling.
[d] Either WRAT Arithmetic or the mean score of WJ-III Calculation and Math Fluency.

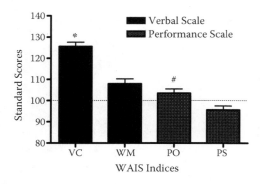

Figure 18.1 WAIS Index scores. *Significant difference from WM score; #Significant difference from PS score (ps < .001).

Although their mean PIQ score was significantly lower than their mean VIQ, the mean PIQ was still in the average range. Similarly, all academic skills were in the average range, with the lowest score in math computation. All mean academic scores were nevertheless significantly lower than would be predicted by the mean VIQ, including for math ($t_{47} = 8.15$, $p < 0.001$), spelling ($t_{47} = 4.69$, $p < 0.001$) and decoding ($t_{47} = 4.21$, $p < 0.001$). Thus the adults in this sample had "normal" range skills in all areas but may have had difficulty acquiring academic skills at a level commensurate with their full intellectual potential. As such, the group met educational criteria for learning disabilities based on a relative rather than absolute standard. The most pronounced basic academic deficiencies were in arithmetic.

The four WAIS indices are compared in Figure 18.1.* Within the Verbal Scale, the mean Verbal Comprehension Index (VCI) score was in the superior range and significantly greater than the mean Working Memory Index (WMI) score, which was in the average range. Thus, verbal attention and working memory, though intact, were significantly weaker than knowledge-based verbal comprehension and expression, consistent with the high prevalence of ADHD in this sample. Both mean index scores within the Performance Scale were also in the average range. However, the mean Processing Speed Index (PSI) score was significantly lower than the mean Perceptual Organization Index (POI) score. Thus, psychomotor speed was significantly weaker than visuospatial abilities, and all other intellectual clusters. As a group, the NLD sample was slow, irrespective of their general intelligence levels.

---

* PIQ and VIQ were not compared since the sample had been selected for differences between them.

Overall, this NLD group had exceptionally strong verbal reasoning (superior range) but was notably slow in visual-motor processing (lower average range). Working memory and visual-perceptual reasoning were relatively weak, which is consistent with usual visual-perceptual markers for NLD and their high rate of ADHD.

Summary and Thoughts

This sample represents a group with higher overall cognitive ability than described in previous clinical reports of NLD adults. The higher aptitude range permits a glimpse at how intelligence may moderate the functional impact of the NLD deficits. Possibly due to their intellectual strengths, many people in this sample had advanced educational degrees or professions and thereby show that adults with NLD can be successful in these important aspects of life. However, these clients still reported learning problems (more pronounced in math) and other adaptive problems. While depression, anxiety, and social problems were very common, they were not universal. This partial dissociation suggests that the socioemotional and cognitive symptoms of NLD may be distinguishable and to some extent independent in adulthood. By contrast, comorbid ADHD, especially inattentive type, was quite frequent and may reflect common core neurological dysfunction (e.g., right-hemisphere dysfunction). Lastly, processing speed was weaker than all other intellectual ability clusters, perhaps serving as a *marker for poor neurologic integration*. These and other issues are further examined below.

Neurocognitive Data and Intercorrelations

Data on four domains of neurocognitive ability were available for examination, usually within half or more of the sample (i.e., from 24 to 48). Results are presented in Table 18.4, and include: (a) fine motor ability ($n = 24$), assessed by either the Purdue Pegboard test or the Grooved Pegboard test; (b) sustained attention ($n = 48$), assessed by the Conners' Continuous Performance Task (CPT); (c) visuomotor integration/planning ($n = 38$), assessed by the Copy trial of the Rey Complex Figure Task (RCFT); and (d) visual learning/memory ($n = 36$), assessed by the immediate and delayed recall trials of the RCFT.

Regarding fine motor ability, the majority of the sample performed in the average or better range with either hand, similar to what would be expected of a nonimpaired group. However, around 40% performed in clinically problematic ranges for either hand (i.e., low average or worse), suggesting a high frequency of motor speed/coordination weakness in this adult NLD sample. There was no obvious handedness difference in

Table 18.4 Neuropsychological Results

	(n)[a]	Superior % (n)	Average % (n)	Low Average/ Borderline % (n)	Deficit % (n)
Fine-motor Ability[a]					
Dominant hand	24	14 (3)	46 (10)	23 (5)	18 (4)
Nondominant hand	24	4 (1)	52 (12)	22 (5)	22 (5)
			WNL % (n)	Borderline/ Atypical—% (n)	Clinical— % (n)
Conners' Continuous Performance Test (CPT) (overall index)	48		40 (18)	31 (14)	29 (13)
Rey Complex Figure Test (RCFT)					
Copy	38		26 (10)	32 (12)	42 (16)
Delayed	36		11 (4)	44 (16)	45 (16)

[a] Represents the number of clients who were administered the particular test.
[b] Motor ability domain classifications were derived from either the Purdue Pegboard Test (n = 21) or Grooved Pegboard Test (n = 3).

performance, but perhaps this subgroup was too small to detect subtle lateral differences. Visual-motor integration was assessed in most case (38/48) and deficits were more obvious. That is, more than 70% of the tested clients performed below normal limits on the RCFT Copy trial, with about 42% of clients performing in the clinically impaired range. Thus, consistent with their presumed NLD diagnoses, motor and visual-motor weakness were pronounced.

Many clients (about 60% of the total sample) showed evidence of poor sustained visual attention (i.e., borderline or clinical ranges), as measured by the Conners' CPT, with almost 30% performing in the clinically impaired range. This observation is consistent with the high rate of ADHD in the sample. Notably, the Conners CPT has been found to be rather insensitive for measuring ADHD in adults (Solanto et al., 2004); thus, the high positive rate in this sample implies significant impairment. Performances on the immediate and delayed recall trials of the RCFT were also frequently below average, although it is unknown how much of this was due to poor visual learning and memory per se, as many clients also had poor visuospatial planning (RCFT Copy) and visual attention (CPT).

We next performed a series of correlational analyses to examine the associations between key NLD constructs (verbal and nonverbal aptitude discrepancy, social-emotional dysfunction, and math disability).

Scaling considerations limited us to nonparametric correlations (Spearman's rank order), which means that caution is urged in generalizing these results to the NLD population at large. We also limited our correlational analyses to those dependent measures where we had adequate data for the most number of clients. While this strategy increased our confidence in interpreting the correlations, it left us unable to assess potentially meaningful relationships between those variables that were excluded.

Table 18.5 shows the intercorrelations between aptitude scores, academic achievement scores, and social function ratings for most of the sample. All IQ scores and most of the index scores are highly and positively correlated with each other, except for the PSI. The PSI is only mildly correlated with Full Scale IQ and the verbal cluster scores, and showed no significant relationship with WMI or POI.

Regarding academic skills, this NLD population showed a number of unexpected patterns that were sometimes in the opposite direction of the usual associations between aptitude and skills. For example, their reading decoding skills were not significantly related to VIQ and VCI but showed a significant positive relationship with the other *more visual* aptitude cluster scores (i.e., PIQ, POI, as well as WMI). By contrast, math skill showed the opposite pattern and was significantly correlated with verbal aptitudes (i.e., VCI and VIQ) but not with nonverbal reasoning, speed, or working memory. Spelling ability was unrelated to all aptitude measures but was correlated with ability in the other two skill areas. Thus, this sample of NLD adults may have learned basic skills in an atypical manner from the norm or currently relies on different underlying aptitudes in their academic performance.

Next, the relationship between attention and social functioning with aptitude and academic skills was considered. As seen, attention was only minimally associated with academic skills and surprisingly was not significantly correlated with any aptitude cluster. Breadth of social networks was unrelated to all cognitive and skill measures, suggesting that the emotional and cognitive traits of NLD are independent. However, both attention and social functioning data were at the ordinal level of scaling and with restricted ranges. Thus, these results may be a statistical artifact rather than true findings. Nevertheless, the data suggest that the relationship between social and cognitive symptoms of NLD in this sample is, at best, not a powerful one.

Overall, the clients in this sample showed the weaker fine motor, visual-motor integration, and visual-memory functions expected in an NLD population. However, the intercorrelations among intelligence, clusters of academic skills, and other key NLD symptoms yielded a number of unexpected associations. Their slower processing speed appears relatively

Table 18.5 WAIS-III Global Indices and Academic Skills, in Adult NLD

	Aptitude							Academic Skills		
	VIQ	PIQ	FSIQ	VCI	POI	WMI	PSI	Math Ability	Spelling Ability	Decoding Ability
VIQ										
PIQ	.776[a]									
Full IQ	.929[a]	.936[a]								
VCI	.664[a]	.691[a]	.815[a]							
POI	.727[a]	.905[a]	.689[a]	.696[a]						
VMI	.856[a]	.529[a]	.647[a]	.357[b]	.562[a]					
PSI	.327[a]	.485[a]	.400[a]	.310[b]	.240	.168				
Math	.403[b]	.201	.306	.360[b]	.260	.307	.209		.465[a]	.178
Spelling	.142	.064	.082	.154	.065	.159	.146	.465[a]		.572[b]
Decoding	.289	.367[b]	.315	.218	.381[b]	.338[b]	.378[b]	.178	.572[a]	
CPT	.133	.131	.158	.205	.247	.037	.256	.385[b]	.391[b]	.400[b]
Social isolation	.180	.160	.135	.025	.018	.092	.151	.099	.008	.260

[a] Significant at the 0.01 level (2-tailed).
[b] Significant at the 0.05 level (2-tailed).

dissociated from their other nonverbal and attention abilities/disabilities, and is paradoxically associated with mainly verbal integrity. The associations between aptitude and academic skills are also atypical: (a) basic reading is related to nonverbal aptitude and working memory (WM) rather than verbal aptitude, (b) math skills appear primarily mediated by verbal processes, and (c) spelling ability is not significantly correlated with cognitive aptitude (even verbal abilities). This suggests that their underlying approach to learning in the past, or use of cognitive skills in the present, may be different from the norm. Lastly, math level and social relationships are not associated in this adult sample, suggesting relative independence between the emotional and cognitive signs of NLD in this sample.

Cases Studies

These three cases were diagnosed as NLD due to the highly significant differences between their Verbal and Performance IQs during childhood, as well as their learning and social problems and correlated motor and other neuropsychological deficits. Their histories illustrate the divergent developmental paths that individuals with NLD can take, particularly with respect to their adaptive and social outcomes.

Case 1

History   Mr. A is a 20-year-old male, previously diagnosed with developmental delay, LD, ADHD, oppositional defiant disorder (ODD), and most recently, provisional bipolar disorder. He was referred by his lawyer in order to assess how his probable neurocognitive deficits may have contributed to his alleged computer fraud. At the time of testing, he had declined all treatment with medications but was in psychotherapy, and his adoptive parents reported ongoing problems in a wide range of cognitive and functional domains, including adaptive decision making, attention, fine motor skills, and language and math. They also reported that he had problems with recognizing facial expressions and body language, and that he was socially withdrawn, depressed, and often aggressive toward his family.

Mr. A was adopted at birth and the youngest of several adopted children. There was no known history of neuropsychiatric issues in his biological family and no reported overt pre- or perinatal problems, although his adoptive parents recalled him being an "irritable and very active" toddler, prone to accidents. Academic problems in all areas were first noticed in kindergarten and continued throughout his education. First evaluated at age 9, results revealed weaknesses in visual-motor abilities and visual and auditory memory, and he was classified as LD and placed in special education classes. Significant behavioral and mood-regulation problems began

Table 18.6 Mr. A's Longitudinal IQ and Achievement Test Scores

Age	10	20
Wechsler IQ		
Verbal scale IQ	107	95
Performance scale IQ	78	95
Full scale IQ	92	95
Wechsler Indices		
Verbal comprehension	101	100
Perceptual organization	77	101
Processing speed	N/A	86
Freedom from distractibility/working memory	97	86
Woodcock-Johnson Tests of Achievement		
Letter–word identification	106	95
Passage comprehension	111	99
Dictation	97	N/A
Calculation	118	71
Applied problems	100	88

in middle childhood and thereafter remained a continuous feature in his life. These socioemotional problems were severe and included chronic irritability and agitation, general noncompliance with authority figures (e.g., repeatedly running away from home and schools), and occasional explosive and violent episodes (e.g., hitting, kicking, and spitting at family members). He was psychiatrically hospitalized at ages 11 and 13 for control of physical aggression and was enrolled in several residential therapeutic high schools. He had also been treated with individual and family therapy, and antidepressants and stimulants (which he was generally noncompliant with) throughout much of his life.

Data were available from a psychoeducational testing at age 10, which is presented in Table 18.6 along with data from the current evaluation. As shown, Mr. A originally demonstrated extremely poor perceptual-motor abilities (PIQ = 78, borderline range) with significantly greater verbal reasoning aptitude (VIQ = 107, average range; 29-point discrepancy). This pattern, combined with his lifelong social and emotional problems, suggested the presence of NLD to a psychologist consulted by the lawyer and triggered the evaluation during adulthood. However, his Woodcock-Johnson scores indicated academic skills commensurate with, or slightly greater than, his overall intellectual ability, with a *strength* in calculation ability. Thus, his early academic problems may have been more related to his social-emotional difficulties than his lack of academic knowledge.

Ten years later, Mr. A's overall intellectual ability remained in the average range, with weaknesses now clearly apparent in working memory (Letter–Number Sequencing [LNS] 16th percentile), visual scanning (Symbol Search, 9th percentile), and social causal reasoning (Picture Arrangement, 16th percentile). While his early WISC-III scores and more recent WAIS-III tests are not entirely comparable, the discrepancy between his VIQ and PIQ seems to have diminished by virtue of a dramatic increase in perceptual organization abilities (POI: 77 → 101) and a mild decrease in attention/working memory (FDI of 97 → WMI of 86). Regarding academic skills, decreases in age-appropriate knowledge occurred across the board, indicating that he had difficulty maintaining expected levels of academic achievement skills, despite intensive interventions. Most notably, his former strength in calculation became his most apparent weakness.

Despite intact overall intellectual ability, Mr. A showed moderate to severe levels of dysfunction in all neuropsychological domains, most severely in attention (e.g., most CPT-II scores in the markedly atypical range) and executive functions (e.g., D-KEFS Color–Word Inhibition/Switching, 8th percentile; Trails B, < 1st percentile). The pattern implied extensive bifrontal system compromise biased towards the right hemisphere. Visuomotor skills, language, and visual/verbal learning and memory were also significantly depressed, but to a less consistent degree.

Mr. A performed strongly on the WAIS-III Matrix Reasoning subtest (84th percentile). This strength in abstract visual pattern matching is consistent with his strong computer skills.

Behavioral Observations and Outcome He presented with appropriate appearance and grooming but gave suboptimal effort on many tasks and showed impulsive tendencies. The current evaluation took six sessions due to Mr. A's habitual lateness, poor tolerance for extended testing (e.g., he would often ask to stop testing after only 10 to 15 minutes), and his tendency towards tangential speech and behavior (e.g., he needed to be refocused on task frequently).

Overall, the results corroborated his previous diagnoses of ADHD, ODD, and NLD, and were highly consistent with his long-standing deficits in impulse control, academic performance, and socialization. Criminal charges were mitigated, long-term structured residential treatment with psychiatric monitoring was recommended, and he has done remarkably well thus far (i.e., graduating college and improved family relationships).

Case 2

History Mr. B is a 24-year-old male, repeating his first year of law school. He requested neuropsychological evaluation as an aid for educational

Table 18.7 Mr. B's Longitudinal IQ and Achievement Test Scores

Age	14	16	23	24
Wechsler IQ				
Verbal scale IQ	121	119	118	130
Performance scale IQ	99	94	106	121
Full scale IQ	111	107	113	128
Wechsler Indices				
Verbal comprehension			120	129
Perceptual organization			116	125
Processing speed			106	125
Working memory/freedom from distractibility			106	106
Woodcock-Johnson Tests of Achievement				
Broad reading			95	105
Broad math			95	96
Broad written language			99	99

planning. Despite taking 100 mg of Ritalin daily, he still reported being highly distractible and had significant problems with planning, organizing himself, and managing time.

Several features of Mr. B's personal and developmental history were consistent with neuropsychiatric vulnerability and NLD. He was born prematurely (34 weeks), showed delayed walking and toilet training, and showed attention problems, motor problems, and hyperactivity as early as his toddler years. Social and emotional difficulties were pronounced throughout his childhood and adolescence. Psychoeducational and pediatric evaluations at age 12 had reportedly revealed high average verbal skill but relative weaknesses in visuomotor abilities, spelling, math, and handwriting. At that time, his true intellectual potential was estimated to be in the superior range (95th percentile, when tested with the Ravens Progressive Matrices), and he was formally diagnosed with LD, ADHD, and developmental coordination disorder (DCD). Thereafter, Mr. A had received various accommodations throughout most of his education but had not sought supports when he started law school.

Longitudinal IQ data from four evaluations since age 14 are presented in Table 18.7. As these scores show, Mr. B's Verbal IQ consistently fell in the upper high average to lower superior ranges until the current evaluation, where it increased to the very superior range. Similarly, his Performance IQ remained in the average range until the current evaluation, where it increased to the superior range. As such, an early discrepancy of > 20 points between his Verbal and Performance IQs progressively closed to less than 10 points as of the most recent evaluation. Thus, his global intellectual function had finally reached the potential estimated by his Ravens IQ at age 12, and the discrepancy between his verbal and performance abilities appeared to have diminished. As judged by his Wechsler Index scores, improvements in component intellectual abilities occurred across the board, with the exception of working memory (e.g., WAIS-III LNS, 16th percentile), an area of core dysfunction for individuals with ADHD.

Unlike his increasing aptitude scores, Mr. B's performance on the Woodcock-Johnson had remained stable across evaluations and he again earned largely average to high-average range scores. Thus, as is often seen with LD, his academic skill development had not kept pace with his intellectual development. Regarding his specific strengths and weaknesses, performance on the WJ-III Math Fluency subtest was relatively weak (21st percentile, implying residual dyscalculia), while his reading comprehension on the WJ-III (76th percentile) and the Nelson-Denny (Comprehension, 80th percentile; Reading Rate, 92nd percentile) were stronger. In addition, he showed visuomotor integration/planning difficulties on the RCFT copy (qualitatively), weak visual learning and memory (RCFT immediate and delayed recall, 16th and 9th percentile, respectively), as well as more evidence of working memory dysfunction (recall repetitions on the CVLT-II, < 1st percentile). Surprisingly, his most salient intellectual strength was *nonverbal* pattern matching and abstract thinking (WAIS-III Matrix Reasoning, 95th percentile), perhaps consistent with his Ravens IQ at age 12. Both of these strong scores in visual reasoning suggest basically intact visual-perceptual functioning, which is considered weak when compared to his verbal functioning.

Behavioral Observations and Outcome   Mr. B. presented as a young man with appropriate appearance, grooming, and affect. He sometimes arrived late but was fully cooperative. He was also compliant with his pharmacotherapy but still showed residual impulsivity and poor concentration. There were no mood or anxiety symptoms.

Mr. B's profile, consisting of an early VIQ-PIQ discrepancy with social and academic dysfunction and current deficits in arithmetic speed and psychomotor skills, is consistent with the classic NLD profile. His chronic attention and working memory problems are consistent with ADHD. Based on the results and historical data, Mr. B met *DSM-IV* criteria for ADHD/NOS and learning disability NOS. After this last neuropsychological evaluation, necessary accommodations were reinstated (e.g., note-taking services, extended time on tests, supportive counseling) and his medications were readjusted. He did extremely well, eventually graduating with honors and securing a competitive job. Notably, significant social complaints have not been an issue since middle childhood, although he does not have a significant other and often has interpersonal tensions at work and with his family.

Case 3

History   Mr. C is a 27-year-old male who was brought in by his parents for help with long-term planning. He was an unemployed college graduate who had been diagnosed with pervasive developmental delay as a preschooler, and LD and ADHD during school years. Most recently, he was diagnosed with Asperger's syndrome due to his chronic social difficulties, weakness in nonverbal aspects of communication, difficulty adapting to novel situations, and narrow preoccupation with sports.

Mr. C was delivered via emergency C-section and developed meconium pneumonia shortly after birth. Subsequently, Mr. C did not show obvious developmental delays but had febrile seizures at 14 months. At age 6 he had another seizure and was started on antiseizure medications, which he took until age 9. He initially attended regular schools but had social and academic difficulties, and was formally diagnosed with LD and ADHD at 12. Thereafter, he was treated with psychotherapy, stimulants, and antidepressants as needed, and attended specialized schools for the LD (including college).

Longitudinal data from two evaluations since age 11 are presented in Table 18.8. As seen, Mr. C initially showed average verbal aptitude and low-average nonverbal aptitude (i.e., VIQ = 108 and PIQ = 88, respectively). Yet, at that time, his basic verbal academic skills were underdeveloped (decoding and spelling at standard scores of 76 and 80, respectively, but with variable comprehension), while his mechanical arithmetic ability was surprisingly strong (standard scores 101 to 113). As an adult, and following both introduction of medication and remedial education, his overall verbal aptitude had improved greatly (i.e., VIQ = 128, superior to very superior range), while his nonverbal aptitude remained about the same (i.e., PIQ = 92, average to low average). Thus, he was the only one of the three cases with longitudinal data that showed the predicted increase in discrepancy between verbal and nonverbal aptitudes. Basic decoding improved to a standard score (SS) of 92, but underlying phonemic processing deficits were still apparent (i.e., SS = 83 on Pseudoword Decoding), and reading comprehension was average and essentially unchanged. Math remained a relative strength. WAIS-III Index scores showed that, similar to the larger NLD sample, Mr. C's greatest weakness was his slow processing speed (SS = 79), followed distantly by his relatively weak perceptual organization ability (i.e., SS = 97).

Table 18.8 Mr. C's Longitudinal IQ and Achievement Test Scores

Age		11	24
Wechsler IQ			
Verbal scale IQ		108	128
Performance scale IQ		88	92
Full scale IQ		99	112
Wechsler Indices			
Verbal comprehension		NA	126
Perceptual organization		NA	97
Processing speed		NA	79
Freedom from distractibility/working memory		NA	111
Misc. Achievement			
Reading decoding	WRAT (WIAT-11)	76	92
Reading comprehension	Gray Oral (11)	105	101
(Metropolitan)		79	
Numerical ability	WRAT (11)	113	107
(Metropolitan)		101	
Spelling	WRAT (WIAT-11)	80	83

Other tests of emotional processing revealed intact ability to recognize emotional states in pictures and voices, while tests of neuropsychological abilities revealed executive dysfunction (e.g., deficits in organization and planning, and novel problem solving), bilaterally impaired motor dexterity, and impaired sustained attention.

Behavioral Observations and Outcome Mr. C was always on time, cooperative, and appropriately groomed and attired. His speech volume and prosody were sometimes odd, and he could be pedantic, perseverative, and/or tangential. Nevertheless, he showed excellent sense of humor, made good eye contact, and was well related.

Mr. C's interest in sports was judged to be a passion rather than an obsessive preoccupation, and he demonstrated a very wide range of other interests (including theater, literature, and politics). In addition, his thinking was overly rigid and concrete, but he was judged to be too flexible and socially engaged to fully meet criteria for Asperger's syndrome. In many ways, he represented the prototype of what many would consider NLD, including the seizure disorder and birth trauma he shares with most of Mykelbust's original cases. Moreover, like many of those original cases and in our current sample, math was not a weakness but rather his strength. He did also show the common ADHD, here primarily inattentive type, and was being treated for depression and anxiety disorders. Unfortunately, he has still not found a suitable vocation but is trying to develop a business that takes advantage of his copious creativity.

Summary and Thoughts on Case Studies

We examined longitudinal data for three young men with probable NLD and found that all were also diagnosed with ADHD and had some degree of executive dysfunction. Thus, these cases support previous observations of a close association between ADHD and NLD, which is not surprising given the posited importance of the right hemisphere for both (see Stefanatos & Wasserstein for a review, 2001). Moreover, none showed a consistent math deficit over time and these difficulties had little apparent association to social dysfunction. In fact, the best math profile (Mr. C) was seen in the case with the worst social abilities. All had received multiple interventions throughout their lives but showed different outcomes. Psychosocial outcomes, while often negative, were not necessarily so. It was not possible to determine the predictors for success from available information, although we would expect that differences in level of executive function ability may ultimately be most important in enabling people to control impulses and thus maximize their development.

Notably, two individuals exhibited strength in one area of nonverbal function, abstract visual pattern matching, which paradoxically provided a more accurate measure of their intellectual aptitude. This raises questions about the nature of the nonverbal deficits in NLD, and suggests that nontimed measures of nonverbal pattern matching and abstract thinking (i.e., Ravens Progressive Matrices, WAIS-III Matrix Reasoning) may be useful as estimates of intellectual ability in this population.

Last, while Tsatsanis and Rourke (this volume, Chapter 7) suggest that NLD individuals likely evidence increasing discrepancy between their cognitive strengths and weaknesses over time (due to an overreliance on their strengths), only one of these three adults showed the predicted pattern. Instead, in the other two cases, the discrepancy decreased but for different reasons. For one person, the domains that were initially strong became weaker, and for the other person the domains that were initially weak became stronger. Thus, one young man actually made his greatest gains in his weakest areas. This observation suggests that for some individuals, core NLD deficits may represent developmental delays (rather than fixed deficits) or may be responsive to interventions. The differences between the three men again illustrate the inherent variability in adult outcomes for this population. The changing discrepancy patterns also suggest this primary indicator of NLD (i.e., significant verbal/nonverbal aptitude differences) may not be stable throughout life. In view of these findings,

Tsatsanis and Rourke's recommendation that a VIQ-PIQ discrepancy be viewed only as a single indicator of NLD, and interpreted in the context of behavioral, academic and social behaviors, as well as neuropsychological findings, is particularly salient.

Summary and General Conclusions

Review of the historical origins of the NLD indicates that the construct initially emerged as a distinctive *symptom complex* in children with learning disabilities. It was then was regarded as a *syndrome* when the collection of behaviors were considered to arise from specific functional impairments related to right-hemisphere dysfunction and subsequently white-matter deficiency. Relatively little information has been available regarding variations in the developmental course and long-term outcomes of NLD. Without this knowledge, it is unclear which of the core features of NLD, evident at initial diagnosis (usually in elementary school-aged children), remain stable and which are transient or dissipate over protracted periods of time. Without this information, our understanding of the syndrome is incomplete and a determination of potential causal pathways must remain indeterminate or underspecified. Here, we attempted to address some of these issues through an empirically based exploratory study of adults with this poorly understood disorder.

Clinical data were examined for adults presenting to a private neuropsychological clinic with a mean 21-point VIQ-PIQ discrepancy and who also met many of Rourke's criteria for NLD. These clients were predominantly young, white, right-handed, well educated, gainfully employed, and had generally above-average aptitude. We also looked at three case studies for whom longitudinal test results and history were available. Both data sets showed several recurrent findings: (a) ADHD was almost universal, (b) depression and social isolation were common but not universal, (c) the core markers of NLD did not necessarily coexist (but rather seemed fairly independent), and (d) psychosocial outcomes covered a broad range, even in consideration of this selective clinically referred cohort. The group data further suggested that LD in this intelligent NLD sample extended to all basic academic skill areas, not just math, and that individuals appear to learn or use their skills atypically (e.g., verbal skills are more of a determinant of mathematical achievement). Importantly, slow processing speed (and underlying motor slowness or visual-processing slowness), rather than poor visual perception per se, may be the most universal neuropsychological marker. Moreover, only one of the case studies showed the predicted increasing cognitive discrepancy with development.

The importance of slow processing speed in this study converges with other studies that found PSI to be especially relevant for NLD children. For example, Waxman and Casey (2006) summarize evidence suggesting that performance on PSI relative to other WISC-III Index scores was especially meaningful for understanding a subgroup of children with nonverbal processing deficiency they identified in a cluster analysis of 182 WISC-III and WIAT-II (Wechsler Individual Achievement Test–2nd Edition) profiles obtained from children with perceived impairments in cognitive or academic functioning. Moreover, particularly depressed PSI may be a characteristic of an NLD profile irrespective of the degree of VIQ-PIQ difference. While the VIQ-PIQ discrepancy was only 8 points in the Waxman and Casey sample, a pattern of particularly depressed processing speed has also been identified with NLD profiles in children with larger (18 points) VIQ-PIQ discrepancies (Donders & Warchausky, 1997). Since slow processing is not characteristic of all LD (Waxman & Casey, 2006), it therefore may have a special meaning in NLD and needs to be better understood.

In terms of long-term outcome, our study results indicate that the NLD profile does not necessarily imply a very poor prognosis for adaptive behavior and achievement in adulthood. While many (and perhaps even most) NLD adults continued to struggle, results from both the group and case studies illustrate that a proportion of NLD adults do quite well vocationally, educationally, and even socially, especially when they have the benefits of interventions and intellectual strength. Some people in this study were very high functioning, both socially and adaptively, a few even worked in quantitative fields, and most did not have major psychopathology. Indeed, while this cohort represents a clinical sample, the reason for referral (often self-referred) was educational planning rather than concerns regarding social or emotional adaptation.

The results raise important questions regarding the status of NLD as a syndrome. One of the issues emerging from the current dataset concerns the apparently weak coherence of the NLD symptom complex in adults. Some individuals had math problems, some had visuomotor deficits, some had social or emotional problems, but very few had dysfunction in all, or even most, of these target domains. Similar questions have emerged in consideration of findings in children. Thus, it may be more accurate to conceptualize the NLD profile as encompassing a number of possible symptoms or symptom clusters, which may reflect different causal pathways arising out of dysfunction impacting *different* aspects of right-hemisphere function. Based on our adult sample, it appeared that the core markers of NLD (social problems and math problems) were not necessarily associated and that the pattern of symptoms could have a number of different origins. Such issues may underlie the continuing lack of diagnostic consensus.

At best, current conceptions of NLD are polytypic in structure: Individuals regarded as having NLD need not share any single attribute or any formally specified pattern of attributes. Accordingly, the current emphasis on math disability for the diagnosis and characterization of NLD may as much represent a historical consequence of the prolific body of neuropsychological research on subtyping LD children on the basis of patterns of academic performance, rather than the strength of the association of specific math disability with other components of the symptom complex. That is, children who did not have learning problems per se but who still had social or nonverbal processing issues would not have been included in LD subtyping studies that have so influenced current conceptualizations of NLD. Given that the main purpose of developing and validating different subtypes of LD is to construct entities about which we can make generalizations that will facilitate diagnosis and treatment and allow reasoned prognostic assertions, it would be inappropriate to place too much emphasis on specific math disability. Bright adolescents or adults may develop alternative and highly adaptive means to progress in the development of quantitative skills. Alternatively, some children with the NLD profile have broader learning problems that encompass verbal areas of basic academic achievement.

This was an exploratory study with many methodological limits, some of which were discussed. The findings nevertheless raise many questions. What is the relationship between ADHD and NLD? Are there subtypes of NLD with different presentations and prognoses? Can we come up with some diagnostic consensus? What are the predictors of success and the best ways to intervene? In short, we need to go back to the historical roots and recall that the symptom complex probably reflects, directly or indirectly, the influence of right-hemisphere dysfunction, with an anterior-posterior gradient for symptoms, and likely different forms of underlying pathophysiology. Consequently, symptom clusters should be variable depending on the brain areas involved (e.g., anterior or posterior or both, focal or diffuse), and the developmental course should be variable in part depending on the nature of tissue dysfunction (e.g., white-matter transmission difficulties, structural abnormalities, scar tissue, developmental delays of some sort) and in part by the level of function in intact areas and the extent to which these strengths can be recruited in the service of compensating for processing deficiencies. Nevertheless, and importantly, NLD symptoms do continue into adulthood and can take a substantial toll on productive life. It is extremely important that we "not throw out the baby with the bath" but continue to work at better understanding this elusive clinical entity.

References

Cleaver, R. L., & Whitman, R. D. (1998). Right hemisphere, white-matter learning disabilities associated with depression in adolescent and young adult psychiatric population. *Journal of Nervous & Mental Disease, 186,* 561–565.

Denckla, M. B. (1978). Minimal brain dysfunction. In J. S. Chall & A. L. Mirsky (Eds.), *Education and the brain (77th yearbook of the National Society for the Study of Education, part 2).* Chicago: University of Chicago Press.

Donders, J., & Warchausky, S. (1997). WISC-III Factor Index score patterns after traumatic head injury in children. *Child Neuropsychology, 3,* 71–78.

Drummond, C. R., Ahmad, S. A., & Rourke, B. P. (2005). Rules for the classification of younger children with nonverbal learning disabilities and basic phonological processing disabilities. *Archives of Clinical Neuropsychology, 20,* 171–182.

Fisher, N. J., & DeLuca, J. W. (1997). Verbal learning strategies of adolescents and adults with the syndrome of nonverbal learning disabilities. *Child Neuropsychology, 3,* 192–198.

Frith, U., & Frith, C. D. (2001). The biological basis of social interaction. *Current Directions in Psychological Science, 10,* 151–155.

Grace, J., & Malloy, F. (1992). Neuropsychiatric aspects of right hemisphere learning disability. *Neuropsychiatry, Neuropsychology and Behavioral Neurology, 5,* 194–204.

Greiffenstein, M. F., & Baker, W. J. (2002). Neuropsychological and psychosocial correlates of adult arithmetic deficiency. *Neuropsychology, 16,* 451–458.

Grodzinsky, Y. (2003). Imaging the grammatical brain. In M. Arbib (Ed.), *Handbook of brain theory and neural networks* (2nd ed., pp. 551–556). Cambridge, MA: MIT Press.

Johnson, D. J., & Myklebust, H. R. (1967). *Learning disabilities: Educational principles and remedial approaches.* New York: Grune & Stratton.

Klin, A., Volkmar, F. R., Sparrow, S. S., Cicchetti, D. V., & Rourke, B. P. (1995). Validity and neuropsychological characterization of Asperger syndrome: Convergence with nonverbal learning disabilities syndrome. *Journal of Child Psychology and Psychiatry, 36,* 1127–1140.

Lezak, M. D., Loring D. W., Howieson, D. B., Hannay, H. J., & Fischer, J. S. (2004). *Neuropsychological assessment.* New York: Oxford University Press.

Myklebust, H. R. (1975). Nonverbal learning disabilities: Assessment and intervention. In H. R. Myklebust (Ed.), *Progress in learning disabilities* (Vol. 3, pp. 85–121). New York: Grune & Stratton.

Pennington, B. F. (1991). *Diagnosing neurological disorders: A neuropsychological framework.* New York: Guilford Press.

Rourke, B. P. (1975). Brain-behavior relationships in children with learning disabilities. *American Psychologist, 30,* 911–920.

Rourke, B. P. (1987). Syndrome of nonverbal learning disabilities: The final common pathway of white-matter disease/dysfunction? *The Clinical Neuropsychologist, 1,* 209–234.

Rourke, B. P. (1988). Socio-emotional disturbances of learning-disabled children. *Journal of Consulting and Clinical Psychology, 56,* 801–810.

Rourke, B. P. (1989). *Nonverbal learning disabilities: The syndrome and the model.* New York: Guilford Press.

Rourke, B. P. (Ed.). (1995). *Syndrome of nonverbal learning disabilities: Neuro-developmental manifestations.* New York: Guilford Press.

Rourke, B. P., & Finlayson, M. A. J. (1978). Neuropsychological significance of variations in patterns of academic performance: Verbal and visual-spatial abilities. *Journal of Abnormal Child Psychology, 6*, 121–133.

Rourke, B. P., & Strang, J. D. (1978). Neuropsychological significance of variations in patterns of academic performance: Motor, psychomotor, and tactile-perceptual abilities. *Journal of Pediatric Psychology, 3*, 62–66.

Semrud-Clikeman, M., & Hynd, G. (1990). Right hemispheric dysfunction in nonverbal learning disabilities: Social, academic, and adaptive functioning in adults and children. *Psychological Bulletin, 107*, 198–209.

Solanto M. V., Etefia, K., & Marks D. J. (2004). The utility of self-report measures and the continuous performance test in the diagnosis of ADHD in adults. *CNS Spectrum, 9(9)*, 649–659.

Stefanatos, G. A., & Wasserstein, J. (2001). Attention deficit/hyperactivity disorder as a right hemisphere syndrome: Selective literature review and detailed neuropsychological case studies. *Annals of the New York Academy of Science, 931*, 172–195.

Strang, J. D., & Rourke, B. P. (1983). Concept-formation/non-verbal reasoning abilities of children who exhibit specific academic problems with arithmetic. *Journal of Clinical Child Psychology, 12*, 33–39.

Strang, J. D., & Rourke, B. P. (1985). Adaptive behavior of children who exhibit specific arithmetic disabilities and associated neuropsychological abilities and deficits. In B. P. Rourke (Ed.), *Neuropsychology of learning disabilities: Essentials of subtype analysis* (pp. 302–328). New York: Guilford Press.

Strub, R., & Geschwind, N. (1974). Gerstmann syndrome without aphasia. *Cortex, 10*, 378–387.

Voeller, K. K. S. (1986). Right-hemisphere deficit syndrome in children. *American Journal of Psychiatry, 143*, 1004–1009.

Wasserstein, J., Zappulla, R., Rosen, J., & Gerstman, L. (1984). Evidence for differentiation of right hemisphere visual-perceptual functions. *Brain and Cognition, 3(1)*, 51–57.

Waxman, R. S., & Casey, J. E. (2006). Empirically derived ability-achievement subtypes in a clinical sample. *Child Neuropsychology, 12*, 23–38.

Weinberg, W. A., & McLean, A. (1986). A diagnostic approach to developmental specific learning disorders. *Journal of Child Neurology, 1*, 158–172.

Weintraub, S., & Mesulam, M.-M. (1983). Developmental learning disabilities of the right hemisphere: Emotional, interpersonal, and cognitive components. *Archives of Neurology, 40*, 463–469.

CHAPTER **19**

Concluding Thoughts

HOPE SCHREIBER, LORRAINE E. WOLF,
and JEANETTE WASSERSTEIN

Contents

Representing some of the most contemporary developments in the investigation of learning disorders in adults, the chapters collected in this book are by a diverse group of clinicians and researchers. Yet, in their study of brain development, genetics and neuroimaging, diagnostic assessment, outcome, and policy, these writers have utilized new advances in neuroscience and technology to define the purpose and trajectory of their work. In this final section, we would like to review some prevailing themes that emerged throughout the volume and suggest future directions for both research and clinical practice.

The progression of chapters in this book was structured to introduce a life-span perspective, beginning with normal and abnormal developmental models and then tying development to brain models and genetic mechanisms involved in specific learning disorders. We then moved to clinical issues of special interest to neuropsychology, including the varieties of learning disorders, diagnosis, and assessment strategies. We ended with life outcomes of school and work and some topics relevant to policy, areas perhaps less familiar (but no less relevant) to many workers in the field. Our original interest was to explore some aspects of neuroimaging and genetics as they have contributed to our understanding of learning disorders in adults. While all of the authors worked "blind" to the process of the volume as a whole, remarkable consistencies emerged across all of the chapters.

This final chapter will echo the structure of the book, presenting five common themes that arose in many of the chapters: concepts of atypical brain development, heterogeneity versus single core deficit, tensions between clinical versus empirical models, conceptual versus measurement issues in assessment, and longitudinal outcome (including low literacy). By reviewing these ideas, we hope that the unique role neuropsychology can play to improve clinical practice and to facilitate the emergence of new research ideas will become clearer.

Atypical Brain Development

It is not possible to understand neurodevelopmental learning disorders without considering normal as well as atypical brain development (ABD). Sherman sets the stage by highlighting that, rather than simply reflecting a delay in acquisition, core academic skills develop differently in normal and LD populations. Kniele and Gur further this idea by presenting evidence of sexual dimorphism in brain development in learning disorders, deepening our understanding of the increased prevalence of LD in boys versus girls. Gilger and Kaplan then introduce the concept of "atypical brain development," a complex process involving genes, intra-uterine and perinatal factors, postnatal brain growth, and elaboration. It is not only perinatal factors that affect genetically driven brain development throughout the life span but also the elaborate and complex interactions between neurological substrate and environment.

It is tempting to invoke the early nomenclature of "minimal brain dysfunction" (MBD) in the discussion of ABD; however, the terms are quite distinct. MBD refers to an "ill-defined syndrome" (Gilger & Kaplan, Chapter 3, this volume), while ABD refers to a complex set of processes, the underpinnings of which are still in investigation. Quoting Muller's work, Tager-Flusberg and colleagues (Chapter 6, this volume) caution us about the assumptions we may make about atypical brain development from neuroimaging studies:

> It is important to be cautious about the interpretation of findings from brain imaging studies. Neurodevelopmental disorders like SLI and ASD are known to arise from disturbances in brain development, beginning, perhaps, during the early stages of embryonic development. At the same time a brain image taken from either a child or adult with a disorder is the end product of abnormal brain development, and it is not clear whether observed abnormalities in the image are the cause of behavioral symptoms such as impaired language or the result of the atypical delayed developmental pathway that defines the disorder. (Muller, 2004)

Further research will be required to develop and apply the concept of ABD throughout the entire life span.

ABD may also be invoked in our understanding of comorbidity. Gilger and Kaplan argue that the use of the word "comorbidity" may be problematic in considering disorders that are frequently seen together, such as reading and other learning and attention disorders, or psychiatric and learning disorders (also see Schreiber, this volume, Chapter 13). Considering these disorders to coexist leaves open the etiological question: from whence did this collection of symptoms come? Are they inherited independently, are they interrelated, or are they the manifestations of atypical development?

Core Deficits or Heterogeneity?

The search for an underlying explanatory principle or core deficit has traditionally been the goal of many studies of neurodevelopmental disorders. More recently, however, investigators are moving from core deficit hypotheses to an understanding that these conditions are quite heterogeneous in presentation and quite possibly represent multiple subtypes and phenotypic variants. For example, the single-deficit model of behavioral inhibition as the defining core of attention-deficit/hyperactivity disorder (ADHD) (Barkley, 1997) has lately given way to the discussion of subtypes and multiple deficits (Pennington, 2005). The exploration of the role of different executive functions in some types of ADHD and heterogeneity in the phenotypic distribution of such functions suggests that ADHD may in fact be comprised of variable constellations of symptoms or subtypes (e.g., endophenotypes; Nigg, 2005; Doyle et al., 2005; Willcutt, Doyle, Nigg, Faraone, & Pennington, 2005; Stevenson et al., 2005). Delineation of clear subtypes is often complicated by the degree to which symptoms appear to overlap. Exploration of the cognitive heterogeneity of ADHD, as well as family history, "comorbidity," and type of symptom (e.g., predominantly inattentive or hyperactive/impulsive symptoms, executive dysfunction or limited motivation), may be necessary prerequisites to successful endophenotypic studies. Only in this way can more homogeneous groups be formed for neurocognitive or molecular genetic studies (Doyle et al., 2005; Waldman, 2005).

In a similar fashion, reading disorders are often described as having a core deficit in phonemic awareness and decoding based on abnormal performance on tests of these fundamental reading skills and the association of these deficits with discrete brain regions in the left hemisphere. Yet the authors in this volume present new information from genetic and neuroimaging studies that suggests that this focus represents only a beginning in our understanding of such disorders. Grigorenko (this volume, Chapter 4) describes the four candidate genes associated with dyslexia that have recently been identified and that appear to be involved with neuronal migration and axon crossing. She elegantly elaborates the many sources of variance from which gene expression may be derived. Individual difference in reading skill is not only derived from complex genetic mechanisms but also involves consideration of socioeconomic, educational, and environmental factors, she adds.

Compensatory mechanisms that develop over the course of development and through education and remediation may involve efforts to shift reading towards more anterior and right-hemisphere sites (Shaywitz & Shaywitz, 2005). In similar fashion, Gilger and Kaplan (Chapter 3, this volume) suggest that brain plasticity in response to a deficit can actually result in an atypical developmental trajectory. Such atypical development continues into young adulthood, such that even well-compensated adults with childhood histories of dyslexia usually remain slow readers with poor automaticity in reading functions (Daniels, Chapter 5, this volume).

Thus, multiple genetic, developmental, and environmental factors can affect phenotype and lead to heterogeneous presentation in clinical and academic settings. For example, the recent finding where a single gene appears to be related to both reading and ADHD is most interesting in this light (Willcutt et al., 2002). Grigorenko (Chapter 4, this volume) notes it is possible that there is at least a partial overlap between the two groups of genes involved in both disorders. Tager-Flusberg and colleagues (this volume, Chapter 6) also underscore the heterogeneity of specific language impairment and autism spectrum disorders. Here, too, core phenotypic features are not reflective of the wide range of symptoms often observed, nor are they reflective of differing phenotypic presentation depending on whether individuals are of preschool age, school age, or adults.

The heterogeneity of reading and language disorders creates a number of research challenges. Tager-Flusberg and colleagues note that subject heterogeneity has hindered our ability to compare research studies with the intent of drawing generalizations. Clearly, better defined research groups that either reduce or take heterogeneity into account are necessary. When studying genetically complex behaviors, Grigorenko describes two approaches to defining groups in research: the cognitive endophenotype and the syndrome, each of which has its strengths and weaknesses. Others have suggested using phenotypes generated from neuroimaging studies for research samples (Goldberg & Weinberg, 2004). Yet changes observed in functional neuroimaging studies, no matter how groups are defined, are correlational, not causal. Further clarification in how to link patterns of brain activation to the genetic mechanisms of reading disorders may continue to improve our understanding of individual difference (Grigorenko, this volume).

Krueger and Grafman's report (Chapter 8, this volume) of recent structural and functional neuroimaging studies point to parietal involvement using subpopulations of dyscalculic populations. In addition, fMRI studies of other well-defined genetic conditions associated with dyscalculia, velocardiofacial syndrome, and fragile X, showed hypoactivation in a parietofrontal network. Yet they too note that neuroimaging studies remain limited due to the heterogeneity of dyscalculia and its association with other disorders.

Tager-Flusberg and colleagues point to the need to more accurately define subtypes in the heterogeneous disorders they study, specific language impairment and autism spectrum disorders: "Investigating brain abnormalities within different subtypes may yield more consistent findings within and across studies; and, in turn, neuroimaging studies may help to define different subtypes on the basis of neurobiological profiles rather than behavioral profiles" (e.g., this volume, Chapter 6, p. 146). Heterogeneity in the clinical world is described by Schreiber, who has observed a high frequency of psychiatric disorders in postsecondary students referred for neuropsychological evaluation of learning disorders, and their families. A raised index of suspicion for coexisting disorders may indeed be appropriate in the clinical world, state Gilger and Kaplan. In addition, a better understanding of the nature of such associations would be helpful for both assessment and treatment.

A number of authors suggest new, combined strategies to better understand the subjects of their study. Gilger and Kaplan note that future dyslexia research should include multiple measures so to capture the complexity of their subjects' strengths and weaknesses. From a clinical perspective, Mapou echoes this orientation, noting that comprehensive assessment is necessary to rule out other salient disorders and to identify associated disorders. Tager-Flusberg, Lindgren, and Mody (Chapter 6, this volume) describe a growing methodological trend to combine EEG, MEG, and fMRI to improve spatiotemporal characterization of brain activity of subgroups of specific language impairment and autism spectrum disorders. Diffusion tensor imaging methods have promise in better defining normal and disrupted neural connectivity, they note, and when combined with fMRI may be helpful in better understanding neurodevelopmental disorders. Simos et al. (2005) also discuss the need to improve spatial sensitivity and temporal resolution in neuroimaging in the study of children with dyslexia. Their solution involves use of magnetoencephalography (magnetic source imaging) with which they track brain circuits involved with reading in normal and problematic early readers to better outline the developmental course leading to atypical activation patterns in older children with reading difficulties. Thus, the authors point to a number of promising trends involving multiple technologies and well-defined research groups, coupled with an appreciation of the current limits of our technological know-how. The linking of instruction and remediation to changes in brain activation in poor readers presents promise in understanding those individuals who do not respond well to such intervention. In addition, it suggests that "quality instruction does impact brain function" (Simos, 2006, p. 609).

The Clinical–Empirical Dialectic

Clinicians working with neurodevelopmental disorders have long understood that learning disorders are heterogeneous in their presentation. Surely many are relieved to find research efforts validating their clinical perspective. The current trend of shifting away from neuroanatomical localization toward a systems perspective of brain function, and the embracing of complex concepts of genetic transmission and epigenetic processes, clearly foster this viewpoint. The clinical experience is replete with evaluations of clusters of symptoms, some of which appear to be "as expected" per research and others that are not. The individual variety of presentation can be of spectacular proportions, as those in clinical practice are well aware. More often than not, the profiles of individual patients do not conform to the group findings of strictly defined research populations. This may particularly be the case when assessing adults, since there is so little empirical research to turn to. The ongoing tension between such clinical observation and empirically based or evidence-based assessment can create fertile ground for further understanding of neurodevelopmental disorders as clinician observations inform research and vice versa.

Following the pathways led by empirical research can aid the clinician in syndrome identification and provide guides for treatment. Conversely, the clinician can assist researchers in developing focused questions, which may explain the "unexpected" variability in clinical populations. The pursuit of an evidence-based approach has been more recently suggested as appropriate for assessment as well as treatment. Hunsley and Mash (2005) suggest consideration of factors beyond reliability and validity, to include utilization of appropriate normative groups, and choice of instruments with adequate sensitivity and specificity. By comparing the consistency of neuropsychological data with data from other sources such as clinical history, patient's complaints, academic and vocational history, reports of significant others, neurodiagnostic tests, and medical records, for instance, an operational estimate of ecological validity of such data may be obtained (Sbordone, 1996). For example, evidence-based approaches may better assist in using test data to predict outcome. To date, there is limited rigorously designed evidence-based research available to help us understand the developmental trajectory of those individuals with LD who do and who do not pursue higher education. Weinstein, Wolf, and Schreiber (Chapter 17, this volume) further discuss the limits of our knowledge in how to use neuropsychological testing to predict future vocational performance in professionals with LD.

Assessment: Concepts versus Measurement

More than any other neuropsychological disorder, the conceptual definition of learning disability is inextricably bound with its measurement. The original definitions were formulated in 1977 when the U.S. Department of Education established both a process and a set of criteria to guide school districts in the identification of students with "unexpected underachievement." This concept assumes that academic skills are typically commensurate with native intelligence and that this relationship can be reliably measured. By definition, the student with a learning disability is performing academically at a level that would not be expected given his or her age, grade, and innate potential and in the absence of sensory, socioeconomic, or educational deprivation. Thus, unexpected academic failure, which is conceptualized as inherent in the individual and rooted in neurobiological causes, is central to the definition of LD.

The *Diagnostic and Statistical Manual of Mental Disorders* (4th ed., *DSM-IV*) adopted this language in the diagnostic criteria for specific academic disorders. Disorders of learning are diagnosed when academic achievement "is substantially below the expected given the person's chronological age, measured intelligence, and age-appropriate education" (APA, 1994, p. 46).

Further, the *DSM-IV* recommends administration of standardized ability and achievement tests followed by a comparison of scores to determine whether there is a discrepancy. The *International Classification of Diseases and Related Health Problems (ICD-10)* "Diagnostic Criteria for the Diagnosis of Specific Reading Disorder" goes further in stating that a reading disorder, for instance, is defined as follows: "A score on reading accuracy and/or comprehension that is at least 2 standard errors of prediction below the level expected on the basis of the child's chronological age and general intelligence" (World Health Organization, p. 176). Thus, the three most common assessment paradigms focus on defining LD as a statistical discrepancy between ability and achievement.

However, many disagree as to the psychometric validity of the discrepancy definition of LD (Siegel, 1988, 1989; Stanovich, 1999; Francis et al., 2005; also see Kelman & Lester, 1997 for a thorough discussion of this). Siegel and Smythe (this volume) have argued this point. Several recent consensus and congressional reports (summarized in Fletcher, 2004) strongly critiqued continued use of the discrepancy analyses to determine eligibility for special education. The most recent reauthorization of Individuals with Disabilities Education Act (IDEA) in 2004 (codified in August of 2006, www.ed.gov/policy/speced/guid/idea/idea2004.html) removes the mandate for IQ discrepancy as a means to classify students with LD but recommends (a) a broader assessment of cognitive skills related to academic development, and (b) a response to targeted intervention within the general education environment. Siegel and Smythe note that that assessment of learning disability in adults must move beyond simple psychometrics and reliance on criteria such as the IQ-achievement discrepancy. Concentration on assessment of component skills such as phonological processing has proven to be valuable in the evaluation of reading. Yet when learning disorders are viewed as complex neurodevelopmental entities, as they are in this book, a circumscribed evaluation may not be sufficient at times. Furthermore, none of the major diagnostic classification models, including *DSM-IV, ICD-10*, and IDEA, specifically address identification of learning disorders in adults.

In many instances, the clinical setting may guide the questions we wish to ask in an assessment; adults and students may be referred to different sorts of settings depending on the level of complexity of the referral question. Furthermore, the qualities and constraints inherent in such settings have resulted in different research questions being asked, even among our authors. Mapou points to the empirical basis of comprehensive evaluation of adults with learning disorders, and notes there is no one right way to diagnose LD in adults. Rather, he refers to the complexity of the process, one based on the needs of the client. It may use testing data, the relationship of some pieces of data to others, the history and environment in which the individual functions, and our knowledge of brain function. This view is echoed by Wolf and Kaplan (this volume) in discussing the assessment of regulatory deficits, by Grigorenko in her discussion of varieties of reading disabilities, and by Schreiber in her discussion of coexisting psychiatric disorders.

Certainly, the context in which evaluation takes place, the nature of the referral question, and the intended effect of the evaluation are all important. Seidman (2006a, 2006b) has similarly suggested that ADHD may best be assessed through different intensities of assessment depending on the needs of the student, client, or patient. He notes that screening may focus the assessment and referral questions, while an intermediate level of evaluation may address coexisting disorders such as LD, psychiatric disorders, and emotional disturbance. A comprehensive evaluation may add those features that allow the student or patient to seek accommodation and may allow the individual to learn more about how he or she functions. In particular, when there is a discrepancy between one's appraisal of how one thinks one should function and one's ability to actually do so, such an evaluation becomes more pressing. This enhancement of self-knowledge, according to Seidman (as well as Weinstein, Wolf, and Schreiber, Chapter 17, this volume), can lead to a realistic appraisal of one's strengths and weaknesses, improvement in the understanding of family members or significant others about the nature of the disorder, and a reduction in the tendency for others to blame the individual for "lazy" or "irresponsible" behavior.

As echoed by Wolf and Kaplan, and by Weinstein, Wolf, and Schreiber, the ultimate goal of such an evaluation is to improve self-control, regulation, and "metacognitive strategies" to manage the disorder, and to improve self-esteem and feelings of mastery. Assessment is also often the key to educational or work-related services and accommodations, as discussed by Gregg and colleagues (this volume) and by Macurdy and Geetter (Chapter 16, this volume). Yet there are no clear guidelines for what constitutes an appropriate level of assessment, as most agencies echoed the requirements of the IDEA. In light of the new reauthorization, as note Siegel and Smythe, new criteria need to be developed for adults. We assert that the staged assessment approach outlined by Seidman for ADHD is also appropriate for adults with learning disorders. Neuropsychologists are expert in evaluating the unique cognitive processes as required in the new IDEA, but more importantly can provide detailed information about the behavioral effects and long-term implications of such impairments (Proctor-Weber & Golden, 2006), as well as tie such findings to current research.

Longitudinal Research and Outcome in Adulthood

Few would dispute the importance of longitudinal research to better understand changes in phenotype of neurodevelopmental disorders throughout development and into adulthood. Bernice Wong (1994) has described one major benefit from longitudinal research for individuals with learning disorders: verification of hypotheses concerning particular developmental patterns. Gogtay et al. (2004), among others noted in Kniele and Gur (Chapter 2, this volume), tracked structural images of 13 children over 10 years, demonstrating maturational patterns of myelogenesis and synaptic pruning occurring concurrently. Particularly as we learn more and more about normal development, hypotheses about atypical developmental trajectories will be easier to test. In addition, the importance of enhancing our knowledge of the sexual differentiation of brain structure, function, and neurophysiology could improve our understanding of why males and females differ in prevalence and perhaps phenotype of LD. Kniele and Gur refer to their excitement about advances in genomics and behavioral endophenotypes as they may contribute to our understanding of sex differences.

Developmental trajectories into adulthood of many LDs were addressed by the authors. In their study of NLD, Tsatsanis and Rourke (Chapter 7, this volume) suggest that some neuropsychological deficits may worsen in adulthood, particularly those related to social skills, communication, clumsy behavior, and daydreaming. Visuospatial problems originating in childhood continue to be present in adulthood, as noted in a large longitudinal study (Spreen & Haaf, 1986). However, Wasserstein and colleagues (Chapter 18, this volume) did not find pervasive impairment in their case studies, and, although sometimes present, psychopathology was not universal. Differences in diagnostic procedures, LD definitions, IQ, and socioeconomic make-up of samples may account for some of the differences. Associated psychopathology also may be present in adulthood in some individuals. Schreiber (Chapter 13, this volume) notes that coexisting disorders were frequently present in postsecondary students referred for evaluation of learning disorders or ADHD. To her eye, a better understanding of the nature of the association between psychiatric and neurodevelopmental disorders seems important for treatment and outcome with this group. Daniels (Chapter 5, this volume) describes a typical developmental trajectory for individuals with reading disorders as they enter adulthood; limited automaticity tends to be the rule, in contrast to difficulties characteristic of childhood such as impaired phonological skill. Krueger and Grafman (Chapter 8, this volume) suggest that longitudinal studies could be used to track organism-environmental interaction throughout development into adulthood for dyscalculia; such focus could easily be beneficial in application to all learning disorders.

Thus, it is only through developmentally oriented, longitudinal work that we may better grasp effective intervention and remediation of learning disorders. Gilger and Kaplan (Chapter 3, this volume) note that while intensive remediation could perhaps improve neuronal communication to some degree, compensatory, more intact, brain systems may improve reading skill over time. The subsequent appearance of diffuse clinical presentations in adulthood suggests to them that comprehensive evaluation and treatment focusing on many symptoms would obviate the failures involved in more circumscribed interventions. Tager-Flusberg, Lindgren, and Mody (Chapter 6) note the recent introduction of brain-imaging measures to chart effectiveness of treatment or intervention programs. They quote Tallal (2004), who hypothesizes that "remapping" brain areas may be possible, presupposing the persistence of plasticity throughout the life span. Outcome studies addressing effectiveness of interventions in adulthood for LD are limited. The presence of well-established compensatory strategies may confound such work, suggest Tsatsanis and Rourke. In children, phonologically based reading intervention led to development of neural systems in both anterior and posterior brain regions (Shaywitz & Shaywitz, 2005). Reading fluency is a critical skill (National Reading Panel, 2000), yet many adults with dyslexia do not achieve it. Furthermore, some professionals may attain a competence in decoding words frequently seen in their own fields but continue to have difficulty decoding less familiar words or learning a foreign language (Downey, Snyder, & Hill, 2000; Sparks, Ganschow, & Pohlman, 1989; Ganschow & Sparks, 1986). Young adults from the Connecticut Longitudinal Study, followed since they were age 5, who were persistently poor readers were accurate at reading high-frequency words but less accurate at low-frequency and unfamiliar words (Shaywitz & Shaywitz, 2005). Similarly, Gregg and colleagues (Chapter 15, this volume) note the need for investigation of adult writers' skills in a variety of types of tasks, with and without accommodations. In this way, a better understanding of how to effectively "enhance" the writing of adults with learning disorders may be achieved.

Understanding of the natural history of each such learning disorder can provide guidance to the clinician as an individual travels through development. Knowledge about variations in outcome based on age, coexisting disorders, interaction with various environments, gender, socioeconomic status, and other demographic variables can help the clinician predict potential pitfalls and anticipate difficulties in a way that enhances the well-being of the patient or student. Rey-Casserly and Bernstein (Chapter 14, this volume) describe individuals from their practice who transition from high school to college. A successful transition is not just about academic success but also about the adjustments to the entire adult world of work, relationships, and becoming a member of a community. Such success appears to them to be related to "adequate self-regulatory capacities as these are expressed in behavioral flexibility and modulation, in self-control, in appropriate social comportment, and in independence in thinking and reasoning."

Low Literacy in Adults

Only a small subset of adults with learning disabilities are found in colleges and universities. In postsecondary academic contexts, individuals who have any sort of reading comprehension or fluency problem are far more likely to be identified than those who do not attend college. Such individuals represent a far larger group, are heterogeneous, and are underserved (Gerber, 2006). Gerber notes that the research currently available is not systematically conceived, does not easily inform practice, and does not reflect the varied demographic characteristics in race/ethnicity, socioeconomics, gender, and age represented by this group. He concludes that our "islands of knowledge" are limited; only through a more thorough, rigorous, and diverse research agenda, with evidence-based practice in mind, can education and intervention respond well to the populations in need.

Conclusions

Our authors have often expressed both appreciation and caution about the effects of neuroimaging and genetic technologies on our understanding of neurodevelopmental disorders. Thomas Kuhn (c1972) has discussed shifts in scientific paradigms, where one belief system may supplant another as evidence accrues over time. At the present time, it is not so much that one belief system about how the brain works and develops is supplanting another; it is more that layer upon layer of complexity has been added to our understanding. In this way, both the questions being asked and the tools being used are changing. This is a work in progress.

In this climate it is no accident that in 2004 the National Institutes of Health (NIH) (2004) launched the NIH Blueprint for Neuroscience Research, "inspired by recognition that certain themes in neuroscience cross institute and Center boundaries and relate to the prevention and treatment of a broad range of nervous system disorders." In this endeavor, NIH reported a wish to focus on neurodegeneration, neurodevelopment, and plasticity. By reflecting on the themes discussed by our authors, it is not too difficult to address each of these priorities. The need for further focus on adult development, effective interventions for adults with learning disorders, and exploration of aging issues in individuals with potentially vulnerable brains is quite clear. The NIH Blueprint for Neuroscience Research also noted awareness of a schism between basic neuroscience research and clinical research. More interdisciplinary endeavors will be encouraged. Efforts to form large shared databases of brain-imaging data and to increase the number of common protocols in brain research may be of help (Kennedy, Heselgrove, & McInerney, 2003) in ongoing research. Indeed, the benefits of cross-fertilization between genetic and neuroimaging scientists has been underlined by Grigorenko in this volume.

Such shifts in the research community can certainly benefit clinical practice. Macurdy and Geetter suggest that a collaborative effort to enlarge the available knowledge base about what works for adults with learning disorders in both academic and specific work settings can better facilitate the possibility that adults with LD will have an equal opportunity to succeed in a variety of contexts. In addition, the genetic, neuroimaging, and neurobehavioral databases are becoming robust enough to support new definitions of LD that are not solely psychometrically dependent. Improved definitions of LD and implementation of empirically supported evaluation, remediation, accommodation, and policy are no small matter, and certainly much work lies ahead. We hope this volume has moved us forward one small step toward this end.

References

American Psychiatric Association. (1994). *Diagnostic and Statistical Manual of Mental Disorders* (4th ed.). Washington, DC: Author.

Barkley, R. A. (1997). Behavioral inhibition, sustained attention and executive functions: Constructing a unifying theory of ADHD. *Psychological Bulletin, 121*, 65–94.

Boylan, K., Bieling, P., Marriot, M., Begin, H., Young, L., & MacQueen, G. (2004). Impact of comorbid anxiety disorder on outcome in a cohort of patients with bipolar disorder. *Journal of Clinical Psychiatry 65*, 1106–1113.

Downey, D., Snyder, L., & Hill, B. (2000). College students with dyslexia: Persistent linguistic deficits and foreign language learning. *Dyslexia, 6*, 101–111.

Doyle, A., Faraone, S., Seidman, L., Willcutt, E., Nigg, J., Waldman, I., et al. (2005). Are endophenotypes based on measures of executive functions useful for molecular genetic studies of ADHD? *Journal of Child Psychology and Psychiatry, 46*, 774–803.

Fletcher, J. M., Coulter, W. A., & Rischl, D. J. (2004). Alternate approaches to the definition and identification of learning disabilities: Some questions and answers. *Annals of Dyslexia, 54*, 304–331.

Francis, D. J., Fletcher, J. M., Steubing, K. K., Lyon, G. R., Shaywitz, B. A., & Shaywitz, S. E. (2005). Psychometric approaches to the identification of LD: IQ and achievement scores are not sufficient. *Journal of Learning Disabilities, 38*, 98–108.

Ganschow, L., & Sparks, R. (1986). Learning disabilities and foreign language difficulties: Deficit in listening skills? *Journal of Reading, Writing, and Learning Disabilities International, 2*, 305–319.

Gerber, P. J. (2006). Low-literate adults with learning disorders. *Thalamus, 24*, 42–54.

Gogtay, N., Giedd, J. N., Lusk, L., Hayashi, K. M., Greenstein, D., Vaituzis, A. C., et al. (2004). Dynamic mapping of human cortical development during childhood through early adulthood. *Proceedings of the National Academy of Sciences, 101*, 8174–8179.

Goldberg, T. E., & Weinberg, D. R. (2004). Genes and the parsing of cognitive processes. *Trends in Cognitive Sciences, 8*, 325–335.

Hunsley, J., & Mash, E. (2005). Introduction to the special section on developing guidelines for the evidence-based assessment (EBA) of adult disorders. *Psychological Assessment, 17*, 251–255.

Kelman, M., & Lester, G. (1997). *Jumping the Queue: An Inquiry into the Legal Treatment of Students with Learning Disabilities*. Harvard University Press, Cambridge, MA.

Kennedy, D. N., Haselgrove, C., & McInerney, S. (2003), MRI-based morphometric analysis of typical brain development. *Mental Retardation and Developmental Disabilities Research Reviews 9*, 155–160

Krishnan, K. (2005). Psychiatric and medical comorbidities of bipolar disorder. *Psychosomatic Medicine, 67*, 1–8.

Kuhn, T. S. (c1972). *The structure of scientific revolutions* (2nd ed., enlarged). Chicago: University of Chicago Press.

Muller, R.-A. (2004). Genes, language disorders, and developmental archaeology: What role can neuroimaging play? In M. L. Rice & S. F. Warren (Eds.), *Developmental language disorders: From phenotypes to etiologies* (pp. 291–328). Mahwah, NJ: Lawrence Erlbaum.

Nigg, J. (2005). Neuropsychological theory and findings in attention-deficit/hyperactivity disorder: The state of the field and salient challenges for the coming decade. *Biological Psychiatry, 57*, 1424–1435.

NIH Blueprint for Neuroscience Research: Tools, Resources and Training. (2004). Retrieved October 1, 2007, from http://neuroscienceblueprint.nih.gov/.

Pennington, B. (2005). Toward a new neuropsychological model of attention-deficit/hyperactivity disorder: Subtypes and multiple deficits. *Biological Psychiatry, 57*, 1221–1223.

Proctor-Weber, Z., & Golden, C. (2006). *Neuropsychological approach for classifying adults seeking post-secondary accommodations*. Poster presented at the International Neuropsychological Society annual conference, January 1–4, Boston, MA.

National Reading Panel (2000). *Report of the National Reading Panel*. Washington, DC: National Institute of Child Health and Human Development.

Sanovich, K. E. (1999). The socioeconomics of learning disabilities. *Journal of Learning Disabilities, 32*, 350–361.

Sbordone, R. (1996). Ecological validity: Some critical issues for the neuro-psychologist. In R. Sbordone & C. Long (Eds.), *Ecological validity of neuro-psychological testing*. Delray Beach, FL: Grove Press.

Seidman, L. (2006a). Neuropsychological functioning in people with ADHD across the lifespan. *Clinical Psychology Review, 26*, 466–485.

Seidman, L. (2006b). *Neuropsychology and neurobiology of ADHD across the life span*. Paper presented at the 34th annual meeting of the International Neuropsychological Society, Boston, MA.

Shaywitz, S. E., & Shaywitz, B. A. (2005). Dyslexia (specific reading disability). *Biological Psychiatry, 57*, 1301–1309.

Siegel, L. S. (1989). IQ is irrelevant to the definition of learning disabilities. *Journal of Learning Disabilities, 22*, 469–479.

Siegel, L. S. (1988). The discrepancy formulae: Its uses and abuse. In: Shapiro, B. K., Accardo, P. J., & Capute, A. J. (Eds.), *Specific Reading Disability: A View of the Spectrum* (pp. 123–135).

Simos, P., Fletcher, J., Sarki, S., Billingsley, R., Francis, D., Castillo, E., et al. (2005). Early development of neurophysiological processes involved in normal reading and reading disability: A magnetic source imaging study. *Neuro-psychology, 19*, 787–798.

Simos, P., Fletcher, J., Denton, C., Sarkari, S., Billingsley-Marshall, R., & Papanicolaou, A. (2006). Magnetic source imaging studies of dyslexia inter-ventions. *Developmental Neuropsychology, 30*, 591–611.

Sparks, R., Ganschow, L., & Pohlman, J. (1989). Linguistic coding deficits in foreign language learners. *Annals of Dyslexia, 39*, 179–195.

Spreen, O., & Haaf, R. G. (1986). Empirically derived learning disability subtypes: A replication attempt and longitudinal patterns over 15 years. *Journal of Learning Disabilities, 19*, 170–180.

Stevenson, J., Asherson, P., Hay, D., Levy, F., Swanson, J., Thapar, A., et al. (2005). Characterizing the ADHD phenotype for genetic studies. *Developmental Science, 8*, 115–121.

Tallal, P. (2004). Improving language and literacy is matter of time. *Nature Reviews Neuroscience, 5*, 210–219.

Waldman, I. D. (2005). Statistical approaches to complex phenotypes: Evaluating neuropsychological endophenotypes for attention-deficit/hyperactivity disorder. *Biological Psychiatry, 57*, 1347–1356.

Willcutt, E., Pennington, B., Smith, S., Cardon, L., Gayan, J., Knopik, V., et al. (2002). Quantitative trait locus for reading disability on chromosome 6 is pleiotropic for attention-deficit/hyperactivity disorder. *American Journal of Medical Genetics, 114*, 260–268.

Willcutt, E., Doyle, A., Nigg, J., Faraone, S., & Pennington, B. (2005). Validity of the executive function theory of attention-deficit/hyperactivity disorder: A meta-analytic review. *Biological Psychiatry, 57*, 1336–1346.

Wong, B. (1994). The relevance of longitudinal research to learning disabilities. *Journal of Learning Disabilities, 27*, 270–274.

World Health Organization. (1993). *The ICD-10 Classification of Mental and Behavioral Disorders: Diagnostic Criteria for Research*. WHO: Geneva, Switzerland.

Index

O